The Human Polity

A Comparative Introduction
to Political Science

Fifth Edition

Kay Lawson
San Francisco State University

Houghton Mifflin Company
Boston   New York

Editor in Chief: Jean Woy
Sponsoring Editor: Katherine Meisenheimer
Senior Project Editor: Kathryn Dinovo
Senior Manufacturing Coordinator: Marie Barnes
Marketing Manager: Nicola Poser
Marketing Assistant: Laura McGinn

Cover image: Robert Stanton. Copyright © Tony Stone Images.

Part and chapter opening image: Chad Baker/Getty Images.

Printed in the U.S.A.

Library of Congress Control Number: 00-133828

ISBN: 0-618-04364-0

1 2 3 4 5 6 7 8 9-VHG-06 05 04 03 02

For James Spencer Wallace

Contents

PART THREE

Acting in Politics

PART FOUR

Governing Nation-States

Preface

Where were you on September 11, 2001? You probably know and so do I. I was sitting at my desk, working on what was planned as a more thorough revision of *The Human Polity* than had ever been done before. Then the news arrived and that was the end of work for that day. When I went back to my desk, the whole world had changed, and the changes I had planned for this, the fifth edition, were clearly not enough. The destruction of the World Trade Center towers by terrorists had ramifications that would affect every single chapter. This was indeed going to have to be a very serious revision.

And so it is. While keeping to the original new plans, I added others to take account of what had happened. At the same time, I was determined to adhere to the book's mission, that is, to offer a comprehensive introduction to political science. *The Human Polity* describes the nature of the discipline, explains the ways in which political scientists study politics, and offers introductory treatment of all the major topics we normally think of as constituting political science.

New To This Edition

In addition to incorporating reference wherever appropriate to how the world has changed since September 11, 2001, this edition of *The Human Polity* is characterized by very extensive changes in the order and content of the book. Chapter 1 now combines former Chapters 1 and 2: It explains the idea of a human polity, offers examples of how the progress of globalization affects individual lives, and gives an overview of the subjects, subfields, methods, and some of the major concepts of political science.

The next five chapters provide new perspectives and new information regarding the major political ideologies; the relationship between politics and culture; and the ways in which individuals, groups, and parties act in politics at the national level. Chapter 7 combines familiar and new topics: It discusses the actors in international politics at greater length than before, plus three of the issues that concern them most, beginning with one never covered before and now impossible to omit: defense against terrorism. Chapters 8 and 9 offer new scholarship and new examples for familiar topics: the work of legislatures, executives, and bureaucrats. Chapter 10 is a new chapter on public policy, giving special attention to the issues of health, education, and the distribution of wealth. Chapters 11 and 12 take a fresh look at the judiciary and systems of law and at subnational governments. Chapter 13 is almost entirely new, greatly expanding the discussion of international government (within regions and worldwide) and placing the growing importance of this topic in historical context. Chapter 14, on political and economic globalization, gives greater attention to the agents of that major transformation of our era.

Globalization now replaces interdependence as the basic theme in the book. The two are, of course, closely related. But there is a difference, and the fifth edition tries hard to make that clear. More than ever, we are compelled to accept that there are problems we can resolve only in unison with the citizens of other states. Yet working out the compromises, the treaties, and, finally, the institutions of international governance that will make the world one in which fairness and equity is maintained—and wars are avoided—is now also more difficult than ever. Globalization poses new problems for individuals as well as for governments: Even as we continue to give our first loyalties to the separate nation-states that lay claim to our citizenship, we must somehow learn to think of ourselves as members of a human polity, a political community to which we all belong merely by virtue of living together on the globe. Reading this edition will, it is hoped, help in this important transition.

Another new feature, the "Questions to Consider" added at the end of each chapter, will allow students to consider these larger topics, as well as review the key points and problems raised under every topic.

Popular Features Retained

As in earlier editions, examples and contemporary scholarship are used to highlight important points and clarify difficult concepts, but in this edition an extra effort has been made to use the best and most recent scholarship for every subject as well as to use examples from recent events with which students may be familiar, intermixed with those less familiar that may pique their curiosity and interest. As before, a few of the examples are personal, drawing from my own experience or asking the students to reflect on their own, as a way of helping readers realize the relevance of topics and issues they might otherwise regard as remote or arcane.

That world of politics is ever more complex. But I have continued to believe that we can respect the complexity of modern politics and at the same time write about it clearly, using a familiar vocabulary and explaining new terms in a context that makes their meaning immediately comprehensible and easy to remember.

Thus, as before, the style of *The Human Polity* is one of informal but respectful dialogue between author and reader. Direct questions are occasionally posed in the text in order to stimulate the students' interest and to prompt them to apply their steadily increasing knowledge of political science to the more familiar experiences of their own lives. Students who take this opportunity to "talk back" to the author will find that as a consequence they are better prepared to enter into class discussions and to recall what they have read. Both normative and practical problems are raised throughout the book, in a manner intended not only to inform but also to encourage students to form their own opinions and make their own recommendations for change.

All the topics treated in the fourth edition are discussed in this edition as well. Those familiar with previous editions need not worry: every topic is still here—and much more besides.

Also as before, the *Instructor's Manual with Test Items,* written by W. D. Kay of Northeastern University, provides a chapter outline, a chapter overview, questions for class discussion, and an annotated list of additional readings for each chapter. The test items include essay questions for each chapter and approximately thirty-five multiple-choice items per chapter. A computerized test generation program containing all the printed test items is also available.

Acknowledgments

This book is itself always the product of interdependence. Once again I have leaned heavily on the work of Paul Andersen, who helped with both the third and fourth editions as well and whose Internet research skills are nothing short of remarkable. Jennifer Ramos also gave extremely valuable and timely help for this edition. The excellent work of former assistants—Tina Nasseri, Dana Polk, and Lori Smersfelt for the fourth edition; Janet Ciarico, Andrea Rommële, Ann Loepfer, and Regan Fordyce for the third edition; Marisa Kelly for the second edition; Andrea Bonime, Robin Davis, Mark Dorfman, Paula Fleming, Lynne Laidlaw, Adrienne Levey, James McGuire, Alan Vlautin, and Cynthia Witman for the first—lingers here and there throughout the book, perhaps now harder to trace but still deeply appreciated.

It is also a pleasure to thank the following reviewers, whose thoughtful comments and careful critiques have helped to guide the manuscript's development:

Clement E. Adibe, DePaul University
Robert W. Compton Jr., Western Kentucky University

Rekha Datta, Monmouth University
Victoria Mantzopoulos, University of Detroit Mercy
Mary M. McKenzie, Grossmont College
A. P. Simonds, University of Massachusetts at Boston

Once again, a new edition owes a great deal to the support of family and friends. To the former I have been glad indeed to welcome the addition of James Spencer Wallace, to whom it gives me great pleasure to dedicate this edition. Dedicating books to grandchildren (the fourth edition was dedicated to his brother, Trevor) is not just an act of sentimentality—I am quite convinced there is no better support for any intellectual activity than the sheer delight of turning it off from time to time and chatting cheerfully with beloved children, and no better way of keeping faith in the capacity of the human polity to overcome its distressing woes than to welcome its brand new members into your arms and share your thoughts and hopes with them.

Finally, as always, I willingly take responsibility for the book's faults but insist on my share of any praise for its merits. I hope the effort that I and others have given to making this new edition a lively and interesting introduction to the ever-changing world of politics and political science will seem well worthwhile, especially to the students for whom *The Human Polity* is their introduction to political science, and that the book may help all its readers find their ways through the present parlous and difficult times.

Kay Lawson

PART ONE

The Work of Political Science in an Era of Globalization

CHAPTER 1

Political Science in an Era of Globalization

POLITICAL SCIENCE AND THE HUMAN POLITY

Today the world of nations is more interdependent than ever. Increasingly, our lives and welfare depend on developments beyond our nation's borders, however secure those borders may be and however strong the social and economic systems within those borders. The need to preserve and replenish the limited resources of our planet while meeting the massive energy demands of advanced civilization, and the need to develop and expand this civilization while protecting it from the destructive havoc our own technology has made possible, are needs we can meet only collectively and cooperatively. Defending humanity everywhere against the threat of terrorism is a task we all must share. We can no longer comfortably assume that "we" means "we Americans" or "we Swiss" or "we Japanese" when such matters are to be resolved. More and more often, "we" means "we humans," and "our" problems, resources, and efforts are those of the species, not of any single nation-state. We live in the human polity.

Polity is a word with several meanings. It can mean a state or any society that has an organized government. More generally, it refers to a "body politic"—that is, any group of persons who have some form of political relationship with one another. The *human polity* is a polity in the second sense. It includes all the people presently living on the planet who have become so interdependent that they now constitute a body politic.

However, the *human polity* is made up of separate polities in the first sense of the word, too—individual nation-states. It is to these states that most people pledge their loyalty. For this reason, the capacity of human beings to interact effectively across national boundaries depends very much on what goes on inside those boundaries. If the citizens of individual polities are able to address their internal problems efficiently, equitably, and cooperatively, then they will be better able to address the problems that extend into the international arena. On the other hand, citizens of individual polities that suffer from severe internal conflict and dissent, inequitable distribution of inadequate national resources, inappropriate or outmoded political institutions, and/or exploitative intervention by other polities in their own affairs inevitably find it difficult to function effectively in the world at large.

Studying political science means studying polities and the human beings who live in them at all levels. It means learning the facts we have about them and raising the questions that still do not have answers. It means thinking about the impact individuals and groups, organizations and institutions, cultures and economies, and war and peace have on the nature of polities— and the impact polities have on them. It is a very large subject and one that is very important to us all.

However, every subject and every job has a beginning, and every beginning has a beginning, too. We can only do so much in one book, in one semester. We can only begin. This is an introduction to political science. It is, furthermore, a comparative introduction, because that is what it must be now, now that we live in the human polity, as well as within our own nation-states.

But what does referring to the whole world as a human polity really mean? Is it just an idea, or are we talking about something we can feel and observe in our own lives? In this chapter we will discuss the subjects of political science, its subfields, its methods, and some of its most important concepts. But first of all, we are going to take a look at some of the human beings who have learned, for better or for worse, that they do indeed live in the human polity.

We begin in Russia, about five years after the fall of communism. At that point, the new interconnectedness of the human polity was producing some wonderful payoffs for Oleg Polumordvininov, a Russian citizen who was selling his Japanese customers electronic space heaters and other appliances he bought in Vladivostok, and for his fellow trader Alexandr V. Levin, who bought Russian pig iron, lead concentrate, and raw materials to sell in Japan and who was also selling Japanese consumer goods, forklifts, trucks, and electronics in Russia. Capitalism had come to Russia, and they were both doing pretty well. Said Mr. Levin, "When you succeed, wealth multiplies very quickly." [1] Nikolai Panchenko, a compatriot of theirs, was also pleased with the massive political change he had witnessed as a young man: He now lived in a "colossal, turreted, walled-off brick mansion" complete with enormous bedrooms, a sauna and swimming pool in the basement, stained glass windows upstairs, and a marble entrance hall with a massive crystal chandelier. Under communism, he and his father sold consumer goods, but that was an illegal activity then, and Mr. Panchenko Sr. spent nine years in prison for selling sheepskin hats and nylon raincoats. Mr. Panchenko Jr., on the other hand, was now running his own food store, selling car parts, and importing various consumer goods from Europe—and all his new activities were completely legal.[2]

That was a very nice change for the Panchenkos and today they still have many successful counterparts. However, not everyone fared so well, then or now. Take the case of Viktor Popov, one of the world's leading experts in cell biophysics. For him, the arrival of capitalism meant that his laboratory had less than 5 percent of the funding it used to have, with "no money for equipment, for new journals, for computers." To supplement their incomes, he and fellow scientists were tutoring American high school students during the summer.[3] Or consider the plight of Yefim and Olga Hayut, young doctors in Tver, Russia, who earned a combined monthly salary of 1,000 rubles in 1994. The elimination of virtually all price controls by Russian President Boris Yeltsin in 1992 had reduced the value of this income, formerly sufficient to feed the Hayuts and their two children, to the equivalent of less than $10 a month. "Our profession will always be needed," said Yefim, "but I'm not sure this profession will always be able to feed me."[4]

Vera Simyonova, a cleaning woman, was sure hers was no longer feeding her. Simyonova was never wealthy, but the food packages and other state

Jeff Danziger © *The Christian Science Monitor News Service* (www.csmonitor.com)

assistance she used to receive from the old, centrally controlled economic system now no longer came her way. Her income of 200 rubles was far below the poverty line of 1,900 rubles a month. To support herself and her mentally handicapped son she was forced to go, with hundreds of others like herself, to the outdoor market in the town of Tishinsky every day to try to sell whatever personal belongings she could, including canned food in her cupboard left over from the days of subsidized prices. Simyonova was not a fan of capitalism, nor even of democracy: "Under Brezhnev," she says, referring to the days when hard-liner Leonid Brezhnev was the Soviet leader, "everything was cheap. We could live." [5]

The lives of these Russian citizens illustrate the impact on individual lives of the sharp shift to free market practices and an ever more globalized economy that took place throughout the human polity after the fall of communism in 1989–1990. Economic liberalization, including drastic cuts in public spending and extensive privatization of state-owned firms, proceeded at a rapid pace, while overall productivity took a sharp dip.[6]

More recently, Russia has experienced a spurt of economic growth, but the desperate inequalities persist. And it is individuals who continue to suffer, none more so than the children. Eleven-year-old Oleg Mukhin lives with several friends in a hollow beneath the platform of Moscow's Vikhino railway station, having run away from his family in the central Russian city of Orel when he was only seven. He lives by begging, stealing, and taking help from charity and social action groups. He is far from alone—the Moscow Interior Ministry rounded up over 29,000 street children in 2001 and sent most of them "home." Most leave again—Oleg has been returned to his family twice. Some say there are over a million now on their own in post-Soviet Russia.[7]

Yet as the lot of the most defenseless worsens, other deprived Russians may be learning and applying valuable new post-Communist skills. When threatened with layoffs, wage cuts, and canceled benefits, engineer Anna Smirnova led the 230 workers at her machine-building factory 200 miles northeast of Moscow on a wildcat strike, refusing to accept the advice of their old-style Machine Builders Union just to try to "work things out on a personal level with plant management." Across Russia, independent trade unions are growing and beginning to achieve results.[8]

The Russian story also illustrates how rapidly and unevenly the transformations that are taking place in the human polity are changing human lives. Public opinion polls show that collectively the Russians still scarcely know what to make of it all. Although two-thirds of Russian voters still support the idea of democracy and over 80 percent think it is important to elect the country's leaders and to have freedom of expression and the press, only 12 percent are satisfied with the way democracy is developing and over 70 percent think the Soviet Union should not have been dissolved.[9]

Eastern Europeans share some of the ambivalence of the Russians about the impact the rest of the world is now having on their lives. Efforts to make these nations' economies globally competitive have led to cuts in government welfare spending. Women have been especially hard hit: Not only have many child care centers been closed and maternity leaves curtailed, but women workers in the public sector have been laid off in disproportionate numbers as the number of government employees has been reduced.[10] Freedom of the press has led to more fashion magazines and home improvement guides encouraging women to think of themselves as consumers rather than workers, as well as to the rapid growth of pornography. Most of the new democratic parliaments are almost exclusively male.

It should be remembered, however, that women's role was far from idyllic under communism. Although in those days women entered the labor force en masse, they still spent nearly three times longer on household tasks than men and held the lower skilled and lower paid jobs. In Hungary, they earned on average only 72 percent of what men were paid for equal work. And although Polish men still kissed women's hands when introduced, they almost never dirtied their own by sharing household tasks when married.[11]

Furthermore, today there are some interesting signs of change. In Poland, some women are becoming owners of small businesses, women academics have succeeded in changing the law calling for their mandatory retirement at

American workers protest losing their jobs as their factory closes owing to global competition.
Mark Richards/PHOTOEDIT

age 60 and have begun to introduce women's studies courses in their class-rooms, and women's magazines now run stories advising readers, "Don't be afraid of success." [12]

These changes in the lives of Russians and Eastern Europeans are obvious examples of the complex and growing interdependence of nations and of individuals within the human polity. However, the brave new world of globalization is not connected just by one-way streets. We are all involved. When the immigrant population grows, as citizens in other nations seek to leave intolerable poverty or political oppression behind, the receiving nations are profoundly affected, and not always generous in their welcome. Far-right movements and parties may prosper as local citizens, fearing competition for scarce jobs, turn against the new arrivals and look for ways to keep others out. Wealthy democracies may turn miserly: "Democracies don't like sacrifices, or the politicians who demand them. . . . Democracies don't want their comfort or profits interfered with." [13]

But isolationism is tricky when jobs and profits depend on exports. When Republican Mark Sanford represented the First District of South Carolina in the U.S. House of Representatives, he was well aware that one-third of the gross domestic product and one-third of the jobs in that district depended on foreign trade. "Most of the people in my district," said Sanford, "would say we need to stay connected with the rest of the world." [14]

Staying connected helps, and the freer trade that is also part of globaliza-

BOX 1.1
**Globalization in
Small-Town and
Rural America**

Of the 2,400 employees the copper mines of the Phelps Dodge Corporation in Grant County and Hidalgo County, New Mexico, used to employ, all
but 700 have been laid off. That's bad enough, but businesses that serve
the mines have had to let another 400 workers go, and unemployment in
the county is up to 14 percent, with stores "closing fast." The nearby town
of Loving used to have two pool halls, two bars, two cafes, and a barber
shop among its many businesses; now it has one bank and a hair salon.

Some communities find a way to shift to new sources of income. Brady,
Texas, may have lost much of its income from wool, but hunters still come
to town to hunt game in its well-stocked woods. Silver City, New Mexico,
is counting on museums and antiques shops to attract enough tourists to
fill in part of the gap left by the fall in demand for its copper. Suffering
peanut farmers in Floresville, Texas, are selling out to subdividers eager to
turn the little town into a bedroom community for nearby San Antonio.
Where there's a will, there may be a way. Then again, there may not.

Source: Peter T. Kilborn, "Changes in World Economy on Raw Materials May Doom Many
Towns," *New York Times,* 16 Feb. 2002, 1. Copyright © 2002 The New York Times Company.
Reprinted by permission.

tion is obviously good news for consumers and industries now able to buy
commodities and raw materials from abroad at lower prices. But what helps
you may not be so great for me: Australian wool is cheaper than New Mexican wool, copper from Latin America sells at prices well below those that
miners in Arizona can offer and still make a profit, and Canadian potash is
beating out that from the United States.[15]

Furthermore, when economies falter and recessions come along, the impact of globalization is multiplied. Japan's economic woes have not helped
Americans deal with their own—just ask Tommy and Wanda Quick of Loving County, Texas, who raise angora goats: "The whole wool business is
shot. Every Japanese man wanted a mohair suit. It comes from angora
goats." But no one in Japan wants them anymore, and now Mr. Quick plans
to sell his 125 goats for meat.[16] And in small communities it isn't just the
producers who are hurt when local wool—or copper, potash, oil, or cotton—becomes noncompetitive globally. See Box 1.1.

THE SUBJECTS OF POLITICAL SCIENCE

Thus, as globalization proceeds, the existence of the human polity becomes
ever more palpable, ever more present in all our lives. Not only do we need
to understand this new reality, we also need to understand how it affects
our understanding of just about everything else. Subjects that were hitherto

treated matter-of-factly only as they applied to "us," the citizens of a particular nation, now simply cannot be understood if we put the same old blinders on. An educational system that seemed good enough ceases to be so if it ranks far behind those of other nations, whose citizens compete with ours in this brave new world. Never mind political science; there is *nothing* we do—fighting cancer and AIDS, defending human rights, paying fair wages while earning an honest profit, taking care of our children and the aged, building better roads and bridges, producing more food per acre, selling more cars per month, you name it—that we don't do better when we consider how others are doing the same thing in other lands. How much is a new alternative fuel car made in Japan going to cost on the world market? Better find out before you go into the business in Detroit. Interested in improving child care facilities in your community? Better read up first on how they do it in France.[17] We members of the human polity can now learn from each other as never before. And in many cases, failure to do so is dangerous indeed.

Nowhere is the need—or the danger that comes from failing to serve it—greater than in the study of political science.

Political science is an American subject; Americans invented it as it exists today, and the United States has by far the most practitioners. But the subject matter of political science can no longer be adequately treated by referring to a single nation, even the most powerful in the world, even the one with the most political scientists. Consider, if you will, the first eleven topics we will cover in this book, chapter by chapter: ideology; culture; individual political behavior; political action in groups, in parties, and at the international level; government action in legislatures and administrations; domestic and foreign policymaking; judiciaries; and the special roles of local and provincial governments. In the past, ten of these topics could have been and often were considered purely in national terms—and the eleventh, political action at the international level, would have meant little more than talking about the activities of diplomats and spies and would normally have been given a few paragraphs in an optional final chapter, "international relations." Two separate chapters, as you will find here, one on international and regional governments, and the other on political and economic globalization, would have been unthinkable and unnecessary.

Before the sun set in New York City on September 11, 2001, those of us watching television or listening to the radio that day, wherever we lived on the planet, had heard over and over again "the whole world has changed." It was true; everyone in the world now had to take the threat of terrorism more seriously—even nations that had been fighting terrorist groups for decades, even Osama bin Laden, who later happily confessed he was surprised how successful the attack had been. The nature of international relations, of warfare, of espionage, of civil liberties and judicial due process, of nationalism, of U.S. patriotism, of religious tolerance, and of hope for democracy—all had changed, instantly. But as overwhelming and sudden as they were—

overwhelming in part *because* they were so sudden—these changes were caused by and taking place within changes of far grander scope that had been going on for over twenty years. Globalization did not take place in an instant; globalization is not an accomplished fact (and may never be), but globalization is the force that brought religious fanaticism angry new adherents by the thousands if not millions, the network that made training and weapons easy to acquire, the banking system that could be used to transfer the needed funds, the worldwide web of communications that told all who would listen how wide the gap between those who had and those who did not really was. Globalization did not invent terrorism, but globalization did produce September 11. Globalization is not a force only for evil, far from it, but neither is it a force only for good. We cannot study the subjects of political science inside the ivory tower of nationalistic pride, not any more.

At the same time, as my Franco-American sister-in-law likes to say when the world around her turns a touch hyper, "*du calme.*" Stay calm; don't get carried away. We members of the human polity are all connected as never before, but we all have our own lives, and our own polities, as well. Most of us live within many layers of politics. Neighborhood associations, local government, county or cantonal authorities, state and regional leaders, and the nation-state are still the primary political forces determining our lives, telling us what to do and what not to, sometimes even doing as we collectively have asked them to do. Not unheard of, but still very rare, is the businesswoman who has to change her way of doing business because an international court told her to; not unknown, but nonetheless unusual, is the soldier who is compelled to serve in an international peacekeeping force. Ancient ideologies and ethnic cultures still often guide our hearts and our thoughts, and thus our political behavior. Our political opinions form close to home, and indeed very often at home, and our ability to express them with a modicum of political power usually depends on constitutions and electoral rules no international body devised. Interest groups have more power over policy at home than abroad; parties elect national leaders; most laws, and all the more powerful ones, are made in state and national legislatures; bureaucrats do their work under national flags, watched over by the stern or benevolent photos of national leaders; public policy is mostly domestic; and each nation has its own legal culture, even as it draws heavily on the examples past and present of others.

We cannot lose sight of the ways in which the political life of different peoples varies, and indeed much of the delight in studying the subjects of political science lies in remarking them. Although we may be in closer contact and competition with our fellow occupants of planet Earth, and more dependent on them for our very survival than ever before (as are they on us), we still know which police officer to obey, which rascal to vote out of office on election day. Knowing the kind of police *we* have, the legal code that governs *us*, the elective and appointive offices that constitute *our* constitutional system, and indeed all the rich panoply of our own political life and government, that too is the subject matter of political science.

In this book we seek to place the near within the context of that which has hitherto seemed far. Because most readers will be American, we use mostly American examples. Because all readers, including Americans, are presumably interested in and enlightened by knowing how others carry out similar activities, we include many specific non-American examples. Because we all live in the human polity in an era of globalization, we stress the international dimensions of every topic.

THE WORK OF POLITICAL SCIENCE

Of course you don't have to be a political scientist to think about the subject matter of political science—everyone who reads a daily newspaper or listens to the evening news does that. What makes a scholarly discipline is not only what is studied. A discipline is organized, it has methods, and it usually has its own vocabulary and concepts. Political science is no exception, and these three topics will be the focus of the remaining pages of this chapter.

The Subfields of Political Science

Political science is the study of politics. This means the work of political science is to seek the answers to a number of important questions: What attitudes and values produce political conflict and dissent? What political organizations are active in the struggle to achieve political consensus? What is the nature of the socioeconomic; relationships inside a polity? How adequate are resources to meet needs; how equitably are resources distributed; and how are material interests pursued, protected, or changed by the course of public policy? What are the constitutional structures and the decision-making procedures of each nation, and how well suited are they to that nation's needs? What internal structures and procedures exist for the debate and resolution of problems with other nations? What assistance is available from international agencies and the international community at large?

Political science does not have all the answers to these questions, but it does have some, and, what is more important, it has the means of finding others. Becoming a political scientist means joining a community of people who work on just these sorts of questions.

Like politics itself, the work of political science has developed over the centuries, expanding and subdividing. Scholars, critics, playwrights, correspondents, and poets have been observing and commenting on political processes since pen was first put to paper (or stylus to tablet). Confucius wrote on moral and ethical issues relevant to the concept of authority as early as 500 B.C.E. In 450 B.C.E., Herodotus' history of the Persian Wars included his reflections on the issue of tyranny versus the rule of law, and Aristophanes wrote *Lysistrata*, an antiwar play, in 412 B.C.E.

Over the years the focus of political studies has changed and expanded. The subfields of political science have multiplied accordingly. To our original study of political philosophy (now more commonly termed *political theory*) we have added, one by one, constitutional law, public administration, international relations, American government, comparative government (by which we really mean the study of foreign governments), political behavior (the study of political attitudes as well as political acts), political economy, political organizations, and urban politics. In addition, some of us devote most of our time to studying and developing the methodology of political science, while others are interested in newer, less well-established areas of study such as *biopolitics* (the study of how the physical characteristics and conditions of political actors may sometimes influence their behavior).

The Methods of Political Science

How do political scientists do their work? They often begin with very ordinary activities: They read what other people have to say, they follow current events, they note what appear to them to be certain interesting tendencies, they wonder why such things are happening, and they wonder what will happen next. What makes a political scientist different, however, is the capacity and the will to make systematic inquiries into a political puzzle. The political scientist does not simply say, "Hmm, I see by the paper that our president has vowed to save the American worker from the competition of cheap foreign imports while at the same time protecting the principle of free trade. That's a good trick," and turn the page. The political scientist tries to solve the puzzle such a statement presents.

But what is that puzzle? When we stop to think about it, this statement, like almost every statement about politics, is replete with puzzles. Think about it for a moment. An American president promises to save American workers while encouraging the freedom of international trade that threatens the livelihood of many of them. What do you think is puzzling about that promise? (Write your answer.) Does it seem to you that what you just wrote is the only possible answer? In fact, we all differ in how we perceive political reality, and thus in how we formulate the puzzles it poses. Just consider some of the possibilities:

1. What puzzles me is what endangered workers think about this announcement. Did this president win the steelworkers' vote? Is he likely to do so again?

2. What puzzles me is how the *president* can do anything to save jobs. Isn't it the work of the legislature to make the laws and of the president to carry them out?

3. What puzzles me is why the president suddenly made this nod to the protectionists. He has always been strongly committed to free trade. Is it because an election is coming up, or has he decided the effects of foreign competition are so harsh they require a serious change of direction?

4. What puzzles me is the perennial conflict between policies that help, in the short term, to solve a national problem, and long-term policies that seem necessary if we are ever going to have a human polity that is economically stable and at least minimally responsive to the needs of human beings everywhere. Must we always sacrifice the needy of another nation to care for the needy at home?

5. What I don't understand is how the president can act as if all the trade treaties we have made with various nations can simply be set aside at will. Are our agreements no longer worth the paper they are written on?

6. What puzzles me is what the impact of protectionism—if that is the policy we really adopt—is going to be on those nations whose economies depend on cheap exports to the United States. Will our policies destabilize those economies, and, as a consequence, those polities? Will there be other effects in international relations stemming from these changes?

As you can see, how we formulate our puzzles makes a big difference in the questions we ask and in the work we need to do to find answers to them. Not all political scientists study the same subfield, and not all of them puzzle about political phenomena in the same way. Some kinds of questions interest you, other kinds interest me, and across the room our good friend Bob is probably thinking about this same problem in some entirely different way —or simply doesn't care at all. How we formulate the problems we wish to study as political scientists also has some relationship to the subfields that interest us. Wondering about how workers will react at the polls or about whether or not policy statements are governed by upcoming elections are questions about political behavior as well as about American government. Those interested in constitutional law might worry about presidential interference in the legislative domain, and so might political scientists whose studies are concentrated in American government or public administration. The philosophical tone of the fourth puzzle suggests the work of political theorists, but political economists might want to claim this puzzle as their own since it stresses the relationship between politics and economics, whereas those interested in comparative politics will appreciate the focus here and in puzzle number six on the internal affairs of other nations. Arguing for the validity of international treaties suggests an interest in international affairs, as does considering the impact of the president's decision on the welfare of foreign states.

The way we puzzle over political phenomena does more than reveal which subfields of political science are likely to interest us most. It is also strongly related to our method of inquiry and the approach we take in our quest for an answer. There are six main approaches to the study of politics: (1) behavioral, (2) structural-functional, (3) historical, (4) philosophical, (5) documentary, and (6) predictive.

■ **Studying Political Behavior.** The **behavioral approach** to politics means focusing on how individuals act politically and seeking explanations for that behavior within those individuals. Behavioralists are not especially interested in what the rules say or what philosophers recommend about political action. They want to know what human beings really do when they act politically—that is, when they discuss politics, vote, contact government officials, demonstrate, riot, or otherwise act out their political convictions.

Once political scientists have what seems to them to be reliable evidence about the facts of political behavior, they want to know what motivated that behavior. What does the actor feel, believe, or think about politics that caused him or her to act in that particular way? Sometimes the behavioralist carries the inquiry another step: What factors seem to be associated with having those particular feelings, beliefs, and opinions? Does growing up in a certain kind of home or having a certain kind of job influence what kind of a political actor a person will be?

How can this kind of information be gathered? A key method for the behavioralist is survey research—that is, research that studies a large number of individuals, finding out, by asking them, about their political behavior (voting, joining groups, writing letters, and so on). Such research permits the acquisition of a great many answers, often in simple, uniform format (*yes, no, often, one, two . . . five*), and these answers may in turn be subjected to statistical analysis, permitting the researcher to draw far-reaching conclusions about political behavior and its causes with considerable confidence. In the United States we know, for example, not only the characteristics most commonly associated with voting but also what other kinds of political participation voters engage in, how much more likely they are to do so than nonvoters, and what difference various kinds of voter registration arrangements are likely to make in voter turnout.[18] Such knowledge does not always tell us what to do next, but it does give us an important part of the factual base we need.

The behavioral approach is appropriate when the puzzle at hand requires and permits the accumulation of information about human behavior and its motives. It helps if that data can be gathered in discrete but uniform bits, permitting statistical analysis. The study of the personality of a single political actor, however, may be as important—and is every bit as "behavioral"—as the study of hundreds of voters.

■ **Studying Political Structures and Functions.** When political scientists adopt the **structural-functional approach,** they focus on the important political roles established in a society, what functions they perform, and how the carrying out of these roles influences the quality of life. Structural-functionalism is an approach that was first developed by anthropologists looking for ways to free themselves from Western biases when studying non-Western cultures. It soon became clear to such scholars that different structures might well perform different functions in different societies. For example, religious institutions might have the function of conducting seasonal ceremonies to ensure that planting and harvesting are done at the appropriate times of the year as well as the functions of setting codes of interpersonal behavior and guiding believers to presumed eternal happiness. Even where familiar political structures seem to be missing, closer observation might reveal that very familiar functions are still being performed, although through other structures. There may be nothing that calls itself a political party, but when the members of the club Mr. X belongs to are busily asking everyone to vote for him, while those in the club Ms. Y belongs to are equally active on her behalf, then at least one of the key functions of parties—campaigning on behalf of chosen candidates—is not neglected.

The structural-functional approach helps us focus on what is really happening. It tells us to look at structures objectively: What are their role occupants really doing? It reminds us that certain functions are probably being performed even when persons with positions inside the structures normally responsible for them are not doing the job: Someone is creating political issues, someone is choosing the leaders, someone is making rules for society, someone is carrying them out, someone is deciding disputes arising under those rules. Who is doing what, in what office or role, and with what effect?

Structural-functionalists are often accused of finding functions for every structure that exists and thereby implicitly defending that structure, no matter how unfortunate its effects. Where others might study the Spanish Inquisition as an example of religious intolerance, for example, the functionalist might consider it an interesting illustration of how religious bodies can take over the government functions of making and carrying out the laws and settling disputes. But this does not mean the functionalist *approves* of the takeover. Understanding how particular structures perform essential functions is obviously important, regardless of our opinion of their worth. Furthermore, if in fact we strongly disapprove of what is being done by persons within a particular structure, knowing what they offer to those who support them (i.e., what functions they fulfill) is essential before we offer our recommendations for replacing the structure within which they work. Practicing structural-functionalists may have a bias (or may not), but the method itself seems reasonably neutral.

A further testimony to the continuing usefulness of this mode of analysis is the rapid growth of a "new" subfield in political science, known as the "new institutionalism." Institutions are, of course, structures. However, in political science as in botany, a rose by any other name sometimes does smell sweeter, whatever William Shakespeare may have had to say on the subject.[19]

■ **Studying Political History.**   One criticism often leveled at the two approaches we have considered so far is that they are not useful for considering political change. Behavioralists rely on opinion polls that may be useless two days after they are taken. How many Russians do you suppose felt exactly the same about the likelihood of their nation making a peaceful change to a capitalistic market system before, during, and after the attempted coup d'état by old-guard Communists in 1991? The structural-functionalist determination that a structure does or does not perform a particular function may be equally shortsighted. The role of the Guinean Confederation Générale du Travail, an early trade union in what later became the west African nation of Guinea, changed with dramatic speed when that union staged the first successful strike by black workers in west Africa. Shortly thereafter, the trade union became the nation's leading political party.[20] In such cases, goes the critique, what is missing is any allowance for change. An approach to politics that does not find a way to take into account the inevitability of change can never get more than a fleeting hold on the slippery facts of political reality.

Studying politics as the result of history does not suffer from the same problem. It begins with an interest in change. The question this approach asks first and foremost is: What are the causes of a significant change in a political system? Specifically, what are the events that led up to that change, and which of these were significant in producing that change? In recent years this approach has often taken the form of "path dependence" theory. As Paul Pierson explains, this theory makes "a few key claims," such as "specific patterns of timing and sequence matter; starting from similar conditions, a wide range of social outcomes may be possible; large consequences may result from relatively 'small' or contingent events; particular courses of action, once introduced, can be virtually impossible to reverse; and consequently, political development is often punctuated by critical moments or junctures that shape the basic contours of social life." The difference between path dependence theory and ordinary political history is its emphasis on "increasing returns," i.e., on "self-reinforcing or positive feedback processes." Proponents of this approach believe they can show that there are "formative moments" and "it is not only a question of what happens but also of when it happens."[21]

Note that in the effort to find the roots of major change, the student of political history inevitably asks and answers numerous questions that could properly be considered the work of the behavioralist and the structural-functionalist. What sets this approach apart is its commitment to the study of structures, functions, behavior, and events *over time*.

■ **Studying Political Ideas.**   The **philosophical approach** to the study of politics focuses on the meanings of political life. Like the behavioralist approach, this mode of study is closely associated with a single subfield of political science, in this case *political theory* (so-called even though theory is in fact used in every subfield of the discipline). Typically, the political theorist is interested in general questions relevant to politics. What are the limits on the exercise of political power, if any? What are the various meanings of *representation* in the political arena? Can the apparent conflict between economically sound versus humanely caring public policy ever be resolved?

All such questions have specific applications. When we argue about whether any conditions exist under which investigative agencies like the FBI should be allowed to tap private telephones, we are arguing about the limits that should be imposed on political power. If we are angered when one of our senators votes his or her conscience, even though that vote is contrary to known popular opinion in our state, we are expressing an opinion about the meaning we prefer to see given the concept of representation in the political arena. The controversy over whether or not the American public debt can be reduced while maintaining programs for social welfare reflects the eternal conflict between good budget management and social responsibility in the making of public policy.

The political philosopher seldom makes more than passing reference, however, to specific problems illustrative of the more general question under consideration. The emphasis in this approach to the study of politics is on examining the work of other philosophers who have grappled in a useful— or at least an interesting—way with the topic at hand and then endeavoring to deduce one's own logical conclusions. Sometimes this form of study involves simply allowing the comments of accepted classical authors, carefully selected, to make the desired point. In other cases, political scientists using this approach make their own arguments, backed up by authoritative citations. Sometimes the theorist's chief object is to offer a new interpretation of a classic text. In other cases, the object is to draw together the comments of several political philosophers on a particular matter of interest to the political scientist.

Because they place so much emphasis on political ideas—their own and others'—political philosophers are often criticized for having too little awareness of the real world, for worrying too much about what should be and too little about what is. But, in fact, all political scientists have values that guide the work they do. The political philosopher differs in placing greater emphasis on general ideas and values and in keeping alive the arguments for and against their application.

■ **Studying Political Documents.** The art and practice of reading **political documents**, from constitutions to campaign speeches, is one of the oldest forms of political science—and currently one of the least appreciated. Political scientists have learned the hard way that documents cannot always be trusted as guides to political practice. Constitutional and statutory law, treaties, party statutes and platforms, leaders' speeches and memoirs, records of legislative proceedings, authorized biographies, judicial decisions, and newspaper accounts of political happenings are among the forms of the written word that political scientists have discovered they must approach with caution. They offer rich lodes of information about politicians' intent and officeholders' official commitments, but often only fragmentary evidence of motivation and practice, and they are sometimes replete with self-serving distortions of the truth.

Even a constitution, the "highest law of the land," is not always to be trusted as an infallible guide to reality. No constitution did a better job, on paper, of protecting democratic principles than did that of the Union of Soviet Socialist Republics (USSR), yet nothing in that constitution could effectively block Joseph Stalin from transforming the Soviet government into an instrument of personal tyranny. Similarly, Adolf Hitler came to power under the terms of the well-respected constitution of the Weimar Republic of Germany.[22] Democratic nations have also shown surprising gaps between constitutional theory and political practice. Charles de Gaulle refused to take power in France in 1958 until he was assured that he would have the right to rewrite that nation's constitution, yet only four years later he blithely put through a major constitutional change (direct election of the president) by popular referendum, in bold contravention of his own prescribed method of constitutional amendment.

Nevertheless, studying political documents remains an important and useful mode of inquiry in political science. As long as such pronouncements are not openly repudiated or revised, any violation of their provisions invites attention and protest. Political scientists who explicate the meaning of such materials may well make the fact of such violation clear for the first time and provide a means of holding officials accountable to their word—and to their words. Or they may simply make clear how ambiguous certain key clauses in important documents may be, such as the wording of the idea of maintaining the separation of church and state, contained in the First Amendment to the U.S. Constitution.[23]

Furthermore, we need to ask how much sense it makes to accord greater credibility to forms of evidence other than official documents. Why believe an unofficial commentator more readily than an official one? Are not nonofficials sometimes just as strongly motivated to distort the truth as those in authority? And why believe that the spoken word, even when uttered in the sheltered confines of the personal interview, is necessarily more reliable than words committed to the greater permanence and accessibility of print? The fact is that political truth is difficult to come by, and we need every useful method we can devise to track it down.

■ **Studying the Political Future.**   In a sense, every political scientist studies the future, and all the approaches thus far discussed can be applied to the study of the future. Our interest in politics is sharply honed by our desire to be prepared for what might be coming next. But some political scientists take the responsibility to make well-founded predictions about the feared or hoped-for events of the future more seriously than do others.

Efforts to predict the future must necessarily be based on our knowledge of the past. We cannot predict the future from the present—not if we use that term literally. How much does any of us know about what is happening right now? We need time to acquire information, organize it, assimilate it, and make sense of it—and by then the present will be the past. However, the time-honored certitude that "the past is prologue" has been shaken by the course of events in the late twentieth and early twenty-first centuries. Too often and too obviously the past has proved an untrustworthy guide. Soviet suppression of eastern European revolutionary movements in Hungary in 1956 and in Czechoslovakia in 1968 would never have led us to expect the USSR would offer active support to new movements to overthrow the state in those two nations in 1989. Periodic angry denunciation of the NATO pact and its members by members of the Warsaw Pact of the eastern bloc did little to prepare us for the day in 1992 when many of the latter would seek to join the former, having dissolved their own alliance the year before. And although some engineers knew the internal structure of the World Trade Center towers would not be able to withstand temperatures above a certain level, and some intelligence agents knew a great deal about the plans of some terrorist organizations, what actually happened on September 11, 2001, was beyond anyone's power to predict. Even the perpetrators were amazed.

Our species' capacity for rapid change that shatters old patterns of political relationships forever—a capacity that seems to have grown only stronger as we move gingerly into the new millennium—has been a major stimulus to the effort to find ways to use information about the past more systematically to predict the future. One such way is by building **models.**

What is a model? Scratch fifty political scientists and you will probably find fifty different definitions. Let me try to offer a fifty-first here, one that encompasses most of what is said in the other fifty. To begin with, a model is an imitation of something that is, or that is thought to be, or that might someday be. It is an *ideal* in the Platonic sense—that is, a representation of the essence of the subject, not the best possible version. Thus, a model is also a simplification. It does not tell the whole truth about a subject, nor does it purport to do so.

Models are not used only in the study of the future. They can be used in all the approaches of politics that we have looked at so far. Models, as any child putting together a toy spaceship can tell you, can be material objects. The models of political scientists, however, almost never are. They are abstract—verbal, mathematical, or diagrammatic descriptions or imitations of reality. For example, political scientists have formulated verbal models of political development, trying to help us understand how the relationship between political and economic factors will affect a nation's ability to develop and to modernize. Some development models suggest that modernization requires the centralization of political power, others stress the need for a division of labor (leading to a division of political power), and still others argue that development will never take place until the poor nations of the world free themselves from dependency on richer nations whose only goal is to continue to exploit them.[24]

Statistical models are used to predict electoral outcomes, among other things. Suppose you had wanted to know what the chances were that the National Action Party (PAN), led by Vicente Fox, might actually take the presidency of Mexico away from the Institutional Revolutionary Party (PRI) for the first time in the history of either party in the presidential election of July 2, 2000. Given the PRI's tight grip on power since its founding as the National Revolutionary Party in 1929, often helped along by clear-cut instances of electoral fraud, almost no one believed it could happen. It was true that in recent years the PRI had been carefully engineering limited and local victories for PAN in order to maintain the image, however dubious, of Mexico as a multiparty democracy. But power in Mexico means controlling the presidency, and the PRI had no intention of handing that crown to a rival. Yet somehow Fox took 42.5 percent of the vote, and PRI candidate Francisco Labastida took only 36.

The result surprised Labastida, most Mexicans, and most of the rest of the world, but it probably would not have surprised political scientists who knew how to gather data and use statistical models, had they put their best skills to work before the election. Had they done so, they would have found out as much as possible about public opinion on the issues of the day, the degree of support each candidate was able to gather from key groups, the amount of money they were spending, and any other quantifiable variable their statistical model told them should be given due consideration. If their work were well done, they would have known that Mexicans were increasingly ready to say they had little or no confidence in any of the major national institutions; that the issue of corruption was at the top of their concerns; and that Fox was attracting a very large number of adherents, some of whom were making extremely generous campaign contributions, which were added to already ample public monies. They would have known that the illiteracy rate was declining and the urban population growing, both bad signs for the PRI, always strongly dependent on the uneducated rural population. And they would have noted that older voters with higher incomes and a strong interest in politics were now more likely to vote, whereas the PRI had always been most effective in turning out the poor and the politically disengaged.[25] All of these findings could then have been fed into a computer, weighted as their model (based on earlier elections) directed, and made to produce an informed prediction. They would probably have been right.

Rational choice theory is a kind of modeling that is both verbal and mathematical. It uses the model of the game to predict the political future. Any game has players who play to win, rules, and information. Rational choice theorists use this model and imagine politicians as players; international treaties, laws, and electoral systems as rules; known political conditions as information; and desired political outcomes as what the players are trying to win. Using this model, they attempt to deduce the decisions the players will make to move rationally toward their goals. As you have probably guessed, the major objection to this form of modeling is its strange assumption that human beings are always rational actors. Others have argued that the values inherent in this perspective "feed into growing public cynicism about government and lead to a conservative policy agenda" as well as that it is an approach that disdains the "messy" world of democratic politics, which is always "fraught with emotion, ideology, and self-interest."[26]

Yet another kind of modeling, one that is both verbal and diagrammatic, is found in **political systems analysis,** a form of analysis suitable for the study of whole nations.[27] Studying whole nations as political systems means treating them as structures with interdependent parts and exploring the relationships among those parts. Citizens do not come into the political system untouched by life—we have all been shaped by our "nonpolitical environments" as well as by the dominant political culture and patterns of political socialization. Once we take on the identity of "member of a polity," we inevitably find some way of letting those in positions of authority know what we think of their performance. We may do this simply by keeping quiet, thereby letting the government know that its work is at least being tolerated, if only for the time being. Or we may provide more substantive "inputs," expressing our "support" (for example, by voting to reelect the same men and women to office again and again, or by paying our taxes without protest) or making "demands" (for example, by forming new pressure groups or parties, or by using those that exist to carry our wishes for different policies into the arenas of power). Those who receive these inputs, the "authorities," convert them into "outputs" by making and enforcing policies, laws, and decisions, or simply by passing on information. Citizens are expected to obey the laws, suffer punishments for criminal offenses, accept the rewards good government brings, and, in democracies, show their approval or disapproval in the next election. The systems loop is complete; the spiraling history of the political system continues on its way.

Some critics have argued that the systems model overemphasizes the interdependence of the parts of any given political system and fails to distinguish among parts that are more or less important to ensuring the successful functioning of the whole system. Today the chief deficiency of the systems model would seem to be its failure to deal with the interdependence of different political systems and of their citizens, and the difficulty of transferring this preeminently national model to the international arena.

How good are the methods of political science? Do they really work to solve political puzzles? That depends on what you mean by work. If you mean, "Are political scientists able to figure out what is really going on behind the superficial appearance of political phenomena?" the answer is, "Yes, quite often." But if you mean, "Can they come up with lasting solutions to the puzzles of politics?" the answer is almost certainly, "No." As we have already had occasion to point out, political life is both complex and constantly changing. One plus one is likely to remain two for all eternity, but the factors causing political phenomena to take the form they do may well disappear and be replaced by others—or they may not. What is most likely to happen as a result of a political scientist's work on a puzzle is that the puzzle will become a little less puzzling—at least for a while.

The Concepts of Political Science

When an aspect of our experience interests us, we begin to develop language for talking about it. The words we choose are not important in themselves. We might decide to call the people who decide disputes "munchkins" or "sweethearts" instead of "judges." What is essential is that a name, once we settle on it, should always refer to the same aspect of our experience. The *concept* is important—in this case, the idea that some people have the job of making authoritative decisions in disputes between other people.

Some names, as in the preceding example, refer to concepts or phenomena that we have little or no trouble recognizing. We can see them and touch them. We can confirm their existence *ad lapidum*—that is, in the same way we can confirm the existence of a stone, by looking at it, touching it, picking it up, or giving it a kick. (Most of these are not seriously recommended when verifying the existence of judges.) Other concepts are more difficult or even impossible to confirm through single sensory perceptions. We develop an awareness of what seems to us an important component of the nature of reality, and we pick what seems like a good name for it. That way we can at least talk about it and describe it more carefully. We may discover that we were wrong. The divine right of kings to rule, the unseen hand of the free market, and the biological inferiority of women and of nonwhite races are all examples of concepts that have been developed, explored, found inadequate, and abandoned by most social scientists.

The study of politics is rich with language about concepts.[28] Some political scientists argue persuasively that our discipline is still too young for us to have achieved full agreement on the concepts we use and the language we employ. However, we do agree on the meanings of many important terms and are unanimously persuaded that these terms refer to phenomena that really do exist. We cannot review them all, but here we consider nine: organization, institution, state, power, authority, legitimacy, equality, freedom, and order. The first three denote ways of talking about structures, the next three are concepts that deal with relationships of control, and the final three have to do with the quality of life inside a polity.

As used in the social sciences, structure is a set of patterned role relationships. Any time human beings interact by adopting specific roles and carrying out those roles in a specific way, they have created a structure. An **organization** is a body of persons working together in a structured way to achieve a specific purpose. In the case of a political organization, that purpose is political. Interest groups, political parties, candidates' campaign organizations, revolutionary movements, and even terrorist groups are examples of political organizations. Political organizations may be long lived or short lived, large or small, important or unimportant. Such seemingly nonpolitical organizations as flower clubs, hobby associations, and poetry reading groups may find themselves temporarily politicized under certain circumstances. If the park in which the city's finest chrysanthemums are grown is threatened by the extension of the freeway, the members of the flower club may find themselves devoting much of their time to lobbying the state legislature and engaging in various tactics to enlist public opinion on their side. Under these circumstances, the club will have become, for the time being, a political organization.

When a structure becomes an institution, its activities are widely viewed as helping to meet one or more of the basic needs of a society. An **institution** is a structure with established, important functions to perform; well-specified roles for carrying out those functions; and a clear set of rules for governing the relationships between the people who occupy those roles. Organizations may be institutions, but not all are—and not all institutions are organizations. The members of an organization may have a common purpose, but they may not be viewed by society as having an important function; the people working through an institution may have a common and important function to perform, but they may not have a common purpose. A single political party is an organization; political parties, collectively, may or may not have the status of institutions in a given polity. If they are routinely expected to carry out important functions such as recruiting political leaders in a particular way, political parties in that system have achieved the status of institution.

Any given institution may be wholly or partly political, or absolutely non-political. Courts, legislatures, civil services, and political parties are examples of wholly political institutions. Most institutions are at least partly political; when the occasion arises, they will engage as institutions in the political process. Many of the world's corporations, trade unions, and educational and religious institutions routinely commit a portion of their resources and attention to attempts to influence political decisions.

It is wrong to imagine all institutions as fixed, rigid, ossified structures. Effective institutions are the ones that can adapt successfully to changing conditions. The Catholic church is an example of an institution that has maintained power for centuries by making effective adaptations to changing conditions—it is interesting to note in this regard that although the first instinct of the Vatican was to dismiss the scandal of widespread pedophilia by priests in the U.S. church as a purely American aberration, it rather quickly came to understand that the problem would have to be dealt with at the top, and very seriously. The Communist parties of eastern Europe that came tumbling down soon after the Berlin Wall fell are examples of institutions that did not respond to signs that change was essential, or did so too little, and too late. What about the British monarchy? Is this an institution that is failing, as the British public becomes ever more aware of the deficiencies not only of some members of the royal family, but also of the high cost to themselves, the taxpayers, of maintaining an institution that the citizens of so many other nations find, at best, amusingly archaic?

A **state** is a structure that has the legal right to make rules that are binding over a given population within a given territory. As such, it has geographic as well as political characteristics. A state is a political institution, but it differs from other political institutions in having sovereignty—that is, it has the power to make decisions that cannot be overruled by any other body. This definition may seem reasonable and clear enough, but in practice the term *state* is often very ambiguous, especially with regard to the question of sovereignty. There is no better example of this ambiguity than the practice of referring to the constituent units of the federal system of government in the United States as *states*. These units were never sovereign states—although some of them nearly met the conditions of that definition in the few years between the Declaration of Independence and the adoption of the present Constitution.

Political philosophers from Niccolo Machiavelli to Robert Nozick and John Rawls have grappled with the question of what constitutes a state, and what its powers over the individual should be. Machiavelli understood that much would depend on the cleverness of the leader, and did his best to offer instruction for maximizing that person's power.[29] Contemporary philosophers argue about how much power the state should properly have: Rawls has argued that the state has an obligation to help the disadvantaged, providing free education and health care, but Nozick is much more conservative: "[A] minimal state, limited to the narrow functions of protection against force, theft, fraud, enforcement of contracts, and so on is justified; any more extensive state will violate persons' rights not to be forced to do certain things, and is unjustified."[30]

The idea that a state is always sovereign poses new and special problems today. As Steven Krasner points out, "the concept of states as autonomous, independent entities" never was fully grounded in fact, and is rapidly disappearing today "under the combined attack of monetary unions, CNN, the Internet, and nongovernmental organizations."[31] To this list must be added the need some states have felt to cede some of their powers to a supranational body, such as the European Union, which has now evolved to the point where it routinely expects its interdependent member states to obey its collective decisions in matters reaching far beyond simple economic pacts. Most of the member states' constitutions do not allow for this infringement on the sovereignty of the state, but their silence on the matter does not make the change any less real.[32]

The constitutions of some African states (Ghana, Guinea) have clauses permitting sovereignty to be ceded to a larger African body, because when those states first achieved independence it was hoped that a larger African state would be formed in the near future. The Organization of African Unity was formed in 1963, but not as a state; as we will see in Chapter 13, it has only very recently returned to the idea that it should evolve into a larger African state (renaming itself the African Union in July 2001). At the other end of the spectrum are certain geographical entities that are called states only by legal definition and international courtesy. Lesotho, Monaco, and Panama are "states" that remained under the nearly absolute power of a neighboring or surrounding state long after achieving legal independence.

Although some have argued that the nation-state is now obsolete, others have made more convincing arguments that although existing state borders will continue to break down as "self-defined" ethnic groups become the "basic building block of the coming international order," eventually such new states will "recombine with other states and peoples . . . as voluntary members of a new association."[33] Most scholars today agree that however changed its role and its composition may be, the state itself will survive.

■ Concepts That Deal with Relationships of Control.

We are usually ready to endorse such glib comments as "Power is the very heart of politics." In fact, however, the concept of **power** is one of the most difficult to define and understand. For Karl Marx power derived from the economic ascendance of the ruling class, but for sociologist Max Weber the key variable was the organization, particularly the modern bureaucracy.[34] Robert Dahl pointed out three common fallacies in the analysis of power. The "lump-of-power" fallacy is the mistaken assumption that power comes in lump sums and cannot be shared, so all one needs to ask is: Who's in charge? "Confounding power with resources" is what we do when we take literally such aphorisms as "Money is power." Money may be a resource on which power rests, but the two are different entities. Finally, "confounding power with rewards and deprivations" happens if we look beyond the powerful act to its ultimate consequences for the people it has been exercised for or against.

One consequence of a law calling for lower defense expenditures may mean fewer jobs in California, but "reducing the number of jobs" is *not* power.[35]

Power.   What, then, *is* power? Dahl suggested that power means getting others to comply "by creating the prospect of severe sanctions for noncompliance."[36] He quotes Harold Lasswell and Abraham Kaplan to the same effect: "It is the threat of sanctions which differentiates power from influence in general. Power is a special case of the exercise of influence: it is the process of affecting policies of others with the help of (actual or threatened) severe deprivations for nonconformity with the policies intended."[37] By "sanctions" all three authors mean any severe reprisal, including war; they do not mean simply placing embargoes on the importation or exportation of certain goods.

Examples are not hard to find. When Adolf Hitler forced significant changes in the foreign policy of the British Prime Minister Neville Chamberlain by making clear the devastation he was prepared to wreak, that was power. When President Franklin Roosevelt persuaded the U.S. Supreme Court to stop declaring New Deal legislation unconstitutional by threatening to induce Congress to increase the number of justices so he could "pack" the Court with fellow liberals, and the Court promptly ceased to find that kind of legislation questionable, that was power.

Thus defined, power involves two parties and two steps. In the first step, party A threatens unpleasant consequences if party B acts or does not act thus and so. In the second step, party B acts as party A wishes *because* party A has made the specified threat. It is a relationship of control. Sometimes the power relationship is interestingly reciprocal. The 1995 decisions of the British to withdraw troops from Northern Ireland and of the Irish Republican Army to end its acts of guerrilla warfare were clearly both made in partial response to the continued "deprivations" the other had threatened and imposed.

Dahl's formulation seems to place chief emphasis on the *threat* of sanctions. In today's world, however, power is all too frequently achieved only when threats have been carried out, and even then the results can be ambiguous. Iraq withdrew from Kuwait in 1991 only after the Gulf War had taken some 100,000 Iraqi lives; the subsequent imposition of sanctions short of war have all but closed that nation's economy down and created "horrific rises in infant mortality, malnutrition and disease," but they have not sufficed to remove Saddam Hussein from power or change his policies significantly.[38] Most commentators on the war in the Balkans believe that a major reason it became such a long, drawn-out, and bloody affair was because so often the threats made by the United States, by the North Atlantic Treaty Organization, by the European Community, and by the United Nations were either not carried out or were carried out with such minor damages that neither Serbs nor Bosnians, Christians nor Muslims found the

"At least we always know who's in charge around here."
© The New Yorker Collection 1983 W. B. Park from cartoonbank.com. All Rights Reserved.

sanctions sufficiently compelling.[39] Not every leader or nation yields to even the most believable threats, as the refusal of Afghan leaders to turn over the Al Qaeda terrorists to Americans after the bombing of the World Trade Center towers despite the perfectly credible and eventually executed threat of bringing U.S. wrath down on their own heads. The fierce resistance so long waged by the fighters for Chechen independence inside the boundaries of contemporary Russia is another recent example.

Authority. **Authority** is the right to exercise the power and influence of a given position that comes from having been placed in that position according to regular, known, and widely accepted procedures. We sometimes speak of "the authorities" as if they were remote figures, self-created, hopelessly beyond our reach. It is a misuse of language, however, to confuse those who usurp political power by means of force or trickery with those who have obtained such power by accepted means. In a democratic system, accepted means are normally either elections or appointments by elected officials. The furor over malfunctioning voting machines and the intimidation of black voters in the contested presidential election of 2000 was a furor about authority: Were the accepted means really being followed?

Whatever one's personal judgment in that matter may have been, the words of Denis Diderot are still apropos: The authority of a government, he said, "is not a piece of private property but a public good, which consequently can never be taken away from the people, to whom alone full ownership of it essentially belongs."[40]

Of course different nations have different ideas and practices regarding how authority is to be acquired. An Indian president must be elected by an electoral college consisting of the elected members of the Indian Parliament and the state legislatures, by means of a complicated system of weighted voting. An Australian aboriginal headman comes to his office through traditional paths of kinship. A French judge must have studied for and passed a competitive exam; only those who do best will receive appointments from the Ministry of Justice. A Japanese prime minister must win the approval of the leaders of all factions of the party that wins the most seats in the Diet, Japan's legislative body.[41]

A sign that significant change is taking place in any country is a shift in the rules for authorizing access to political power. The declaration of American revolutionaries that British agents had no authority to collect taxes from subjects who were not represented in British decision-making processes initiated a set of changes leading to the formation of a new nation. Some older inhabitants of the African continent have witnessed an amazing series of changes in the procedures for authorizing leadership. The precondition for attaining the right to rule in many parts of Africa has shifted over the last century from (1) place in the kinship lineage to (2) position as representative of foreign conquerors to (3) good behavior as "native administrator" (the title given African chiefs willing to serve as agents of colonial rule) to (4) "reasonableness" and "representativeness" (when leadership shifted to Africans who represented key groups that were willing to make the transition to independence on colonial terms) to (5) number of votes (in the early days of independence) to (6) having the backing of armed strength (as the first military coups took place and/or personal dictatorships were established), and back again to (7) number of votes (when the military returned power to civilian hands or other leaders, keen to reduce corruption and improve the nation's eligibility for foreign aid, forced the dictators out of office and reestablished democratic elections).

Legitimacy.   **Legitimacy** means having the approval of others. It is the condition of being regarded as correctly placed in a particular role and as carrying out the functions of that role correctly (whether or not one is actually doing so). **Political legitimacy** means having widespread approval for the way one exercises political power: "The governed not only acknowledge the power of their governors but the ruled feel that the power wielders ought to have power and they ought to be obeyed."[42] Under normal circumstances, authority gives legitimacy to power; it is possible, however, to have authority—to have come into power by accepted means—but to lack legitimacy.

If jurists are viewed as ruling in accord with their own political bias, the legitimacy of the system is placed at risk. Here a demonstrator holds the U.S. flag upside down after the U.S. Supreme Court ruled in favor of George W. Bush in the contested race of 2000 for the American presidency.
© Rob Crandall/The Image Works

If a president is seen as failing to take adequate steps to resolve an economic crisis, such as a wildly fluctuating financial market or a seemingly unending recession, he or she may lose legitimacy without losing authority. If jurists rule in accord with their own political bias—as many believed the Florida Supreme Court justices who ruled on behalf of Albert Gore and the U.S. Supreme Court justices who ruled on behalf of George W. Bush did in the 2000 election fiasco—they risk losing legitimacy, however correctly authorized to perform their functions.

The authority to rule and the power to rule legitimately may rest in different hands. If a king is insane, a grateful people may permit the cardinal to rule and grant his orders legitimacy. In some circumstances, no duly constituted authority may be able to take charge when leadership is required. Isolated survivors of catastrophes accept as legitimate the orders of someone whose directions make sense and save lives; they will worry later about who should be "authorized" to take charge of the little polity they may be forced to create.

Standards of legitimacy do not always change with standards for achieving authority. When Communist political systems were established in the nations of eastern Europe, the new rulers placed strong emphasis on single-party rule, centralized at the top. As long as they remained in power, gaining a position of authority was possible only by working through that single party and receiving its approval for one's candidacy, which would then be uncontested in the pro forma election that followed. The new rulers also worked hard to change their nations' standards of legitimacy, stressing the importance of reducing ethnic rivalries and eliminating organized religion (which had often played a powerful role in the earlier political systems). To all appearances, their efforts were successful, or largely so. Yet as soon as the Communist systems began to crumble and fall, both ethnic identity and religious guidance resumed their former function as legitimizing agencies. In post-Communist states, the various peoples who originally formed these polities are now once again granting legitimacy on the basis of answers to the age-old questions: Is this leader one of ours? Does he or she come from the same ethnic group and have the same religious faith? In the former Yugoslavia, the answers to these questions have assumed such overriding importance that hundreds of thousands of lives have been lost when the answer seemed "wrong" and the questioners have had the armed might to insist on *their* standards of legitimacy.[43]

In any case, the distinction between legitimacy and authority is an important one to keep in mind. When the exhortation "Question authority!" is widely uttered and widely followed, existing authorities are in danger of losing their legitimacy. When the people authorized to rule lose legitimacy, the chances are good that an attempt will be made to replace them with others; if a change in the basis of authority is required to replace the people who have authority, that change may well be made. On such foundations do revolutions rise.

■ **Political Concepts Regarding the Quality of Life.**   Politics is a fascinating subject in and of itself, but the reason most of us care enough about the subject to study it is both more personal and more global. We are well aware that the quality of the life we lead together is strongly influenced by the quality of our politics. We rely heavily on political processes to organize our interactions with one another. We know we need one another to live and prosper, but we do not always find that aspect of the human condition entirely satisfactory. Three questions in particular are likely to concern us here: How different are we, or should we be, from one another? How free from control by one another are we, or should we be? How peaceful, stable, and orderly can we make our interactions with one another?

Puzzling over these questions has given rise to the concepts of equality, freedom, and order. Although these terms refer to qualities of daily life that, in practice, are inextricably meshed, I will endeavor here to treat them one by one.

Equality.   Contemporary political systems nearly all give at least lip service to some version of the happy thought that all men are created equal. Some even go so far as to include women in this blessing. Rational observers may protest that there are obvious differences, from birth, in the physical and intellectual abilities of human beings.[44] However, despite this "dilemma of difference," most of us are willing to grant that there are important ways in which we all *are* created equal, if we focus not on our abilities but our needs. All of us need shelter, food, sleep, safety, various forms of social responsiveness (love, sex, affection, kindness, respect), and interesting activity. We may even agree that this fundamental **equality** in neediness should be more important in determining the role of government than innate or acquired differences in abilities.

Political equality means an equal right to participate in the political process and to be treated fairly by it. When Oliver Cromwell's momentarily victorious troops sat around the campfire on the fields of Putney during the English Civil War, debating the order of the future society they intended to establish, one eloquent soul argued for political equality (as opposed to basing the right to vote on the possession of property) on the grounds that government affects everyone. "Verily," he said, "I do believe that the poorest he that is in England hath a life to live as the richest he."[45] In the seventeenth century such a notion was nothing short of radical, and in the twenty-first century its implications are still not accepted everywhere. The right to vote and the right to hold office are hemmed in by numerous restrictions, and equal treatment under the laws is routinely denied women, children, aliens, and racial and religious minorities in various parts of the world.

Social equality is the right to be treated as a social equal, at least with respect to one's basic characteristics and needs. When governments attempt to outlaw discrimination in housing, jobs, and education on the basis of race, religion, or sex, they are asserting that such differences do not make some persons more socially worthy than others. Constitutional provisions that forbid governments to grant titles of nobility; laws that establish egalitarian standards of salutation ("citizen," "comrade"); and judicial rulings that limit the right of private associations to grant or deny membership privileges

Slums and high-rise housing in Caracas, Venezuela. Such inequities in status and prosperity are met throughout the world.
Peter Menzel/Stock, Boston LLC

are all motivated by the belief that government has a role to play in ensuring that if we cannot all be truly equal socially, our differences of rank will nevertheless not be permitted to extend to painful extremes.

Are governments properly concerned with fostering **economic equality**—that is, with ensuring that every citizen has approximately the same amount of material goods? That controversial question is often sidestepped by arguing that government is responsible only to provide equality of opportunity in the economic domain—that the goal of economic equality is sufficiently served when government sees to it that opportunities to get the necessary training and education are equal and that there are enough jobs for everyone. After that, goes the argument, natural and acquired inequalities in ability should be allowed to have whatever effect they may in producing unequal economic rewards. Others argue that such an approach will never eliminate the suffering of the poor and that governments must assume a greater role by carrying out rigorous taxation, land redistribution, or other policies designed to limit the growth of private fortunes.

Freedom.   It is impossible to determine what government's role should be in ensuring any form of equality without confronting the concept of **freedom**. Any political measures taken to make us more equal are likely to make us both more and less free: more free to pursue some measure of happiness, less free to disregard the welfare of others while pursuing our happiness. But what is freedom? The Old English word *freo,* from which the word *freedom* comes, meant "not in bondage, noble, glad, illustrious." Even today the word carries a connotation of pride, of a sense of personal accomplishment in the fact of not being in bondage. Thus *freedom* means something more than *liberty,* which suggests simply the absence of constraint. In practice, however, the two terms are often used interchangeably.[46]

There is general agreement today that it is the responsibility of all governments to keep their citizens free, in the sense of "out of bondage." At the same time, most people would agree that there are times when governments must limit individual liberty. The question is: Where shall the line be drawn? No one has argued more eloquently for maximizing individual freedom than John Stuart Mill, whose nineteenth-century essay *On Liberty* provides the classic defense of liberty as the guarantor of human progress. Only when men and women are free to explore and propound any idea they wish can there be a hope of discovering truth, said Mill, for only in the struggle against error can truth emerge. He went so far as to regret the "universal recognition" of any particular truth, because there is no better "aid to the intelligent and living apprehension of a truth [than] is afforded by the necessity of explaining it to, or defending it against, opponents."[47] Mill was also keenly aware of the threat posed to liberty by what seemed to him to be an excessive concern with political equality. If all are given an equal vote, politicians will simply comply with the will of the majority, however uninformed or misguided that will might be. There "ceases to be any social support for nonconformity."[48] According to Mill, "Eccentricity has always abounded when and where strength of character has abounded; and the amount of eccentricity in a society has generally been proportional to the amount of genius, mental vigor, and moral courage which it contained. That so few now dare to be eccentric, marks the chief danger of the time."[49]

Like equality, freedom comes in various forms. Political freedom means the freedom to dissent without fear of punishment. Social freedom means the freedom to behave as one wishes. Economic freedom means the freedom to acquire and dispose of one's personal wealth without hindrance. None of these freedoms is absolute in any land, but the extent to which each is protected varies enormously from nation to nation, and from time to time. It is an unending debate, one that often pits one kind of freedom against another, and different nations arrive at different resolutions. Governments in underdeveloped nations are sometimes so determined to maintain political stability that they use brutal means to stifle the free expression of ideas while at the same time encouraging a shift to greater economic freedom in order to stimulate the livelier competitiveness essential for joining a capitalistic global economy. In a series of military governments, Nigeria has allowed crop prices to be determined by the market (abolishing price-fixing commodity boards), reduced the number of commodities requiring import licenses from seventy-four to sixteen, deregulated the banking system and foreign exchange market, and set up a privatization committee to sell off state-owned enterprises. But it also banned all political parties and any political assembly, severely restricted freedom of the press, and did nothing at all about the fact that women do not receive equal pay for equal work, are often denied commercial credit, and receive less than one-third the education given to men. Some European polities, on the other hand, prefer limiting economic freedoms to ensure that the gap between rich and poor does not become too great while taking freedom of expression, even for the most "dangerous" opinions, absolutely for granted.[50] How would you characterize your own nation in this regard?

Order. The problem of balancing government's responsibility to aid the needy with its responsibility to protect individual freedom is compounded by our need for order, stability, and personal security. Our life as a social, interacting species requires us to organize our relationships with one another, to create **order** out of chaos, and to develop some ability to predict what will happen next. As Cornelius Castoriadis has pointed out, even revolutionary movements, challenging the established social order, seek to establish order within their own ranks, and posit themselves as the very "embodiment of a new institution of society."[51] Order is essential, yet it is often difficult to establish without sacrificing other desired conditions. In particular, the quest for order often gets in the way of the quests for equality and freedom.

Consider, for example, the fact that one way order is achieved is through the division of labor; certain persons are authorized to perform certain functions. Inevitably, some functions prove more essential than others to the collective good, and it is likely that those functions will come to be better rewarded than others, which means the loss of whatever socioeconomic equality may have existed. A hierarchy of jobs evolves, including the job (usually at or near the top) of making decisions binding throughout the society—that is, the job of political leadership. Creating this job inevitably means creating institutions of government, which, aside from their more positive functions, provide the means by which those leaders, if left unchecked and so inclined, can suppress their subjects' most cherished personal freedoms.

Although such problems can be mitigated by careful wording of constitutions and laws, the possibility of overresponding to the need for order is never fully absent. The danger is especially present in times of pervasive fear.

The era of McCarthyism in the United States during the early 1950s was an example, when the fear of the spread of communism was so strong some would have eliminated important freedoms of speech and expression altogether. Some would say the fear of terrorism after the attacks of September 11, 2001, threatens to bring another such era to the United States, a possibility we will consider in Chapter 7.

As should be apparent by now, the nine concepts we have examined are strongly interconnected, and it is often difficult to discuss one without entering into a discussion of the others.[52] But on the whole, the language of political science is not difficult. As in any field, efforts to tackle new problems or improve our understanding of old ones can lead us to create new words (neologisms) that no one really needs. But most of the terms are already familiar to you, as you will discover. (For those who occasionally need help, see the Glossary at the end of the book.)

Political scientists have been working hard to improve our methods of inquiry and to acquire a body of significant and readily applicable knowledge, and much of this book is devoted to summarizing the knowledge political scientists have acquired. Our work is not done, but then, if it were, what would be the fun of studying how to do it?

SUMMARY AND CONCLUSION

The human polity is the world of politics. In a time of increasing globalization and international interdependence, we have all become members of a global body politic as well as citizens of individual nation-states. This means that the only way we will be able to cope with the problems of today's world is to study not only our own nation's politics but those of other nations as well, and the relationships among nations.

Political science is the study of politics. Politics is a means of organizing collective human activity. The city-state, the empire, the nation-state, and the United Nations are four of the more complex forms of that kind of organization, but politics has been with us ever since human beings first began living and working together. Today, politics is part and parcel of nearly all human interactions, and political power is constantly expanding.

The scope of political science is vast, and the puzzles of political science are all interrelated. Political scientists need one another's work, and that work is divided into subfields. Political theory, constitutional law, public administration, American government, and comparative government are some of the oldest. More recent additions include political behavior, international relations, methodology, political economy, political organizations, and biopolitics. These may or may not endure; political science changes and evolves.

Men and women constantly make observations about what interests and perplexes them about politics. Political scientists treat these observations as puzzles and set to work to understand them. To do so, they use various approaches, singly or in combination: behavioralism, structural-functionalism, political history, the study of ideas, the study of documents, and models to predict the future.

Political scientists commonly use three kinds of concepts in their work: those that name kinds of structures (such as organization, institution, state); those that name relationships of control (such as power, authority, legitimacy); and those that name certain qualities of daily life that are subject to political determination (such as equality, freedom, order).

An organization is a body of persons working together in a structured way to achieve a specific purpose. An institution is a structure with established functions to perform, roles for carrying out those functions, and rules for how to do so. A state is a structure that has the legal right to make rules that are binding over a given population within a given territory.

Power is a relationship in which control is achieved by threatening and sometimes carrying out severe sanctions for noncompliance with the power holders' wishes. Authority is the right to exercise the power and influence of a given position that comes from having been placed in that position according to accepted procedures. Legitimacy is the condition of being regarded as correctly placed in a particular role and as carrying out the functions of that role correctly. Political equality means an equal right to participate in the political process and to be treated fairly by it. Political freedom means the freedom to dissent without fear of punishment. Political order is the organization of our relationships with one another within a polity.

The language of political science is, by and large, clear and familiar. It is certainly possible to discuss the subject matter of political science clearly—and that is exactly what this book attempts to do in the chapters that follow.

QUESTIONS TO CONSIDER

1. Why is it important to study political science in the context of a changing world?
2. What positive and negative effects of globalization can you think of besides those mentioned in this chapter?
3. Name a puzzle about the world of politics that intrigues you. Which subfield/s of political science does it belong to and which method of those discussed here might be most appropriate to use in studying it?
4. Of the nine concepts of political science discussed in this chapter, which seems the most important to you, and why?

SELECTED READINGS

Beetham, David. *The Legitimation of Power* (Atlantic Highlands, N.J.: Humanities Press International, 1991). Provides an introductory discussion of the concept of legitimacy in contemporary politics.

Castiglione, Dario and Iain Hampsher-Monk. *The History of Political Thought in National Context* (New York: Cambridge University Press, 2001). A team of international contributors explores the relationship between the history of political thought as a discipline and the politics, history and culture of the various nations discussed, which include the United Kingdom, the United States, France, Germany, Italy, and the new democracies of central and eastern Europe.

Cohen, Mitchell and Nicole Fermon, eds. *Princeton Readings in Political Thought* (Princeton, N.J.: Princeton University Press, 1996). A survey of writings on western political thought, each of which has influenced current society and politics.

Edelman, Murray J. *Constructing the Political Spectacle* (Chicago: University of Chicago Press, 1988). An early and now classic examination of political psychology, symbolism in politics, and sociolinguistics.

Freeden, Michael. *Rights* (Minneapolis: University of Minnesota Press, 1995). Examines the evolution of the concept of rights in relation to politics.

Harrison, Lisa. *Political Research: An Introduction* (New York: Routledge, 2001). Covers the key issues involved in doing research in politics, assuming no prior knowledge of the subject. Distinguishes between quantitative and qualitative research and explains why both are useful.

Johnson, Janet Buttolph, Richard A. Joslyn and H. T. Reynolds, eds. *Political Science Research Methods*, 4th ed. (Washington, D.C.: Congressional Quarterly Press, 2001). An examination of political science research techniques, using case studies and ranging from formulation of the questions posed to techniques of statistical analysis and observation.

Lasswell, Harold D. *The Analysis of Political Behavior: An Empirical Approach* (New York: Oxford University Press, 1947). One of the early explanations of behavioralism, by a leading practitioner.

Monroe, Alan D. *Essentials of Political Research* (Boulder, Colo.: Westview Press, 2000). This introductory text explores what one needs to know to be "an effective consumer of scientific research" as well as how to conduct one's own research projects. It contains numerous examples and exercises, presented in an informal style.

Parsons, Wayne. *Public Policy: An Introduction to the Theory and Practice of Policy Analysis* (Gloucestershire, U.K.: Edward Elger, 1995). A detailed study of the theory and practice of public policy; provides a good introduction to the role of government.

Robertson, David, ed. *A Dictionary of Modern Politics: A Comprehensive Guide to the Complex Ideology/Terminology Which Surrounds the World of Politics* (New York: Taylor and Francis, 2002). Includes over 500 definitions and explains ideas and institutions frequently referred to in the media but not always understood by the nonspecialist.

WEB SITES OF INTEREST

1. Political Resources on the Net
   http://www.politicalresources.net/
   Listings of political sites available on the Internet, sorted by country, with links to parties, organizations, governments, media, and more from all around the world.

2. International Forum on Globalization
   http://www.ifg.org
   An alliance of sixty "leading activists, scholars, economists, researchers and writers" representing over sixty organizations in twenty-five nations, focusing on the consequences of globalization as it affects democracy, human welfare, local economies, and the natural world.

NOTES

1. Mark M. Nelson, "Russia's Far East Attracts Intrepid Western Investors," *Central European Economic Review* 2, no. 2 (Spring 1994): 14. As the title of the article suggests, the opportunities Polumordvinov and Levin have depend in large part on the presence of foreign investors—and investments.

2. Lee Hockstader, "Spending Russia's New Money: Lavish Mansions Are Sprouting Next to Communist-Era Hovels," *Washington Post,* 23 June 1994, A18. Not all the rich new capitalists were newly rich; see John Pomfret, "In E. Europe, Old Comrades Are New Rich," *Washington Post,* 30 April 1994, A1, a news story about the ability of former Communist Party members to make the shift to the free enterprise system. ("People who made it in the old regime are going to make it in the new one too.")

3. Michael Specter, "Russia's Elite Scientists Turn High School Tutors," *New York Times,* 25 July 1994, A1.

4. Carey Goldberg, "Husband-Wife Doctors Join Russia's Poor," *Los Angeles Times,* 25 Jan. 1992, A1, A6.

5. Margaret Shapiro, "Moscow's Hard-Luck Flea Markets," *Washington Post,* 15 Feb. 1992, A1, A35.

6. Terence Roth, "Gap Widens Between Winners and Losers," *Central European Economic Review* 2, no. 2 (Spring 1994): 5–7.

7. Fred Weir, "Russian Runaways Find Few Willing to Help Them," *Christian Science Monitor,* 19 Dec. 2001, 7.

8. Fred Weir, "Russia's Bold New Proletariat," *Christian Science Monitor,* 6 Sept. 2001, 6.

9. Michael McFaul, "Ten Years After the Soviet Breakup: A Mixed Record, an Uncertain Future," *Journal of Democracy* 12, no. 4 (2001): 87–94.

10. "The Human Rights Watch Global Report on Women's Human Rights," *Human Rights Watch* (August 1995): 307, 316.

11. Barry Newman, "Women in Poland Find Little Liberation in Shift to Democracy," *Wall Street Journal,* 19 Nov. 1993, 1.

12. Newman, "Women in Poland," pp. 1, A11. Two interesting studies of the impact of globalization on women elsewhere are Saskia Sassen, "Women's Burden: Counter-Geographies of Globalization and the Feminization of Survival," *Journal of International Affairs* 53, no. 2 (Spring, 2000): 503–24 and Ritu Dwan, "Gender Implications of the 'New' Economic Policy," *Women's Studies International Forum* 22, no. 4 (8 July 1999): 425–29. The entire issue of the latter journal is devoted to the study of the different meanings of globalization for women living in different contexts.

13. William Pfaff, "The Complacent Democracies, The International Community and the War in the Former Yugoslavia," *New York Review of Books,* (15 July 1993): 17. The United States, for example, spends only about 1 percent on foreign aid, the lowest percentage of gross national product that any of the developed nations disburses. *Christian Science Monitor,* 5 May 1995, 1, 5.

14. George Moffett, "Despite Threats, America Turns Its Gaze Inward," *Christian Science Monitor,* 5 June 1996, 1, 10.

15. Peter T. Kilborn, "Changes in World Economy on Raw Materials May Doom Many Towns," *New York Times,* 16 Feb. 2002, A1.

16. Ibid., loc. cit.

17. And the French might well find it helpful to ask Americans about how to give women and minorities a fairer chance at the really good jobs in their economy and government.

18. Michael M. Gant and Norman R. Luttbeg, *American Electoral Behavior: 1952–1988* (Itasca, Ill.: Peacock, 1991), and Steven J. Rosenstone and John Mark Hansen, *Mobilization, Participation and Democracy in America* (New York: Macmillan, 1993).

19. William Shakespeare, *Romeo and Juliet,* act 2, sc. 2, lines 43–44.

20. Claude Rivière, *Guinea: The Mobilization of a People,* trans. Virginia Thompson and Richard Adloff (Ithaca, N.Y.: Cornell University Press, 1977).

21. Paul Pierson, "Increasing Returns, Path Dependence, and the Study of Politics," *The American Political Science Review* 94, no. 2 (June 2000): 251–67.

22. On the Soviet constitution, see Robert LeFevre, *Constitutional Government in Soviet Russia: The Constitution of the USSR* (New York: Exposition Press, 1962). On that of the Weimar Republic, see Herbert Kraus, *The Crisis of German Democracy: A Study of the Spirit of the Constitution of Weimar* (Princeton, N.J.: Princeton University Press, 1932).

23. See, for example, Robert S. Alley, *School Prayer: The Court, The Congress, and The First Amendment* (Amherst, N.Y.: Prometheus, 1994).

24. Samuel H. Beer, *Modern Political Development* (Boston: Little, Brown, 1966), p. 25; Immanuel Wallerstein, *The Modern World System*, vols. 1 and 2 (New York: Academic Press, 1980).

25. Joseph L. Klesner, "The End of Mexico's One-Party Regime," *PS, Political Science and Politics* 34, no. 1 (March 2001): 107–14.

26. Max Neiman and Stephen J. Stambough, "Rational Choice Theory and the Evaluation of Public Policy," *Policy Studies Journal* 26, no. 3 (1998): 449–65.

27. The concept of the political system has been most fully developed by David Easton in *A Framework for Political Analysis* (Englewood Cliffs, N.J.: Prentice Hall, 1965). See also his *An Analysis of Political Structure* (New York: Routledge, 1990). For another, more imaginative use, see Karl W. Deutsch, *The Nerves of Government* (New York: The Free Press, 1966).

28. Andrew Heywood, *Political Ideas and Concepts: An Introduction* (New York: St. Martin's Press, 1992).

29. Niccolo Machiavelli, *The Prince* (Cambridge: Cambridge University Press, 1993), written in 1513.

30. Robert Nozick, *Anarchy, State and Utopia* (New York: Basic Books, 1974), p. ix, cited in Will Kymlicka, *Contemporary Political Philosophy* (Oxford and New York: Oxford University Press, 1990), p. 97.

31. Stephen D. Krasner, "Sovereignty," *Foreign Policy* 122 (Jan./Feb. 2001): 20–29.

32. The French, who are perhaps more likely than other peoples to insist on a rational match between what they say and what they do, added an appropriate sovereignty-ceding amendment to their constitution before voting to ratify the EC's Treaty of Maastricht in 1992.

33. Graham E. Fuller, "Redrawing the World's Borders," *World Policy Journal* 14 (Spring 1997): 11–21.

34. Martin N. Marger, *Social Inequality: Patterns and Processes* (Mountain View, Calif.: Mayfield, 1999), p. 205.

35. Robert A. Dahl, *Modern Political Analysis,* 4th ed. (Englewood Cliffs, N.J.: Prentice Hall, 1984), pp. 20–22.

36. Ibid., p. 41.

37. Harold Lasswell and Abraham Kaplan, *Power and Society: A Framework for Political Inquiry* (New Haven, Conn.: Yale University Press, 1950), p. 76; quoted in Dahl, *Analysis*, p. 47, n. 5.

38. "Iraq and the West: When Sanctions Don't Work," *The Economist* (8 April 2000): 23–25.

39. *Wall Street Journal,* 28 July 1995, A1, A4.

40. Denis Diderot, *Political Writings* (Cambridge: Cambridge University Press, 1992), pp. 8–9. From volume one of the *Encyclopedie,* first published in 1751.

41. Zoya Hasan, S. N. Jha, and Rasheeduddin Khan, *The State, Political Processes and Identity: Reflections on Modern India* (New Delhi: Sage, 1989); M. J. Meggitt, "Indigenous Forms of Government Among the Australian Aborigines," *Tot De Tall-, Land-en Volkenkunde* 6, no. 120 (1964): 163–80; Mary L. Volcansek and Jacqueline Lucienne Lafon, *Judicial Selection: The Cross-Evolution of French and American Practices* (New York: Greenwood Press, 1988), p. 110; and Percy R. Luney Jr. and Kazuyuki Takahashi, *Japanese Constitutional Law* (Tokyo: University of Tokyo Press, 1993).

42. Frank L. Wilson, *Concepts and Issues in Comparative Politics: An Introduction to Comparative Analysis* (Upper Saddle River, N.J.: Prentice Hall, 1996), p. 9.

43. Robin Alison Remington examines the role played by rising nationalisms in contemporary Bosnia in "Bosnia, The Tangled Web," *Current History* (Nov. 1993): 364–69.

44. Kenneth Baynes, "Equality and Difference in Democratic Theory," in Ron Bontekoe and Marietta Stepaniants, *Justice and Democracy: Cross-*

Cultural Perspectives (Honolulu: University of Hawai'i Press, 1997), pp. 51–60.

45. C. H. Firth, ed., *The Clarke Papers: Selections from Papers of William Clarke,* vol. 1 (Westminster, U.K.: Nicholos and Sons, 1891), p. 301.

46. Lyman Tower Sargent, *Contemporary Political Ideologies: A Comparative Analysis,* 9th ed. (Belmont, Calif.: Wadsworth, 1993), p. 61. Sargent points out the word *right* also often means *freedom,* referring to specific legally guaranteed freedoms (although it can also mean a basic human or natural right).

47. John Stuart Mill, *On Liberty* (New York: Appleton-Century-Crofts, 1947), p. 43.

48. Ibid., p. 74.

49. Ibid., p. 67.

50. "Nigeria: Anybody Seen a Giant?" in "Nigeria Survey," *The Economist* (21 Aug. 1993): 6–7, and Adrian Karatnycky, *Freedom in the World: The Annual Survey of Political Rights and Civil Liberties* (New York: Freedom House, 1994), pp. 434–37.

51. Cornelius Castoriadis, *Political and Social Writings, Volume Three, 1961–1979: Recommencing the Revolution: From Socialism to the Autonomous Society,* originally published 1973, 1974, and 1979, ed., trans. David Ames Curtis (Minneapolis: University of Minnesota Press, 1993), p. 263.

52. These nine are, of course, only a fraction of the total number of concepts with which political scientists routinely deal. Here I have provided the beginning of an initiation into the language of political science. Throughout the rest of this book, other terms and concepts will be introduced as they are needed.

PART TWO

Shaping Political Thought

Political Ideologies

Sometimes the political questions we ask ourselves are explicit and specific. What is our government's role in providing free education? What policy goals besides the immediate one of fighting terrorism may have been served when the U.S. government gave itself greater powers to wiretap personal conversations, arrest and hold noncitizens without bringing them immediately to trial, and otherwise regulate internal security after the bombing of the World Trade Center in September 2001? What was the role of the international community, if any, in forcing Hugo Chavez from power in Venezuela in April 2002 — and in bringing him back to power two days later? Sometimes, however, we find ourselves thinking about politics in much broader terms, asking much more fundamental and far-reaching questions. Why has our political system taken the form it has? What would be the ideal political system? Would the ideal system be ideal for all peoples, or just for us? How could an ideal system be established?

When we try to find answers to these more fundamental questions, we are involved in an age-old quest, the search for a system of political beliefs. If we are concerned enough to do a little research, we will find a few well-formulated ideologies from which to choose, such as conservatism, liberalism, and socialism. If we are looking for something radically different from the status quo, we may explore the tenets of some of the more extreme ideologies, such as fascism or a branch of religious fundamentalism. Or perhaps the insights of contemporary feminism will seem to cover more of the problems we must deal with today — or the passions of ethnic nationalism will strike us as more relevant than any more comprehensive world view. Some of us will shop around, picking up an idea that makes sense here, another that seems exciting there, and gradually piece together a more or less coherent but still very personal view of political reality and possibilities. Not all of us will become *ideologues.*

WHAT IS AN IDEOLOGY?

Ideology is a word with almost as many definitions as there are people using the term. Most scholars would agree that an ideology attempts to offer answers to at least the first two questions just cited: How have our political systems taken the form they have, and what would be the ideal political system? Beyond this, there is little consensus. Some scholars argue that an ideology must be "accepted as fact or truth by some group," but others believe individuals can have personal ideologies, unshared and unadvertised.[1] Some think an ideology always claims "a monopoly of truth" and thus seeks to "explain everything and in so doing [will] refuse to tolerate rival views or opposing theories," whereas others believe most ideologies leave room for some opposition and point out that in fact a key component of liberalism is its insistence on the importance of the open competition of points of view.[2] Some think an ideology must be revolutionary to merit the name: "The ideologue is a revolutionary, dedicated to the overthrow of the existing system and concerned above all with the means by which this can be accomplished."[3] Others suggest that it is possible for an ideology to be simply a defense of the status quo (in which case its doctrine presumably suggests that the answers to the first and second questions are one and the same and that the other questions are without interest).

A little empirical work suggests that in each of these various controversies "others" are right. Individuals do develop personal, idiosyncratic ideologies; listen to any talk show for an hour or so if you are in doubt. Most ideologies are not entirely closed systems of thought, nor do their supporters claim they are—the very multiplicity of meanings we give to the words *conservative, liberal,* and *socialist* testifies to how far from closed these three dominant ideologies have been.

Similarly, not all ideologies preach revolution. Once a socialist system has been established, socialist ideologues can become strong defenders of the status quo—and of course the chief object of conservatism can be to make sure that nothing changes. (On the other hand, even conservatives can be change oriented when the present system appears unsatisfactory to them and their goal is to establish a more orderly or more libertarian political system.)

Saying that an ideology can be personal or shared with a group, open or closed, and revolutionary or defensive is all well and good, but it does not give us our own working definition; it simply tells us what to leave out of that definition. Let us approach the problem more assertively: An **ideology** is a comprehensive set of beliefs and attitudes about social and economic institutions and processes. It offers a critique of the existing system and a view of the ideal system. Where these differ, it suggests the means for moving from the existing to the ideal. It also presents a theory of human nature and, thereby, of human potentiality and of the need for particular modes of social control.

These various characteristics of all ideologies will become clearer as we discuss specific examples. But before we proceed, note the word that is missing from the preceding paragraph: *political.* All ideologies that merit the name deal extensively with political questions; all ideologies are, in some sense, political ideologies. But not all ideologies are predominantly political ideologies. Because they are comprehensive systems of beliefs and attitudes, they usually have as much to say about economic and social relationships as they do about matters purely political—or even more. When we talk about *political ideologies,* we usually mean that we are stressing the political aspects of ideologies. In this chapter we will be looking at the political tenets of seven systems of belief. Although we will consider some economic and social factors, keep in mind that the range of each ideology considered is far wider than the focus of this discussion permits us to show.

Furthermore, the most important ideas incorporated in the systems of belief that we will be examining are ideas that were conceived long ago. Indeed, most of them have been on the philosophic agenda ever since men and women first began to consider whether the system under which they lived was necessarily the best of all possible systems. On the other hand, political *ideologies* as we know them today did not fully emerge until relatively recent times. The major intellectual, economic, and social upheavals of the past three hundred years have both forced and enabled more of us to take the questions of ideology seriously and to seek new hope in the promise these systems of thought hold for creating a better world.

Finally, we should be aware from the outset that not all these ideologies have shown equal concern for the question that provides the theme of this book, global interdependence. Most of them have something to say, however, about what the relationship between polities should be. Indeed, their approaches to this problem reveal some of the most intriguing and significant differences among them, as I will try to make clear in what follows.

Conservatism

Conservatism is well named. The conservative believes first and foremost in conserving what exists, in the idea that "the accumulated wisdom and experience of the countless generations gone is more likely to be right than the passing fashion of the moment."[4] Thus, conservatives have a certain bias in favor of the existing political system. If change is needed, it should be approached very cautiously: "Man's hopes are high, but his vision is short. Efforts to remedy existing evils usually result in even greater ones."[5]

The conservative view of human nature is not entirely positive and is definitely nonegalitarian. Conservatives believe that some people contribute more than others to society and should therefore be more honored by society.[6] One such honor is the right to positions of political authority. If ordinary people are given the power to rule themselves, they are likely to be intolerant of anyone who does not fit the common mold and to sacrifice the protection of minority rights in order to ensure majority rule.[7] Personal liberty is the individual right conservatives hold most dear, but this does not mean that everyone must be left to pursue his or her own interests with no restraint: "The result will be self-indulgence, anarchy, and a turn toward totalitarianism."[8] It makes sense to use the power of government to support traditional moral standards because "genuinely ordered freedom is the only sort of liberty worth having: freedom made possible by order within the soul and order within the state."[9] But the individual must not, in "the mindless assertion of appetite," depend on the state for security; to do so is to abdicate to the power of the state, to become part of a mass society, and to risk falling prey to tyranny. Self-determination means, on the contrary, "achieving the appropriate fit between personal character and the society's institutional requirements."[10]

Conservatives are divided on the question of international interdependence. Respect for the past and for established institutions, combined with the belief that each nation is an organic whole in which everyone has a place and function, leads naturally to a strong sense of patriotism, if not outright nationalism.[11] Some conservatives do tend to see other nations as threatening the values, confidence, or security of their own land and are likely to place greater trust in military might and action than in seemingly endless diplomatic negotiation.

At the same time, however, conservatives do not entirely deny the fact of interdependence. The staunch defense of imperialist ventures that European conservatives have advanced has traditionally been based on their assertion of the responsibility of the more advanced nations to bring the blessings of civilization to those less fortunate. Such a view emphasizes the dependence of others rather than interdependence, but most contemporary conservatives are willing to go a step further. The need to defend one's own system against external enemies makes it desirable to have external friends. It is important to give aid and comfort to allies, to keep them as allies, and to prevent them from becoming the friends of one's enemies.

Conservatives are sometimes viewed by others as unbending and incapable of compromise, but on many matters they show themselves to be far less dogmatic than supporters of other ideologies. They do not, for example, specify particular institutional forms of government as necessarily better than others, nor do they believe that those who rule must follow a consistent program of domestic and foreign policy. For the conservative, it is far more important that the basic principles of conservatism (order, continuity, loyalty, protection of individual freedoms, piety, and nationalism) be maintained and that those who rule exercise practical wisdom in ensuring that they are. In that sense, conservatives are among the most pragmatic of political thinkers. Andrew Heywood goes so far as to say that "conservatism is the most intellectually modest of political ideologies . . . [it] has prospered because it has been unwilling to be tied down to a fixed system of ideas."[12]

■ **The Development of Conservatism.**   Although conservatism must now contend with a multitude of other ideologies, it is fair to say that for centuries almost all significant thought on political affairs manifested these key characteristics of conservatism. The ideas of conservatism are found in some of the earliest recorded efforts to prescribe political order. Chinese philosophers decided over three thousand years ago that it "was the gentleman's duty to exercise benevolent rule over the small men," that they themselves had worked out "man's most perfect system of government and society," and that the beauties of peace could be "expressed through the word 'flat': no disturbances in the realm, the village, or the home."[13] Confucius (551–479 B.C.E.) gave even greater emphasis to the need for benevolence but never doubted that the superior man (*chun tzu*) must rule and the commoner

Conservatives maintain that "the accumulated wisdom and experience of the countless generations is more likely to be right than the passing fashion of the moment." Contemporary conservative leaders include French and U.S. presidents Jacques Chirac and George Bush, here meeting at the U.N. Conference on Financing for Development (March 2002).
© Reuters NewMedia, Inc./CORBIS

(*hsiao-jen*) must bow before his authority: "The people [should be] like grass, the ruler like the wind."[14]

Similarly, conservative principles informed the thought of Plato (427–347 B.C.E.), who believed that in the ideal state authority rests in the hands of the philosopher-king, an enlightened despot assisted by almost equally enlightened "guardians." Both the Stoics (members of the dominant school of political thought in Greece and Rome as these city-states took on the attributes of empires) and the early Christians argued that human beings were basically equal but stressed nevertheless the duty of obedience to a divinely ordered government.[15] Augustine (C.E. 354–430) saw a firm government as the only possible earthly corrective to the sinful nature of humankind since its fall from grace; for Thomas Aquinas (1225–1274) the highest law was God's law, and a just king was one who ruled according to that law.[16] In the period of the Renaissance and Reformation, writers such as Bodin, Grotius, Machiavelli, Richard Hooker, and Thomas Hobbes all insisted that the state was sovereign and absolute.

However, by the time of Hooker (1553–1600) and Hobbes (1588–1679), new ideas were beginning to challenge even the most fundamental beliefs of conservatism. The Protestant Reformation seemed to threaten not only the Roman Catholic church but also the divine right of monarchs to absolute ascendancy in civil matters, a power given the blessings of that church. When theological radicals began to raise disturbing doubts, conservative appeals to order and obedience were used to defend royal authority against political dissidents as well as against those who wished to establish a new religion.

Nevertheless, the intellectual ferment continued into the seventeenth and eighteenth centuries and reached its climax in 1789, when the French Revolution brought about the collapse of an entire feudal, agrarian, and aristocratic order. British statesman and writer Edmund Burke (1729–1797) watched in horror as an established order crumbled and a new system emerged. This arch-conservative believed society is an organism to which everyone belongs and that institutions that have evolved within that organism, in response to national characteristics and conditions, could no more be casually cut away without jeopardy to the life of that organism than could the internal organs of any other creature.[17]

Across the Atlantic a new nation, the United States, was being forged after its own revolution. Yet many of the Americans who had accepted the idea that armed overthrow of an oppressive Britain was unavoidable nevertheless wrote in the conservative tradition. John Adams, Alexander Hamilton, and Fisher Ames all warned against carrying revolution to the dangerous point of establishing a mass democracy. As the nation did in fact slowly but inexorably democratize, leading conservatives like Daniel Webster feared that the extension of the right to vote would inevitably endanger the right to property. Southern conservatives had a different concern; in *Sociology for the South* (1854), George Fitzhugh saw the relationship between master and slave as one between natural leader and follower, a relationship "of mutual good will," in which the "whole life of the slaveholder" is spent in "providing for the minutest wants of others, taking care of them in sickness and in health." [18]

Defense of slavery was no more viable a stand than the effort to forestall democratic government had been, but toward the end of the nineteenth century, as the Western world became increasingly industrialized and great fortunes were amassed, conservative authors found a new and more popular cause, the glorification of the acquisition of wealth. An Englishman, Herbert Spencer, preached the doctrine of Social Darwinism—that is, that social and economic competition was natural, part of the process of ensuring that the fit should survive, and on the whole better for society even if it meant suffering for those less fit. The American clergyman Russell H. Conwell was more optimistic and believed that everyone could gain. "It is your duty to get rich," he told his countrymen.[19]

As should by now be clear, the substance of conservatism shifts with time and place. That which is to be protected varies according to the threats that are posed. In the early twentieth century, the welfare state became the favored target and conservatives fought for the rights of workers and employers to continue to make their own contracts, without risk of intervention by a state bent on protecting workers. U.S. President Herbert Hoover insisted even after the Great Depression of 1929 and his failure to win reelection in 1932 that "voluntary agencies" were the answer to the suffering caused by widespread unemployment. "I do not feel," he said, "that I should be charged with lack of human sympathy for those who suffer. . . . I am confident that our people have the resources, the initiative, the courage, the stamina, and the kindliness of spirit to meet this situation in the way they have met their problems over generations."[20]

At present, some of the most powerful parties in Europe and North America express the typical conservative concern for preserving traditional institutions (especially family, church, and nation-state) and traditional values (especially hard work, personal responsibility, and patriotism).[21] The U.S. Republican Party, the British Conservatives, and the French Neo-Gaullists are all examples of this kind of party. In many nations, the writings of neoconservative scholars and journalists are given close attention and neoconservative organizations and clubs have formed, sometimes to support such parties, sometimes to demand that conservative principles be carried further than the practical politicians are willing to do.[22]

Liberalism

The chief difference between conservatism and **liberalism** is the view each takes of human nature. Where the conservative is at best cautiously hopeful that the ordinary person will, in a well-ordered state, manifest the admirable characteristics of loyalty, patriotism, and piety, the liberal takes a much more egalitarian view. The liberal believes that human beings—all human beings—are capable of reason and rational action, but that they are often caught in difficult situations in real life. People are not born equal, but everyone has the capacity to live a satisfactory and productive life if given the chance. An essential role of government is to ensure that all citizens have the opportunity to develop their skills and abilities, whatever they may be.[23]

Such a view of human nature virtually guarantees that the liberal will be optimistic about the possibility of improving a particular political system and will expect the ordinary citizen to play an important role in bringing about such an improvement. The liberal is seldom a revolutionary, however, and never imagines that progress is inevitable. Given the positive attributes of human nature, it is worthwhile to try, but the outcome is uncertain.

Furthermore, progress cannot and should not be forced on an unwilling populace. The responsibility of people in power is to make it possible for all men and women to exercise reason, work for a better life, and make their own important choices. The liberal hopes that their choices will be wise, but individual liberty includes the right to make choices that work against one's own interests.

Liberalism, as may begin to be clear, is a difficult and sometimes ambiguous creed. It suggests that government should intervene to "help" but never to "curb freedom." In practice, it is often difficult to accomplish the one without the other. Liberalism says that ordinary men and women are entitled to satisfactory lives, but that individual liberties, including the right to prosper from one's efforts, should not be curtailed. This same ambivalence is apparent in the liberal approach to the question of interdependence, both among individuals and among nations. People and polities are interdependent and must show a humane concern for one another, but at the same time the individual person or state has the right to pursue individual interests. When these goals conflict, liberals (like conservatives) are content to look for pragmatic solutions according to the circumstances rather than to spell out one specific way to establish the ideal social system.

■ **The Development of Liberalism.**   The liberal view of human nature also had its early proponents. At a mass funeral in 430 B.C.E. for warriors killed in the Peloponnesian War, Pericles asserted the Athenian belief that everyone is capable of free and rational deliberation. "If few of us are originators, we are all sound judges of a policy. The great impediment to action is, in our opinion, not discussion, but the want of that knowledge which is gained by discussion preparatory to action." [24] Some three hundred years later, the Stoic orator Marcus Tullius Cicero (106–43 B.C.E.) argued that "there is no difference in kind between man and man," that reason "is certainly common to us all," and that this quality not only "raises us above the level of the beast" but makes us capable of figuring out the "principles of right living" that have been implanted in us by "nature." [25] And in China in the fourth century B.C.E. the philosopher Mencius taught that "every human being can become a sage-king"—that is, that anyone can gain the wisdom needed to rule. [26]

The argument that everyone has the right to exercise independent judgment in at least some domains of life, and sufficient reason to do so adequately, was strongly advanced by the Protestant Reformation. Although the Judeo-Christian tradition had always stressed an element of free choice (virtue consists in willing and believing in the right, not simply giving in to force or custom), the Protestants went further. Believers could figure out for themselves how to achieve personal salvation by relying on the sacred writings of the church, so long as these scriptures were explicated by trained theologians. If they could manage that, argued such liberal Protestant philosophers as John Locke (1632–1704) and Jean Jacques Rousseau (1712–1778), then they could certainly judge for themselves as well in the matters of worldly affairs. In fact, both Locke and Rousseau were sure that they had done so in the past. Both believed that men and women had once lived in a "state of nature" and had decided to improve their lot by making a social contract, an agreement to create a political society and thus to order human affairs more satisfactorily.[27] They argued, however, that a contract is binding only as long as all parties adhere to its terms and only on condition that individual rights and liberties were maintained. If they were not, then the ones who governed had "put themselves into a state of war with the people, who are thereupon absolved from any further obedience."[28]

If the term *contract* strikes you as interestingly businesslike, you have picked up a clue to the reason the ideas of Locke and Rousseau and their various followers proved to have such wide appeal in the eighteenth and nineteenth centuries. The massive transformations in people's relationships that took place with the decline of feudalism, the birth of capitalism, and the onset of the Industrial Revolution stimulated the adherents of liberalism (as it had those of conservatism) to develop their arguments into a more formal ideology. What did these changes have to do with liberal thought? As Box 2.1 shows, they produced conditions that made the tenets of liberalism newly appealing—both to the worker seeking a freer and better life than could be found in agriculture and to the industrial employer seeking freedom of investment and a mobile labor force.

This era of new appreciation for liberal values produced its own crop of ideologues. David Hume (1711–1776), Adam Smith (1723–1790), Jeremy Bentham (1748–1832), and John Stuart Mill (1806–1873) spoke variously of "the greatest good for the greatest number," the benevolent guidance of "the unseen hand of the market" (or "laissez faire economics"), and "utilitarianism," but the underlying message was the same: Pursuing individual interests freely and rationally would lead to the best of all social systems. The role of government was to protect the weak while leaving the strong as free as possible to carry out their business.[29]

As we have already seen, the dual responsibility liberals assign to government is often difficult to fulfill, and as the Industrial Revolution went forward the humming machinery set up by the strong seemed to drown out the faint cries of the weak. Sweatshops, child labor, and intolerable working conditions became the order of the day. But was all this really liberalism in action? Some early twentieth-century liberals such as John Dewey claimed that it was not, that the plight of the common citizen had been forgotten by those who were in power and made the subject of revolutionary rabble-rousing by those who were not, whereas the true liberal stood resolutely for trust in reason, belief in progress, sympathy for the downtrodden, and protection of individual liberty. Others, such as sociologist Leonard Hobhouse and economist John Maynard Keynes, began to argue that under the new

BOX 2.1
**How the Decline
of Feudalism
Stimulated the
Rise of Liberalism**

1. Evolving human technology and science, combined with the wealth accumulated from successful warfare, made it possible for Europeans to engage in global exploration and conquest.
2. Lands newly conquered, farmed by peoples newly conquered (often slaves), provided highly profitable crops.
3. The move into new environments stimulated human inventiveness.
4. High profits provided capital for investment in the development of new inventions to make new kinds of goods out of new kinds of raw materials.
5. The result was the large-scale development of machined goods— the Industrial Revolution— and of a new workplace, the factory.
6. Because factories tended to cluster where the import and export of goods was easiest, required workers, and paid workers more than they could earn in agriculture, more people moved to the city and urbanization accompanied industrialization.
7. As workers moved off the farm, old communal bonds loosened and broke; individual workers moved out on their own, seeking a freer and better life, but often found only long hours of labor in a confined and dangerous setting.
8. At the same time, a new freedom beckoned those with capital to invest. If government could be kept from interfering, there seemed to be no limits to capitalist entrepreneurship. Any human need might be met with a new product, and any amount of wealth might be acquired by meeting those needs.
9. The new era's promises of progress, freedom, and the redistribution of wealth appealed to almost everyone but were unequally kept. The tenets of liberalism addressed both the hopes and the disappointments that were so keenly felt.

circumstances a more interventionist role for government in the economy was essential, that laissez faire economics could no longer ensure the conditions in which true liberal values could flourish. Still others clung to the belief that Smith was right, that the market, if not disturbed by wrong-headed reformism, would ultimately resolve all inequities, and that this was what liberalism most essentially meant.

By and large, the latter interpretation of liberalism has prevailed in Europe, but in the United States the problem of assigning a fixed meaning to the term has been yet further compounded over the past few decades. In the first half of the twentieth century, the Dewey-Hobhouse-Keynes interpretation of what it means to be a liberal clearly prevailed and won new adher-

BOX 2.2
**How the Word
Liberal Came to
Have Opposite
Meanings in the
United States and
Europe**

Classical liberalism says government must "help" the unfortunate and yet must also "protect freedom."

Some early liberals placed the emphasis on the freedom of the market and gave less attention to helping the poor. Contemporary European liberals have followed this tradition.

Other early liberals placed the emphasis on helping, and saw protecting freedom more as a matter of protecting individual liberties of speech and association. Contemporary American liberals have followed this tradition.

Contemporary Americans who place great emphasis on the freedom of the market think of themselves as conservatives. Because they disagree with contemporary Americans who call themselves liberals, they never think of themselves as liberals at all. Nevertheless, Europeans call this kind of conservative a liberal. And Americans call the European kind of liberal a conservative.

Now is that perfectly clear?

ents, particularly under the leadership of presidents Franklin Roosevelt, Harry Truman, and John Kennedy. Gradually, however, the word *liberal* has been slowly stripped of almost all its meanings except the idea of "sympathy for the downtrodden" and "government interventionism"—in short, the welfare state. In the increasingly market-oriented United States, *liberal* is now often used as a critical term to deplore the beliefs of those whom most Europeans would probably call "social democratic"—and the Americans who use it that way often have beliefs that most Europeans would say are "liberal" (but that they themselves call "conservative"). If you find this confusing, rest assured that so do Americans and Europeans who try to talk to each other about liberalism. Box 2.2 suggests that the problem has its amusing side; however, the inability of the world's most powerful and most consistently interdependent economic powers to develop a common usage of so vital a term no doubt does impede the ability of their citizens to understand one another and may not really be so laughable.

However, despite the present semantic confusion and oversimplification, the ideas of liberalism—*all* the ideas—still find their supporters as a new century begins. Political parties and groups that accept existing economic and constitutional structures but nevertheless struggle to enhance minimum standards of living and individual rights, to foster popular participation in policymaking, or to fight for consumer protection are all examples of the contemporary staying power of liberalism. And as we have shown, those who are in favor of eliminating excessive government regulations are also really in the liberal tradition.

The leading conservative parties of today have brought Hume, Smith, Bentham, and Mill into their own pantheon. When European journalists refer to past U.S. presidents George Bush and Ronald Reagan, or to House Speaker Newt Gingrich, as economic liberals, they are not confused—they are right.

Socialism

For socialists, the most important characteristic of human nature is each individual's natural sociability. Socialists believe that human beings readily engage in cooperative social activity when given a chance. Unfortunately, some individuals have selfishly established structures of control that make it impossible for this natural cooperative instinct to flourish. These structures have become progressively more oppressive, causing ever greater human suffering. The ideology of **socialism** evolved out of concern for the suffering caused by human exploitation of other humans.

Socialists have traditionally been critical of existing social systems, certain that better systems could be established and determined that an important characteristic of any new system would be the limitation, if not complete abolition, of private property. The possibility of acquiring unlimited private property, argues the socialist, has stimulated the greed that causes some people to exploit others and at the same time causes the people who are exploited to endure their lot, hoping thus to obtain a better share of the world's goods. The only solution is to enlarge the public domain dramatically, establishing a community in which the land, the factories, and perhaps all the means of production are owned by the state. The state itself should be controlled by the workers, who should use their new power to guarantee a job and a fair share of the national largesse to every citizen. Above all, human want and suffering must not be allowed to continue.

The word *socialism* covers a wide range of beliefs. Despite their agreement on the need to eliminate suffering by limiting private property, socialists disagree sharply on such matters as whether revolutionary methods will be required to set up the ideal system; whether a socialist revolution will necessarily be worldwide; what conditions make revolution possible; how extensive the limitations on private property should be; how large the ideal socialist community should be; and what roles, if any, government and the state should play.

■ **The Development of Socialism.**   Although in most respects a conservative, Plato recommended the abolition of private property, at least among the ruling class (his guardians "will not rend the community asunder by applying that word *mine* to different things"). Similar themes can be found in the writings of some medieval philosophers such as Tommaso Campanella and Sir Thomas More, and in the arguments of early dissenters such as Oliver Cromwell and Gerrard Winstanley.[30]

The actual practice of various forms of socialism was also widespread long before the doctrine was articulated by Western philosophers. The small community in which land and its produce are collectively owned is in fact the oldest form of social organization and continues even today among some indigenous peoples such as the Quechua of Peru and the Paez of Colombia.[31]

Here again, the development of early musings and matter-of-fact practices into a well-articulated ideology begins with the Industrial Revolution. The same forces that compelled conservatives to formulate their ideas in defense of traditional ways, and liberals to express their belief that freedom and social justice could be combined, produced conditions that stimulated socialists to organize their thoughts and set forth manifestos of their widely ranging beliefs. Those who began the process have come to be known as *utopian socialists*. The French philosopher Henri Comte de Saint-Simon (1760–1825) argued that "the elementary needs of life are the most imperative" and that those "whose work is of positive utility to society"—specifically, scientists, artists, and artisans—should be placed in charge. His countryman Charles Fourier (1772–1837) stressed the importance of community and recommended the formation of small voluntary associations of producers. The Englishman Robert Owen (1771–1858) preached a similar sermon and furthermore practiced what he preached, providing the workers in his textile mills with inexpensive housing, food, and education and urging them to develop their moral and intellectual faculties and to work together for their common good in their own community. The utopian socialists believed the changes they recommended could be effected peacefully and cooperatively, through an evolutionary process.[32]

However, Karl Marx (1818–1883) found such recommendations naive and uninformed. He believed it was a waste of time to appeal to the consciences of the capitalists who profited from the status quo. Marx and his collaborator, Friedrich Engels (1820–1895), developed a much more complex and elaborate version of socialist ideology, which they termed **communism** and others have come to label Marxism.[33] (See Figure 2.1.)

To explain how the present system had developed, Marx took his cue from the dialectical method of G. W. F. Hegel (1770–1831).[34] However, where Hegel saw dialectical evolution taking place in the realm of ideas, Marx found it in material conditions, inventing what others were later to call **dialectical materialism.** Human history was, he asserted, moving through five stages of economic organization: communalism, slavery, feudalism, capitalism and, finally, communism. Each stage was characterized by a different dominant mode of production, and the social system was determined by who owned the means of production. According to Marx, the fourth stage, capitalism, would inevitably be replaced by a fifth, final, and climactic stage

FIGURE 2.1
Marx's Five Stages
of Economic
Organization

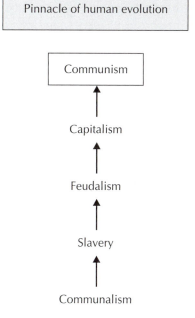

of human evolution, *communism*, in which all the productive advantages of the earlier stages would be retained but control over the means of production would be restored to the people who did the producing, the workers. At this point, Engels claimed, the state would "wither away" and government would consist of no more than "the mere administration of things."[35]

Marx argued that a chief feature of the three intermediate stages between primitive communalism and communism was that society was divided into two classes, those who owned the means of production and those who did not. The owners used their power not only for immediate economic gain but also to establish a political system that would endorse and defend their economic control over others. Class struggle was the inevitable by-product of noncommunal control of the means of production. The state and the dominant political ideology were merely the *superstructure* erected on a base of economic power: "The ruling ideas of each age have ever been the ideas of its ruling class."[36]

According to Marx, the final transition, from capitalism to communism, was inevitable. Capitalists would be certain to carry the exploitation of labor to the point where no one would be able to buy the goods produced, the market would shrink, the less aggressive capitalists would be forced into the ranks of the ever more exploited proletarian workers, and the workers would become aware that their only recourse was to abolish the system of private property. Because capitalism had become an international network of greed and exploitation (the Marxist viewpoint on the nature of interdependence in a capitalist world), the revolution would spread from nation to nation. The triumph of communism would be complete. "Let the ruling classes tremble. . . . The proletarians have nothing to lose but their chains. They have a world to win." [37]

Coming as it did at the height of the abuses of the Industrial Revolution, **Marxism** has had a powerful appeal from the start. Following its precepts, Vladimir Lenin (1878–1924) and his fellow Marxists worked to bring about the Russian Revolution of October 1917, adapting the Marxist prescription to fit the Russian reality. Lenin's major contributions to Marxist theory were the propositions that a Communist revolution was possible even in a state that, like Russia, had been only partially industrialized; that imperialism extended the life of capitalism by developing supplementary markets and a new source of cheap labor and material; that the revolution would have to be the work of a small "vanguard" party of dedicated and informed revolutionaries who would take it upon themselves to act in the interests of the proletariat at first; and that the first stage of the revolution would produce a socialist system, in which the apparatus of the state would still be necessary, whereas true communism (and the withering away of the state) would appear only when it was finally possible to introduce the formula of "from each according to his ability—to each according to his needs." [38]

Lenin agreed with Marx that as soon as the spark of revolution was ignited in one country, the Communist revolution would become international. But his successor, Joseph Stalin (1879–1953), countered that "socialism in one nation" was possible—a necessary adjustment given the apparent reluctance of workers elsewhere to follow the Russian example.[39] Stalin also proceeded to establish one of the most ruthless dictatorships of the twentieth century, making imitation of the Soviet model less and less likely. His own successor, Nikita Khrushchev (1894–1971), attacked the "cult of the individual" that Stalin had set up and accepted the idea that communism could take different forms in different states.[40] The final attempt to adjust the meanings of communism in the Soviet Union proved to carry within it the seeds of the downfall of the entire political system. When Mikhail Gorbachev came to power on March 11, 1985, he introduced the idea of *perestroika* ("restructuring"), which included plans for economic reform, technological modernization, improved living standards, and, most significantly, the principle of *glasnost. Glasnost* means "openness," and by including it in *perestroika,* Gorbachev was saying that the Soviet version of Communist ideology should henceforth include a much greater readiness to hear all points of view. The Soviet people responded with enthusiasm, and for a time it seemed the new leader's hopes that the deeply suffering Soviet economy could be brought back to life by strong injections of personal liberty might be well founded. But the medicine proved stronger than the system itself could bear, and the 1991–1992 collapse of the Soviet Union was the result.

At the same time that the cult of the individual was being repudiated in the Soviet Union under Khrushchev, the People's Republic of China was establishing its own experiment with communism under the ever more personal guidance of Mao Zedong (1893–1976). The need to build a strong military arm while raising the level of consciousness of vast numbers of illiterate and uneducated peasants prompted Mao to make his own contributions to Communist dogma. It was Mao who explained how guerrilla warfare could be an instrument of political change as well as a tool of military takeover, how a "massline" of action could be developed by reconciling what the masses will support with what the party thinks they should support, and how economic backwardness could be overcome by encouraging the people to draw on their own common sense and experience rather than relying on foreign models.[41]

The years following Mao's death in 1976 were characterized less by ideological development than by a general relaxing of ideological rigor, combined with a repudiation of the worst forms of repression endured during Mao's reign. But relaxation was not to be overdone. In 1979, the party reminded the people that everyone must uphold the four fundamental principles of Chinese communism: socialism, single-party leadership, the dictatorship of the proletariat, and Marxism-Leninism as modified by Mao Zedong. And when mass demonstrations on behalf of democratic reform were held in Tiananmen Square in Beijing and elsewhere throughout the nation in 1989, the response was a brutal massacre that left hundreds of peaceful demonstrators dead and the watching world appalled. Post-Tiananmen developments in the Chinese political system will be discussed in later chapters; here we conclude this brief look at Chinese communism by noting that over 1 billion people—or approximately one out of every five presently living persons—are still living under this form of Communist ideology.

At its height, communism was the official ideology of sixteen nations, ranging alphabetically from Albania to Yugoslavia, and geographically from Cuba to North Korea, and exerted a strong influence in the political systems of many other nations, where Communist parties kept the dogma alive and constantly sought the means to take control.[42] However, as the number of Communist nations and parties grew, so did the laments of those socialists who saw little if any similarity between the ideology they believed in and the practice of the so-called Communist states. Calling themselves **democratic socialists** or just plain socialists (and called revisionists or rightwing counter-revolutionaries by Soviet Communists), they developed a much more moderate form of socialist ideology.

One of the earliest and most effective democratic socialist movements was the Fabian Society, founded in 1888 in England by Beatrice Webb (1858–1943) and Sidney Webb (1859–1947). This group of concerned students and intellectuals rejected the idea of a desperate conflict that could be ended only by a workers' revolution but did believe that the owners of capital had become "merely the recipients of profits, interest and rent" always seeking to stifle competition and that they should be replaced by hired managers, permitting profits not needed for reinvestment to be used to address public needs. The Fabians' approach was to use reason and argument; their members wrote a series of essays that had considerable influence, and the society, which continues to the present day, played a key role in the formation of the British Labour Party.[43]

In other nations of western Europe, similar groups of intellectuals broke away from Communist parties too closely aligned with the Soviets and formed their own labor or socialist parties. These more moderate socialists usually have the following beliefs in common:

1. Contemporary society is based on the class struggle.
2. The ideal society is one in which workers control the state.
3. Revolution is not essential to achieve that ideal.
4. The chief task is to organize the working class, develop its consciousness, and give it a voice in local and national government.

Such socialist parties have taken power in several European polities and shared in coalition governments in others. Their records of accomplishment are mixed, but they distinguish themselves from their former Communist cousins in one important respect: They always make unambiguously clear their willingness to submit to the results of democratic elections, whatever those results may be.

Several more contemporary ideologies also fit unambiguously into the broad domain of socialist thought. *African socialism,* a body of thought developed by African writers and leaders in the postcolonial years, incorporates a desire to maintain the traditional communalism of small African polities with the more modern concern to wrest power from an oppressive class and restore it to the working class. In Tanzania this non-Marxist socialism is known as *ujamaa* ("familyhood") and has been written about extensively by that nation's former president, Julius Nyerere.[44] The Israeli *kibbutz,* a settlement in which all property is collectively owned and all labor collectively employed, yet the power of the collectivity is nonetheless limited by "the individual's legitimate and essential autonomy," is perhaps the closest modern version of the anarchist socialist's dream of a self-sufficient community.[45]

What, then, does socialism mean today? Shortly after the fall of commu-

Gerhard Schroeder and Tony Blair, two European leaders of democratic socialist parties, shown at the December 7, 2002, meeting of the European Summit. Democratic socialists believe that if everyone is given a voice in government, socialist goals can be attained without revolution.
© Nice-Matin/Imapress/The Image Works

nism in the Soviet Union, a conference of American professors attempted to formulate an answer. Socialism means, they decided, that there will be "(1) no exploitation of man by man, (2) a comprehensive guarantee of social-economic rights, (3) concern for equality, (4) collective ownership, and (5) communal participation in the disposal of resources."[46] More recent developments have led some to argue that ideological demands for a fully socialist system are now out of the question—"there is no alternative to mixed economies, with ever-changing relations between public and private sectors, and with social minimums and safety nets," says Arno Mayer. Along these lines, John Roemer recommends a new form of mixed economy, one he calls "market socialism" in which money will be divided into two forms: "commodity money" to be used for ordinary consumer goods and "share money" that would be distributed equally and used only for buying ownership rights in firms.[47]

In any case, the socialist dream is far from dead, and as the dust of do-it-yourself democratization and marketization raised in the post-1989 revolutions slowly settles we are likely to see more and more systematic efforts to bring this ideology into keeping with contemporary reality. It is still too soon to say whether any of these efforts is likely to prove a sure and certain guide to the Moldavian mother, the Romanian mayor, or the Polish deputy who must meanwhile face the challenges of the present.

Fascism

Conservatism, liberalism, and socialism are all concerned with the problem of how a political system can best serve the needs of the citizens who compose it. They may all become distorted in practice into apologies for systems of exploitation, but all at least give lip service to the idea that what matters most is the lot of the citizen. Not so fascism. **Fascism** is predicated on the belief that what matters most is the nation itself. This ideology begins with the argument that citizens can prosper only when the nation prospers, but it carries this argument so far that the fate of the citizens becomes secondary to that of the nation they live in. Fascism is nationalism carried to the extreme.

Like conservatives, fascists think that some human beings are naturally better than others, but for fascists being better is not a matter of social class or circumstance but of race and nationality: If one person is better than others, it is because that person belongs to the "right" race or is a citizen of the "right" nation. There are, however, two qualities shared by all humankind. In the first place, all human beings are motivated by their emotions, not by their reason. According to the French historian Ernest Renan (1823–1892), later quoted approvingly by Benito Mussolini, the fascist leader of Italy during World War II, "To expect reason directly from the people and through the people is a chimera." [48] Second, everyone is struggling to survive. The quest for self-preservation motivates us all. For the fascist, this fundamental human condition does not suggest the need for cooperative arrangements, acknowledging our interdependence and seeking the fairest possible distribution of the world's goods. On the contrary, the fascist agrees with Adolf Hitler that in such a world, "if men wish to live, then they are forced to kill others. . . . On earth and in the universe force alone is decisive. Whatever goal man has reached is due to his originality plus his brutality. . . . Struggle is the father of all things in this world." [49]

Given these characteristics of humanity, the greatest good that could be achieved would be for superior people to put themselves in the service of an organization that would permit them to engage in this perpetual struggle on the best possible terms. Such an organization is the fascist state, engaged in perpetual warfare. If the present system is such a state, there is no higher destiny than to commit oneself to its service. If it is not, the individual's task is to help bring that state into being. In serving their nation, fascists serve themselves, because only thus are they able to protect themselves from others, and only thus can they hope to impose their own dominion in a world where everyone is engaged in a ruthless battle to take the largest possible share of life's rewards, regardless of the needs of others.

The fascist state is characterized by absolute discipline ("No dogma! Discipline suffices," was Mussolini's slogan in the early days), by a ruling party, and above all by submission to the leader. Glorification of the leader is carried to the ultimate extreme: "Mussolini is always right," was one of the ten points in the Italian Fascists' Decalogue, and under Hitler the German National Socialist Party (the Nazis) stated that "the authority of the Führer is complete and all-embracing; it unites in itself all the means of political direction, it extends into all fields of national life, it embraces the entire people, which is bound to the Führer in loyalty and obedience."[50] In such a system all human interactions, including economic exchange, come under the sway of the state and the leader. Industry is nationalized or heavily regulated, not to benefit the workers but to benefit the nation (hence the German term *national socialism*). One Italian fascist wrote that "there cannot be any single economic interests which are above the general economic interests of the State." All industry is to be organized into "corporations"—guilds composed of employers and employees who work in the same branch of industry. "Through these corporations the State may at any time that it deems fit, or that the need requires, intervene within the economic life of the individual to let the supreme interests of the nation have precedence over his private, particular interests, even to the point where his work, his savings, his whole fortune may need to be pledged, and if absolutely necessary, sacrificed."[51]

■ **The Development of Fascism.**   Although fascism has roots in the thinking of nineteenth-century nationalists and in the work of Friedrich Hegel, it did not come into its own until after World War I, when fascist movements emerged in both Italy and Germany. Although these nations had been on opposite sides in that struggle, both faced similar conditions afterward: high rates of inflation, high rates of unemployment, and large numbers of veterans returning from the war who had to be reassimilated into a peacetime economy. In fact, such conditions were endemic in western Europe at the time, but Italy and Germany had two further characteristics in common that other nations were fortunately spared: Neither had been a nation for very long (Italy was unified in 1861, Germany in 1871), and in each nation a young fanatic with the ability to move others with powerful oratory stood ready to capitalize on the situation and use it as a means of raising himself to power. Mussolini and Hitler were able to persuade both the angry workers and the industrialists frightened by that anger (and the talk of socialism that accompanied it) that the answer to the problems of Italians and Germans alike was a fascist state.

Although there are numerous historical parallels for fascist practice, the Italians and Germans were the first to elevate such practices to the heights of "philosophy." Since World War II, no nation has openly espoused fascism, but numerous groups and parties have openly or indirectly done so. Many

Far-right movements have been on the rise in Europe. Here German neo-Nazis parade past the Brandenburg Gate in Berlin on March 12, 2000, chanting anti-foreigner slogans and expressing support for Austrian far-right leader Joerg Haider on the anniversary of the 1938 Nazi annexation of Austria.
AP/Wide World Photos

of these organizations are found in the industrialized nations of Europe, in small far-right parties or groups whose leaders call for racial purity, fanatic nationalism, and undeviating loyalty to themselves. The appearance—and terrorist activities—of neo-Nazi groups in Germany itself has dismayed the world and the vast majority of German citizens (although German judges have been criticized for being unduly lenient with cases brought to court).[52] The National Front party in France, headed by far-right extremist Jean-Marie Le Pen, bases its appeal to voters on a stridently anti-immigrant campaign, claiming that most of France's economic problems are the result of the large number of Arab workers admitted during the full-employment era of the 1960s and early 1970s. Le Pen's blatant racism (which he constantly reiterates and just as constantly denies) brings him public condemnation; however, throughout the 1980s and most of the 1990s his party was the leading party of protest for disillusioned Frenchmen and women, and the vote for this modern version of an ugly past steadily climbed, reaching as high as 15 percent.[53]

Highly disciplined rightwing terrorist movements seeking to undermine democratic states, secret paramilitary groups defending dictators from those who would assert constitutional rights, and religious cults insisting that the divinity of their leaders legitimizes their denial of basic individual rights and liberties to their followers are other sad reminders that fascist principles can still find expression.

IS AN *ISM* ALWAYS AN IDEOLOGY?

Conservatism, liberalism, socialism, and fascism are all commonly accepted as ideologies. They meet the terms we set out at the beginning of this chapter: An ideology is a comprehensive set of beliefs and attitudes about social and economic institutions and processes. It offers a critique of the existing system and a view of the ideal system. Where these differ, it suggests the means for moving from the existing to the ideal. It also presents a theory of human nature, and, thereby, of human potentiality and of the need for particular modes of social control.

Today, however, political thought is moving in new directions—or moving with surprising passion in directions that are very, very old. Feminism, ethnic nationalism, and religious fundamentalism are three ways of thinking about politics that have achieved remarkable importance in the past few decades, often making our more conventional approaches seem out of date, perhaps irrelevant. More recently, environmentalism (or ecologism) has been seen by some as itself a new kind of ideology.[54]

To what extent are these newly powerful *isms* true ideologies? To what extent are they simply effective ways for groups to assert threatened or never-realized identities or to fight for goals that have assumed new urgency in the minds of many?[55] The only way to find out is to put them to the test, one by one, examining the beliefs and attitudes of each and determining whether these do in fact constitute "a comprehensive set of beliefs and attitudes about social and economic institutions and processes." Here we make that effort with the first three: feminism, ethnic nationalism, and religious fundamentalism. Keep in mind that even if we find that one or more is not a true ideology, each of these ways of thinking about politics has nonetheless assumed enormous importance in recent years.

Feminism

To begin with, we may say that all feminists believe that women are at least the equals of men, that they deserve equal inclusion in society, and that they have been denied that status for centuries of human history.[56] Such a belief is, of course, profoundly political, if not in itself fully ideological. In fact, early feminists were not seeking to create a new ideology; they wanted to modify those that did exist, especially liberalism and Marxist socialism, in ways that would make them inclusive of women. Those who worked in the liberal tradition typically stressed the need for women as well as men to gain greater individual rights and equality of opportunity. One of the earliest liberal feminist tracts was *A Vindication of the Rights of Women* by Mary Wollstonecraft, published in 1779; another was Harriet Taylor's *The Enfranchisement of Women* on which her husband, John Stuart Mill, based his own *The Subjection of Women* (which, of course, things being as they were, became far better known).[57] In the twentieth century, Betty Friedan (*The Feminine Mystique*, 1963) and Alice S. Rossi ("Sentiment and Intellect," 1970) have been among those also identified as liberal revisionists.[58]

Others have approached the problem of the oppression of women from the perspective of Marxist socialism. In theory at least, Marxism also gave some attention to the oppression of women from the very beginning: Friedrich Engels, Karl Marx's collaborator (see above, pp. 58–59), explained in 1884 how in a class society women were oppressed in the home just as the proletariat (presumably male) was outside the home, both by the ruling bourgeoisie.[59] More contemporary Marxist feminists include Claudia von Werlhof, interested in all workers who are either unpaid (mostly women) or earning only subsistence wages (men and women, mostly in the Third World); and Maria Mies, who has studied the impact of capitalist roles and technologies on poor rural women in India.[60]

If all feminists could be identified as revisionist liberals or Marxists, we could stop right here and say, sorry, this may be very important, but it is not a distinct ideology. But feminism has gone far beyond such revisionism. Often incorporating liberal and/or Marxist insights, contemporary feminists have placed more and more emphasis on themes all their own, particularly the idea of the **patriarchal** social system. The oppression of women by men precedes all other forms of oppression, they argue. "It is the hardest form of oppression to eradicate" and "causes the most suffering to its victims."[61] When we come to understand the oppression of women we will, suggests Shulamith Firestone in *The Dialectic of Sex*, be able to understand racism, classism, and all other forms of oppression. Thus, for example, Suzanne Pharr explains the oppression of gay men and lesbian women in feminist terms; she argues that by denying lesbians and gay men the fundamental civil rights that heterosexual women are allowed, heterosexual men ensure that most women will accept and depend on the patriarchal family structure.[62]

Other feminists have combined Marxist and patriarchal modes of interpretation, noting, for example, how patriarchy has for so long given men control of women's property, or pointing out how control over women's labor enhances men's control of all productive resources.[63]

Also not normally found in the more conventional ideologies (although not unknown in contemporary socialist thought) is the poststructural, deconstructionist approach of some feminists. As early as 1952, when she published *The Second Sex* in Paris, Simone de Beauvoir saw the importance of challenging not only current definitions of women and women's roles, but the very idea of the concept "woman"—"Are there women?" de Beauvoir asked.[64] Contemporary feminist poststructuralists are convinced that only by challenging (deconstructing) all established categories (structures) of social identity, including race, class, and gender, can we hope to break free of the confines of patriarchal language and practice.[65]

Insistence on the impossibility of separating oppression based on race and class from that based on gender is another poststructuralist feminist theme. Those who hope to understand and eradicate any form of oppression, feminists say, must pay attention to the structural factors that intersect to create sex, class, and race inequality.[66]

As the foregoing summary suggests, contemporary feminism has moved well beyond mere amendment of earlier modes of thought. Its critique of all existing political systems as profoundly patriarchal, its goal of specieswide egalitarianism, and its insistence on the interconnectedness of all forms of oppression summon up its own view of an ideal world.

Feminism also suggests how to effect change. Although most feminists seem to agree that the contemporary state is profoundly suspect, they emphasize that it is important nevertheless to change the policies of existing political systems. Joyce Gelb has examined how feminists in Britain, the United States, and Sweden have worked within their respective "political opportunity structures" to struggle for labor force equality, higher welfare benefits, better child care, and other specific policies relevant to women's condition.[67] Mary Hawkesworth has looked at feminist studies of substantive policy domains, commenting on the shift "from the critique of bias in existing programs to the formulation of proposals for alternative, equitable policies" in the areas of "health, housing, welfare, education, employment, equal protection, occupational safety, defense, foreign policy, development, abortion, reproductive rights, reproductive technology, rape prevention, sexual harassment, domestic violence, criminal justice, divorce, privacy, and pornography."[68]

Although many feminists thus seek specific short-range ameliorative reforms, all appear to agree that in the long run a more basic change must be made. For women and other oppressed persons to achieve equality, nothing less than a revolution is required. But it is a revolution of understanding, of consciousness, of meaning. Those who share these problems and these views must meet, discuss, write, and talk to others. International gatherings are particularly important so that no one will forget the many forms that patriarchy and related forms of oppression take across the globe. For most feminists, the concept of interdependence takes a negative form at the level of the state, as patriarchically dominated systems interact to maintain oppression, but a positive form at the level of the individual, as women meet from across the globe in forums such as the United Nations' periodic conferences on women, to share their histories and their insights and to move toward fundamental and global transformations in the way the human polity thinks about oppression.

Feminism thus clearly meets the criteria we have laid out to define what constitutes an ideology. Can the same be said for ethnic nationalism and religious fundamentalism?

Ethnic Nationalism

As the breakup of the former Soviet empire took place, we began to see the resurgence of another way of viewing politics: ethnic nationalism. We were forced to relearn something we really already knew—that modern *states* have often been formed out of many separate *nations*. And remembering this has compelled us to review and sharpen some of our definitions: A **nation,** says Ernest Gellner, is a category of persons with shared attributes, such as language, history, customs and traditions, and/or the fact of sharing a specific territory. What matters is not so much the attribute itself but the importance the members of the group attach to it. What makes a nation is the fact that "the members of the category firmly recognize certain mutual rights and duties to each other in virtue of their shared membership in it." [69]

Nationalism is the belief that the interests of one's own nation must take precedence over those of any individual, any group, any other nation, and— when they are in conflict—those of the state itself. For some authors, it is important to distinguish between the "good" nationalism of those who pursue individual freedom and the "bad" nationalism of those who unscrupulously assert the interests of one's own nation at the expense of others.[70] In practice such a distinction depends very much on the subjective views of the observer.

A **nation-state** is a polity in which sovereignty is coterminous with the sense of nationhood; everyone who lives within that political system feels he or she belongs with all the others nationally as well as politically. In fact, however, nations and states are *not* always coterminous. Indeed, probably every nation-state in the world has certain pockets of **subnationalism,** that is to say, there are groups within that nation-state whose members feel so strong a loyalty to one another it is as if they were all members of a nation within the larger nation-state. Such groups may or may not be located in a single geographical area within the official nation-state.

Ethnic nationalism is subnationalism based on ethnicity. **Ethnicity** is a shared perception that one's own group is distinctive, usually based on "a sense of common experience . . . continuity through biological descent and the sharing of common social and cultural conditions . . . at the heart of ethnicity is the feeling of *being special.*" [71]

In the case of ethnic nationalism, the domination that is resented may or may not have been originally established by imperial conquest, but it is always regarded as imposed by persons who are "not like us." The cases of the former republics of the Soviet Union and the warring nations of the former Yugoslavia, so constantly before us in the news, have reminded us forcefully that peoples may accept common statehood with others for many long years without losing this sense of ethnic distinctiveness, without ceasing to dream of the day when the balance of power will shift and permit the establishment of a separate nation-state.[72]

The political upheavals of the final decade of the twentieth century gave new life to old dreams. The changes have been immense: Henry Teune estimates that about half the world's population is now "living in a radically different kind of political system than that into which they were born."[73] In some cases changing borders and systems have been peacefully accommodated but examples of the contrary are not hard to find.[74] Militant and violent ethnic nationalism has raged in the Indian states of Punjab, Kashmir, and Assam; in Sri Lanka; in Nigeria; in Uganda; in Somalia and Rwanda. Ethnic subnationalism combines with religious subnationalism to fuel the continuing furies of the Middle East and of the United Kingdom. Pockets of ethnic nationalism pit the Basque people against the Spanish and the French, Native Americans against the government of the United States, and bastions of white supremacists against newly majoritarian South Africa. Many Canadians of French descent in francophone Quebec are firmly committed to a peaceful but nevertheless angry and determined struggle to establish an independent state, while rebellious Chechens in Russia seek the same goal by violent means, waging a desperately mismatched battle against the vastly superior military power of the dominant state.

Ethnic nationalism is thus a driving force for political change in our times.[75] Long-established states are breaking up, or appear on the point of doing so, and the magnitude of suffering and death caused by these struggles sometimes threatens to overwhelm our capacity to hope. If the world is becoming ever more interdependent, how can we be moving so passionately apart, at such enormous cost?

These are extremely important questions, questions to which we will often return in this book. But right now we have a simple (some might say, a colder) task; we need to decide if ethnic nationalism is an ideology. The definition we have adopted suggests that it is not. Nationalism is, as we have seen, one of the important "beliefs and attitudes" in both conservatism and fascism, and in the latter it has commonly taken the form of ethnic nationalism. But one conviction, no matter how passionately and desperately held, cannot be said to constitute an ideology. Look at the ethnic nationalists just listed. What common views regarding human nature or social and economic institutions and processes do the anachronistic white supremacists of South Africa and the Native Americans of the United States share? The Rwandan Tutus and the Quebecois autonomists? The Sri Lankan Tamils and the members of the Basque terrorist group known as the ETA? The beleaguered Chechens with any of the others? All these groups have a keen sense of personal oppression, but we would be hard put, would we not, to find a common definition of "oppression" that would fit them all. All are caught in the grip of the same passion for control of their own destinies, but they have no agreement among themselves about what means to use to achieve that control or what form that ideal destiny would take. Nationalism is, says Michael Freeden, "a plastic structure," capable of reflecting, often effectively and forcefully, the "complexities of its broader host containers," that is, the world's established ideologies. But if we attempt to view it as an ideology standing on its own, Freeden insists, and we would agree, "its ideational paucity comes to light."[76]

None of this is to deny that ethnic nationalism is a powerful force, and one to which we must pay more attention (as indeed we will in later chapters). We need to develop ways of assessing when the grievances so deeply felt merit the compassion of the human polity, when they are at any rate reasonable given the natural human need to possess and assert an identity, and when they bespeak nothing more than selfish unconcern for the rest of us. Above all, we need to find ways to put an end to the misery this passionate conviction so often leads human beings to inflict on themselves and others. Nevertheless, there is no need to label this particular *ism* an ideology.

Religious Fundamentalism

For some authors, insistence on a religious identity has little to distinguish itself from insistence on ethnicity or race—it is simply one way of asserting rights, especially for members of a minority group.[77] But as we will see, religious fundamentalism is much more than the assertion of a religious identity. It is a complex body of thought, particularly difficult, as we will also see, to classify either as "an ideology" or "not an ideology."

Many religions—Christianity, Islam, Judaism, Sikhism, Hinduism—have lent themselves to the growth of fundamentalist thinking, although such thinking is never shared by all the followers of any of these religions. Furthermore, fundamentalists do appear to share a set of values across the lines of their religions. Do these shared values constitute an ideology? Let us take a closer look at what contemporary scholars of this phenomenon have found.

Niels C. Nielsen points out that fundamentalists everywhere believe that truth is to be found in the sacred texts of their religion, that in respecting that truth they live "in a well ordered world," but that "the tradition that guarantees them religious truth is threatened."[78] For Robert Frykenberg, other shared characteristics are the division of the world into true believers and unbelievers, the sense of being a specially chosen people, the belief in a preordained destiny that includes the creation of a new heaven on earth, the conviction that sinister opposition is at work (or will be soon) to attempt to prevent the inevitable millennium, and that conversion means an "altogether total transformation, a complete and drastic change."[79]

Such beliefs clearly have their implicit political connotations, as do the three traits John H. Garvey finds in all fundamentalist movements; they are all, claims this author, conservative, popular, and practical. Protestant fundamentalists in the United States and Ulster; Muslim fundamentalists in Iran, Pakistan, Sudan, and Nigeria; and Orthodox *haredi* Jews all *conserve* long-established texts and traditions as guides to their behavior. All have interpreted these texts in a simple and nonhierarchical fashion, stressing the "fundamentals" and explaining them in ways everyone can understand, producing "a kind of stripped-down religion that travels light and fast" that gives them their potential for *popular* mass appeal. All, finally, offer a great deal of *practical* advice about how to conduct oneself in daily life, with detailed instructions regarding matters of "dress, diet, ritual, socialization and contact with modern culture."[80]

But fundamentalists share more explicitly political beliefs as well. If all truth can be found in the sacred texts, this includes, for the fundamentalist, truth about how to set up a government. Ann Mayer cites the Ayatollah Khomeini's insistence that "the entire system of government and administration, together with the necessary laws, lies ready for you. . . . There is no need for you, after establishing a government, to sit down and draw up laws, or [to] . . . run after others to borrow their laws. Everything is ready and waiting."[81] What waits for the fundamentalist Muslim is the Shari'a, drawn from the Qur'an and the Sunna; what waits for the fundamentalist Jew is the *halakha*, rabbinic interpretations of biblical law; what waits for Christian fundamentalists are the words of their god via the prophet Moses and the evangelists.[82]

Furthermore, although the political programs thus derived are not all the same, they do move in similar directions. All imagine and seek to establish a society in which the modern, secular division between public and private is abolished. In such a state, all behavior would be governed by religious precepts and further, within that state, by the *same* religious precepts. Freedom of religious choice is not a value for those who firmly believe their own contains all truth, nor are other individual liberties, such as the right to political dissent or the right to determine most of one's own behavior autonomously. The religious state will issue and enforce rules governing sexual behavior, family life, education, and business affairs.[83] For the fundamentalist, "God shows concern for everyday matters, such as jobs, food, clothes, travel and repair of automobiles" and the religious state knows what that god requires, and sees to it that he is obeyed.[84]

The means of moving toward this ideal state vary, but such variance seems to depend on the circumstances in which different fundamentalist groups find themselves. Some, such as fundamentalist Sikhs mindful of the political autonomy that Southeast Asian Hindus find in Hindustan and Muslims in Pakistan, seek to be granted a separate state; others, such as the Amish or

Religious fundamentalists, such as Osama bin Laden, believe all social and economic institutions must be closely governed by religious precepts and are willing to work by whatever means seem possible to move toward that end.
© AFP/CORBIS

the original Mormons in the United States, seek an enclave of their own within the larger state; some, such as the New Christian Right in the United States or the *haredim* parties in Israel, seek to transform the dominant state so far as possible by making specific policy demands (for example, the teaching of creationism in U.S. public schools, the granting of greater powers to the rabbinic courts in Israel); and others seek nothing less than the takeover of entire existing states, whether by revolution, as in Iran, or via a combination of terrorist intimidation and participation in democratic elections, as in Algeria.[85] But none countenances the idea of permanent minority status. All believe a greater day is coming, and with it a greater state.

Thus, contemporary fundamentalism meets many of the terms of our definition of ideology. Today's fundamentalists share a common view of human nature: fallible but susceptible to correction by religious orthodoxy that is strictly maintained by an all-powerful state. They share a belief in strict adherence to moral standards, with strong respect for family, personal honesty, and resistance to drugs and alcohol. They share the conviction that the modern state has lost its way, that social and economic institutions must be closely governed by religious precepts, and that a new day is coming when religious governance will prevail. They share a willingness to work by whatever means seem possible to move toward that end with passionate devotion.

Of course, even though fundamentalists share so many beliefs, *it does not seem so to them.* Any fundamentalists among the readers of this text must by now be thoroughly outraged at having been lumped together with those "others" whose views strike them as so patently erroneous. But the discomfort of the various adherents is not in itself sufficient reason to say fundamentalism is not an ideology. After all, today's democratic socialists do not enjoy being lumped in the same category as Chinese Communists, nor are liberals who stress individual freedoms easy companions of those whose liberalism is confined to the marketplace. Yet the categories *socialist* and *liberal* have meaningful and separate paradigms, however great the diversity within them.

Which brings us back to conservatism. Fundamentalists clearly are, in the general sense of the term, very, very conservative. Is fundamentalism, then, merely an extremist subcategory of conservatism? One could perhaps say so, but then one would probably have to say the same for fascist ideology. However, both fascism and fundamentalism utterly reject, in their very different ways, a core value of conservatism: the importance of personal liberty. It is true that conservatism expects the ideal state to be compelled to place important restraints on that liberty in the interests of order and the maintenance of tradition. But where conservatism accepts and promotes such control by the state with regret and seeks as far as possible to achieve the ends of an ordered world by concentrating on the individual, cherishing "a spirit of character, marked by the virtue of thrift, hard work and prudence," fundamentalists turn joyously in the opposite direction, delighting in submitting their entire lives to the control of higher authorities who themselves are believed to be in touch with the highest of all.[86]

So the answer is yes. Religious fundamentalism is an ideology.

BEYOND IDEOLOGY

Not all the important ideas about politics are contained in the classical or newly evolving ideologies we have discussed in this chapter. Great thinkers about politics have not all developed comprehensive systems of belief.

Indeed, one of the signs of their greatness is often that ideologues of many different stripes have been able to find useful and persuasive ideas in their writings. Studying the history of political thought (normally referred to as "political theory") we discover thinkers and writers, from Socrates to Weber, from Confucius to Habermas, whose ideas about politics have roamed far and wide, and who would be difficult to classify as exclusively conservative, or liberal, or anything else.

Even the classical and other ancient philosophers cannot always be classified as archconservatives. Socrates' dialectical method stressed wisdom and the pursuit of logical truth above the assertion of any single principle. Plato took what some might call a fundamentalist view in his conviction that eternal truths and unchanging realities existed, if only human beings knew how to find them, and his certainty that war is a natural outcome of a state's quest for more territory in order to meet the growing needs of its people, necessitating the maintenance of a "warrior class," provides a familiar justification for modern fascist thought. Like a good liberal, Aristotle argued that those who contributed equally to the good of the polity should be treated equally, and believed that all men were equal in their capacity to govern; on the other hand, however, he acknowledged that in practice some will inevitably emerge as so superior to others that it is impractical to pursue pure equality, and endeavoring to do so will lead only to the rule of the mob.[87]

A similar richness and ambiguity can be found in the work of the great political thinkers of Asia. Although Confucius insisted that rulers were to rule and followers to follow, a cardinal principle of Confucianism is *jen,* meaning benevolence, love, compassion, and sympathy toward others. Mahatma Gandhi's certainty that every individual had the right and duty to economic self-sufficiency is clearly echoed in the socialist credo, however different the means envisaged.[88]

Nor do the world's dominant religions each fall tidily into the category of a single political ideology. It can be and has been argued that the stress on the importance of harmony in Buddhist and Taoist thought risks teaching the peaceful acceptance of dictatorship (be it to the far left or far right), while other religions—Hinduism, Islam, Judaism, and Christianity—have all produced their share of fundamentalists who find support for their beliefs in the written dogma of their creeds. But contrary tendencies are even easier to find within each of the world's major organized religions than within the thought of a single writer on politics. They are not, in themselves, political ideologies.

Finally, we need to distinguish between some terms that are often used in discussing political beliefs and the systems of thought we call ideologies. These terms are *left, right, authoritarian, totalitarian,* and *democratic.* Politically, *left* and *right* are comparative terms, used to locate ideological perspectives in relation to each other. Generally, **left** is used for ideologies that take a positive view of human nature and demonstrate a conviction that change and progress are necessary and possible to improve the human condition. **Right** usually means a more pessimistic view of human nature and a conviction that it is important to maintain tradition and order. It should be fairly obvious that liberalism and socialism and most forms of feminism are on the left, with socialism moving farther to the left as we talk about the more extreme versions, and that conservatism, fascism, and religious fundamentalism are on the right, the latter two on the far right. Figure 2.2 suggests how these spatial designations can be used to compare the six ideologies we have discussed in these pages.

There is nothing wrong with this exercise, provided we do not give it more or less meaning than it has. Placing conservatism, fascism, and fundamentalism on the same side should not cause us to use the terms interchangeably, and the same is also true for liberalism, socialism, and feminism. It is also important to remember that this spatial arrangement refers only to certain characteristics of the ideologies *as ideologies,* not to the practices of political control adopted by people who assume power in the names of those ideologies. Some have argued, for example, that communism and fascism have much more in common than calling one *far left* and the other *far right* suggests. What these commentators are referring to, however, is not the content of the two ideologies but rather the authoritarian practices of rulers who call themselves Communists or fascists. To lump the two together ignores the extremely different principles of leadership in the two ideologies—not to mention all the other significant differences.

Authoritarian and *totalitarian* are two other often-misused terms. Neither refers to a belief system or to an ideology. Both refer to political systems in which political power is concentrated in the hands of a few. An **authoritarian system** is one in which the power of the authorities is virtually unlimited, although this power is not always exercised in all domains. A **totalitarian system** is one in which the authorities not only have unlimited power but attempt to exercise it over all domains of life—it is authoritarianism carried to the ultimate extreme. You will often find, however, that the words are used—incorrectly—to distinguish between capitalist systems ruled by an authoritarian elite (called *authoritarian*) and socialist systems ruled by an authoritarian elite (called *totalitarian*). Both kinds of systems are in fact authoritarian, just as there are both capitalist and socialist democratic systems. Furthermore, capitalist authoritarian systems are not necessarily less concerned about controlling every aspect of their citizens' lives than are socialist authoritarian systems. The control exercised by a Hitler or a Mussolini was every bit as totalitarian as that of a Stalin or a Mao, and in underdeveloped nations that have fallen under dictatorial rule neither the socialist nor the capitalist tyrant is likely to find it physically possible to extend the power of government to every corner of the land.

In this text I will use the term *authoritarian* to refer to all states that are elite controlled and drop the word *totalitarian* altogether. The fact that some

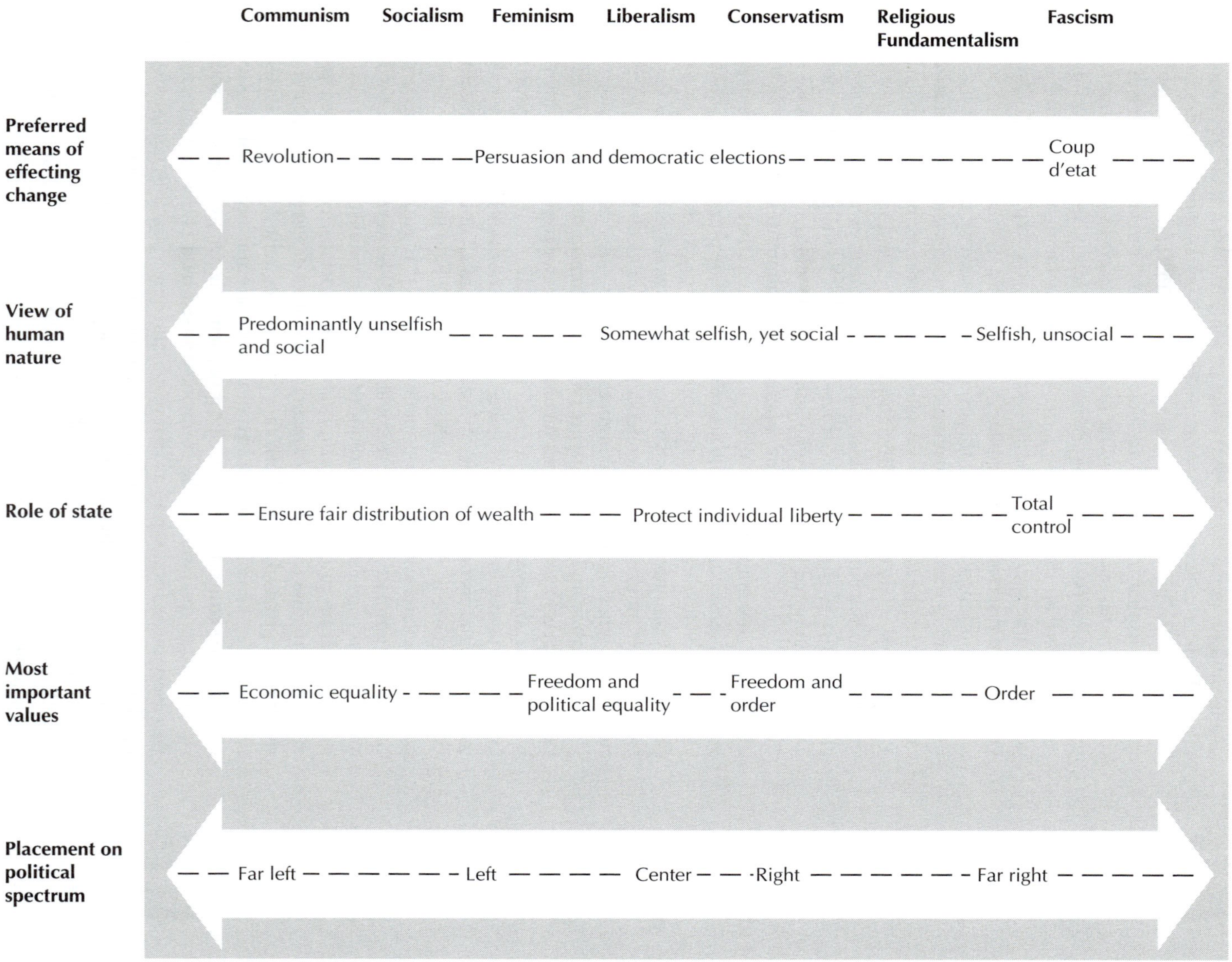

	Communism	Socialism	Feminism	Liberalism	Conservatism	Religious Fundamentalism	Fascism
Preferred means of effecting change	Revolution — — — — — — — — Persuasion and democratic elections — — — — — — — — Coup d'etat						
View of human nature	Predominantly unselfish and social — — — — Somewhat selfish, yet social — — — — Selfish, unsocial						
Role of state	Ensure fair distribution of wealth — — — Protect individual liberty — — — Total control						
Most important values	Economic equality — — — Freedom and political equality — — — Freedom and order — — — Order						
Placement on political spectrum	Far left — — — Left — — — Center — — — Right — — — Far right						

FIGURE 2.2 Key Characteristics of Major Political Ideologies

authoritarian systems carry their tendencies to control the lives of their fellow citizens much farther than do others can be made clear as we proceed. (For that matter, so can the fact that some democracies carry their democratic tendencies much farther than do others.) When it becomes necessary to distinguish between economic systems, we will add such economic terms as *capitalist, socialist,* and *mixed economy.* This leaves us with the semantic problem that *socialism* is both an ideology and an economic system, but that conflation cannot be avoided. As we have seen in this chapter, the very essence of the ideology of socialism is the demand that a specific economic system be established.

In these days when the ideas of democracy seem to have triumphed so dramatically, it may be tempting to think of democracy itself as a political ideology. But it is not. The idea of democracy is both less and more than an ideology. It is less because it is nothing more than a set of rules for choosing leaders who carry out the popular will. The conditions of personal freedom, free elections, and political equality are strongly associated with democracy and help make it possible, but the literal meaning of **democracy** is simply rule by the people. However, although democracy can be reduced to a single idea, that idea is currently more powerful than any of the ideologies we have discussed; it is in this sense that democracy is more than an ideology.

As an ideal, democracy fits comfortably inside at least four ideologies: conservatism, liberalism, socialism, and feminism. Conservatives, liberals, socialists, and feminists are all highly likely to call for democratic practices. Only fascists and religious fundamentalists argue, usually in very different ways, that respecting the will of the people should not be the primary justification for a government.

Of course, whether or not ideologues follow democratic rules once in power is always a question for empirical study. Indeed, the fact that the term is used so loosely in today's world makes it particularly important to keep the true meaning of *democracy* in mind. The fall of Soviet communism is often attributed to the "triumph of democracy," and it is certainly true that the quest for the greater personal freedom associated with democratic processes played an important role in the determination of the nations and republics under Soviet control to seek autonomy. It should not be forgotten, however, that the major cause of the collapse of the Soviet empire was its own mismanagement, both at home and abroad.[89] The effort now to find ways to erect the structures of democratic capitalism on the ruins of this form of socialism is fraught with difficulty and peril, not least of which is the resurgence of unregenerate nationalism in polities that must be able to join the global economy in order to have a hope of independent survival.[90] Furthermore, many have begun to question how effectively the people can be said to rule in nations where voter turnout is so weak, other forms of political participation often ineffective, and special interest control of campaign finance so strong, questions we will return to in Chapters 5 and 6. Whether or not democracy will triumph under these conditions remains an open question, and one that requires our most sober attention.

SUMMARY AND CONCLUSION

An ideology is a comprehensive system of beliefs and attitudes about social and economic institutions and processes. It is an attempt to explain how an existing political system has come into being and to describe the ideal political system. It may be either strictly personal or shared with a group, open or closed, and revolutionary or defensive. An ideology offers a theory of human nature, and thereby of human potentiality and of the need for particular modes of social control. Five major ideologies are conservatism, liberalism, socialism, fascism, and feminism.

Conservatives believe in conserving what exists. They have a nonegalitarian view of human nature, believing that some people are born into a "natural aristocracy" and that those people can best protect the individual liberty of all. Personal liberty is extremely important to conservatives, which helps explain why they often wish to see the power of government reduced. On the other hand, they frequently propose that government power be used to ensure that traditional moral standards are maintained. Conservatives have traditionally believed that it is the responsibility of the more advanced nations to bring the blessings of civilization to those less fortunate and that it is necessary to maintain good relations with allies as a means of protecting one's own system against external enemies. Although conservatives are sometimes viewed by others as incapable of compromise, they take a pragmatic approach to many questions, provided that the end result will further the basic principles of conservatism (order, continuity, loyalty, protection of individual freedoms, piety, and nationalism).

Liberals believe that all human beings are capable of reason and rational action and should be helped by their governments to fulfill their potential. However, although governments should be ready to help, they must never force such assistance on unwilling citizens—it is also an important liberal value to maintain personal freedom. As much as liberals would like to create a more egalitarian society, they are unwilling to invade individual rights to do so. Thus, they hold two beliefs that are in practice extremely difficult to reconcile. Liberals commonly believe in some form of social contract— that is, in the idea that human beings consent to be ruled by others, but only on condition that individual rights and liberties are maintained. If the terms of this contract are not met, the consent to be ruled may be withdrawn. Liberals believe, however, that political change should be made by peaceful, not revolutionary, means.

Socialists believe human beings are naturally sociable and cooperative and that only the establishment of nonsocialist governments and exploitative work arrangements has interfered with these natural instincts. They believe that the solution is to limit or even abolish outright the institution of private property—which, they say, should be owned by a state that is in turn controlled by the workers.

The world has seen many varieties of socialism. The early socialists argued for the abolition of private property or simply acted out that belief by establishing communal ownership of land and other goods. Utopian socialists argued that human beings should and could work together for their common good in small communities. Marxist socialists follow the teachings of Karl Marx and believe that human history is moving inexorably through five stages of economic organization, each characterized by a different dominant mode of production and a different form of class struggle over ownership of the means of production. The final stage will be communism, in which control over the means of production will be restored to the workers, probably by means of a violent revolution. Soviet Communists added to the ideas of Marx the teachings of Vladimir Lenin: that a Communist revolution is possible even in a state that has been only partially industrialized, that only the emergence of imperialism has been able to extend the stage of capitalism, that the Communist revolution is always the work of a small "vanguard" party of dedicated and informed revolutionaries, and that such a revolution leads at first only to a socialist system, in which the apparatus of the state will still be necessary, and only later to true communism. Later amendments to the doctrines of Soviet communism can be seen, from the vantage of hindsight, as the quest for philosophical arguments on behalf of political reforms whose ultimate result was to bring the experiment with the Soviet form of socialism to an end in most of the states in which it had been practiced. Other forms of socialism, as far apart as Chinese communism and democratic socialism, continue to attract adherents.

Fascism begins by arguing that the citizen can prosper only when the nation prospers and ends up placing the fate of the nation above that of its people. Like conservatives, fascists think that some human beings are naturally better than others, but for them being better means belonging to the "right" race or nationality. They think human beings are motivated by their emotions, not by their reason, and by the struggle for survival. Because this is so, citizens should accept the rule of the fascist state, which will permit them to engage in that struggle on the best possible terms. Under fascism, all human interactions—including economic exchange—are necessarily subject to the absolute discipline of the state and its leader.

Feminism is a relatively new ideology that began when women sought to modify liberalism and/or Marxist socialism to fit their needs and found it necessary to move on to formulate the concept of patriarchy and adapt the tools of poststructural deconstructionism. Feminists have a positive view of human nature, and argue for the right of all to share equally in the creation of our collective destiny, but they have a highly negative view of the state. They seek to move toward the ideal society by achieving a better understanding of the causes of all oppression, including that based on class and race as well as gender; they believe all forms of oppression are interconnected. While working for this understanding, often internationally, they also work for policy reform on questions of relevance and concern to women.

Despite the havoc it has wreaked in recent world affairs, ethnic nationalism is too narrow a concept and the values and hopes of those caught in its grip vary too widely for us to term this powerful motive for political behavior an ideology. Religious fundamentalism, on the other hand, meets the definition of an ideology, however profound the differences and the antipathies among its diverse adherents. Fundamentalism views human nature as flawed but susceptible to religious instruction, which can itself produce a heaven on earth when followed without question. It would give the religious state absolute power in all domains and expects true believers to move toward the establishment of such a state by whatever means possible.

Not all political thought is contained in the world's dominant ideologies and in the works of the world's greatest political thinkers—as in the dogma of the world's most powerful religions—ideologues of many different persuasions can find fodder for their beliefs. The history of political thought is not the same as the study of political ideology.

We frequently misuse such terms as *left, right, authoritarian, totalitarian,* and *democratic* as well as the terms that name the ideologues we have studied. Left means taking a positive view of human nature and believing that change and progress are necessary and possible to improve the human condition. Right means taking a somewhat more pessimistic view of human nature and placing greater emphasis on the importance of maintaining order and continuity. Many variations are possible, however, within this simplistic dichotomy.

Authoritarian and *totalitarian* refer to political systems in which political power is concentrated in the hands of a few, the difference being that in a totalitarian system more effort is made to exercise that power in all domains of human existence. *Democracy,* like authoritarianism, is not a political ideology but rather a description of the relationship between citizens and their leaders. The conditions of personal freedom, free elections, and political equality are strongly associated with democracy and help make it possible, but the literal meaning of democracy is simply rule by the people.

Ideology is a system of thought, but we are not all ideologues. For many of us, our political values and beliefs have come to us more subtly and less consciously, evolving naturally as we grow up in and learn the mores of a particular culture. That culture may be national or subnational, or a mixture of the two. Some cultural values are supranational, shared by the citizens of more than a single state. Not all cultural values have political content, but many do. In Chapter 3 we will examine the cultural context of politics and how our shared beliefs help structure our political life together.

QUESTIONS TO CONSIDER

1. Referring to Figure 2.2, name your own beliefs and attitudes regarding how to effect change, the nature of human nature, and the proper role of the state. Then say which of these values is most important to you: economic equality, freedom, political equality, or order. Given your answers, which ideology of those discussed appears to come closest to fitting with your own ideas?

2. What are the main differences between conservatism and liberalism? Between conservatism and fascism? Between liberalism and socialism?

3. Can a man ever be a feminist ideologue? Why or why not?

4. Why is it possible to say that religious fundamentalism is an ideology, but ethnic nationalism is not?

SELECTED READINGS

Daniels, Robert V., ed. *A Documentary History of Communism and the World: From Revolution to Collapse* (Hanover, N.H.: University Press of New England, 1994). A comprehensive study of communism worldwide, including the failure of communism in the Soviet Union.

Girvin, Brian. *The Right in the Twentieth Century: Conservatism and Democracy* (London and New York: Pinter, 1994). An in-depth and historical overview of right-wing political movements worldwide.

Gurr, Ted and Barbara Harff. *Ethnic Conflict in World Politics* (Boulder, Colo.: Westview Press, 1994). Seeks to explain how ethnicity can turn into ethnic nationalism and then into ethnic warfare.

Ollenberger, Jane C. and Helen Moore. *A Sociology of Women* (Englewood Cliffs, N.J.: Prentice Hall, 1992). A clear and useful explanation of the different forms of feminist theory.

Rawls, John. *Political Liberalism* (New York: Columbia University Press, 1993). A collection of lectures by one of today's best known political philosophers, providing an extensive study of liberalism.

Rejai, Mostafa. *Political Ideologies: A Comparative Approach* (Armonk, N.Y.: M. E. Sharpe, 1995). Offers a framework for the comparative study of the major political ideologies.

Schwarzmantel, John. *The Age of Ideology: Political Ideologies from the American Revolution to Postmodern Times* (New York: New York University Press, 1998). Particularly interesting for its examination of how the impacts of new technologies and increased globalization have affected traditional social structures based on heavy industry and thus call into question ideologies directed toward understanding a world no longer with us.

Vincent, Andrew. *Modern Political Ideologies* (Cambridge, U.K.: Blackwell, 1992). There are many useful surveys of contemporary ideologies, but this one is unusual in including environmentalism (or *ecologism*) as a new kind of ideology.

NOTES

1. Lyman Tower Sargent, *Contemporary Political Ideologies,* 5th ed. (Homewood, Ill.: Dorsey, 1961), p. 3.

2. Andrew Heywood, *Political Ideologies: An Introduction* (New York: St. Martin's Press, 1992), pp. 7–8.

3. David E. Ingersoll, *Communism, Fascism and Democracy* (Columbus, Ohio: Charles E. Merrill, 1971), p. 8.

4. F. J. C. Hearnshaw, *Conservatism in England* (London and Basingstroke: Macmillan, 1933), p. 22.

5. Samuel P. Huntington, "Conservatism as an Ideology," *American Political Science Review* 51, no. 2 (June 1957): 456.

6. Sargent, *Contemporary Political Ideologies,* p. 67.

7. Alexander J. Groth, *Major Ideologies* (New York: John Wiley, 1971), p. 88.

8. Kenneth R. Hoover, *Ideology and Political Life,* 2nd ed. (Monterey, Calif.: Brooks/Cole, 1994), p. 41.

9. Russell Kirk, cited in Sargent, *Contemporary Political Ideologies,* p. 67.

10. Hoover, *Ideology,* p. 41.

11. Ibid., p. 40.

12. Heywood, *Political Ideologies,* p. 56.

13. Franz Schurmann and Orville Schell, eds., *Imperial China* (New York: Random House, 1967), pp. xv–xvi.

14. John K. Fairbank, "The Nature of Chinese Society," in Schurmann and Orville, eds., *Imperial China,* pp. 54–55.

15. See R. D. Hicks, *Stoics and Epicureans* (New York: Charles Scribner's Sons, 1910), and Henry Chadwick, *The Pelican History of the Church: The Early Church* (London: Hodder and Stoughton, York, 1967).

16. See Thomas Aquinas, *Treatise on Law, Summa Theologica* (Garden City, N.Y.: Tirage Books, 1969), and Augustine [St. Augustine of Hippo], *City of God,* trans. Henry Bettenson (London: Penguin, 1972).

17. For a commentary on Burke's use of the organic metaphor, see Gerald U. Chapman, *Edmund Burke, The Practical Imagination* (Cambridge, Mass.: Harvard University Press, 1967), chap. 1.

18. George Fitzhugh, *Sociology for the South* (Richmond, Va.: A. Morris, 1854), excerpted in Jay A. Sigler, ed., *The Conservative Tradition in American Thought* (New York: Capricorn Books, 1969), p. 211.

19. Quoted in Sigler, *Conservative Tradition,* p. 24.

20. Herbert Hoover, a speech made 3 Feb. 1931, and reprinted as "Defense of Private Initiative," in Sigler, *The Conservative Tradition,* p. 323.

21. See Peter Steinfels, *The Neo-Conservatives* (New York: Simon & Schuster, 1959).

22. For an interesting discussion of some of the forms of neoconservatism, see Desmond S. King, *The New Right: Politics, Markets and Citizenship* (Chicago: Dorsey, 1987).

23. Heywood, *Political Ideologies,* pp. 21–22.

24. Thucydides, *The History of the Peloponnesian War,* trans. Henry Dale (New York: Harper, 1873), p. 114.

25. Marcus Tullius Cicero, *De Re Publica, De Legibus,* vol. 16, trans. C. W. Keyes (London: William Heineman, 1977), p. 329.

26. *The Book of Mencius* (London: Penguin Classics, 1970), sec. 6b, 2.

27. For Rousseau, the original state of nature was an idyllic state and only its degeneration forced individuals to make an effort to return, through the use of reason, to the condition of freedom and harmony that had once been naturally theirs; for Locke, the social contract was an improvement on the earlier state.

28. John Locke, *The Second Treatise of Government* (New York: Liberal Arts Press, 1952), p. 124.

29. Adam Smith, *An Inquiry into the Nature and Causes of the Wealth of Nations* (London: Methuen, 1961); J. S. Mill, "Utilitarianism," in Mary Warnock, ed., *Utilitarianism and Other Writings* (New York: New American Library, 1974); J. Bowring, ed., *The Works of Jeremy Bentham* (Edinburgh: Wm. Tate, 1843); David Hume, *A Treatise of Human Nature* (New York: E. P. Dutton, 1920).

30. Plato, *The Republic,* trans. F. M. Cornford (London: Oxford University Press, 1941), p. 166.

31. Julian Sherword, ed., *Handbook of South American Indians,* vol. 2 (Washington, D.C.: U.S. Government Printing Office, 1946).

32. For excerpts from the work of Henri Comte de Saint Simon's *New Christianity* (1825), Charles Fourier's *The Theory of Universal Unity* (1822), and Robert Owen's *An Address from the Association of All Classes of All Nations to the Governments and People of All Nations* (1837), see Carl Cohen, ed., *Communism, Fascism and Democracy* (New York: Random House, 1962), pp. 17–

48. For a discussion of utopian socialism in general, see Gordon Graham, *Politics in Its Place: A Study of Six Ideologies* (Oxford: Clarendon Press, 1986), pp. 103–106.

33. For a good selection of the chief writings of Marx and his collaborator Friedrich Engels, see Robert C. Tucker, ed., *The Marx-Engels Reader* (New York: W. W. Norton, 1972).

34. See excerpts from G. W. F. Hegel, *Lectures on the Philosophy of History* (1861), in Cohen, *Communism, Fascism and Democracy,* pp. 57–66.

35. Friedrich Engels, *Anti-Duhring,* 3rd English ed. (Moscow: Foreign Languages Publishing House, 1962), p. 385.

36. Karl Marx and Friedrich Engels, *Manifesto of the Communist Party,* in Lewis S. Feuer, *Basic Writings on Politics and Philosophy of Karl Marx and Friedrich Engels* (New York: Anchor Books, 1959), p. 26.

37. Marx and Engels, *The Holy Family,* cited in Tucker, *Marx-Engels Reader,* p. 41.

38. V. I. Lenin, *State and Revolution* (New York: International Publications, 1932).

39. J. Stalin, *Dialectical and Historical Materialism* (New York: International Publishers, 1940).

40. Nikita Khrushchev, *Crimes of the Stalin Era, a Special Report to the 20th Congress of the Communist Party of the Soviet Union,* Closed Session, 25 Feb. 1956, reprinted in Cohen, *Communism, Fascism and Democracy,* pp. 248–54.

41. Michael Gasster, "The Rise of Chinese Communism," in Gary K. Bertsch and Thomas W. Ganschow, eds., *Comparative Communism: The Soviet, Chinese and Yugoslav Models* (San Francisco: W. H. Freeman, 1976), pp. 117–19. See also *Selected Works of Mao Tse-tung,* vol. 3 (Peking: Foreign Languages Press, 1965), pp. 264–67.

42. Of former Communist nations, only China, Cuba, North Korea and Vietnam can now be counted as Communist and China is undergoing rapid transformation toward market socialism.

43. Charles Funderburk and Robert G. Thobaben, *Political Ideologies: Left, Center, Right,* 2nd ed. (New York: HarperCollins, 1994), pp. 85–86. For excerpts from the work of other leading social democrats, see "Part IV: Democratic Socialism" in H. B. McCullough, ed., *Political Ideologies and Political Philosophies* (Toronto: Wall and Thompson, 1989), pp. 150–71.

44. Barbara Stallings, "External Finance and the Transition to Socialism in Small Peripheral Societies," in Richard R. Fagen, Carmen Diana Deere, and José Luis Coraggio, eds., *Transition and Development* (New York: Monthly Review Press, 1980), pp. 65–66.

45. T. M. S. Evens, *Two Kinds of Rationality: Kibbutz Democracy and Generational Conflict* (Minneapolis: University of Minnesota Press, 1995), p. 27. According to Evens, "the kibbutz has, in noticeable measure, arrived at its ideal of 'order without government'" (p. 29).

46. "Soviet Economic Reform: Socialism and Property," Report of the Thirtieth Strategy for Peace, U.S. Foreign Policy Conference (Muscatine, Iowa: Stanley Foundation), 19–21 Oct. 1989.

47. Arno Mayer, "Past and Prologue," *The Nation* (16 Sept. 1991): 290, and John E. Roemer, *A Future for Socialism* (Cambridge, Mass.: Harvard University Press, 1994). Under Roemer's scheme, on reaching the age of majority, everyone would be given an equal share of coupons; and on each person's death all shares and unspent coupons would revert to the state for redistribution. The market would otherwise function freely, but there would be a far more egalitarian distribution of property than under unrestrained capitalism. For a brief summary, see "A Future for Socialism," *Politics and Society* 22, no. 4 (Dec. 1994): 451–78; for his more recent comments on this scheme see *Equal Shares* (with Erik O. Wright) (London: Verso, 1996).

48. See excerpts from Benito Mussolini, *The Doctrine of Fascism* (1932), in Cohen, *Communism, Fascism and Democracy,* p. 358.

49. From *Hitler's Words,* quoted in Cohen, *Communism, Fascism and Democracy,* pp. 409–10.

50. From Mussolini, *Doctrine of Fascism,* in Cohen, *Communism, Fascism and Democracy,* pp. 349–64, and excerpts from Ernst R. Huber, *Constitutional Law of the Greater German Reich* (1939), in Gould and Truitt, *Political Ideologies,* pp. 123–26.

51. See excerpts from Mario Palmieri, *The Philosophy of Fascism* (1936), in Cohen, *Communism, Fascism and Democracy,* pp. 369–90.

52. Charles Lane and Karen Breslau, "Germany's Furies," *Newsweek* (7 Dec. 1992): 30–32, and *The Economist* (5 Sept. 1992): 55.

53. For the reasons for the party's more recent division and decline, see Chapter 6.

54. Andrew Vincent, *Modern Political Ideologies* (Cambridge: Blackwell, 1992), pp. 208–77.

55. See Valentine M. Moghadam, *Identity Politics and Women: Cultural Reassertions and Feminisms in International Perspective* (Boulder, Colo.: Westview, 1994) for a variety of approaches to this possibility.

56. Jane C. Ollenburger and Helen Moore, *A Sociology of Women* (Englewood Cliffs, N.J.: Prentice Hall, 1992), p. 16. The following discussion draws heavily on Ollenburger and Moore, who note their own indebtedness to Alison M. Jagger and Paula S. Rothenberg, *Feminist Frameworks* (New York: McGraw-Hill, 1984) for their explanation of the different forms of feminist theory.

57. J. M. Todd, ed., *A Wollstonecraft Anthology* (Bloomington, Ind.: Indiana University Press, 1977); John Stuart Mill and Harriet Taylor Mill, *The Enfranchisement of Women and the Subjection of Women* (London: Virago, 1983).

58. Betty Friedan, *The Feminine Mystique* (New York: Norton, 1963), and Alice Rossi, ed., *Essays on Sex Equality by John Stuart Mill and Harriet Taylor Mill* (Chicago: University of Chicago Press, 1970).

59. Friedrich Engels, *The Origin of Family, Private Property and the State* (New York: International Publishers, 1884/1972).

60. Claudia von Werlhof, "Women's Work: The Blind Spot in the Critique of Political Economy," in Maria Mies et al., eds., *Women: The Last Colony* (London: Zed Books, 1988), pp. 13–26, and Maria Mies, "Capitalist Development and Subsistence Production: Rural Women in India," in Maria Mies et al., eds., *Women: The Last Colony,* pp. 27–50.

61. Jagger and Rothenberg, p. 86.

62. Suzanne Pharr, *Homophobia: A Weapon of Sexism* (Inverness, Calif.: Chardon Press, 1988); Andrea Dworkin, *Women Hating* (New York: Dutton, 1974) and *Pornography: Men Possessing Women* (New York: Putnam, 1979); and Charlotte Bunch and S. Pollack, *Learning One Way: Essays in Feminist Education* (Trumansberg, N.Y.: Crossing Press, 1983). Dworkin and Bunch believe heterosexual women are too closely linked to their oppressors to be able to confront them.

63. Juliet Mitchell, *Woman's Estate* (New York: Pantheon, 1971) and *Psychoanalysis and Feminism* (New York: Pantheon, 1974); Heidi Hartmann, *Women and Revolution: The Unhappy Marriage of Marxism and Feminism* (London: Pluto Press, 1981).

64. Simone de Beauvoir, *The Second Sex* (New York: Knopf, 1952). De Beauvoir might well ask: She did far better than her fellow student (and lover), Jean Paul Sartre, when the two of them took an important philosophy exam, but their professors decided nevertheless to award the highest prize (and thereby significant financial aid for further study) to "the man."

65. S. Bordo, "Feminism, Postmodernism and Gender Skepticism," in L. J. Nicholson, ed., *Feminism/Postmodernism* (New York: Routledge, 1990), and R. Tong, *Feminist Thought: A Comprehensive Introduction* (Boulder, Colo.: Westview, 1989).

66. M. B. Zinn, "Family, Feminism and Race in American Society," *Gender and Society,* vol. 4 (1990), pp. 68–83, and Ollenberger and Moore, *Sociology of Women,* pp. 26–27.

67. Joyce Gelb, *Feminism and Politics* (Berkeley: University of California Press, 1989).

68. Mary Hawkesworth, "Policy Studies within a Feminist Frame," *Policy Sciences* 27, nos. 2–3 (1994): 99, 114–15. The entire issue of *Policy Sciences* is devoted to "Feminism and Public Policy," under the guest editorship of Hawkesworth. Other political scientists who have brought a feminist perspective to policy studies in recent years (dates following their names refer to years of publication of key works) include Ellen Boneparth and Emily Stoper (1988); Margaret Conway, David Ahern, and Gertrude Steuernagel (1994); Janet Flammang (1985); Jo Freeman (1989); Joyce Gelb and Marian Lief Palley (1987); Joni Lovenduski (1986); Barbara Nelson (1984); Sue Tolleson Rinehart (1992); Anne Schneider and Helen Ingram (1993); and Dorothy McBride Stetson (1991).

69. Ernest Gellner, "Nations and Nationalism," in Richard K. Betts, ed., *Conflict After the Cold War: Arguments on Causes of War and Peace* (New York: Macmillan, 1994), p. 285. Gellner refers to this as the "voluntaristic" definition of a nation, as contrasted to a "cultural" definition which requires only the sharing of a culture ("a system of ideas and signs and associations and ways of behaving and communicating") and finds merit in both kinds of definition.

70. See, for example, the distinction made by Peter Alter between Liberal Nationalism and Integral Nationalism in "Nationalism: An Overview" in *Nationalism and Ethnic Conflict* (San Diego, Calif.: Greenhaven Press, 1994), pp. 18–25.

71. Louis L. Snyder, *Encyclopedia of Nationalism* (New York: Paragon House, 1990), p. 94.

72. For a comparative examination of the shifting meanings of several of these concepts, see Russell F. Farnen, ed., *Nationalism, Ethnicity, and Identity: Cross National and Comparative Perspectives* (New Brunswick, N.J.: Transaction Publishers, 1994), pp. 45–58.

73. Henry Teune, "Introduction: The 'Problem' of Ethnic Nationalisms," *International Political Science Review* 3 (1998): 231–32.

74. Two examples of studies that seek to explain the factors that turn ethnicity into ethnic nationalism and thence into ethnic warfare are Ted Robert Gurr and Barbara Harff, *Ethnic Conflict in World Politics* (Boulder, Colo.: Westview, 1994), and Subrata K. Mitra, "The Rational Politics of Cultural Nationalism: Subnational Movements of South Asia in Comparative Perspective," *British Journal of Political Science* 25, pt. 1 (Jan. 1995): 57–77.

75. As it was of course in ancient times as well. For a view of the specific historical roots of modern ethnic conflict, see Fred W. Riggs, "The Modernity of Ethnic Identity and Conflict," *International Political Science Review* 19, no. 3 (1998): 269–88.

76. Michael Freeden, "Is Nationalism a Distinct Ideology?" *Political Studies* XLVI (1998): 748–65.

77. Peter Janke, *Ethnic and Religious Conflicts: Europe and Asia* (Aldershot, Maine: Dartmouth, 1994), p. viii.

78. Niels C. Nielsen Jr., *Fundamentalism, Mythos and World Religions* (New York: State University of New York Press, 1993), p. 8.

79. Robert Frykenberg is cited by both Nielsen and Garvey. See Robert Frykenberg and Pauline Kolenda, *Studies of South India* (New Delhi: American Institute of Indian Study, 1985).

80. John H. Garvey, "Introduction: Fundamentalism and Politics," in Martin E. Marty and R. Scott Appleby, eds., *Fundamentalisms and the State* (Chicago: University of Chicago Press, 1991), pp. 15–17.

81. Ann Elizabeth Mayer, "The Fundamentalist Impact on Law, Politics and Constitutions," in Marty and Appleby, *Fundamentalisms and the State,* pp. 110–51.

82. Garvey, "Introduction," p. 19.

83. Nielsen, p. 14.

84. Ibid., p. 10.

85. Garvey, "Introduction," pp. 23–24.

86. Comments on the importance of individual character were made by British Prime Minister Stanley Baldwin in 1924 and are quoted in Hearnshaw, *Conservatism in England,* pp. 30–31.

87. Kenneth W. Thompson, *Fathers of International Thought: The Legacy of Political Theory* (Baton Rouge: Louisiana State University Press, 1994), pp. 28–43.

88. Lawrence Siiring and C. I. Eugene Kim, *The Asian Political Dictionary* (Santa Barbara, Calif.: ABC: Clio, 1985), pp. 76, 80.

89. Michael Kinsley, "Just Why Did Communism Fail?" *Time* (4 Nov. 1991): 98.

90. E. P. Thompson et al., "What's Next?" *The Nation* (23 Sept. 1991): 323–40.

CHAPTER 3

Politics and Culture

Do you get a lump in your throat when you see your country's flag waving in the breeze? Do you care about the plight of the planet more than about any nation-state? Do you have stronger feelings of affiliation with a particular ethnic group than you do with the nation-state in which you live? Would you like to see the United Nations become a stronger body—or a weaker one? Do you think it might make sense to decriminalize the sale and use of marijuana? What is your stand on the issue of abortion? How important do you think it is to maintain the present Social Security program in the United States? Were you rooting for George W. Bush or Albert Gore during the debate over who really won the presidential election in 2000? Which of the ideologies discussed in Chapter 2 made the most sense to you?

The point of all these questions is not to persuade you that you have political attitudes and opinions, but to get you ready for another question: Where did you get them? Why do you have these views about politics? And here's still another question: So what? Your beliefs may be important to you (let's hope they are), but does it make any difference to your political system that you hold the views you do? What about your counterparts in other political systems? Do the views of the Russian or Thai college students on matters of political significance have any impact on their nations' politics?

Perhaps your first instinct is to answer these questions more or less like this:

1. I have the opinions I have because I have given these matters rational thought and have made intelligent decisions.
2. My opinions matter when I vote, because I live in a modern democracy. Most of the time, however, no one besides my mother and my dog pays very much attention to what I think (and neither of them is really all that interested, either).
3. The political opinions of an ordinary citizen who lives in a nation that is not a modern democracy do not matter to anyone.

If these are your answers, then this chapter should give you grounds for rethinking them. First, the good news: Your political opinions (and those of your counterparts in other nations, whatever the nature of their political system) probably matter a great deal more than you think, especially if they are expressed by means other than merely voting. Then the not-so-good news: You may have worked out fine, logical reasons for holding the opinions you do, but chances are you got them in the first place because you were influenced by other forces in your life.

The subject of this chapter is the social and cultural context within which we make our political decisions, and the effect these have on politics. We will explore how different societies, and different groups within societies, develop and disseminate the values that shape political opinions, structures, and policy decisions. Our interest now is in **cultural values**—that is, values shared by a group of people in a given culture. (**Culture** is a word that has many meanings, as a quick trip to the dictionary will remind you; here I am using it to mean the ideas and customs shared by a given people in a given period of time.) Some cultural values are widely shared throughout a polity; others are shared less widely, by specific groups within that polity, or, sometimes, more widely, by groups whose boundaries are larger than that of specific states. In this chapter, we will consider first how cultural values are important at the level of the nation-state, and then how they help create distinctive social identities at the subnational level. We will emphasize the cultural values of ethnicity, race, and religion, but we will also give attention to group balues based on shared class, language, gender, age, or region of residence. Finally, we will examine some of the more important findings in the subfield of political science known as *political socialization,* the study of the processes by which our political values are learned.

THE POLITICAL CULTURE OF THE NATION-STATE

Almost every polity has something that political scientists call a **political culture,** that is, a set of attitudes, beliefs, and values that are widely shared and that permit the members of that polity to "order and interpret political institutions and processes, and their own relationships with such institutions and processes."[1] Of course, the values that compose a political culture may and normally do change over time. A recent study of American values finds, for example, that while acceptance of different ethnic groups and diverse lifestyles has increased in recent years, as has concern for the environment, there has, on the other hand, been a steady decline in the importance attached to obligations to others, to work for its own sake, and to following the conventions of the larger society.[2] But there are also continuities in the U.S. value system: Walter S. Jones points out that Americans continue to be much more concerned about how to protect political and religious liberty than about the capacity of a political system to ensure economic well-being and economic justice.[3]

The political cultures of other nations have also been analyzed and reanalyzed over time. In one study, German citizens were found to have a "detached, practical and almost cynical attitude toward politics," while Mexicans were said to reject bureaucratic authority as "corrupt and arbitrary," and the Italian political culture was described as one of "unrelieved political alienation and . . . social isolation and distrust."[4] These comments are all drawn from *The Civic Culture,* a large-scale comparative study of the political cultures of five nation-states, including the United States and Great Britain as well as Germany, Mexico, and Italy, made in the early 1960s. In this important study, authors Gabriel Almond and Sidney Verba set forth the ideal of a **civic culture,** one in which citizens combine a commitment to moderate political participation with a belief in the legitimacy of officialdom and a mild tendency toward **parochialism,** that is, toward withdrawing into the private sphere. Such an orientation, they argued, serves the citizen and the polity by keeping "politics, as it were, in its place," and ensuring the necessary "balance between governmental power and governmental responsiveness" necessary to maintain a stable democracy.[5]

The question of an ideal political culture is, of course, a normative one. Not everyone has agreed with Almond and Verba that their model of the civic culture is ideal. When belief in the duty and value of political participation is low, especially among the less advantaged groups in a society, the surface calm of the civic culture can be both deceptive and short lived. Great Britain was described by Almond and Verba as a "deferential civic culture" in 1963, but since that time has become subject to sporadic rioting by hitherto politically passive groups ("deferential" according to Almond and Verba). Such groups have felt the impact of reductions in public spending on social welfare, health, and education made under the Conservative government of Prime Minister Margaret Thatcher and not reversed by her successor, John Major, nor his Labour Party successor, Tony Blair.[6]

Dramatic changes have also taken place in the German political culture since *The Civic Culture* was published. In 1963, Almond and Verba found that only 7 percent of their German sample cited "governmental and political institutions" as "the things about this country that you are most proud of." A follow-up study done in 1978, after the memory of the institutions that nation had established during the Nazi regime had had fifteen more years to fade, found 31 percent of West Germans ready to give this answer to the same question.[7] Then came German reunification in 1990, posing immense new problems of national identity: "The new Republic has to . . . recover both the East German past and the past common to both states. . . . Unification entails the coupling, however uneven, of two ideological visions, two political and cultural projects, two different kinds of legitimacy and logic."[8] The evolving political culture of the new Germany includes such dangerous trends as increased hostility to the nation's large Turkish and Romish populations and renewed emphasis on bonds of German kinship.

Italian political culture has also changed significantly at the end of the twentieth century and the beginning of the next. In assessing Italian political culture a key question has been the changing role of the family. In a book published about the same time as the Almond and Verba study, Edward Banfield argued that Italians always put the family and its interests first, regardless of the impact on community or national interests, an interpretation that seemed to explain why Almond and Verba found them so politically alienated and distrustful. In recent decades, however, the role of the family has greatly changed in Italy. Although the divorce rate remains comparatively low, women have acquired more education, the birth rate has fallen, a feminist movement has emerged, and families often need more than one income to make ends meet, so that more and more women have moved into the workforce. At the same time, it has become more difficult for young adults to earn enough to live on their own, so families do, perforce, stay together, but on very different terms. Youth unemployment (ages 15–29) is among the highest in Europe, and although universities are easier to enter than in the past, there are few student grants or cheap student loans. During the 1970s young people were active in leftist party politics and protest movements, far more active than Almond and Verba had found, but this has now been succeeded, says Donald Sassoon, by attitudes of resignation and passivity, and a tendency either to ignore politics or to vote for parties to the right.[9] Alienation may have returned, but such an attitude can now be more reasonably explained by historical and political factors—in particular, the bitterness that follows unsuccessful efforts at reform—than by unusually strong family ties.

Nevertheless, many national political cultures continue to be based in large part on strong family values. In most African and Middle Eastern societies, family ties are not only strong but extensive, including the larger extended family and kinship group as well as the nuclear family (which itself may, in those Muslim communities where polygamy is still practiced, include several wives and their offspring). The sense of identity and loyalty such ties provide fosters a tendency toward political homogeneity: Where traditional family bonds remain strong, say Oladimeji Aborisade and Robert J. Mundt in writing of Nigeria, a "politician may be able to count on the support of literally hundreds of individuals based on actual kinship ties."[10] James A. Bill and Robert Springborg find members of the same family in the Middle East may well join competing parties and groups, but they argue that the "ligaments of kinship" which "run through rival collectivities" help make such societies work, binding such groups "into a working whole [by] softening tensions."[11]

Sometimes the most important value in a nation's political culture is simply pride in shared nationhood, a value we have already discussed in Chapter 2 as *nationalism*. This value is particularly likely to be stressed in the early years of a new nation or when a nation has been through a particularly harrowing period in its history. When France suffered humiliating defeats, both in World War II and in the loss of empire, the insistence by General and then President Charles de Gaulle that French grandeur could yet make its mark in the world brought him strong support—especially as France struggled to keep from being overwhelmed by American wealth and power in the immediate postwar years—and a marked revival of French nationalistic spirit.

Of course, the task of creating a new sense of national unity is often complicated by the presence of groups whose tendency is to give their first loyalty to their own members. At such times, national leaders must find a way to balance the demands of such groups against the need for national solidarity. They cannot simply be ignored; precisely because a value is an opinion to which the holder attaches importance, acting without regard to values widely held in a society is one way to ensure a very brief tenure in office.

However, a wide repertoire of responses is available to those in authority, ranging from outright oppression to nationalistic exhortation to careful and pragmatic efforts to accommodate diversity without allowing it to tear the nation apart. Charles Tilly suggested long ago that when groups become sufficiently powerful to threaten the established leadership, more effort will be devoted to suppressing the group than to meeting its demands.[12] The Serbian and Russian responses to the growing demands of Kosovars and Chechens for political autonomy, escalating from political arrests of individual opposition figures to large-scale military attack, provide recent disturbing evidence of the truth of this analysis.[13]

But the most effective ways for nation-states to develop a shared sense of nationhood when significant differences exist within the polity is to find ways to accommodate those differences—ways that do not undermine the state. It may be possible to reach compromise positions on conflicting values, neither fully pleasing nor fully outraging any single set of sensibilities, as in the Irish decision to delay a referendum on permitting divorce while passing legislation to protect the property rights of persons divorced elsewhere.[14] Sometimes the nation-state seeks to ensure the trust and loyalty of diverse groups by enshrining such compromises in the nation's constitution. In multilingual India, for example, the constitution explicitly recognizes fourteen languages in addition to the principal one, Hindi (although in fact about 1,650 languages and dialects are spoken).[15]

Federal systems, in which the constituent units (states, departments, provinces) have independent power over certain matters (as discussed in Chapter 12), permit different geographical regions to maintain different social norms on the matters under their jurisdiction. (Exactly which norms are protected in such systems is not always crystal clear: Canadians have recently battled over whether or not legislation forbidding businesses in the province of Quebec to use any language other than French on their outdoor signs really comes under the protection of that nation's federal constitution.[16])

Other important constitutional accommodations of conflicting values are clauses that ensure the protection of individual rights and liberties. The Bill of Rights in the U.S. Constitution, the French Declaration of the Rights of Man, the Indian Bill of Fundamental Rights, and the Venezuelan Bill of Rights are all examples of the ways polities attempt to ensure in their constitutions that citizens will be able to live according to their personal values as long as they do not interfere with the rights of others. Such clauses are usually addressed to individual values, but when they refer to matters of religion or language, or to the right of equal treatment under the laws regardless of gender, race, or ethnicity, then they are obviously of major significance for particular organized groups as well.

CULTURAL BASES OF SUBNATIONALISM

In the previous section, our focus has been on the shared culture of a nation-state, and the different ways such polities may seek to repress, limit, and/or accommodate subnational cultural differences that threaten national unity. It is time now to look more directly at the nature and significance of subnational and supranational group cultures. What is the basis for their formation? Such a question, of course, has no single answer. Individuals within a polity may feel themselves separated from their compatriots—and closer to

BOX 3.1
Class

In most social systems, differences in level of income, level of education, and kind of occupation tend to cluster together and to produce, sometimes in combination with differences in the way we talk and dress and the kind of material goods we acquire, a class identity.[17]

Class identity can be a powerful force urging citizens to adopt distinctive political attitudes and beliefs. This is especially likely to be the case when two other conditions are met: First, the members of a class are conscious of that membership, and second, class membership is "bonded" with one or more other group identities.[18] To cite an example of the latter condition, trade unions have often been formed by people who have a sense of common destiny owing to shared social class, as well as by those seeking to improve conditions of employment. Class identity thus becomes bonded with union identity, and the possibility of acting on behalf of the two identities simultaneously gives added power to the members' political action. The Polish trade union *Solidarnosc* was formed by members of the Polish working *class* who were then able to use their years of experience working to defend the always embattled organization to engage in a political struggle of yet greater significance: helping to bring about the downfall of communism in their nation by forming a *party* and successfully campaigning to make their own leader, Lech Walesa, president of the new republic.[19]

Of course, the politicization of class interests is not always a working-class phenomenon. The social and business contacts of the more affluent with one another can also stimulate a sense of shared class, shared values, and shared responsibility to protect those values through political activism. Traditional middle class occupational groups who feel threatened as much by changing social mores as by automation and advanced technology sometimes seek political expression in new political movements, and rising class consciousness among peasant populations has played a key role in the growth of organized and sometimes successful rebel movements.[20]

the citizens of other states—because of such personal characteristics as ethnicity (or race), religious affiliation, class identity (see Box 3.1), gender, age, language, or regional origins. This sense of difference may be present when the polity is first formed, in which case it may constitute one of the chief hurdles to the original establishment of the nation. Or it may develop during the lifetime of the polity, as wars shift national boundaries, as patterns of immigration and emigration change the mix of humanity contained within those boundaries, as the gap between rich and poor grows or declines, as values change regarding gender roles, or as the proportion and health of the aged change.

The significance of group values for the political system can be better understood by looking briefly at two of the key variables—ethnicity and religion—in turn, and then considering two contemporary examples of the impact these forces have had in national and international politics.

Ethnicity and Race

Determining whether a given person belongs to a racial or an ethnic group or not is a highly subjective matter. As Robert J. Thompson and Joseph R. Rudolph Jr. have pointed out, "Ultimately, membership in an ethnic group is largely a matter of ascription. One belongs because one perceives oneself as a member of a group or because others so perceive one."[21] Those who accept membership in a particular group, be it out of passionate conviction or passive acceptance, tend to share more than a single belief or value, and the values they share may well assume political significance. However, the fact that diverse groups share other values as well as nationhood or territory may not suffice to prevent conflict and bloodshed. By the time European colonizers arrived in the late nineteenth century, the Tutsi, Hutu, and Twa peoples of Burundi and Rwanda were already "speaking the same language, believed in the same god, shared the same culture, and lived side by side throughout both countries." But these three groups had come to this fertile region in east Africa from different lands and at different times and they each maintained their sense of ethnic distinctness. The more numerous and more powerful Tutsi were firmly ensconced in power before colonial conquest by the British. In subsequent years, the British policy of administering colonial rule via established rulers greatly increased the inequalities among the three groups and thereby their sense of ethnic difference as well. As Hutu resentment grew in Rwanda, the British changed sides, conniving in the overthrow of the Tutsi monarchy in that nation. As might have been predicted, such a tactic simply exacerbated ethnic tensions. Violence escalated year by year, carrying through the granting of independence and into the widespread slaughter and warfare within and between the two nations in the 1990s.[22]

Not all cases of strongly felt ethnic distinctiveness lead to such dire results, of course. But even where peace is maintained, the views of different ethnic

BOX 3.2
**Race and
Ethnicity in the
United States**

What racial or ethnic group do you belong to? U.S. citizens often refuse to play that game and proudly assert, "I am an American and that's that." Others are hard pressed to give an answer: "Well, my mother's mother was Welsh, and her father was a mixture of English, French, and Norwegian. My father's mother was half Cherokee, one-fourth African American and one-fourth Scottish and his father was part German, part Dutch, and part Indonesian. So you tell me: What ethnic group do I belong to?" But even in so large and heterogeneous a nation as the United States, there are many for whom racial or ethnic identity is a matter of great importance, and whose values and attitudes are shaped by this primary reference group.

TABLE 3.1   U.S. Population Percentages by Race, 1810–2050

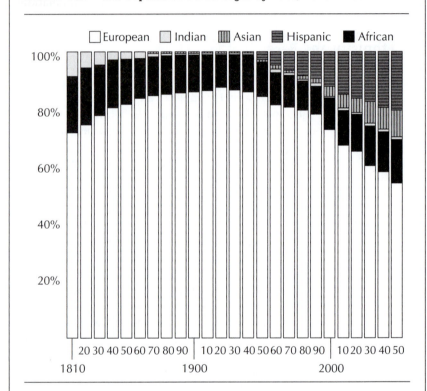

Source: "U.S. Population Percentages by Race, 1810–2050" from "The Dynamic Racial Composition of the United States" by Antonio McDaniel from *Daedalus*, pp. 179–98. Reprinted by permission from Daedalus, Journal of the American Academy of Arts and Sciences, from the issue entitled "An American Dilemma Revisited," Winter 1995, Vol. 124, No. 1.

groups in a single society on such easily politicized issues as the content of schooling, employment services, welfare aid, the standards for promoting individuals to positions of responsibility, and procedures for adjudicating disputes may well run counter to each other, and require constant negotiation.

It is useful to remember that ethnic and racial distinctiveness, rivalry, struggle against oppression, full or partial assimilation into the national ethos, bloodletting, and civil war are not new, nor are they found with any greater frequency in one part of the world than in any other. The Chinese absorption of the Mongol and Tibetan peoples, the struggle of immigrants from former colonies for equal treatment in Great Britain, the determination of the Jewish people in Israel to build a state of their own, the rivalry between the Luo and Kikuyu groups in Kenya, the battle of African Americans in the United States for equality in the land their ancestors were brought to by force, and the treatment of indigenous populations throughout the Americas—different as they may be in other respects—are all manifestations of the conflict between group and national political cultures and the quest for a political resolution of that conflict, be it peaceful and accommodative or harsh and oppressive.

We should also keep in mind that ideas of ethnic and racial *distinctiveness* can be imposed from without. Stephen Cornell and Douglass Hartmann have pointed out that it is "in the interests of Whites to construct a boundary that . . . sets African Americans apart [and] to attach a meaning to that boundary . . . that can justify denying to African Americans the rights of White Americans. Race meets *their* needs." They trace the same process in the thinking of Afrikaners in South Africa.[23]

However, as the history of the last two examples cited suggests, the result of such struggles is not always negative, especially (but not exclusively) when the battle is for fairness and assimilation rather than separatism. Witnessing the suffering endured, often by the innocent on both sides of the divide, inevitably awakens the sense of shared humanity among at least some of the contenders. When peace is won, the national political culture is often strengthened and revitalized as at least some of the values and practices of the newly accepted are absorbed. And those who have gained their rights will have commonly gained as well the satisfactions and self-esteem of those who did not give up until a righteous cause was won.

◼ Religion

Many of the comments made about group distinctiveness based on ethnicity apply with equal force to groups based on religion. Indeed, ethnic and religious characteristics are often bonded, in the sense that the group's identity is based on both, and the line between the two is difficult to distinguish. Catholicism is nearly as important as French ancestry in providing Canada's largest minority population with its sense of group identity. Judaism is a religion, but Jews share an ethnic as well as a religious heritage and constitute important minority populations in numerous countries. Significant Armenian-Christian populations exist in the predominantly Arab-Muslim nations of Iraq and Syria. The second largest ethnic group in the predominantly Malay-Muslim nation of Malaysia is Chinese Buddhist.

There are, however, societies that encompass separate group cultures based exclusively on religious differences. Muslim, Jewish, Buddhist, and Christian communities persist in cultures where the dominant religion is a different one and where the members of the religious minority are similar to the dominant populations in all other respects. In some cases, the religious distinction even arises within the same denomination as separatist sects develop among those who belong to the dominant religious group but practice their religion "with a difference." Members of both the Sunni and Shiite Islamic sects are Muslim, but the incompatibility between these two groups is severe; it played a major role in provoking war between Iraq and Iran and periodically produces armed clashes within nations like Pakistan in which both sects are found.[24]

In other cases, the distinction is not between religions or sects but simply between dramatically different interpretations of the same religion and the significance of its rulings for political affairs. Almost every Algerian is Muslim, but those who believe that the Qu'ran gives women full civil, social, and political rights and those who believe it says that women should remain invisible and in the home are presently in violent conflict. Over 30,000 persons have been killed over that issue in the past few years, including many women whose sole offense was to appear in public in Western clothes or wearing makeup.[25]

Religious values are, almost by definition, nonnegotiable, and the stakes are high. If I believe I will achieve eternal life and happiness by following a certain religious code, I will not be easily persuaded to give it up in the interests of such temporary comforts as peace on earth. Furthermore, the more my religious beliefs are challenged by the dominant culture, the more likely I am to be persuaded that I am being tested. Do I really believe? Then I will endure any hardship rather than sacrifice one tenet of the faith I have chosen. The members of a minority religious group, scorned or perhaps actively oppressed by members of the dominant group, must either break away or develop a strong enough attachment to their religious values to be able to endure the insults and injuries that come their way. It is for these reasons that religious fanaticism is more common in minor sects. Of course, the fanaticism itself makes the group less and less acceptable to the dominant groups in the society. If the boundary between the religious sphere and the political sphere cannot be established and maintained, the result may well be a spiral of increased fanaticism on one hand and increased public condemnation on the other. (See Box 3.3.)

BOX 3.3
**Religion and
Politics in the
United States**

Although churches that hold federal tax-exempt status are forbidden by law from endorsing or actively supporting candidates for public office, parishioners often do receive political guidance along with religious counsel. The relationship between religious identity and politics has always been strong in the United States, and is stronger at certain moments in our history. The 1990s were such a "moment." In 1988, it was considered something of an oddity that two ministers, Jesse Jackson and Pat Robertson, were among the serious early contenders for the presidential nomination of their respective parties, especially when the latter candidate campaigned almost exclusively on the moral issues associated with right-wing evangelicalism.[26] But by 1996, the Christian Right movement had become an even stronger force in U.S. politics, particularly within the Republican Party, and the growing power of this group forced candidates for that party's presidential nomination to demonstrate their good faith to them— in every sense of the word.[27] By the elections of 2000, however, the Republicans sensed that excessive catering to the Christian Right was costing more votes than it was gaining, and backed off accordingly. In that election the power of religion took a new form, one we may call "religiosity" —specific religious beliefs were now less significant, but candidates of both parties insisted on the importance of maintaining strong religious convictions.

IMPACT OF CULTURAL DIVISIVENESS ON THE NATION-STATE: YUGOSLAVIA AND CANADA

The divisions created in societies by ethnicity and race, or by religion, are among the deepest we know. They can, of course, be a source not only of diversity but of important contributions to the strength and creativity of a polity. Different peoples living harmoniously together in a single nation-state already know what it means to live in the human polity and are in that sense inevitably better equipped than more homogeneous peoples to function effectively internationally.

In recent years, however, groups that formerly lived together in relative contentment (or resignation) within the same nation-state have become determined to break apart, or establish new rules for living together. The end of the Cold War has meant the end of polarized conflict between blocs of nations each unified by a common goal of resisting the territorial and ideological encroachment of the other. Peoples whose struggle to maintain separate identities seemed long ago to have been forever submerged in this global battle have reemerged with seemingly undiminished needs to assert themselves and their nationhood. This has been particularly true of peoples whose cultural identity rests most heavily on ethnicity or race. The breakup of the former Yugoslavia and of the former Czechoslovakia as well as the efforts of the Baltic states and of the Chechnyans to establish independence from Russia are obvious examples of how the fall of the Soviet Union has permitted this kind of nationalism to reappear.

Not all ethnic intergroup struggles are clearly related to the end of the Cold War, however. The genocidal attacks of the warring peoples of Rwanda upon one another, the renewed insistence of some Canadians of French descent on the need for a separate state, and the complete transformation of legal and social relationships between white and black South Africans are examples of ethnic struggles that are only indirectly affected, if at all, by the fall of the Soviet Union. Their genesis is in more ancient battles: those of imperialist conquest and the resultant imposition of common nationhood on peoples who would have rather kept apart.

As the mere mention of these examples reminds us, the determination of different ethnic groups to redefine their legal and social relationships with other groups may be amply well motivated. They may also sometimes be peacefully pursued. Why do they sometimes lead to bloodshed and even civil war, and sometimes not? Looking more closely at two very different cases, that of the former Yugoslavia and of Canada, may help us find the answer to that question.

The background of the ethnic disputes in the territory of the former nation of Yugoslavia and in the present nation of Canada have a certain number of points in common. In both cases, national boundaries were determined by conquest and subsequent warfare, ultimately bringing together, not terribly long ago, people of different religions and different languages as well as different ethnic backgrounds. In both cases, the smoldering coals of old resentments have been periodically fanned by leaders seeking political gain, and these resentments have been deeply felt by many members of the general populace. Yet the battle in Canada, while certainly intense and as yet unresolved, has for many years been waged within the confines of the democratic process, whereas in Yugoslavia it has provoked open warfare and even attempted genocide.

To understand the differences, we must go beyond these superficial similarities and back in time—much farther back in the case of Yugoslavia than in that of Canada. The early nations of Croatia and Serbia were two separate groups of Slav settlers in the Balkans. During the Middle Ages, each practiced different forms of Christianity, the Croats becoming Roman Catholics within the Austro-Hungarian empire (beginning with the Treaty of Zagreb in 1102) and the Serbs following the tenets of Eastern Orthodoxy. The spread of the Ottoman empire in the fourteenth century meant the conversion of many in both groups to Islam. This third religion proved particularly strong in Bosnia-Herzegovina, a land in which both Croats and Serbs had settled and over which both ruled at different times. Some historians believe there is no separate Bosnian identity, pointing out that Bosnia had never been an independent state and that even "among Bosnian Muslims themselves . . . there are those who would argue that all Bosnian Muslims are simply Croats or Serbs who converted to Islam."[28] However, religious identity appears to be ascendant for Muslims, whereas ethnic identity as Serb or Croat is at least as important as religion for the self-identification of the Christian populations. Language is also a factor. Although all these peoples speak the same language, they use different scripts (Latin and Cyrillic) for writing it, and there are multiple dialects.[29] (See Figure 3.1.)

The first Yugoslav state bringing these peoples and others together was founded in 1918. In little more than a decade the more numerous Serbs imposed their rule over Croatia in the person of King Aleksander Karadjordjevic, who dissolved parliament and established a personal dictatorship. An underground Croatian resistance movement, Ustashe, led by Ante Pavelic, was formed and in 1934 the king was assassinated. As World War II began, the Yugoslav state was dissolved by Hitler, who gave the Croatian fascist movement, led by Pavelic, a free hand in the slaughter of somewhere between 350,000 and 750,000 Serbs, Jews, gypsies, and dissident Croats. To the extent they could, Serbs retaliated in their own resistance movement, the Yugoslav Army of the Fatherland (often referred to as the Chetniks) combining the pursuit of vengeance against the Croats with their battle against the Nazis. When Yugoslavia was recreated after the war its Communist leader, Marshall Josip Broz Tito (and his successors after his death in 1980), sought to overcome this history, in part by suppressing it, in part by trying to substitute the ideals of Communist egalitarianism for ethnoreligious competition and in part by loosening ties with the Soviets and reforming the tenets of Communist ideology to suit Yugoslav realities. But these efforts proved inadequate, especially as there continued to be different levels of economic development throughout the nation.

The fall of communism brought the Yugoslavs the opportunity to complete a process of separation from the Soviet bloc that was thus already well begun. Even more important, it brought them the chance to break away from each other, once and for all. Croatia and the more northern republic of Slovenia declared independence in July 1991. Each had maintained relatively cohesive religious, ethnic, and geographic identities, and these declarations were accepted by most of the international community. The Christian Serbs, however, were settled extensively throughout most of Yugoslavia and were determined to keep what remained of the nation intact, as well as to fight for the autonomy of Christian Serbian communities within the newly independent states. Muslim peoples, heavily concentrated in Bosnia but living throughout the region, were caught in the middle, whatever their lines of Slavic descent.

The difficulties of untangling this web have been tragically compounded by the readiness of demagogic leaders on both sides to stir up old memories that seemingly had begun to fade away, and to speak as if those guilty of

FIGURE 3.1
The Present
Boundaries of the
Former Yugoslavia

In March of 2002 the leaders of the remaining two republics of Yugoslavia, Serbia and Montenegro, met in Belgrade, officially dissolved the nation of Yugoslavia, and created the new state of "Serbia and Montenegro." In practice, the new state is an "extremely loose confederation" in which the two partners share only a common foreign and defense policy and a few governmental institutions, and provisions have been made to allow for their full separation after three years. Meanwhile, the former Yugoslav republic of Kosovo has become an international protectorate, administered under a U.N. Security Council resolution that specifically reaffirms the "territorial integrity" of Yugoslavia. The actual status of Kosovo is thus highly ambiguous, although in practice the tiny state appears to be moving steadily toward ever greater autonomy.[30]

crimes long past were in fact all the currently living members of the enemy group.[31] In addition, international forces such as the European Community, NATO, and the United Nations, as well as the world's strongest single power, the United States, all proved unable to work out timely, consistent, and realistic plans to avert the civil war that broke out in 1991.[32]

Of course no sooner was that war brought to an end than another subnationalist group in Serbia, the Muslim inhabitants of Kosovo, claimed their own right to independence. Kosovo had been granted considerable autonomy in 1974, in a constitutional revision that gave ethnic Albanians (Muslims) control over local affairs and the Albanian language equal footing with Serbo-Croatian, the language of the Yugoslavs. When Slobodan Milosević became Yugoslav president in 1989, however, he deprived the region of its autonomy, suppressed the Albanian language, and forced Albanians out of state jobs. By 1991, the Kosovo Liberation Army (KLA) had been established. As its claims and sporadic attacks grew stronger, Milosevic launched a counterattack and began forcing ethnic Albanians to leave. By May 1999, more than 90 percent had been expelled from their homes, with an estimated 700,000 Kosovars taking refuge in Albania, Bosnia-Herzegovina, the former Yugoslav Republic of Macedonia, and the Republic of Montenegro. Among the 600,000 forced from their homes but still trying to survive in Kosovo, at least 10,000 had been killed by July of that year. Once again, the international community, led by the United States but under NATO command, felt compelled to intervene, and this time the battle did not end until the relentless bombing of Serbia had forced the Serbs to remove Milosevic from power.[33]

The case of the conflict between the English-speaking and French-speaking populations in Canada is very, very different. First, the *history* of both peoples in this part of the world goes back less than five hundred years, and large-scale settlement began only at the beginning of the seventeenth century. Second, both groups considered themselves colonists for the nations from which they had migrated, rather than independent peoples and states. Third, one group, the French settlers, came under the control of the other after only about 150 years of separate settlement and after only one relatively brief war; the so-called French and Indian wars ended with French defeat in 1759, and in 1763 the French ceded the colony to Britain.[34] A brief rebellion in 1837 was rapidly suppressed. Fourth, in combination, the British and French settlers soon outnumbered and outfought the indigenous residents of what later became the provinces of Quebec and Ontario, particularly the Iroquois and the Algonquins.

Fifth, from the beginning the nation of Canada, established in 1867 when the British granted nearly complete independence to their own compatriots, has been dominated by one contingent, the English-speaking citizens. Although relatively small indigenous Indian and Inuit populations combined with relatively large-scale immigration from other nations in Europe, South-

Nationalism is often at its strongest when small neighboring states populated by persons of different religions battle for territory deemed religiously sacrosanct. Here Arabs and Israelis wave flags to demonstrate on behalf of their seemingly ir-reconcilable demands for land taken from the latter and now held by the former.
Above: © AFP/CORBIS; opposite: Nir Elias/Reuters

east Asia, and Latin America meant that by the end of the twentieth century nearly half of all Canadians were of neither French nor British origin, the politics and government were nevertheless originally formed by and for those of English descent.[35] Newcomers have arrived as individuals, and although some settle in ethnic enclaves (e.g., the Ukrainians and the Dutch), they have accepted Canadian structures as they found them and most have learned to speak English.

Sixth, despite this continued dominance of the English-speaking population, those of French descent have always had a special status as the largest and most cohesive ethnoreligious group, concentrated in a single region and present from the beginning of modern Canadian history. Canada thus has

two official languages, English and French, and the province of Quebec, 80 percent French speaking, has numerous other special dispensations.

A seventh and final crucial difference between the Yugoslav and Canadian cases is that other nations have never attempted to play out their own struggles by waging warfare on Canadian soil (as did Hungary, Turkey, Germany, and the Soviet Union, in the case of Yugoslavia). Although the French have given their North American cousins strong moral support, they have never promised serious military aid for a battle for independence.

In combination, these factors have meant that Catholic French Canadians have really had no choice but to pursue their ends by peaceful means, and English-speaking Canadians had no need to engage in violence to protect their ascendant position. The divisions between these two peoples are, compared to those between Croats and Serbs in the former Yugoslavia, tidy and relatively peaceful. The absence of a history of repeated warfare between British and French-speaking Canadians means there are no memories of recent bloodshed and pillage by the other side that ambitious politicians can exploit to motivate new wars and build new careers. (The Indian and Inuit peoples who remain may have such histories, but they lack the power to form additional contingents in the current battle.)

But make no mistake. The struggle between French- and English-speaking Canadians is serious, ongoing, and very real. Today's French Canadians do not take their religion or their ethnicity less seriously than the embattled peoples of the former Yugoslavia, and they have an extremely strong commitment to maintaining a different language from the majority population. They have often believed this heritage to be threatened by the policies of the national government. But they have been compelled by circumstance, not weakened by faint-heartedness, to wage their battle politically and constitutionally. This battle has not led them back to war, but it could yet lead them forward to secession. It provides ample fuel for occasional flare-ups of demagogic leadership.

The case of Quebec and the French Canadians is an interesting one that illustrates many other points we will make later in this book. We will return to them, and explain the current sources of their discontent as well as English-speaking Canadians' response, more fully later on. But for now, this example, contrasted with the Yugoslavian case, does help us understand some of the reasons why ethnoreligious struggle sometimes leads to bloodshed and sometimes does not. It should help us as well to stifle the impulse to call for simple solutions, insisting that if one set of peoples can find peaceful ways to conduct their battles with one another, others "should" be able to do the same. History has worked for peace in eastern Canada, but for recurrent slaughter in southern Europe. The conditions present in the Yugoslav case cannot be transformed overnight. People raised in battle and the memories of battle cannot be expected suddenly to value peace over revenge and order over victory. An immense task of political resocialization lies before those who seek an end to ethnoreligious strife in this and similarly affected polities.

EXPLAINING COMMITMENT TO A SUBNATIONAL GROUP: IDENTITY THEORY

Stating the racial, ethnic, and religious variables associated with group distinctiveness does not explain why the sense of difference sometimes assumes paramount importance and sometimes does not, inside particular polities. Tracing the different histories of the Canadian and Yugoslav examples tells us that what Cornell and Hartmann call "circumstance and utility" do indeed play an important role in determining when and why one's sense of group membership will become overwhelmingly significant, and what one will be prepared to do about it. Recent investigations into these questions have tried to combine personal and social/historical factors by focusing on the human need for a positive **identity**, considering how a group identity can help meet that need, and why that sometimes seems the only possible way to meet that need. "Political-cultural identity," says P. W. Preston, "is a matter of the creative response of groups to the structural circumstances enfolding the collectivity which they inhabit."[36] In other words, such identities become more important when they are more needed, and they are more needed when they help the members of a group cope with difficult conditions inside a larger polity. Daniel Bar-Tal reminds us that all "individuals strive for positive self-image" and that being part of a group and sharing "group-beliefs" is an extremely functional way of achieving such an image. Because others believe the same thing, "group beliefs arouse high confidence in their content," serve as the frame of reference for other more personal beliefs, and provide the group members with a sense of being united, belonging, and having the strength of numbers.[37] When the members of the group are denigrated by others, perhaps actively oppressed, then group identity becomes an ever-more important way of maintaining individual self-respect and confidence.

The conditions that make accepting and helping to create a powerful group identity appealing are often severe discrimination and repression directed at oneself as a member of that group. In some cases, however, the motivation is the awareness of having lost privileges that were formerly casually associated with group identity. As an example of the latter, Sankaran Krishna ascribes the rise of the Hindu fundamentalist Bharatiya Janata Party to the fear of many Hindus of loss of a "once-great Hindu civilization" swamped by a more democratic and heterogeneous Indian democracy. He suggests the party's appeal has been owing to the relief it offers to those (Hindus) who suffer from "anxieties of identity in a post-colonial society."[38] Similar anxiety regarding a loss of privilege associated with a once-secure identity clearly motivated the Ku Klux Klan to pledge itself to "maintain forever the God-given supremacy of the White Race."[39] Identity theory rightly reminds us that passionate commitment to a group commonly rests on a background of suffering one has undergone as a member of that group—but let us not forget that some suffering is more worthy of our compassion than other suffering.

CULTURAL DISSEMINATION OF POLITICAL VALUES: POLITICAL SOCIALIZATION

As we have already noted, not all cultural values endure, be they widely shared or subscribed to only by narrow groups. The lifetime of a value, however, is not determined by mere chance. Values endure when two conditions are met: (1) They continue to be relevant to objective needs, and (2) they are passed on clearly and persuasively by those who hold them to those who do not. Here we will focus on the second condition, the inculcation of values—a process known as **socialization**. Because we are interested in values that have political content, we will confine our study to **political socialization**.

Political socialization means the process by which we acquire our political opinions, beliefs, and values. Very shortly after my grandson Trevor came into the world, he lifted his head and looked around as if demanding to be told what this was all about. It was only with great restraint that I decided it was perhaps just a bit early to tell him he was now a citizen of the human polity. But only a little bit too soon. The world begins to teach us lessons about politics earlier than you might think. There is no better way to understand that truth—or to grasp what political socialization is all about in practice—than to explore your own memory. Take a moment to answer the following twelve questions:

1. What is your earliest political memory? What is the first political event you can recall? How did you learn about that event? What feelings did you have about it?

2. Was politics a subject for discussion in your home when you were a small child? If so, who talked about it? Did they talk to you about it directly? How would you characterize the general tone of such discussions? Interested or apathetic? Positive or negative? Factual or emotional?

3. Did the adults in your family vote? Did they tell you how they were voting? Did they themselves vote the same way?

4. Did anyone in your family take an active role in politics? What kind of role? Working for a political party or an interest group? Talking or writing to government officials about a problem requiring public action? Running for elective office or helping in someone else's campaign? If so, were you yourself involved in any way in that effort?

5. Do you know all the words to your country's national anthem? When and where did you first learn this song? Can you remember how you felt when you were first able to sing it?

6. What are some of the subjects your teachers in elementary school and high school covered when they taught you about the government of your country? About its history?

7. When did you get into your first political discussion? Who was it with? How did you feel about it?

8. Did you ever find that you were a minority of one in a political discussion with fellow students? How did you feel about that situation? Have you ever joined with fellow students in trying to persuade someone else to adopt a particular political opinion?

9. Do you watch the news on television, listen to it on the radio, or read it in the newspaper? If so, do you think you can tell how the newscaster or reporter feels about the political event he or she is reporting? If so, do you usually feel the same way?

10. Do you pay attention to political campaigns? Do you try to figure out the character of political candidates as well as the content of their messages? Do you sometimes make up your mind how you will vote (or how you would vote) on the basis of such assessments?

11. If you have a job (or have had one in the past), have you ever discussed politics with coworkers? How did it make you feel to find you were in agreement? In disagreement?

12. How important do you think it is for people in love to have the same ideas about politics? If you are in love, do the two of you ever talk about politics? Do you tend to agree or disagree? Have you changed any of your political beliefs because of the ideas and arguments of the person you love?

By taking the time to probe for the answers to these questions, you have begun to get a good sense of how you personally were socialized to have the political beliefs you do. You can probably also see that political socialization is a complex, layered process. We do not learn about politics all at once, and no one receives only a single set of socialization messages from a single agent or institution. By looking at the most powerful agents of socialization—family, school, peers, media, and politics itself—we can learn a bit more about how political socialization really works.

Political Socialization by the Family

The family is almost always the most important agent of political socialization, even in homes where politics is never discussed. Adult family members (especially mothers and fathers, but aunts, uncles, and grandparents can also play important socialization roles if they live in the same household) guide children in the development of basic personality traits, attitudes, and values. Such guidance may be deliberate and benevolent or haphazard and even cruel, but because family members are in more or less constant contact with one another, and because the emotional ties between them are strong, the family inevitably plays the key role in the early socialization of the child.

Socialization within the family need not be "about politics" in order to include political socialization. It can be indirect as well as direct. As we are taught that certain general personality traits are desirable, we develop a personality that will have specific political as well as social proclivities. Tamar Liebes and Rivka Ribak found that different patterns of interpersonal communication within Israeli families were related to the political attitudes children developed and their level of commitment to political participation. Particularly important was the distinction between families that believed that conflicts should be minimized and even suppressed in the interests of harmony and those that believed they should be "resolved through clear representation and fair debate of diverse points of view."[40] Did your family emphasize obedience, responsibility, and orderliness? Or were you taught that discussion, independent thought, and having the courage of your convictions were more important?[41]

Whether by direct or indirect means, the family has been shown to play an important role in one's choice of partisan affiliation. (See Box 3.4.) Children often have "strong positive or negative feelings concerning candidates as a result of parental suggestion," and in one study over 50 percent of American, British, and German children chose the same party as their parents (American Democratic parents appeared to be the most influential; 70 percent of their children chose the Democratic Party as their own, while 20 percent opted for Independent and only 10 percent chose the Republican Party).[42] In families where there is no conflict between the parents on that subject, parental influence is at its strongest, and the likelihood of such congruence is even greater in families where parents and their grown children have similar occupations, incomes, levels of education, and religion.[43]

The quality of family life also influences other forms of political behavior. Several studies gathered recently by Constance Flanagan and Lonnie Sherrod suggest that "a family ethic of social responsibility" helps build a sense of civic commitment, especially for daughters, and that adolescents who are encouraged to engage in volunteer work carry that ethic forward into adulthood.[44] On the other hand, Sai-Wing Leung has shown how Chinese children in postwar Hong Kong families were taught to avoid politics altogether as a way of avoiding trouble, given the facts of British domination, a powerful neighboring Chinese government, and the confusing alternative taken in Taiwan. As one of them later recalled, "adults did not want to talk about the Chinese government or the Taiwanese government; regarding the colonial government, they treated it as nonexistent."[45]

Political Socialization by the School

Education is a second major force in political socialization. Political leaders in every part of the world have recognized the importance of the schools in developing loyal and productive citizens, and have worked to bring education under the control of the state. Thus, almost every school in the world, be it public or private, is required to function in accordance with an elaborate body of statutory law that prescribes (at least in part) the content of its curriculum, the training required for its instructors, and the standards established for admission and graduation. Is the course you are reading this book for meeting one of your requirements for graduation? Chances are good that the program making it so was reviewed at some level of your university's administration for its compliance with state educational policy.

This does not mean that the only purpose of the political socialization you receive in school is to ensure your loyalty to the system. Societies vary in the extent to which they insist that the schools perform such a function. In any case, numerous forces are at work in the average public school—curriculum, teachers, classroom rituals, extracurricular activities, and the attitudes of fellow students—and only the most rigorously authoritarian system is capable

BOX 3.4
**Teaching Children
About War**

1. Mother to 3-year-old son: "War is when many people are fighting. They fight all at the same time. War is not nice. We don't like the fighting." "Peace is when people everywhere like each other and get along. The people share. They don't hit each other nor hurt each other."

2. Father to 5-year-old son: "War is when two groups of people disagree so much that they are willing to kill other people to try to prove their point."

3. Mother to 6-year-old son: "[War is] when countries disagree and fight with each other. [Peace is] when countries are *not* fighting with each other."

4. Mother to 7-year-old daughter: "War is when two groups of people get mad at each other and stop trying to talk to one another. Then they start fighting each [other] and people on both side[s] get killed. The war isn't over until enough people on one side are killed and the other side can take over. When we think of peace we think of quiet, restful times. But I think peace is more than that. If two people are being noisy but they are having fun together and feel good about themselves— they are being peaceful. I think peace can be a lot of work to get— because peace is when people work hard to talk about their differences and work them out so that they can cooperate instead of fighting. If people are peaceful we don't waste time fighting and things are right so that good things can happen between people."

5. Mother to 10-year-old daughter: "[War is] fighting with words, attitudes and ammunition (guns, bombs, and knives). When you sisters fight and then refuse to speak to each other and fix your problem that is silent war. Peace is communication: [being] able to work, live and play together. Peace is restful and safe like our home. Peace is where love is: giving in to each other and preferring one another like Jesus taught us with his life."

6. Father to 12-year-old son: "War is armed aggression by one country on another. It is not abstract, one country fighting another. Real people are getting killed or maimed. War isn't fun or a contest: it's life and death and it should not be entered into lightly. Peace is the absence of war. It's toleration of others' opinions. Hopefully it's even cooperation and respect between different ways of life."

Source: Judith A. Myers-Walls, Karen S. Myers-Bowman, and Ann E. Pelo, "Parents as Educators about War and Peace," *Family Relations* 42 (January 1993): 66–73. Copyrighted 1993 by the National Council on Family Relations, 3989 Central Ave. NE, Suite 550, Minneapolis, MN 55421. Reprinted by permission.

Note: The war in question was the 1991 conflict in the Persian Gulf.

Saying the pledge of allegiance. Political socialization often takes place in the schoolroom.
Shirley Zeiberg/Photo Researchers Inc.

(or desirous) of ensuring that all these forces operate to inculcate the same set of political attitudes and values.

How do all these different forces influence a student's political choices? The curriculum is where we are most likely to find an emphasis on political indoctrination, or, more benignly, on civic training.[46] A person who is politically indoctrinated is simply given all the "right" answers, but a person who receives civic training learns the rules for playing the nation's political game, whatever that game might be. A citizen in an authoritarian regime is likely to find the emphasis on indoctrination; a citizen in a democracy normally receives a higher quotient of civic training.

Some of the tools of indoctrination in the schools include reciting a pledge of allegiance, raising and lowering the flag, working under the photograph of the smiling president or emperor, and singing patriotic songs. Such rituals work to develop a sense of awe, devotion to the state, commitment to collective activity, and a feeling of belonging to a larger community. The Chinese schoolchild is taught that the prodemocracy demonstrations in Tiananmen Square in 1989 were "the activities of hoodlums and counter-revolutionaries who attacked the army and killed many brave soldiers."[47] However, every political system includes some indoctrination of children, even the most democratic. Needless to say, such indoctrination does not always "work." Carol Seefeldt argues, for example, that the daily recitation of a pledge of allegiance in a democracy too easily becomes a meaningless ritual; she suggests it is more important for schoolchildren to be involved in the school community, taking part in setting rules as well as obeying them and seeking ways to change them democratically when they are not fair.[48]

Seefeldt's recommendation fits within the approach of civic training. So do the conclusions of Miranda Yates and James Youniss in their recent study of a year-long service learning program for black urban adolescents who were required to help in a local soup kitchen as part of their high school curriculum. Participants came to believe they had a personal responsibility to help enact social change, and furthermore that their actions could make a difference, that they could "help shape the political and moral directions of the nation." Alumni interviews several years later persuaded Yates and Youniss that such experiences have enduring consequences; effective civic training inculcates participatory commitment as a personal value for life.[49]

In any case, the balance between the two forms of socialization in the schools is always subject to change, not only from nation to nation, but sometimes from community to community. There is some evidence, for example, that children in lower-income settings in the United States are more likely to be taught that "politics is conducted by formal governmental institutions working in harmony for the benefit of citizens" (stress on indoctrination), while those in more affluent communities "encourage a belief in the citizen's ability to influence government action through political participation" (stress on civic training). Similarly, girls attending British private schools, including those from lower-income families whose tuition is paid by scholarship, have higher levels of interest in politics, trust in the political process, belief in the stability of the political system, and knowledge of local politics than girls attending state schools. They are also more likely to anticipate being politically active in the future.[50]

Political Socialization by Peers

The study of political socialization has concentrated very heavily on what happens during childhood and adolescence, but more and more attention is now being paid to patterns of adult socialization. We do not spend our youth being taught how to think about politics and our adulthood acting out these acquired beliefs. We continue to be influenced by others, either to hold fast to our old points of view or to come to a different understanding of the world of politics.

Peers are a good example of a lifelong force for political socialization. We find them in the sandbox, at school, on the assembly line or in the office, in clubs, and eventually in retirement homes. They may be friends we have chosen, fellow students, or coworkers we do not particularly like but with whom we must perforce spend a great deal of our time. Sometimes they are peers only in the limited sense that we are all "grownups." Authority figures—the boss, the landlord, the military commander—may continue to shape our political choices for us in adult life as they did in childhood.

How influential our peers will be depends in part on how we feel about them and in part on how much attention they give to political questions. It also depends on the nature of the times and the personal circumstances of those involved. If the society is in an era of change, as when a nation is recovering from a devastating war, or if our personal circumstances have changed significantly from what they were in the past, as when we gain or lose a fortune, we are more likely to be susceptible to the influence of our peers, seeking contemporary guidance in a strange new world. On the other hand, when we move with others like ourselves into new situations, these accompanying peers sometimes help us maintain the values we had in the past. A high-ranking New York City official riding on a bus filled with New York African American leaders about to join the 1995 Million Man March on Washington, D.C., said, "All black men ought to be supporting this. We have a lot to overcome in this country. I'm here because I feel we ought to support each other." His words were directed to his peers—others like himself who had moved up economically and might be at risk of losing touch with the less fortunate members of their race.[51]

How much our political values are shaped by the values of our peers depends not only on the content of those values and the quality of those peers but also on the social context we live in. Peers may be the least or the greatest of the socializing forces in our lives.

Political Socialization by the Media

The socializing forces we have discussed so far are what can be called **proximate forces**—that is, forces we encounter in person as we live with our family, go to school, or interact with others in a wide range of social settings. Human beings are also socialized by **nonproximate forces**, however—agents with whom we have no direct personal contact. One such force is the mass media, and by far the most important source of news and information is television.

Americans now average nearly 52 hours of television watching per week (for American children, the figure is 28 hours a week, and 54 percent have a television set of their own in their bedrooms). Our addiction to television has reached the point where one scholar, Mary A. Hepburn, suggests that it is time to redesign our model of socialization. She argues that not only are

FIGURE 3.2
The Cultural
Formation of
Political Values

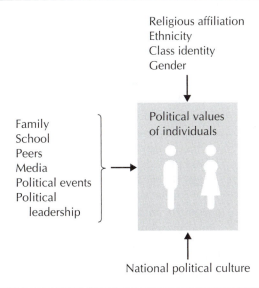

Religious affiliation
Ethnicity
Class identity
Gender

Political values
of individuals

Family
School
Peers
Media
Political events
Political
   leadership

National political culture

the media the prime socializing force operating directly on individuals in our society but they also socialize all the other socializing agents (see Figure 3.2).[52]

The fact that studies have found that 57 percent of television programs contain violence tells us something about the nature of that socialization, but so does the content and format of actual news broadcasts. As Hepburn says and we all know, significant public issues are seldom covered in depth on TV. News stories are presented between commercials, hard news is mixed with human interest vignettes, and recurrent loud music themes inform us that although what we are watching is "exciting" it is also "entertaining." When we are switched without warning from scenes of human devastation to those of happy drinkers of soft drinks, how can we believe we should take the former seriously, possibly even try to do something about them? Answer: we cannot.

The commercial needs of the publishing and broadcasting companies, and the level of interest and comprehension of most audiences, combine to ensure that we normally acquire only the most fragmentary understanding of local, national, and world events, and must rely on reporters and commentators to tell us what they "mean."

This is not to suggest, however, that the news media are always in the business of handing out ready-made political opinions. Indeed, in the United States and in many other Western nations there is a strong tradition of journalistic impartiality that prevents reporters from taking sides on controversial issues or introducing their own biases into straight news stories. A number of exceptions to this rule, however, are tacitly allowed. The news media in the United States, for example, seldom hesitate to show a strong bias in favor of national interests over the interests of other nations; they often present those who take action on behalf of unfamiliar or unpopular political opinions as eccentric, amusing, or contemptible; and they permit their reporters to use adjectives—or, in the case of television anchors, gestures—that help to convey the "correct" interpretation of the event being reported. Such exceptions to the rule of journalistic impartiality are particularly likely during a time of national crisis—we need only hearken back to the coverage of the events of September 11, 2001. At such a time, the American people would probably be deeply shocked by any effort to achieve impartiality; they expect the media to be "on our side," 100 percent.

Of course, not all news is conveyed on news programs—much of it is now presented on talk shows on radio and television. Although such conversational shows normally discuss news that has already been presented in more conventional ways, in fact, many citizens first learn of important events by listening to or watching their favorite talk show hosts and their guests. In these settings, the media escape most of the restrictions imposed on conventional news, and their hope of attracting viewers (and selling the products advertised on commercial breaks) stimulates them to stress entertainment values—which in turn inevitably means highlighting issues that arouse emotional response and discussing them emotionally. Yet nearly all of the questions discussed have a political component, and the net result is a powerful new form of political socialization. Is listening to and watching talk shows a good way to form opinions rationally, considering all the facts? If not, does it matter?

The Internet gives citizens who have access to it the possibility of obtaining more detailed news; however, we know full well that that is not the purpose of most "surfing."

In any case, it is not hard to understand why the world's more authoritarian systems insist on absolute control over radio, television, and the press, and in some cases over all forms of the printed word. When the rulers of Myanmar refused to accept the result of democratic elections in 1990, they engaged in numerous killings, "disappearances," and acts of torture to suppress opposition—but they also took great care to maintain absolute control of all six newspapers published in the nation as well as all its radio and television networks.[53] Unfortunately, an almost endless number of similar examples could be cited from around the world.

Political Socialization by Political Events

Not all our political opinions are secondhand. We pay attention to what we are taught or advised to think about politics by our families, textbooks, teachers, peers, and the news media, but we are also directly influenced by

Algerian women wave prodemocracy banners and demonstrate against the Muslim fundamentalists seeking to keep all women in traditional roles. When the world of politics impinges directly on individuals, changing their destinies, powerful socializing forces are at work.
AP/Wide World Photos

the world of politics. We may get our information about a political issue or event from one of the socialization agents already cited and still adopt our own distinctive attitudes about the facts presented, regardless of what we are advised to believe. In some cases, we move out into the political world ourselves and form our opinions on the basis of direct experience.

In times of peace, children are rarely socialized directly by political reality but receive its impact indirectly through attention to other socializing agents: family, school, peers. But even though filtered through such a lens, a major event like the assassination of a president may have as strong an effect on children as on adults. Studying schoolchildren's reactions to the death of President John F. Kennedy, Roberta Sigel found that they responded to the event with emotional reactions very similar to those of adults. They felt grief, sympathy for the family, shame (that "this could happen in our country"), and anger; they lost their appetites, had headaches, and had trouble going to sleep—and they reported all these reactions with just about the same frequency as adults.[54]

Long-term warfare, on the other hand, directly and painfully socializes all those in its path, including the children of the world. In the years between 1985 and 1995, between 4 and 5 million children were physically disabled by acts of war, more than 5 million were moved into refugee camps, and more than 12 million were made homeless. Children are themselves often drafted as combatants, sometimes as human minesweepers and sometimes even as spies. Not surprisingly, those who have been forced to play such roles are often unable to readapt to civilian life. Psychiatrist Daya J. Somasundaram, who works at Jaffna General Hospital in Sri Lanka, a nation of continuing internal warfare in recent years, says that for such children "normal living becomes sort of dull." They develop, he says, a "tendency to sudden, aggressive outbursts—throwing things, assaulting people . . . these experiences go deep and become a permanent part of the personality."[55]

Other observers have noted the impact that political crises can have on the way young adults will later interpret political events and on the choices they are likely to make in the voting booth. Thus, American voters who came of age in the midst of the Great Depression are more likely than others to make political decisions on the basis of economic factors, whereas those who reached maturity during the height of the Vietnam War are more concerned with issues of war and peace. French citizens who came of age around the time of the massive student demonstrations of 1968 that brought the nation to a standstill and forced serious changes in its educational system are often referred to as *soixantehuitards* or "nineteensixtyeighters"—the term has come to mean not only those who took an active part in that year's massive and eventually nationwide protest movement, but anyone of that age group who shows a tendency to reject the status quo and to insist on the need for reform. In Britain, the conservative beliefs of former Prime Minister Margaret Thatcher were more attractive to those who came of voting age in the relatively prosperous mid-1980s than to those who joined the political arena in the more difficult years just before.[56]

Of course, the world of politics sometimes impinges powerfully and directly on citizens of all ages, changing their views forever. The individual drafted to fight in wartime, or forced to donate the family's livestock to the cause of guerrilla insurgents, or arrested in a case of mistaken identity—or simply summoned to appear at the tax agency's office—may well have a different opinion of the political process after such a direct experience of "how it really works." The change may be a positive one. The military experience may produce a veteran more patriotic than the draftee; the guerrilla movement may succeed and introduce land reforms that give the farmer whose livestock was confiscated a sense of commitment to a glorious cause; judicial procedure may establish innocence with impressive speed and efficiency—and it is even possible that the tax agency will graciously acknowledge that the original payment was correct. But whether positive or negative, direct experience in politics and government does function as a force for political socialization.

The forces of family, school, peers, media, and political events are not the only forces of political socialization, nor do they act separately on us. We can never be sure when the messages of one agency will be stronger than those of another in shaping how we respond to the political present.[57] But we *can* seek to be conscious of where we have learned our opinions and try to reevaluate them from time to time in the light of the best knowledge we may have gained since their original inculcation.

SUMMARY AND CONCLUSION

The culture that we live in powerfully shapes the political values we hold dear. Family, school, peers, media, and political events all exert a strong influence on our attitudes and opinions regarding the world of politics, and so do our religious, ethnic, class, and other group identities—including that of national citizenship. When political values are bonded with cultural values, they have an added strength; we do not take lightly the efforts of any individuals or institutions to prevent us from living our lives according to those values. For this reason, our leaders, our institutions, and other nations interested in maintaining successful relations with us must give such values careful consideration and response, or risk the loss of legitimacy, political alienation, social unrest, and possibly even revolution or war. The formation of cultural values and their significance for the political process are summarized graphically in Figure 3.2.

Conflicting cultural values can trouble international relations in time of peace as well as in time of war. In some cases, problems develop because the parties involved do not even recognize that they are operating on different normative assumptions. In most African systems, great emphasis is placed on one's responsibility to take care of other members of one's extended family, if one is in a position to do so. In most European systems, great emphasis is placed on hiring the most qualified candidate for any job, regardless of that person's family ties. When African and European management teams attempt to work together on a development project, misunderstandings and recriminations over hiring practices are highly likely if both sides have not understood and resolved this fundamental difference in cultural values.

As the nations of the world grow more interdependent, will our cultural values grow more similar? Probably. After all, socialization can take place across national boundaries as well as across the diningroom table or the village well. The process is complex, as a simple personal example may serve to illustrate. When I am invited to a home in west Africa, I am unlikely to be offered kola nuts—but when my host passes the bowl to his other guests, he is now likely to be aware that I may find the omission disturbing and to take the trouble to explain to me that it is not the tradition to include women in this practice. I myself, aware of the many courtesies that have been extended to me, may be able to put my Western feminist instincts on hold, yet feel compelled to make a point of including his wife in the political discussion we are having, whether she is interested or not. What is happening in such a case? Several persons whose cultural values are not the same are interacting. Although we disagree, we listen to each other and we are unavoidably socializing each other. It is unlikely that no change is taking place.

Then again, how desirable is it that the same values should be shared throughout the whole human polity? What if one of the values we come to share might be respect for one another's differences? Or might some values be called *requisite* values for humanity? Perhaps there really are values that must be universally held if there is to be any hope at all of harmonious resolution of the problems we confront—and share—in the human polity.

QUESTIONS TO CONSIDER

1. What is the political opinion you have that you care most about, believe in most fervently? See how many persons, events, or media reports you can name that *may* (just possibly?) have influenced you to have that opinion.
2. What are the dominant opinions and values that are shared in the political culture of your nation? How well do they fit your own opinions and values?
3. Consider one of the cultural groups in your nation (to which you may or may not belong). What factors have given this group its sense of difference from others?
4. Why did cultural divisiveness lead to war in the former Yugoslavia, and not in Canada, at the end of the twentieth century?

SELECTED READINGS

Aaron, Henry J., Thomas E. Mann, and Timothy Taylor, eds. *Values and Public Policy* (Washington, D.C.: The Brookings Institution, 1994). Essays discussing how values are formed and can mediate the effects of public policies.

Almond, Gabriel and Sidney Verba. *The Civic Culture* (Boston: Little, Brown, 1963). This is the classic study of political culture, focusing on political attitudes and democracy in Italy, Mexico, the United Kingdom, and West Germany. See also their edited volume, *The Civic Culture Revisited* (Newbury Park, Calif.: Sage, 1989).

Coyle, Dennis J. and Richard J. Ellis. *Politics, Policy and Culture* (Boulder, Colo.: Westview Press, 1994). The authors argue that politics, policies, and preferences cannot be understood without a consideration of culture.

Howe, Carolyn. *Political Ideology and Class Formation: A Study of the Middle Class* (Westport, Conn.: Praeger, 1992). An analysis of theories and opinion data on the political ideology of the middle class.

Inglehart, Ronald, Miguel Bassanez, and Alejandro Moreno. *Human Values and Beliefs: A Cross-Cul-*

tural Source Book: Political, Religious, Sexual and Economic Norms in 43 Societies (Ann Arbor: University of Michigan Press, 1998). Provides a wealth of information about the values and beliefs of people all over the world on such topics as politics, economics, religion, family life, and gender roles. Analyzes differences in terms of age, gender, economic standing, and education.

Putnam, Robert D. *Bowling Alone: The Collapse and Revival of American Community* (New York: Simon & Schuster, 2000). Examines over 500,000 interviews of Americans conducted in the final quarter of the twentieth century and documents the increasing disengagement of Americans not only from the public sphere, but from informal and private social relations as well.

Renshon, Stanley and John Duckitt, eds. *Political Psychology: Cultural and Cross-Cultural Foundations* (New York: New York University Press, 2000). Explores how cultural and political psychology shapes a wide range of contemporary political issues, ranging from international and cross-cultural conflicts to cultural diversity, human rights, social stratification, and cultural shifts in the course of political change.

Schatzberg, Michael G. *Political Legitimacy in Middle Africa: Father, Family, Food* (Bloomington: Indiana University Press, 2001). An innovative work examining deeply ingrained views of government and its relationship to citizens as revealed in metaphors found in the popular press in eight African nations.

Sigel, Roberta, ed. *Political Learning in Adulthood: A Sourcebook of Theory and Research* (Chicago: University of Chicago Press, 1989). Eleven chapters by noted specialists in political socialization, with extensive reference guides to sources in this area of study.

WEB SITES OF INTEREST

1. Political Culture Questionnaire
   http://www.pitt.edu/redsox/pol.cul.html
   Register your thoughts regarding the U.S. system of governing and what is happening to it; receive a summary of current results from this ongoing survey (by e-mailing redsox@vms.cis.pitt.edu).

2. World Values Survey
   http://wvs.isr.umich.edu/
   A worldwide investigation of sociocultural and political change covering more than sixty-five societies on all six inhabited continents.

NOTES

1. This definition combines those used in Ian McLean, ed., *The Concise Oxford Dictionary of Politics* (Oxford, U.K.: Oxford University Press, 1996), p. 379, and by Ann L. Craig and Wayne A. Cornelius, "Political Culture in Mexico: Continuities and Revisionist Interpretations," in Gabriel Almond and Sidney Verba, eds., *The Civic Culture Revisited* (Boston: Little, Brown, 1980), p. 340.

2. Henry J. Aaron, Thomas E. Mann, and Timothy Taylor, eds., *Values and Public Policy* (Washington, D.C.: The Brookings Institution, 1994), p. 5.

3. Walter S. Jones, *The Logic of International Relations,* 7th ed. (New York: HarperCollins, 1991), p. 53.

4. Gabriel Almond and Sidney Verba, *The Civic Culture* (Boston: Little, Brown, 1963), pp. 308–11.

5. Ibid., pp. 338–40.

6. Almond and Verba, *Civic Culture,* p. 315; Desmond S. King, *The New Right, Politics, Markets and Citizenship* (Chicago: Dorsey, 1987), pp. 121, 198.

7. David B. Conradt, "Changing German Political Culture," in *Civic Culture Revisited,* p. 230.

8. Anne-Marie Le Gloannec, "On German Identity," *Daedalus* 124, no. 2 (Winter 1994): 133–34.

9. Donald Sasson, *Contemporary Italy: Economy, Society and Politics since 1945* (London and New York: Longman, 1997), pp. 107–27.

10. Oladimeji Aborisade and Robert J. Mundt, *Politics in Nigeria* (London and New York: Longman, 1999), p. 82.

11. James A. Bill and Robert Springborg, *Politics in the Middle East* (London and New York: Longman, 1999), p. 76.

12. Charles Tilly, *From Mobilization to Revolution* (Reading, Mass.: Addison-Wesley, 1978), p. 122.

13. For an interesting view of the complexities of the Chechnyan case, see Anatol Lieven, "Nightmare in the Caucasus," *Washington Quarterly* 23, no. 1 (Winter 2000): 145–59.

14. *New York Times,* 8 Jan. 1995, 4.

15. *World Encyclopedia of the Nations: Asia and Oceania* (New York: Worldmark Press, 1988), p. 92.

16. Barry Came, "A Grievance Upheld," *Maclean's* 106, no. 18 (3 May 1993): 26.

17. Standard works on the problem of class include Karl Marx, "Manifesto of the Communist Party," in Robert C. Tucker, ed. *The Marx-Engels Reader* (New York: Norton, 1978), pp. 469–500; "The Class Struggles in France," in ibid., pp. 586–93; and "The Eighteenth Brumaire of Louis Napoleon," in ibid., pp. 594–617; Max Weber, "Class, Status, Party," in H. H. Gerth and C. Wright Mills, eds., *From Max Weber: Essays in Politics* (New York: Oxford University Press, 1946), pp. 180–95; and Thomas Humphrey Marshall, *Class, Citizenship and Social Development: Essays* (Garden City, N.Y.: Doubleday, 1964). For a contemporary summary and analysis, see Berch Berberoglu, *Class Structure and Social Transformation* (Westport, Conn.: Praeger, 1994).

18. On the question of class consciousness, see Clem Brooks, "Class Consciousness and Politics in Comparative Perspective," *Social Science Research* 23 (June 1994): 167–95.

19. Lawrence Goodwyn, *Breaking the Barrier: The Rise of Solidarity in Poland* (New York: Oxford University Press, 1991), pp. ix, xxvi–xxvii. Goodwyn argues that the shared experiences of the activist members of Solidarnosc were more important in bringing success than all the "documents of written exhortation—leaflets, public demands, organizing appeals, and the like" that others produced in their support (xxvii).

20. For an interesting study of a recent peasant revolt, see Neil Harvey, *The Chiapas Rebellion: The Struggle for Land and Democracy* (Durham, N.C.: Duke University Press, 1998). A recent example of a political party formed by both farm and working-class interests in an effort to protect cherished values and defy "technocratic decrees" is the Hunt-Fish-Nature-Tradition party of France, whose members are as resistant to modern environmentalist values as they are to the automation of the traditional agricultural and artisan labor they represent. (*L'Express,* 5 Mar. 1992, 60–62.)

21. Robert J. Thompson and Joseph R. Rudolph Jr., "Ethnic Politics and Public Policy," in Dennis L. Thompson and Dov Ronen, eds., *Ethnicity, Politics and Development* (Boulder, Colo.: Lynne Rienner, 1986), p. 32.

22. Peter Ulvin, "Ethnicity and Power in Burundi and Rwanda: Different Paths to Mass Violence," *Comparative Politics* 32, no. 3 (April 1999): 253–71.

23. Stephen Cornell and Douglass Hartmann, *Ethnicity and Race: Making Identities in a Changing World* (Thousand Oaks, Calif.: Pine Forge Press, 1998), pp. 150–51.

24. Akbar S. Ahmed, *Living Islam: From Samarkand to Stornoway* (New York: Facts on File, 1994), pp. 49–51.

25. Nora Boustany, "Targets of Opportunity," *Washington Post National Weekly Edition* (13–19 Mar. 1995): 17; "If Islamists Rule Algeria," *The Economist* (25 Feb. 1995): 98. See also Karima Bennoune, "Algerian Women Confront Fundamentalism," *Monthly Review* 46 (Sept. 1994): 26–39.

26. For the Robertson campaign, see *New York Times,* 7 Sept. 1987, 7; 14 Sept. 1987, 1; 15 Sept. 1987, 19; 30 Sept. 1987, 20.

27. James A. Barnes, "Rightward March?" *National Journal* (6 Aug. 1994): 1847–51.

28. Robin Alison Remington, "Bosnia: The Tangled Web," *Current History* 92, no. 577 (Nov. 1993): 364–69. I have drawn extensively from this useful article; the quote comes from p. 366.

29. Ian D. Armour, "Nationalism vs. Yugoslavism," *History Today* 42 (Oct. 1992): 11–13.

30. Joanne Mariner, "Serbia and Montenegro—and Kosovo?" March 18, 2002, at http://writ.news.findlaw.com/mariner/20020318.html.

31. Svetlana Slapsak, "Trains, Times Lost Forever," *The Nation* (31 May 1993): 740.

32. *Wall Street Journal*, 28 July 1995, A1–A4. For a discussion of the belief held by many Muslims that international reluctance to interfere effectively came from the fact that "[the West] does not want a viable Muslim nation in Europe," see Akbar S. Ahmed, "Ethnic Cleansing: A Metaphor for Our Time?" *Ethnic and Racial Studies* 18, no. 1 (Jan. 1995): 18.

33. "Kosovo: The Jerusalem of Serbia," from the Web site of the *Washington Post*, http://washingtonpost.com/wp-srv/inatl/longterm/balkans, 19 Oct. 1999; John Kifner, "Inquiry Estimates Serb Drive Killed 10,000 in Kosovo," *New York Times*, 18 July 1999, 1; and U.S. Department of State, "Erasing History: Ethnic Cleansing in Kosovo," report accessed at http://www.state.gov/www/regions/eur/rpt_9905_ethnic_ksvo_exec.html as of 19 Oct. 1999.

34. The French and Indian wars were actually a struggle between the British and the French for control of that part of North America that later became the Canadian provinces of Quebec and Ontario; the struggle began as the two European peoples sided with different Indian tribes engaged in battle—hence the name.

35. The word *Indian* is the official term used in Canada, although *Native American* would of course apply there as well as in the United States.

36. P. W. Preston, *Political/Cultural Identity: Citizens and Nations in a Global Era* (London: Sage, 1997), p. 1.

37. Daniel Bar-Tal, "Group Beliefs as an Expression of Social Identity," in Stephen Worchel, J. Francisco Morales, Dario Paez, and Jean-Claude Deschamps, *Social Identity: International Perspectives* (London: Sage, 1998), pp. 93–114.

38. Sunkaran Krishna, "Constitutionalism, Democracy and Political Culture in India," in Daniel P. Franklin and Michael J. Baun, eds., *Political Culture and Constitutionalism: A Comparative Approach* (Armonk, N.Y. and London: M. E. Sharpe, 1995), p. 175.

39. Quoted in Bar-Tal, op. cit., p. 98.

40. Tamar Liebes and Rivka Ribak, "The Contribution of Family Culture to Political Participation, Political Outlook and Its Reproduction," *Communication Research* 19, no. 5 (Oct. 1992): 618–41. The quote is on p. 620.

41. For another interesting study in this regard see Vesha V. Godena, "Hidden Tendencies and Unintentional Impacts in Family Socialization: The Example of Authoritarian vs. Non-Authoritarian Family Socialization Type," Research Notes, *Journal of Comparative Family Studies*, XXII, no. 3 (Autumn 1991): 359–66.

42. Stanley W. Moore, James Lare, and Kenneth A. Wagner, *The Child's Political World: A Longitudinal Perspective* (New York: Praeger, 1985), p. 135, and Russell J. Dalton, *Citizen Politics*, 2nd ed. (Chatham, N.J.: Chatham House, 1996), p. 201.

43. Steven A. Peterson, *Political Behavior: Patterns in Everyday Life* (Newbury Park, Calif.: Sage, 1990), p. 157. (Peterson offers an excellent general summary of socialization scholarship.)

44. Constance Flanagan and Lonnie Sherrod, "Youth Political Development: An Introduction," *Journal of Social Issues* 54, no. 3 (1998): 447–56.

45. Sai-Wing Leung, *The Making of an Alienated Generation: The Political Socialization of Secondary School Students in Transitional Hong Kong* (Brookfield, Vt.: Ashgate, 1997), p. 28.

46. This distinction was first made by Richard Dawson and Kenneth Prewitt in 1969, in their book, *Political Socialization* (Boston: Little, Brown). They characterized the first as teaching "a specific political ideology which is intended to rationalize and justify a particular regime," and the second as teaching "how a good citizen participates in the political life of [the] nation" (pp. 147–48).

47. Clive Harber, "International Contexts for Political Education," *Educational Review* 43, no. 3 (1991): 247.

48. Carol Seefeldt, "The Pledge of Allegiance in Pub-

lic Schools," *Education Digest* 55, no. 1 (Sept. 1989): 62–63.

49. Miranda Yates and James Youniss, "Community Service and Political Identity Development in Adolescence," *Journal of Social Issues* 54, no. 3 (1998): 495–512.

50. For the British research, see Michael H. Banks and Debra Roker, "The Political Socialization of Youth: Exploring the Influence of School Experience," in *Journal of Adolescence* 17, no. 1 (Feb. 1994): 3–15. The U.S. study is by Edgar Litt, "Civic Education, Community Norms, and Political Indoctrination," in Roberta S. Sigel, ed., *Learning About Politics: A Reader in Political Socialization* (New York: Random House, 1970), pp. 328–36. See also Michael H. Banks and Debra Roker, "The Political Socialization of Youth: Exploring the Influence of School Experience," *Journal of Adolescence* 17 (1994): 3–15.

51. See "Black Gentry Vows to Stay in Step," *New York Times,* 17 Oct. 1995, A13.

52. Mary A. Hepburn, "The Power of the Electronic Media in the Socialization of Young Americans: Implications for Social Studies Education," *Social Studies* 89, no. 2 (March/April 1998): 71–76.

53. Charles Humana, *World Human Rights Guide,* 3rd ed. (New York: Oxford University Press, 1992), pp. 55, 57.

54. Roberta Sigel, "An Exploration into Some Aspects of Political Socialization: School Children's Reactions to the Death of a President," in Sigel, *Learning About Politics,* pp. 152–72.

55. Molly Moore, "Victims in a Warring World: Millions of Children," *International Herald Tribune,* 18 Apr. 1995, A4.

56. A. T. Russell, R. J. Johnston, and C. J. Pattie, "Thatcher's Children: Exploring the Links Between Age and Political Attitudes," *Political Studies* 40 (Dec. 1992): 742–56.

57. For two interesting illustrations of this fact, see Katharine Cutts Dougherty, Margaret Eisenhart, and Paul Webley, "The Role of Social Representations and National Identities in the Development of Territorial Knowledge: A Study of Political Socialization in Argentina and England," *American Education Research Journal* 29, no. 4 (Winter 1992): 809–35, and Tamar Liebes, "Television, Parents, and the Political Socialization of Children," *Teachers College Record* 94, no. 1 (Fall 1992): 159–64.

PART THREE

Acting in Politics

CHAPTER 4

The Individual in Politics

Powerful forces shape our political life: institutions, ideologies, social pressure, and economic conditions. Even those of us who live in democratic systems often tend to assume that we have no way, as individuals, to influence the course of politics. We vote because we think we should, not because we believe our single vote can possibly change very much. If we want to bring about serious change, we usually try to do so in the company of others who agree with us; we join a group, a political party, or a social movement. We may try to prepare ourselves for a kind of employment that we hope will bring benefits to others, but usually we plan to do that work within an organization. We like to read about great men and women who have made a difference by following their dreams, but we imagine such exploits are unique, and perhaps no longer possible.

However, even in today's densely populated and increasingly complex world, the individual retains the capacity for meaningful political action. A Chinese student standing strong and firm against the advancement of a tank containing soldiers ordered to crush the demonstration he and his fellows have organized may attract the world's amazed respect and sympathy and thereby give courage to those who are determined to carry on the battle for democracy. A Latin American journalist may persist in telling the world of her government's repressive acts even after she herself is imprisoned and tortured, and thus force changes in that nation's way of dealing with political dissent. An African American social worker who never misses a meeting of his city's board of supervisors nor an opportunity to speak on behalf of those he serves may influence the decisions of that body more than even he can tell.[1]

Individual political acts may be positive or negative—a dedicated artist may find the means to make the public newly aware of an endangered civil liberty or a religious fanatic may engage in a suicide bombing that kills many innocent persons and further enflames relations between states—but the point is the same: Individuals can make meaningful changes in the course of human history.

Sometimes the individual's act is meaningful only because other individuals are performing the same act simultaneously. Even then, however, if there is no organized cooperation, it is still individual political behavior that is influential. Individual voters, acting in unwitting concert, can change the composition of parliaments and the content of national policy. Individual citizens, each responding to specific internal promptings as well as to the exhortations of others, can form a jury that issues a verdict so patently unfair that riots break out, costing many lives and millions of dollars of damage. Individual persons, acting alone, sometimes *can* change the world.

Furthermore, even when individual actors are not interested in change, their political behavior can still be significant. The same kinds of personal action that we use to try to bring about change (voting, protesting, testifying) can be used with equal effectiveness to prevent change. The reelection of an incumbent president, a deluge of telegrams protesting a government's announced intention to send troops abroad, or the passionate testimony of a series of unacquainted and unorganized witnesses against a proposed new law or the appointment of a high official are all individual acts that can shape our collective destinies by preventing change rather than bringing it about.

Finally, even when individual political actions have no significant impact on the polity at large, they may still be very meaningful to the individual actor. Your grouchy grandfather might decide (as mine did) to send his Social Security check back to the government, muttering, "I've decided I don't believe in it." A Croatian tour director in Dubrovnik might decide, after the Serbs have leveled his apartment building, the hotel where he works, and a portion of the ancient city whose wonders provided him his livelihood, that the best thing to do is move his family and his skills to Italy. Or a soldier in the army of the Ivory Coast might opt not to reenlist because he is unhappy with the way the army is used for domestic chores (road building, peace keeping), even though his fellows are all persuaded that the relatively good pay makes a second tour of duty attractive. In all these cases, individuals have made and acted on choices that are at least partly political but that are also atypical and attract very little attention. Such choices are unlikely to have any noticeable impact on the political system, but they can be very significant for the individual actors who make them. There are, then, at least three good reasons to study the individual political behavior of ordinary citizens: (1) It can change the course of government, (2) it can prevent the course of government from changing, and (3) it can have a profound significance in the lives of individual actors.

In this chapter we will consider, first, individuals' motives for behaving as they do in the political arena; second, the variety of political acts they perform; third, the most common act of political behavior, the vote; and fourth, factors that enhance or reduce a citizen's opportunity to take part in politics.

INDIVIDUAL MOTIVES FOR PARTICIPATION IN POLITICS

Did you vote in the last election, or do you know someone who did? Then ask yourself this question, "Why did I (or my friend Elmer Endicott) vote the way I (he) did?" Stop for a moment and give that question a brief answer—write it down.

Even if you wrote down something whimsical ("My mother told me to," or, "Elmer always votes for the loser"), your answer almost surely contains some information about your own or Elmer's motives for voting that particular way ("My mother's work as city manager has given her a lot of insight into political matters," or "Elmer has a strong sense of sympathy for political underdogs"). People may be motivated by their attitudes, opinions, interests, or values. To understand behavior—to know how significant it is to the individual actor, to be able to predict how likely it is to change or remain constant, and to get a sense of the goals it is intended to achieve—we need to understand the motives behind that behavior. It makes a great deal of difference what blend of attitudes, opinions, interests, and/or values guides the political actor, as the following discussion should make clear.[2]

Attitudes

Some of our acts are motivated by general, often unverbalized feelings about certain kinds of objects. Such feelings are **attitudes,** which are based on our underlying opinions, interests, or values. If we sense, rightly or wrongly, that a candidate shares our ideas on matters we deem important, we may well vote for that candidate. When we act on this basis, we may be scarcely aware of the particular attitude in question or how it has guided us in making our choice. If we are asked to explain why we voted as we did, we may feel hard pressed to answer. Perhaps we will be able to bring the relevant underlying motive to the surface and say something like, "I voted that way because I think maintaining free enterprise is important," or, "I think it is more important to reduce crime than to pamper criminals; that's why I voted for candidate X." Or we may be unable to say anything more specific than, "I don't know; it just felt like the right thing to do."

Opinions

As commonly used today, the word *opinion* covers a wide range. Sometimes what we mean by "my opinion" is really "my belief"—I truly believe that something is true (although of course I may be quite, quite wrong). To say that we believe something suggests that we have given the matter some serious, conscious consideration. We may, of course, be entirely wrong in our beliefs. A belief is not the same as knowledge. We normally do not say we absolutely *know* something unless we have verified it by methods that seem to us to be reliable (even then we might be wrong), but we can believe all manner of strange and untrue things, and different people can have absolutely opposite beliefs. One person may firmly believe that allowing business corporations to pay lower taxes will increase capital investments, which will produce more jobs and more affluence for all. Someone else may believe just as firmly that the same procedure will simply increase profit margins for the rich and deprive the government of funds it needs for maintaining the national security and the general welfare.

Not all beliefs become opinions: Perhaps you believe that just passing laws guaranteeing homosexuals equal rights to employment opportunities will not have the desired effect, without really caring whether it does or not. But if the subject is one that we care about, be it personally or intellectually, we often tend not to let the fact that we might possibly be wrong hold us back; our belief becomes our opinion.

On the other hand, opinions can be ideas we have that we ourselves would not dignify as beliefs. We know we don't always have good reasons for thinking as we do, but still, that's what we *do* think: "It's just my opinion," we say in self-defense, or, to others, "Well, I suppose you're entitled to your opinion." Although we may try to base our opinions on our beliefs and our beliefs on knowledge, utterly ungrounded opinions nevertheless often guide our political behavior every bit as powerfully as those based on what we think are "the facts."

Interests

Another word with multiple meanings is **interest.** Here we are concerned with only one of those meanings, a clearly identifiable personal stake in a decision or the outcome of an event. If a proposed policy will clearly affect our personal fortunes, most of us respond to it differently from the way we would respond to a policy that will not impinge on our interests. Just consider, for example, how you—or your parents or your fellow students—respond when the news media report the introduction of a bill in the legislature that would change the terms for issuing government-sponsored student loans.

The government may follow several policies that affect our interests in conflicting ways—just as a candidate may make some promises we like and others we are not so sure about. When making up their minds, voters all over the world must find a way to distinguish between—and choose between—individual interests and the interests of larger groups to which they belong. When South Africa made its transition to democracy and President Nelson Mandela promised a peaceful, multiracial society in which there would be significant redistribution of wealth from the affluent white minority to the impoverished black majority, some whites recommended boycotting the first election in 1994 and a few went so far as to form militia movements and to engage in terrorist bombings. But the large majority of the minority group decided otherwise. Economic sanctions against South Africa had been lifted, and the nation was rapidly becoming a respected member of the international community. Furthermore, Mandela had promised to move in a cautious and conciliatory manner. Even if redistribution policies were followed, most members of the white minority reasoned that their own interests would now be better served by helping to make the transition as peaceful as possible. They opted to take part in the election, some of them voting for candidates of Mandela's own party, the African National Congress.[3]

Values

Values are yet another motive force in political decision making. A **value** is a serious and deeply held normative principle with wide applicability. "Our values," says Russell Dalton, "tell us what is important, to ourselves and society, and provide the reference standard for making our decisions." [4] In the example just given, suppose you were a member of the white South African community. You might then have chosen to vote on the basis of your personal values, not your interests. In that case, you might have voted for Mandela's party because one of your highest values was racial equality, or majority rule, even though you believed that supporting such principles was in fact contrary to your own interests. Or you might have joined those who refused to vote altogether, on the grounds that whoever won, the election was arranged to ensure the defeat of white supremacy, your most cherished value, beside which questions of material gain seemed unimportant to you.

A Mix of Motives

Most of us base our political decisions (and indeed, all our decisions) on a complex blend of attitudes, beliefs, opinions, interests, and values. If asked, we usually claim that our choices are based on our beliefs and our values. We like to think we know the facts, or enough of them to warrant our having beliefs, and we also like to think that we have carefully chosen our values, know what they are, know how to resolve conflicts among them, and know how to act accordingly. It is not always so, however. Stop and consider your own views on a current issue of importance—for example, the advisability of relying on nuclear energy as an alternative source of power. When you express yourself on this topic, are you doing so on the basis of your attitudes, your beliefs, your opinions, your interests, or your values?

MEASURING MOTIVES

Although we ourselves cannot always be sure why we decide as we do, others still want to know our motives for our political decisions—and we ourselves want to know how our fellows think, and why, as well as what they actually do in the world of politics. The kinds of motives that receive the most attention are opinions and values.

Measuring Opinions

Opinion polls are studies of the opinions of a representative sample of the general public, or of a specific group. Such polling is subject to a multitude of criticisms, many of them perfectly sound. To begin with, because such

Rob Rogers reprinted by permission of United Features Syndicate, Inc.

studies must be based on a random sample to be roughly accurate, they may and often do include those who have no opinion on the question at hand as well as others who simply create one in a hurry in response to a pollster's inquiry. Very rarely is any effort made to determine the intensity with which the opinion is held, or the effort any individual may have made (beyond voting) to convey that opinion to those who have the political power to act on it. Serious distortions can be introduced just in the way the question is asked: "When did you first start believing the Florida recount in the 2000 presidential election was hopelessly flawed?" Questions that interest the writer may be posed, questions that interest the respondent may never get asked. Journalists may try to find the answers to questions that require serious research and about which ordinary citizens have little or no information by taking a poll. (When we stop to think about it, we know perfectly well that asking a random sample of the population whether or not Kosovo should be a separate state, welfare recipients cheat, or O. J. Simpson was guilty of murder is a very poor way to seek the truth or decide what policy should be.)[5]

Yet despite these and other valid criticisms, such statistical reporting is a great improvement over older methods of determining "public" opinion (see Box 4.1). Indeed, the very term is out of date: We now know full well that there is never a single public opinion, that opinion is always divided and conflicting, and now we can find out just exactly what percentages of the population sampled think what. Furthermore, such data can be analyzed

BOX 4.1
Can Polls Be Trusted?

Not all polls are accurate measures of public opinion. Indeed, not everything called a poll really is one. Humphrey Taylor, president of a polling business, suggests some important points to keep in mind:

1. An unexpected poll finding is more surprising, and hence more "newsworthy," than one that confirms what other polls also report. Bad (i.e., inaccurate) polls are more likely to be surprising and therefore more likely to be reported.

2. Bad polls are cheaper than good polls. A survey of 600 people is less expensive than a survey of 1,250. A poll with very few questions is cheaper than one with more questions. High-quality sampling and interviewing cost more than poor quality. And so on. If the media report findings regardless of their quality, why spend money on better polls?

3. One-day "instant" polls are much less accurate than polls conducted over three or four days because of all the people they miss. But, the media love them because they are the "first with the news" about public reactions to events.

4. 900-number straw polls are not polls. The people who are watching the TV shows and choose to phone in their answers are often very different from the population as a whole.

5. Poll results are the answers to questions and are therefore critically dependent on the wording and, sometimes, on the order of the questions. Never interpret the results without reading the questions carefully.

6. Opinion on most issues is more complicated than a yes/no to one or two questions. Polls inevitably simplify and categorize. To really understand public opinion on any issue— from abortion to economic

over time, by income or occupational categories, or into various other subcategories, to answer a wide variety of questions.

Opinion polls can also perform important services in a democracy. The system of representative democracy as presently practiced does not provide any systematic means for keeping those in power informed between elections of the will of those who have elected them. Political parties, pressure groups, and other political movements normally provide selective and limited input to elected representatives, who need to know how opinions are divided at least in order to plan future campaign strategy, if not for the more noble goal of showing some respect for that opinion while in office. Parties and groups themselves need to know the public's views on the leaders and issues they support. Challengers to officeholders wonder if their alternative

BOX 4.1
(continued)

policy— it is necessary to review the answers to a variety of questions addressing the issue in different ways.

7. A poll is valid only for the population surveyed and for the time of the survey. Surveys of adults, registered voters, or likely voters will all yield different answers.

8. Focus groups are not polls. Getting eight to ten people in a room to talk together has many uses, but it does not provide a measure of public opinion, as surveying a representative cross-section of people does.

9. Electronic town halls are not polls; they are not even a national version of the New England town-hall meeting. For that, tens of millions of people would have to participate, and there would have to be a comprehensive debate on each issue, with all major points of view discussed before a vote was taken.

10. Candidates' polls are often misleading. Polls are leaked not to inform but to influence the media and the public.

11. Polls really don't predict, they just measure. Good polls report what a representative cross-section of the public (or of likely voters) say when interviewed. The only reason that pre-election polls "predict" elections is that most people tell the interviewers how they think they will vote and then actually vote that way. But some people change their minds, and some of those who say they will vote don't. The difference between intentions and behavior, not sampling error, is the main reason why polls sometimes get it wrong.

Source: *National Review* (19 Oct. 1992): 48. © 1992 by National Review, Inc., 150 East 35th Street, New York, NY 10016. Reprinted by permission.

views or programs will find a receptive audience. Polls help answer these and other questions.

Opinion polling is also proving to be extremely important as a tool for monitoring the impact on people's lives of the global shift away from Communist rule to free market economies. Seeing this massive transformation as nothing more than the long-overdue introduction of democracy and personal freedom is clearly simplistic, and polls have helped the outside world understand the confusion and disillusionment of those who welcome their new liberty but not the sometimes desperate hardship that accompanies it. It may be disappointing to learn that five years after the revolution, 71 percent of Hungarians said they were either worse off or no better off than in the Communist era and that in Russia, 27 percent believe the takeover by Boris

Yeltsin was "a tragic event with ruinous consequences for the country and its people," whereas, at the other extreme, only 7 percent say the coup was "a victory of the democratic revolution"—but it is important to have this kind of sobering evidence of how difficult it is to make such a massive change.[6]

In any case, popular readiness to answer such inquisitive surveys varies from community to community, from nation to nation, and from time to time. Scots prefer to keep their opinions to themselves, and if pressed may find it amusing to mislead the self-important scholars who come their way. Americans used to feel offended if they had not been consulted, and when asked would try to answer as honestly as they could, but have lately been less forthcoming: The Gallup Organization reports that only 60 percent of those contacted will now cooperate, whereas the figure used to be 80 percent.[7] And, of course, questions that make sense in one polity may make none at all in another. Daniel Lerner long ago discovered a classic case when he began an interview by asking a Turkish peasant what he would do if he were president: "'Me,' exclaimed the astonished man, 'How can I . . . I cannot . . . a poor villager . . . master of the whole world.'"[8]

Studying Values

In recent years there has been a growing interest in the study of values. Some writers, beginning with Ronald Inglehart in 1977, have argued that in the latter decades of the twentieth century, basic values have shifted in modern political democracies. Although many citizens continue to form their values (and hence their opinions and their behavior) around the familiar cultural norms of modern society—economic achievement, individualism, innovation, and progress—others have developed new and different values. In particular, they are significantly less interested in material gain; they are, in the term coined by Inglehart and adopted by many, **postmaterialists.** What they care about most is not economic prosperity but "giving people more say on the job or in government decisions, or protecting freedom of speech or moving toward a less impersonal, more humane society."[9]

One reason for this shift is that a certain level of economic prosperity has been achieved in advanced societies: "They still contain poor people, but most of their population does *not* live under conditions of hunger and economic insecurity." Another reason, paradoxically, is that greater economic prosperity is now harder to achieve than heretofore: There are "diminishing returns from economic growth" in these societies and hence individuals are less likely now to achieve dramatic upward mobility (some do; many do not). Many (not all) of those who find their way forward blocked have therefore turned their thoughts (and their values) elsewhere. They are more concerned by "quality of life" issues; they are more likely to insist on their and their compatriots' right to individual self-expression than on the right to a better job.

Furthermore, Inglehart and co-authors Miguel Basanez and Alejandro Moreno now say that growing postmaterialism is itself just one component of a yet broader change, which they characterize as a shift from modernization to postmodernization. "Postmodernization is," they say, "transforming basic norms governing politics, work, religion, family and sexual behavior." In politics, the new norms have meant, they argue, a declining emphasis on social class conflict and an increasing focus on such issues as environmental protection, abortion, ethnic conflicts, women's issues, and gay and lesbian emancipation. Postmaterialism is particularly strong on the political left, they claim, and has helped account for the growing skepticism of leftists regarding "the desirability and effectiveness of state planning and control, a growing concern for individual autonomy, and a growing respect for market forces."

These are large claims, and they have not gone uncontested or unstudied. Although there is now considerable evidence that significant numbers of citizens in contemporary advanced societies do fit the model, it has also become very clear that the earlier enthusiasts' certainty that the values of postmaterialism/postmodernization were rapidly sweeping away the old norms altogether was unwarranted. Postmaterialists co-exist with materialists; postmodernization with modernization.[10] And most of us still care quite a bit about material gain.

MODES OF INDIVIDUAL PARTICIPATION

Whatever their opinions and their values, individuals have a wide range of choices open to them in contemporary societies when they contemplate taking part in politics. To understand how extensive the choices are, we can divide any citizenry into five participatory types: those who are utterly apathetic about politics, those who are interested but nonparticipatory, those who are moderately participatory, those who are highly participatory, and those who are paid participants.

The **apathetic** pay as little attention as the world (and their television) permits and refuse to answer polls. The **interested but nonparticipatory** pay quite a bit of attention, but neither talk to others much about politics nor vote nor take any other active part in politics; for them, politics is strictly a spectator sport.[11] If they answer a telephoning pollster, or give in to a family member's insistence and vote, they are acting out of character; they'd rather just watch.

The **moderately participatory** may not pay much more attention to the substance of politics, or even as much, as those who are interested but nonparticipatory, but they do engage in some forms of political action, perhaps nothing more than talking to others about politics (and thereby entering the public debate, however minimally) and voting. They may, once in a while, sign a petition presented to them, or send it on to others via e-mail. In recent years, the Internet has provided a new avenue for moderate participation, as candidates and political organizations set up chat rooms and other opportunities for registering one's views casually, without commitment.

Although they are rarely numerous in any society, the **highly participatory** are active in a wide range of ways. They almost certainly vote. They may spend a great deal of time sending out e-mail and otherwise registering their views on the Web. They are also the ones who write letters to or go to see those officials who have or appear to have political power, who donate money to groups working for causes they believe in, who join community organizations or political movements, and who volunteer to work in political campaigns. When sufficiently aroused, they march or picket in political protest demonstrations. They may even engage in illegal behavior, surreptitiously or as an act of public **civil disobedience** on behalf of a cause they believe in.

Finally, **paid participants** are persons who engage in political behavior for a price. Lower level workers may be paid to gather signatures to get a new party or an initiative measure on the ballot, to distribute leaflets, stuff envelopes, or make canvassing telephone calls. Higher paid lobbyists and political consultants earn far larger sums by pressuring political officials or designing and carrying out all stages of a political campaign (on lobbying, see Chapter 5; on campaigns, see Chapter 6).

Sometimes a single issue can provoke nearly every form of active participation by individuals. The debate over the 1991 nomination to the U.S. Supreme Court of a man accused by a respectable law professor of sexual harassment led to a wave of telegrams and letters addressed to U.S. senators, a march on the Senate, the formation of angry coalitions, and an apparent increased determination on the part of many women to use the vote in order to elect more members of their own sex to positions of power.[12] Similarly, Florida's failure to achieve an acceptable count of its votes on November 7, 2000, provoked a steady stream of letters, contributions, petitions, and demonstrations on both sides; gave vote counters and recounters paid work; and stimulated demands for a revote made by many of those who had been unfairly turned away from the polls or who believed their votes had not been properly tallied.

Sometimes persons who disagree with each other on many other issues will find themselves making common cause and using common means to seek a particular political response. Thus advocates of free speech, "sexpositive" feminists, and persons openly engaged in producing pornographic materials have all sought to defend pornography, whereas feminists who believe pornography inflicts harm on individuals have been joined by those who attack all forms of what they call sexual "deviance," including homosexuality.[13] Such spontaneous coalitions of concerned individuals may bring together persons who would rather not be seen in each others' company—but can nevertheless have a powerful effect in stimulating new legislation or working to prevent its enactment.

New ways to bring about higher levels of participation are constantly being sought and tried. Although there is not much evidence of its efficacy yet, one of the more interesting of such attempts has been the use of pop musicians, comedians, and other entertainment figures to encourage young people to take part in partisan politics. The British Organization Rock the Vote, endorsed by all three major parties, launched an all-out effort in that nation to raise youth registration and voting by offering a series of events featuring major pop celebrities. What was their purpose? Martin Cloonan and John Street see it as something more than public relations. They point out evidence that British youth are actually quite interested in politics, but not party politics, and that the key sponsors of Rock the Vote were a bank, a brewer, and an insurance company. In general, they see this movement as an effort to stimulate brand loyalty in politics as in consumer products, to protect the British music industry, and to reinforce "a more passive, consumerist politics."[14] Those who respond to such a campaign would presumably never go beyond the level of moderately participatory; Rock the Vote has no interest in rocking the boat.

There are, of course, a seemingly endless number of efforts to stimulate and direct voter interest and participation on the Internet. Almost all candidates and parties now maintain their own Web sites, and many individuals and groups are eager to post their political views as well. In addition, nonpolitical entrepreneurs sometimes seek to serve presumed voter interests in order to attract visitors to their sites (and their advertisements). One of the more successful Web sites during the 2000 U.S. presidential campaign was www.selectsmart.com, a site that asked visitors to answer a set of questions regarding their views on the issues and then told them which presidential candidate's positions most closely matched their own. America Online developed a similar site, www.presidentmatch.com.[15]

PARTICIPATION BY VOTING IN ELECTIONS

The most common act of individual participation in politics is to vote. It seems a simple act: just register, then walk in on election day and mark your choice. But, as Americans learned in the presidential election of 2000, it is not that simple at all. That election demonstrated to a surprised and embarrassed nation that "marking your choice" and having it counted correctly depends, above all, on having the right technology. American voting machinery in many states had fallen nearly half a century behind the times, as was discovered in Florida when the race there became so close that state law mandated a recount and the recounting procedures uncovered all the problems associated with using "punchcard" ballots. This cumbersome and untrustworthy method of preparing data for computer entry had been abandoned in almost every other domain of government, business, and research 30 to 40 years earlier.

However, even when the machines work properly, to understand how individuals participate in politics by voting we must look at other related topics, in particular at voter turnout and at electoral systems. Achieving effective participation by voting depends not only on whether or not citizens vote, but also on the nature of the institution that makes voting possible.

Voter Turnout

One of the most puzzling—and, for some, one of the most distressing—facts about voting is how very few citizens take part in this relatively easy form of political behavior in the United States. Voter turnout in the United States is low by any standards, and certainly low comparatively; in modern democracies, only Switzerland has a worse record for average turnout (see Table 4.1). Voter turnout in presidential elections in the United States has decreased steadily in recent years, with the exception of 1992, when the first candidacy of independent Ross Perot helped produce a temporary 4 percent boost in the figures (see Figure 4.1).[16] Voting in nonpresidential elections is marked by even lower turnout; in the 1994 congressional elections, only 36 percent of those eligible voted and the rate in municipal elections has at times fallen even lower.

What explains this phenomenon? Not only is the answer hard to determine, but the question is one that has caused considerable dispute among political scientists. For some authors, social demographics tell us all we need to know. Having little education, being young, having a low income or being unemployed, belonging to a minority racial group, and living in the South are all demographic factors that have been associated with nonvoting in the United States. For others, the partisan compatibility of voters' views on the issues with those they ascribe to the parties or the voters' retrospective evaluations of party performance in office have stronger explanatory value (see Table 4.2). Still others have looked at factors possibly associated with lower U.S. turnout from a comparative perspective, asking if voter turnout varies significantly between richer and poorer nations or between larger and smaller nations. The answer was a disappointing "no," but the same researchers did find what appears to be a strong link between voter turnout and the competitiveness of electoral politics. They studied 805 elections across the world and found that "In the 542 elections where the largest party won less than half of the votes turnout was a full 10 percent higher than the 263 elections where a single party won over 50 percent of the pop-

FIGURE 4.1
U.S. Turnout
by Year
(in Percentage)

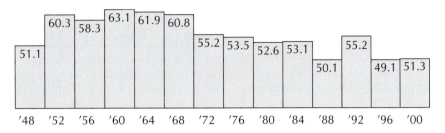

Source: Federal Election Commission, http://www.fec.gov./elections.html.

ular vote."[17] Elections in a two-party system like the U.S. inevitably tend to fall into the second category.

However, in recent years the debate regarding low turnout in the United States has centered on the question of registration laws. The first serious investigation into the possibility that a more lenient and less complex registration system would mean better turnout was made by Raymond Wolfinger and Steven Rosenstone (1980), but they discovered that even if all voters were allowed to register right up to election day, registration offices were kept open during regular working hours and in the evening or on Saturday, and absent civilians were permitted to register by mail (in ten states, only military absentee registration was then permitted), U.S. turnout rates could be expected to increase by less than 10 percent.[18]

Some ten years later G. Bingham Powell Jr. spread his net considerably further, making a broadly comparative study and including psychological attitudes and other institutional factors, as well as registration laws in his effort to explain varying rates of turnout. He found that provoting attitudes were stronger in the United States, but that registration laws gave the United States a 14 percent disadvantage.[19]

For Powell the American party system was almost equally to blame (a 13 percent disadvantage), but in a study published the following year, Frances Fox Piven and Richard A. Cloward insisted that registration was the key: 40 percent of Americans eligible to register and vote were not registered—and so could not vote. Furthermore, voting rates of registered voters were higher, they showed; indeed, by that standard (counting the turnout rate of the registered) the United States tied with the Netherlands and Germany for seventh place.[20] They pointed out that the United States is the only major democracy where "government assumes no responsibility for helping citizens cope with voter registration procedures." In Switzerland, Italy, Germany, Austria, France, Sweden, Great Britain, Belgium, and Canada, the government itself takes the responsibility to register voters (keeping track of all residents and sending them the necessary papers).[21]

TABLE 4.1   Ranking of Average Turnout in the 1990s in 163 Nations

Rank	Country (Number of Elections)	Vote/VAP%	Rank	Country (Number of Elections)	Vote/VAP%
1	Malta (2)	96.7	46	St. Lucia (1)	76.8
2	Seychelles (1)	96.1	47	Brazil (2)	76.7
3	Uruguay (1)	96.1	48	Philippines (2)	76.7
4	Indonesia (2)	90.2	49	Slovakia (1)	75.9
5	Italy (3)	90.2	50	Cape Verde (2)	75.6
6	Angola (1)	88.3	51	Burundi (1)	75.4
7	Iceland (2)	88.3	52	Palestinian Authority (1)	75.4
8	Uzbekistan (2)	86.2	53	Republic of the Congo (1)	75.3
9	Antigua and Barbuda (1)	85.6	54	Netherlands (1)	75.2
10	South Africa (1)	85.5	55	Armenia (1)	74.9
11	Albania (4)	85.3	56	Nicaragua (2)	74.8
12	Czech Republic (3)*	84.8	57	Vanuatu (2)	74.6
13	Greece (3)	84.7	58	Norway (1)	74.5
14	Costa Rica (2)	84.6	59	Sri Lanka (1)	74.1
15	Belgium (2)	84.1	60	Croatia (2)	73.5
16	Israel (2)	83.2	61	Monaco (1)	73.2
17	Sweden (2)	83.2	62	St. Vincent and The Grenadines (1)	73.2
18	Bosnia and Herzegovina (1)	82.8	63	Germany (2)	72.7
19	Bulgaria (2)	82.8	64	Tajikistan (1)	72.4
20	Australia (3)	82.7	65	United Kingdom (2)	72.4
21	Azerbaijan (1)	82.5	66	Finland (2)	71.5
22	Kuwait (2)†	82.5	67	Macedonia (1)	71.2
23	Mongolia (3)	82.3	68	Nepal (2)	71.2
24	Chile (1)	81.9	69	Ireland (2)	70.2
25	Western Samoa (2)	81.9	70	Panama (1)	70.1
26	Grenada (2)	81.5	71	Taiwan, Republic of China (4)	70.1
27	Maldives (1)	81.5	72	Republic of Korea (2)	70.0
28	Andorra (2)	81.3	73	St. Kitts and Nevis (2)	69.6
29	Denmark (2)	81.1	74	Suriname (2)	69.5
30	Dominica (2)	80.6	75	Togo (3)	69.1
31	Slovenia (2)	80.6	76	Trinidad and Tobago (2)	68.8
32	New Zealand (3)	80.4	77	Belize (1)	68.7
33	San Marino (1)	80.3	78	Malawi (1)	67.9
34	Mauritius (1)	79.8	79	Bahamas (1)	67.6
35	Austria (3)	79.6	80	Iran (2)	67.6
36	Turkey (2)	79.4	81	Algeria (2)	67.1
37	Palau (1)	79.3	82	Hungary (2)	66.9
38	Papua New Guinea (1)	79.2	83	Barbados (2)	66.7
39	Spain (2)	79.0	84	Mozambique (1)	66.4
40	Argentina (3)	78.9	85	Ecuador (3)	66.2
41	Aruba (2)	78.5	86	Ukraine (2)	65.1
42	Portugal (2)	78.4	87	Burma (1)	64.6
43	Ethiopia (1)	77.4	88	Kazakhstan (1)	64.3
44	Cyprus (2)	77.3	89	Moldova (1)	64.1
45	Romania (2)	77.2	90	Namibia (1)	63.8

Rank	Country (Number of Elections)	Vote/VAP%	Rank	Country (Number of Elections)	Vote/VAP%
91	Guyana (1)	63.7	128	Uganda (1)	50.9
92	Honduras (1)	63.5	129	Central African Republic (1)	50.3
93	Malaysia (3)	63.4	130	Venezuela (1)	49.9
94	Latvia (3)	63.1	131	Nauru (1)	49.7
95	Bangladesh (2)	63.0	132	Ghana (2)	49.0
96	Belarus (1)	63.0	133	Poland (2)	48.2
97	Federated States of Micronesia (1)	63.0	134	Tanzania (1)	47.9
98	Thailand (3)	62.5	135	Dominican Republic (3)	46.2
99	Kiribati (1)	62.0	136	Paraguay (1)	45.4
100	France (2)	60.6	137	Chad (1)	45.1
101	Georgia (2)	60.6	138	USA (4)	44.9
102	Solomon Islands (1)	60.6	139	Botswana (1)	44.6
103	Luxembourg (1)	60.5	140	Cameroon (1)	44.4
104	Tunisia (1)	60.3	141	Jamaica (1)	44.1
105	Lebanon (2)	60.2	142	Haiti (2)	42.9
106	Benin (2)	60.1	143	Mauritania (1)	42.5
107	Canada (2)	60.1	144	Kenya (1)	40.9
108	Lithuania (2)	60.1	145	Ivory Coast (2)	39.9
109	Fiji (2)	59.9	146	Pakistan (3)	39.8
110	Guinea (1)	59.9	147	Singapore (2)	39.4
111	Lesotho (1)	59.6	148	Switzerland (1)	37.7
112	Sao Tome and Principe (2)	59.6	149	Zimbabwe (2)	37.3
113	India (2)	59.2	150	Sierra Leone (1)	36.8
114	El Salvador (2)	59.1	151	Yemen (2)	36.8
115	Syria (1)	58.0	152	Sudan (1)	36.2
116	Peru (2)	57.3	153	Niger (2)	35.6
117	Federal Republic of Yugoslavia (3)	57.2	154	Jordan (1)	34.7
118	Japan (4)	57.0	155	Guinea-Bissau (1)	32.1
119	Mexico (3)	56.8	156	Zambia (2)	32.0
120	Bolivia (2)	56.2	157	Colombia (3)	31.6
121	Estonia (3)	56.0	158	Guatemala (3)	29.6
122	Gambia (2)	56.0	159	Egypt (2)	27.7
123	Russia (2)	55.0	160	Senegal (1)	26.8
124	Liechtenstein (2)	54.7	161	Burkina Faso (1)	26.7
125	Madagascar (1)	54.1	162	Djibouti (1)	26.3
126	Morocco (1)	51.8	163	Mali (1)	21.9
127	Kyrgyzstan (1)	51.2			

*Czech Republic includes elections in Czechoslovakia in 1990 and 1992.

†Women are excluded from the franchise in Kuwait.

Key: VAP = voting age population

Source: "Voter Turnout from 1945 to 1997: A Global Report on Political Participation," from International Institute for Democracy and Electoral Assistance, 1997, pp. 14–15. Reprinted by permission of International IDEA.

TABLE 4.2

Percentage of U.S. Electorate Who Reported Voting for President, by Party Identification, Issue Preferences, and Retrospective Evaluations, 1996

Attitude	Voted	Did Not Vote	Total	(N) *
Electorate, by party identification				
Strong Democrat	89	11	100	(201)
Weak Democrat	72	28	100	(260)
Independent, leans Democratic	69	31	100	(164)
Independent, no partisan leaning	52	48	100	(100)
Independent, leans Republican	77	23	100	(150)
Weak Republican	79	21	100	(225)
Strong Republican	96	4	100	(198)
Electorate, by issue preference				
Strongly Democratic	84	16	100	(76)
Moderately Democratic	73	28	100	(99)
Slightly Democratic	64	36	100	(170)
Neutral	73	27	100	(434)
Slightly Republican	70	30	100	(266)
Moderately Republican	82	18	100	(235)
Strongly Republican	90	10	100	(241)
Electorate, by retrospective evaluations of performance				
Strongly Democratic	76	24	100	(21)
Moderately Democratic	80	20	100	(119)
Leans Democratic	74	26	100	(212)
Neutral	75	25	100	(155)
Leans Republican	75	25	100	(67)
Moderately Republican	79	21	100	(97)
Strongly Republican	86	14	100	(87)

*Numbers are weighted.

Source: Paul R. Abramson, John H. Aldrich, and David W. Rhode, *Change and Continuity in the 1996 Elections* (Washington, D.C.: Congressional Quarterly Press, 1998), p. 87. Copyright © 1998 by Congressional Quarterly, Inc. Reproduced with permission of Congressional Quarterly, Inc. via Copyright Clearance Center.

Nonetheless, those who focus on specific registration laws in the United States continue to say it is obvious they are not the problem: Glenn E. Mitchell and Christopher Wiezien, following roughly the same methodology as Wolfinger and Rosenstone, concluded that despite some differences twenty years after the original study, it remained true that overall liberalizing rules regarding such matters as closing dates and the hours the registration offices are open would have little effect on rates of turnout.[22]

The record of the National Voter Registration Act, otherwise known as the motor-voter act, lends substance to this claim. Passed in 1993, this law requires states to permit registration when one applies for or renews a driver's license, to permit registration by mail, and to make forms available at certain public assistance agencies. This would seem to have been a good step in the right direction, yet voting rates have not improved, and Michael D. Martinez and David Hill have presented data suggesting the new law

Voter registration during the Million Man March on Washington, D.C., October 16, 1995. Despite several recent improvements, U.S. laws still make registration more difficult than in other major democracies.
© Teake Zuidema/The Image Works

actually "appeared to slightly increase the class and racial inequality in state elections."[23]

Furthermore, Ray Teixera points out, registration laws in the United States have in fact been liberalized in many other ways in recent years, with no visible overall effect on turnout. Bilingual registration materials have been made more available, registration by mail is much more widely permitted, state residency requirements have been sharply reduced (now normally a month or less), closing dates have been moved closer to the election, and standards for absentee registration are much easier to meet—and nonetheless, not only has turnout not increased but the turnout rates of those registered to vote have also been falling.[24]

Looking beyond registration laws, Teixera does find another statutory law partially to blame: the election calendar. Elections are now more frequent, and in particular gubernatorial elections are now rarely held at the same time as presidential elections and this appears to have a moderately depressing effect on turnout. But the real answers, Teixera's data suggest, are in changing individual-level characteristics of citizens, specifically "a substantial decline in social connectedness, as manifested in a younger, less married, and less church-going electorate and a generalized withdrawal or disconnection from the political world, manifested most dramatically by declining psychological involvement in politics and a declining belief in government responsiveness." [25]

Focusing on the attitudes of those who are eligible to register and vote but do not choose to do so does seem the more promising approach. Demographic variables may tell us what groups are less likely to vote but none (well, few) of us can change our gender or our race, and many find it very hard indeed to improve their socioeconomic status. Registration laws are pretty clearly not the villain, although Americans still have not tried the European tactics of making registration a government service or opening the polls on Sundays. Perhaps the answer is really very simple: In order to be better voters, Americans need better and more trustworthy candidates, better and more responsive government, and a better sense of social connectedness to one another.[26] (Of course a simple answer does not necessarily mean a simple solution.)

The Electoral System

So far we have been stressing what makes individuals *want* to vote, which is a behavioral question. But it is also important to consider the *institution* that makes voting possible, which is a structural question (see Chapter 1). This institution is the *electoral system,* a structure that seldom receives the attention it deserves. We know that elections can be burdened with more issues than a legislative session, bring about judgments more far reaching than those of a court, attract more attention to qualities of leadership than a presidency, and sometimes stir up battle spirit as fiercely as any army. But we tend to act as if their existence and their characteristics were all preordained, immutable. We tend to forget that every election is the product of an electoral system, and further, that any electoral system is itself the entirely changeable product of fallible human beings, often guided at least in part by the desire to serve their own political fortunes.

What is an **electoral system?** The term is sometimes used simply to indicate how many offices are to be contested and how votes are to be cast and counted, but we will use it here in its broader sense to include all the rules and regulations governing the vote.

Every nation has some form of electoral system, but the opportunities for meaningful participation on the part of the would-be voter vary enormously according to the kind of system in effect. In a single-party dictatorship, elections may be held merely for ceremonial purposes, with no competition allowed. Or competition may be allowed within the party, as several candidates, all expressing their loyalty to the ruling party, are permitted to compete for a particular constituency's legislative seat.

It is not unusual for a nation to have two electoral systems—one dictated by law that calls for fair elections at specified times with full competition, and a second, determined by tradition and the actual distribution of political power, that allows for infrequent and irregular balloting, rigged in advance. The military coup makes a mockery of any electoral system, even one rigged to keep a single party in power, although some have argued that when coup follows upon coup, as has been the case in several African and Latin American nations, *that* is the nation's electoral system.

Furthermore, even where the electoral system is fair and scrupulously carried out, great variations are possible. There are, for example, important differences, worth taking a moment to understand, between the three main ways the vote is translated into legislative seats in most Western democracies: *plurality, majoritarian,* and *proportional representation.*

■ **Plurality Election in a Single-Member District System.** The system most commonly used in the United States for state and congressional offices is election by plurality in a single-member district. Under this system, the voters in each electoral district (also called a *constituency*) choose one person to fill a specific post, be it state legislator or representative to Congress. Whoever gets the most votes (a plurality, which is not necessarily a majority) is elected. Americans often call such a system *winner-take-all*; the British, using a racing metaphor, call it *first past the post* (or FPTP). In practice, it is used nationally by only four major democracies: Canada, the United States, the United Kingdom, and India. However, nearly all the nations formerly colonized by Britain and now seeking political development also use this system, bringing the total to 68 (or 32 percent) of the 212 independent states and related territories. Other nations use either some form of proportional representation (65, or 31 percent of the 212), or a combination of systems.[27]

The main objection to a winner-take-all system is that it produces far greater discrepancies between the vote and the actual allocation of seats than other systems. The *deviation from proportionality,* or *DV,* is calculated by subtracting the percentage of votes a party has received from the percentage of seats it has in the legislature; for example, in the 1997 elections to the British House of Commons, the Labour Party gained 44.4 percent of the votes but 65.4 percent of the seats; its DV was +21.[28] David Farrell has ranked 37 democratic nations for disproportionality over recent elections and has found that the four using FPTP rank 26th, 32nd, 35th, and 37th, respectively (the United States, Canada, the United Kingdom, and India, respectively).[29]

■ **Majoritarian Election.** To avoid the drawbacks of the plurality system, some nations with single-member districts require the winner to have a majority. This may mean scheduling a runoff election if no candidate wins over 50 percent of the vote on the first ballot. In French legislative elections, any candidate with more than 12.5 percent of the vote may take part in the runoff, held two weeks later, and in the race for the French presidency, when the

Russian women cast their votes in Russian presidential elections in the village of Yadromino, March 26, 2000. The new Russian electoral system makes it possible for many candidates to compete for the presidency, and the outcome is no longer certain as it always was in the past.
© AFP/CORBIS

"single district" is the nation at large, only the top two candidates will be present at the second ballot.

Such a system encourages minor parties to participate—one can never be certain which candidates will make it into the runoff—and thus provides individual voters with a wide choice, but at the same time it ensures strong support (usually an absolute majority) for the winner of the runoff.

A third variation designed to maximize the chances of majoritarian support while maintaining single-member districts is the *instant runoff vote* system, used in Australia for its lower house, in Ireland to elect the president and in London to elect the mayor, and in a number of American towns. In this system each voter *ranks* the candidates. When the votes are counted, if no candidate has a majority of first-choice rankings in the district, then the candidate who is ranked first the least often is eliminated, and the votes of those who preferred this candidate are assigned to the persons they ranked second. If this doesn't produce a majority for one candidate, the process is repeated; eventually, of course, the process of elimination means that one candidate *will* have a majority. Again, individual voters benefit by having a wide choice to begin with and by knowing that their votes (including, if need be, their second and third choices) have been thoroughly taken into consideration. Collectively, everyone benefits by knowing that the most preferred candidate has been selected. He or she may in fact be "everyone's second choice" but can never be a widely hated figure who has won only a slim plurality.

■ **Election by Proportional Representation.** *Proportional representation* (often referred to by its initials, PR) requires multimember districts. Each district chooses several representatives, and each political party offers the voters a list of its candidates for those posts. In some nations, such as Belgium, the voter can vary the order of the candidates on the list; in others, as in Switzerland, the voters have multiple votes that they may spread around as they wish among the lists. In the simplest and most usual version, however, each voter casts one vote for one party list and the parties are then awarded seats according to the proportion of the vote they received. If a party gets 40 percent of the vote, the top 40 percent of its list is elected. But of course real life is seldom that tidy, and in practice it is necessary to have some kind of formula for determining how to assign the seats. The two most common formulas used are the *largest remainder* and the *highest average* systems (see Box 4.2). Whatever formula is used, the goal is to assign seats proportionately to the vote. Minor parties with very few votes may thus get a seat or two in the legislature and do not necessarily feel encouraged to drop out or to combine with other small parties just because they are not doing well.[30]

Although PR gives voters the maximum amount of choice and ensures a legislature that is not only closely keyed to the actual vote but also one that is much more fully representative of all points of view, it can also have the effect of making it difficult to form majorities behind a government program. In the Netherlands, for example, where a party needs only .67 percent of the total vote to gain a seat in the 150-member parliament, "governments are formed more on the basis of post-election negotiations in smoke-filled rooms, rather than as a result of clear electoral mandates."[31] To avoid this effect, other nations using proportional representation normally require a party to obtain at least 5 percent of the vote in order to be entitled to any representation. Establishing such a threshold has helped the new political systems in eastern Europe reduce the number of parties actually taking seats in their new parliaments, despite the amazing proliferation of parties in the first years of their transition to democracy: Eighty parties competed in the 1992 Czechoslovakian elections; that same year, there were 131 parties in Poland.[32]

■ **Mixed Electoral Systems.** It is possible to use both systems in the same polity. The Germans, for example, elect 664 deputies to their legislature, the Bundestag, by a dual procedure: Half are elected in direct balloting in their

BOX 4.2
How Proportional Representation Works: The "Largest Remainder" and "Highest Average" Systems

The largest remainder system, common in Latin America, works like this: Say that in a five-seat district 100 votes are cast: Blue 38, Red 32, White 17, Green 13. Each 20 votes (100 ÷ 5) get one seat. Any seats left go to whoever has the most votes remaining. Result: Blue 20 + 18) gets two; Red (20 + 12) one; White (0 + 17) one; Green (0 + 13) one. Hardly proportional. And see how small parties are favored. Had White and Green merged, the joint "Lime" party's 30 votes would have earned only one seat.

Bigger districts are fairer. Say that there are ten seats. Blue gets four; Red three; White two; Green one. And if White and Green had merged, "Lime" would still get three. Fair enough? In either case, "swings and roundabouts" even out the national result— but still with a bias to small parties.

The highest-average formula widely used in Europe allocates seats, one by one, to whichever party thereby shows the highest votes-per-seat. To do this, divide the party votes by 1, 2, 3 and so on, then pick out the highest five (or ten or whatever) figures from the resultant matrix, below. The winning figures are shown in **bold** for a five-seat district (the seat-number is indicated by a superscript figure), plus five more in *italics* for a ten-seat one:

	Blue	Red	White	Green
÷ by 1	**38**[1]	**32**[2]	**17**[4]	*13*
÷ by 2	**19**[3]	**16**[5]	*8.5*	*6.5*
÷ by 3	*12.7*	*10.7*	*5.7*	4.3
÷ by 4	9.5	8	4.2	3.2
Seats won:				
Five-seat	two	two	one	none
Ten-seat	four	three	two	one

Small parties suffer: Were there only three seats, Blue would get two, Red one, White and Green none (where "Lime" would have got one). With eleven, even Red would get a fourth seat, Green still only one. But larger districts are usually fairer than small. The divisors can be varied: Scandinavian countries divide by 1.4, 3, 5 and 7, which aids medium-sized parties.

BOX 4.3
An Unusual Variation: The Single Transferable Vote (Ireland)

A few countries use the single transferable vote, in multimember districts.

Say that there are five seats. The "quota" for election is then one-sixth (sic) of the total votes cast, plus 1. Voters number candidates in order of preference from 1 to 5.

First preferences are counted. Only Fergus O'Fail gets a quota. He is elected, and his "surplus" votes are shared out, in due proportion, among those candidates who were his backers' second choice. That brings Nuala O'Fail up to a quota. She is in, so share out her surplus votes.

No one gets a quota? Out goes the bottom name, Sean Gael, and *all* his votes are shared among those voters' second choices. Still no quota? Out too goes now-bottom Patrick Gael, and all his votes are shared. Now Liam Gael is over the top. Share out his *surplus* votes. And so on.

Result, say: two Fianna Fail, two Fine Gael and one Labour. But note: These are individuals— party people, but maybe not the ones the bosses most fancied.

Even with its districts of only 3–5 members, Ireland's STV produces quite proportional results nationally.

respective constituencies, while the other half are selected proportionally from party lists of candidates in each of the *Länder* (states). Similarly, the Spanish senate is elected by simple plurality, but its lower house by the highest average version of proportional representation. Italy, long known for its most elaborately "fair" system of proportional representation, switched to a system that is 75 percent plurality, 25 percent proportional representation.[33]

It is also possible to have multimember districts without using proportional representation, as is done in many polities at the local level; the candidates getting the most votes win the available seats on the city council or the county board. Such a system has been used in several American cities in an effort to increase minority representation without reverting to district elections (see below, pp. 155–56).[34] More unusual multimember districts without proportional representation have been used for the Irish legislature and the Japanese parliament (for the Irish case, see Box 4.3).

The range of choice is indeed wide and confusing, and there are no simple decision-making rules for nations wondering which method will work best.[35] Although some political scientists have customarily argued that proportional representation tends to produce fragmented and unstable government, they almost always cite the case of postwar Italy, where numerous other factors contributed to produce those conditions (and where a single party, the Christian Democrats, nevertheless stayed in power until 1994!), and do not look at the stable and effective coalition governments other nations, such as those in Scandinavia, have managed to produce using the same system. Similarly, single-member districts do not always close out minor parties altogether, although they do have a strong tendency to do so.

Proportional representation is definitely the fairest system, in the sense of assuring that the distribution of seats matches the distribution of votes as closely as possible. However, other arguments in its favor are shaky. In order for it to favor minorities and women, or other underrepresented groups, these groups must win positions high on existing parties' lists or form parties of their own.[36] And PR may or may not improve voters' trust in their political systems; on this point the studies are still too few and too uncertain.[37] We also need to know more about the effects of mixed electoral systems.

Initiative and Referendum

So far we have been talking about ways the institution of an electoral system can offer citizens an opportunity to participate in the choice of representatives to lawmaking bodies. But elections can be devoted to other offices and to matters other than the choice of representatives. A polity's electoral system might include provisions for the **initiative,** enabling citizens to vote directly on specific proposals for new legislation. The only requirement is that a certain number of citizens (usually at least a specified percentage of the population that voted in the previous election) sign a petition within a specified number of days (frequently ninety days) proposing that a question be put on the ballot for everyone to vote on.

Somewhat more common is the **referendum,** a provision enabling a group of citizens, following procedures similar to those for an initiative, to "refer" a piece of legislation passed by the government to the voting public. Only if a majority approves does the legislation actually become binding. Some issues must automatically be made subject to such a procedure; state laws, for example, often require that school bonds be placed on a referendum ballot.

Another version of the referendum is found in systems that allow the executive branch of the government, under certain conditions, to rule by referendum—that is, to take a new proposal directly to the people. This kind of referendum is permitted in the French constitution and was a favorite device of former president Charles de Gaulle, who frequently staked his political life on a referendum vote, telling the French to vote for his proposal or accept the consequences—his own resignation. The inevitable result was that he won every single referendum vote except the last one he tried.[38]

It is often taken for granted that electoral systems allowing initiatives and referenda provide for more participation than those that do not, and there are many who urge the adoption of a national initiative system in the United States. The matter is not quite as simple as it looks, however. It is no easy job to gather large numbers of signatures for a petition in a short period of time, and some observers have suggested that well-financed groups have an even greater advantage when this system of lawmaking is used than when laws are made by ordinary legislative processes. Such groups are far better able to hire the workers needed to gather the necessary number of signatures and to bombard the general public with the political advertising likely to persuade them to vote "correctly" than are less wealthy groups. It is also pointed out that debating complex issues in the public arena, without the benefit of careful deliberation by experienced representatives, makes the initiative and the referendum prime targets for demagogic politicking—that is, for appeals based on emotional sloganeering rather than on full and rational discussions of the issues.[39]

Other Electoral Opportunities to Participate

Other opportunities to participate by voting may include **recall elections**, held when a sufficient number of voters petition for a special election to vote on removing an official (usually an elected official) from office. The grounds for demanding a recall vary from genuine *malfeasance*—that is, acting contrary to law or failing to carry out the terms of office—to simple public discontent with the policies or style of the offending incumbent.[40] Other, more constructive options for participation include the election of such executive officers as attorney general and controller, the election of judicial officers, such as lower court judges in many states of the United States, and the political party primary election.

The *party primary* is a special form of election indeed, almost unique to the United States. (Belgium has a roughly comparable system, and in some nations with runoff elections the first election is referred to—not really correctly—as the primary election.) Although party primaries in the United States are set up and monitored by state governments, many of them are closed, which means that only the voters who have registered as supporters of the party are allowed to vote. This makes sense, because the supporters are not voting for a government official but simply for a candidate to run as the nominee of a private organization, the political party. On the other hand, the right to choose nominees for office has such far-reaching effects for all citizens that many states have adopted the institution of the *open* primary as a way to encourage greater individual participation in the political process. Still other states have continued to allow the party to control its own nominations (by internal party elections known as *caucuses*). This too makes sense: Why should persons who have taken no part in party affairs be allowed to tell the party which person it should run for office? As we will see in Chapter 6 it can also be argued that adoption of the primary, far from strengthening democracy, has served so to weaken political parties as agencies of linkage between citizen and the state that the net effect of this unique institution is actually antidemocratic.

ACCESS: HOW WELCOME IS INDIVIDUAL PARTICIPATION?

The factors we have considered so far do not exhaust all the ways individuals are stimulated to participate in politics—or to stay at home. We conclude by examining five other conditions that help determine how meaningful the concept of democratic citizenship is in actual practice.

Limiting the Electoral Option: Impersonal Restrictions

In every nation there will be electoral provisions or customs that have the effect, sometimes deliberate, of limiting individual opportunities for participation in politics. Some of these are impersonal—that is, they apply to everyone, with no apparent discrimination. Requiring citizens to have lived in their constituency for a certain period of time before registering and then again before voting can curb participation, as we have seen. Making absentee ballots difficult to acquire or placing polling stations in out-of-the-way locations will make participation harder for some persons than for others, but no particular person or group is openly targeted for discouragement. Purging the voting lists of the names of anyone who has not voted within a certain period of time makes it harder for chronic nonvoters to change their ways.[41] Calling political meetings without public notice or holding important political discussions in settings where women or minorities or persons of lower economic status are made to feel unwelcome is another way that access to politics is limited, although no one has posted a "No Trespassing" sign.

Indirect elections are another technically impersonal means of limiting the right to participate in elections. An election is indirect when only those who have already been elected to another post are entitled to vote. The ordinary citizens of a French village, for example, elect their municipal council, but only the council members can choose the mayor. And until 1916, U.S. senators were indirectly elected, by state legislatures.

Electoral systems that mandate constituencies too large to permit effective organization by minority groups on behalf of their own interests—the majority population will almost inevitably win, even if the district has multiple representatives, as on a city council—are another way some individuals find themselves thwarted when trying to bring their particular interests into the public domain, even though there is no apparent discrimination in the law. Considering these untoward effects has prompted renewed interest in *district elections,* a system whereby a city is divided into several single-member districts, one or more having a large majority of what is, citywide, a minority population.

Although this procedure does work to increase minority representation, it is often criticized as divisive, especially when carried out on the basis of race. However, David Epstein and Sharyn O'Halloran find that "a race-neutral approach to districting will probably result in a minimization of minority influence on public policy, as minorities do still face significant difficulties in gaining office." [42]

Limiting the Electoral Option: Personal Restrictions

Other structured restrictions on the right to vote have been clearly directed at specific groups. Not all of these arouse our indignation. We normally tend to accept the idea that children, criminals convicted of serious crimes, the legally insane, and noncitizens should be kept off the electoral rolls. Yet even some of these restrictions are, in fact, debatable. The states of Maine, Massachusetts, and Vermont permit prison inmates to vote, as does the nation of Canada, but in thirty-five American states even persons who are not in prison but are on probation or parole are denied that right. [43] The question of whether or not to allow noncitizens to vote is also not always easily resolved. Is a nation that has encouraged large numbers of foreigners to cross its borders in order to assure the existence of a labor force willing to take the lowest-paying and most physically exhausting jobs really within its rights to deny this population the right to vote? [44] What about a refugee population, forced into that status by the takeover of their own land by others? Are these people "aliens" in the ordinary sense? Should they have the right to vote?

One of the most consistently applied personal restrictions on the right to vote has been on the basis of race or ethnic origin. In the United States such electoral laws have been designed to keep African Americans from voting. Often thinly disguised as impersonal limitations—such as literacy laws, poll tax requirements, and the infamous *grandfather clause* (if your grandfather voted, you could vote without having to pass the literacy test, a stipulation impossible for former slaves to meet)—such devices were used in practice against only one group of citizens, African Americans, and consequently are properly classified as personal limitations. [45]

Today a changed climate of opinion and the Voting Rights Act of 1965 make it more difficult to devise such restrictions, but the practice has not been entirely eliminated, and important battles for minority voting rights are

French National Front presidential candidate Jean-Marie Le Pen delivers a speech in Paris, May 1, 2002. Le Pen's message is overtly racist and demagogic, but modern democracies permit all points of view to be expressed, counting on the wisdom of the voters. In this multi-candidate election, the excessive fragmentation of the left allowed Le Pen, with 18 percent of the vote on the first ballot, to make it into the runoff; however, at that point moderately conservative candidate Jacques Chirac won by 82 percent of the vote.
© Reuters NewMedia Inc./CORBIS

still being waged. The questions involved are not always simple to resolve. If, for example, a city draws voting district lines so as to dilute the strength of a racial minority, should members of that group have the right to insist they be redrawn to concentrate their strength and thereby assure them of representation on the elected governing body at issue? The Hispanic community of Los Angeles argued "yes" in 1991 and won their case in the courts.[46] But when President Bill Clinton proposed Professor Lani Guinier for the position of assistant attorney general for civil rights a mere two years later, the fact that Guinier had urged the adoption of other, milder electoral system reforms to ensure a modicum of representation for minority groups provoked such outraged opposition to her nomination that it was speedily withdrawn.[47] Should electoral systems be reformed to increase the importance of the vote of disadvantaged groups whose ballots may otherwise be entirely submerged in purely majoritarian polling systems? Why? Why not?

Freedom to Form Political Groups

Access to appropriate political groups depends partly on the willingness of citizens to form such groups and partly on the attitude of those in power toward their formation. The second factor can be troublesome even in polities where the political culture includes respect for the constitutional principle of "freedom of association." Serious limitations on this right have been imposed at certain moments in U.S. history on groups seen as offering a dangerous threat to the democratic form of government, such as the American Communist Party. Even today, requiring political parties to meet difficult tests of "significant support"—such as filing petitions signed by a number of people equal to a large percentage of the number that voted in the previous election—and setting early closing dates for such petitions to get candidates listed on the ballots is another way of limiting participation. Such restrictions are particularly hard on new parties trying to get organized for the first time.[48]

In other systems, constitutional or statutory limitations on individuals' rights to form and join political associations have been motivated more clearly by the simple determination of those in power to *stay* in power. Alberto Fujimori, the former president of Peru, stunned his nation and the international community by establishing "emergency" rule with military support, closing down Congress and the courts, and placing leaders of the opposition party APRA under house arrest.[49] In the nation of Georgia, a former Soviet republic, individuals who join groups loyal to former President Zviad Gamsakhurdia, ousted in 1991 by opposition forces, face repression and harassment and their demonstrations are brutally dispersed by government forces. The Moroccan government forbids the formation of any party seeking to contest elections under an Islamic banner.[50]

Freedom to Join Existing Groups

The right of individuals to participate in political groups is not simply a matter of such groups having the right to exist, nor even of the groups' right to conduct its activities without repression. There is also the question of whether or not individuals are allowed to join the groups of their own choice. Here two rights are likely to come into conflict: the right of private groups to determine their membership for themselves and the right of individuals to join whatever groups they wish. Americans have decided that political parties cannot deny membership on the basis of race but they still allow private social groups, which frequently engage in influential political lobbying, to maintain discriminatory membership practices.[51] Membership in the Communist Party of China, which is a requirement for almost all the most desirable jobs in that nation, is viewed as a privilege, not a right, and is granted only to citizens who have met a long list of personal and performance criteria. Being denied membership in powerful political groups can obviously be more than personally offensive; it can mean the difference between a life of affluence and authority and one of the cruelest poverty and powerlessness.

Access to the Cultural Prerequisites for Political Participation

The ability to participate also depends in large measure on having access to the skills of participation and developing the confidence that one can engage in such activities effectively. The extent to which any person possesses such characteristics will vary enormously from individual to individual, no matter what the political system does. Nevertheless, political systems do enact laws that help determine their citizens' access to education and to political information. We looked at the social context of political action in Chapter 3, but it is worthwhile to point out here that governments play a powerful role in determining what that social context shall be. If the government ensures me a free education, at least to some minimal level; helps maintain an economy that increases my chance of gainful employment and thereby of a life of positive involvement in my community; and protects the news media's right to free expression and thereby my right to full political information, the likelihood of my being able to participate in my nation's politics is inevitably enhanced. Political structures—be they rules, institutions, or other means of imposing systematic patterns on our relationships with one another—have far-reaching effects, often beyond the intent of those who introduce them.

An interesting case in point here is the effect colonial powers have sometimes had in raising the political aspirations of their subjects for political freedom by introducing them to Western literature on the subject. The career of Mahatma Gandhi of India is a good example of this phenomenon—it was in the course of receiving a British education that Gandhi developed his passion for achieving Indian independence and thereby ensuring his compatriots the same rights and liberties his teachers had taught him existed elsewhere.

SUMMARY AND CONCLUSION

In this chapter we have considered individuals' motives for participating in politics; the variety of political acts they perform; different aspects of voting; and, in broader terms, the question of access: How welcome is individual participation in politics?

There are important but often misunderstood differences among attitudes, beliefs, opinions, interests, and values— the motives for individual political behavior. Opinions and values are the motives that have been most often measured in recent years, and although polling techniques can be flawed, the random sample poll is a useful tool not only for research but for democracy. Individuals adopt different modes of participation, depending on the opportunities open to them but also upon their own interests and propensities.

The reason for low voter turnout in the United States is not such a mystery—not when we compare what other nations with higher turnout have done to facilitate and encourage voting and not when we consider growing rates of disenchantment among American citizens. Achieving effective participation by voting also depends on the nature of the electoral system adopted. The three main types are the single-member district with plurality election, majoritarian election, and proportional representation, but many variations are possible.

The right to participate in politics is limited in many ways in many lands: There are both personal and impersonal restrictions on the right to vote, as well as limitations on the right to form political groups, to join existing groups, and to acquire the cultural prerequisites for taking part in politics.

Although our emphasis throughout has been on conditions that enhance or obstruct participation, it is important that before quitting our subject we note that there is another side to this coin, and that is the role individuals are *constrained* to play, whether or not they choose to participate. The laws governments make, with or without their citizens' consent, require a great deal of obedient responsiveness. Like it or not, we are all caught up in the world of politics in one way or another. We pay our taxes, obey traffic regulations, fulfill military obligations, conform to safety regulations, and otherwise comply with the rules imposed on us—or suffer the consequences, when our failure to do so is noted and the laws are fairly enforced. This other side of the individual's role in politics, the "subject" role, will receive more attention in later chapters, when we consider the national and local institutions that make the rules we are expected to obey. Our emphasis here has been on the part we as individuals can play in influencing the rules those institutions make. We turn now to the natural sequel to that topic—the part we can play as members of political organizations.

QUESTIONS TO CONSIDER

1. Name a belief of yours. Is it based on knowledge? Is it also an opinion of yours (do you care about it)? Do you have any opinions that you know are not really based on knowledge?
2. Invent a biased question for an opinion poll about a political matter. Now invent an unbiased one about the same subject.

3. Which of the five "participatory types" does your own political behavior fit best? Is that okay with you? Why or why not?

4. How is access to participation in politics sometimes limited? Are any of these limitations found in your own society?

SELECTED READINGS

Dalton, Russell J. *Citizen Politics,* 2nd ed. (Chatham, N.J.: Chatham House, 1996). Compares citizen participation, value orientations, and elections in the United States, Great Britain, Germany, and France.

Flanigan, William H. and Nancy H. Zingale. *Political Behavior of the American Electorate,* 10th ed. (Washington, D.C.: Congressional Quarterly Press, 2002). Analyzing data from the extraordinary 2000 elections, Flanigan and Zingale ask not only who votes and why but also how economic and social characteristics influence individuals' political behavior and the changes that have taken place in American politics over the past fifty years.

Gastil, Raymond P. *Freedom in the World* (New York: Freedom House, 2001). An annual comparative assessment of the state of political rights and civil liberties in 192 countries and 17 related and disputed territories. Useful not only for human rights specialists but also for those interested in what "access" to politics actually means in practice throughout the world.

Ginsberg, Benjamin and Alan Stone, eds. *Do Elections Matter?* (Armonk, N.Y.: M. E. Sharpe, 1996). Questions the connection between the election choices of voters and policy decisions of politicians once they are elected.

Girard, Michel, ed. *Individualism and World Politics* (New York: St. Martin's Press, 1999). An international team of scholars explores the theoretical and methodological problems related to the individualistic perspective in international relations and the role of exceptional or ordinary individuals in different spheres of international politics.

Kuklinski, James H., ed. *Citizens and Politics: Perspectives from Political Psychology* (New York: Cambridge University Press, 2001). A collection of studies in which different scholars address the question of citizens' political competence from different perspectives in contemporary political psychology: emotions, cognitive reasoning, values, basic political attitudes, and ideologies.

Lijphart, Arend. *Electoral Systems and Party Systems: A Study of Twenty-Seven Democracies* (Oxford, U.K.: Oxford University Press, 1994). A comprehensive study of electoral systems, including how they influence election results and legislative representation.

Lipset, Seymour M. and Stein Rokkan, eds. *Party Systems and Voter Alignments: Cross-National Perspectives* (New York: Free Press, 1967). An early and still often cited effort to compare voting behavior across nations.

Marcus, George E., W. Russell Neuman, and Michael MacKuen. *Affective Intelligence and Political Judgment* (Chicago: University of Chicago Press, 2000). Conceptualizing habit and reason as "two mental states that interact in a delicate highly functional balance controlled by emotion," the authors study political behavior ranging from party identification to symbolic politics to negative campaigning.

WEB SITES OF INTEREST

1. Proportional Representation Library
http://www.mtholyoke.edu/acad/polit/
damy/prlib.htm
Information on proportional representation elections, including beginning readings, as well as in-depth articles, an extensive bibliography, and a guide to related Web sites.

2. Center for Voting and Democracy
http://www.fairvote.org/
This nonpartisan and not-for-profit organization supports fair elections and studies how voting systems throughout the world influence participation, representation, and governance.

NOTES

1. For some interesting examples of "dedicated community activists," see Janny Scott, "The Ultimate Volunteers," *New York Times*, 4 Sept. 1994, 1QU.

2. For interesting recent studies of the relationship between these kinds of variables and our political behavior, see James H. Kuklinski, ed., *Citizens and Politics: Perspectives from Political Psychology* (New York: Cambridge University Press, 2001), and Michel Girard, ed., *Individualism and World Politics* (New York: St. Martin's Press, 1999).

3. Tom Maslund, "No News Is Good News," *Newsweek* (15 May 1995): 37, and Richard Stengel, "White Right," *The New Republic* 212 (29 May 1995): 14, 16.

4. Russell J. Dalton, *Citizen Politics: Public Opinion and Political Parties in Advanced Industrial Democracies*, 2nd ed. (Chatham, N.J.: Chatham House, 1996), p. 89.

5. For other reasons poll data may be misleading, see "All Polls Are Not Created Equal," *U.S. News and World Report* (28 Sept. 1992): 24–25 and chap. 3, "The Anatomy of a Public Opinion Poll," in Gary W. Selnow, *High-Tech Campaigns: Computer Technology in Political Communication* (Westport, Conn.: Praeger, 1994), pp. 27–43. On the other hand, in chap. 4, pp. 45–66, "Technical Advances in Polling," Selnow shows how technology has revolutionized polling in recent years, improving its precision.

6. Robin Knight and Victoria Pope, "Back to the Future," *U.S. News and World Report* (23 May 1994): 40–43, and Lee Hockstader,

"Three Years Later, Russians Revising View of Coup Plotters," *Washington Post,* 21 Aug. 1994, A34.

7. Daniel Schorr, "Washington Notebook," *The New Leader* 75 (4 May 1992): 3.

8. Daniel Lerner, *The Passing of Traditional Society, Modernizing the Middle East* (Glencoe, Ill.: The Free Press, 1958).

9. Ronald Inglehart, *The Silent Revolution* (Princeton, N.J.: Princeton University Press, 1977). The quote here given and others following are from Ronald Inglehart, Miguel Basanez, and Alejandro Moreno, *Human Values and Beliefs: A Cross-Cultural Sourcebook* (Ann Arbor: The University of Michigan Press, 1998), pp. 9–13.

10. Dalton, op.cit., pp. 89–110.

11. On this point: A suggestive study discovered that 42 percent of the American public listens regularly to a talk show where public issues are discussed, but only about 4 percent has had the experience of speaking on the air themselves. See *The Vocal Minority in American Politics* (Washington, D.C.: Times Mirror Center for the People and the Press, 1993), cited by Sidney Verba, "The 1993 James Madison Award Lecture: The Voice of the People," *P.S.: Political Science and Politics* 26, no. 4 (Dec. 1993): 679.

12. *New York Times*, 9 Oct. 1991, A1, and 13 Oct. 1991, 34.

13. David Futrelle, "The Politics of Porn," *In These Times* (7 Mar. 1994): 14–17.

14. Martin Cloonan and John Street, "Rock the Vote: Popular Culture and Politics," *Politics* 18, no. 1 (1998): 33–38.

15. Rebecca Fairley Raney, "Sites That Measure Candidates' Views Against Your Own," *New York Times,* 23 Dec. 1999, D7.

16. According to Curtis Gans, director of the Committee for the Study of the American Electorate, nonmajor party voting increased by one-third in 1992, as compared to 1988, and most of that vote went to Ross Perot. (Interview, 9 Nov. 1992.)

17. *Voter Turnout from 1945 to 1997: A Global Report on Political Participation* (Stockholm, Sweden: International Institute for Democracy and Electoral Assistance, 1997), p. 33.

18. Raymond Wolfinger and Steven Rosenstone, *Who Votes?* (New Haven, Conn.: Yale University Press, 1980), p. 73; Steven J. Rosenstone and Raymond E. Wolfinger, "The Effect of Registration Laws on Voter Turnout," in Richard Niemi and Herbert Weisberg, eds., *Controversies in Voting Behavior,* 2nd ed. (Washington, D.C.: Congressional Quarterly Press, 1984), pp. 66–67.

19. G. Bingham Powell Jr., "American Voter Turnout in Comparative Perspective," *American Political Science Review* 80, no. 1 (Mar. 1986): 17–41.

20. Frances Fox Piven and Richard A. Cloward, *Why Americans Don't Vote* (New York: Pantheon Books, 1987), pp. 15, 17–19.

21. Russell B. Dalton, *Citizen Politics in Western Democracies* (Chatham, N.J.: Chatham House, 1988), p. 39. See also William J. Keefe, *Parties, Politics and Public Policy in America,* 7th ed. (Washington, D.C.: Congressional Quarterly Press, 1994), p. 193. Only Australia, Belgium, and Italy legally require citizens to vote, inflicting minor penalties on those who do not.

22. Glenn E. Mitchell and Christopher Wiezien, "The Impact of Legal Constraints on Voter Registration, Turnout, and the Composition of the American Electorate," *Political Behavior* 17, no. 2 (1995): 179–202.

23. Michael D. Martinez and David Hill, "Did Motor Voter Work?" *American Politics Quarterly* 22, no. 3 (July 1999): 296–315.

24. Ruy A. Teixera, *The Disappearing American Voter* (Washington, D.C.: The Brookings Institution, 1992), pp. 26, 29.

25. Ibid., pp. 54, 57.

26. Two recent studies presenting data underscoring the importance of attitudes are Robert A. Jackson, Robert D. Brown, and Gerald C. Wright, "Registration, Turnout and the Electoral Representativeness of U.S. State Electorates," *American Politics Quarterly* 26, no. 3 (July 1998): 259–87, and Richard J. Timpone, "Structure, Behavior and Voter Turnout in the United States," *American Political Science Review* 92, no. 1 (March 1998): pp. 145–58. Timpone says (p. 154), "Election-specific forces also were found to have a substantial influence on electoral participation in the United States, underscoring *the importance of politics* in the fundamental act of political participation." (Italics added). Not *too* surprising, is it?

27. Andrew Reynolds, *Electoral Systems and Democratization in Southern Africa* (Oxford and New York: Oxford University Press, 1999), p. 91.

28. In the same election the Liberal Democrats had 17.2 percent of the votes and only 7.2 percent of the seats—its DV was therefore −10.0. Patrick Dunleavy and Helen Margetts, "The Electoral System," *Parliamentary Affairs* 50, no. 4 (October 1997): 733–49.

29. David M. Farrell, *Comparing Electoral Systems* (London: Macmillan, 1997), Table 7.1, pp. 146–47.

30. For a strong defense of proportional representation, see Douglas J. Amy, *Real Choices, New Voices: The Case for Proportional Representation Elections in the United States* (New York: Columbia University Press, 1993).

31. Farrell, op. cit., p. 79.

32. *International Herald Tribune,* 5 June 1992, 7.

33. Martin Jacques, "The Godmother: Italy's Meltdown—and Ours: Crisis of Government Credibility," *The New Republic* (20 Sept. 1993): 23–27.

34. Variations on this system include limited voting (LV) and cumulative voting (CV). For an explanation of these two versions and their relative effect on minority representation, see David Brockington, Todd Donovan, Shaun Bowler and Robert Brischetto, "Minority Representation under Cumulative and Limited Voting," *The Journal of Politics* 60, no. 4 (November 1998): 1108–25.

35. For recent studies of the variety of electoral systems possible, see Farrell, op. cit., Arend Lijphart, *Electoral Systems and Party Systems: A Study of*

Twenty-Seven Democracies 1945–1990 (Oxford, U.K.: Oxford University Press, 1994), and Joseph F. Zimmerman, "Alternative Voting Systems for Representative Democracy," *P.S.: Political Science and Politics* 27, no. 4 (December 1994): 674–77.

36. Farrell, op. cit., p. 153, and Karen Beckwith, "Comparative Research and Electoral Systems: Lessons from France and Italy," *Women's Politics* 12, no. 1 (1992): 7.

37. Regarding the question of PR and women, see Susan A. Banducci, Todd Donovan, and Jeffrey A. Karp, "Proportional Representation and Attitudes about Politics: Results from New Zealand," *Electoral Studies* 18 (1999): 533–55.

38. Henry W. Ehrmann and Martin Schain, *Politics in France,* 5th ed. (New York: HarperCollins, 1992), pp. 213–19.

39. For a good discussion of the advantages and disadvantages of instituting a national initiative and referendum, see Thomas E. Cronin, *Direct Democracy: The Politics of Initiative, Referendum and Recall* (Cambridge, Mass.: Harvard University Press, 1989), pp. 157–95. See also Bruno S. Frey, "Direct Democracy: Politico-Economic Lessons from Swiss Experience," *American Economic Review* 84, no. 2 (1994): 338–41.

40. See Peter McCormick, "The Recall of Elected Members," *Canadian Parliamentary Review* (Summer 1994): 11–13, for an argument in defense of this institution and a recommendation that it be adopted in Canada.

41. George M. Anderson, "Voting Rights and the Poor," *America* (26 Sept. 1992): 180–96. In Arizona and New Mexico, states that purge every two years, those who vote only in presidential elections are sure to find their names removed from one such election to the next.

42. David Epstein and Sharyn O'Halloran, "Measuring the Electoral and Policy Impact of Majority-Minority Voting Districts," *American Journal of Political Science* 43, no. 2 (April 1999): 367–95.

43. Andrew L. Shapiro, "Giving Cons and Ex-Cons the Vote," *The Nation* (20 Sept. 1993): 767.

44. This question was raised some time ago about Mexican farmworkers in the United States (see George C. Kiser and Martha Woody Kiser, eds., *Mexican Workers in the United States: Historical and Political Perspectives* [Albuquerque: University of New Mexico Press, 1979]), but at present majority opinion appears to be moving in the opposite direction. In 1992 the same question was raised by the European Economic Community, and it now appears likely that resident aliens will be given the right to vote in local elections in Europe long before a similar change is made in the United States.

45. Beck and Sorauf, *Party Politics in America,* pp. 208–12.

46. *Los Angeles Times,* 11 Dec. 1990, B1, B4, and B8 Jan. 1991, B1.

47. John L. Safford, "John C. Calhoun, Lani Guinier, and Minority Rights," *P.S.: Political Science and Politics* 28, no. 2 (June 1995), and Anthony Lewis, "Depriving the Nation," *New York Times,* 17 Sept. 1993, A17. For a general discussion of this issue as it affects Hispanics, see Linda Chavez, "Hispanics, Affirmative Action and Voting," *Annals of the American Academy of Political and Social Science* 523 (September 1992): 75–87.

48. The best source for information on state laws limiting the rights of political parties, particularly the rights of new parties to get on the ballot and of minor parties to *stay* on the ballot is *Ballot Access News,* published privately by editor Richard Winger, Box 47026, San Francisco, CA 94147.

49. *Los Angeles Times,* 7 April 1992, A1, A14.

50. Adrian Karatnycky, *Freedom in the World: The Annual Survey of Political Rights and Civil Liberties 1994–1995* (New York: Freedom House, 1995), pp. 260, 415.

51. The "white primary" was a system that allowed Democratic Party organizations in the American South to deny African Americans the right to participate in their primary elections, on the grounds that parties were private organizations. This had the effect of disenfranchising African Americans altogether, since at the time the Democrats entirely dominated the South's electoral politics and whoever won the primary was sure of election to office. The Supreme Court ruled, in *Smith v. Allwright* (1944), that political parties played too important a role in the nation's political fortunes to be considered private organizations, and the "white primary" was accordingly ruled illegal.

Organizing for Politics: The Group

Jogging contentedly around the familiar track, a middle-aged American runner is startled to see a fellow jogger arrive with a poster: "Save Our Track. Sign the Petition." After completing her twenty laps, she trots over to see what is going on. The track is on the grounds of a school for the deaf and blind that is being sold to the local university. The school for the handicapped has always allowed the public to use the track; the university refuses to make any such promises. Fearful of being excluded, the alarmed joggers meet at the home of one of their number, choose a name (East Bay Community Track and Field Association), elect a president and a recording secretary, gather dues, distribute leaflets, write letters to city council members and state legislators, and arrange for a meeting in the mayor's office with representatives of the university. The smiling university attorney now assures them there will be "no problem." Continued public access to the track will be permitted. Three days later they have this promise in writing.

In this example of organizing for politics, the joggers form an interest group spontaneously as a way to use political means to meet nonpolitical needs.[1] This is a common beginning for interest groups, but not the only way to organize for political purposes. Let's look at another example.

Labor costs are seriously reducing profits, the chairman of a rapidly expanding Japanese electronics firm reports to his governing board. It is his view that government unemployment benefits are unrealistically generous, stimulating workers to hold out for higher wages. After heated discussion, the board resolves to attack the matter through the Unemployment Policy Committee of the Nikkeiren (Japanese Federation of Employers' Associations), to which the company has belonged since its formation in 1948. If the government expects to continue to receive the backing of Japanese business, declares the chairman, it must take steps to reward that loyal support. No one on the board appears to disagree.[2]

In this case, what is happening? A nonpolitical group (a business corporation) is itself a member of a political group (the employers' federation). When the members of the nonpolitical group decide to take political action, they may do so through the exterior group, drawing on the larger group's expertise and numerical strength to pressure the government for change. Their success in doing so will depend on their ability to persuade the other members in the federation that this is an appropriate path to pursue. Sometimes, however, belonging to an existing political group is not a satisfactory way to organize for one's own political purposes. Consider the next example.

Fascinated by politics and determined to devote his life to the struggle for his people's freedom, a student newly arrived in London from an African colony under British dominion soon assumes a leadership role in the activities of the West African Students' Union in London. His work in organizing international conferences brings him to the attention of the leaders of the United Gold Coast Convention, the strongest political party in his native land, and he responds to their request to come home and take the post of general secretary. Soon, however, he finds himself in disaccord with the other leaders of the party, who move too slowly and too cautiously for his taste. Quietly, he helps a friend form a Youth Study Group, which brings together young men and women eager to wage a more active struggle against colonialism. When this organization becomes strong enough, he aids in its transformation to the Convention People's party, breaks with the UGCC, and leads the new party to electoral victory—and the Gold Coast to independence as the new nation of Ghana.[3]

This third example is the true story of the early political career of Kwame Nkrumah, the former president of Ghana. So far we have looked at three ways individuals use political groups to accomplish their ends: They may form a group spontaneously, they may belong to a nonpolitical group that in turn belongs to a political group, or they may work within one political group to develop the strength to form another group more suitable to their purposes. But we have not yet considered the way most of us work through political organizations—that is, we simply join the one that suits us best, stay with it, and gradually come to accept its goals as our own. Those goals may vary from the most ordinary to the most extreme. Our last example falls into the extreme category.

When Wafa Idress was a child, living in the Al-Am'ari refugee camp in the West Bank, her widowed mother would not let her go to school during the time of fierce battles between Palestinians and Israelis, from 1987 to 1993, afraid that she might herself want to join in protests against the Israelis. Her three brothers all joined the Fatah faction, the group supportive of Palestinian president Yasser Arafat. Wafa was not religious, did not wear the chador, and loved a good time. But she was also very angry, and this anger grew as violence returned to Palestine in 2002. She became a paramedic, giving first aid to injured Palestinians and she herself was hit by Israeli rubber bullets and attacked by Israeli soldiers as she went to work. "She used to come and tell us about the children who were shot and killed during confrontations," said her sister-in-law. And finally it became too much for Wafa. She would no longer be kept from taking an active part in her country's battle for autonomy. Somehow she found the means to carry a bomb into a West Jerusalem shopping street popular with strollers and set it off, killing herself and one Israeli, injuring more than 100 others. She had joined the Intifada at last, and her own mother approved: "She is a hero; my daughter is a martyr."[4]

The forms that political organizations take vary as greatly as the routes that individuals follow to join them. The spontaneous, short-lived interest group, the permanent lobby, the political party, and the revolutionary movement mentioned in these examples only begin to suggest the range of political organizations found throughout the world. In fact, since a **political organization** is "any organization that is not itself a government agency but whose main purpose is to affect the operation of government," the subject is too vast to be covered in a single chapter.[5] Our solution is to discuss **interest groups** and **violent revolutionary groups** in this chapter and **political parties** in the next chapter, Chapter 6. All are political organizations, of course, and the differences among them are not always easy to identify. But there are distinctions.

An **interest group** is an organization that seeks to affect the operation of government by using peaceful means to persuade key persons in government to act in accordance with the group's interests. The first two cases discussed in the opening pages of this chapter are examples of interest groups. A **violent revolutionary group** is an organization that seeks to achieve change in government policy—or to change the government altogether—by violent means; the fourth case tells of such a group. A **political party** is an organization that nominates and campaigns on behalf of candidates seeking office in an existent government through popular election; the third case describes the beginning of a new political party.

Although at any given moment in its life, a political organization is usually easily identified as an interest group, a political party, or a violent revolutionary organization, that same organization may well have begun as a different type, and may yet change again. Interest groups may become violent revolutionary groups when they despair of achieving their objectives by peaceful means; revolutionary groups, once successful or partially so, may change themselves into political parties; political parties may be forced underground by government repression and become violent revolutionary groups—or may lose so many elections at such great expense that they abandon the quest for office and become ordinary interest groups, exerting peaceful pressure on those who do win control of the government. Many other permutations are possible. Normally, it is the leaders of political organizations who choose the form (and when to change it), basing their choice on their values, their skills, their experience, and what they believe most likely to work for pursuit of the group's particular goals in its particular circumstances. Rank and file members—or potential members—may or may not be consulted.

INTEREST GROUPS

Most of this chapter will be devoted to the study of interest groups. We will consider the benefits they offer to those who join them, the nature of their organizational apparatus, the goals toward which they are directed, and the tactics they employ. We will also devote an entire section to an important problem posed by some interest groups today: their growing ability to substitute themselves for constitutional government.

Benefits to Joiners of Interest Groups

Individuals must be motivated to combine with others before group action can be effective in influencing government. No one joins a group without seeking some kind of reward. Robert Salisbury has suggested that individuals join groups seeking one of three kinds of benefits: material, solidary, or purposive.[6]

■ **Material Benefits.**   Material benefits are goods and services made available to group members. Salisbury points out that members may join a group to improve their supply of these benefits either directly or indirectly. A group exercising political pressure to keep access to a jogging track is pursuing a material benefit directly. But a group trying to change government unemployment benefits so that businesses may employ workers at lower wages and thus retain greater profits for owners is pursuing such a reward indirectly.

■ **Solidary Benefits.**   Others join groups less for what they can get materially than for the good feelings they get from joining. For some, these "good feelings" are **solidary benefits.** Joining the group gives these people a sense of belonging, a chance to socialize with others, or improved social status. Some of the men and women at the Gray Panthers' annual picnic may be there just to help raise funds for the lobbying efforts of this activist senior citizen group, but for most the opportunity to have a good time in congenial surroundings with others who share their interests may well be the primary motive for attendance. And the chance to go to the picnic may well have brought them into the Gray Panthers in the first place.

■ **Purposive Benefits.**   Some groups offer their members another kind of "good feeling" reward: **purposive benefits.** Working on behalf of a value or cause they believe in can give some members so much satisfaction that they need seek no personal rewards. Groups fighting for such causes as human rights (the International League for the Rights of Man), environmental safeguards (Friends of the Earth), and consumer protection (the British Public Interest Research Centre) are likely to attract members in search of this kind of reward.

The categories are far from discrete. Individuals may join a group for a combination of motives, and groups may offer a combination of rewards. Suppose, for example, that one summer evening you are sitting at home watching the local news on television, after spending a hard, boring day at a temporary job doing data entry—a job you have taken just to earn some money for school expenses. Suddenly you see some familiar faces on the television screen. It is your good friend Angela and her boyfriend Jerry. Then suddenly Jerry is being knocked down by some very tough-looking characters, and Angela is being roughly shoved away. You sit up straight, pay close attention, and learn that your friends were peacefully marching in front of city hall for a cause they believe in—one that you yourself happen to think is worthwhile and important. The people who assaulted them do not agree, and furthermore seem to have little or no respect for other people's rights of free expression. Before you know it, you are on the phone to Angela and Jerry, offering your support. The next night you attend a meeting of their group, and for the rest of the summer you are one of its most ardent members, joining in all its activities. You scarcely mind that boring job anymore, you have so much to think about. Your coworkers are impressed when they see you being interviewed on television during the group's next major demonstration. The group itself likes your work so much that they offer you a paid staff position for the following summer.

What were your rewards? Were they material, solidary, or purposive?

Rewards also vary with intensity of membership. Many groups consist of a handful of activists, backed up by lists of supporters—who are merely all the people who have ever sent in a membership form, with or without a check attached. Active participation by the great majority of the members of interest groups is rare: "A relatively small number of people with strong collective concerns follow through on those attitudes by taking collective action," says Paul E. Johnson.[7] Grant Neeley and Antony J. Nownes find that activists in interest groups are more likely to be motivated by a sense of duty and commitment, plus a desire for expressive benefits. In Salisbury's terms, we would say they seek purposive and solidary benefits.[8]

One reason so many of those who believe in a group's cause take no active part is that, as Mancur Olson pointed out long ago, it is entirely possible for individuals to reap some of the rewards of interest group membership without being a member. **Collective benefits** are benefits that go to all the members of a polity whether they helped work for them or not. Olson called this the **free-rider** problem: The nonparticipants take a free ride on the backs of the hard-working few, and reap the collective benefits. It is often the most difficult problem for a group that is determined to attract and maintain a mass membership.[9]

However, it is also true that some groups deliberately limit the number of active members, either because they prefer a cohesive core to a larger and more heterogeneous group beset by factionalism or because by making membership a privilege and an honor they increase the readiness of those who belong to be generous in donations of time and money.

How Organized Is the Interest Group?

Interest groups vary not only in the kind of benefits they offer to their members but also in the degree to which there is a formal organization devoted to political action. Drawing on the work of others and observing groups in action today, we can identify seven levels of interest group organization.

Amorphous groups are groupings of individuals who share an interest and act on its behalf in a way that indirectly affects government policy, even though they do not see themselves as taking any action that might be called political.[10] **Spontaneous** groups are groups of unorganized individuals who act together politically and deliberately, but in unconventional and often violent fashion.[11] Student demonstrations in France, race riots in Great Britain, and wildcat strikes in the United States all fit into this category, as long as they begin without the participation of any formal organization. Only slightly more organized are the **nonassociational** groups, which make occasional representations to government officials on behalf of unorganized—or loosely organized—individuals who share a particular demographic characteristic. Mexican Americans who testify in favor of bilingual education but do not organize an ongoing group around that issue or around their own ethnic identity provide an example of this level of group activity.

At a fourth level of organizational complexity are **institutional** groups. These are subgroups *within* such institutions as churches, business corporations, and armies. They take special responsibility for the institution's political interests by such tactics as lobbying individual government officials, testifying at hearings, and placing advertisements to arouse public support. When public agencies, officially part of the government, assume the guise of interest group, lobbying another part of government (the legislature or the chief executive), they may be seen as a particular kind of institutional group.

Fifth are **associational** groups, those fully organized groups that are formed specifically to represent the interests—political or other—of their members. These are the groups we most commonly think of when we speak of interest groups. Trade unions, business federations, professional associations, neighborhood associations, political action committees (PACs), and ethnic associations all fit here. Most of this chapter is devoted to their activities.

Sixth are **ad hoc coalitions.** An ad hoc coalition is a temporary organization created to allow several political organizations (which may be any combination of interest groups, parties, or other political organizations) to pool their resources in a joint effort in which all are temporarily interested. When various women's groups, such as the National Organization for Women, the National Council of Jewish Women, the League of Women Voters, and the General Federation of Women's Clubs, engage in collective lobbying on behalf of specific issues and then disband to pursue their more distinctive interests, they are creating ad hoc coalitions. Other groups particularly likely to form coalitions among themselves include environmentalists and business organizations.[12] Sometimes ad hoc coalitions bring together unlikely partners, known as "Baptist-bootlegger" coalitions, a term derived from the days of prohibition, when Baptists favored staying "dry" on moral grounds and bootleggers knew their lucrative businesses depended on keeping the sale of alcohol illegal. Similarly, wealthy mining companies sometimes join environmentalists in demanding strict protective regulations that they know their poorer competitors would be unable to meet.[13] Marie Hojnacki has shown that groups are more likely to form such temporary alliances when their members have strong expressive (purposive) motives, when they believe an alliance is "pivotal" to success, and when they perceive a strong organized opposition.[14]

Social movements may be called a seventh form of interest group, although they are in reality a kind of organization that is very difficult to classify. Such groups are interested in the reform of entire polities, normally on behalf of its least privileged members. If they employ—as many do—violent means, then they fall into the category of violent revolutionary groups; the Shining Path of Peru is an example. If they work primarily—as many do—via political parties, then they fall into that category; a principal example here are the Green movements in many western European nations. But if they avoid the use of violence and enter partisan politics only intermittently and tangentially, then even though they may grow to dimensions that threaten to break its bounds, they still fit better in our present category, the interest group. Social movements are often inspired by religious thought—the Christian Right in the United States, liberation theologists in Latin America—but not always, as we see in the examples of environmentalist movements, the feminist movement at its height in the 1970s, the Polish trade union movement *Solidarnosc,* and the U.S. civil rights movement.[15] And they too are often found working in the international arena, as we will make clearer in Chapter 7, where we discuss the work of International Nongovernmental Organizations (INGOs).

The Goals of Interest Groups

Interest groups may also be distinguished according to the purposes for which they work. Some work only on behalf of the immediate interests of their members, others on behalf of causes that their members believe will benefit all (or a significant portion of) humankind. Some work for a single purpose, others for a wide range of causes that seem to them to fit under a common rubric.

■ **Special Interest Groups and Public Interest Groups.** The most common goal of interest groups is to serve the "special interests" of their members. In almost every nation of the world, groups that focus exclusively on the interests of business, labor, or agriculture are among the best organized and most powerful of all. The Colombian National Association of Manufacturers (ANDI), the American Federation of Labor–Congress of Industrial Organizations (AFL–CIO), and the German Farmers League (*Deutscher Bauernveband*) all work for interests that are found worldwide and that tend to make strong representations to government wherever the most minimal freedom of assembly is protected. Other special interest groups, like the Quebec Teachers Federation, the Akhil Bharatiya Vidyarthi Parishad (India's largest student organization), and the Original Cherokee Community Organization, are also found around the globe; teachers, students, and members of oppressed minorities very often form groups to pursue their particular goals. Other kinds of groups, such as the Anti-Vivisection League or the Ku Klux Klan, are more truly "special."

In their efforts to influence government, special interests often struggle against each other. The Pacific Coast Federation of Fishermen's Associations, a group representing West Coast commercial fishermen, believed the livelihood of its members depended on maintaining the terms of the 1973 Endangered Species Act. However, the National Endangered Species Reform Coalition, an ad hoc coalition of 185 U.S. groups and companies, including major timber, mining, ranching, and utility interests, believed that same piece of legislation was seriously jeopardizing their ability to meet *their* economic needs. In 1995, both groups were actively lobbying Congress, the one to maintain and the other to remove major provisions of that act.[16]

Other groups organize for causes they claim are in the public's interest, not their own. The Sierra Club, the Consumer Federation of America, The Center for Science in the Public Interest, and the National Center for Tobacco Free Kids are American examples of groups that claim the identity of **public interest group**.[17]

Claiming such a status is clearly a good way to discourage opposition, but the question of when a group's goals are truly in the public interest is not always simple to resolve. The nineteenth-century British Union for the Abolition of Vivisection clearly worked for its members' special feelings about animal welfare but that meant working as well against research many others considered essential for human welfare. Contemporary animal protection leagues have also been accused of neglecting basic human needs—for example, the economic well-being of Inuit (Eskimo) families engaged in whaling—in their concern to protect other species. (Perhaps you have seen the bumper sticker showing a picture of a concerned whale pleading, "Save the Humans.") Such cases require careful study and, finally, a normative choice to determine where the public interest truly lies.

■ **Single-Issue Groups and Multiple-Issue Groups.**   Another distinction to be made between groups is the number of goals a group works toward. Some groups focus on single issues, others attack a broad range of political problems that they believe are linked to their members' interests. Large business federations, such as Italy's Confindistria or India's Chambers of Commerce and Industry; labor organizations, such as the Nigerian Trade Unions Congress or the American AFL–CIO; and some public interest groups, including Common Cause and the League of Women Voters, regularly undertake a program for government action that covers a wide range of topics. (Common Cause began in 1970 with a wide-ranging list of issue areas, including antiwar action, government reform, urban concerns, welfare, and the environment, but soon learned it would be more effective with a more limited agenda. Since then it has emphasized the reform of political procedures and institutions.)

Other groups, such as People for the Ethical Treatment of Animals (PETA) or the National Rifle Association (NRA), confine themselves to a single issue.[18] Multiple-issue groups are sometimes accused of having too broad an agenda, but single-issue groups are often criticized for taking too little interest in the larger concerns of government, supporting or attacking government officials strictly according to the actions they take in their one area of concern.

Another criticism of single-issue groups is that their members become so passionate about the single cause that they forget the importance of *aggregating interests* in a wide-ranging program for social change, with the result that those who might be political allies—be it on the left, right, or center—and thus helpful to one another, become competitors for public attention and resources, hurting each other's causes and accomplishing less for their own than cooperative tactics would permit.

The Tactics of Interest Groups

How *do* interest groups work to achieve their goals? To answer that question, we need to consider both **pressure methods,** the means groups use to exert pressure on government, and **pressure points,** the levels and branches of government that groups seek to influence.

■ **Pressure Methods.**   The means of influencing government that is most often associated with interest groups is **lobbying.** In practice, however, groups have a large arsenal of methods at their command, and lobbying itself can take many forms. Waylaying the public official in the lobby of his or her workplace is still a lively art, and making personal offerings ranging from simple lunches to lavish gifts to outright bribes, another time-

OLIPHANT © UNIVERSAL PRESS SYNDICATE. Reprinted with permission. All rights
reserved

honored way of doing this kind of business, has by no means vanished from
the globe.

The **campaign contribution** is now a leading means of gaining access to
elected officials in the United States. When successful candidates owe their
election in significant part to financial assistance during the campaign, they
usually know they are in debt, and know that such debts must be repaid with
appropriate policy decisions or appointments. "The campaign contribution is pervasive," says Daniel Lowenstein, "It is present in legislators' talks
among themselves, in their meetings with lobbyists and in lobbyists' evaluations of their own tactics and strategies. . . . Are contributions the only consideration in the legislative deliberations? Of course not. Are they the dominant consideration? Probably not in most cases. But they are always there,
and their effect can never be isolated or identified with precision." [19]

Although elected officials commonly deny that contributions influence
their decisions, the contributors themselves are often more forthcoming.[20]
Thus when asked whether he thought the $1.3 million worth of financial
support his savings and loan firm had provided for various Democratic political campaigns had influenced the recipients to take up his cause, Charles
H. Keating Jr. answered candidly, "I want to say in the most forceful way I
can: I certainly hope so." [21] Others are more discreet: W. Henson Moore,
head of the American Forest and Paper Association, not only raised over
$100,000 for George W. Bush, but also recruited other CEOs to do the

same. He offers a more modest interpretation of the quid pro quo: "We get a chance to educate George W. on the issues facing our industry."[22]

Although some PACs clearly expect one party to be more responsive to its donations than the other, in fact the money tends to follow power as well as partisanship. Candice J. Nelson has shown that the amounts contributed by PACs of all kinds to House Republican chairs during the 1996 election cycle were significantly greater than the amounts contributed during the 1994 cycle, when those same Republicans were minority members of their committees.[23] Focusing on a single industry, Table 5.1 notes the balanced contributions of the tobacco industry to both parties from 1979 through 1992, and the upturn in contributions to the Republican Party when that party took control of Congress in 1994.

How could so much money go to the candidates from private interests? After all, under campaign finance law in the United States, any group wishing to contribute money or services to a candidate must create a political action committee (PAC) and that committee must make detailed disclosure of

TABLE 5.1
Bipartisan Campaign Contributions: The Case of Tobacco, 1979–2000

		Total	Democrats	Republicans
1979–1990	PACs	$6,102,903	$3,087,399	$3,011,804
1991–1992	PACs	$2,298,950	$1,278,644	$1,020,106
	Soft Money	$2,807,739	$923,364	$1,884,375
	Individual Contributions	$624,439	$269,560	$348,960
	Total	**$5,730,328**	**$2,471,568**	**$3,253,441**
1993–1994	PACs	$2,281,716	$1,149,067	$1,132,649
	Soft Money	$2,518,563	$356,150	$2,162,413
	Individual Contributions	$342,979	$132,804	$209,875
	Total	**$5,143,258**	**$1,638,021**	**$3,504,937**
1995–1996	PACs	$2,769,519	$667,098	$2,101,421
	Soft Money	$6,901,559	$1,064,680	$5,836,879
	Individual Contributions	$653,010	$159,000	$493,800
	Total	**$10,324,088**	**$1,890,778**	**$8,431,560**
1997–1998	PACs	$2,340,002	$647,421	$1,691,581
	Soft Money	$5,470,542	$837,219	$4,633,323
	Individual Contributions	$616,269	$197,275	$418,994
	Total	**$8,426,813**	**$1,681,915**	**$6,743,898**
1999–2000	PACs	$1,132,859	$351,790	$771,819
	Soft Money	$2,920,149	$237,500	$2,682,649
	Individual Contributions	$420,962	$116,500	$304,462
	Total	**$4,473,970**	**$705,790**	**$3,758,930**

*Based on FEC data downloaded 6/1/00. Totals include contributions to federal parties and candidates.

Source: http://www.opensecrets.org/news/tobacco/tobacco.htm., as of 5 December 2000. Reprinted by permission of Center for Responsive Politics.

BOX 5.1
Political Action Committees and the FEC

This page, one of many from one of many forms, provides an example of the kind of disclosures all PACs must make to the Federal Elections Commission.

DETAILED SUMMARY PAGE
of Receipts and Disbursements
(Page 2, FEC FORM 3)

Name of Committee (in full)

Report Covering the Period:
From: To:

I. RECEIPTS	COLUMN A Total This Period	COLUMN B Calendar Year-To-Date	
11. CONTRIBUTIONS (other than loans) FROM:			
(a) Individuals/Persons Other Than Political Committees			
(i) Itemized (use Schedule A)			11(a)(i)
(ii) Unitemized			11(a)(ii)
(iii) Total of contributions from individuals			11(a)(iii)
(b) Political Party Committees			11(b)
(c) Other Political Committees (such as PACs)			11(c)
(d) The Candidate			11(d)
(e) TOTAL CONTRIBUTIONS (other than loans)(add 11(a)(iii), (b), (c) and (d))			11(e)
12. TRANSFERS FROM OTHER AUTHORIZED COMMITTEES			12
13. LOANS:			
(a) Made or Guaranteed by the Candidate			13(a)
(b) All Other Loans			13(b)
(c) TOTAL LOANS (add 13(a) and (b))			13(c)
14. OFFSETS TO OPERATING EXPENDITURES (Refunds, Rebates, etc.)			14
15. OTHER RECEIPTS (Dividends, Interest, etc.)			15
16. TOTAL RECEIPTS (add 11(e), 12, 13(c), 14 and 15)			16
II. DISBURSEMENTS			
17. OPERATING EXPENDITURES			17
18. TRANSFERS TO OTHER AUTHORIZED COMMITTEES			18
19. LOAN REPAYMENTS:			
(a) Of Loans Made or Guaranteed by the Candidate			19(a)
(b) Of All Other Loans			19(b)
(c) TOTAL LOAN REPAYMENTS (add 19(a) and (b))			19(c)
20. REFUNDS OF CONTRIBUTIONS TO:			
(a) Individuals/Persons Other Than Political Committees			20(a)
(b) Political Party Committees			20(b)
(c) Other Political Committees (such as PACs)			20(c)
(d) TOTAL CONTRIBUTION REFUNDS (add 20(a), (b) and (c))			20(d)
21. OTHER DISBURSEMENTS			21
22. TOTAL DISBURSEMENTS (add 17, 18, 19(c), 20(d) and 21)			22

III. CASH SUMMARY

23. CASH ON HAND AT BEGINNING OF REPORTING PERIOD	$	23
24. TOTAL RECEIPTS THIS PERIOD (from Line 16)	$	24
25. SUBTOTAL (add Line 23 and Line 24)	$	25
26. TOTAL DISBURSEMENTS THIS PERIOD (from Line 22)	$	26
27. CASH ON HAND AT CLOSE OF THE REPORTING PERIOD (subtract Line 26 from 25)	$	27

FE8AN079PDF

expenditures both directly to candidates and independently on their behalf. (Box 5.1 shows one of the many pages in one of the many forms any "Authorized Committee" must submit to the Federal Elections Commission.)

Until the spring of 2002, the answer was "soft money," meaning the various loopholes permitting groups to give unlimited sums to the parties and to spend "independently" on behalf of preferred candidates themselves. In the 2000 campaign the practice reached new heights, with the establishment of "leadership PACs." Such PACs, established as early as three years before the election, did not bear the candidate's name, and, when set up as intrastate PACs in states such as Tennessee and Virginia that impose no or all-but-meaningless limits on the size or source of contributions, permitted interested "super-donors" to donate as much as they pleased.[24] (See Box 5.2.)

When the Feingold/McCain Campaign Finance Law was passed in March 2002, Congress appeared to be making an effort to eliminate such contributions: The new law prohibits unions, corporations, and nonprofit groups from paying for broadcast advertisements "if the ads refer to a specific candidate and run within 60 days of a general election or 30 days before a primary" and has also imposed new limits on how much money such groups can give to political parties (see Chapter 6).

However, despite some effort at reform, the loopholes for group spending remain very large indeed. In the first place, PACs can still buy broadcast ads. They must use "hard money," that is, money coming in under federal limits, but those limits have now been raised (individuals can now contribute up to $95,000 to all federal candidates, political parties, and political action committees, whereas formerly the limit was $50,000). And the new law has done nothing to limit the practice of *bundling*. Bundling means gathering numerous maximum contributions and passing them on to candidates in a single envelope. The Enron Corporation, to cite a now-notorious example, gathered $499,600 in contributions from individuals and $280,043 in contributions from political action committees; its accounting firm (Arthur Andersen) gave even more ($527,761 from individuals and $640,499 from PACs) and its law firm (Vinson and Elkins) was a not-very-distant third ($343,300 from individuals and $194,563 from PACs). As one author pointed out, the new law bans only the soft money the companies gave or spent directly.[25]

Interest groups also help candidates with campaign expenses by making in-kind contributions, such as polls the group conducts on issues salient to voters (an especially welcome gift), training for candidates and campaign officials, and transportation for candidates. Such contributions are counted at fair market value by the FEC; however, the PAC itself may have in-house capacities to provide them far more cheaply than they could be bought by the candidate. The PAC is thus able to "max-out" (show the candidate it has given the maximum possible) or at least come far closer to its maximum contribution limit per candidate, at far less cost to itself.[26]

When the government official who has received campaign help from interest groups wishes to cooperate, be it out of innocent agreement or simple avarice, he or she will be more likely to be able to persuade others to go along if a majority of the general public is on the same side as the donor. The health and insurance industries that were opposed to the plans for health care reform by the Clinton administration were estimated to have spent over $40 million in campaign contributions, but also another $60 million in advertising, public relations, and lobbying, in their efforts to defeat that plan.[27]

BOX 5.2
**The Leadership
PAC Game**

[Leadership] PACs are not only offering a way around the spending limits. They are also fostering a new breed of superdonors, who are funneling tens and sometimes hundreds of thousands of dollars into candidate-controlled accounts— vastly in excess of the $1,000 limit on contributions.

Take the network of PACs set up by former Tennessee Governor and GOP hopeful Lamar Alexander. Alexander's federal PAC, the Campaign for a New American Century, raised and spent more than $4 million in 1997 and 1998. The PACs are limited to contributions of $5,000 per election—five times the $1,000 cap on donations from individuals to candidates.

But this is peanuts compared with the money that flowed into Alexander's nonfederal accounts. The Campaign for a New American Century has state affiliates in both Tennessee and Virginia, where the $5,000 cap doesn't apply and where state laws impose virtually no limit on the size or source of a contribution.

Alexander set up yet a third nonfederal PAC, dubbed We the Parents, also headquartered in Virginia. Together, his three state PACs had raised $4.5 million as of Jan. 1. That brings Alexander's total pre-election fund raising to $8 million, none of which will count toward his overall spending limit— despite his intent to take public money.

Source: Eliza Newlin Carney, "Rules? What Rules? A Guide to Loopholes," *National Journal* (29 June 2002): 1258. Copyright © 2002. Reprinted by permission of National Journal.

More recently, lobbyists working for timber, mineral, and cattle interests, who find that environmentalist concerns make it ever more difficult to develop the natural resources crucial to their industries, have helped form citizen activist antienvironmental organizations "because," says a proindustry strategist, "citizen's groups have credibility and industries don't." Samantha Sanchez describes People for the West as such a group; while it describes itself as "a grassroots campaign supporting western communities" it fights to preserve an 1872 mining law that gives mining companies cheap access to mineral-rich public lands and it receives "about 96 percent" of its $1.7 million budget from its corporate sponsors.[28]

Of course, since time immemorial effective lobbying has also meant spending a great deal of time preparing the arguments and documentation that will help the cooperative official get the necessary agreement of other officials. Legislators "value the technical and political information the lobbyists provide" and successful lobbyists seek to become such trusted sources of high-quality credible information that they create a dependency.[29] Web sites are used extensively to keep such information readily accessible.

Another older form of lobbying, writing letters, has taken a new form, as groups with the money to do so may now hire lobbying firms to generate what appears to be "grassroots lobbying." One of the first such efforts was undertaken by the Coalition to End Abusive Securities Suits, which hired the Wexler Group, a Washington lobbying firm, to ask companies and associations first to join the coalition and then to ask their members and employees to write to Congress, using packets of sample letters and computer disks supplied by the firm. E-mail makes it easy for those solicited by such means to comply. Other such firms have used mass mailings of preprinted post cards and have even used phone banks to call potential supporters, transferring the calls to congressional offices when consent is secured.[30]

Interest groups with limited funds may not be able to make serious campaign contributions, send lobbyists to meet with elected officials often enough to make an impact, or hire professionals to reach those whom they wish to influence. Such groups are likely to organize their own e-mail campaigns, hold demonstrations, call for product boycotts, wage strikes, advertise to limited target audiences in the cheaper media, write books, stage various events to attract the attention of the news media, and use whatever means they can afford to call public and official attention to their cause. Student movements, from the Free Speech Movement of the 1960s in the United States to the Brazilian Youth Corps of Popular Action to the French students protesting educational reforms proposed by a rightwing government in early 1992, have moved into the streets with alacrity on behalf of a wide range of causes. Similarly, environmentalists have staged many kinds of theatrical events, from sailing into nuclear test zones to burying automobiles, in their efforts to arouse public interest and concern. Gays and lesbians frequently use parades and other low-cost demonstrations to convince the general public of their right to the same civil liberties enjoyed by heterosexual citizens.[31] As was first shown in Seattle in December 1999, the meetings of the World Trade Organization are now sure to attract a large number of demonstrating activists drawn from environmentalist groups, trade unions, senior groups, women's groups, and any other group convinced that the advance of free trade and globalization is working not for them, but against them.[32]

■ **Pressure Points.** The choice of means is often closely linked to the second tactical question, the choice of whom or what to pressure. Interest groups seek to bring influence to bear on those capable of making a difference. This may mean working at any level of government, including the international, but most groups still focus primarily on national or subnational agencies.[33] In the U.S. presidential system, the separation of the legislative and executive branches and the increasing power of the executive, combined with the declining importance of political parties, means that groups must develop numerous points of access to be effective in promoting government actions they desire or in blocking actions they deplore. The successful group

An interest group at work. Here German members of Greenpeace have locked themselves in a cage outside the French embassy in Bonn to protest France's renewal of nuclear testing in the Pacific. The banner in the background reads: "You can stop our ships, but not our resistance!"
Reuters/Ulli Michel/Archive Photos

stays on good terms with the bureaucrats and congressional aides who draft legislation relevant to its interests, with the members of Congress who vote on it, with the members of the executive branch who counsel the president on such matters, and with the bureaucrats who see to the actual implementation of the policies adopted.[34]

In a parliamentary system, on the other hand, access to individual deputies and to members of the executive branch is very often through the political parties that play such strong roles in this form of government. In Great Britain, the close ties between the business interests of Great Britain and the Conservative Party, and between the labor unions and the Labour Party, mean that each kind of group has a vested interest in seeing the party it trusts take power. The business interests of Germany and the Christian Democratic Party have also always been close, as have business and the Rally for the Republic (the party whose leader, Jacques Chirac, was elected president in 1995) in France. French groups have also linked themselves to the strength of the presidency under the Fifth Republic by working with the Social and Economic Council, which includes in its membership more than 200 delegates from trade unions, agricultural associations, business organizations, and professional groups.[35] In a highly centralized state such as France, bureaucratic ministries exercise great power and will also be the direct focus of industry efforts to influence policy.[36]

In Japan, it is important for business to maintain good relations with the Japanese Ministry of International Trade and Industry (MITI), although the powers of that agency often prove limited in practice. Unrestrained by antitrust laws, Japanese firms are permitted to unite in massive holding companies, known as *zaibatsu* and typically consisting of a conglomeration of banks, insurance companies, and manufacturing concerns. The Mitsubishi zaibatsu, "the most tightly knit, largest and most powerful" of Japan's eight major industrial groups consists of about 185 individual companies, and produces 9.5 percent of all Japanese corporate profits.[37] Such major business interests are able to offer strong incentives to high-level government officials and party leaders, incentives that may take the form of direct bribes or, more commonly, of the practice of *amakudari,* which means "descent from heaven" and refers to the fact that bureaucrats from the ministry often take comfortable positions with these firms when they leave the government. Thus their power has often proved more than a match for any efforts the MITI might make to direct their destinies.[38]

How Well Do Interest Groups Do Their Work?

What role do interest groups play in strengthening individual polities? Political scientists, like the general public, seem to be of two minds on this subject. Some have argued that all politics consists of the struggle among groups and the best system is the one that best protects the rights of free association and intergroup bargaining. Groups serve the interests of individuals far better than individuals are capable of serving themselves, say these political scientists, and those who find no suitable group should form one for themselves. Groups that are able to influence governments deserve to do so; they have shown the strength of their cause on the battleground of politics.[39] This theory of the relationship between groups and government is called **pluralism.**

More recently, the tendency has been to focus on groups as Non-Governmental Organizations (NGOs) and as social movements, and to see them collectively as forming **civil society.** Those who take this approach tend to be even more optimistic about the role of groups than the pluralists. In the works of such writers as Zygmunt Bauman, Ulrich Bech, Allan Schaniberg with Kenneth Alan Gould, and Michael Walzer, we find groups operating independently and often benevolently, making governments pay attention in ways that political parties and their elected representatives have proved themselves no longer capable of doing. They struggle, say these theorists, less over controlling the means of production than over the cultural components of societies, less over the distribution of resources than over how to bridge social gaps, and less over the distribution of goods than over the distribution and reduction of risks, such as those associated with damage to the environment.[40]

Other political scientists, however, have been far less optimistic. *Elite theorists* trace their intellectual roots to the work of the late sociologist C. Wright Mills, whose book, *The Power Elite,* charged that effective control of power in the United States was in the hands of the wealthy and other powerful groups in society. In response to the pluralists, elite theorists pointed out the difficulties many underrepresented groups face in attempting to organize, given lack of time, energy, or political freedom (or all three), as well as the particular advantages the better-organized groups may have had in achieving that status.[41] Government oppression may be sustained by the more powerful segments of public opinion; in states where women, racial minorities, or immigrant workers are openly denied equal rights with other citizens, the control of the dominant groups over the shaping of public opinion can sometimes lead even the oppressed to believe their treatment is inevitable and just.

On the other hand, interest groups that seek support for "acceptable" causes may find that almost any tactics they use to gain their ends are tolerated, if not officially approved. Vigilante groups, whether composed of cowboys lynching horse rustlers in the Old West of the United States, armed guerrillas executing drug dealers in Medellín, Colombia, or revolutionary crusaders meting out summary justice to discredited leaders in post-Communist Romania, are an example of groups using illegal means to accomplish socially approved ends.[42] Even when the ends accomplished are not acceptable to a broader public, illegal means may be tolerated and even abetted by agencies officially responsible for their elimination. Under the ultraconservative leadership of J. Edgar Hoover, the U.S. Federal Bureau of Investigation not only failed to curb the known illegal activities of the Ku Klux Klan but even helped the Klan organize forty-one chapters in North Carolina.[43]

Finally, said some antipluralists, even people who are able to achieve significant roles in effective and well-established pressure groups are not necessarily adequately represented in the political process. After all, citizenship means a concern for national policy and practice that extends beyond the range of one's liveliest personal interests. Short-term personal interests may indeed be best served by joining specific groups, but for the broader concerns and responsibilities of true citizenship, a broader, more all-encompassing form of political organization, such as a social movement or a political party, is required.

Nor have elite theorists been overwhelmed by the later cheerful assessments of civil society. Eva Etzioni-Halevy, John Higley and Michael Burton, and Thomas Dye and Harmon Zeigler have all reminded us that even as agendas may change, elites continue to control and exercise power, and certainly not always benevolently on behalf of the disadvantaged. Although most of these authors acknowledge—and some stress—that committed elites often play a key role in the preservation of democracy, they point out that the growing interdependence among politicians and the leaders of business, unions, voluntary organizations, and social movements has, to a considerable extent, weakened earlier linkages between elites and underprivileged groups (e.g., between labor leaders and the lower-paid workers of a nation). For Etzioni-Halevy, this condition exacerbates inequality and insecurity; for Dye and Zeigler it can even be seen as reducing democracy to empty ritual.[44]

A SPECIAL PROBLEM OF INTEREST GROUP BEHAVIOR: EXTRACONSTITUTIONALISM

Let us introduce the problem of extraconstitutional behavior by interest groups with an example. In Colombia, the Catholic church is one of the largest landowners and 90 percent of Colombians are Catholic. This makes the church a powerful force and ensures that its views on matters political are given close attention. The church has almost exclusive control of education, is a strong voice in determining social welfare policies, and has periodically influenced the government to engage in severe persecution of the minority Protestant population. There are reform-minded progressives within the Colombian Catholic hierarchy, but whether conservatives or progressives are dominant, the fact remains that state policy in such matters is determined by clerical rather than secular leadership.[45]

As this example suggests, sometimes certain groups grow so powerful that they usurp the power of constitutionally established governments. Extraconstitutional power is exercised when groups external to the government are able to exert *so much pressure* on the agents of government that the government has—or believes it has—*no choice but to comply.* In such cases the decision-making powers of government have been appropriated by powerful interests, and the government itself—that is, those persons who occupy all the constitutionally prescribed posts in government—no longer governs, or at least not exclusively. Now it often simply carries out the decisions made elsewhere. The two kinds of groups that have most commonly assumed this degree of political power are business and organized religion. A third force now increasingly likely to fit this category is the media.

Business as an Extraconstitutional Force

The power of business to set government policy varies according to the kind of political system, the kind of economic system, and the nature of the popular culture, but it is found throughout the world. This is not a new phenomenon, although it has accelerated a great deal in our own century, and particularly since World War II. Even before the outbreak of World War I, major German industrial and financial leaders who had established close ties with Kaiser Wilhelm II were able to persuade him of the importance of raising the level of German armaments to unprecedented heights. These industrialists included the armaments manufacturer Friedrich Alfred Krupp, who "made good use of Wilhelm's favorite idea that Germany needed a strong army." [46] A similar relationship between Japanese shipping interests and the Japanese imperial government during the 1870s helped account for the rise of the Mitsubishi Company whose power to resist government regulation (see p. 181) has made it another borderline case of extraconstitutionality. [47]

Even fully socialized systems have not proved to be immune to extraconstitutional business influence. In true socialist systems (in contrast to mixed economies or socialist democracies), *business,* in the sense of independent commercial interests, ceases to exist; the state assumes control of the means of production, and the business of business (like all economic planning) is done by employees of the state. The state-employed managers are expected to remain subordinate to the state. However, if they nevertheless manage somehow to make policy on their own, they are assuming an extraconstitutional role.

Does it ever happen? Of course it does. Until the fall of communism in most of the former Soviet bloc, the evidence was hard to find simply because political infighting in such systems received so little publicity. [48] However, once the old system began to crumble, it became apparent that in fact one of the main reasons for the fall of Communist regimes was public disgust with the use party officials made of the system for their own personal aggrandizement. And as Russia transformed itself into a mixed economy, the old habits persisted. According to Pavel Voshchanov, a spokesperson for Russian President Boris Yeltsin, when party leaders realized a market economy was inevitable, they began setting up independent commercial ventures for themselves as early as 1988. Voshchanov claimed that "the managing department of the Central Committee alone had control of more than sixty major facilities, with a total value of 1.3 billion rubles ($18.6 million). Much more belonged to those groups on the lower levels—the provincial, city and district party committees." [49] According to a U.S. observer, Yeltsin issued decrees facilitating the process by which "yesterday's Communist bureaucrats [were] simply converting themselves into the CEOs and owners of the Russia of tomorrow."[50] Today these new "robber barons" often hold public office and appear to many to have made a mockery of the nation's fledgling party system.

Similar processes are at work in China, where senior party and government officials who benefit from nepotism, favoritism, and corruption are known as "princelings" by a resentful population. As China seeks to encourage free enterprise within the context of the continuing authoritarian rule of the Communist Party, some efforts have been made to bring such corruption to an end, but other forms are ready to take their place. Some authors claim that the ancient system of *guanxi* (relationships) that has always controlled Chinese interpersonal relationships is taking a peculiarly modern form as party bureaucrats reveal confidential information to vendors with whom they have close relationships or allow them to ignore rules others must obey, all in exchange for favors that range from invitations to visits abroad to outright money bribes.[51] China has an unusually elaborate system for contending against such crimes. But when the criminals are themselves members of the government, who will guard the guards?

Another way private business may have an undue influence on government policy is simply to refuse to play—that is, to take its money and its business elsewhere when the home government is not to its liking. When Britain's Labour Party took power in 1945, it stimulated a flight of British capital into other nations' economies. The party itself was later to estimate that between 1947 and 1949 over £645 million (approximately $2.4 billion) left Britain. Less than half of that was actually invested elsewhere; the remainder was simply "hot" money, "quitting Britain because its owners disliked the Labour Government's policy . . . or were engaged in currency speculation."[52] When socialist regimes fight back by imposing heavy penalties for transferring money out of the nation, private business may refuse to make significant levels of investment altogether, preferring to wait for an expected change of command back to procapitalist hands. In either case, the expected high levels of unemployment are likely to impose strong pressures on the government to modify any policies the private sector finds repugnant.

In contemporary times, the capacity of modern business to withdraw its marbles from the national game is greatly heightened by the emergence and development of the **transnational corporation** (TNC, sometimes referred to as the multinational corporation, or MNC). The TNC is a cluster of businesses located in several different nations but owned and managed by the same people. Although they may have headquarters in a single nation (the United States and Japan are the first- and second-largest centers of transnational corporations), they carry out important management as well as production activities around the globe.[53]

TNCs are in some ways reminiscent of **cartels,** associations of businesses formed in the early twentieth century to establish national or international monopolies over particular raw materials or manufactured goods. However, despite their power, cartels depended in part on being able to maintain supportive economic and fiscal policies in the nations where they were headquartered. They were thus vulnerable to shifting political fortunes and the concomitant fluctuations in national policy. The modern TNC differs from the cartel in that it is more interested in expanding its profits than in establishing a monopoly, and it is a far more independent network of investment, research, productive, and distributive institutions. (For further discussion of TNCs, see Chapter 7.)

Organized Religion as an Extraconstitutional Force

It is important to be clear that when organized religion takes over—or plays a dominant role in—the functions of the state, its behavior as an interest group is not necessarily extraconstitutional. Many nations have decided either to establish outright *theocracies* or to give organized religion a strong constitutional role in governance. A **theocracy** is a state ruled by clergy, priests, or other religious leaders. The ancient kingdom of Tibet was a theocracy until it was compelled to become part of China in 1965. The Dalai Lama, a person chosen in accordance with religious traditions and ceremonies as the reincarnation of his predecessor, ruled with the assistance of two prime ministers, one a monk and the other a layman, plus a four-member Bka'-shag (Council of Ministers) to supervise home affairs, foreign affairs, defense, and economic affairs. The remaining structures of government, including a bicameral legislature, were similarly divided between religious leaders and lay persons. The Dalai Lama was the final authority in all matters. He decided what laws should be promulgated and what officials appointed to high office. Today the Dalai Lama has many of the same political powers, but owing to Chinese conquest of Tibet these can be exercised only over the Tibetan refugee community in India, and only with the concurrence of the host nation.[54]

Small-scale Christian theocracies have also often existed within nation-states, such as the sixteenth-century Protestant community under the leadership of Huldreich Zwingli, a Protestant reformer who regarded the population as a Christian congregation under the rule of God, entitled to defend itself even by aggressive warfare in order to prevent interference by nearby Catholic cantons. In the same century, John Calvin established his version of the perfect Protestant community in nearby Geneva, excommunicating and banishing all Catholics who did not submit to his regime. Two hundred years later, Moravian communities were set up by Count Nikolaus Ludwig von Zinzendorf throughout Europe and the United States. In 1849 the Provisional State of Deseret was set up by Mormons in a territory that now makes up most of Utah, California, Arizona, Nevada, and Colorado. However, disappointed by their unsuccessful application for statehood in 1850 and widespread opposition to their practice of polygamy (now engaged in by only some 30,000 "rogue Mormons"), the group moved slowly but steadily toward its present identity as one Christian sect among many, although it continues to place a very great emphasis on political activity.[55]

Although absolute theocracies are now hard to find, numerous contemporary states, including Israel and most Islamic polities, have decided to combine the religious and the secular in a more or less seamless web of regulation; here again, there is nothing unconstitutional in the role of organized religion. The Islamic religion, founded in the seventh century B.C.E., has consistently been closely associated with political governance. In the sixteenth century, when the Ottoman empire was at its peak and the rule of Islam extended from deep inside what is now Iran, across Asia Minor and north Africa, across the European Balkans, and up to what is now Austria, the sultan's power to rule was based entirely on his role as caliph, successor to the Prophet of God, overlord of all the Muslims. In contemporary Islamic states, which cover most of the same territory, excluding Israel and all southern European states except Turkey, but now including Iran, Pakistan, and Afghanistan, the tradition of combining the state and religion remains strong and often appears to be growing stronger.[56] Countries with mixed religious populations, such as Nigeria, have permitted states within them to adopt Islamic law (the Shari'a).[57] In such polities, the law is interpreted by religious guides, know as *imams,* who are normally appointed, promoted, and paid their salaries by the state; there is no separate religious clergy. Under the rule of the Taliban, Afghanistan became a true theocracy.[58] Although the abuse of human rights in that nation, especially those of women, aroused horror throughout the rest of the world and many Muslims insisted that the religious precepts followed were a gross distortion of the rulings found in the Koran, religious dominance in Afghanistan was the law of the land and thus definitely not extraconstitutional.[59]

In other polities, however, the dominant tendency today is to assert that church and state are separate entities, at least in constitutional theory. Nevertheless, religious groups within the state may seek to impose religious dogma as state practice. Sometimes, as in Algeria and Egypt, the state fights back rigorously against efforts of the dominant religion (in these cases, Islam), to take over the state, but the very effort to do so can lead to other problems of individual liberties: The rights of those seeking to establish religious control of the state may be invaded or the state may make such important concessions to the dominant religion that the rights of others to practice their own beliefs — or to follow no system of religious belief whatsoever — become severely limited. In Algeria, the military intervened in 1992 to prevent what would have been an entirely legal takeover of the government — via free elections — by the FIS (Front Islamique du Salut) and then subsequently denied it the right to take part in the political process.[60] In Egypt the repressive use of emergency law to restrict the activities of Islamic fundamentalists in Egypt may have done more to stimulate than to eliminate terrorist activity by such believers against the state, and has furthermore helped erode private rights to the point where it is now sometimes used to silence anyone who speaks against the state.[61] A case in point is the 2001 imprisonment of the internationally distinguished Egyptian sociologist, Saad Eddin Ibrahim, for daring to form a research team to investigate electoral fraud in that nation.[62]

In other cases, the relationship between a dominant religion and a constitutionally secular state has been more ambiguous. The relationship between church and state has been particularly interesting in Mexico, where 92.2 percent of the population is Catholic.[63] After that nation achieved independence from Spain in 1821, the Catholic church found itself both weakened and strengthened. The church was weaker because it was, after all, a Spanish institution, which meant not only that anticlericalism became in a sense patriotic, but also that many bishops, monks, and nuns returned to Spain. It was stronger because despite these difficulties, it was an older and better-established institution than the new government itself. By linking itself to conservative politicians and working hard to maintain internal unity on political questions, it has managed to establish and maintain strong ties with government leaders, and constitutional restrictions on its power are often simply ignored or circumvented. For example, the Mexican constitution states that education is a function of the state, except when delegated to private schools with a nonreligious format—but the church in fact administers an elaborate school system of its own without government interference. Seminarians are required, like everyone else, to fulfill a year of military service—but in practice, these are weekend training sessions at the seminary. Officially, all church property belongs to the state—but local communities are allowed to designate land for the construction of churches, and these arrangements are normally sanctioned by the government. Priests were forbidden from appearing in public in clerical dress—but did so anyway.[64] Constitutional changes made in 1992 ostensibly reinforced limitations on the church, especially in the holding of openly political meetings, but by permitting the recognition of all churches as legal entities these changes "effectively legitimized the church's institutional role" and had the effect of "allowing the church a greater part in nonspiritual matters."[65]

Even in states where the official exercise of religion is forbidden or socially frowned upon, religious political activism has proved possible. Poland's Roman Catholic church was an interesting case in point in the years leading up to the overthrow of the Communist regime. Antigovernment forces such as the trade union *Solidarnosc* and its supporters consistently used attendance at Catholic ceremonies—most dramatically during the 1979 visit of the first Polish pope, John Paul II, to his homeland—as a means of demonstrating their political convictions. The church in turn functioned as a mediator, strongly supporting *Solidarnosc* and the people's right to free assembly and freedom of expression but at the same time seeking to induce all the contending forces—authorities, workers, and peasants—to settle their disputes without violence. The Polish church was the one agency the state would allow to speak on behalf of the dissenting population, a role that gave it definite extraconstitutional power; it was, according to Mirella Eberts, "the most powerful institution in the country" at the end of the Communist period.[66]

After the revolution, the church sought to consolidate and extend its power, even though it was not long before a majority (60 percent) of Polish citizens were telling pollsters that the church's influence in public life had become "excessive." Aided by the sympathies of the first postrevolution president, Lech Walesa (whose own rise to power from underground labor leader to chief executive owed much to the church), the church succeeded in reintroducing religious instruction in the public schools in 1990 and ensuring the passage of an antiabortion law in 1993. The election of Social Democratic candidate Aleksander Kwasniewski as president in 1995 brought a few changes in the opposite direction. Public schools continued to give religious instruction, but the abortion law was liberalized in 1996. A new constitution in 1997 and a new Concordat between church and state in 1998 sought to set out the rights and duties of the church, and the limits upon them, more clearly than before. But while insisting on all citizens' rights to religious freedom (including the right not to practice any religion), these documents nonetheless granted the Catholic church privileges and promised it levels of state support that churches normally do not have in Western democracies. Thus the church remains a powerful public force, but no longer extraconstitutionally.[67]

The Media as an Extraconstitutional Force

Another institution that now plays a very specialized role in extraconstitutional politics is the media. It is true that even in nations where freedom of expression is protected and the media are relatively free to publish and broadcast what they wish, there are usually some restrictions on their right to publish seditious, licentious, or libelous materials.

Nevertheless, broadcast agencies and the press often interpret events and structure public opinion so as to leave elected governments no effective choice but to make—either directly or indirectly—the recommended response. One of the most striking examples took place during the Vietnam War, when Walter Cronkite, the most respected American television news anchor of the 1970s, saw wire service reports that persuaded him it was time for the United States to withdraw from that struggle and hosted a documentary in which he openly called for no further increase in U.S. involvement and for immediate negotiations with the enemy. His comments were widely regarded as creating the first major impetus for shifting opinion in Congress as well as among the general public. As other leaders of the media followed suit, the support for government policy fell away slowly but surely, and U.S. withdrawal became first possible, then inevitable.[68] A few years later, the double role of the media in revealing the Watergate scandal *and* guiding the formation of public opinion about the event was similarly apparent and dramatic.[69]

Subsequent years have not lacked for further examples, and the power of the media to shape our public life is now widely recognized and analyzed. For Timothy E. Cook, writing about the United States, "the news media now form an intermediary political institution," and as such, they play an ambiguous but extremely powerful governmental role. On the one hand, they are always strongly focused on "the events, ideas, preoccupations, strategies, and politics of powerful officials" and this "enables the news media to be not merely political but governmental." Yet at the same time they are always also focused on what will keep their audience interested, which sometimes propels them in the opposite direction; American news, says Cook, vacillates "widely between news that deeply reinforces the officials' aims and news that undercuts them." In a further complication, political actors inevitably "shape their activities to accord with the production values of the news, and politics follows in turn."[70]

Cook's point regarding the media's need to keep their audience interested is an important one. Although here we treat the media separately from other businesses, we certainly should not forget that the private media (that is, non-public-broadcasting systems or publications) are themselves businesses, or, as Robert Picard calls them, "communication firms," and as such depend on the continued good will of their CEOs and their advertisers.[71] Keeping an audience is not just a matter of pride; it is a matter of money.

The business interests of mass media have become particularly problematic in democratizing nations. John A. Lent finds that in many of the new democracies of Asia the newly privatized media are often more interested in developing ardent consumers than ardent democrats. In particular he faults "mass communication formulas that trivialize or commercialize important issues, corrupt the electoral process, and generally dehumanize society as a whole."[72]

But whether their goal is democratization or the maintenance of authoritarian control, political leaders are never helpless pawns of the media. When those in power fear negative media response, they may decide that their only alternative is to exercise firm control over the media, either by limiting its access to news of government actions or by engaging in direct censorship. The method of limiting access has been used in free societies, for example, by U.S. President Ronald Reagan during the 1983 invasion of the small nation of Grenada, by U.S. President George H. W. Bush during the Gulf War in

1991, and by NATO in Kosovo in 1999.[73] And in the administration of George W. Bush, Defense Secretary Donald H. Rumsfeld was often similarly slow to grant full journalistic access to reports covering the war in Afghanistan and the confrontations between Israelis and Palestinians in the Middle East.[74]

Of course, exercising firm control over the media is yet more common in nations under authoritarian rule: The few foreign reporters allowed to stay in Serbia during the war in Kosovo saw almost nothing the government did not wish them to see, and the well-controlled Serbian media guaranteed that the same would be true for their own people. Perhaps, as Flora Lewis claimed at the height of the war in Kosovo, "the absolute controller of information is clearly personal emotion . . . the Serbian expatriate community in France . . . had access to all the terrible news that turned the rest of Europe against the Serbian regime, even to the point of reluctantly going to war, and they refused to believe it. They believe Belgrade, they say, because they are Serbs and Serbs must stick together."[75] Yet state control of the Serbian media had begun long before the war in Kosovo and must have been an important factor in ensuring that that kind of self-deluding loyalty would be in place, even among expatriates.

Be that as it may, the fact that leaders everywhere do sometimes succumb to the temptation to exercise such censorship serves to underline the power of the media. But here again, the case is interestingly ambiguous: If in the course of exercising a constitutional *right* (freedom of expression) the media, for whatever reasons and in service of whatever cause, effectively limit the ability of elected officials to carry out their constitutional *duties* as they see fit, are they themselves acting unconstitutionally? And can state efforts to restrain them in the exercise of their freedom ever be viewed as constitutionally defensible?

Although business, religion, and the media are the three kinds of interest groups that most commonly and most powerfully usurp roles assigned constitutionally to the structures of government, they are certainly not the only institutions that try to play that role. All powerful interest groups, including educational institutions, professional associations, trade unions, public agencies, or so-called public interest groups, may attempt to carry pressure politics to the point where it is in effect itself making policy within the domain that affects it, and may succeed. Furthermore, some agencies within the government itself may make so strong an effort to influence other government agencies (directly and via the public) that they themselves sometimes appear to be going beyond their appropriate constitutional limits. Consider, for example, the efforts (and expenses) of the Public Relations Division of the U.S. Department of Defense, which not only sends high-ranking officers to argue before legislative and other governmental bodies for its budgetary needs but also maintains a continuous flow of news releases, film clips, and public exhibits to keep the American public supportive of those needs. To some, this public relations effort appears an entirely appropriate exercise of the constitutional powers of the military; but others do not agree. What do you think?

VIOLENT REVOLUTIONARY ORGANIZATIONS

As the whole world learned again on September 11, 2001, when terrorist attacks leveled the two towers of the World Trade Center in New York City and destroyed a large section of the Pentagon in Washington, D.C., killing thousands in the process, not every group works peacefully to achieve its means. Some decide only violence will accomplish the ends they seek. Terrorism and revolution are not the same thing. Not every revolutionary organization uses violence to pursue its goals. In politics, a **revolution** is any fundamental change in the political organization of a polity. An extremist political party, a fundamentalist religious organization, or a group of idealistic intellectuals seeking world government may all be bent on accomplishing such fundamental change, yet draw the line at the use of violence. However revolutionary their goals, such groups nevertheless fall into the category of interest group (see earlier) or political party (see Chapter 6). Groups that are willing to use violence to achieve revolutionary change—perhaps by turning the clock backward, perhaps by inventing a "brave new world"— must be treated as a case apart. We will look at three subtypes: the terrorist group, the guerrilla organization, and the military mutiny.

Terrorist Groups

Those who study terrorist behavior have sought to distinguish among the fanatical true believer, the simple criminal who conceals a desperate quest for personal gain in the rhetoric of a cause, and the paid employee of a nation-state that has adopted the sponsoring of terrorist acts as a means of achieving foreign policy goals.[76] But more and more frequently now, the terrorist acts not as an isolated fanatic or criminal and not as any government's hired hand, but rather as a member of a *terrorist group*.

Terrorist groups are organizations that attempt to change the operation of one or more governments by using isolated and unpredictable acts of violence to induce fear of the consequences of *not* changing. Sometimes the attempt is made to instill fear in government officials, sometimes in ordinary citizens, and sometimes in both simultaneously (for example, by attacks on representatives of government in public places). If the focus is the ordinary citizen, the hope may be that the frightened populace will organize in more conventional ways to pressure the government to comply with the terrorists' demands. Leftwing terrorist groups sometimes operate on the principle that their activities will cause such widespread government repression of civil liberties in the course of efforts to end the terrorism as to arouse support for a

BOX 5.3
**And in the
Twenty-First
Century?**

During the 1970s, 8,114 terrorist incidents were reported around the world, resulting in 4,798 deaths and 6,902 injuries. During the 1980s, the number of incidents increased nearly fourfold, to 31,426, with 70,859 deaths and 47,849 injuries. From 1990 to 1996, there were 27,087 incidents, causing 51,797 deaths and 58,814 injuries. The number of deaths due to acts of terrorism varies from year to year, but there is a clearly increasing trend. Between 1970 and 1995, on average, each year brought 106 more incidents and 441 more fatalities.

Source: Jessica Stern, *The Ultimate Terrorists* (Cambridge, Mass.: Harvard University Press, 1999), p. 6.

popular revolution. Rightwing terrorists may entertain the hope that their activities will produce a military takeover, establishing a government more likely to function in accord with their values; many of the French rebels who launched terrorist attacks in the early 1960s in a vain attempt to prevent the granting of independence to Algeria were themselves military men.[77]

On the other hand, terrorist groups also often form around a political goal that is not identifiable as left or right: the goal of national autonomy.[78] What the Irish Republican Army, the Basque Homeland and Liberty movement, and the Palestinian Liberation Organization all have had in common, when operating as terrorist organizations, is the passionate desire to free themselves from what they consider to be intolerable foreign domination, to occupy a homeland of their own, and to exercise popular sovereignty. It should always be kept in mind that such a group may pursue its goals on behalf of an ungrateful populace that would much rather maintain present arrangements, or work for change peacefully, than see the use of violent means.[79] Terrorism has been a mode of demanding change since time immemorial, but has clearly experienced a resurgence in recent years, in the number of incidents, in the skillful deployment of limited resources, and in the degree of damage and mayhem inflicted on civilian populations (see Box 5.3). What steps can and should be taken to reduce this peril? Punishing the perpetrators of these heinous acts as swiftly and severely as is consistent with the rule of law, radically improving security both at the site of likely targets and by building international antiterrorist alliances, studying sociopsychological explanations of the small group dynamics that can turn discontent into hatred and hatred into violence, *and* giving thoughtful consideration to the substantive issues that terrorists raise are not mutually exclusive activities. Indeed, combining all four approaches may be the only answer likely to work.

The last two both tend to receive short shrift, however. Governments and media often prefer to insist that terrorist acts are simply "incomprehen-

Captured Al Qaeda members are marched away from their stronghold in the Tora Bora mountains of Afghanistan (December 17, 2001). The first—but not the only—step in fighting terrorism is to capture and punish the perpetrators.
© Reuters NewMedia Inc./CORBIS

sible," and to work together to raise the need and demand for revenge, and even for acts of war. Such an approach is not only likely to lead to excessive bloodshed and serious violation of human rights but is also unlikely to eradicate terrorism. We must also work harder to understand how leaders of small groups can persuade their followers to accept such outrageous means, even to the point of sacrificing their own lives on suicide missions, and then carry them out. Of the September 2001 bombings, Martha Crenshaw said, "You had to have a small group of people who worked together, who knew each other and trusted each other. . . . What keeps them fighting is what keeps soldiers in a platoon fighting. They don't want to let their buddies down."[80] In this case, the hijackers who carried out the attack were older than is usual for terrorists, better educated, more middle class. What went on inside their groups to make such men accept such a destiny? Or are these signs that the phenomenon finds its strength outside the group—does it mean, as Stuart Grassian has wondered, that rage against the United States is now "endemic to a culture"?[81]

Finally, difficult though it may be when we have suffered at the hands of terrorists, we also need to pay more attention to the substantive complaints that have been made. These may be hard to understand. Americans in particular seem to find it very hard to imagine what it means to the people of other cultures to see our values swamping their own, even as the global gap between our wealth and their dire need grows. But unless Americans learn to empathize with such feelings among the poor but peaceful populations of the world, they are dangerously unlikely to be able to take, in time, the necessary steps to keep those feelings from turning, in some persons, to the unforgiving hatred that leads to terrorist attacks. As the new war on terrorism makes clear, we are very far from eliminating the quest for change by terrorist violence. (See Figure 5.1.)

Guerrilla Warfare Organizations

> We began to grow more conscious of the necessity for a definitive change in the life of the people. . . . The struggle shall be long and harsh, and its front shall be in the guerrillas' hide-out, in the cities, in the homes of the fighters . . . in the massacred rural population, in the villages and cities destroyed by the bombardments of the enemy. They are pushing us into this struggle; there is no alternative; we must prepare it and we must decide to undertake it.[82]

So spoke Che Guevara, the idealistic Latin American revolutionary who helped bring Fidel Castro to power in Cuba and then lost his life in revolutionary struggle against an oppressive dictatorship in Bolivia. Like Guevara, many guerrilla warfare leaders believe nonviolent means have proved to be inadequate to end the suffering of oppressed peoples. Violence becomes the necessary last resort. *Guerrilla warfare* is similar to the activity of terrorist groups in that it too seeks to inspire fear, and thereby change, and in that the perpetrators are highly unlikely to have either the personnel or the weaponry necessary for confronting an entire army openly. But there are important differences. Guerrilla warriors tend to establish headquarters away from urban centers and to set up institutions of alternative government, including those for education and health as well as military training. They are ready, they claim, to take over the established government altogether, not merely to compel change or to bring it down. They use standard military weapons as well as the equipment of the urban terrorist. They normally try to visit acts

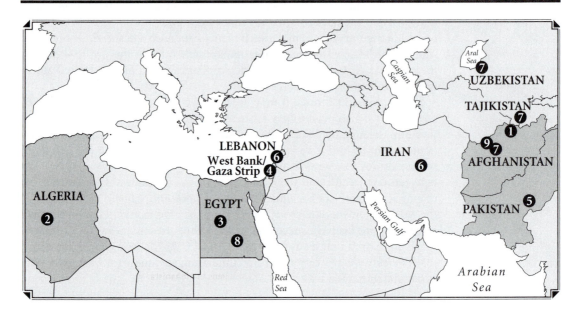

FIGURE 5.1
The Terrorist
Groups and
How They
Interlink

1   AL-QAEDA (The base)
Founded in late 1980s by Osama Bin Laden to organize Arabs who had fought in Afghanistan.
Helped to finance, recruit, and transport Sunni Islamic extremists.

Aims: To spread Islamic fundamentalism and destroy US interests in the Middle East.

Supporters: Probably has several thousand members, but acts as a focal point for many other organizations. Many supporters based in Afghanistan.

2   ARMED ISLAMIC GROUP (GIA)
Founded in 1992 after the Algerian government voided elections in which the Islamic Salvation
Front won a clear victory.

Aims: To overthrow secular Algerian government.

Supporters: GIA probably has around 1,000 members. Algerian government has accused Iran and
Sudan of supporting the organization.

3   AL GAMA'A AL-ISLAMIYYA (Islamic Group)
Founded in late 1970s. Egypt's largest militant group.

Aims: To overthrow the Egyptian government and replace it with an Islamic state.

Supporters: At its peak probably had several thousand members, but many are now in prison or
abroad.

4   HAMAS (Islamic Resistance Movement)
Founded in 1987 from Palestinian branch of the Muslim Brotherhood. Loose structure with some
members working in social organizations or fundraising, others working secretly.

Supporters: Thousands of supporters in West Bank and Gaza Strip. Receives funding from Palestinian expatriates, Iran, supporters in Saudi Arabia and other moderate Arab states.

FIGURE 5.1
(continued)

5 HARAKAT UL-MUJAHEDDIN
Previously known as Harakat al-Ansar. Based in Pakistan with members active mainly in Kashmir. Now led by Farooq Kashmiri, but previous leader, Faziur Rehman Khalil, signed the Bin Laden fatwa calling for attacks on US.

Supporters: Several thousand in Kashmir, Pakistan. Has access to mortars, machine guns, rockets, and explosives. Receives financial support from Saudi Arabia and from Pakistanis and Kashmiris.

6 HEZBOLLAH (Party of God)
Also known as Islamic Jihad, Revolutionary Justice Organisation. Founded by radical Shia muslims in Lebanon.

Aims: Destruction of Israel.

Supporters: Thousands of supporters in the Bekaa Valley, southern Lebanon and Beirut. Allied with Iran.

7 ISLAMIC MOVEMENT OF UZBEKISTAN
Based mainly in the Ferghana Valley, eastern Uzbekistan. Strongly opposed to the secular regime of President Islom Karimov.

Supporters: Several thousand fighters based in camps in Afghanistan and Tajikistan.

8 AL-JIHAD
Also known as Islamic Jihad. Founded in late 1970s and now very close to Bin Laden.

Aims: To overthrow Egyptian state and form Islamic government. 1981: Assassination of President Anwar Sadat of Egypt.

Supporters: Several hundred members, many now in prison. Egypt claims it is supported by Bin Laden.

9 ABU SAYYAF GROUP
Based in southern Philippines. The smallest and most radical of Islamic separatist groups. Many members trained in Afghanistan.

Supporters: Believed to have about 200 core fighters, with another 2,000 supporters [in] the Middle East.

Source: "The Terrorist Groups and How They Are Interlinked" adapted from "Linked and Dangerous: Terror Inc" by Nick Fielding from *The Sunday-Times,* 23 Sept. 2001. Copyright © Times Newspapers Limited, London, 2001. Reprinted by permission.

of violence only on those identified as the enemy or as persons who actively aid the enemy, and they are more likely to seek and even to expect (but not necessarily to get) widespread popular support for their activities. They make themselves easier to join.

The Military Mutiny

The *military mutiny* is a short-lived organization, usually led by high-ranking officers, who seek to accomplish a coup d'etat, the overthrow of the civilian government by force of arms. Such mutinous organizations within the military may be motivated by private or public goals, or a combination of the two. Private grievances may include dissatisfaction with levels of pay, promotion policies, or perceived inadequacies in state support for the military. The Ghanaian army's overthrow of Kwame Nkrumah was said to have been motivated in part by the fact that the president's Own Guard Regiment received better pay and equipment than the regular army. As one of the leaders of the coup wrote later, "One day [the regular soldiers] were to pay for their electricity; the next day they were to lose their training allowances; the following day they were to lose their travelling facilities. We all wondered what was happening to us." [83]

However, even when private complaints help motivate the takeover, the military always has public purposes as well. Military men live in a military culture and often come to hold nonmilitary ways in considerable contempt. Politicians may appear to them to be universally corrupt, demagogic, and inefficient. Personal qualities that can be tolerated in affluent, established nations become more difficult to endure in poor young nations, such as those of Africa after World War II, where coup succeeded coup with sometimes bewildering speed. In such a setting, the army often believes it has the training, the skills, and the values to set things right—that is, to establish stability and order, national unity, and rapid modernization. Yet once in power, its lack of institutionalized contact with the general population and its habit of resolving issues by force of arms often leads to a government more oppressive and more corrupt than any civilian government that may have preceded it. The abuse of human rights by the Haitian military junta after taking power in 1991 is a case in point.[84]

SUMMARY AND CONCLUSION

Political organization exists throughout the human polity. Even where participatory politics is banned or confined to state-sponsored directive structures, the human need to articulate and act on behalf of shared interests will find a way to make itself felt by those in power. Types of organization may be as rudimentary as the East Bay Community Track and Field Association or as complex as a transnational finance corporation, as supportive to government as the latest "Committee to Re-Elect the President" or as hostile as the Red Brigades; as long lasting as the American Democratic Party (which traces its origins back to the original struggle over ratifying the Constitution) or as short lived as an ad hoc coalition to seek asylum for a poet who is a political refugee from his homeland; as close to the grassroots as the Potrero Neighborhood Merchants Association for Fairer Taxes or as remote from its membership as the Coalition on National Priorities and Military Policy, a group whose policy decisions are made, like those of most public interest groups, by a narrow leadership corps. The role of groups in democracies is sometimes analyzed as pragmatic and largely beneficial (pluralists), an essential and largely benign supplement to other political organizations (writers on civil society), or dangerously likely to be dominated by the selfish interests of their own leaderships (elite theorists). But in any case, wherever human beings congregate, groups will form, and sometimes become so strong they usurp the policymaking roles a nation's constitution prescribes for particular government institutions and political organizations such as parties. The power of the business world to move beyond such constitutional limits varies according to the kind of political system, the kind of economic system, and the size of the business in question. Transnational corporations, giant businesses that operate in several nations at once, may be able not only to control the relevant policymaking in those nations but also to substitute their own decision-making processes altogether. Religious interests sometimes control political processes constitutionally, but in states where the religious and the secular are constitutionally separate, churches are nevertheless often permitted to carry out activities that any strict reading of the constitution and the statutory laws would show to be illegal. In socialist states organized religion may play a mediating role between the state and forces of dissent, thereby exercising an extraconstitutional influence on government policy. The media (another kind of business) are a third force now ever-more capable of compelling elected governments to enact or disavow policies in order to maintain or regain public approval, regardless of their own will or that of those who elected them.

Not every group works peacefully to achieve its means. Terrorist groups, guerrilla organizations, and the military mutiny are all different forms of violent revolutionary organization. Terrorist groups use violence to induce fear of the consequences of *not* changing. Guerrilla groups use it in an effort to take over the established government altogether and normally try to limit their attacks to those seen as the enemy or as persons who actively aid the enemy. The military mutiny is a short-lived organization, usually led by high-ranking officers, who seek to overthrow the civilian government by force of arms.

The forms of political organization we adopt inevitably influence the quality of life within individual nation-states and in the human polity at large. How well we are able to conduct our affairs, individually and collectively, depends to a large extent on how well our interests are articulated, compromised, and conveyed to those in power. When some interests are labeled out-of-bounds without fair hearing; when political organization takes the form of nontargeted rioting; when groups fall under the sway of leaders who use their resources for ends contrary to those of the membership; or when intragroup and intergroup compromises prove impossible to reach and maintain, the damage done will extend beyond those citizens whose interests are immediately affected. For unaccommodated interests, when they are seriously held, rarely dissipate, and the means used by the people who hold them to seek satisfaction are likely to grow progressively more disruptive to the entire political system. Nor do the disturbances that stem from failures of political organization necessarily stop at national borders. One of the chief causes of conflict in the human polity at large is the migration of un-resolved internal disputes into the international arena, as representatives of the unaccommodated seek living space, material wealth, personal dignity, or whatever collective good they believe they cannot find in adequate supply at home.

QUESTIONS TO CONSIDER

1. Think of an interest group you might join (maybe you already have). What benefits are likely to come to you from membership in this group? Are these material, solidary, or purposive, or some combination? Which of the seven kinds of organization named in this chapter seems to describe your group's organization best?
2. How would you characterize the role of interest groups in your nation—as pluralistic, as responsible members of a civil society, or as purely elit-ist? What evidence could you give for your answer?
3. Find a non-mainstream media Web site and see what it has to say. Did you learn anything new? If not, keep trying until you do. How sure are you that this new information is accurate?
4. Is it ever a good idea to consider the substantive issues that terrorists raise, even as we concentrate on their capture and punishment? Why or why not?

SELECTED READINGS

Cigler, Allan J. and Burdett A. Loomis, eds. *Interest Group Politics,* 6th ed. (Washington, D.C.: Congressional Quarterly, 2002). An examination of how interest group politics have changed in recent years, covering such topics as how environmental groups are using the Internet as an organizing tool, corporate lobbyists as political actors, and interest groups and gridlock.

Ginsberg, Benjamin and Martin Shefter. *Politics by Other Means: Politicians, Prosecutors and the Press from Watergate to Whitewater* (New York: W. W. Norton, 1999). Addresses the long-term significance of the rise of the politics of scandal and

the decline of electoral competition, arguing that as long as scandals dominate the political agenda, voters will continue to be repulsed by the political process and the government's political effectiveness will be increasingly weakened.

Manzetti, Luigi. *Institutions, Parties and Coalitions in Argentine Politics* (Pittsburgh: University of Pittsburgh Press, 1994). How special interests' competition for resources has prevented long-term political and economic stability in Argentina.

Marquand, David and Ronald L. Nettler. *Religion and Democracy* (Oxford, U.K.: Blackwell, 2000). A study of the growing political power of organized religion that raises an all-important question: Is it an ally or an enemy of pluralist democracy?

Mitchell, Neil J. *The Conspicuous Corporation: Business, Public Policy and Representative Democracy* (Ann Arbor: University of Michigan Press, 1997). Considers why, despite political advantages of business in the policy process, economic power does not always translate into political power and examines the activities of business in politics, the strength of interests opposing business, and business policy failures in the United States and the United Kingdom.

Petracca, Mark P. *The Politics of Interests: Interest Groups Transformed* (Boulder, Colo.: Westview Press, 1992). A study of how and why people form interest groups and the role they play in the United States.

Rosenblum, Nancy L., ed. *Obligations of Citizenship and Demands of Faith: Religious Accommodation in Pluralist Democracies* (Princeton, N.J.: Princeton University Press, 2000). An interdisciplinary and comparative exploration of the place of religion in contemporary public life, offering new perspectives on the proper bounds between church and state in pluralist democracies.

Walker, Jack L. *Mobilizing Interest Groups in America: Patrons, Professions and Social Movements* (Ann Arbor: University of Michigan Press, 1991). A theory of interest group formation and maintenance emphasizing strategies and modes of mobilization.

WEB SITES OF INTEREST

1. Center for Responsive Politics: Lobbyist Database
   http://www.opensecrets.org/lobbyists/index.asp
   A search engine allowing access to the amounts spent on lobbying by companies, labor unions, and other organizations in the United States.

2. The Media Ownership Chart
   http://www.mediachannel.org/ownership/
   Provides data regarding control of media by multinational corporations; raises questions regarding impact on news coverage, entertainment culture, and freedom of speech and democracy.

NOTES

1. Such groups often decline almost as spontaneously as they form, once the crisis is past. The East Bay Community Track and Field Association never met again after its victory was won.

2. Jon Woronoff, *Japan as Anything but Number One* (Armonk, N.Y.: M. E. Sharpe, 1991), p. 159.

3. Kwame Nkrumah, *The Autobiography of Kwame Nkrumah* (Edinburgh: Thomas Nelson, 1959), pp. 40–83.

4. "Palestinians Hail a Heroine; Israelis See Rising Threat; Suicide Bomber Elicits Pride and Fear," Washington Post Foreign Service (31 Jan. 2002), p. A20.

5. This is the definition adopted by the members of the organized section on Parties and Other Political Organizations of the American Political Science Association.

6. Robert Salisbury, "An Exchange Theory of Interest Groups," in Robert Salisbury, ed., *Interest Group Politics in America* (New York: Harper & Row, 1970), pp. 47–55. In this now classic work, Salisbury adopted a set of distinctions first made by Peter B. Clark and James Q. Wilson in "Incentive Systems: A Theory of Organizations," *Administrative Science Quarterly* 6 (Sept. 1961): 129–66.

7. Paul E. Johnson, "Interest Group Recruiting: Finding Members and Keeping Them," in Alan J. Cigler and Burdett A. Loomis, eds., *Interest Group Politics,* 5th ed. (Washington, D.C.: Congressional Quarterly Press, 1998), p. 42.

8. Grant Neeley and Anthony J. Nownes, "Activists, Contributors, and Volunteers: The Participation Puzzle," *Southeastern Political Review* 26, no. 2 (June 1998): 279–92.

9. Mancur Olson, *The Logic of Collective Action* (Cambridge, Mass.: Harvard University Press, 1965). For more recent discussions of the phenomenon, see both Johnson, op. cit., and Neeley and Nownes, op. cit., as well as Jeffrey M. Berry, *The Interest Group Society,* 3rd ed. (New York: Longman, 1997).

10. When Soviet consumers during the Stalinist years refused to spend their money on theatrical productions burdened with heavy political content and thereby forced the government to provide more entertaining fare, they were acting, claims David Lane, who invented the term, as an amorphous interest group. David Lane, *Politics and Society in the USSR* (New York: Random House, 1970), p. 251.

11. This type and the following three are drawn from Gabriel Almond and G. Bingham Powell Jr., *Comparative Politics: A Development Approach* (Boston: Little, Brown, 1966), pp. 75–76. These authors use the word *anomic* to describe the groups we have here termed *spontaneous.* Although they say such groups lack "any set of regulating values or norms" (which would justify calling them anomic), in fact many of the examples they cite are groups that might claim with considerable justification that they are simply fighting for the avowed values of the society— racial justice, equitable distribution of the nation's wealth, patriotism, and so on. In any case, such groups usually defend some values, and so are not normless, as the term *anomic* would imply. *Spontaneous* is a better term for this kind of organization.

12. For environmentalist coalitions, see Chapter 4 in Margaret E. Keck and Kathryn Sikkink, *Activists Beyond Borders: Advocacy Networks in International Politics* (Ithaca, N.Y.: Cornell University Press, 1998). For collective business lobbying in the European Union, see Bert Pijnenburg, "EU Lobbying by *ad hoc* Coalitions: An Exploratory Case Study," *Journal of European Public Policy* 5, no. 2 (June 1998): 303–21.

13. David Vogel, *Trading Up: Consumer and Environmental Regulation in a Global Economy* (Cambridge, Mass.: Harvard University Press, 1995), pp. 20–21.

14. Marie Hojnacki, "Interest Groups' Decisions to Join Alliances or Work Alone," *American Journal of Political Science* 41, no. 1 (Jan. 1997): 61–87.

15. The last two have, of course, been strongly infused with Christian thought, but cannot be said to have been inspired or formed by it. For a study of social movements, see Cyrus Ernesto Zirakzedeh, *Social Movements in Politics: A Comparative Study* (Essex, U.K.: Addison-Wesley-Longman, 1997).

16. Timothy Egan, "Industries Affected by Endangered Species," *New York Times,* 13 April 1995, A7.

17. For a recent review of consumer group activities, see Stephen Brobeck, ed., *Encyclopedia of the Consumer Movement* (Santa Barbara, Calif.: ABC-CLIO, 1997).

18. Kelly Patterson, "The Political Firepower of the National Rifle Association," in Cigler and Loomis, op. cit., pp. 119–42; Carol Matlack, "Animal-Rights Furor," *National Journal* 23 (7 Sept. 1991): 214; and Joan Biskupic, "NRA, Gun-Control Supporters Take Aim at Swing Votes," *Congressional Quarterly Weekly Report* 49, no. 10 (9 Mar. 1991): 604–607.

19. Quoted in Robert K. Goidel, Donald A. Gross, and Todd G. Shields, *Money Matters* (Lanham, Md.: Rowman and Littlefield, 1999), p. 53.

20. Perhaps the best exposé to date of the role of campaign contributions in acquiring positive government response from both Republican and Democratic elected officials exists in the form of a videotape of a television show. In 1997 the Public Broadcasting Service aired "Washington's Other Scandal" on its program *Frontline,* hosted by Bill Moyers. This revealing tape, # FROL-9705, is available from PBS Home Video.

21. Herbert E. Alexander and Rei Shiratori, eds., *Comparative Political Finance Among the Democracies* (Boulder, Colo.: Westview, 1994), p. 6.

22. Eliza Newlin Carney and Peter H. Stone, "To Associate or Not to Associate," *National Journal*

(8 May 1999): 1237. This article is one in a set of articles in this issue, entitled "Money Machine."

23. Candice J. Nelson, "The Money Chase: Partisanship, Committee Leadership Change, and PAC Contributions in the House of Representatives," in Paul S. Herrnson, Ronald G. Sahiko, and Clyde Wilcox, eds., *The Interest Group Connection: Electioneering, Lobbying, and Policymaking in Washington* (Chatham, N.J.: Chatham House, 1998), pp. 52–64.

24. Mark J. Rozell and Clyde Wilcox, *Interest Groups in American Campaigns* (Washington, D.C.: Congressional Quarterly Press, 1999), pp. 100–101, and Eliza Newlin Carney, "Rules? What Rules? A Guide to Loopholes," *National Journal* (8 May 1999): 1258.

25. Richard L. Berke, "For Some, A Bigger Role," *New York Times*, 21 March 2002, A1, A30.

26. Rozell and Wilcox, op. cit., pp. 106–07.

27. Sven Steinmo and Jon Watts, "It's the Institutions, Stupid! Why Comprehensive National Health Insurance Always Fails in America," *Journal of Health Politics, Policy and Law* 20, no. 2 (Summer 1995): 364.

28. Samantha Sanchez, "How the West Is Won: Astroturf Lobbying and the 'Wise Use' Movement," *The American Prospect* (March-April 1996): 37.

29. Paul S. Herrnson, Clyde Wilcox, and Ronald G. Shako, "Interest Groups at the Dawn of a New Millennium," in Paul S. Herrnson, Ronald G. Shaiko, and Clyde Wilcox, *The Interest Group Connection: Electioneering, Lobbying and Policymaking in Washington* (Chatham, N.J.: Chatham House, 1998), p. 329.

30. Jane Fritsch, "The Grass Roots, Just a Free Phone Call Away," *New York Times*, 23 June 1995, A1, A11.

31. Hans Johnson, "Creative Protests: From Street Theater to Fasts, Activists Keep Finding Fresh Ways to Promote Gay Rights," *Advocate* 811 (9 May 2000): 24. See also Daryl Lindsey, "AIDS Activists Change Their Act," *Salon* (25 June 2001). http://www.salon.com/news/feature/2001/06/25/aids/

32. John Nichols, "Raising a Ruckus," *The Nation* (6 Dec. 1999).

33. We will explore group activity in the international arena in later chapters. For a preview, see Vogel, op. cit.

34. In a study with interesting implications for the focus of group efforts, Benjamin Ginsberg and Martin Shefter suggest that the focus of political battles in the United States has now shifted away from parties and elections to the media, congressional investigations, and judicial proceedings. See their *Politics by Other Means: The Declining Importance of Elections in America* (New York: Basic Books, 1990).

35. William Safran, *The French Polity*, 3rd ed. (New York: Longman, 1991), pp. 110–24.

36. See, for example, James A. Dunn Jr., "The French Highway Lobby: A Case Study in State-Society Relations and Policymaking," *Comparative Politics* 27, no. 3 (April 1995): 275–95.

37. "Mitsubishi: The Diamonds Lose their Sparkle," *The Economist* (9 May 1998): 67.

38. Alfred A. Marcus, *Business and Society: Ethics, Government, and the World Economy* (Homewood, Ill.: Irwin, 1993), pp. 256–57.

39. Arthur F. Bentley, *The Process of Government: A Study of Social Pressures* (Chicago: University of Chicago Press, 1908); David Truman, *The Governmental Process* (New York: Knopf, 1951); and Robert A. Dahl, *A Preface to Democratic Theory* (Chicago: University of Chicago Press, 1956).

40. Zygmunt Baumunt, *Intimations of Postmodernity* (London: Routledge, 1992); Ulrich Beck, *Risk Society* (London: Sage, 1992); Allan Schnaiberg and Kenneth Alan Gould, *Environment and Society* (New York: St. Martin's Press, 1994); Michael Walzer, "Rescuing Civil Society," *Dissent* 45 (1999): 62–66.

41. Michael Margolis, "Democracy: American Style," in Graeme Duncan, ed., *Democratic Theory and Practice* (Cambridge, U.K.: Cambridge University Press, 1983), pp. 125–26. See also C. Wright Mills, *The Power Elite* (Oxford, U.K.: Oxford University Press, 1957).

42. Douglas Farsh, "Vigilantes Retake Slums of Medellín," *Washington Post*, 7 Dec. 1991, A17.

43. Michael Parenti, *Democracy for the Few* (New York: St. Martin's, 1988), p. 144.

44. Eva Etzioni-Halevy, *The Elite Connection* (Cambridge: Polity Press, 1993); Eva Etzioni Halevy,

"Elites, Inequality and the Quality of Democracy in Ultramodern Society," *International Review of Sociology* 9 (1999): 239–50; Thomas Dye and Harmon Zeigler, *The Irony of Democracy,* 10th ed. (Belmont, Calif.: Wadsworth, 1996); John Higley and Michael Burton, "Elites, Mass Publics and Democratic Prospects in Post-Industrial Societies," *International Review of Sociology* 9 (1999): 221–37.

45. Daniel H. Levine, *Religion and Politics in Latin America: The Catholic Church in Venezuela and Colombia* (Princeton, N.J.: Princeton University Press, 1981).

46. Hans Jaeger, "Business and Government in Imperial Germany, 1871–1918," in Keiichiro Nakagawa, ed., *Government and Business* (Tokyo: University of Tokyo Press, 1980), p. 142.

47. Takeaki Teratani, "Japanese Business and Government in the Takeoff Stage," in Nakagawa, *Government and Business,* pp. 58–59.

48. In one of the few works by a disillusioned Communist to reach a worldwide audience prior to 1989, *The New Class,* Milovan Djilas (a Yugoslavian official who defected to the West in the 1950s) asserted that all Communist bureaucrats, including those in managerial roles in industry, were directing public policy in their own, not the nation's, interests. They were able to give themselves, said Djilas, "special privileges and economic preference because of the administrative monopoly" they held in various economic enterprises, in sports and humanitarian organizations, and in other branches of the government bureaucracy. Milovan Djilas, *The New Class* (New York: Praeger, 1957), pp. 39, 46.

49. Pavel Voshchanov, "The Secret Business of the Communist Party," *World Press Review* 38 (Jan. 1992): 22.

50. *Los Angeles Times,* 1 Mar. 1992, A1, A12. For an interesting discussion of elite continuity before and after the fall of communism, see Stephen White and Olga Kryshtanovskaya, "Russia: Elite Continuity and Change," in Mattei Dogan and John Higley, *Elites, Crises, and the Origins of Regimes* (Lanham, Md.: Rowman and Littlefield, 1998).

51. Walter L. Keats, "Corruption and the China Trade," *China Business Review* (January/February 1988): 30. For a case study of an effort to bring down one family of "princelings," see Steven Mufson, "Web of Intrigue in Chinese Steel Firm Probe," *Washington Post,* 16 Mar. 1995, A29. For a full and interesting explanation of the original meanings of the term *guanxi,* see Duran Bell, "Guanxi: A Nesting of Groups," *Current Anthropology* 14, no. 1 (Feb. 2000): 132.

52. "Challenge to Britain," Labour Party Policy Statement, 1953, p. 6, cited in A. A. Rogow, *The Labour Government and British Industry, 1945–1951* (Ithaca, N.Y.: Cornell University Press, 1955), p. 36. See also Sidney Pollard, *The Wasting of the British Economy* (New York: St. Martin's, 1982), p. 88.

53. The U.S. share in the "outward stocks" of foreign investment has in fact been on the decline while that of Canada, Germany, Japan, and Switzerland have been rising. Charles W. Kegley Jr. and Eugene R. Wittkopf, *World Politics: Trend and Transformation,* 3rd ed. (New York: St. Martin's, 1989), p. 163.

54. C. W. Cassinelli and Roben B. Ekvall, *A Tibetan Principality: The Political System of Sa Skya* (Ithaca, N.Y.: Cornell University Press, 1969), p. 5; Claude B. Levenson, *The Dalai Lama* (London: Unwin Hyman, 1988), p. 115; and A. Tom Grunfeld, *The Making of Modern Tibet,* rev. ed. (London: M. E. Sharpe, 1996). Grunfeld offers a particularly well-balanced study, making clear that Chinese conquest has brought improvements in health, in education, and in the conditions of women and of the poor, but also political domination as well as heavy control over religious practices.

55. Leonard J. Arrington and Davis Bitton, *The Mormon Experience: A History of the Latter-Day Saints* (New York: Knopf, 1979), pp. 105, 114; Richard N. and Joan K. Ostling, *Mormon America: The Power and the Promise* (San Francisco: HarperCollins, 1999); and Kenneth L. Woodward, "A Mormon Moment," *Newsweek* (10 Sept. 2001): 46–51.

56. It can be argued, however, that the current increasing religiosity in Arab states reverses a trend toward ever-greater secularity that had been steadily developing in the 1980s. See, for example, Fouad Ajami, "The Arab Inheritance,"

Foreign Affairs 76, no. 5 (Sept.-Oct. 1997): 133–48.

57. Norimitsu Onishi, "A Nigerian State Turns to the Koran for Law," *New York Times,* 8 Dec. 1999, A4.

58. Barnett R. Rubin, "Afghanistan Under the Taliban," *Current History* 98, no. 625 (Feb. 1999): 79–91.

59. And even today, some former soldiers of the Taliban still believe the jihad (holy war) is not over: "when the country is threatened by infidels, we are ready to start the holy war again. I still believe in jihad," said one such true believer at the end of 2001. Dexter Filkins, "The Legacy of the Taliban Is a Sad and Broken Land," *New York Times,* 31 Dec. 2001, A1.

60. Martin Stone, *The Agony of Algeria* (New York: Columbia University Press, 1997).

61. Mamoun Fandy, "In Egypt, Rising Fundamentalist Threat," *Christian Science Monitor,* 19 June 1992, 19. For the predicament faced by secular states with large militant Islamic minorities, see Charles P. Wallace, "Muslim Tide Rising in the East," *Los Angeles Times,* 8 Aug. 1992, A1.

62. Mary Anne Weaver, "Mubarak Regime Is Now on Trial in Egypt," *New York Times Magazine* (17 June 2001).

63. Roderic Ai Camp, *Politics in Mexico: The Decline of Authoritarianism* (New York: Oxford University Press, 1999), p. 85.

64. Claude Pomerleau, "The Changing Church in Mexico and Its Challenge to the State," *The Review of Politics* 43, no. 4 (Oct. 1981): 540–59, and Anthony Gill, "The Politics of Regulating Religion in Mexico: The 1992 Constitutional Reforms in Historical Context," *A Journal of Church and State* 41 (1999): 761–95.

65. Camp, op. cit., p. 137.

66. Mirella W. Eberts, "The Roman Catholic Church and Democracy in Poland," *Europe-Asia Studies* 50, no. 5 (1998): 817–43.

67. Ibid.

68. Robert M. Entman and David L. Paletz, "The War in Southeast Asia: Tunnel Vision on Television," in William C. Adams, ed., *Television Coverage of International Affairs* (Norwood, N.J.: Ablex, 1982), pp. 181–98.

69. Gladys Engel Lang and Kurt Lang, *The Battle for Public Opinion: The President, the Press and the Polls During Watergate* (New York: Columbia University Press, 1983).

70. Timothy E. Cook, *Governing with the News: The News Media as a Political Institution* (Chicago and London: The University of Chicago Press, 1998), pp. 62, 111, and 115.

71. Robert G. Picard, "Media Concentration, Economics, and Regulation," in Doris Graber, Denis McQuail, and Pippa Norris, *The Politics of News, The News of Politics* (Washington, D.C.: Congressional Quarterly Press, 1998), pp. 193–217.

72. John A Lent, "The Mass Media in Asia," in Patrick H. O'Neil, ed., *Communicating Democracy: The Media and Political Transitions* (Boulder, Colo.: Lynne Reinner, 1998), p. 168.

73. For Grenada, see *Facts on File,* 4 Nov. 1983, 830, and Gerry O'Sullivan, "Against the Grain," *Humanist* 522, no. 3 (May 1991): 39–42. For the Gulf War, see *New York Times,* 17 Jan. 1991, A15, and 18 Jan. 1991, A7, O'Sullivan, op cit., and Debra Gersh Hernandez, "The Media's Impact on the Military," *Editor & Publisher* no. 19 (13 May 1995): 14. For Kosovo, see Flora Lewis, "A Very Special Relationship," *Index on Censorship* 3, (1999): 22–27.

74. David Shaw, "Rumsfeld OKs Principles for Media Access to Troops," *Los Angeles Times,* 19 Oct. 2001, A1.

75. Lewis, op. cit.

76. David E. Long, *The Anatomy of Terrorism* (New York: The Free Press, 1990). See especially Chapter 2, "Understanding Terrorist Behavior," pp. 15–27.

77. William Rosenaw and Linda Head Flanagan, "Blood of the Condor: The Genocidal Talons of Peru's Shining Path," *Policy Review* 59 (Winter 1992): 82–85; Marc Fisher, "Attacks by Skinheads on Asylum Seekers Unnerve Germans," *Washington Post,* 11 Oct. 1991, A22.

78. For a discussion of separatist terrorism in the developed world, see pp. 66–70 in Adrian Guelke, *The Age of Terrorism and the International Political System* (London and New York: Tauris Academic Studies, 1995).

79. Of course, as we have already seen in the case of Quebec, other separatist groups have found it

possible to pursue their goals by peaceful means; not every group seeking national autonomy should be automatically classified as terrorist.

80. Quoted by Jodi Wilgoren in "A Terrorist Profile Emerges that Confounds the Experts," *New York Times*, 15 Sept. 2001, A2.

81. Quoted in ibid.

82. Quoted in Andrew Sinclair, *Che Guevara* (New York: Viking, 1970), pp. 21, 94.

83. A. K. Ocran, *A Myth Is Broken* (Harlow, U.K.: Longman, 1969), p. 43, cited in Robert Pinkney, *Ghana Under Military Rule 1966–1969* (London: Methuen, 1972), p. 2.

84. Nancy Ely-Raphel, "Human Rights Situation in Haiti," *U.S. Department of State Dispatch* 5, no. 29 (18 July 1994): 484. Unfortunately, the departure of the military does not always mean a reversal of patterns of abuse; see the story of the assassination of a prominent opposition figure several months after the U.S. overthrow of the junta in *New York Times*, 30 Mar. 1995, A3.

CHAPTER 6

Political Parties

In the summer of 1948, a young political-scientist-to-be sat by the radio, holding her breath and listening to the third roll call of the Republican convention. On the first two ballots, Ohio Senator Robert A. Taft and former Minnesota Governor Harold E. Stassen had prevented New York Governor Thomas E. Dewey from getting a majority of the votes. After the second ballot, the anti-Dewey forces had asked for a recess. Now they were back, ready to go. Had they worked out a coalition to stop the New Yorker, or were they giving up? As the voice of the leader of each state's delegation came over the airwaves calling out that state's vote, the avid listener wrote down the numbers for each candidate, adding them as she went along. When one of them suddenly shot past the magic number of 548, she was able to shout, loud and clear, "It's Dewey!" a whole millisecond before the roar of a cheering crowd came out of the little brown box on the table beside her. Her math was as fast as anyone's that summer afternoon, long before calculators and computers were in common usage. Undistracted by the sight of flashing electronic bulletins or frantic reporters and delegates milling about, her mind filled with images of what a convention ought to look like, she experienced a sense of instant participation in U.S. political party life, via the media. It was wonderful.

Or imagine this: In the summer of 2004, a political-scientist-to-be sits by his combination television and home computer, holding his breath and watching the images on his screen, listening to the voices he hears, his hands poised above his keyboard. The images shift. Here are several men and women arguing animatedly around a table over which a sign reads, "Democratic Program Committee." Here is a convention hall of Democratic delegates watching, on more screens, the men and women arguing. Here is an attractive older woman, the well-known governor of a southern state, carefully explaining what is to happen next. Now a question appears on the screen about the important issue of public policy the committee has been discussing, followed by four possible replies. The governor's voice says, "You have one minute to type in your response, delegates and telepollsters." After only a moment's thought, our hero forthrightly types, *c*. At the end of 60 seconds, the screen shows the tally: how many and what percentage of all American voters registered to vote prefer policy choice *a*, *b*, *c*, or *d*; how many delegates at the convention make each choice; and the totals for each, with the winning response outlined in bright red.

Now cut back to the Program Committee, so viewers can see its members looking at the results on their own large screen. Back to the governor: "Ladies and gentlemen, the Program Committee will now continue its deliberations. Thanks to you, the committee knows what the Democratic delegates prefer and what the nation at large prefers on this important issue. But the final decision is their own. As soon as we know what they have decided, we will let you know." Cut for the commercial. Our political-scientist-to-be, one of those chosen to be part of the random sampling of the "nation at large," heaves a contented sigh and sits back in his chair. He has a feeling of instant participation in U.S. political party life, via the media. It is wonderful.

Although the media can and do give us such moments, and have done so now for many, many years, their interaction with the U.S. political party system is fraught with controversy and, some would even say, with peril to democracy. But political parties have not yet been taken over entirely by the media, even in the United States, and other questions also require our attention. In this chapter we will consider the following topics: the difference between parties and interest groups, the functions parties are expected to perform, how parties begin, how they are organized, who their members are, how they choose their candidates, how they prepare their campaigns, how they use the media to carry out their campaigns (and how the media use them), how they try to carry out their programs once in government, the types of parties and party systems, and, finally, the role of political parties today.

POLITICAL PARTIES AS A UNIQUE FORM OF POLITICAL ORGANIZATION

In Chapter 5 we identified three kinds of political organizations: interest groups, political parties, and violent revolutionary organizations. Why do political parties deserve a category—and here, even a chapter—of their own? In particular, what makes them different from an interest group?

Three characteristics, two always present and a third commonly so, distinguish the **political party:**

1. The members of a political party, not content with trying to persuade the government to act in a particular way, instead always seek to *place representatives in the government.*
2. To accomplish this goal, *the party nominates candidates to stand for election* in its name.
3. The political party almost always claims that, if successful, it will *exercise power on behalf of the general public.*

Sometimes interest groups seek to place their representatives in the government (by appointment to advisory boards, for instance, or to other important offices), put up independent candidates for elective office, and claim to act on behalf of the general public. Unlike interest groups, however, political parties never fail to manifest the first two of these three characteristics. And when an interest group assumes all three features, it is no longer a separate organization interested in pressuring government. It is an organization interested in taking part in government; it is a *party* to the action.

THE FUNCTIONS OF POLITICAL PARTIES

What is a political party's job? In practice, political parties have performed a surprisingly wide range of functions, from providing holiday turkeys for the poor to making and carrying out a nation's foreign policy. Most commonly, however, parties are expected to conform to a somewhat more limited job description. Four functions appear on almost everyone's list of what a party does, or should do: leadership recruitment, interest aggregation, campaigning, and governing. We will treat each of these in greater detail later in the chapter; here we simply offer brief explanations of each.

Leadership Recruitment

Even in eras when parties are widely scorned and other groups and individuals perform many of the functions formerly ascribed to them, the political party is still likely to be the structure that identifies potential leaders, brings them to public attention, and secures them the support necessary for taking public office. As we shall see, however, this is not always the case in the United States.

Interest Aggregation

A second major function of parties is aggregating interests—that is, serving as mediator for a wide range of politicized demands. To do this, parties must set up procedures that permit different points of view—different *interests*—to be presented, discussed, compromised, and *aggregated*. To find out what these interests are, they now rely heavily on polls, but study groups, issue-oriented clubs, and representatives invited to serve on platform committees all also help, as do party meetings at all levels. The final speeches and programs must be decided by the leaders and it is always an open question (one well worth asking) how well they really reflect—and aggregate—the various concerns of the different groups whose support is being courted and to what extent they actually cater mainly to special groups of more affluent supporters (the question of whether they really mean what they say can be answered later; see "Governing").

Campaigning

Political parties normally play an important role in helping their candidates campaign for office. Even in today's world of mass media, political consultants, and direct mail advertising, the parties still play a part in ensuring that voters are registered, that they know the differences among the candidates, and that they know when and where to vote on election day. Where parties are strong, as in most western European nations, they may assume full responsibility for their candidates' campaigns, calling in media advisers, pollsters, and other professional experts only as they see fit.

Governing

Finally, the elected officials of victorious parties are usually expected to run the government, and in doing so to make an effort to translate the party's program into legislative bills, and thence into law. As noted, this is where push comes to shove: Do victorious parties really do all they can to carry out their programs? Do they make realistic and defensible adjustments to new political realities? Do they abide by the laws of the land?

Of course, parties do not always perform these four functions, and when they do, they do not always perform them to citizens' satisfaction. To understand the limitations on parties' ability to do the job we wish they would—and that they always promise to do—we need to go back to the beginnings (see Box 6.1).

THE ORIGINS OF POLITICAL PARTIES

The earliest political parties found their genesis in the legislative branches of governments. Even today, some political scientists insist on the legislative connection of parties: A party is "any organization which nominates candidates for election to a legislature," says Fred Riggs.[1] It is, however, perhaps more exact to say that both legislatures and parties owe their existence to the decline of autocratic rule (see Box 6.1).

What causes new parties to develop in modern times? Maurice Duverger prefers to keep the focus on the legislature. New parties, he says, form either inside or outside the legislature for the purpose of taking control (in part or entirely) of the legislature.[2] Access to the legislative arena will sooner or later be a central goal of almost any new party, but still Duverger's answer to our question may be a bit too simple. For one thing, it seems to suggest that parties are created out of whole cloth: "I think I'll form a party," said the disgruntled politician, and he did. In fact, most new parties evolve from other groups. The French Rally for the Republic, known in its early days as the Union for a New Republic, was formed out of a collection of groups and individuals who had very little in common other than the conviction that only Charles De Gaulle could save France from the crisis that its battle with Algerian rebels and rebelling French generals had produced.[3] Other parties began as trade unions (most of the socialist parties of Europe), as mutual aid

BOX 6.1
**The Transition
from Autocracy
to Party Politics**

- The king (or any autocrat) names a council of trusted advisers to assist him.
- The council becomes more and more powerful, perhaps because the king becomes more and more dependent on the resources it commands, perhaps because its members personally dominate a weak-willed monarch.
- The council bargains for and achieves a measure of power independent of the king's (to set taxes, say, or to raise armies), thus becoming a rule-making legislature.
- Factions develop within the legislature, differing on how and for what purposes it should exercise its power.
- Members of these factions seek external support for their side.
- Motivated by the hope of finding more such external support, the monarch and the legislators agree to the principle of elected legislators.
- The right to vote for legislators is extended to more and more of the populace, for the same motives elections were begun in the first place.
- Specific groups within the legislature set up external organizations to assist them in persuading the electors that the public interest will be served by their reelection.
- Challengers set up counterorganizations to persuade electors that the public interest will be better served by substituting their candidates for the incumbents.
- The external organizations outlive the candidacies of the legislators they first support.
- The leaders of the external organizations begin to make their own decisions about which candidates the organization will support — that is, *political parties seek to place their representatives in government by nominating candidates to stand for election in their names, claiming that power so won will be exercised in the public interest.*

associations (many African political parties began as ethnic societies), as agricultural cooperatives (the party that brought political independence to the Ivory Coast began as a group of farmers worried about prices), as underground study groups (the Communist Party of the Soviet Union), as youth groups (the Guatemalan Revolutionary Party was founded by student activists), and as revolutionary movements (the Cuban Communist Party).

Sometimes a group sets up a party while maintaining its own separate identity. The Christian Democratic parties of Europe, heavily backed and guided by the Roman Catholic church, are prime examples. Often new parties begin when old parties divide, as in the cases of Italy's Socialist Party of

New parties may begin when old parties divide, especially in multiparty systems where it is not difficult to get a new party on the ballot. In the French presidential elections of 2002, Jean-Pierre Chevenement was the candidate of the Citizen's Movement, a group that had broken away from the French Socialist Party in order to campaign for a democratic socialist program that retained more elements of traditional socialist concerns.
© Stephane Benito/Imapress/The Image Works

Proletarian Unity and the short-lived "Bull Moose" (Progressive) Party in the United States, which broke away from the Republican Party in 1912.

At least as important as the setting for a new party's origins are the reasons for forming a new party. Some have suggested that new parties begin in times of systemwide crisis. Not all important crises have produced new parties, however, and some parties have begun when no crisis was apparent, so such an explanation does not take us very far. An important factor seems to be the original organizers' belief that it will be useful to form a new party— that is, the conviction that the resources are available to achieve an acceptable degree of success and that success through this party is the best means to improve the status quo. Considering the motives of the leaders of any new party, as well as the conditions of the political system in which it is being formed, is a good way to figure out why a new party has been born.

PARTY ORGANIZATION

The nature of parties, and the reasons for forming a new party, have much to do with the way parties are organized. A political party is formed by individuals who want to acquire or maintain power in government and who seek to gain that power by convincing large numbers of citizens that the organization's candidates will serve as their representatives if elected. Such a commitment puts the political party in a special predicament, which can be summarized in two questions: How can an organization represent "the people" unless it is open to the people and responsive to them? How can an organization subject itself to the fluctuating interests, fleeting passions, and unsophisticated methods of a constantly shifting band of uninformed enthusiasts and still get anything done? In a sense, the whole idea of a participatory organization is a contradiction in terms: the more participation, the less organization; the more organization, the less participation.

Is this conflict between the two goals to which all parties claim to be devoted unavoidable? Robert Michels thought it was, and furthermore was convinced that the battle was dramatically uneven, with participation always sacrificed to efficacy. Organization means oligarchy ("who says organization, says oligarchy"), claimed Michels, and he documented this "iron law of oligarchy" with a convincing study of European parties, in which he depicted the members as apathetic, hero-worshiping, transient, and incompetent and the leaders as egotistically persuaded of their own indispensability—a set of characteristics many have claimed to find in parties in the United States as well.[4]

Other observers have agreed with Michels. Moisei Ostrogorski, who studied American parties of the early twentieth century, went so far as to claim that the pretense of mass participation in fact lessened the opportunities for true participation. By admitting the "mob," Ostrogorski said, parties set up conditions that made it impossible to arrive at decisions in party meetings. The true work of the party was thus always done by the "wire-pullers," usually "the ward secretary surrounded by his ring of associates concocting the business of the party behind the scenes."[5]

Maurice Duverger provided grounds for a more positive view in his analysis of parties. If a party admits members freely but then requires their close affiliation, including payment of dues and attendance at meetings; if communication links are strong throughout the party structure; and if final decision-making powers are located at the top of the party in the hands of leaders chosen on the basis of their ability to perform important duties rather than on the basis of personal status, then, Duverger suggests, parties can hope to meet their dual obligation to be both representative and effective.[6] However, very few parties in the United States or elsewhere live up to these high standards.

Duverger's emphasis on centralized control is worth further consideration. At first we might imagine that decentralized organizations, where more decisions are made at or near the base, would be closer to the popular will. After all, authoritarian political systems are highly centralized, while the more democratic nations place greater stress on local government. The case of political parties makes clear, however, that decentralizing power is not always synonymous with democratizing power. The party bosses of city "machines," be they in New York or Marseilles or Singapore, have shown that local leaders can rule as autocratically as any national figure—if not more so—because they have fewer interests to accommodate and fewer potential rivals. Even where the boss can no longer rule singlehandedly, any power left to local parties has tended to fall into very few hands. The decentralized party is only one step away from oligarchy, claimed Samuel Eldersveld, after studying local party activity in Detroit, Michigan. It is a *stratarchy*—that is, an organization with many levels (strata), at each of which power rests in the hands of a few.[7]

Even Michels, however, recognized that the participatory impulse cannot be forever denied, that "the democratic currents . . . are ever renewed" even if they "break ever on the same shoal" of oligarchy.[8] Parties that allow power to become excessively concentrated inevitably face a falling away of support, especially if their followers become convinced that the power so concentrated is no longer being exercised in their interest. The German Green Party emerged to protect the environment, but its members insisted that improving the environment means improving the political environment as well—that is, ensuring more democracy at the base—and the new party introduced a number of rules in the effort to prevent the rise of oligarchy (for example, the principle of *leadership rotation*—that is, the rule that no one should stay in elected office more than a single term).[9] Yet more recently this same party has found it necessary to modify the rules intended to protect internal democracy in order to have greater continuity of leadership and programs.[10]

Other parties have sometimes attempted to resolve the dilemma of effectiveness versus participation by offering a kind of sham participation. The classic example is the old Soviet party congress, where all decisions were made in advance but a gathering of disciplined party activists could somehow be motivated to meet periodically and give their enthusiastic and unanimous consent. A case could also be made that contemporary American or Canadian political conventions—or the annual meetings of the large central committees of European parties—provide very little more in the way of serious participatory input.[11] In many nations the average party militant simply works hard for candidates others have chosen, an observation that brings us to our next topic: the nature of party membership.

THE MEMBERS OF PARTIES

Ask a Chinese citizen if she belongs to a political party and she might be puzzled by the suggestion that there might be more than one political party to join. She will know for a certainty whether or not she belongs to the one party that has power: the Chinese Communist Party. But ask an American if he belongs to a political party and he is very likely to say, "Well, what exactly do you mean by *belong*, my friend?" What does it mean to belong to a party? Closeness of affiliation is not always easy to measure across cultural boundaries. Attending discussion meetings, learning party history, contributing a fixed amount of one's earnings to the organization, and enrolling one's children in an affiliated youth club may constitute a remarkably high level of commitment to a party in Great Britain but would reflect a simple regimen of self-interest in China, where most education and employment opportunities are strongly correlated with membership in the Communist Party (see Table 6.1).

Duverger, as interested in this question as in forms of organization, named four levels of membership: sympathizers, adherents, militants, and propagandists.[12] A more common set of categories for membership in European parties today is simply supporters, adherents, and militants.

The *supporter* always (or almost always) votes for the party's candidates; the *adherent* joins the party formally, filling out a membership blank and paying dues; the *militant* can be counted on to work actively for the party, performing such mundane chores as stuffing envelopes and distributing leaflets as well as preaching the party's cause at every opportunity. "Talk to a Communist about anything, and in ten minutes you will know the Communist position on that matter," a member of a different party in France commented, sounding more than a little jealous.[13] But in the United States there are subtle cultural biases against open proselytizing on behalf of any party, and a "party card" is likely to be little more than a receipt for a contribution. Individuals can work militantly on behalf of particular candidates without concern for party affiliation (their own or the candidates'), and interest group members have been known to swamp party meetings, from local club to national convention, in order to win party support for their cause while making little or no promise of reciprocal loyalty to the party.

Party membership in the sense of becoming an adherent is generally in decline, even in the European nations where it has been strongest in the past (see Table 6.2) and even as the size of electorates (the number of qualified

TABLE 6.1
Advantages of
Party Membership
in China

	CPP	Non-CPP
Education		
< 3 years primary	0.89%	4.57%
3 years primary	1.20	2.35
Primary graduate	10.03	14.39
Junior high	29.57	38.19
Senior high	18.64	23.97
Professional school	15.15	8.52
Community college	12.07	4.23
University	12.45	3.77
Job type		
Laborer	15.75	65.47
Office worker	38.96	19.19
Factory manager or director	5.81	0.55
Official	16.65	1.01
Professional or technical	22.83	13.79
Sector		
Private	0.09	1.45
Collective	7.93	24.28
State	91.76	73.76
Nature of employment		
Temporary	0.80	2.47
Contract	0.14	1.55
Permanent	99.05	95.98

Source: Bruce J. Dickson and Maria Rost Rublee, "Membership Has Its Privileges: The Socioeconomic Characteristics of Communist Party Members in Urban China," *Comparative Political Studies* 33, no. 1 (February 2000): 94. Copyright © 2000. Reprinted by permission of Sage Publications.

voters) has grown.[14] Jeremy Richardson argues that new interest groups and social movements are taking the place of parties now for citizens; that we have become "*consumers* of participation and activism" and that "a market" of participatory activities has now developed to meet our needs. There is now, he says, "a wide range of participatory organisations offering 'tailor made' opportunities for political activism. 'Brand loyalty' has decreased at the very time that new 'products' have arrived on the market-place." Richardson points out that the breadth of coverage offered by parties may make them the less desirable choice for citizens determined to donate their time or money to support a single issue, even though democratic theory calls for citizenship that is concerned about the public good more generally.[15]

However, although the global tendency seems to be for lower levels of *adherence,* membership in the sense of offering *support* by voting consistently for the same party seems to have experienced a recent resurgence, according to Anders Westholm and Richard Niemi. They find "high levels of partisan transmission across generations" (that is, we still tend to vote as our parents did) as well as "high continuity of partisanship over time" (we tend to continue to vote the same from one election to the next).[16] Yet it is also true that

TABLE 6.2

Decline of
Party Membership
in Europe

Country, Year	Electorate	Total Party Membership	Membership as % of Electorate
Austria			
1980	5,186,735 (79)	1,477,261	28.48
1990	5,628,099	1,334,554	23.71
1999	5,838,373	1,031,052	17.66
Belgium			
1980	6,878,141 (81)	617,186	8.97
1989	7,039,250 (87)	644,110	9.15
1999	7,343,464	480,804	6.55
Czech Republic			
1993	7,738,981 (92)	545,000	7.04
1999	8,116,836	319,800	3.94
Denmark			
1980	3,776,333 (81)	275,767	7.30
1989	3,941,499 (90)	231,846	5.88
1998	3,993,099	205,382	5.14
Finland			
1980	3,858,533 (79)	607,261	15.74
1989	4,018,248 (87)	543,419	13.52
1998	4,152,430 (99)	400,615	9.65
France			
1978	34,394,378	1,737,347	5.05
1988	36,977,321	1,100,398	2.98
1999	39,215,743 (97)	615,219	1.57
Germany			
1980 (west)	43,231,741	1,955,140	4.52
1989 (west)	48,099,251	1,873,053	3.89
1999	60,762,751	1,780,173	2.93
Greece			
1980	7,059,778 (81)	225,000	3.19
1990	8,050,658	510,000	6.33
1998	8,862,014 (96)	600,000	6.77
Hungary			
1990	7,824,118	165,300	2.11
1999	8,062,708 (98)	173,600	2.15
Ireland			
1980	2,275,450 (81)	113,856	5.00
1990	2,471,308 (89)	120,228	4.86
1998	2,741,262 (97)	86,000	3.14

voters do not always support their own parties: In 2000 13 percent of U.S. Democrats reported to pollsters that they voted either for Bush (11 percent) or Nader (2 percent), and 9 percent of the Republicans said they voted either for Gore (8 percent) or Nader (1 percent).[17] Even high levels of party identification do not always mean electoral success, as the U.S. Democratic Party has discovered time and again, especially in presidential races.[18]

Related to the question of closeness of affiliation is the question of reason

TABLE 6.2
(continued)

Country, Year	Electorate	Total Party Membership	Membership as % of Electorate
Italy			
1980	42,181,664 (79)	4,073,927	9.66
1989	45,583,499 (87)	4,150,071	9.10
1998	48,744,846 (96)	1,974,040	4.05
Netherlands			
1980	10,040,121 (81)	430,928	4.29
1989	11,112,189	354,915	3.19
2000	11,755,132 (98)	294,469	2.51
Norway			
1980	3,003,093 (81)	460,913	15.35
1990	3,190,311 (89)	418,953	13.13
1997	3,311,190	242,022	7.31
Poland			
2000	28,409,054 (97)	326,500	1.15
Portugal			
1980	6,925,243	296,123	4.28
1991	8,222,654	417,666	5.08
2000	8,673,822 (99)	346,504	3.99
Slovakia			
1994	3,876,555	127,500	3.29
2000	4,023,191 (98)	165,277	4.11
Spain			
1980	26,836,500 (79)	322,545	1.20
1990	29,603,700 (89)	611,998	2.07
2000	33,045,318	1,131,250	3.42
Sweden			
1980	6,040,461 (79)	508,121	8.41
1989	6,330,023 (88)	506,337	8.00
1998	6,601,766	365,588	5.54
Switzerland			
1977	3,863,169 (79)	411,800	10.66
1991	4,510,784	360,000	7.98
1997	4,593,772 (95)	293,000	6.38
United Kingdom			
1980	41,095,490 (79)	1,693,156	4.12
1989	43,180,573 (87)	1,136,723	2.63
1998	43,818,324 (97)	840,000	1.92

Source: Peter Mair and Ingrid van Biezen, "Party Membership in Twenty European Democracies, 1980–2000," *Party Politics* 7, no. 1 (2001): 15–16. Reprinted by permission of Sage Publications Ltd. and the authors.

for affiliation. The distinctions used by Robert Salisbury to categorize the motives of those who join interest groups—material, solidary, or purposive (see pp. 168–69)—do not fit quite as well for the study of those who join political parties. Other motives are clearly at work, such as a sense of loyalty (be it to a particular candidate or to the organization itself), and the pursuit of power—that is, the pleasure some take simply in being in a position to control the action of others (which, of course, is something one does gain in winning a position of party leadership or, better yet, public office). Thus, for parties a different list is required. There are motives that are purely *personal* (here we may include the material and solidary motives mentioned by Salisbury, but also the pure joy of exercising power over others); motives that have to do with one's *loyalty* to others; and, finally, the motive of *political conviction* (similar to the Salisbury notion of purposive motivation). As in the case of interest groups, it is of course possible and indeed likely that a person will have more than one kind of motive for joining a political party.[19]

Some have suggested that a briefer list covers all the motives of party members: They are either *amateurs* (sometimes called purists), motivated by conviction, or *professionals* (sometimes called realists), motivated by the quest for some form of personal gain. Those who make this simple distinction nearly always favor the professional, who keeps his eye on the doughnut of success rather than on the hole of ideological purity. Ordinary citizens, however, sometimes naively wonder if party politics really suffers more from the intrusion of idealistic newcomers than from the cynical tactics of battle-weary veterans. In any case, amateurs have a way of eventually becoming professionals, especially in parties that know how to welcome and use their energy and enthusiasm at the outset.

Besides asking how closely affiliated members are and studying their reasons for joining, it is also important to consider what kinds of people join particular parties. Is the membership of the party a heterogeneous microcosm of the nation itself? The Democratic Party of the United States, the Rally for the Republic in France, the Congress Party of India, and the Partido Revolucionario Institucional of Mexico are all examples of parties that have succeeded in attracting supporters from all their nation's major social categories.

Or is the party composed predominantly of the members of a single ethnic group (such as the predominantly Kikuyu Kenyan African National Union), a single religious organization (the fundamentalist Sokkagakkai of Japan), a single language group (the Swedish People's Party in Finland), or a single class (the Peasant Party of Romania)? The problem of communal parties has assumed new significance in recent years with the resurgence of ethnic nationalism in the new political systems of eastern Europe. Even when the overriding aim of an ethnic party is simply to protect its own peoples—as with the Hungarian Party in Romania, the German Minority Party of Poland, and the Movement for Rights and Freedoms (of ethnic Turks) in Bulgaria—the dangers of excessive fragmentation in newly forming democracies is very real.

It is also interesting—and sometimes alarming to those who support pluralist democracy—to consider shifts in the membership base of extremist parties on the left and right. Analysts of party development in Western Europe have been particularly struck by the recent rise of new rightwing parties: the Austrian Freedom Party, the Swiss People's Party, the Belgian Flemish Block, and the Norwegian Progress Party, as well as the continued activism of the Italian Northern League, the Danish People's Party, and France's National Front. What these parties have in common is the conviction that democracy can be based only on "a culturally, if not ethnically, homogenous community; that only long-standing citizens are full members of civil society; and that society's benefits should only accrue to those members of society who, either as citizens or at least taxpayers, have made a substantial contribution to society." Their members are typically politically disenchanted and anti-immigrant; they tend to hold stronger sway among blue-collar workers, younger voters (especially first-time voters), and males, but "a significant number of white-collar voters, professionals and other segments of the unemployed" has also joined their ranks.[20]

THE SELECTION OF CANDIDATES

"Did he jump or was he pushed?" The question can be asked about individuals found at the top of party organizations as well as about murder mystery victims found at the bottom of cliffs. It is often unclear whether those who become candidates for office do so because of special characteristics that permitted them to make the jump or because they were pushed (or pulled) by others eager to recruit a winner. An extrovert personality possessed of a strong intelligence and an equally strong appetite for power may be able to build a personal organization capable of seizing the nomination. On the other hand, control over a party's nominating processes may fall into the hands of a single autocrat (as Francisco Franco controlled the Spanish Falange) or a powerful lobby (as the railroad interests controlled California party politics at the turn of the twentieth century)—or simply remain the domain of its established leaders. In fact, in most cases the would-be candidate's personal traits and others' recruitment efforts interact so subtly that no one can be certain which is decisive.

In the United States, personal traits are perhaps more important than elsewhere, owing to the candidate-centered nature of the electoral system. Paul S. Hernnson says that to be a candidate in the United States, the would-be nominee must have *strategic ambition,* "the combination of a desire to get elected, a realistic understanding of what it takes to win, and an ability to assess the opportunities presented by a given political context."[21]

However, personal traits clearly count elsewhere as well. For John Gaffney, the key may lie in the command of political discourse, especially in the ability to create the kind of image the citizens are looking for, whether or not that image corresponds or conforms to the private person.[22] Stefan Stern also believes in the importance of personal style: "Leaders in the future will be quieter, more conversational, more ordinary, and more like the average person—rather like former British prime minister John Major."[23]

Personal circumstances also count, in the United States and elsewhere.

OLIPHANT © UNIVERSAL PRESS SYNDICATE. Reprinted with permission. All rights reserved.

Leaders usually come from higher socioeconomic backgrounds than do their followers, although what constitutes higher socioeconomic status may vary from culture to culture. Having been a tribal leader was very important to someone seeking to lead an African party well into the latter half of the twentieth century, although such a qualification was usually combined with other, more modern indices of success, such as wealth, occupation, and education. Kwame Nkrumah took a chiefly title, Osagyefo, on assuming political leadership in Ghana, but he had also nearly completed the course of study for a Ph.D. in the United States.

Leaders also have usually grown up in more politicized homes than followers, have adopted a partisan identification at an earlier age, and are readier to adopt their parents' partisan affiliation. They have a stronger sense of political efficacy (more likely to be a result rather than a cause of assuming leadership roles), hold views more uniformly in accord with the party's positions, and possibly are more neurotic than followers. (Fortunately for the followers, the evidence is mixed on this final point.)[24]

Rising to the top ranks of a political party, however, has at least as much to do with factors external to the individual. If a nation is divided and the party wishes to reach beyond such divisions, it must seek a leader who is not strongly identified with a particular subgroup, or else set up a council of leaders drawn from all the important groups. If the electoral system offers a better chance to centrist candidates than to ideologues of either extreme, the parties are likely to choose their candidates accordingly.[25] On the other hand, if standing as a candidate is personally risky, as it may be in unstable societies where electoral defeat can bring imprisonment or exile, the party may well seek out its most committed firebrands. If the party has no chance of winning, it is also more likely to urge the nomination of candidates of great ideological purity.

The presence or absence of major political issues also influences the kind of nominee a party seeks. If a particularly sensitive issue is at the forefront, the candidate's past and present pronouncements on that matter must be carefully reviewed. If the nation is in need of a drastic change in economic or foreign policy, the party may search for someone charismatic—that is, someone who has the gift of embodying the nation both at its traditional best and in its desired future state. The party formed to support French military hero Charles De Gaulle in 1958 was a dramatic case in point. More recent examples include Lech Walesa in Poland and Vaclav Havel in Czechoslovakia, two men who achieved prominence in the past in ways that lent them political legitimacy in a post-Communist world.

The Green Party of the United States chose Ralph Nader, a long-time consumer advocate, as its candidate in the 2000 election. Although votes for Nader clearly cost Democratic candidate Al Gore the election, Nader's insouciant reply when reminded of this, was, "Votes for Al Gore cost me the election."
© William Waldron/The Image Works

Finally, the kind of leader a party chooses rests to a large extent on the nature of the party's nominating procedures. In some nations, such as England and France, the top party leadership has the right to "parachute" candidates in—that is, to give the nomination to someone who does not even live in the electoral district where the contest is being waged. In single-party systems it is common practice for the national party leadership to form a national list of candidates without specifying districts at all. (In such cases, being named to the list is tantamount to being elected.) Where local control is the rule, one must still ask whether final power rests in the hands of a small committee (as in Germany, Norway, and Sweden), is shared by all who pay dues (as in Belgium), or is distributed among all those who choose to attend the appropriate meeting and identify themselves as partisans (as in party caucuses in those U.S. states that do not choose delegates to the national convention by primary). Experience suggests that the lower the level of the party hierarchy involved in choosing the nominee, the more the candidate will represent local and special interests and the less he or she will adopt stances on national issues that attract wide popular support. Because candidates who cannot attract wide popular support are rarely winning candidates, we are back to the problem we encountered earlier: How can a party represent its followers and still do its job?

PREPARING THE CAMPAIGN

Preparing the campaign means more than finding the right candidates—or letting the candidates "find" the party. To do their job, parties also need money and a strategy. The latter includes a plan for developing a program, but also developing and deploying the technological expertise that constitutes so large a part of today's campaign.

Raising the Money

In the 2000 campaign, U.S. parties raised and spent $877 million.[26] It remains to be seen if new campaign finance reform laws passed in March 2002 will lower that sum for subsequent elections. In the United States, most of the money spent on political campaigns is raised by soliciting contributions and this is true for the parties as well as for the candidates and their own organizations. Public funding of campaigning is extremely limited: The federal government provides public funding for presidential candidates, but even in that race those who want such help during the primary season can apply only for matching funds and must have raised at least $5,000 in twenty states in contributions of $250 or less to be eligible at all. Public funding for the chosen nominees is given as direct grants: In 2000 the Republican and Democratic candidates each received $67.6 million and each party was given $13,512,000 to help cover its convention costs.[27] However, once the candidate accepts public funding, his or her own campaign spending must be limited to that amount, which means that to have any hope of success the nominees must be supported by independent spending by individuals and political action committees (see Chapter 5) on a massive scale. Over $3 billion was spent on federal elections in 2000, and of that amount over $500 million was spent by or for the presidential candidates.[28] Presidential candidates who do not accept public funding are free to spend as much as they wish of their personal fortunes. But few candidates have the fortunes making this a realistic option.[29] Thus the name of the game is still: political contributions.

Until the campaign finance reforms of March 2002, the political parties played an extremely important role in gathering such contributions. And even though their role has now been weakened by the elimination of "soft money" (unlimited large contributions from corporations, unions, and individuals), they are still important players in the money game, and likely to remain so. In the first place, "hard money" (money in the form of legally limited contributions to the parties) has always been a more important part of each major party's treasury than "soft money," particularly in the case of the Republican Party.[30] Indeed, one of the key reasons for the continued importance of parties, despite growing voter disaffection, is that they are able to raise and spend so much money. The Republican National Committee took the lead as early as 1962, when it first began making large-scale appeals by direct mail and collected $700,000. The Democrats were not long to catch on but have never been able to match the Republicans; by 1990, the Republicans were able to raise $207.2 million (86 percent in individual contributions); the Democrats $86.7 million (64 percent in individual contributions).

Another reason the parties are still important in the money game is that U.S. federal law still permits state and local party committees to accept up to $10,000 per year, per individual, to spend on voter registration and get-out-the-vote drives. Although prior to the 2002 reforms the amount was unlimited, this is still a significant sum, particularly if the Federal Elections Commission continues to rule that grassroots campaign materials (signs, buttons, party newspapers, bumper stickers, and sample ballots telling voters how to vote) are all permissible so long as the emphasis appears to be on the party rather than the candidate.[31]

In many nations, parties need not "raise" money; they merely have to figure out how to make good use of that which is given them by the state.[32] In France a party receives up to 6 million francs (about $1.2 million) for its presidential candidate's campaign expenses, provided that candidate gains at least 5 percent of the vote on the first ballot. State funding is the most important source of funding for Norwegian parties and helps to make the parties roughly equal in resources. However, in Norway as in most nations where large-scale public financing is practiced, the party's share depends in part on how well it does in the vote, a practice that, as Alan Ware points out, "inevitably has a conservatizing effect in helping to protect currently large parties."[33]

Germany has followed a path all its own, and a tortured one at that, having decided six times that its legislation concerning political finance was unconstitutional (and perhaps about to do so decide again as I write). Having first decided that the direct financing of parties with public funds was unconstitutional, the German Supreme Court then ruled that it was acceptable for the state to reimburse the costs of campaigns for any party receiving 0.5 percent of the vote or more, a ruling particularly advantageous to smaller parties.[34] In its sixth revision, however, it ruled that all parties should receive compensation proportionate to the percentage of the vote they gained but never more than the equivalent of all they had raised on their own.[35]

Whether funds are raised or publicly given (or both), parties around the globe have sometimes engaged in fund-raising practices that break the laws in their respective nations. Two of the most flagrant cases developed (1) in Italy, where the revelation of massive kickbacks to ruling parties in exchange for public works contracts resulted in an indignant public's voting to cancel all public funding to the parties, and (2) in Japan, where the discovery of extremely large unreported "contributions" (i.e., bribes) to Liberal Democratic Party members of that country's parliament and cabinet ministers by individuals gaining illegal tax benefits brought about the fall of several prime ministers and eventually of the party itself (temporarily).

Developing a Strategy

Of course, parties must also decide what to do with the money they raise. In addition, they need to plan the overall campaign. Determining the party's strategy depends on what role the party expects to play and what needs it expects to have. In nations where parties maintain control over their own nominations and are publicly funded and where paid advertising is kept to a minimum or forbidden, it is possible for parties to begin by formulating their programs. Individuals who hope to gain the nomination may work hard to influence the program, but technically the program comes first, candidate selection second. Where parties do not control the nomination, as in U.S. presidential elections and most state-level elections, a party's own program-building activity will be much less meaningful; the program that counts will be that of the candidate who wins the nomination.

How do parties and candidates know what to put in their programs? The question itself is a sign of how much party politics have changed over the years—or at least how much our thinking about them has changed. In the past, it would have been assumed that they decided what they believed in and said so. But we are no longer so naive, and neither are the politicians (if they ever were). The art and science of figuring out what to say and where to say it is now highly dependent on a most sophisticated technology. According to David Selnow, the "twin engines" that "drive the political information machine" are public opinion polls and the database. But the engine that drives both of these, as Selnow also makes clear, is the modern computer.[36] Contemporary polling requires carefully crafted questionnaires, the selection of an appropriate sample of the population, and a complex process of data collection. Building a database means taking poll results and sorting out the electorate by almost every possible personal and political characteristic, including age, race, income, education, gender, partisanship, and point of view on every conceivable question of the day—and, more and more important, proclivity to vote.

It is the computer that makes polling possible; it is the computer that creates the database out of the poll results. It is, of course, still a human being who tells the computer what to do. However, the guiding precept for that human being is now almost always the same: Figure out how to maximize the chances of the candidate. The goals of the candidate and the party cannot credibly be changed beyond all recognition, but emphasis can certainly be placed on those positions that best fit the voters' current desires. Different positions—on different issues—can be emphasized in different communities, over different media. The point is to win.

Does this mean doing everything possible to attract as many votes as possible? The answer may seem obvious, but in fact, it is "no." As Paul Herrnson points out, "It makes more sense for candidates to allocate scarce campaign resources in the direction of large groups that vote in relatively large numbers than to direct those resources toward small groups that have low levels of voter turnout."[37] The tendency to ignore the habitual or probable nonvoter is now carried very far in the United States; according to Marshall Ganz, "As of election day, 63 percent of registered voters will not have been contacted by anyone. If, as is typical, only 60 percent of the eligible electorate [is] registered, 78 percent of the eligible voters in the district would never be contacted." Ganz does not accept this fact as calmly as other observers have; he believes that those who are not targeted to receive campaign messages are more likely to be of lower socioeconomic status than those for whom the message is designed and claims that "the introduction of the new political technologies has crippled the American attempt to combine equal voice in politics with unequal resources in economics."[38] Whether or not this is so, it seems unquestionable that the new technologies do not contribute to the democratic goal of rule by *all* the people.

Not every nation has gone as far as the United States in the direction of unrestrained targeting by computer science. Consultants and advertising agencies are widely employed, but in most nations the parties themselves and their leading candidates resist turning control fully over to such specialists.

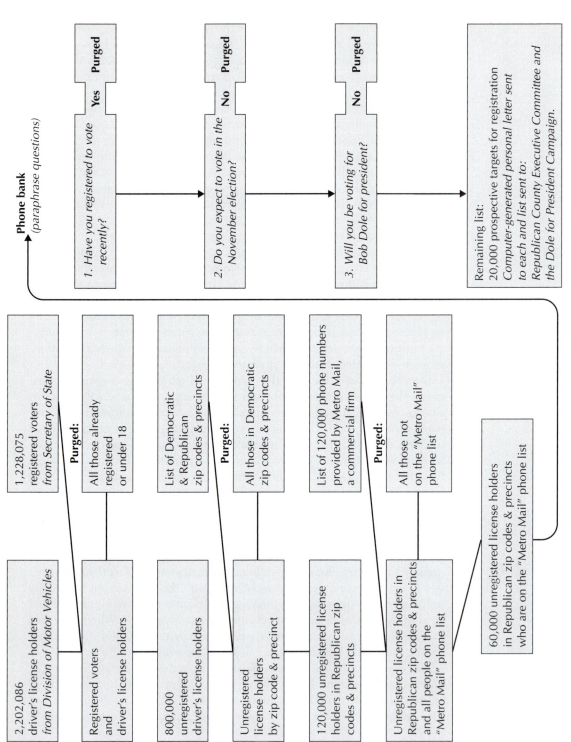

FIGURE 6.1 How Computer Targeting Permits Focused Voter Registration

Parties in Austria incorporate outside consultants into internal decision-making structures in a formal and controlled fashion; parties in Germany and the Netherlands seek to develop in-house expertise—and some parties, such as the Swedish People's Party in Finland, the New Zealand National Party, the Austrian and German Green parties, and most Danish parties, are openly reluctant to use the new technologies at all, and try to do without them as much as possible.[39]

EXECUTING THE CAMPAIGN: PARTIES AND THE MEDIA

Once everything is in place, the next step is to get the messages of the party's candidates to the voters. The candidate, his or her surrogates (persons who are close enough to serve as personal representatives of the candidate, such as a husband or wife, a sister or brother, or a grown child), other known political figures who support the candidate and are not currently running for office, and selected volunteers all put in long, grueling days speaking to as many groups, visiting as many institutions as time and energy permit, and, especially in more local campaigns, going door to door.

Most important of all, however, and more important every year, is the campaign conducted via the media. Getting the media to cover the candidate's speech to the national meeting of the Businesswomen's Club or her visit to the workers in a garment factory is far more important than the immediate response of the businesswomen or the factory workers. However, the media have some very special characteristics that must be taken into account by the parties. To understand the special new relationship between these two powerful forces, we need to consider the evolution of the media over time as well as how parties and media use each other today and, finally, how citizens respond to media presentations of politics.[40] In the following pages we use the United States, where the new relationship is much more prevalent than in other nations, as our example. However, the same forces may be seen at work across the globe.

How Party Politics Became a National Entertainment

The main medium of communication in the early United States was the newspaper, and the first newspaper was entitled *Publick Occurances Both Forreign and Domestick*. It was published in Boston on September 25, 1690, with the announcement that it would reappear "once a month (or if any Glut of Occurrences happen, oftener)"—and then never appeared again.[41] But the precedent was set, and when other newspapers began to appear they too gave much of their space over to "Publick Occurances," including, of course, party politics. In fact, many of the early papers were published by political parties, some with the incumbent president's blessing.[42]

To achieve a large circulation and thereby attract sufficient advertising revenue to stay in business and make a profit, newspapers had to be interesting to the masses. This soon came to mean offering "stories" stressing the more sensational events of the day, a focus that carried into political reporting as well. Political scandals, violence, and corruption sold more newspapers than tame accounts of the debates in Congress. In the twentieth century the invention and rapid spread of radio and then television suggested new ways the political news could be shaped to entertain, and thus to maximize audience numbers and advertising revenue (see Box 6.2). In 1956, the National Broadcasting Corporation recognized the considerable entertainment value of the political convention and began giving both parties' nominations extensive coverage. In 1960, televised debates between Democratic candidate John Kennedy and Republican candidate Richard Nixon were credited with playing a major role in the victory of the former—but also with attracting unusually large audiences. The spread during the 1970s of the more colorful system of choosing convention delegates by primaries rather than by closed caucuses also played a role in stimulating television coverage of the parties.

Another turning point came in the early 1970s during Richard Nixon's tenure as U.S. president. The Watergate scandal was the beginning, suggests Adam Gopnik, of the transformation of the American press to an "aggression culture." Since then, the media has seemed ever more determined to search out and report the most unpleasant aspects of every campaign, every candidate's personal life, every elected politician's tenure in office. This is not, says Gopnik, a matter of a free and independent media doing its job; the media "remained big, profit-seeking businesses, and journalists, whatever else they might be, were employees of those businesses . . . it was not ideological purity that was demanded so much as, simply, 'stories,' and those stories sounded better if they were tough."[43] Thomas Patterson agrees, pointing out that whereas in 1960 evaluative references to Kennedy and Nixon were only 25 percent unfavorable, by 1992 references to candidates Clinton and Bush were more than 60 percent negative.[44] (Historian Bernard A. Weisberger reminds us, however, that the present emphasis on aggressive reporting is not new, that George Washington was accused of "pusillanimous neglect" of the public welfare, Andrew Jackson was termed a murderer for having ordered several summary executions while a general, Mary Todd Lincoln was reported as having revealed military secrets to the Confederacy through indiscreet correspondence, Ulysses Grant was termed a "drunken Democrat . . . besmeared with the blood of his countrymen," and Franklin Roosevelt was routinely accused of "dragging the country down the road to socialism"—and all this in public print.[45])

BOX 6.2
Milestones in the Development of Modern Campaign Communication in the United States, 1952–2002

1952 Richard Nixon's "Checkers" speech; first use by presidential candidates of televised spot advertisements.

1957 Supreme Court rules that broadcasters may not be held liable for content of campaign commercials.

1959 Enactment of exemptions to equal-opportunities provision of the Communications Act of 1934.

1960 First televised presidential debate; publication of the first *Making of the President* book, transforming press coverage of election campaigns; first use of election-night network news projections.

1961 First live televised presidential press conference.

1964 Redefinition of libel in *New York Times v. Sullivan;* first televised presidential adversary commercial; formation of News Election Service, permitting news organizations to acquire timely vote returns.

1968 First year of extensive coverage of national nominating conventions by networks; first use of exit polling by CBS.

1969 Publication of Theodore White's *The Selling of the President, 1968,* describing candidate control of campaign communication; attack by Spiro Agnew on the liberalism of the "northeastern establishment" press.

1972 Presidential primary process changed by Democratic Party reforms; Federal Elections Campaign Act takes effect.

1976 Federal Communications Commission reinterpretation of candidate debate regulation; spending limitations in effect during the presidential general election for the first time; network news offers regular primary night news coverage.

1980 Exit polls used to project election results; extensive political advertising by political action committees.

1984 Networks reduce coverage of nominating conventions.

1988 Networks stop predicting the outcomes of elections before all polls have closed.

1992 Presidential candidates appear on talk shows and accept questions from callers. Independent candidate Ross Perot uses half-hour paid commercials to explain his program.

1994 Full Republican program reprinted in *TV Guide.*

2000 Extensive use of Web sites and targeted e-mail lists.

Source: Adapted from Richard Joslyn, *Mass Media and Elections* (Reading, Mass.: Addison-Wesley, 1984), p. 6, plus recent additions. Reprinted by permission of The McGraw-Hill Companies.

The first televised political debate. Senator John F. Kennedy and Vice President Richard Nixon debate the issues in the 1960 presidential campaign. Kennedy's superior use of the still-new medium was a key factor leading to his victory six weeks later.
© Bettmann/CORBIS

How Parties Use the Media

In any case, it is true that most media are profit-making businesses seeking to entertain, and this basic fact strongly influences the ability of parties and politicians to convey their messages to potential voters, and the ways they seek to do so. Four avenues are open to parties and their candidates seeking to reach the electorate via the media, although not all are open to all parties in all nations. First, they may take advantage of the free time specifically allocated to them in most nations of the world (but not in the United States). Second, they may pay the media to carry their messages, in the form of paid advertising, although this is carefully limited or prohibited altogether in most nations, and is nowhere else so widely practiced as in the United States. Third, they may seek to attract the media to give them free coverage, using a variety of means. Fourth, they may themselves use the kind of media that permit them to go directly to the voters.

■ **Free Time.**   In many nations, the government requires the media to allocate free time to candidates for office, and these allocations go to the parties, not to individual candidates. The media in Denmark and the Netherlands must give equal time to all parties, while those in Germany, France, and Israel must allocate time according to the proportion of the vote a party received in the past election (in Great Britain, the two main parties are entitled to equal time and other criteria are used for allocating time to the smaller parties).[46] Since almost all nations except the United States limit the amount of time that can be purchased (France does not allow any political advertising whatsoever on the broadcast media), the provision of such time is an important determinant of the nature of the campaign.

The United States has never required the media to provide free time, although efforts to ensure fair access for a wide range of points of view have been made. Such regulations have included the **equal-time provision** (if a station gives or sells time to one candidate for a specific office, it must give or sell equal time to all of the candidates for the same office), the **fairness doctrine** ("reasonable time must be given for the expression of opposing views if a highly controversial public issue is discussed"), and the **right of rebuttal** (persons attacked on radio or television "in a way that damages their reputation" have the right to reply). None of these measures has been as effective as hoped by their proponents and the fairness doctrine was discontinued as a regulation in 1987. Instead of providing ample time to all candidates and points of view, U.S. broadcasters often try to stay within the rules by curbing the amount of time given to all.

■ **Paid Political Advertising.** Wherever it is allowed, paid political advertising consumes a very large share of candidates' and parties' budgets. Since 1976, major-party candidates in general U.S. elections have spent over half their total campaign budgets on preparing and buying political ads for television; by the end of the century the proportion was up to 75 to 80 percent.[47]

The 2000 election broke all records, however: Early estimates were that total spending must have gone over $200 million; in fact, it was at $623 million by the time that ill-fated election was over.[48] (Just think how many brand-new voting machines that money might have bought!)

The parties and their candidates have also become ever more devoted to the use of negative advertising. The first Clinton campaign used negative advertising to focus on President Bush's policies, not on his character—and to attack the press itself! In the latter case, the ad boasted of Clinton's abilities to stand up to the false attacks made against him by the media.[49] Bush made much freer use of negative advertising, as did Dole in 1996, forcing Clinton to develop rebuttal stories and ads; Clinton's strategists believed that "a charge left unrefuted is a charge the public will believe."[50] In the 2000 campaign, candidates Bush and Gore largely left it up to their parties and supportive interest groups to carry out the negative campaign, preferring to promote their own virtues; nonetheless, 54 percent of all TV advertising in federal races that year was negative.[51]

"NEVER MIND MY CONSTITUENTS — HAVE YOU POLLED THE NETWORKS?"

© Cole/Rothco

■ **Free Coverage.**   A third way for parties and candidates to use the media is to attract free coverage. Government officials running for reelection or seeking to help those they wish to see win are at a great advantage, since they can often find ways to make campaigning look like the business of government. But even they, and certainly those who are not in office, will work hard to produce interesting political "stories" that can be told quickly and vividly. It is not enough for the candidate to offer a brilliant new solution to one of the nation's most pressing and complex problems. Such a solution would have to address the complexity of the problem, and that would probably be very time consuming and boring. Much more likely to gain the desired coverage is the well-designed *photo opportunity* combined with the well-prepared *sound bite*. A few seconds allowing the candidate to be filmed surrounded by adoring senior citizens at the annual picnic will bring out the television crews far more effectively than the preparation of a 200-page proposal to improve care for the elderly. The result, of course, is that very little substantive information is conveyed. According to Gary Selnow, the technology of the camera has "made it easy for news organizations and attractive for audiences to supplant abstract thought with concrete images. This highly visual and video-oriented society invests more in the illusion of television images than in the substance of reasoned analysis."[52] However true such an accusation may be (and indeed it is hard to deny), the parties have certainly been more than willing to play along.

Sometimes the second and third methods, paying and attracting the media, are actually combined. It is now more and more common in the United States for news broadcasts during election seasons to discuss political commercials as news. Some of these broadcasts are critical and analytical, providing "another viewpoint or interpretive mode for this form of direct, unmediated candidate to voter communication," but in general, one study of "adwatches" finds, reporters and journalists rarely analyze the claims made in the ads—and in every case, the ads themselves are used, a form of free coverage that can only delight those who paid for getting them on the air or in the print media in the first place.[53]

Getting free coverage on cable television is also increasingly important, permitting as it does access to smaller but more homogeneous audiences than does network television and thereby enabling the parties and candidates to send out better targeted messages, at lower costs.[54]

But the most striking development in the effort to achieve free coverage has been the ever-accelerated use of the Internet. Every campaign and every interest group with a political agenda now has its Web site, updated regularly. But Web sites must be visited to be effective, and parties don't like to wait for reporters to ask. The Net means they don't have to. The major U.S. parties now make extensive use of e-mail lists categorized for different media markets, and use them to spin and respin the daily campaign news for media consumption not only farther than the eye can see but also faster than the phone can ring. In the 2000 campaign there were four major "epicenters" of electronic spin: the Gore camp in Tennessee, the Bush camp in Austin, and the Republican National Committee and the Democratic National Committee in Washington.[55] (See Box 6.3.)

■ **Direct-Contact Media.** *Direct-contact media* is the term Gary Selnow has given to media that allow the parties to go directly to the voters.[56] Direct mail and the telephone are familiar forms of such contact; the use of e-mail lists of individuals fitting a category of voters likely to be receptive to the party or the candidate's message is another. Setting up Web sites and publicizing them via other media can also lead to direct contact. Although in this case voters must take the initiative, they do use such sites to register, to contribute money or offer volunteer work to campaigns they support, and to seek information about issues and candidates.[57]

BOX 6.3
The Virtual Campaign, 2000

On Labor Day weekend 2000, just as the presidential campaign was shifting into high gear, the Gore-Lieberman "war room" in Nashville faced a meltdown unthinkable even a few years ago. The computer system's server went down, isolating the press operation from the outside world. The fax machine was no help: In the 2000 race, "blast-faxing" was out, and both campaigns had shifted to mass e-mailing to influence the media with 'round-the-clock rapid response. Unable to get online, the Gore team couldn't fight back against Bush e-mails. As a team of tech-savvy twenty-somethings— the core of Gore's research and communications operation — waited impatiently, Information Technology Director Steven Berrent rerouted their Internet connections through a dial-up line on his desktop computer. After a precious twenty minutes, the electronic battle against the Bush team in Austin resumed.

Welcome to the virtual campaign, where wonks rely on techies to get out the spin du jour. Electronic rapid response at Gore's Nashville office took place in the jeans-and-sweatshirts environment of what's known as "the cage"— a walled-off section containing some fifteen researchers from around the country, none of them older than 30, most fresh from college. As one Gore staffer described it, the cage "has a certain air around it of monkhood— they're constantly studying up." Yet the atmosphere could at times be loud and raucous, as staffers got caught up in the excitement of back-and-forth rapid response. The cage denizens worked long hours, day in and day out, trawling the Web or rifling through piles of clippings for information on Gore policies, Bush's record, or whatever else their specialized area of research was. They were the brains— and often the voice— of the Gore campaign.

Source: Chris Mooney, "The Virtual Campaign," reprinted with permission from *The American Prospect* 11, no 23 (November 6, 2000): 36. The American Prospect, 5 Broad Street, Boston, MA 02109. All rights reserved.

How the Media Use the Parties and the Candidates

Journalists and broadcasters follow candidates for office everywhere they go, sponsor frequent polls in order to keep their readers up to date on who is ahead, and do their best to give the campaign all the qualities of a long and intensely exciting horse race.[58] Personal qualities and histories are explored for dramatic, even melodramatic, effect, and no aspect of a candidate's life is considered out of bounds, as Americans discovered more completely than many of them could bear (or, at first, *believe*) during the Clinton-Lewinsky scandal and the eventual Clinton impeachment. Even in more normal times, family life is often given inordinate attention. As Ann Grimes has noted, "One of the bigger myths in Presidential politics is that because he has an adoring wife who is willing to function as an elbow ornament, [the candidate] has a viable family life and a good marriage," and, further, that such assets will make a difference in how successful he will be in office if elected.[59] "I always accuse him of marrying me to give himself a respectable image," said Betty Ford of former President Gerald Ford.[60]

However, other motives besides providing entertainment are at work in determining what political news the media will present and how they will offer it. "Freedom of the press belongs to the man who owns one," says the cliché, and in choosing what to present, media producers and reporters may well be guided by the very normal desire to please the boss. The "boss" is now likely to be more difficult to argue with, more powerful, and more distant. Most owners of media own more than one agency, controlling either several examples of the same type or different agencies of different types. One radio chain, Chancellor/Capstar, controls 400 radio stations, 25 cable companies account for 88 percent of that medium, and 10 corporations control 128 TV stations, including the majority of the prime stations in the largest markets in the nation. The same person or company may own a community's only newspaper, only television station, and only radio station, thereby controlling all the important information sources, and the situation is not significantly better in large cities: In the Chicago metropolitan area, containing over 6 million people, three companies control among them two prime TV stations, 16 radio stations, and the dominant newspaper, the *Chicago Tribune*.[61]

Concentration enhances power, and that includes the power to control the presentation of political information. Media owners and chief executives are the ones who hire media editors and producers, and they make a point of hiring men and women who agree with them. Their political control is not just a matter of personal political bias; large media firms have political agendas of their own, such as decreasing government regulation—particularly those regulations that would get in the way of their own further growth and concentration. Their owners may even have political aspirations. Italian Prime Minister Silvio Berlusconi began his political career as chairman of the multimedia Fininvest firm: "His close relations with [then] Italian prime minister Bettino Craxi allowed him to skirt Italian broadcasting regulations and develop a media empire that ultimately helped him win Craxi's job."[62]

Although editors and journalists tend to have a spread of political affiliations comparable to those of the rest of the nation, owners are more likely to underrepresent the left and fall somewhere between centrist and archconservative. This political tendency, with some exceptions, is found from nation to nation and from the smallest to the largest media establishment.

Do journalists nevertheless find ways to introduce their own partisan biases into their reports? In a five-nation study (the United States, Britain,

BOX 6.4
**Survival Tips for
Watching Political
Ads on Television**

1. Be aware that the ad is designed to create an emotional response. Think about what mood the ad is trying to create, particularly with music and images.
2. Engage your intellect to examine the ad critically. Is there something that doesn't sound right? Does the ad raise more questions than answers?
3. Don't assume the commercial's information is accurate. Misleading and just plain untruthful ads often get on the air.
4. Don't figure that ads give you all the information you need. If you rely on political advertising to make a decision at the polls, you could be taken for a ride. Get more information from other sources: the *Voters' Pamphlet,* news coverage of the campaign, or knowledgeable friends whom you trust.

Source: Jeff Mapes, "Do Campaign Ads Really Work?" *The Oregonian,* 30 Oct. 1994, A1. Reprinted with the permission of the publisher.

Germany, Sweden, and Italy), Thomas Patterson found evidence that journalists' own partisan beliefs affect their news decisions, especially in determining what approach they will take to a story. He offers the example of a story on tightening air-quality standards, where he found "left-of-center journalists were more likely to emphasize the resultant improvements in air quality while right-of-center journalists were more likely to focus on the costs to business of higher standards."[63] He found bias most pronounced among German journalists, least among American and Swedish journalists, but never fully absent.

In any case, even when the presentation of partisan news is not biased, we should beware, say Dan Nimmo and James E. Combs, of imagining we can learn the truth about politics simply by following media reports. They suggest that the development of mass communication means the development of group fantasies about the nature of reality and argue that perhaps the required skills for citizenship are not those taught in civics texts—being interested and motivated to engage in political discussion and activity, acquiring political knowledge, being principled, and reaching choices by rational thinking—but rather learning how to assess dramatic performances, fantasy themes, rhetorical visions, and melodramatic rituals. Such skills might inspire us to demand more not only of parties, candidates, and journalists in the election melodrama but of ourselves as well.[64] (See Box 6.4 and, the next time you watch a political commercial, see if you can use some of the techniques recommended there.)

How Citizens Are Affected by Mediatized Political News

Whether or not—and how—we are influenced by mediatized political news when forming our political judgments depends in the first place on having access to the media. For some members of the human polity, the first problem is not how to defend oneself against biased news, but how to get the news at all, in any form.

Remarkable new technologies are now in place to aid the spread of communications of all forms. Communications satellites, first used to present the news in the 1980s, are now being launched at the rate of over eighty new systems per year. Fiber-optic cables are providing even better quality and more accessible two-way communication ability. Digital compression makes it possible to have more channels in the same radio frequency space, and is much cheaper than sending programs by satellite.[65] The Internet provides "virtual television" as well as printed political news. Cable television has shown remarkable growth and diversity, ranging from extremist programming on the left or right to the unhurried, carefully balanced, and noninterventionist direct reporting of C-SPAN.[66] Fax machines, satellite television, computer modems, and radio talk shows have come to China and other nations where only a few years ago color television was a rarity.[67] The Pan African News Agency, located in Senegal on the west coast of Africa, has installed satellite and Internet communications systems to take the place of telegraph and radio links that were often incapacitated by desert dust storms or heavy rains.[68] The telecommunications industries of the European states are coordinating their own information highways.[69]

It would seem as if any group, anywhere, including political parties, should be able to reach any spot on the globe where there is any form of receiver. Furthermore, these new technologies not only make television more widely available, they also extend the reach of the alternative media, thereby permitting the presentation of political news that is more substantive, more opinionated, and more interactive than that normally found on television.

There is, of course, a catch. Not all parties have the financial resources to use this technology and not all citizens have the receivers to find out what is being beamed at them. Citizen response to political news is heavily influenced by economic and social limits to access, and the disparities are great. Internet use is an example: As of January 2001, 80 percent of American households had personal computers and 100 million were on line, but in Africa only 11 of the continent's 43 nations had full Internet service and even in those nations access was severely limited by poor or nonexistent phone service, while in China it can still cost as much as $600 to get a telephone installed. As of 1997, 24 million of the world's 40 million users lived in the United States.[70]

When we do get the news about partisan politics, what does it mean to us?

The question of media impact is a difficult one, and not always what one might reasonably expect: Although the media faithfully reported every detail of former President Bill Clinton's year-long involvement in a scandal regarding sexual misconduct and obstruction of justice, public support for his performance as president held in the mid-60-percent range—and actually rose above that even as the House of Representatives voted to impeach him and the Senate conducted an impeachment trial.[71]

We ourselves seldom know how the media is affecting us. Ask yourself exactly what role the media played in your own choice in the last presidential election, and chances are you will be hard put to say. We have a few clues, little more: There is, for example, considerable evidence that U.S. citizens rely heavily on candidates' ads to "get some sense of what a candidate is like"; when asked, 62 percent either completely or mostly agree that "I often don't become aware of political candidates until I see their advertising on television." On the other hand, 74 percent say that news reports give them a better idea of where a candidate stands on the issues than do the ads, and 65 percent prefer news reports to ads for getting an "idea of what a candidate is like personally."[72] Those with Internet access can and do sample candidate and party Web pages, as well as political news sites not affiliated with any candidate or party, but many apparently do so only to find others who agree with them, or reasons to continue to support a candidate or a cause.[73]

One reason we ourselves often do not know what role the various kinds of media play in helping us make distinctions between the parties or among the candidates, is that the media seldom if ever reach us "unmediated." A medium is "an intervening thing through which a force acts or an effect is produced." The campaign news comes to us filtered not only through the commentaries of print and broadcast journalists but also through those of our friends and associates and our own "personal, moral and normative concerns." A long-term news narrative (e.g., Watergate, the Anita Hill case, Clinton-Lewinsky, even the Enron hearings, and certainly the terrorist attacks of September 11, 2001, and their complicated aftermath) becomes, Regina Lawrence and W. Lance Bennett remind us, "a subject of conversation in homes, classrooms, offices, golf courses and car pools across the country" and this communal process "may well be more important to people . . . than the fragmentary issue or approval shifts that are the objects of so much concern in simpler models of media politics."[74]

Another sign of limited direct media impact is the fact that although those who pay attention to media coverage of campaigns tend to be better educated, more interested and active in politics, and more partisan, they do not appear to remember much of what they watch, listen to, or read about. Studies in which television viewers have been interviewed show extremely limited recall. Two hours after a television network news show, viewers can normally remember only one of the twenty or so stories usually presented. News stories that focus on personalities and domestic news items are "better recognized and better recalled than standard political news."[75] In the United States, citizens do somewhat better at retaining personal information about candidates, including how well they are doing in the horse race. And they remember best of all favorable information about the candidates they prefer.

Thus, although it is obviously true that the media are a powerful force in shaping our ideas about the nature of political reality, political scientists still have a long way to go in determining how much influence they really have and under what circumstances that influence will be in the direction they themselves may expect or desire. Be it out of cleverness or stupidity, integrity or inattention, principles or stubbornness, we just don't always think what they tell us to think.

PARTIES IN GOVERNMENT

The idea that modern governments are run by political parties has been so widely accepted that the term *party government* has assumed the status of a concept, one that means government that is organized by the parties or, more specifically, the process whereby the leader of the party winning the most votes takes the top leadership role (be it president or prime minister), works with the advice of a cabinet formed of members of his own party or of other parties that have agreed to work with him, and sees his party's program translated into legislative bills, supported by party members or allies in the legislature, and made into the law of the land. But is party government really possible today?

In multiparty systems it is often necessary to form a ruling coalition by inviting leading members of different parties to take cabinet posts, thereby ensuring the support of their followers. When the parties take strongly different stands on major issues of the day, this can be a far from simple matter to resolve. No modern nation offers a better example of the intricacies of forming ruling coalitions than Italy, a nation in which the conservative Christian Democrats managed to remain in power for nearly forty years after World War II by the constant reshuffling of cabinet posts. In the late 1970s the party engineered the formation of a *minority government*, with cabinets composed of representatives of parties that had, altogether, only a minority of seats in the Chamber of Deputies—the Communists, with 228 seats, could have brought the government down at any time but agreed to abstain in exchange for an unofficial but nevertheless significant say in all major issues. In 1981, as the Communist vote was declining, the involvement of the Christian Democrats in a major political scandal forced them to share power with the small Radical Party to stay in power, and then, in 1983, it was the turn of the socialists to lay claim to a larger share of the pie,

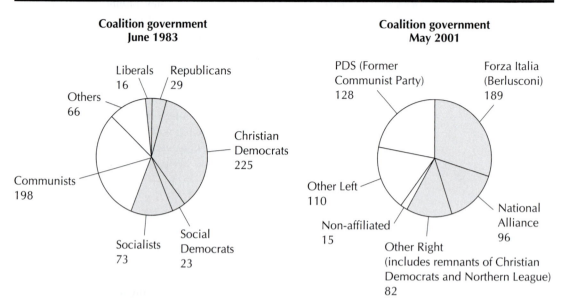

**Coalition government
June 1983**

Liberals
16

Republicans
29

Others
66

Christian
Democrats
225

Communists
198

Socialists
73

Social
Democrats
23

**Coalition government
May 2001**

PDS (Former
Communist Party)
128

Forza Italia
(Berlusconi)
189

Other Left
110

National
Alliance
96

Non-affiliated
15

Other Right
(includes remnants of Christian
Democrats and Northern League)
82

The worldwide decline in Communist Party fortunes, the fall of the scandal-ridden Christian Democrats in the early 1990s, the growth of antiimmigrant feeling, the power of personal wealth in new forms of political campaigning, the growth of concern for the environment, and a new electoral system have changed the names of the players in Italian coalition politics in the past two decades—but rightwing coalitions stay in power nonetheless.

FIGURE 6.2

Multiparty
Coalitions in the
Italian Chamber
of Deputies in
1983 and in 2001

claiming and winning the prime ministership. In 1992, the legislative vote gave the four-party coalition that had been in power only 48 percent of the vote, and it was several weeks before the new cabinet could be formed.[76]

Accumulating scandals and the ever-more obvious and widespread power of the Mafia forced the Christian Democrats out of power altogether in 1994, when they won only 16 percent of the vote.[77] The new government was composed of three new center and center-right parties (Forza Italia, the Northern League, and the National Alliance), and it too was plagued by scandal and intercoalition squabbling, bringing it to an early demise. In 1996, the Italians formed their fifty-fifth government (cabinet) since the war, bringing in center-left as well as rightwing parties in the hope of having a strong enough majority to be able to move toward constitutional changes designed to end the chronic instability from which Italy has suffered so long.[78] The shifting division of power among Italian parties is shown in Figure 6.2.

The Italian example is an interesting one because it is so often cited as proof that multiparty systems inevitably produce excessive fragmentation and are likely to lead to corruption as well. In fact, however, almost all of the world's party systems are multiparty (even in "two-party" United States and Great Britain, minor parties do exist and do sometimes win office, especially at the local level), and of course not all governments are unstable and corrupt. Nor are two-party systems exempt from these deficiencies: In 1993, the elected members of the opposition party in one of the world's few genuine two-party systems, that of Jamaica, refused to attend the sessions of that country's parliament on the grounds that the election that year had been so marked by fraud and corruption as to be invalid.[79]

As the Italians seem to recognize, government instability is likely to be a function of factors other than the number of parties—indeed, some argue that the absence of significant choice in a party system is more likely to produce discontent and instability than the difficulties of forming a government representative of a wide range of perspectives.

Even in different constitutional systems, however, effective party government is far from easy to establish. If the system allows for the separation of powers—and if electoral results sometimes place the legislative and executive branches of the government in the hands of different parties, as in the United States—then party government is possible only if each branch is run by well-disciplined party loyalists, with policy outcomes the result of interparty as well as interbranch compromise.

As power shifts in today's more centralized governments from legislative to executive hands, the leaders of political parties are often hard pressed for means to assert control over their one elected representative in the executive branch (the president or prime minister), his or her numerous appointees, and the army of bureaucrats who remain in government regardless of the changing winds of politics. Furthermore, the party itself may be so beholden to its major donors, and so burdened by the chores of fund raising for the next election, that its own elected officials may find it increasingly difficult to obey the law themselves, especially laws that say things like "no fund raising on federal property."[80]

TYPES OF PARTIES

Is it possible, after considering all the different characteristics of political parties, to discern distinct types of parties? In the interests of organizing the knowledge we have and making it easier to use in the effort to acquire further knowledge—the fundamental reason for setting up any typology—several authors have tried to do so. Some have striven to combine organizational, membership, and leadership variables, classifying parties according to the nature of internal power relationships among leaders, activists, and followers. Thus, Maurice Duverger identified two types: **mass parties,** with large, dues-paying memberships, centralized, bureaucratic leadership, and strong communication links running throughout the organization; and **cadre parties,** with small, loosely affiliated memberships, a co-opted elite leadership with limited control over the base, and weak communication links.[81]

Another way of classifying parties that attempts to combine organizational, membership, and leadership variables is linkage theory. In *Political Parties and Linkage: A Comparative Perspective,* I distinguished among **participatory, policy-responsive, clientelistic,** and **directive** parties. Participatory parties aid their members to participate directly in policymaking processes; the candidates and the program are chosen by the militants, and any elected representatives of the party take the program militants seriously and make every effort to turn it into the law of the land. **Policy-responsive parties** work to ensure that policy is made in the interests of their supporters but are not directly guided by their own members. **Clientelistic parties** make sure their followers receive certain material benefits for their support but do not encourage them to express opinions on matters of policy. Finally, **directive parties** link voters to government by helping the government maintain coercive or educative control over its subjects.[82]

For other authors, the most important determinant of party type has been the way the party performs the function of aggregating interests. Seymour Martin Lipset and Stein Rokkan identified four important political cleavages in modern times: church versus state, center versus periphery, workers versus employers, and rural versus urban. They argued that twentieth-century political parties had been formed around those cleavages and that these earlier origins created enduring party systems.[83] In a simpler typology related less to the question of those interests a party aggregates than to how it does this task, Gabriel Almond and James Coleman divided parties into three types: pragmatic-bargaining, ideological, and particularistic. The **pragmatic-bargaining party** aggregates interests through negotiations, which reach unconcernedly across conflicting values. The **ideological party** is a party of true believers who gradually rally others to their cause; such parties do not aggregate interests so much as pursue a single set of values. The **particularistic party** also minimizes interest aggregation, identifying as it does completely with the interests of a specific social group.[84]

A party type (in this case, not placed in a larger typology) that seems particularly relevant to many today is the **catchall party,** identified by Otto Kirchheimer as a party that makes concrete, pragmatic short-range promises to fulfill the immediate interests of as many voters as possible.[85] More recently, Jean Charlot has written of the **party of electors,** which places great emphasis on finding out what voters want and attempting to carry out their wishes—a combination, perhaps, of the policy-responsive party and the catchall.[86] But Peter Mair and Richard Katz do not think parties are very interested anymore in catching all of us. They see a new kind of party emerging, which they call the **cartel party** and which they say consists of leaders who collude with other parties simply to ensure the survival of them all.[87]

TYPES OF PARTY SYSTEMS

The term **party system** is really just a short way of saying "political system defined by the number of parties that operate within it." Studying the type of party system a nation has usually means trying to see how the number of parties a nation has influences the kind of political system it has.

Does it matter how many parties a nation has? In looking at the question of the possibility of party government earlier (see pp. 241–43), we have already suggested that little relationship seems to exist between the number of parties and the capacity of parties to organize government effectively. Here we turn to other possible relationships. For example, it is almost always assumed that the existence of a single-party system inevitably means authoritarian politics, sometimes defended on the grounds of the need for concerted struggle against the twin forces of oppression and underdevelopment, as in Vladimir Lenin's passionate defense of the single party in prerevolutionary Russia.[88] Other, more recent founders of single-party systems, such as former African presidents Julius Nyerere of Tanzania, Sékou Touré of Guinea, and Kwame Nkrumah of Ghana, argued that the resources of new nations were too limited to permit the luxury of multiple parties. In such states, they claimed, all those trained in the skills of leadership must be put to work, not divided into active victors and inactive and contentious losers. They carried the argument to the point of insisting that only the single party permits true democracy, since only it provides a structure that allows all interested and able participants to take part in government.[89]

In recent years, arguments in favor of single-partyism are rarely heard, particularly as the International Monetary Fund has made the adoption of a multiparty system one of its conditions for "structural adjustment" prior to the receipt of large-scale loans and aids. Such artificially induced multipartyism may, however, take strange and not particularly democratic new forms, as in the Ivory Coast, where the ruling party stays in power after having permitted the creation of a tame opposition fragmented into forty different parties, a pattern some of the remaining single-party states (such as Kenya, Uganda, Tanzania, Malawi, Zambia, Zaire, Guinea-Bissau, Mozambique, and Angola) are also expected to adopt.[90]

The Ivory Coast example is an extreme case of what some have labeled the **hegemonic party system,** a system in which more than a single party exists but one party has established hegemony—that is, pronounced and continuing dominance—over all the others. In China, small parties that are scarcely distinguishable from special interest groups are tolerated but rigidly excluded from sharing power with the ruling Communist Party. In contemporary South Africa, the African National Congress has been described as "dominant but not monolithic" and its opposition as "fragmented, regionally based, and co-opted at the center"—clearly a hegemonic party in the making.[91]

Hegemonic parties do not last forever, although it sometimes seems as if they will. The example of the Italian Christian Democrats, discussed earlier, is a case in point; the long but finally terminated tenure of the Liberal Democratic Party of Japan is another (although that party has recently returned to power).[92] The Partido Revolucionario Institucional of Mexico maintained power for many years, sometimes allowing smaller parties such as the Partido de Acción Nacional (PAN) to win local office, but never more—until suddenly the PAN won the presidency and took power in 2000.

Another useful distinction is that made by Giovanni Sartori between party systems of **moderate pluralism,** in which numerous parties are only moderately differentiated from one another ideologically, and **polarized pluralism,** in which parties are ideologically separated by vast distances.[93]

On the whole, the party systems that appear to function most equitably are the ones in which political power is neither so concentrated as to make authoritarian rule all but inevitable nor so dispersed as to make any government at all difficult to establish and maintain—that is, a party system consisting of a moderate number of parties that are moderately antagonistic toward one another. Despite a strong American bias to the contrary, there is no evidence to suggest that having only two parties is necessarily better than having several, nor is there any guarantee that a moderately multiple party system (say, two to six "significant" parties) will in fact produce an equitable system. Certainly, multiparty systems can establish governments as exclusionary as any single-party system—witness the case of South Africa during the years of apartheid—and "two-party" systems can be as incapable of effective rule as any other—witness the United States at the outbreak of the Civil War or during the height of the Watergate era or, some would say, at the end of the twentieth century. The fairness, stability, and efficacy of any political system clearly depends on far more than the number of political parties active in its electoral arena.

THE ROLE OF PARTIES TODAY

Political parties are held in low esteem in most nations today. They are viewed as selfish, dishonest, biased, and incapable of recruiting leadership of the quality citizens feel they deserve. Leftists imagine that parties work only for the elite members of society; elitists are certain they are the ignorant instruments of mobocracy.

The fact is that parties have almost always been held in contempt, and yet they continue to exist, be formed, and be reformed. If we dislike them so, why do we keep them? James Madison faced part of the answer squarely in Federalist Paper No. 10, when he recognized that the one thing worse than factionalism was a state that denied its citizens freedom of assembly.[94] The late shah of Iran acknowledged another aspect of the power of party when he formed a state-run party, the Rastakhiz, in a belated attempt to create a structure for rallying supporters. Charles De Gaulle discovered twice in his life that the forces of party could be stronger and more enduring than those of personal charisma. Both his retirements—in 1953 and in 1969—were hastened by the machinations of party. In 1980, independent candidate John Anderson found how little enthusiastic public response counted for in the United States without the multiplier effect of a major party's nomination; in 1992, independent Ross Perot, supported by millions of Americans but not by an organized party, lost heart for the battle and dropped out early in the race, only to announce in 1995 that he would try again, this time with a real political party of his own (despite the fact that to place a single candidate on the ballot in all states, a new party in the United States must collect over 750,000 signatures).[95]

Fully understanding why we keep forming institutions in which we place so little faith, however, requires sorting out two matters that are commonly confused. First, we do *need* political parties. We have already reviewed the reasons parties are formed in the first place and the many functions they traditionally perform. Second, we are not satisfied with the *kind* of parties we get. Few observers of political parties deny that they are guilty, at least on occasion, of all the sins of which they have been accused.

For some, the answer to this dilemma is simple: Reform the parties. Efforts at reform, however, often either place the powers of party in the hands of the reformers, who soon begin to perpetrate the very abuses they swore to eradicate, or else rob the parties of much of their capacity to perform their appropriate functions. The latter problem has been particularly pronounced in the United States, the Western nation in which political parties are the most severely regulated.

Why is it so difficult to devise reforms that work? Part of the answer lies in the connection between parties and power. Party leaders want to win elections in order to obtain specific rewards. Obviously, not all the men and women who seek such rewards do so at unreasonable cost to others. But then again, what seems reasonable to me may well strike you as self-serving and exploitative. As long as we have no universal agreement on the rightful distribution of power and the resources it commands, and as long as mere human beings stay in charge of political parties, we must expect that their performance will continue to be disappointing to many.

However, another part of the answer may lie in the fact that we may have been too quick to assume we know the procedures that make democracy work, including how best to organize and regulate our parties. Is it true that parties are impossible to reform, or have we simply not yet given the problem sufficient attention? Despite the fact that political parties are capable—at least in theory—of providing wide-ranging programs and popularly selected candidates and thereby giving citizens a serious link to all the work of their governments, our general dissatisfaction with their performance may soon reach the point of no return. But when we seek to organize in a way to reach our governments on behalf of more than a single cause, what alternatives do we have?

SUMMARY AND CONCLUSION

Political parties are a unique form of political organization, characterized by their effort to place representatives from their own membership in office, which they do by nominating candidates to stand for election in their name. Their principal functions are leadership recruitment, interest aggregation, campaigning, and governing.

Parties began inside legislatures as factions developed among those elected to office but did not reach full development until organizations outside the legislature were created to persuade electors to vote for the members of a particular group. New parties often begin in a time of crisis, but there must always be individuals who believe that it will be useful and possible to form a new party (even if they are wrong!).

Internal democracy is extremely difficult to establish within a political party because of the typical characteristics of members, leaders, and organizations themselves. Decentralizing power does not mean eliminating oligarchic control; it can even make it easier for local oligarchs. Nevertheless, the effort to democratize parties seems to be an unending one, most recently epitomized by the new Green parties of Europe.

Party members may be supporters, adherents, or militants. The motives for joining parties may be summarized as personal objectives, loyalty, and political conviction; as in the case of interest groups, individuals may have more than one kind of motive. Some parties attract members from every sector of society, whereas others focus on the members of a particular ethnic group, religion, or language group. Candidates are chosen by a very wide range of methods throughout the world, and different qualifications are sought according to the conditions of the campaign to come.

Preparing the campaign requires raising funds and developing a strategy; in both cases, modern technologies play an ever-more important part. Carrying out the campaign is now done mainly via the media. To understand the role of the media in modern politics, it is important to understand the history of the media as a business enterprise, their consequent dependency on attracting as large an audience for their advertisers as possible, and the effect this need has had on their presentation of political news, including political campaigns. Parties and candidates gain access to the media via legally required free time, paid advertising, free coverage, and direct-contact media. Media reporters and editors use political news to attract as large an audience as possible and also to meet the demands of the owners, who may have specific political agendas of their own. Citizens have lately shown increasing interest in alternative media, such as the Internet and cable television, but still tend to gather a large portion of what information they have about politics from paid ads, especially in the United States.

Once in government, the elected representatives of parties do not necessarily rule. They may be hampered by divided government, by their inability to form a governing coalition, by their own corrupt behavior, and/or by the excessive power of the civil service.

There are different types of parties as well as different types of party systems, but no consistent relationships exist between the kind or number of parties and their honesty or effectiveness. The fairness, stability, and efficacy of any political system depend on many other factors. Parties themselves are inevitably disappointing; we need them to make democracy possible, yet they are formed to gain power, and those who seek power have their own motives for doing so. Perhaps the only answer is to learn to accept our need for these puzzling and annoying organizations and give more serious attention to how to make them work for us and our democracies.

QUESTIONS TO CONSIDER

1. Pick a political party in your nation. How well would you say it performs the function of recruiting leaders (especially candidates)? Give examples of how it has done this job well or badly, considering not only the persons recruited but the methods by which the recruitment process was carried out.
2. Find a Web site or a local headquarters of the party you have chosen, and see if you can find out when and how that party first began.
3. What do you think of the idea of public financing of political compaigns? What are good arguments for it, and good arguments against it?
4. Do you pay attention to political ads during a campaign? If not, why not? If so, do you do so critically, or just absorb what they have to say? Would it be a good idea to banish paid political advertising from the media? Why or why not?

SELECTED READINGS

Beck, Paul Allen with Marjorie Randon Hershey, *Party Politics in America,* 10th ed. (New York: Longman, 2002). This basic text provides careful and readable coverage of the key topics in the study of U.S. parties.

Dalton, Russell J. and Martin P. Wattenberg. *Parties Without Partisans: Political Change in Advanced Industrial Democracies* (New York: Oxford University Press, 2000). Discusses changes in the roles parties play today in twenty industrial democracies and the impact these changes are having on representative democracy.

Duverger, Maurice. *Political Parties. Their Organization and Activity in the Modern State.* Trans. Barbara and Robert North (New York: John Wiley and Sons, 1954). One of the first comprehensive, comparative studies of political parties, with chapters on organization, membership, leadership, and the nature of party systems.

Gaffney, John, ed. *Political Parties and the European Union* (London: Routledge, 1996). Fifteen case studies and four general discussions regarding the relationships between individual European parties and the institutions of the European Union.

Hofstadter, Richard. *The Idea of a Party System: The Rise of Legitimate Opposition in the United States, 1780–1840* (Berkeley: University of California Press, 1972). One of the most interesting analyses of U.S. party history, tracing the slow legitimization of the idea of a competitive party system, as it reached fruition during the presidency of Martin Van Buren.

Katz, Richard S. and Peter Mair, eds. *How Parties Organize: Change and Adaptation in Party Organizations in Western Democracies* (London: Sage Publications, 1994). Case studies of political party organization drawn from the United States and eleven European nations.

Lawson, Kay, ed. *How Political Parties Work: Perspectives from Within* (Westport, Conn.: Praeger, 1994). A collection of case studies illustrating the difficulties of achieving internal party democracy, the relationship between leadership and organization, the ways internal organization affects parties' performance, and how external events can cause change in their internal organization.

Michels, Robert. *Political Parties* (New York: Dover Publications, 1915). The classical study of the rise of elite control (oligarchy) in all political organizations, even in those political parties most strongly dedicated to democratic procedures.

Selnow, Gary W. *Electronic Whistle-Stops: The Impact of the Internet on American Politics* (Westport, Conn.: Praeger, 1998). The author shows the speed and efficiency of the new "electronic whistle-stop" (the Internet, targeted e-mail, etc.) in politics. Although far more efficient than the original whistle-stop tour (when campaigners on trains made unscheduled stops in backwater towns and the whistle blew to summon the populace), the effects are not always as intended.

Shea, Daniel M. and Michael John Burton. *Campaign Craft: The Strategies, Tactics, and Art of Political Campaign Management* (Westport, Conn.: Praeger, 2001). An updated guide to modern American political campaign communication, including specific voter contact techniques.

Ware, Alan. *Political Parties and Party Systems* (Oxford, U.K.: Oxford University Press, 1996). A comparative introduction to the study of parties and party systems, with an emphasis on the parties of Great Britain, France, Germany, Japan, and the United States.

WEB SITES OF INTEREST

1. Richard Kimber's Political Parties, Interest Groups and Other Movements Around the World
http://www.psr.keele.ac.uk/parties.htm
Links to Web sites of political parties, interest groups, and social movements, organized by country.

2. International Foundation for Election Systems Election Guide
http://www.ifes.org/eguide/elecguide.htm
Provides an election calendar and information on electoral structures, parties, and candidates. Also gives links to country election authorities and summaries of election results, including voter turnout.

NOTES

1. Fred Riggs, "Comparative Politics and Political Parties," in William J. Crotty, ed., *Approaches to the Study of Party Organization* (Boston: Allyn & Bacon, 1968), p. 51.
2. Maurice Duverger, *Political Parties,* 2nd ed., trans. Barbara and Robert North (London: Methuen, 1959), pp. xxiii–xxxvii.
3. Jean Charlot, *L'U.N.R.* (Paris: Armand Colin, 1967), pp. 37–38.
4. "These former believers, these sometime altruists, whose fervent hearts aspired only to give themselves freely, have been transformed into sceptics and egoists whose actions are guided solely by cold calculation." Robert Michels, *Political Parties,* trans. Eden and Cedar Paul (New York: Dover, 1959), p. 209. The quotation comes from page 401.
5. Moisei Ostrogorski, *Democracy and the Organization of Political Parties,* vol. 1 (New York: Anchor, 1964), p. 177.
6. Duverger, *Political Parties,* pp. 4–202.
7. Samuel Eldersveld, *Political Parties, A Behavioral Analysis* (Chicago: Rand McNally, 1964), pp. 98–117.
8. Michels, *Political Parties,* p. 408.
9. Donald Schoonmaker, "The Challenge of the Greens to the West German Party System," in Kay Lawson and Peter Merkl, eds., *When Parties Fail: Emerging Alternative Organizations* (Princeton, N.J.: Princeton University Press, 1988), pp. 41–75, and Horst Mewes, "A Brief History of the German Green Party," in Margit Mayer and John Ely, eds, *The German Greens: Paradox Between Movement and Party* (Philadelphia: Temple University Press, 1998).
10. Thomas Poguntke, "Goodbye to Movement Politics? Organizational Adaptation of the German Green Party," *Environmental Politics* 2, no. 3 (Autumn 1993): 379–404; Thomas Scharf, *The German Greens: Challenging the Consensus* (Oxford, U.K.: Berg, 1994); see especially Chapter 5, "The Organization of the Greens: The Failure of the Grassroots Democratic Model at Local Level."
11. For a study of this question in Canada, see John C. Courtney, *Do Conventions Matter? Choosing National Party Leaders in Canada* (Montreal and Kingston: McGill-Queen's University Press, 1995).
12. Duverger, *Political Parties,* p. 82.
13. From a personal interview with a party militant, June 1978.
14. Richard S. Katz, "Party as Linkage: A Vestigial Function?" *European Journal of Political Research* 18 (1990): 143–61, and Richard Katz et al., "The Membership of Political Parties in European Democracies, 1960–1990," *European Journal of Political Research* 22 (1992): 329–45.
15. Jeremy Richardson, "The Market for Political Activism: Interest Groups as a Challenge to Political Parties," *West European Politics* 18, no. 1 (Jan. 1995): 116–39. See also Kay Lawson and Peter Merkl, eds., *When Parties Fail: Emerging Alternative Organizations* (Princeton, N.J.: Princeton University Press, 1988).

16. Anders Westholm and Richard G. Niemi, "Political Institutions and Political Socialization: A Cross-National Study," *Comparative Politics* 15, no. 1 (October 1992): 25–41.

17. Stephen J. Wayne, *The Road to the White House, 2000* (New York: Palgrave, 2001), pp. 286–87 (Table 8–3).

18. William J. Keefe, *Parties, Politics and Public Policy in America*, 7th ed. (Washington, D.C.: Congressional Quarterly Press, 1994), p. 144.

19. This reformulation of Salisbury's list is based on Kay Lawson, "Toward a Theory of How Political Parties Work," in Kay Lawson, ed., *How Political Parties Work: Perspectives from Within* (Westport, Conn.: Praeger, 1994), pp. 288–91.

20. Hans-Georg Betz, "Exclusionary Populism in Western Europe in the 1990s: Electoral Success and Political Impact." Paper prepared for the United Nations Research Institute for Social Development (UNRISD) Conference on Racism and Public Policy, September 2001, Durban, South Africa.

21. Paul S. Herrnson, "United States," in Pippa Norris, ed., *Passages to Power: Legislative Recruitment in Advanced Democracies* (Cambridge, U.K.: Cambridge University Press, 1997), pp. 187–208.

22. John Gaffney, "Imagined Relationships: Political Leadership in Contemporary Democracies," *Parliamentary Affairs* 54 (2001): 120–33.

23. Stefan Stern, "John Major, Your Time Has Come," *New Statesman* (26 June 2000): 23.

24. Useful studies include Barbara Kellerman, *Political Leadership* (Pittsburgh, Pa.: University of Pittsburgh, 1986); Bryan D. Jones, ed., *Leadership and Politics: New Perspectives in Political Science* (Lawrence: University Press of Kansas, 1989); and John W. Gardner, *On Leadership* (New York: The Free Press, 1990). See especially Chapter 14 in Gardner.

25. See Chapter 4 of this book for a discussion of electoral systems.

26. Wayne, op. cit., p. 26.

27. Stephen J. Wayne, *The Road to the White House, 2000: The Politics of Presidential Elections*, postelection ed. (New York: Palgrave, 2001), pp. 41–43.

28. Wayne, op. cit. p. 26.

29. Steve Forbes spent $16.5 million of his own fortune in 1995; although front-runner Robert Dole raised and spent $21 million in the same time period, $2 million of that sum was spent on the costs of raising funds so as to qualify for matching funds under the terms of federal law. Stephen J. Wayne, *Road to the White House 1996* (New York: St. Martin's Press, 1996), p. 45; *International Herald Tribune*, 7 Feb. 1996, 3.

30. Alison Mitchell, "Vote Is 60 to 40," *New York Times,* A1 and A30. Note particularly the graph on p. A30.

31. Federal Election Commission, *Campaign Guide for Corporations and Labor Organizations* (Washington, D.C.: Federal Election Commission, 1994), pp. 45–51. FEC publications are available free of charge and may be obtained by dialing 800-424-9530 or (for immediate fax delivery) 202-501-3413.

32. Herbert E. Alexander and Rei Shiratori, *Comparative Political Finance Among the Democracies* (Boulder, Colo.: Westview, 1994), pp. 3–5.

33. Alan Ware, ed., *Political Parties: Electoral Change and Structural Response* (Oxford, U.K.: Basil Blackwell, 1987), p. 18.

34. David P. Conradt, *The German Polity*, 4th ed. (White Plains, N.Y.: Longman, 1989), pp. 123–24.

35. Arthur B. Gunlicks, "The New German Party Finance Law," *German Politics* 4, no. 1 (April 1995): 101–21.

36. Gary Selnow, *High-Tech Campaigns: Computer Technology in Political Communication* (Westport, Conn.: Praeger, 1994), pp. 13–14.

37. Paul S. Herrnson, "Field Work, Political Parties, and Volunteerism," in James A. Thurber and Candice J. Nelson, eds., *Campaigns and Elections American Style* (Boulder, Colo.: Westview, 1995), p. 154.

38. Marshall Ganz, "Voters in the Crosshairs: Elections and Voter Turnout," *Current* (May 1994): 4–10.

39. Shaun Bowler and David M. Farrell, eds., *Electoral Strategies and Political Marketing* (New York: St. Martin's Press, 1992), pp. 226–28.

40. Semantic note: *Media* is the plural form of *medium*. When we say "the media," we normally mean the **communications media,** referring in

particular to newspapers, magazines, radio, and television, but also to films and recordings, to the Internet, and to the newer uses of the telephone, radio, and television (jointly referred to as *tele-communications*).

41. Bernard Rochco, "The Evolution of News Content in the American Press," in Doris A. Graber, ed., *Media Power in Politics* (Washington, D.C.: Congressional Quarterly Press, 1984), p. 8.

42. "Jefferson and Jackson sponsored party newspapers that, without pretense of impartiality, gave readers the view from the White House." Bernard A. Weisberg, "The Press and the Presidents," *American Heritage* 45 (Oct. 1994): 24.

43. Adam Gopnik, "Read All About It," *The New Yorker* 70 (12 Dec. 1994): 86, 92. Some of the works cited by Gopnik include John Anthony Maltese, *Spin Control: The White House Office of Communications and the Management of Presidential News* (Chapel Hill: University of North Carolina Press, 1994); David L. Protess et al., *The Journalism of Outrage: Investigative Reporting and Agenda Building in America* (New York: Guilford, 1991); and Mark Wahlgren Summers, *The Press Gang: Newspapers and Politics, 1865–1878* (Chapel Hill: University of North Carolina Press, 1994).

44. Thomas E. Patterson, *Out of Order* (New York: Knopf, 1993). See also William Glaberson, "The New Press Criticism: News as the Enemy of Hope," *New York Times,* 9 Sept. 1994, sec. 4, 1.

45. Weisberg, "Press and the Presidents," p. 22–24.

46. Lynda Lee Kaid and Christina Holtz-Bacha, eds., *Political Advertising in Western Democracies: Parties and Candidates on Television* (Thousand Oaks, Calif.: Sage, 1995), pp. 14–15.

47. Judith S. Trent and Robert V. Friedenberg, *Political Campaign Communication: Principles and Practices* (Westport, Conn.: Praeger, 2000), p. 339.

48. Terence Smith, "Ad Wars," transcript of *The NewsHour with Jim Lehrer,* Public Broadcasting System, October 18, 2000, and Steve Rabinowitz, Ken Goldstein, and Jon Krasno, "Political Advertising Nearly Tripled in 2000 with Half-a-Million More TV Ads," 14 March 2001. http://www.polisci.wisc.edu/tvadvertising. (The title of the latter piece is misleading, as the authors use the nonpresidential race of 1998 as a basis for comparison.)

49. Bruce I. Newman, *The Marketing of the President: Political Marketing as a Campaign Strategy* (Thousand Oaks, Calif.: Sage, 1994), p. 113.

50. Gerald M. Pomper et al., *The Election of 1992: Reports and Interpretations* (Chatham, N.J.: Chatham House, 1993), p. 85.

51. Rabinowitz et al., op. cit.

52. Selnow, *High-Tech Campaigns,* p. 143.

53. Terence Smith, op. cit., and Lynda Lee Kaid, Mitchell S. McKinney, John C. Tedesco, and Kim Gaddie, "Journalistic Responsibility and Political Advertising: A Content Analysis of State and Local Newspaper and Television Adwatches," *Political Advertising Research Reports* 4, no. 1 (Nov. 1999): 1–4.

54. Selnow, *High-Tech Campaigns,* p. 140.

55. Chris Mooney, "The Virtual Campaign," *American Prospect* 11, no. 23 (6 Nov. 2000): pp. 36–39.

56. Ibid.

57. Roberta Ann Johnson, "Cyberspace and Elections," *Peace Review* 13, no. 3 (Sept. 2001): 417–23.

58. Richard M. Perloff, *Political Communication: Politics, Press and Public in America* (Mahwah, N.J.: Lawrence Erlbaum, 1998), pp. 315–19.

59. Ann Grimes, "The Making of a Bachelor President," *New York Times,* 6 Oct. 1991, sec. 4, 17.

60. Ibid.

61. Dean Alger, *Megamedia: How Giant Corporations Dominate Mass Media, Distort Competition and Endanger Democracy* (Lanham, Md.: Rowman and Littlefield, 1998), pp. 121–23.

62. Robert G. Picard, "Media Concentration, Economics and Regulation," in Doris Graber, Denis McQuail, and Pippa Norris, eds., *The Politics of News, the News of Politics* (Washington, D.C.: Congressional Quarterly Press, 1998), pp. 193–217.

63. Thomas E. Patterson, "Political Roles of the Journalist," in Graber, McQuail, and Norris, op. cit., pp. 17–32.

64. Dan Nimmo and James E. Combs, *Mediated Political Realities* (New York: Longman, 1983), p. 69.

65. Carla Brooks Johnston, *Global News Access: The*

Impact of New Communications Technologies (Westport, Conn.: Praeger, 1998), especially Chapter 3, "Global Village Media."

66. On C-SPAN, see Lou Prato, "Politics in the Raw," *Washington Journalism Review* (Sept. 1992): 35–38.

67. Xiao-huang Yin, "China's Gilded Age," *Atlantic Monthly* (April 1994): 42.

68. *New York Times,* 1 Oct. 1994, A2.

69. Bruce Barnard, "A Revolution in the Making," *Europe* (Oct. 1994): 20–22.

70. Johnson, op. cit., loc. cit. and Johnston, op. cit., loc. cit.

71. Regina G. Lawrence and W. Lance Bennett, "Rethinking Media Politics and Public Opinion: Reactions to the Clinton-Lewinsky Scandal," *Political Science Quarterly* 116, no. 1 (2001): 425–46.

72. *The People, the Press and Politics 1990* (Washington, D.C.: Times Mirror Center for the People and the Press, 1990), p. 133, cited by William J. Keefe, *Parties, Politics and Public Policy in America,* 7th ed. (Washington, D.C.: Congressional Quarterly Press, 1994), p. 142. Although a majority of Canadians believe that ads "may sometimes play a useful role," one-third of those polled would do away with them altogether, and 77 percent believe there should at least be limits on party advertising. Andre Blais and Elisabeth Gidengil, *Making Representative Democracy Work: The Views of Canadians* (Toronto and Oxford: Dundurn Press, 1991), pp. 113–26.

73. Judith S. Trent and Robert V. Friedenberg, *Political Campaign Communication: Principles and Practices,* 4th ed. (Westport, Conn.: Praeger, 2000), pp. 344–45.

74. Lawrence and Bennett, op. cit., p. 446.

75. V. Price and E. J. Czilli, "Modeling Patterns of News Recognition and Recall," *Journal of Communication* (1996): 55–78.

76. *International Herald Tribune,* 7 April 1992, 1.

77. For the 1994 shift, see Mark Donovan, "The Politics of Electoral Reform in Italy," in Pippa Norris, ed., *The Politics of Electoral Reform,* special issue of *International Political Science Review* 16, no. 1 (Jan. 1995): 47–64; David Henderson, "Little Joy for the Italian Left," *New Statesman and Society* (1 April 1994): 10; David I. Kertzer, "Italy Produces a Ballot-Box Revolution," *Baltimore Sun,* 3 April 1994, 1E+; and Mario Sznajder, "Heirs of Fascism? Italy's Right-Wing Government: Legitimacy and Criticism," *International Affairs* 71, no. 1 (January 1995): 83–102.

78. *International Herald Tribune,* 1 Feb. 1996, 5, and 2 Feb. 1996, 1, 11.

79. Basil Wilson, "Fifty Years of Party Politics in Jamaica," *Everybody's* (July 1993): 15–18. Jamaica has had only two parties for over fifty years but has also had frequent periods of instability, particularly during the 1970s.

80. Nancy Gibbs and Michael Duffy, "Legal Tender," *Time* (17 March 2000). Gibbs and Duffy report the explanation then President Clinton offered, "Sometimes there is a difference between what is legal and what ought to be done," an unusual statement by the leader whose responsibility it is to execute the law.

81. Duverger, *Political Parties,* pp. 4–202.

82. Kay Lawson, ed., *Political Parties and Linkage: A Comparative Perspective* (New Haven, Conn.: Yale University Press, 1980). The chapters in this volume provide examples by different authors of all these types.

83. Seymour Martin Lipset and Stein Rokkan, *Party Systems and Voter Alignments: Cross-National Perspectives* (New York: Free Press, 1967). See also Stein Rokkan, *Citizens, Elections, Parties* (Oslo: Universitets Forlaget, 1970) and, for a more recent and more elaborate typology based on the Lipset-Rokkan version, Daniel-Louis Seiler, *De la comparison des partis politiques* (Paris: Economica, 1986). Although all this work is based on types of cleavages rather than types of parties, it clearly has relevance here.

84. Almond and Coleman, *Politics of the Developing Areas,* pp. 43–45.

85. Kirchheimer, "Transformation," in La Palombara and Weiner, *Political Parties and Political Development,* pp. 177–200.

86. Jean Charlot, "Catch-allism Revisited," paper presented at "Party Politics in the Year 2000," Manchester, U.K., January 1995.

87. Richard S. Katz and Peter Mair, "Changing Mod-

els of Party Organization and Party Democracy: The Emergence of the Cartel Party," *Party Politics* 1, no. 1 (1995): 5–28.

88. V. I. Lenin, *What Is to Be Done?* (New York: International, 1929).

89. Sékou Touré, *L'Action Politique du Parti Démocratique de Guinée* (Conakry, Guinea: Imprimerie Nationale, n.d.); Julius Nyerere, *Freedom and Unity* (London: Oxford University Press, 1967); and Kwame Nkrumah, *Consciencism* (London: Heinemann, 1964).

90. Victoria Brittain, "Democracy Takes a Few Steps," *World Press Review* (August 1991): 14–16.

91. Alexander Johnston, "South Africa: The Election and the Emerging Party System," *International Affairs* 70, no. 4 (October 1994): 721–36.

92. For interesting studies of several hegemonic parties, see T. J. Pempel, ed., *Uncommon Democracies: The One-Party Dominant Regimes,* (Ithaca, N.Y.: Cornell University Press, 1990).

93. Giovanni Sartori, *Parties and Party Systems: A Framework for Analysis* (Cambridge, U.K.: Cambridge University Press, 1976), pp. 127 and 179.

94. Alexander Hamilton, James Madison, and John Jay, *The Federalist Papers* (New York: Mentor Books, 1961), pp. 77–84.

95. *New York Times,* 28 Sept. 1995, A11.

Acting in International Politics

Once upon a time, when we were young and not so foolish, my husband, our small son, and I spent a year living on a boat moored on the Seine, in the heart of Paris. The boat was one of several small but livable craft rented out to an international community of young people like ourselves, newly arrived in Paris, ready for adventure and unwilling to move into any of the dingy apartments we could otherwise afford. In the midst of this enthusiastic group lived one middle-aged woman, the mother of a young Englishman, who had come along to "keep boat" for him. She, unlike the rest of us, was less than thrilled with her accommodations. She didn't mind the low ceilings, the butane heaters, or even the way the dishes rattled in the galley every time a barge went by. But she was sure she would never be able to bring this nautical home up to her own standards of cleanliness. "Because you know, my dear," she told me in her haughtiest British tones, there in the middle of Paris, "foreigners are always so dirty."

Here's another story, this time from one of my husband's classes. A student said he'd like to take a class from him again the next semester. How nice, my husband said, but he would be on sabbatical leave, writing a novel while in France. "France?" said the student, "Why go there if all you want to do is write? I've never been there, but it's got to be better here."

Well, some of us are never foreigners, at least in our own eyes. And some of us do not need to visit distant places to know that home is good, better, best. Either we never travel, or when we do we move through the world so immersed in our own sense of nationhood that we never really see the world at all. Such uncompromising chauvinists go beyond patriotism. They believe not only that their nation is the best nation, but that it is the only one that really matters. In some cases, they suffer from xenophobia, the fear or hatred of anything foreign or strange.

Other citizens, however, are more and more aware that however much they care about their own nation, it does not constitute the whole world, and indeed, it cannot function well unless its officers and its citizens remain constantly aware of that.

The events of September 11, 2001, brought that fact home not only to many Americans, but also to many persons in other nations who had been equally ready to ignore international affairs as much as possible. Now most of us know that even if we are unable or unwilling to travel abroad, we should nevertheless make an effort to follow international events, to observe how our own leaders deal with foreign affairs, to keep foreign affairs in mind when voting, and to offer support to groups pursuing international goals of which we approve.

Citizens who accept these responsibilities are actors in international politics, whether or not they ever own a passport. And of course many of us are even more active, earning our livings by working for international organizations, private or public, at home and abroad. In this chapter we will focus first on these two kinds of actors, considering several of the kinds of activi-

When hijacked planes crashed into and destroyed two towers of New York's World Trade Center on September 11, 2001, citizens of democratic nations throughout the world were given a heart-rending reminder of the interdependence of nations and the importance of paying attention to international affairs.
Najlah Feanny/Stock, Boston LLC

ties they engage in, then on the issues that concern them most, and finally on two specific kinds of actors—international judges and national warriors—who seek to bring ultimate resolution to the worst dilemmas of our shared international life. As we shall see (and indeed already know, all too well), not all the activities of those who act at the international level are benign, and not all that they do helps to further their own fortunes, those of their nations, or those of the world at large.

One further word of introduction: This chapter is the final chapter of four that make up Part Three: Acting in Politics. This is not the place to discuss international and regional government organizations in detail; they will be the subjects of Chapter 13. Here we are still behavioralists, trying to understand what political actors do, and why. The structures they must work in—or struggle against—will receive our full attention in Parts Four and Five.

This book is dedicated to the principle that all nations, and all their citizens, matter. The human polity is the composite of all the world's polities. But is there really such a thing as "the human polity"? Is there a whole that is greater than—or at least different from—the sum of the parts? By the end of this chapter I hope we will be in a better position to assess the extent to which the citizens of the world may be starting to conceive of themselves as global compatriots—rather than just themselves, the good guys, versus the others, the dirty (or primitive, or pagan, or warmongering, or fanatical, or oppressive) *foreigners*.

ACTORS SHAPING INTERNATIONAL POLITICS

Who participates in international politics? The answer that first comes to mind is a simple one: individual nations. But it is more and more common for private groups as well as nation-states to work actively in the international sphere, and even nations must act through individuals. Who, then, are the key actors in international politics? We look now at four of the many types: private citizens and elected officials, diplomats and spies, international nongovernment institutions, and international business. These four sets of actors are among the most important forces determining the direction of international politics at any given point in time.

Private Citizens and Elected Officials

In a certain sense, all of us are actors in international politics. We may act openly, taking part, for example, in a letter-writing campaign denouncing the continued imprisonment of a Chinese dissident or telephoning the office of a chief executive to say how deeply we approve or disapprove of an act of war. But our private acts also help influence the course of world events. The decisions an individual consumer makes about whether to take her vacations by air, train, or car have their impact, however small, on whether or not the United States will decide to upgrade its railway system to European standards by importing a rapid train system from France, Japan, or Germany (at present the three leaders in this industry). The vacationers who crowd aboard the first tourist boat sailing to mainland China from Quemoy are telling the world how greatly changed now are relations between China and Taiwan, separated in 1949—and making another forward step in the development of more peaceful relations.[1] Your own readiness or reluctance to serve in your nation's military forces must be taken into account when your nation's leaders calculate their preparedness to use military means to secure the ends they seek. And did you or your family buy UNICEF cards to send greetings during the holidays last year?

Similarly, the acts of a wide range of public officials help shape the course of international relations. Local politicians, for example, may work hard to create conditions that will convince foreign investors to establish production facilities—and create jobs—in their communities, even when they would prefer to do so without the foreign capital. Jyoti Basu, chief minister of the Indian state of West Bengal, recently toured the United States and Europe with twenty-seven of Calcutta's top industrialists to publicize the city's political stability, skilled workforce, local democracy, falling birthrate, and rising literacy. A lifelong Communist who has held his office for eighteen years, the 82-year-old Basu has accepted the pressures of global capitalism. "I am forced to do certain things," said the minister, conceding that, given present circumstances, "when PepsiCo came here and took over a sick company . . . it was very good. I'm not interested in their drinks but they've done good work in Punjab with food processing."[2]

Legislators and executives at the provincial level can also be significant actors in international relations. They can create conditions that foster or impede the development of export commodities, the demand for imported goods, the growth of defense industries, the willingness to accept refugee populations, or the establishment of cultural ties. National legislators perform all these roles as well, and often have the further responsibility of approving treaties, declaring wars, and appropriating the funds to carry out a nation's international commitments. As we have already noted, chief executives normally play a leading role in establishing as well as executing foreign policy, aided by a more or less vast bureaucratic apparatus devoted to that task. Nor is it uncommon for judges to have their say in this domain, ruling the terms of particular treaties valid or invalid, or judging the behavior of citizens lawful or unlawful according to its conformity with international agreements that have become the law of the land.

In short, among the various participants in international affairs, members of the world's executive branches and departments still hold the lead in making and carrying out the decisions that shape relations among nations. In doing so, however, they customarily rely on two other sets of actors whose work deserves closer scrutiny: the members of the diplomatic corps and their sometimes shadowy colleagues, the officers of the world's intelligence agencies.

Diplomats and Spies

The job of the diplomat changed a great deal during the twentieth century. One hundred years ago, the work was by and large a gentleman's game, played according to extremely formal rules by the frequently aristocratic representatives of chief executives who were themselves often autocratic potentates, accountable to no electorate. At the same time, existing modes of transportation and communication meant that diplomats were taken more seriously by their hosts as national spokespersons. It was impossible for other senior government officials to engage in impulsive globetrotting or to pick up a telephone and check out the information they were given by another nation's diplomats or by their own overseas representatives through their slow-moving couriers' pouches. Negotiations were often carried out in the greatest secrecy, and lip service at least was given to the idea that a diplomat's word of honor was as good as his bond.

■ **The Changing Role of the Diplomat.** The contrast between such conduct and the round-the-clock exchanges between the world's major leaders after the terrorist attacks on the United States in September 2001 could scarcely be greater. However, these changes in international diplomacy had begun long before this epochal event. The spread of democratic institutions, the development of much more efficient means of transportation and communication, and the emergence of the new and more compelling issues of interdependence discussed in the previous section had already deeply changed the world of the diplomat. For the past half-century the public has been much better informed about diplomatic exchanges, and chief executives or other high-ranking officials have been ever more likely to serve as their own diplomats. When Richard Holbrooke, the American ambassador to the UN, paid a call in October 2000, on Vojislav Kostunica, the new leader of Yugoslavia shortly after the deposition of Slobodan Milosević—and when Russian President Vladimir V. Putin wrote to newly elected U.S. President George W. Bush right after the latter's election, proposing broader Russian-American cooperation and naming the issues on which such cooperation could be profitable to both—the world was receiving important signs of the changed relationships between the United States and two of its former adversaries, but the new style of widely publicized high-level diplomacy illustrated by these two contacts had long been in place.[3]

One result of the change has been some lessening of the significance of the role played by resident diplomats, who now may engage in a number of public relations tasks that would have seemed beneath their dignity in other days—putting in dutiful appearances at trade fairs, football games, and television talk shows. However, lower level diplomats, in residence or sent from the home office, still have crucial roles to play. Less likely to capture media attention, they are the ones who can carry out the delicate preliminary negotiations that permit distinguished visitors to arrive at agreements later on, as in the quiet discussions undertaken by teams of North and South Korean diplomats to help their nations take the first step toward renewed dialogue in 1998.[4] And in a smaller nation unlikely to attract high-powered visitors, it is still the local embassy that may make a powerful difference not only in international relationships but also in the fortunes of that nation. The example of the work of the U.S. embassy in the very small nation of Belize during the three-year term of Ambassador Carolyn Curiel—concluding agreements on narcotics, legal assistance, and extradition; building schools and wells; and offering important help with conservation efforts—is only one case among a multitude.[5]

■ **Diplomacy by Third-Party Nations.**   Another difference in today's diplomatic game is the role of *third-party nations* in disputes between other nations. It is now much more common for nondisputing nations to take a major role in international conflict resolution. Sometimes those outside the conflict consider themselves implicated in the dispute and seek to interfere in order to produce a satisfactory outcome. More and more often, however, the motive for outsiders to intervene is broader than immediate self-interest; it rests on the understanding that global issues affecting everyone are at stake.

The visits of U.S. secretaries of state to the Middle East over the past two decades provide a good case study for several of these developments. The persistent efforts of George Shultz, James A. Baker, Warren Christopher, Madeleine Albright, and Colin Powell to find solutions for the points of discord between Israel and the Arab states offer excellent examples of the high-ranking statesman or woman serving as diplomat, of a third-party nation (the United States) taking part in the diplomatic negotiations between two other nations, and of the tendency to conduct some kinds of diplomacy far more openly than in the past. In recent years it has also provided an interesting insight into how the activities of diplomats may be shaped, not only by their own governments but also by other interests within the nations they represent. While seriously pursuing peace negotiations, recent U.S. administrations have at the same time put more and more emphasis on "dollar diplomacy" in the Middle East, seeking to improve U.S. business opportunities in the area and to launch projects such as Partnership for Growth, an economic agreement initiated with Egypt in 1995 in order to increase U.S. investment there, boost contacts between the two countries' private sectors, and intensify trade flows.[6] Of course, diplomats have always been involved in questions of international trade as well as questions of war and peace, but the ever-growing global economy makes the link between the two clearer now than ever before.

This link is very apparent in the meetings of the Group of Seven, commonly referred to as G-7, an annual meeting of the prime ministers and presidents of the world's largest industrial nations. The agenda of these summit meetings always includes many matters of economic concern with global significance, such as the development of an international telecommunications system or the creation of a worldwide emergency fund for nations on

Diplomacy by heads of state: Here Japanese Prime Minister Junichiro Koizumi and South Korean President Kim Dae-jung shake hands as they meet in Seoul, March 22, 2002, to discuss ways to promote friendship between their historically often contending nations during the 2002 World Cup soccer tournament (held in both nations).
AP/Wide World Photos

the verge of bankruptcy.[7] Furthermore, the same top executives, or their very close seconds-in-command, are now more and more likely to meet one another as well at the periodic meetings of the World Trade Organization (both the G-7 and the WTO will be further discussed in Chapter 13).

■ **Gathering Intelligence.**   However, to deal effectively with one another, the diplomats of the world's nations must be well informed about one another's national conditions, policies, and plans. Of course, some of that information is readily acquired, either by specialists at home or by experts in the diplomatic corps abroad. A trip to the library, reading the newspapers, paying a few friendly visits, or simply making an open request for the facts may be all that is necessary. However, when relations between nations are unfriendly or when the information in question concerns the military materiel and procedures necessary to maintain security against foreign attack or internal subversion, the inquiring party is likely to encounter a formidable wall of secrecy. In the sometimes strange language of international relations, gathering information about another nation is called gathering *intelligence.* (If the other nation would prefer that the information not be known and it must therefore be gathered by covert means, the attempts to acquire it are called *espionage*.)

Whether operating openly or covertly, *intelligence agencies* do not, by their nature, seek publicity. We may know that such agencies exist—the U.S. Central Intelligence Agency (CIA), the British Secret Intelligence Service, the Mossad, Israel's intelligence agency, the Australian Security Intelligence Organization (ASIO)—but we seldom know exactly what they are really doing, or failing to do. The proclivity of intelligence agencies for secrecy is closely related to another of their characteristics: a readiness to operate outside the law, be it domestic or international, if conditions appear to them to warrant it. Under international law, for example, sovereign states are expected to respect each other's territorial integrity and political independence, but this principle is often set aside, and spies may be and often are employed not only to discover but also to foil enemy plans.

More difficult problems with the ethics of intelligence operations occur when the agency slips free from control by a nation's elected officials. The Inter-Services Intelligence agency of Pakistan is an example. Although Pakistan was not a combatant, this agency played a key role in transferring foreign monies into the Afghan Islamic resistance forces during Afghanistan's war with the Soviet Union and then helped the Taliban militia take power. It also helped Kashmir nationalists fight for independence from India even as Pakistan's Prime Minister, Nawaz Sharif, was working hard to normalize relations with India.[8]

But Pakistan's leaders have not been alone in losing full control over their nation's intelligence activities. Part of the problem rests in the difficulty many nations have in being certain just what such an agency should be allowed to do. The tangled history of the CIA over the past thirty years is a case in point. The revelation that agents of the CIA regularly planned and carried out assassinations, bombings, and other violent activities, up to and including the overthrow of popularly elected governments, stimulated public condemnation in 1974 and a number of congressional investigations. These led to the formation in 1976 of two additional oversight committees, one in each house, and to the passage in 1978 of the Foreign Intelligence Surveillance Act, insisting that federal warrants be issued before electronic surveillance could be used in suspected cases of foreign espionage, terrorism, and sabotage.

By 1981, however, the year Ronald Reagan came to office, public opinion had shifted again and the new administration's determination to "revive" the CIA met with strong approval. The agency steadily regained some of its former liberty of action and its reputation as "an aggressive Cold War weapon." It also resumed the practice of hiding some of its more delicate and controversial operations from Congress itself, including its involvement in the Iran-Contra scandal (the secret and illegal transfer of profits made from the sale of arms to Iran to guerrilla groups fighting the established government in Nicaragua) in the mid-1980s. The scandal caused by the revelation of these activities and the agency's failure to prepare the government or the nation for the collapse of the Soviet Union and the consequent revolutionary change in the politics of Europe undermined the agency's newly restored reputation.

Once again, however, the agency made a comeback. Democratic President Bill Clinton promoted the position of agency director to a cabinet-level post, insisting that that official should play a stronger role in setting national security policy and at the same time making clear his approval of industrial espionage. Now it was believed that the battle for economic supremacy had replaced the Cold War and that the secrets to be discovered were to be found in the business world. At the same time, the agency launched a new effort to improve its standing in Congress, asking its agents to develop better personal ties with members of that body, and to educate themselves regarding their "special interest areas."[9]

Nonetheless, criticism of the CIA continued. Report followed report, none of them complimentary.[10] Then on May 7, 1999, in the course of its determination to help bring the Serbian government to accept independence of Kosovo, the U.S. Air Force dropped two 2,000-pound satellite-guided bombs on Belgrade—but these particular bombs fell not on a military target but rather on the Chinese embassy, killing three persons. The investigation that followed pinpointed the fact that the CIA had not updated the targeting database on which the Air Force relied; it also stressed that a major problem in this and other failures, a problem often noted and never adequately addressed, was the woefully inadequate coordination among the various intelligence agencies of the nation (including the Defense Department, National Security Agency, National Reconnaissance Office, and the FBI).[11]

But before an adequate overhaul could be effected, September 11, 2001, brought the attack on the Pentagon and the World Trade Center. This stunning success by terrorist forces raised many questions about the work of U.S. intelligence forces. Why had the CIA not known about and prevented the attack? Why was there so much reliance on distant technology and so little on the "old-fashioned" use of agents, men and women who could join in and blend with the enemy, learning plans and tactics at first hand (the spending ratio for technical intelligence and human agents had become roughly 7 to 1, despite constant reminders from some that "spy satellites are unable to see through roofs")?[12] Why *were* the CIA and the FBI so poor at sharing information developed independently with one another? And why on earth had this agency been so slow to move on the basis of the information that it *did* have in advance?[13]

In the immediate aftermath, corrective steps were once again taken, this time with a historically unparalleled sense of urgency. Although military action could and would be used to ferret out the terrorists abroad and punish nations that sheltered them, it would have to be combined with vastly

BOX 7.1
**Not All Spies
Are Scary**

In 1999 U.S. agents in Miami arrested five members of a Cuban spy ring, codename the "Wasp Network," who were assigned the task of securing defense secrets and sowing discord among Cuban exiles in Florida. They were expected to infiltrate the Pentagon's Southern Command, based in Miami and centered on Latin America.

According to their lawyers, however, any sentences meted out should be light, because these spies were just not very good at the job. One of them admitted that he never obtained any classified materials, and his coded reports to Havana consisted of little more than "a painfully detailed description of the street location of Southern Command, with a list of neighboring bus routes." His Cuban-based superior wrote back in disgust, "Results of the penetration are nil."

improved intelligence at home. It was indeed a new kind of war, one in which the relative importance of intelligence had increased a thousandfold. Very quickly, the CIA and the FBI were given greatly increased budgets, powers of wiretapping and preventive detention never extended before, instructions to employ even "unsavory foreign agents" and to provide much better language training to their own, and, finally, the obligation to report to a new White House agency, the Office of Homeland Security, one of whose most important duties would be to ensure they shared information fully with one another.[14]

International Nongovernmental Organizations

Our third set of international actors, private international nongovernmental organizations (INGOs) seeking to improve the human condition by attacking particular problems, are now more and more active internationally, steadily gathering recognition and support. As Peter J. Spiro noted nearly ten years ago, "Environmentalists, human rights activists, women, children, animal rights advocates, consumers, the disabled, gays, and indigenous peoples have all gone international. . . . These groups have developed distinct agendas at the global level, and . . . are working with increasing sophistication to further these interests in international institutions."[15] The phenomenon has become even more pronounced in the past decade. Their number now exceeds 17,000, and scholars find not only that such groups are "increasingly important actors in international arenas" but also that they are ever more likely to work together in multisector alliances and to be broadly accepted as useful partners by international organizations.[16] According to their most optimistic supporters, they are slowly but surely creating a global civil society.[17] Other supporters are more cautious, wondering if the groups are sufficiently accountable; consultations by INGO leaders with their own memberships or with those nonmembers whose interests they claim to represent are often infrequent and superficial, with no structures in place to ensure internal, democratic decision making.[18] Others see their efforts as naive and sometimes dangerous, especially when they stage mass demonstrations against such agencies as the World Bank and the IMF, which those observers see as indispensable "handmaidens of today's specifically international species of capitalism." [19] Some suggest their net effect is not as great as imagined, especially when compared to transnational businesses: "The United Fruit Company had more influence in Central America in the early part of the 20th century than any NGO could hope to have anywhere in the contemporary world." [20] And still others find that they are, just like groups at the national level, a mixed bag, neither all good nor all bad, in their intentions and effects.

International nongovernmental organizations employ a variety of methods to bring pressure to bear—publishing reports, showing up at international meetings, staging demonstrations to arouse public opinion, and, ever more important, forming networks of activists and supporters on the Web. The International Crisis Group, founded in 1995 to help the international community "anticipate, understand and act to prevent and contain conflict," has attracted over 1 million visitors a year to the "concise, policy-oriented" reports it puts up on its Web site (www.crisisweb.org) about various trouble spots in the world.[21]

Not all INGOs work by bringing pressure on others; some go directly to work on the problems they discern. Organizations such as the Grameen Bank in Bangladesh and Accion International in Latin America serve as *microlenders,* providing small loans to borrowers, often rural women, who would never be welcome in an ordinary bank but who can, with as little as $25, start up a paying business. The Microcredit Summit Campaign (MSC), an international lobbying group on behalf of the lenders, asserts that about 14 million poor people have received such loans.[22] (For more on how it works, see Box 7.2.) Other INGOs, such as TechnoServe, supply direct aid to small businesses and farmers in underdeveloped nations around the world.[23]

International nongovernmental organizations sometimes develop such impressive ability to reach the poorest and neediest that government aid programs funnel their assistance through them. Although some observers point out the danger to such groups of being co-opted by officialdom, thereby losing their legitimacy as independent and effective agents of social transformation, the groups themselves tend to welcome the opportunity to expand their funding and effectiveness.[24]

The Microcredit Summit Campaign is an international lobbying group for microlenders, agencies that make small loans to poor borrowers and have repayment rates of over 98 percent. Here's an example of how it works: Pakmogda Zarata runs a restaurant in a marketplace near Ouagadougou, the capital of Burkina Faso, one of Africa's poorest countries. Perhaps "restaurant" is an exaggeration— she serves only cooked rice. But by taking out a series of small loans from the local branch of the Féderation des Caisses Populaires du Burkina Faso, the country's main microlender, Ms. Zarata has been able to buy rice wholesale rather than retail, and her profits are now sufficient to allow her to employ seven people, pay her children's school fees, and ride around town on a second-hand motorcycle.

Repayment is often at a higher rate than other lenders achieve because the number of loans is limited and the next borrower will not receive a loan until a previous one has been repaid: "Peer pressure makes sure that default rates are minimal." Another version of microlending that encourages repayment in urban communities where peer pressure is less effective is "stepped lending." Under this system, if the borrower repays promptly she can ask for a larger loan: "The better her credit record becomes, the more she can borrow."

International Business

In recent years private business enterprises have taken an increasingly active role in international politics, bringing corporate interests into the international arena either individually or in the form of transnational corporations (TNCs).[25] New TNCs are now being formed on an almost daily basis by mergers that cross national boundaries, such as that between Chrysler and Daimler-Benz, and old TNCs are extending their reach by buying into companies strong in new technologies that operate overseas, a recent favorite tactic, for example, of Japan's enormous Mitsubishi Corporation.[26]

The growth of TNCs has been speeded up in recent years by the numerous and dramatic changes taking place in so many governments since the fall of the Berlin Wall in 1989. The relationship between TNCs and regime change is reciprocal. International business interests have strongly influenced the decisions of the international funding agencies that are so actively shaping the new economies; the investment opportunities thus produced have in turn revolutionized the international business world. The rush to privatize has opened investment opportunities to businesses as well as to individuals. The readiness of new regimes to welcome foreign owners as well as investors has led to the building of new plants in cities never before considered as likely sites for such construction.[27] At the same time, the liberalization of trade means that it is often not necessary to build such plants in order to be multinational—key steps in the production and distribution of many products are now routinely "outsourced" to entrepreneurs in other lands, where lower wage costs and "less restrictive" labor practices contribute to higher profits.

One of the most interesting developments is the new link between some TNCs and large-scale international development banks (IDBs), such as the World Bank and the International Monetary Fund. (Two others with major funding are the International Finance Corporation, affiliated with the World Bank, and the Inter-American Development Bank.) The announced mission of such banks, which are put together by the governments of nation-states and financed by taxpayers, is to help less-developed nations (LDCs) out of chronic poverty. Each year they generate about $30 billion in contracts.

Such contracts are more and more likely to go to private entrepreneurs rather than to the governments concerned. "The Cold War's demise removes the philosophical underpinnings for the earlier support of government intervention," says one former top official of the World Bank. By this he means that it is no longer necessary to make loans directly to governments to keep them from "going Communist." In addition, the banks are now beginning to align themselves more openly with private investment funds in the First World, serving as advisers and sometimes entering into cofinancing of projects that are likely to bring those private investors profits as high as 25 percent a year.[28] To understand how this process works, read Box 7.3.

The competition for TNC investment monies has also had a profound effect on First World nations, now engaged in sometimes drastic recreations of themselves. New Zealand is an interesting example. Now completing a massive privatization program, the state has sold so many of its formerly state-owned enterprises to TNCs that over half of the nation's stock market capitalization is foreign money. Attracting foreign investors has meant downsizing the labor force and reducing workers' rights and services "that were once taken for granted." The Employment Contracts Act of 1991 gives employers in New Zealand the right to negotiate directly with employees; since its adoption, "union membership has plunged 38 percent through layoffs."[29]

The growing presence of business in the international arena—and the effects of this presence on the less advantaged—is the subject of a great deal of concern and anger. Richard J. Barnet has written one of the most scathing attacks on the effect TNCs are having on the economy and labor force of the United States. Outraged by the fact that "the world's 358 billionaires have a combined net worth of $760 billion, equal to that of the bottom 45 percent of the world population . . . the average CEO in the United States now brings

BOX 7.3
**International
Development—
Of What
for Whom?**

The Inter-American Development Bank is owned by forty-six nations. Its mission is to reduce the chronic poverty of Latin America, and it lends billions of dollars to private businesses in those nations. In the fall of 1995 the bank entered into a "first-of-its-kind" alliance with a group of private investors, including Lloyd M. Bentsen, U.S. Secretary of the Treasury in 1993 and 1994 and a former governor of the bank, now a private businessman. The alliance will provide a "billion-dollar investment fund banked by giant corporations and pension funds. They hope to realize profits of as much as 25 percent a year by investing in Latin American power projects, telecommunications systems and toll roads." The agreement with the Inter-American Development Bank will include "information sharing and possible co-financing," according to Mr. Bentsen. Many of the managers of the investment group formerly held high positions in this or other international development banks (IDBs), including the World Bank.

Jerome Booth, head of emerging markets research for a private bank, points out that the fund's natural emphasis on profit seeking may distort the kind of development pursued. He believes that banks like the Inter-American Development Bank should just be "in the business of helping development of countries, typically things like water, sanitation, health and education, not toll roads, telecommunications or power stations."

The bank's president, Enrique V. Iglesias, recognizes that the new alliance could pose some problems. He promises that the bank will "prod Mr. Bentsen's fund to follow its lead and invest in the region's neediest countries. But he . . . fears 'money will only flow to the best projects' since Mr. Bentsen's fund's stated intention is to make 80 percent of its investments in the region's six richest countries."

Louis T. Wells, professor of International Management at Harvard Business School, says, "It's going to be questioned in the host country where somebody is going to say we could have raised this money a lot cheaper. It's an interesting dilemma."

Donald Strombon, a business consultant in Washington, D.C., isn't worried. He says forming links with the IDBs is good business: "The multilateral development banks do $30 billion a year in contracts awarded by borrowers, and . . . give out another $4–$5 billion in consulting contracts. It's a very sizeable market."

Moeen Qureshi, a former top official of the World Bank and identified as the "brains" behind the new alliance, agrees with Strombon and points out the advantages of working through an IDB: "The risk is lower with the presence of a multilateral institution. Governments will think twice about reneging on an obligation where a public institution is involved."

Source: Drawn from Jeff Gerth, "In Post-Cold-War Washington, Development Is a Hot Business," *New York Times,* 25 May 1996, pp. 1, 6.

home about 149 times the average factory worker's pay . . . an estimated 18 percent of American workers with full-time jobs earn poverty-level wages; [and] since 1973, the number of American children living in poverty has increased by 50 percent," Barnet puts the blame squarely on the "stateless corporations" of the world, who are, he says, just "walking away from the enormous public problems their private decisions create for American society." Gone are the good old days when "big companies created tens of millions of well-paid jobs, provided health care and pensions, and brought women and minorities into the work force." Now "a global pool of bargain labor is available to companies making virtually anything" and "about a third of the jobs in the United States are at risk to . . . low-wage workers . . . elsewhere." Strikes don't work anymore—"Management now wields the more credible threat: Take it or we leave" and only 12 percent of the U.S. workforce in private industry is now organized for collective bargaining. American workers in the "superstar" category "bring home a fortune every year," but the median earnings of the professional class and most entertainers are staying flat, and the real wages of low-ranked workers like janitors, bank tellers, and back-office employees in brokerage houses have fallen 15 percent or more. Layoffs and CEO salaries are up, often in tandem. The corporate share of federal income taxes fell from 23 percent in the 1950s to 9.2 percent in 1991 as TNCs improved their competitiveness by going "stateless" and basing their accounting operations in tax havens abroad.

Barnet does not offer any easy cures. He thinks the dependency of both political parties and their leaders on "the obscenely expensive, never-ending campaign that now defines American politics" means that even in the United States free elections are not enough to guarantee that those chosen will be able to carry out their programs (he cites the failures of Clinton's health-care reform and job creation programs, which he ascribes to the "medical-industrial complex" and the bond market, respectively). Furthermore, it is hard to get the message out, says Barnet: "[The] rage and the fury found almost everywhere . . . is directed almost exclusively at government because the mainstream media . . . never target global corporations as major contributors to the nation's socio-economic woes, and because even if they did, the business behemoths would seem beyond reach." [30]

A. G. Kefalas agrees that the TNCs now have amazing power, surpassing that of the nation-state, and describes them as "at the center of the entire world-reshaping scheme." But Kefalas has hopes that Barnet does not seem to share. He outlines three ways of looking at TNCs—pessimistic, optimistic, and melioristic (it can get better)—and tends to take a point of view somewhere between the second and the third positions. International businesses are, Kefalas says, "a potent and potentially valuable force that must be integrated into" the process of building a new world order that brings "a more equitable distribution of material wealth." He is confident the nation-states of the world "share the goals of establishing world security, increasing world productivity, stabilizing the world populations, sustaining economic growth, creating equitable conditions for development and promoting world monetary stability," and he is sure international business possesses "great potential for facilitating the accomplishment of these goals." Kefalas therefore recommends recognizing such businesses as "full-fledged partners" in the work at hand, and he urges the businesses themselves to "engage in a process of self-assessment in order to bring [their] philosophies, policies, and operating procedures in line with the idea of an interdependent world of diverse but unified societies." [31]

The ideas of Kefalas are reassuring; those of Barnet are tough to take, but note that both writers agree that we are giving too little attention to the power these giants now wield over our lives and those of others.

CONTEMPORARY ISSUES OF INTERNATIONAL POLITICS

The issues of international politics that attract the attention and action of the wide range of actors discussed above—and sometimes must be resolved by the actors discussed in the following section—vary over time. Not very long ago, many Americans would have said the most important issue was how to keep their nation's involvement in the international arena to an absolute minimum; isolationism was on the march. Today an issue that most citizens thought about rarely if at all, defense against terrorism, has taken priority. Other issues of great concern, such as the dangers of arms proliferation and ethnic nationalism, are now seen at least partly in terms of their connection to the fight against terrorism. The issues of human rights and a deteriorating environment remain extremely important and activist groups and official organizations are working hard to ensure we do not let them slip away as the new battle demands so much of our attention.

Although it is normal for the saliency of certain issues to rise and fall in international relations, what is unusual now is that the issue of terrorism was brought to the fore not by the act of another nation-state, but by individuals joined together by fundamentalist religious beliefs of a particularly virulent nature, individuals who are said to reside in some sixty nations of the world, and who are actively condemned by the leaders of almost all those nations, even those not on particularly good terms with the United States.

Other crises and controversies in international politics, however, have been—and no doubt will continue to be—brought about by the policies of nation-states. When Iraq invaded Kuwait in 1990 and when the United States led a concerted retaliatory attack on Iraq in 1991, the participant nations knew they were making trouble for other polities. When arms were taken up in 1992 by Russians against Chechnyans (and vice versa) and by Serbs against Croats (and vice versa), everyone knew the effect on international relations would be painful and direct.

In these cases, national policies involved acts of war. In other cases, however, international controversies have developed owing to national policies that applied directly only to domestic matters. Sometimes the international response is deliberately sought: The decision of the Clinton administration to place a 100 percent tariff on thirteen Japanese luxury cars in 1995 was intended to force Japan to open its market to American cars and car parts.[32] But even policies that seem not to be related to international relations at all—such as those that govern labor-management relationships, redistribute land, break up monopolies, or seek to stimulate small business—can have a lasting influence on the role a nation plays in the world economy, and thus on the fortunes of other nations that depend on the global marketplace.

But whether a nation's policies are focused on foreign or domestic affairs, whether they are openly belligerent or only indirectly influential on other nations' destinies, the growing interdependence of individual polities has so extended the scope of international politics that almost *any* course of action undertaken by a single nation will have some influence on the well-being of one or more other nations. This fact of life in the human polity remains true today, despite the emphasis on one issue that pits nearly all the nations of the world against a band of believers whose loyalty to an extremist religious dogma is far greater than that to any nation-state.

We turn now to a closer look at some of the key issues of great concern in global politics today, beginning with terrorism, turning next to human rights, and ending with a look at an issue that will not go away even if our attention is elsewhere: the dangerous decline in the quality of our natural environment. Our examination of all three issues can be only brief and indicative of their seriousness; it cannot hope to be comprehensive.

Defense Against Terrorism

As we have said, almost all crises in international relations have been caused by national policies that have caused other nations to respond; they were inter-*nation*-al. Terrorism, however, operates on a multitude of levels: It is interhuman, intergroup, *and* international. Members of a group strike out against individuals in an effort to battle against whole nation-states. The victims turn to their national leaders, and to international leadership, to wage the battle in return.

After September 11, 2001, how that battle should in fact be waged became the central issue not only in the United States but in other nations as well, many of which had suffered often or occasionally from terrorism before, but never in the context of a worldwide struggle.[33] It became apparent almost immediately that it is one of the most complex the human polity has ever faced. We certainly cannot do it full justice here, and must limit ourselves to some of its principal components: first, how difficult it is to determine and apply the correct means, and second, how high a cost it can demand, in both money and loss of liberty, to do so.

■ **Means of Defense: Hard to Know, Hard to Apply.**   The difficulties in waging war against terrorism are staggering. In the case of the Osama bin Laden terrorist network, the enemy spread itself out in a hidden web across the world before striking and sheltered its headquarters in an impoverished land whose greatest asset to the terrorists, besides a leadership sharing their extreme fundamentalist version of Islam, was a harsh and mountainous terrain.

Bombing whole mountains to smithereens is, to say the least, impractical.[34] Cruise missiles, high-technology reconnaissance aircraft, manned bombers, and special ground forces are likely all to be needed, yet may not be sufficient. Because not all the terrorists in a network will be in the same country, other means must also be employed, although here too there are uncertainties. Freezing accounts of known or probable funders of terrorism is unlikely to stop those who believe in the cause from finding ways to finance its operations. Ears already filled with hate messages based on religion are likely to be all but deaf to contradictory propaganda; hearts filled with that kind of zeal will not necessarily beat faster when offered the material rewards of simple bribery.

A war against terrorism is also a defensive war at home. It is very difficult to know where and how this enemy will strike and with what means. Every kind of attack requires a particular kind of defense. Improved airport and airplane security is little help against biological warfare, especially if the materials and expertise have already made it through customs. Antibiotics and vaccinations are no cure for renegade nuclear weaponry outside the control of any state.[35] Posting photos of suspected terrorists is not likely to help block computer hackers capable of destroying vital communication networks and bringing both the defense effort and economic life to a standstill.[36]

Furthermore, the international nature of terrorism means not only that a wide variety of very disparate tactics must be used, but also that these tactics must be deployed in international concert. Existing agencies such as the United Nations and Interpol, the international police agency representing 178 nations, have important roles to play, but both organizations have suffered from inadequate funding and limited trust among their members; the common cause of fighting terrorism may ameliorate those problems, but that will take time, if it occurs at all.[37]

In the fight against the Osama bin Laden network, the emphasis at first was thus on building other, more limited and more numerous alliances. Bilateral alliances, widely varying in nature and extent of commitments promised, were speedily formed between the United States and an unprecedented range of "friends," new and old. Even a partial list reveals how truly the events of September 11, 2001, did create a brand new world. Beginning with an apparently unreserved and total commitment from the United Kingdom, the United States also secured agreements, strong or shaky, wide-reaching or rigorously limited, with states far beyond its usual allies: those formerly part of the Soviet Union, such as Russia herself but also Uzbekistan, Tajikistan, Kazakhstan, Turkmenistan, and Kyrgyzstan; moderate Arab states like Jordan and Egypt; not so moderate Arab states like Saudi Arabia and Sudan; non-Arab states with large Muslim populations like Indonesia and the Philippines; and other mixed states like Pakistan, India, and China, whose battles with each other seriously complicated any effort to join in a coalition of interest to all.[38]

■ **Costs of Defense: In Money, In Liberty.** Although the question of how best to wage the battle effectively lends itself to a multitude of debates, the issue of defense against terrorism is also an issue about *costs*. There are two broad categories of costs: the *monetary* and what we may call the *civil*.

In the first rush to counterattack, many of the important internal debates regarding the proper distribution of limited funds were set aside in the United States and in threatened nations. The money flowed: In the United States the federal government immediately approved $40 billion of emergency appropriations to aid in recovery and $15 billion to the airline industry.[39] But the costs would go far beyond such allocations. In the first place, an economic recession, already underway and, as usual, extending across Europe once established in the United States, immediately accelerated and deepened.[40] The terrorists' main target had been well chosen. The World Trade Center really was a world trade center, and the loss of output caused by its sudden disappearance radiated outward across the globe. Airline travel, brokerage transactions, and retail sales all nose-dived.[41] The World Bank predicted that a slump in tourism, lower commodity prices, and falling foreign investment would make the burden especially heavy on poor nations, countries with little or no safety nets.[42] Abrupt downturns were registered in Latin America as the prices of basic exports like oil, copper, zinc, steel, and foodstuffs plummeted.[43]

But if all the threatened nations had to worry about was money, how nice that would be. For after all, the number of those who accepted the radical preachings of the terrorists were, on a global scale, very few, perhaps, according to one estimate, not more than 50,000, and once the known bank accounts and other assets of the terrorists were seized, the donations of money funneled by supporters into the cause by those who sympathized with them but did not join the network directly were likely to be insignificant compared to the wealth of Western nations. It is true that the old math of conventional warfare did not apply to the original attacks, but eventually the battle of the purse would be won, and the costs of doing so considered well worthwhile.

But there are costs that have nothing to do with dollars, pounds, or euros. The *civil* costs of fighting so insidious and invisible an enemy were apparent almost overnight. Although heightened security measures such as checking airline baggage and suspicious packages anywhere were widely accepted as only sensible, other limitations on personal freedoms were more questionable.

The U.S. Congress expanded the power of law enforcement and intelligence agencies to use Internet surveillance of e-mail and other electronic communications; Great Britain, where terrorist activities had long been periodically disrupting the nation, considered issuing compulsory identification cards and some Americans suggested their country should do the same; Germany, in many respects a bastion of personal freedom after post–World War II reforms, removed a constitutional provision forbidding the government from banning any group, even one advocating terrorism, that described itself as religious or faith-based.[44] Censorship was threatened: "Americans . . . need to watch what they say, watch what they do," said White House Press Secretary Ari Fleischer when a comedian made an unwelcome comment on a late-night TV talk show.[45] And censorship was applied: Journalist Dan Guthrie was fired by the publisher of *The Daily Courier* in Grants Pass, Oregon, for writing a column criticizing President George W. Bush's actions immediately after the attack.[46] Strikers whose cause might well be legitimate were condemned for daring to walk out in the midst of a national crisis.[47] Racial profiling by police officers and other state officials, a method that had recently come under serious attack in the courts, now shifted its focus from black to brown, and was accepted by many as unavoidable. Most serious of all, openly racist and violent acts were committed against Muslims or those who might be Muslims, and such acts were not always subject to punishment.[48]

How far must and can a free people go in trusting those who would protect them by watching them, arresting them if they happen to "look suspicious," and casually setting aside supposedly inviolable civil liberties? Can democracy be protected by weapons hitherto considered outside the democratic arsenal? Supreme Court Justice Sandra Day O'Connor summed up the problem: "First, can a society that prides itself on equality before the law treat terrorists differently than ordinary criminals? And where do we draw the line between them? Second, at what point does the cost to civil liberties from legislation designed to prevent terrorism outweigh the added security that that legislation provides?" Admitting these were "tough questions" she suggested, "It is possible, if not likely, that we will rely more on international rules of war than on our cherished constitutional standards for criminal prosecutions in responding to threats to our national security."[49] Others were less calm. Mark Rasch, a former federal prosecutor opposed in partic-

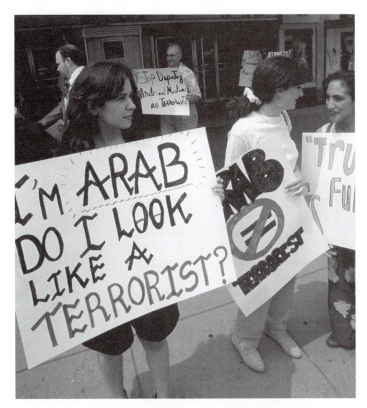

An Arab American woman angry at the treatment given her fellow Arabs after the bombing of the World Trade Center on September 11, 2001. Unless care is taken, one of the costs of fighting terrorism can be the loss of important civil liberties.
Paul Conklin/PHOTOEDIT

ular to excessive surveillance, was frankly appalled: "We're going to look back on this a year from now and ask, 'What the hell were we thinking?'"[50]

Finally, what about the costs of the challenge to Americans' sense of nationhood? There was, of course, a tremendous upsurge in patriotism in the United States after the attack. But there was also a special kind of national anguish. One of the most interesting phenomena for the rest of the world to observe during these traumatic days was the utter unpreparedness of most Americans to recognize themselves as widely hated. Somehow it seemed that Americans—so pragmatic, realistic, and down to earth in most respects—had convinced themselves not only that they were safe in pursuing their own ends without much regard for the rest of the world, but that they were, without the shadow of a doubt, the finest people on earth.[51] Of course, a certain proportion must have had a glimmering that American prosperity depended not only on American hard work, but also on the advantages that go to the citizens of the nations that lead in global economic competition—and that the factors that had put the United States in the lead were neither all of America's own making nor always nobly conceived and carried out. Certainly most knew, in any case, that there were large populations living in ever more desperate poverty. It seems odd, in retrospect, that there was so little understanding that the American style of life, adopted so eagerly by immigrants and by followers in other Western nations, could nevertheless be deeply offensive to many—and such a strong conviction that in any case it could never be seriously threatened. The word that dominated the American news on September 12, 2001, told it all: "incomprehensible."

Slowly, however, a few bold souls began to suggest that in the midst of the suffering and the anger, there might be, nonetheless, a lesson to be learned. We would, said one columnist, "have to become serious in addressing the needs of the most desperate nations. . . . Desperate populations are beating at our doors and are menacing our ease of life. We have to care."[52]

But perhaps this development belongs on the other side of the ledger. Was the terrible shock to the happy sense of unquestionable superiority held by Americans and so many other Westerners really a *cost?* Or was this perhaps the one great *gain* to come from the events of September 11, 2001?

Protection of Human Rights

Another major issue demanding action in contemporary international politics is the violation of human rights by governments who imprison, torture, and execute their own citizens. Often these citizens' only offense is political dissent; sometimes they are simply members of another ethnic group or religious sect. The military weapons and methods now available to control domestic populations have made tyranny more fearsome than ever before; even the most determined band of dissidents is a poor match for the strength of the modern police state. When dictatorships are ruthless in the execution of policies designed to eliminate protest, the only hope of their oppressed citizenry is likely to be appeal to more powerful external forces—that is, to other nations and to world opinion.

The Universal Declaration of Human Rights, adopted in Helsinki, Finland, in 1975, states that "everyone has the right to life, liberty and security of person." The exercise of political power to deny these basic rights is certainly not a new phenomenon in human history, but the scale of punishments meted out to those who attempt to exercise such rights has reached truly horrifying proportions as this era's technological efficiency is exhibited in the instruments and strategies of oppression. China's swift and bloody suppression of the student-led democracy movement in 1989 deeply dismayed a watching world, as did the revelations that in the Philippines Ferdinand Marcos had ordered some 50,000 persons to be arrested, detained, and, in many cases, tortured and killed.[53] Elsewhere—out of camera range, as it were—other appalling events have been taking place in the past quarter of a century. Over 500,000 people were killed by the Indonesian army, assisted by gangs of youths belonging to a fundamentalist Muslim party, in the nine months following the attempt of dissidents to overthrow the government in 1965. In Cambodia under Khmer Rouge rule (1975–1979), between 1 and 3 million people were killed in a series of purges that began with the highest officers of the preceding government and worked steadily downward through lower officials, intellectuals, teachers, students, members of ethnic minorities, and finally even members of the current government who were considered less than 100 percent loyal to the leadership. The numbing statistics go on: Up to half a million killed in Uganda during the eight-year rule of President Idi Amin (1971–1979); 5,000 political opponents killed in a single Ethiopian city in a three-month period (November 1977–February 1978); more than 80,000 killed in Burundi in the spring of 1972; 11,712 noncombatants killed in El Salvador during 1981; as many as 20,000 persons described as "the disappeared" in Argentina between 1976 and 1984; about 20,000 Hindu Tamils killed in Sri Lanka since 1983; over 25,000 persons killed from 1980 to 1992 in the fighting between members of the Sendero Luminoso (Shining Path) guerrilla movement and three successive Peruvian governments; and approximately 800,000 Tutsi people and known moderate Hutus slaughtered by Hutu warriors over the course of about 100 days in Rwanda in 1994.[54]

Every one of these numbers is made up of a series of individuals—of human lives. A man or woman or child woke up, considered the day ahead, got dressed, ate whatever breakfast was available, and sallied forth to death. Such assassinations and massacres are not only committed outside anything that can be called the law, they are for the most part entirely unwarranted even on grounds of fear of opposition. Whole ethnic groups or social classes are labeled undesirable. Their most innocent and nonpolitical members are killed indiscriminately along with the dissenters—and of course those who have dissented have frequently done so only by means that would be considered legitimate and fair in politics that respect human rights. Furthermore, these figures—far from complete—say nothing of the even greater numbers of people who are imprisoned and tortured by such governments. Nearly half of the 184 nations that make up the United Nations are believed to be holding in prison people whose only offense is their beliefs or origins. In the period 1997–2000, over 150 nations were accused of torture or ill treatment by state agents, and deaths from torture were reported in over 80 countries.[55]

Such wholesale contempt for human life and liberty is a major issue in international relations today, and a wide range of international remedies has been sought. Declarations and covenants abound: The Nuremberg Charter, the Geneva Conventions, the International Covenant on Civil and Political Rights, the American Convention on Human Rights, the African Charter on Human Rights, and the European Convention on Human Rights are the six most widely cited. Although their high-sounding language may seem a weak defense against ruthlessness on the scale we have just reviewed, these covenants provide the necessary definitions and distinctions on which to base more substantive intervention. (For example, they set standards for fair trials, for legal use of the death penalty where serious crimes have been committed, and for "acceptable" killings during times of war and other armed conflicts.) The UN Human Rights Commission is devoted to the protection of human rights, and regional organizations such as the European Parliament, the Inter-American Commission on Human Rights, and the African Commission on Human and Peoples' Rights have also sent fact-finding missions and published reports identifying abuses of human rights.[56]

Reports, however, do not stop bullets—or machetes—and unfortunately those who violate human rights often seem more capable of action than those who seek to stop them. The United Nations, for example, was widely criticized for doing nothing at all to stop the genocide in Rwanda. In March 1999 the Secretary-General of the United Nations appointed an independent commission to study the failure and in December the commission published its report, stating flatly that "The United Nations failed the people of Rwanda during the genocide in 1994."[57] Ten of its recommendations, published on a UN Web site, are in Box 7.4. But will this report make a difference?

It must also be recognized that appalling as the conditions described above may be, there is far from unanimous agreement that the international community should assume responsibility to act in this domain. Stopping genocide is one thing, but for outsiders to insist that women should have rights equal to those of men or that maiming is an intolerably cruel punishment for criminal behavior is another. Nations that permit what appear to others to be unconscionable violations of human rights frequently argue, first, that it is a violation of their national sovereignty for others to interfere and, second, that what looks like a human rights violation to you may be absolutely in accord with indigenous customs and traditions, as well as essential for maintaining law and order.[58] And even nations that pride themselves on protecting human rights at home and abroad may find their own law enforcement officers guilty of violating those rights: The many well-documented cases of police brutality in the United States may be taken as an example.[59]

There are, nevertheless, ways to correct human rights abuses that sometimes work. INGOs devoted to questions of human rights, such as Amnesty International and Human Rights Watch, and individual journalists working for sympathetic publishers or networks can do a great deal to arouse public opinion and help free individuals unfairly imprisoned or bring malefactors to justice. National leaders who have ordered wide-scale persecution

BOX 7.4
**Ten Recommenda-
tions of the Inde-
pendent Inquiry
into the Actions
of the United
Nations During
the 1994 Genocide
in Rwanda**

1. The United Nations— and in particular the Security Council and troop contributing countries— must be prepared to act to prevent acts of genocide or gross violations of human rights wherever they may take place. The political will to act should not be subject to different standards.

2. The early warning capacity of the United Nations needs to be improved, through better cooperation with outside actors including NGOs and academics, as well as within the Secretariat.

3. Efforts need to be made to improve the protection of civilians in conflict situations.

4. Further improvements in the security of UN and associated personnel, including local staff, are necessary. Consideration should be given to changing existing rules to enable the evacuation of national staff from crisis areas.

5. Cooperation between officials responsible for the security of different categories of staff in the field needs to be ensured.

6. An effective flow of information needs to be ensured within the UN system.

7. Further improvements should be made in the flow of information to the Security Council.

8. The flow of information on human rights issues should be improved.

9. National evacuation operations must be coordinated with UN missions on the ground.

10. Further study should be given to the possibility to suspend participation of the representative of a Member State on the Security Council in exceptional circumstances such as the crisis in Rwanda.

Source: "Report of the Independent Actions of the United Nations During the 1994 Genocide in Rwanda," 15 Dec. 1999, 1–69. http://www.un.org/News/ossg/rwanda_report.htm. Reprinted by permission of the United Nations.

of specific groups can now be accused of crimes against humanity and brought to trial before the U.N. War Crimes Tribunal. This procedure, used in the cases of former Chilean leader Augusto Pinochet and former Yugoslav ruler Slobodan Milosević, inevitably provokes the defense that national sovereignty is being violated, and some also fear that the procedures being developed may "encourage vendettas against former officials and heads of state."[60] Others note such procedures have yet to be shown to have any noteworthy deterrent effect on other leaders guilty of similar offenses. But Payam Akhavan reminds us that "in contrast with the gloom that encircled those seeking justice in the not-so-remote past, even these modest and early glimmerings of international criminal justice may be dramatic and transformative."[61]

However, when whole populations have been complicit in wrongdoing, even a change in the political system is unlikely to suffice to bring those culpable to justice. The problem becomes one of simple overload: No criminal system can deal fairly with vast numbers of guilty persons, affording each the luxury of a fair trial, and probably no political system could achieve national reconciliation if justice were in fact done in every case when the number of victims is so great. At those times the only answer may be a new quasi-judicial institution, the *truth commission*. At least 14 nations—Uganda, Bolivia, Argentina, Zimbabwe, Germany, the Philippines, Uruguay, Chile, El Salvador, Rwanda, Brazil, Haiti, Guatemala, and South Africa—have established these commissions to deal with horrific histories that cannot just be set aside. Such commissions seek to document and acknowledge "a past history of human rights violations that took place within a specified period of time." They do not normally have prosecutorial powers to bring cases to trial.[62]

Such an approach may seem far too benign to outraged outsiders. But, as Audrey Chapman and Patrick Ball point out, "Official acknowledgment of abuses can support the credibility of victims' suffering and help restore their dignity . . . [and the process] at least imposes the punishment of shame."[63] The commissions are also expected to determine the major causes of the violence and make recommendations regarding what to do to ensure there will be no repetitions of the past.

Protection of the Environment

One reason the whole world must become more active in resolving the problem of environmental degradation is that the whole world seems to be guilty of creating the problem. Pollution and consumerism have resulted in the destruction of 90 percent of the coral reefs in the Philippines; the total fishing catch off the northwest coast of the United States has fallen 32 percent since the 1970s; Brazil, China, and India are shifting to the feedlot system of ranching, developed in the West and guaranteed to present a major threat to soil, air, and water quality owing to accumulated animal wastes; the birthrate in Uganda (and in many other nations) is more than seven children per woman; and smog is so bad in Beijing, New Delhi, Jakarta, Bangkok, and Tehran that breathing is literally bad for the health.[64]

The problems are severe almost everywhere. Among the industrialized nations they appear to be worst of all in the former Soviet republics of Eastern Europe, where four decades of failing to meet even the most minimal requirements for protection of land, air, and water have produced an environmental nightmare. The list of Soviet sins is long and includes permitting soil overexploitation and erosion, uncontrolled management of dangerous

Polluting a sacred river: Here one of the many sewage pipes for the city of Varanasi, India, dumps the city's waste directly into the River Ganges. The Ganges is India's most sacred and at the same time most polluted river. (December 6, 2001)
AP/Wide World Photos

waste, unreliable treatment of water waste, and lack of concern as air quality in urban and industrial conglomerations steadily deteriorated. The five republics of Kazakhstan, Uzbekistan, Turkmenistan, Kyrgyrzstan, and Tajikistan were "treated from the outset as a reservoir of natural resources and manpower" for the rest of the nation and suffered even more grievous neglect and misuse of land and waterways.[65]

Unfortunately, the situation has improved very little since these nations took responsibility for their own destinies after the fall of the Soviet Union. Encouraged by multinational oil companies and eager to make a profitable transition to capitalism, Kazakhstan, Uzbekistan, and Azerbaijan are endangering local ecosystems by large-scale oil drilling in the shallow waters of the Caspian Sea; Uzbekistan makes massive use of fertilizers and pesticides to intensify its cotton production; the Aral Sea is drying out; desertification spreads across the land. In Russia herself, the first state committee on the protection of the natural environment, established in 1988, was disbanded in 2000; its functions were assigned to the ministry of natural resources, "whose role is precisely to exploit those resources."[66]

Although such problems must receive the attention of individual nation-states, the forces that create them and the socioecological disasters they produce affect the entire world, and the international community has been taking an ever more active collective role in addressing the issue of environment degradation. Much of that work is done by the United Nations, which conducts research and fact-finding missions, tries to raise global consciousness of the importance of these problems, and works to bring its members together in international meetings where common ground can be found and agreements reached on the remedies required.

To address the problems in Eastern Europe, both in the former Soviet Union and in the other nations composing the Soviet bloc, the UN's Organization for Economic Co-operation and Development created an Environmental Program for Central and Eastern Europe (EAP) in April 1993. The EAP recommended that responsible actors in the region "pursue policies and projects that lead to both economic returns and environmental improvement." Recognizing and supporting the forces of economic change, it urged reliance on market-based instruments to achieve cost-effective reductions in pollution, and hoped that increasing economic stability and growth would encourage governments and industries to take the steps necessary to improve the environment. Five years later it found significant improvements, but admitted that in some nations these improvements were owing more to falling output as economies declined (fewer industrial emissions to contaminate the environment) than to growth-inspired investments in cleaner and more efficient technologies. It estimates another twenty years may be necessary before "countries wishing to accede to the European Union . . . meet all current EU environmental requirements" and found the problems in the former Soviet Union nations particularly resistant: "Throughout the region, there is growing recognition that the often-rapid pace of liberalization and privatization has not been matched by the development of institutions necessary to support a well-functioning market economy."[67] Eric Freyfogle has drawn the larger lesson: Reliance on market-based tools to fight pollution is dangerous, he argues, unless it fits into "a larger scheme of environmental policy that has as its principal aim not the promotion of markets, but the achievement and maintenance of a healthy land."[68]

Of course, the United Nations also monitors environmental problems on a global level, and seeks to work out solutions that can be applied worldwide.[69] One such important effort was the Conference on Environment and Development (UNCED), popularly known as the Earth Summit, held June 13–14, 1992, in Rio de Janeiro, Brazil. The meeting brought together 178 national delegations (including 117 heads of state) to study the key problems of the environment: global warming, overpopulation, pollution, and endangered species. The conference produced an Earth Summit treaty with twenty-seven nonbinding "principles" for the good management of the resources of the planet; Agenda 21, a program of action containing 800 measures from which each country could choose its own priorities; and three considerably more specific agreements concerning the exploitation of forestlands, maintaining biodiversity, and reducing atmospheric pollution.[70]

The Rio pact was an important advance, with one important exception: The United States refused to sign the biodiversity agreement, claiming it imposed unacceptable restraints on U.S. biotech industries. It was the only nation represented at Rio to refuse to sign, but although many Americans found this refusal shameful, in late 2000 the United States was once again the major opponent to another pact, this time the Kyoto Protocol on global warming. At the meetings held in The Hague in the Netherlands, the United States refused to sign unless changes were made to the agreement to ease its effects on U.S. businesses. This time the negotiations broke up altogether.[71]

It may seem to some that only greedy industrial polluters (and governments excessively responsive to such forces) resist efforts to protect the world's environment. There is, however, another side to the story, one well articulated by Ramahandra Guha. This angry historian and anthropologist from Bangalore argues (and he is far from alone) that "the people who are the most vocal in defense of nature are those who most actively destroy it." He is referring to Westerners, and in particular to American tourists and scientists, who ardently support international conservation efforts to preserve vacation lands and wilderness areas for the sake of their own pleasure and fun, or for science. Guha calls this "environmental imperialism," especially when it is directed at such overseas sites as African animal parks. Such conservationists are, he points out, citizens of nations that make the heaviest use of nonrenewable resources in order to drive their cars and run their household machinery, but they nonetheless demand that "indigenous tribal people or fisherfolk . . . vacate the forest or the ocean" so that they may enjoy their holidays "in communion with nature."[72]

Conservationists reply that they are fighting for environmental protection on the home front as well and are not oblivious to the contributions that excessive U.S. consumerism has made to the degradation of the environment. The only way to slow global warming, the most serious challenge not only to the global environment but to the very life of the planet, is to reduce the use of fossil fuel, and Americans "use five times more per capita than the average earthling," points out American conservationist Bill McKibben.[73]

ACTORS RESOLVING INTERNATIONAL CONFLICTS

The actors in international politics may be private citizens, groups, elected officials, diplomats, or secret agents. They may work individually or within complex organizational structures. In any case, their behavior—where it is not purely careerist and self-serving—is likely to be guided by respect for two often contradictory principles: the rule of law and the rule of superior force. In international relations guided by respect for law, the final appeal in any dispute is properly made to the World Court, where the principles of international law are developed and applied. In relations between nations that are governed by respect for superior force, the final appeal is likely to be to strength in battle—to warfare. The net result of the world's mixed adherence to these two principles is the web of power relationships at any given time: victor to defeated, colonizer to colonized, superpower to satellite, peer to peer.

International Lawmaking

The international actor guided by respect for the rule of law must sometimes make a difficult choice between national and international law. If the two are in conflict, the choice is very likely to be made in favor of the national law; at the present time, the surest protector of the cultural identity and military security of any state remains that state itself. Yet even the most resolutely autonomous state can no longer help but recognize the need for a modicum of global social order. New conditions that threaten the internal order of all nations but can be solved only on a global scale—such as international terrorism, control of outer space, exploitation of marine resources, the need for restraints on transnational corporations, the removal of landmines, and pollution of the biosphere—force the evolution of new international law. Conditions that have recurred throughout history but are now deemed intolerable—such as executive leaders who order ethnic cleansing campaigns or other large-scale massacres of subgroups in their own nations—also demand significant innovations in international law and in the willingness of the international community to enforce it.

One of the clearest signs of how well this new reality is now understood appeared in 1994 when the writers of the new Russian constitution expressly included treaties and customary international law in their domestic legal system. In areas such as human rights, the writers of the constitution formulated Russian domestic law by making direct reference to international law.[74] It is also significant that early in 2001 President Bill Clinton signed the treaty establishing an international criminal court, despite objections of some conservatives in Congress and a long-standing caution on the part of the United States against signing any international pacts appearing to invade the principle of national sovereignty.[75]

Thus the body of international law continues to grow, gradually receiving greater and greater acceptance. The International Law Commission, an auxiliary of the United Nations General Assembly, has taken on the job of codifying international law in a wide range of fields. More specialized groups, such as the International Labour Organization and the Intergovernmental Maritime Consultative Organization, have helped to spell out accepted principles of law in their respective domains. Drawing from established customs, generally accepted principles of law, and specific treaties or conventions, the writers of international law have established rules to govern relations between nations. These rules cover such matters as the recognition by states of one another's sovereignty (including the granting of diplomatic immunity), the establishment of frontiers on land and water, the acquisition and loss of territory, the human rights of aliens and citizens, the making of treaties, the responsibilities of international organizations, the arbitration of third parties in international disputes, the conditions for the legal use of force, and the conditions governing nuclear testing.

Warfare: Resolution by Force

> Now, God be thanked who has matched us with His hour
> And caught our youth, and wakened us from sleeping,
> With hand made sure, clear eye and sharpened power
> To turn, as swimmers into cleanness leaping.
> Glad from a world grown old and cold and weary.
> Leave the sick hearts that honour could not move,
> And half-men, and their dirty songs and dreary,
> And all the little emptiness of love![76]

What causes human beings to prefer to settle disputes by the use of armed force? Theoreticians of war suggest almost as many plausible explanations as there have been wars. We will consider only the following condensed list, giving each rationale for war the name of the author or scholar most commonly associated with it.

■ **The Rupert Brooke Argument.** War provides an opportunity to exercise some of the finer human qualities not called for in peacetime: self-sacrifice, courage, heroism, and devotion to a cause larger than oneself. The lines of poetry cited above and written by Rupert Brooke during World War I summarize this point of view.

■ **The Hobbesian Argument.** War is the natural condition of humankind; the state of nature is a time of "war of all against all."[77]

■ **The Clausewitz Argument.**   War is the continuation of politics by other means. This often-cited argument from the early nineteenth century reads in full: "War is not a mere act of policy but a true political instrument, a continuation of political activity by other means. What remains peculiar to war is simply the peculiar nature of its means."[78]

■ **The Freudian Argument.**   Humankind is innately, genetically predisposed to aggressive behavior as a way of discharging accumulated stress, asserting leadership, supplanting parents or breaking free of the restraints they impose, or relieving boredom.[79]

■ **The Marxist Argument.**   War is a way of acquiring economic benefits from other states. The victors acquire access to raw materials, living space, cheap labor, expanded markets.[80]

■ **The C. Wright Mills Argument.**   War is a way to acquire economic benefits from one's own political system. The industrialists who make war-related materials and the professional warriors who seek an opportunity to prove their worth combine forces in a "military-industrial complex" to manipulate public opinion and pressure elected officials to take the path of war.[81]

■ **The Margaret Mead Argument.**   War is a cultural habit that, once learned, is passed on from generation to generation. If children are taught to engage in simulated acts of violence, exposed to stories in which violence plays an important part (whether they are told by grandmothers or broadcast on television sets), and encouraged to emulate the bellicose acts of their elders, their society will tend to settle conflicts with other states by means of war.[82]

Beyond Arguments: The Control of War

It is impossible to state with certainty what causes war, but we can say with considerable confidence that the Hobbesian argument is wrong. There is a good deal of evidence that earlier societies were, on the average, less warlike than so-called modern states—that the incidence and severity of wars has, paradoxically, increased with the evolution of civilization. This phenomenon seems to be related to the development of fixed settlements and the consequent need to assert and expand control of territory. The technological advances that began in the fifteenth century have steadily improved (if that is the word) the capacity of humans to slaughter one another and have led to ever-greater expenditures on arms and ever-greater numbers of men and women serving in the military. Thus, it is no surprise that by far the greatest share of the work of diplomats, regional organizations, and the United Nations is devoted directly or indirectly to the attempt to avoid, limit, or end wars.

Although idealists have long argued that the best way to avoid wars is to promote pacifism ("what if they gave a war and nobody came?"), for most of the twentieth century war theoreticians tended to take a tougher stance and recommend two approaches that countenanced and indeed encouraged preparedness.[83] The first approach was to encourage the widespread development of the power to make war in the hopes of ensuring a balance of power between would-be combatants, thereby making both sides hesitant to make the first move. Then, after World War II and the development of nuclear bombs, it became fashionable to speak of *deterrence* rather than balance of power. The idea of being able to prevent war by building such a massive and threatening arsenal of nuclear weapons that no one would dare attack seems at first fundamentally different from the idea of establishing a power equilibrium. But in practice deterrence theory seems to have become balance-of-power theory written in megatons. For forty years the two major superpowers relied on the fact of each other's power as well as their own; because the Soviet Union had its own arsenal of nuclear weapons, the United States could count on it to understand the probable meaning of particular American advances in defensive or offensive weaponry and to be suitably "deterred"—and vice versa. Other nations accepted the argument and sought either to shelter under the protective wing of one of the superpowers or to develop their own deterrence force.

Even before the collapse of the Soviet Union, however, it was quite clear that balanced nuclear power might deter nations from engaging in nuclear warfare but had little or no impact on their willingness to engage in conventional warfare. Once that event took place, the dissolution of the Warsaw Pact, the withdrawal of Soviet armies from Eastern Europe, the reunification of Germany, the breakup of the Soviet Union into separate states, the emergence of the United States as the world's single remaining superpower, and the fracturing of polity after polity into warring factions of nationality versus nationality, guerrillas versus regular army, and ins versus outs changed the nature of warfare drastically.[84]

The stockpile of weapons so zealously built up in the name of deterrence did not disappear at the Cold War's end, despite various disarmament treaties that had been put in place, and was in fact becoming ever more dangerously dispersed. India, Pakistan. and Israel are known to have nuclear weapons and none of them has signed the Comprehensive Test Ban Treaty (CTBT). North Korea, Iran, Iraq, and Libya are also suspected of either

	1992	1993	1994	1995	1996	1997	1998	1999	Total 1992–99
United States	11,231	12,332	9,524	12,481	10,582	12,135	11,279	11,366	90,929
United Kingdom	6,341	6,164	5,247	5,364	6,217	6,191	3,392	3,900	42,816
France	1,292	913	782	2,189	3,109	5,981	6,166	2,200	22,632
Russia	3,053	2,968	2,345	2,956	2,358	2,308	1,953	2,000	19,940
China	1,174	1,256	670	766	643	1,049	514	300	6,372
Germany	235	685	893	876	429	105	514	600	4,336
Italy	117	0	223	219	107	630	0	0	1,296
All Other European	2,114	1,484	2,456	2,518	2,465	3,253	1,953	1,800	18,043
All Others	1,292	1,256	1,116	1,204	1,179	944	719	500	8,211
Total	26,848	27,056	23,257	28,573	27,090	32,597	26,489	22,666	214,576

Source: Richard F. Grimmell, "Conventional Arms Transfers to Developing Nations, 1992–1999" (Washington: Congressional Research Service, August 18, 2000), p. 51.

TABLE 7.1

Arms Deliveries to Developing Nations, by Supplier, 1992–1999 (in millions of constant 1999 U.S. dollars)

having already produced a nuclear bomb (North Korea) or being actively involved in a program designed to do so (Iraq was considered two years away from producing such a bomb at the time of the Gulf War and fended off UN weapons inspectors after 1991).[85]

Perhaps even more alarming was the shocking proliferation of conventional arms, the kind of weaponry most likely to be used in terrorist activities. By 1990, the United States had become the biggest supplier of weapons to the Third World and to the Middle East (the areas most likely to harbor terrorist groups), and since then it has not dropped from its lead position. (See Table 7.1.) In 1999 U.S. sales were at $11.4 billion, while those of all other nations were $11.3 billion, combined. Despite the risks to themselves ever more obviously entailed, First World nations, struggling to overcome high rates of unemployment and negative balances of payment, have shown little sign of imposing voluntary curbs on one of their most profitable exports: the instruments of death.

In this new situation, a primary question throughout the 1990s was what role the remaining superpower should play. Should the United States become the peacekeeper for the entire world? Was it in that country's interest to assume that role? Was it in the interests of the international community? Should a facade of UN—or NATO—alliance building be maintained as a cover for U.S. power and a clear statement of international consent to its use? And if the United States did assume that role, what should be the criteria—and the goals—of its interventions in disputes between other nations, or, more and more likely, between different groups in the same state? What about its own well-known hunger and capacity for economic expansion—could the United States (or any nation, for that matter) be trusted, once peace was made, not to exploit the chastened nation for its own economic

gain, as it invited leading U.S. business men and women to invest in the lucrative work of rebuilding? Next, what about the means to be employed in
keeping (really, *restoring*) peace? Obviously, the first efforts should be directed toward a negotiated peace, but when negotiations failed, then what?
Large-scale bombing from impervious heights, all but ensuring the deaths of
thousands of innocent civilians? Or a slogging ground war that would endanger the lives of thousands of the peacekeepers? Finally, to what lengths
would the peacekeepers go? Would they take whatever measures necessary
to achieve their ends, or would they stop when losses of men—or of public
support for the endeavor—became unacceptable?

The Gulf, Bosnian, and Kosovo campaigns appeared to demonstrate that
U.S. intervention would be at least superficially cloaked in the robes of international alliance, that bombing from a safe height (or sending missiles
from an even safer distance) was the preferred means, and that the extent of
the effort to be made would be evaluated and reevaluated throughout the
course of each incursion. American casualties would be kept to an absolute
minimum; when the Gulf War seemed to demand more sacrifice than Americans would support, the answer was to halt the attack and seek, in vain, to
accomplish the same ends by imposing sanctions on the regime of Saddam
Hussein in Iraq.[86] In Kosovo there were no American military casualties at
all during the bombing, and postwar reconstruction was turned over to the
United Nations.[87]

And then came September 11, 2001. Within a single day the nature of warfare changed again, even more radically. Not since the United States dropped
atomic bombs on Hiroshima and Nagasaki at the end of World War II had
so many civilians been the target of a single act of war—and the 1945 bombing had taken place after long years of grueling battle between military
forces in an open and declared state of war. Then, the objective was military
victory to be followed by striking an honorable peace. However, when the
objective is to root out terrorism, peace pacts may be worked out with those
who formerly harbored the perpetrators, but the terrorists themselves, once
captured, can expect to be treated not as erstwhile enemies, but as criminals.
Furthermore, the acts of terror of September 11 were not a result of a war
between nations, or within a nation. It was a war of a widely dispersed group
of fanatics, hidden from sight, against the world's greatest power. Most dramatic of all was the change in weaponry on the part of the attackers: commercial airplanes filled with high-octane fuel and a worldwide propaganda
campaign. A great nation was to be brought to her knees, trembling in terror, on a very low budget.

The damage done was in fact horrific, and provoked a kind of immediate
counterattack that was also unique, at least in part. As we have seen, it employed the familiar tactic of forming a wide alliance, but this time that alliance was to include those never consulted or much considered in earlier

missions. It also used the tactic of bombing from above the clouds, but put special troops on the ground as well. It reached into the scientific and public health communities for as high-powered a response to biological warfare as they could muster, fast. It unleashed a flood of patriotic propaganda not seen since World War II (which meant never before seen by most of those on the receiving end).

Whatever the eventual military outcome, it seems clear that for a long time to come the role of global policeman will be one the United States will be unable—and now, perhaps, reluctant—to abandon. Even as a domestic recession makes it yet harder to care for the neediest at home, U.S. resources are likely to be stretched and stretched again to meet the demands of this new kind of warfare.

The immediate threat of terrorism will no doubt be eliminated—or nearly so—and what then shall we say of modern warfare and the actors who wage it? At this writing, we can only pose more questions, and not just to Americans, not just to Westerners. Do we members of the human polity, across the world, believers or nonbelievers in all the various religions, now find ourselves at the beginning of a new long, hard era of limited freedoms, heightened fears, extravagant military budgets, diminished attention to social needs, and growing hatred of others unlike our selves? Or is it possible a significant majority of us at least will be inspired—wherever and however we live—to take a sharper and more honest look at our own beliefs and where they have led us? Now that we see the price to be paid by everyone on the planet if we cannot change, will we be willing to both improve our understanding of one another and ourselves and to develop the skills that permit peaceful negotiation and settlement of disputes? Increased diplomatic contact, cultural exchanges, better codified international law, and intergovernmental organizations that work on substantive problems before they become the basis for war of any kind are remedies that have been proposed time and again; are we ready to put them to work?

SUMMARY AND CONCLUSION

Contemporary issues of international politics are multiple and complex. Defense against terrorism, the protection of human rights, and the ever more serious need to protect our environment are only a few of the problems requiring our urgent, global attention.

Attention is paid by a wide range of actors. Private citizens and elected officials work within their own nations to find remedies that will work at home to ameliorate problems found across the globe. Diplomats and secret agents pursue the quest for international solutions while at the same time seeking to maximize national advantage. Interest groups pursue their own goals in international arenas, sometimes persuaded that doing so is in the interest of all those who wish for a better world, sometimes purely selfishly. Lawyers steadily clarify and augment the body of law that gives us a means of resolving our international disputes peacefully and fairly. Soldiers and scientists seek to improve the means of waging war successfully.

Of course, none of this is enough. Our problems are immense, and the amazing events of recent years have not lightened our load. Although we turn now, in Part Four, back to the level of the nation-state, in the final two chapters of this book we will look at the institutions of international governance and the economics of globalization. Furthermore, if this chapter has done its job, we will not forget, while working at the level of the state, that now more than ever what we do in our own polities profoundly affects life in the polity we all must share.

QUESTIONS TO CONSIDER

1. Pick an issue in international affairs that seems important to you. Draft a letter, stating your opinion about that issue and the reasons for it, and find out to whom you might send it. (Maybe you will decide to send it, and thereby become a political actor in international affairs—or maybe you already are one.)
2. In the discussion regarding the role of TNCs today, which author makes more sense to you, Barnet or Kefalas, and why?
3. How do you respond to the argument that "what looks like a human rights violation to you may be absolutely in accord with indigenous customs and traditions, as well as essential for maintaining law and order"?
4. Is periodic warfare inevitable in relations between nations? Why or why not?

SELECTED READINGS

Burgerman, Susan. *Moral Victories: How Activists Provoke Multilateral Action* (Ithaca, N.Y.: Cornell University Press, 2001). Considers how human rights activists can successfully exert international pressure and change oppressive state behavior, using the cases of El Salvador, Guatemala, and Cambodia as examples.

Chen, Lung-chu. *An Introduction to Contemporary International Law: A Policy-Oriented Perspective* (New Haven, Conn.: Yale University Press, 2000). Introduces all major aspects of contemporary international law, using a policy-oriented perspective of international law not as a fixed set of rules but as an ongoing process of decision making through which the members of the world community identify, clarify, and secure their common interests.

Clark, Ann Marie. *Amnesty International and Changing Human Rights Norms* (Princeton, N.J.: Princeton University Press, 2001). Traces the efforts of Amnesty International to increase awareness of popular human rights and strengthen international law against torture, disappearances, and political killings. Clark believes this group's "strenuously cultivated objectivity" accounts for its ability to be critical of all governments violating rights and to offer persuasive interpretations of abuses according to international standards.

Drache, Daniel, ed. *The Market or the Public Domain: Global Governance and the Asymmetry of Power* (New York: Routledge, 2001). A collection of studies focused on the idea that we are witnessing "the return, reconstitution and redeployment" of the public domain and that new institutions of governance for a globalizing world must and will be devised.

Forsythe, David P. *The Internationalization of Human Rights* (Lexington, Mass.: Lexington Books, 1991). Discusses the protection of human rights in international law, the United Nations, the Organization of African States, the United States, and private international organizations such as the Red Cross.

Keck, Margaret E. and Kathryn Sikkink. *Activists Beyond Borders: Advocacy Networks in International Politics* (Ithaca, N.Y.: Cornell University Press, 1998). Examines transnational politics as carried out by networks of activists who coalesce and operate across national frontiers, often exercising particularly strong influence in the areas of human rights and environmental politics.

Orlin, Theodore E., Allan Rosas, and Martin Scheinen, eds. *The Jurisprudence of Human Rights Law: A Comparative Interpretive Approach* (Syracuse, N.Y.: Syracuse University Press, 2000). Studies the reasoning of various national, regional, and international courts and tribunals in arriving at human rights rulings.

Talbott, Strobe and Nayan Chanda. *The Age of Terror: America and the World After September 11* (New York: Basic Books: Yale Center for the Study of Globalization, 2001). Eight historians and policymakers examine the impact of the events of September 11, 2001, on U.S. policy decisions.

Vig, Norman J. and Regina S. Axelrod. *The Global Environment: Institutions, Law and Policy* (Washington, D.C.: Congressional Quarterly Press, 1999). Leading American and European academic experts on environmental politics, international law, and sustainable development policies assess the institutions, regimes, laws, and policies in place for the protection of the global environment.

WEB SITES OF INTEREST

1. United Nations International Law
   http://www.un.org/law/
   Provides links to various international tribunals as well as international law commissions of the United Nations.

2. Center for International Environmental Law
   http://www.ciel.org/
   A not-for-profit law firm providing legal services relevant to international and comparative environmental law and policy around the world.

NOTES

1. Craig S. Smith, "A Tourist Boat Signals Less Turbulence in China-Taiwan Ties," *New York Times*, 2 Jan. 2001, A9.

2. Hamish McDonald, "The Big Switch: Calcutta's Ruling Communists Give Capitalism a Chance," *Far Eastern Economic Review* (29 June 1995): 58–61.

3. "Eyes on Kosovo, Again," *The Economist* (28 Oct. 2000): 35, and Michael Wines, "In Letter to Bush, Putin Urges Wider U.S.-Russian Cooperation," *New York Times*, 25 Jan. 2001, A7.

4. *Le Monde*, 14 April 1998, 4

5. Carolyn Curiel, "The Serpent in the Camera," *New York Times*, 8 Feb. 2001, A31.

6. Leon Hadar believes the new stress on trade (over aid) is owing to the nature of U.S. electoral politics; he claims those elected to power work to serve "the interests of the most powerful and skillful players in the political game in Washington, those who can deliver votes, raise funds, and manipulate the media." According to Hadar, this means paying particular attention to Saudi Arabia, a wealthy nation whose purchases of U.S. goods can "create jobs in key electoral states" and to Israel, a nation befriended by Jewish-Americans whose votes are critical, often in the same states. "Muddling Through in the New World Disorder—and in the Middle East," *Journal of Palestine Studies* 23, no. 4 (Summer 1994): 62–68.

7. Nigel Tutt and Orla Ryan, "Gore Opens G-7 Meeting with Promise of Open U.S. Telecom Market," *Electronics* 68, no. 5 (13 March 1995): 12; David E. Sanger, "International Business: Big Powers Plan a World Economic Bailout Fund," *New York Times,* 8 June 1995, 1.

8. Amin Saikal, "Pakistani Intelligence Agency Is Fueling the Fire of Conflict," *International Herald Tribune,* 30 June 1999, 8.

9. Ray S. Cline, *The CIA Under Reagan, Bush and Casey* (Washington, D.C.: Acropolis Books, 1981); Scott D. Breckinridge, *The CIA and the U.S. Intelligence System* (Boulder, Colo.: Westview, 1986); Rhodri Jeffreys-Jones, *The CIA and American Democracy* (New Haven, Conn.: Yale University Press, 1989); Steve H. Hanke, "Common Cause: What's This New Love Affair Between President Clinton and the CIA?" *Forbes* 155, no. 8 (10 April 1995): 7.

10. See *Preparing for the 21st Century: An Appraisal of U.S. Intellgence,* The Commission on the Roles and Capabilities of the U.S. Intelligence Community, March 1, 1996.

11. Pamela Hess, "Secret CIS Document Spelled Out Intelligence Failures," *United Press International,* 15 May 2000.

12. See, for example, Lock K. Johnson, "Spies," *Foreign Policy* (September/October 2000): 18–25.

13. Jane Perlez and David E. Sanger, "Powell Says U.S. Had Signs, But Not Clear Ones, of a Plot," *New York Times,* 3 Oct. 2001, 1, B3. Much about a growing terrorist network was known by the general public as well—or at least by those who were paying attention. See, for example, the detailed and well-documented series of articles "Holy Warriors: A Network of Terror" that the *New York Times* ran January 14–16, 2001. For after-the-fact commentary on CIA failures, see Matthew L. Wald, "Hints of Day of Terrorism Went Unheeded by Officials," *New York Times,* 3 Oct. 2001, B2, and James Risen, "In Hindsight, CIA Sees Flaws That Hindered Efforts on Terror," *New York Times,* 7 Oct. 2001, A1, B2.

14. Alison Mitchell, "House Votes for More Spy Aid and to Pull in Reins on Inquiry," *New York Times,* 6 Oct. 2001, B5; Tim Weiner, "To Fight in the Shadows, Get Better Eyes," *New York Times,* 7 Oct. 2001, sec. 4, p. 1; Elizabeth Becker and Tim Weiner, "New Office to Become a White House Agency," *New York Times,* 28 Sept. 2001, B5.

15. Peter J. Spiro, "New Global Communities: Non-governmental Organizations in International Decision-Making Institutions," *Washington Quarterly* 18, no. 1 (1994): 45–56.

16. L. David Brown, Sanjeev Khagram, Mark H. Moore, and Peter Frumkin, "Globalization, NGOs and Multi-Sectoral Relations," *Working Paper No. 1* (The Hauser Center for Nonprofit Organizations and the Kennedy School of Government, Harvard University): July 2000, pp. 1–37.

17. Paul Wapner, *Environmental Activism and World Civic Politics* (New York: State University of New York Press, 2000).

18. Eva Etzioni-Halevy, "Linkage Deficits in Transnational Politics" *International Political Science Review* 23, no. 2 (April 2002): 203–22.

19. "Anti-Liberalism Old and New," *The Economist* (21 Oct. 2000): 92.

20. Stephen D. Krasner, "Sovereignty," *Foreign Policy* (Jan./Feb. 2001): 20–29.

21. "Net Effect: Global Politics and Economics on the Web," *Foreign Policy* (Nov./Dec. 2000): 104.

22. "Africa's Women Go to Work," *The Economist* (13 Jan. 2001): 43.

23. "Technoserve World," newsletter of Technoserve (Summer 2000).

24. Michael Edwards and David Hulme, "NGO Performance and Accountability in the Post–Cold War World," *Journal of International Development* 7, no. 6 (1995): 849–56. See also Roger Charlton and Roy May, "NGOs, Politics, Projects and Probity: A Policy Implementation Perspective," *Third World Quarterly* 16, no. 2 (1995): 237–55.

25. In the best of all semantic worlds, we would recognize that transnational corporations are also INGOs, albeit profit-seeking ones. However, scholarly usage forbids us to call them that; the acronym of choice is TNC. (As you may have noticed, the first qualification for the study of international relations today is an ability to master the acronyms. It isn't fair to change them in midstream, and so we will stick with TNC. But TNC used to be MNC, the multinational corporation. Think about the difference between *multi* and *trans*. What does it tell you about the process of globalization that it has seemed necessary to make *this* change?)

26. "Chrysler's Troubled Marriage," *New York Times,* 9 Jan. 2001, A24, and "Japanese Companies: Another Shopping Trip," *The Economist* (21 Oct. 2000): 73.

27. "Coca-Cola Moves to Broaden Business in the Soviet Union," *Wall Street Journal,* 30 Aug. 1991, A3.

28. Jeff Gerth, "In Post-Cold-War Washington, Development Is a Hot Business," *New York Times,* 25 May 1996, 1, 6.

29. *Wall Street Journal,* 2 Oct. 1995, R16, R22.

30. Richard J. Barnet, "Stateless Corporations: Lords of the Economy," *The Nation* 259, no. 21 (19 Dec. 1994): 754–57. Barnet also points out that the world's 200 largest corporations now control more than one-fourth of the world's economic activity. This article is drawn from Richard Barnet and John Cavanagh, *Global Dreams: Imperial Corporations and the New World Order* (New York: Simon & Schuster, 1994).

31. A. G. Kefalas, "The Global Corporation: Its Role in the New World Order," *National Forum* (Fall 1992): 26–30.

32. *New York Times,* 17 May 1995, A1. See also *World Press Review* 42 (July 1995): 4.

33. European nations such as Britain, France, Spain, and Germany have had considerably more experience with terrorism than the United States, owing to such groups as the Irish Republican Army, the German Maoist Red Army Faction, and the Basque separatists (E.T.A.). See Niall Ferguson, "The War on Terror Is Not New," *New York Times,* 20 Sept. 2001, A31.

34. Douglas Frantz with Raymond Bonner, "Web of Terrorism," *New York Times,* 23 Sept. 2001, A1, B4. Also Douglas Jehl, "Pilots Are Running Out of Targets to Drop Bombs On," *New York Times,* 10 Oct. 2001, B2.

35. Sheryl Gay Stolberg, "Some Experts Say U.S. Is Vulnerable to a Germ Attack," *New York Times,* 30 Sept. 2001, 1, B3; William J. Borad and Melody Petersen, "Nation's Civil Defense Could Prove to Be Inadequate Against a Germ or Toxic Attack," *New York Times,* 23 Sept. 2001, B12.

36. Barnaby J. Feder, "Trying to Plan for the Unthinkable Disaster," section on "The Role of Technology," *New York Times,* 17 Sept. 2001, C2.

37. Ronald K. Noble, "Invest in Global Policing," *New York Times,* 15 Sept. 2001, A23; Tim Weiner, "The Building of a Network That Is Global and Reliable," *New York Times,* 23 Sept. 2001, B7; Serge Schmemann, "Annan Urges New Methods to Fight Terrorism," *New York Times,* 25 Sept. 2001, B3.

38. Timothy Garton Ash, "A New War Reshapes Old Alliances," *New York Times,* 12 Oct. 2001, A23; Stephen Kinzer, "5 Ex-Soviet Asian Republics Are Now Courted by the U.S.," *New York Times,* 10 Oct. 2001, B7; Patrick E. Tyler and Celia W. Dugger, "Powell's Message: America's Courting of Pakistan Will Not Come at India's Expense," *New York Times,* B3.

39. Laura D. Tyson, "Financing the Fight Against Terrorism," *New York Times,* 8 Oct. 2001, A21.

40. Edmund I. Andrews,"America's Economic Cloud Extends Across Europe," *New York Times,* 28 Sept. 2001, W1.

41. Leslie Wayne and Leslie Kaufman, "A Body Blow to the Economy," *New York Times,* 16 Sept. 2001, sec. 3, p. 3.

42. Joseph Kahn, "World Bank Says Poor Nations Will Suffer Worst Economic Toll," *New York Times,* 2 Oct. 2001, B4.

43. Clifford Krauss, "Economic Pain Spreads from U.S. Across Latin America," *New York Times,* 14 Oct. 2001, A3.

44. John Schwartz, "Privacy Debate Focuses on F.B.I. Use of an Internet Wiretap," *New York Times,* 13 Oct. 2001, B6; Sarah Lyall, "Britain May Require ID Cards for All," *New York Times,* 28 Sept. 2001, A8; Alan M. Dershowitz, "Why Fear National ID Cards?" *New York Times,* 13 Oct. 2001, A23; Steven Erlanger, "Shocked Germany Weakens Cherished Protections," *New York Times,* 1 Oct. 2001, B1.

45. Richard Reeves, "Patriotism Calls Out the Censor," *New York Times,* 1 Oct. 2001, A25.

46. Bill Carter and Felicity Barringer, "In Patriotic Time, Dissent Is Muted," *New York Times,* 28 Sept. 2001, A1, B8.

47. Steven Greenhouse, "Some Unions Find It a Difficult Time to Strike," *New York Times,* 5 Oct. 2001, A20.

48. William Glaberson, "Racial Profiling May Get Wider Approval by Courts," *New York Times,* 21 Sept. 2001, A16; Sam Howe Verhovek, "Americans Give in to Race Profiling" *New York Times,* 23 Sept. 2001, 1; Bob Herbert, "A Look in the Mirror," *New York Times,* 17 Sept. 2001, A15.

49. Linda Greenhouse, "In New York Visit, O'Connor Foresees Limits on Freedom," *New York Times,* 29 Sept. 2001, B5.

50. Quoted by Schwartz, op. cit.

51. It was not, Richard Reeves reminded us, a new idea. About 170 years ago Alexis de Tocqueville, visiting from France, remarked that Americans "have an immensely high opinion of themselves and are not far from believing that they form a species apart from the rest of the human race." (Quoted in Reeves, op. cit.)

52. Anthony Lewis, "The Inescapable World," *New York Times,* 20 Oct. 2001, A21.

53. Mel Gurtow, *Global Politics in the Human Interest* (Boulder, Colo.: Lynne Rienner, 1988); *Time International* (22 June 1992): 19.

54. Amnesty International, *Political Killings by Governments* (London: Amnesty International Publications, 1983), pp. 15–25; *International Herald Tribune,* 22 June 1992, 1, 4; *Time International* (22 June 1992): 38; "Report of the Independent Inquiry into the Actions of the United Nations During the 1994 Genocide in Rwanda," 15 Dec. 1999, 1–69. http://www.un.org/News/ossg/rwanda_report.htm.

55. "Torture—A Modern Day Plague," News Release from *Amnesty International Publications* (18 Oct. 2000): 1–3.

56. For a sober and thoughtful study of the problems facing the most recently created of these organizations, see Claude E. Welch Jr., "The African Commission on Human and Peoples' Rights: A Five Year Report and Assessment," *Human Rights Quarterly* 14, no. 1 (February 1991): 43–61.

57. "Report of the Independent Inquiry into the Actions of the United Nations During the 1994 Genocide in Rwanda," 15 Dec. 1999, 1–69. http://www.un.org/News/ossg/rwanda_report.htm.

58. For a good, recent discussion of the problems involved in justifying intervention, see Mahmood Monshipouri and Claude E. Welch, "The Search for International Human Rights and Justice: Coming to Terms with the New Global Realities," *Human Rights Quarterly* 23, no. 2 (May 2001): 370–401.

59. Human Rights Watch, *Shielded from Justice: Police Brutality and Accountability in the United States* (New York: Human Rights Watch, 1998).

60. Marguerite Feitlowitz, "Prosecuting Latin America's Dirty Wars," *Dissent* (Spring 1999): 33–40. Both arguments were used by Yugoslavians, even after Milosević had been removed from power. See Carlotta Gall, "A Rocky Meeting in Belgrade for War Crimes Prosecutor," *New York Times,* 24 Jan. 2001, A4.

61. Payam Akhavan, "Beyond Impunity: Can International Criminal Justice Prevent Future Atrocities?" *American Journal of International Law* 95, no. 1 (January 2001): 7–31.

62. See Jennifer Widner, "Courts and Democracy in Postconflict Transitions: A Social Scientist's Perspective on the African Case," *American Journal of International Law* 95, no. 1 (January 2001): 64–75, for a study of the role of the regular courts and of such commissions in the aftermath of large-scale conflicts in Africa.

63. Audrey R. Chapman and Patrick Ball, "The Truth of Truth Commissions: Comparative Lessons from Haiti, South Africa and Guatemala," *Human Rights Quarterly* 23, no. 1 (Feb. 2001): 1–43.

64. Tim Weiner, "Terrific News in Mexico City: Air Is Sometimes Breathable," *New York Times,* 5 Jan. 2001, A1, and Michael Renner, "Overview: The Triple Health Challenge" in *Vital Signs 2001: The Trends That Are Shaping Our Future* (New York: W. W. Norton, 2001), pp. 17–24.

65. Philippe Rkacewicz, "Environmental Disaster in Eastern Europe," *Le Monde Diplomatique,* July 2000.

66. Ibid.

67. Organization for Economic Cooperation and Development, *Environmental Trends in Transition Economies, OECD Policy Brief* (October 1999): 1–8. http://www.oecd.org/publications/Pol_brief/.

68. Eric T. Freyfogle, "The Price of a Sustainable Environnment," *Dissent* (Spring 1998): 37–43.

69. For comments on two UN initiatives other than the one discussed below, see "The U.N. Convention on the Law of the Sea: A Chronology," *U.N. Chronicle* (March 1995): 10–12, and Michael Stocking, "The Quest for World Environmental Cooperation: The Case of the UN Global Environmental Monitoring System," *Journal of Development Studies* 31, no. 2 (Dec. 1994): 368–70.

70. *Le Monde,* 16 June 1992, 1, 14. See also "The 'Earth Summit' on Population," *Population and Development Review* 18, no. 3 (Sept. 1992): 571–82.

71. Ross Gelbspan, "Disgrace at The Hague," *The Progressive* (Jan. 2001): 8–9.

72. Ramachandra Guha, "The Paradox of Global Environmentalism," *Current History* 99, no. 640 (Nov. 2000): 367–70.

73. Bill McKibben, "Too Hot to Handle," *New York Times,* 5 Jan. 2001, A21.

74. Gennady M. Danilenko, "The New Russian Constitution and International Law," *American Journal of International Law* 88, no. 3 (July 1994): 451–70.

75. "A Step Toward International Justice," *New York Times,* 3 Jan. 2001, A18. More recently, the Bush administration argued for a clause giving "a 100 percent ironclad guarantee that no American servicemen will be investigated by the court," but settled for one that ensured U.S. peacekeepers would not be prosecuted for the first twelve months of the court's existence (expecting this deferral to be renewed annually). Glenn Kessler, "Concerns Over War Crimes Not New," *Washington Post,* July 2, 2002, p. A09, and Colum Lynch, "U.S. Drops Demand for War Court Immunity," *Washington Post,* July 11, 2002, p. A1.

76. Rupert Brooke, "1914," in *Collected Poems of Rupert Brooke* (New York: Dodd, Mead, 1915).

77. Thomas Hobbes, *Leviathan* (Oxford, U.K.: Basil Blackwell, 1960).

78. Carl von Clausewitz, *On War,* ed. and trans. Michael Howard and Peter Paret (Princeton, N.J.: Princeton University Press, 1976), p. 87.

79. Roy L. Prosterman, "The Study of Lethal Human Conflict," in Farrar, *War,* pp. 14–17. It should be noted that Prosterman rejects all of these explanations except the quest to assert leadership: "Together, the frustrated, status-protecting, ideology-affirming leaders, and the obedient, ideology-accepting followers, make war" (p. 18). Prosterman also identifies Freud with the Hobbesian argument, but elsewhere Freud argued along the lines described here, in a fashion more consistent with his general trend of analysis.

80. Karl Marx, "The German Ideology," in Robert C. Tucker, ed., *The Marx-Engels Reader* (New York: W. W. Norton, 1972), pp. 115–16.

81. C. Wright Mills, *The Power Elite* (New York: Oxford University Press, 1956).

82. Margaret Mead, "Alternatives to War," in Morton Fried, Marvin Harris, and Robert Murphy, eds., *War: The Anthropology of Armed Conflict and Aggression* (Garden City, N.Y.: Natural History Press, 1968), pp. 215–28.

83. For a recent summary of the effort to promote peace by nonviolent strategies, see Peter Ackerman and Jack DuVall, *A Force More Powerful: A Century of Nonviolent Conflict* (New York: St. Martin's, 2000).

84. Don M. Snider and Gregory Grant, "The Future of Conventional Warfare and U.S. Military Strategy," *Washington Quarterly* 15, no. 1 (Winter 1992): 203–28.

85. "The World's Nuclear Arsenal," *BBC World News,* 2 May 2000. http://news.bbc.co.uk/hi/english/world/newsid_733000/733162.stm

86. Thomas L. Friedman, "The War Saddam Won," *New York Times,* 6 Feb. 2001, A25.

87. David Ransom, "Globocops," *New Internationalist* 330 (December 2000): 9–11. Mary Kaldor claims that at the start of the twentieth century there were roughly eight military casualties of war for every civilian casualty, but that at the start of the present century the ratio has been reversed. (*New and Old Wars,* New York: Polity Press, 1999). For the role of the UN in postwar Kosovo, see "United Nations Governance of Postconflict Societies," *American Journal of International Law* 95, no. 1 (Jan. 2001): 76–85.

PART FOUR

Governing Nation-States

CHAPTER 8

Making the Laws

Do you remember your first day in college? Chances are you spent most of that day trying to figure out the rules. All kinds of rules presented themselves to you: rules about which pieces of paper you had to have, where to exchange them for other pieces of paper, where to put your things, where to put yourself. Some rules were more compelling than others: If you are a young man receiving a government-backed loan for your education, you may have been required to demonstrate that you had registered for the draft in order to receive that aid. Other rules were given quietly and following them was clearly optional: You learned without being told that there was or was not a specific way to dress, to talk, perhaps even to sit and look about. In any case, there you were, an independent human being with the ability to decide for yourself which rules to follow and which to reject. Once you had sorted it all out, made your decisions, followed some rules to completion ("Here is the check for my tuition"), adopted others as a pattern for your behavior ("I will be in my botany class by 8:10 every Monday, Wednesday, and Friday morning"), and rejected others ("I don't care what the others do, I'm going to wear the clothes I have and that's that"), chances are life began to seem a little bit easier. You knew what you were doing.

What you went through in those first few days tells you a great deal about the role of rules in our lives—including the role of those rules we call laws. A rule is a guide to behavior. It may be a regulation established by persons in authority, a principle of conduct that one sets for oneself, or simply something that normally happens ("As a general rule, Americans eat three meals a day"). A law is a rule of the first category: a regulation established by persons in authority. But not all such regulations are laws. A law is a regulation established by *public* authorities and backed by the collective power of the polity to which it applies. It is, in effect, a *plan*—a decision to handle a particular problem in a particular way—and a *commitment*, made by the entire polity when they acquiesce in the authority of those making the plan, that the plan will in fact be carried out. Because it is so strongly backed, it is the most powerful kind of rule. We have the power to act contrary to the law, but we do so at our peril.

The polity for which a particular law is made may range from the smallest village to the nation-state. (The uncertainty of enforcement of international law places it in a special category, as we have seen and will discuss further in Chapter 11.) At the lowest level are local ordinances, sometimes referred to collectively as municipal law. "The charge to the university for providing police protection at university events shall be $50 per hour per officer" is a rule set by officeholders (perhaps a council, a board, a mayor, or a sheriff) who have been granted the authority to make such rules throughout a governmental domain (a village, township, city, or county), either by other officeholders or by statute.

Laws are made at all levels of government, and rules having the force of law can be made by any branch of government. We think of the legislative branch as the lawmaking branch of national government, and quite rightly so; thus, the work of legislatures will be the central topic of this chapter. However, legislators are not our only national lawmakers; rules issued by executives also have the force of law, although they may be called by a different name. "I have ordered the National Guard to remain on twenty-four-hour duty at all campuses of the university where disturbances have been reported" is a rule set by a chief executive. Such a rule is often called a decree but may also be called an ordinance, an executive order, or a decree law.

The pronouncements of judges are more likely to be rulings than rules, but these too can have the force of law. "The right of students to use notes in university examinations is not protected by the First Amendment; there was, therefore, no violation of the Constitution in the university's decision to withhold the degree" is a ruling, which is to say, an interpretation of a rule (such as a clause in a constitution, law, ordinance, decree, or executive order) that affects the applicability of the rule. A nation's constitution is a set of rules that has precedence over all other rules. The constitution and judicial rulings about the meaning of the constitution are together called constitutional law.

Some rules have the force of law even when made outside government. "Henceforth the party's policy is that only those veterans with three or more years' membership in the party shall be eligible for educational benefits" is a rule that may have the force of law if the party in question has unrestrained power to tell the legislature what laws to write and pass (as has often been the case in single-party governments).

Finally, some rules are written to be laws from the very beginning. When the U.S. Congress passed Title IX, a federal statute prohibiting sex discrimination and promoting gender equality in American schools, that bill, once signed by the president and entrenched in the U.S. code, became part of the law of the land: "No person in the United States shall, on the basis of sex, be excluded from participation in, be denied the benefits of, or be subjected to discrimination under any education program or activity receiving federal financial assistance."[1] The result was a wide range of improvements in the educational opportunities of women (see Box 8.1). Laws like Title IX can be reversed only by other, subsequent laws, or by rulings of the U.S. Supreme Court that they are in some way contrary to the U.S. Constitution.

This chapter is about the making of those rules that are called laws or that have the force of law. Our primary emphasis will be on how laws are made in legislatures, but our functional approach (see Chapter 1) helps us recognize that other governmental and even extragovernmental bodies also make rules or rulings that have the force of law. Thus, we will also consider how executive and judicial agencies make law and will end with a few words about how laws are sometimes shaped by extragovernmental bodies.

BOX 8.1
**A Law at
Work: Changes
Attributed to
Title IX in
Increasing Equal
Educational
Opportunity**

- For American colleges and universities, women now constitute majorities in college enrollment and completion, and are the majority of recipients of bachelor's and master's degrees. The proportion of women graduating from college today is now equal to that of men, with both at 27%. In 1971, only 18% of young women completed four or more years of college, compared to 26% of young men. By 2006, women are projected to earn 55% of all bachelor's degrees.

- In graduate and professional fields, women have had new opportunities to advance and broaden their education, and have made significant inroads in specialty fields. In 1994, women earned 34% of all U.S. medical degrees, compared to 1972 when only 9% of U.S. medical school degrees went to women. Women also earned 39% of all U.S. dental degrees in 1994; in 1972 they were only 1% of the graduates. In 1994, women accounted for 43% of all U.S. law school degrees, up from 7% in 1972. Of all doctoral degrees awarded to U.S. citizens in 1994, 44% went to women, compared to 25% in 1977.

- There are more female faculty members now than in 1972, with women constituting 37.9% of faculty members at two-year public colleges, and 19.5% at private four-year colleges and universities. In 1972, women held 10% of all academic positions.

- In athletic participation, an area that has received the lion's share of media attention, there has been a fourfold increase in participation since 1971, with more than 100,000 women competing in intercollegiate events. Currently, women constitute 37% of all U.S. college athletes, compared to 15% in 1972. Recent data show that there are 2.4 million high school girls, taking part in various sports, representing 39% of all high school athletes, more than a fivefold increase. In 1971, they totaled 300,000, or 7.5%. Studies have shown that values learned from sports participation, such as teamwork, leadership, discipline, and pride in accomplishment, are important attributes as women increase their participation in the workforce, as well as their entry into management and ownership positions in higher numbers than ever before. For example, 80% of female managers of Fortune 500 companies have a sports background. Also, high school girls who participate in team sports have been found to be less likely to drop out of school, smoke, drink, or to have unwanted pregnancies.

Source: Leslie Gladstone and Gary Galemore, "Sex Discrimination in Education: Overview of Title IX," *CRS Report for Congress 97–954 GOV,* Congressional Research Service, January 14, 1998.

LAWMAKING IN THE LEGISLATURE

A legislature is an institution in which individuals gather with the primary purpose of making laws. It need not be an elected body, although it often is. It need not be a permanent body convened periodically; sometimes it is, sometimes it is not. A legislature is established every time a tribal chief, king, military commander, or the highest potentate in a theocracy summons some of the elders, nobles, senior officers, or higher clergy (respectively) to help work out policy on a matter of politywide concern. When Sultan Mahmud II, leader of the Ottoman Empire, established an advisory body known as the Supreme Council of Judicial Ordinances in 1838 and gave it the job of preparing and discussing new regulations, that was a legislature.[2]

The more familiar form of a modern legislature, however, is a permanent, periodically convened institution composed of officials elected for a limited term for the express purpose of making laws, such as the German Bundestag, the British House of Commons, the Japanese Diet, the French National Assembly, the Mexican National Congress, and the U.S. Congress. Even in this category there are numerous variations. The legislature's relationship to the executive branch and the individual legislators' relationships with their constituents vary significantly from polity to polity. Other differences include the number and nature of the individual houses of the legislature, the power of committees, and the customs and mores of the particular legislature — all relatively minor variations that will take considerably less of our time to understand.

THE RELATIONSHIP BETWEEN LEGISLATIVE AND EXECUTIVE POWER

In the United States, with its tradition of separation of powers, legislative power is distinct from executive power, at least in constitutional theory. But this kind of system, known as a presidential system, is very different from a parliamentary system, and parliamentary systems are in fact much more common around the world. And just to make our job a bit more complicated — and a bit more interesting — there is also a third kind of system, a blend of the other two, a presidential-parliamentary system.

The simplest way to make these differences clear is to describe each of these three systems in turn. Diagrams in Figures 8.1, 8.2, and 8.3 illustrate how each establishes a different relationship between legislative and executive power; they will be easier to understand after reading the text about each system and they will also help you understand that text better. In each diagram, a solid arrow shows the direction of effective control of one body over another and a broken arrow indicates some degree of control, often varying according to political circumstances.

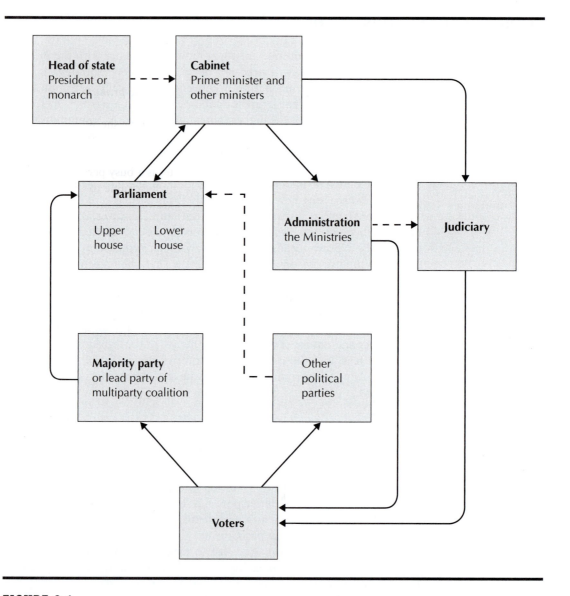

FIGURE 8.1
A Parliamentary
System

The Parliamentary System

In a parliamentary system, the legislature maintains extremely close bonds with the system's executive leadership and has significant power of its own. In fact, the head of the legislature, usually called the *prime minister* or *premier,* is the top chief executive of the land. There may also be a president, but that person will have no significant power; he or she will simply carry out the same, largely ceremonial functions of a king or queen, capable of making a real difference only very rarely, as we shall see.

In a parliamentary system the prime minister is a busy person indeed. His job is to direct the work of the *lower house* (comparable to the U.S. House of Representatives, but more powerful) *and* the work of the *bureaucracy,* including all the departments or ministries of government (sometimes also referred to as the *administration*). To do all this, the prime minister often relies heavily on his *cabinet.* The parliamentary cabinet is, like the U.S. cabinet, composed of the heads of the departments of government, usually called *ministers,* occupants of important appointive posts, such as the head of the national security agency, the top leader in the military forces, or an important prelate in a system where church and state are closely intertwined. The main difference is that these important administrators report to the prime minister, who is the head of the cabinet, and not to a president. This makes the cabinet very important and indeed the cabinet in a parliamentary system is often called the *government,* not because it is in fact the entire government but in recognition of the key role it does play.

Where do parliamentary cabinets come from, and what do they do? In the most typical form, the individual members of the cabinet are chosen by the prime minister but must be approved by the lower house (see p. 311 for the difference between the lower and upper houses of legislatures in parliamentary systems). To become prime minister, one must be a leader (usually the top leader) of a political party. If that party wins a majority of the seats in the lower house of the legislature, its senior leader will be asked to try to "form a government." If he or she can win the approval of the lower house of parliament for the cabinet proposed (and if the party has won the majority of seats in the legislature, such approval is virtually assured), then the new government is established and the party leader in question becomes the prime minister. The cabinet may be formed exclusively of members of parliament (who may or may not be allowed to keep their seats in that body), or it may include some persons who have not been elected to any office whatsoever; the more common pattern is for cabinet members to be members of parliament as well.

In a parliamentary system, the person who asks the party leader to try to form a government is the nation's monarch or president (often referred to as the **head of state**). This is the most important role—or at least the most politically powerful role—that a monarch or a president can play in a parlia-

The European Parliament is one of the world's newest parliaments, and is still quite weak. Here it meets in Strasbourg, France, on January 14, 2002.
Vincent Kessler/Reuters

mentary system; as noted above, most of the functions of the head of state are purely ceremonial. Even in this case, if the party leader leads a party that has indeed won a majority of seats in the lower house, the head of state can only follow a script written by others. Everyone knows that the majority party's leader must be asked to form a government and will succeed in doing so.

In **multiparty parliamentary systems,** however, where it often happens that no party wins a majority of the seats, the ceremonial leader may have an opportunity to exercise a very real influence on the course of events. In such a case it is usually still expected that the leader of the party winning a plurality of seats will be given the first chance to form a government, often by asking leading members of various other parties to take posts in the cabinet in order to form a *coalition* government. Coalitions are also sometimes formed to achieve a semblance of national unity in a time of deep division, as in Israel or in Yugoslavia.[3] But whether mandated by political results or dictated by strategy, in a parliamentary system the coalition cabinet, like any other, must win the approval of the lower house. If it cannot, the same person may be asked to try again with a different cabinet, or the leader of another party may be asked to try. Sometimes a nation's politics are so fragmented that no single leader is considered dominant over all the others in a particular party; in that case, the job of trying to form an acceptable cabinet may be passed on to someone else in the same party. As a general rule, the more difficult it is to form a government (cabinet) that the lower house will accept, the more power will likely be exercised by the monarch or president in a parliamentary system, at least during this difficult period. However, even in cases where it is very difficult indeed to form a new government, the ceremonial leader customarily takes the advice of the nation's most astute and most powerful politicians in deciding whom to ask next.

Once formed, the new cabinet becomes the center of the entire governmental process in a parliamentary system. It assumes primary responsibility for the formulation of new legislation and accounts for the initiation of most new bills. Government bills (bills proposed by the cabinet) typically have precedence over bills proposed by individual members of parliament. In some systems, individual members are not allowed to introduce certain kinds of bills—for example, those that would require additional expense with no provision for additional revenue. At the same time, it is also the duty of cabinet members to see to it that the bills are properly carried out by the appropriate departments or ministries once they become law.

So far, it may appear that once the legislature has approved a cabinet and a government is formed, the ordinary members of parliament will find themselves playing an insignificant role in the making of laws. But such an impression is not correct. Although most bills are initiated by the cabinet and all laws must be carried out through the administrative apparatus the cabinet controls, the members of parliament still have an important role to play in shaping the content of legislation. (We will come back to this in discussing the role of committees.) No bill becomes law without the consent of at least the lower house of the legislature; more commonly, both houses must approve, although the upper house may be overruled by the lower house. Furthermore, it is usually possible for the lower house of a parliament to put an end to the life of any cabinet. The most forthright way of doing so is by calling for a motion of censure or by voting negatively when the government itself calls for a vote of confidence. If a majority of the lower house votes for the motion (or against the government), the government is dismissed—or, in the term more often used, *dissolved*. Sometimes, as in Norway, a single member of parliament may introduce a motion of no confidence; sometimes, as in Greece, a new no-confidence motion may be introduced within six months of a previously failed one only if it has more signatures than necessary for a majority.[4] But almost always a successful motion of no confidence will mean not only that the cabinet must resign but also that the members of the lower house will themselves have to face new elections. Since this is not always politically convenient, members of parliament often prefer to accept partial changes to the cabinet, engineered by the majority party's leadership.

However, if it proves impossible to form a new cabinet that can command a majority, then elections must be held. In parliamentary theory, the vote of the electorate should resolve the dispute on which the government foundered, but this does not always work: Postwar crises in Italian parliamentary government have come about in part because the vote has consistently failed to produce a clear majority for any party or ideologically workable coalition of parties. Between the end of World War II and 1996, fifty-four different cabinets had been installed, and in that year the government "fell" again. Italian President Oscar Luigi Scalfaro, unable to find a parliamentary leader capable of putting together an acceptable new cabinet, was forced to call for new elections. Scalfaro's failure had been more or less expected but was not seen as inevitable, since time and again Italian presidents have managed to engineer a change of cabinet without the need for new elections; there have been only about one-fourth as many legislative elections as cabinet collapses in the same fifty-one-year period since World War II. However, since the fall of the Christian Democratic Party in 1994 after successive revelations of criminal behavior by its leadership, the balance of power among the new Italian parties has made the formation of governing coalitions yet more difficult, with power split among the increasingly popular Democratic Party of the Left (successor to the former Communist Party), the Forza Italia (the right-leaning party of entrepreneur Silvio Berlusconi, twice named prime minister, but also accused of criminal activity), the hard-right National Alliance (successor to the prewar fascist movement of Benito Mussolini), and the almost equally rightwing Northern League, as well as numerous smaller parties (see Chapter 6).[5]

A parliamentary system is, as I am sure you are beginning to see, the very antithesis of a system based on the separation of powers. Even the judicial branch, made up of judges (often, at the highest level, appointed by the prime minister without need for ratification by parliament) and other court officers, is closely linked to the other two branches of government, and sometimes considered part of the administration. In Great Britain, the highest court in the land is a committee of the upper house, the House of Lords (the "Lords of Appeal in Ordinary"), and even its rulings can be—and have been—overruled by legislation passed by the two houses of Parliament. Since the British House of Lords has the power only to delay legislation, not to veto it, and since the majority in the lower house, the House of Commons, commonly votes as directed by the cabinet (unless so unhappy with that body that it helps bring about a dissolution), ultimate power over the judiciary resides in the cabinet in Britain as in most other parliamentary systems.[6]

The parliamentary system is, in fact, predicated on keeping the functions of government tightly interwoven. The link between legislative and executive functions is considered so important that one author has referred to it as the "buckle" that holds everything together and makes the system work.[7]

The Presidential System

A presidential system is characterized by weak ties between the legislative and executive branches and a shifting balance of power between them. The presidential system (see Figure 8.2) functions quite differently from the parliamentary system. It rests on the assumption that placing too much power in the hands of too few is dangerous to the liberty of citizens. The government is therefore divided, on the principle of the separation of powers, into three branches: legislative, executive, and judicial. Each branch is given a separate domain, a separate source of power (the chief executive and the legislators are elected independently, the highest judges are appointed), and the power to correct the abuses of the others. Under such a system the relationship between the executive and legislative branches, which may and often do come under the control of members of opposing parties, is likely to be contentious and fraught with difficulty. Defenders of this system argue that such conflict is a small price to pay to protect the nation against the tyranny that might arise with more concentrated power.[8] But those who prefer parliamentary government point out that that system permits stronger and more representative parties as well as more cohesive government. Christopher S. Allen points out that it also improves voter turnout, eliminates the need for the head of the government to be as well a ceremonial head of state, and makes it possible to get rid of an unsatisfactory chief executive much more efficiently than the present impeachment process.[9]

Whatever side one takes in such a debate, it is important to understand four crucial differences between presidential systems and parliamentary systems: the different sources of executive power, the different roles of the executive in the initiation of legislation, the presence or absence of ceremonial leadership, and the different roles of political parties. Exact procedures vary, but the more usual patterns are as follows.

■ **Source of Executive Power.**   In a parliamentary system, the prime minister is chosen first by a party (as party leader), second by the voters in a particular constituency (as their representative to the lower house of the legislature), third by the ceremonial leader (as a possible head of government), and fourth by the lower house of the legislature (as prime minister in fact). The voters within their constituencies choose the other members of parliament. National legislative elections are always important: They determine the balance of power in both the legislative and executive offices.

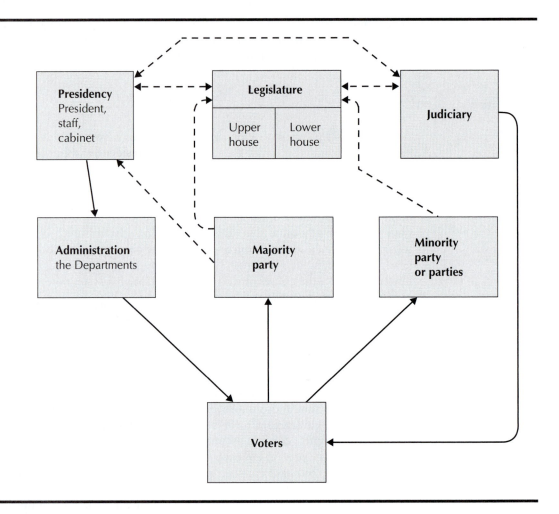

FIGURE 8.2
A Presidential
System

In a presidential system, on the other hand, the president is chosen first by a party (as nominee), and second by the voters of the entire nation (as president).[10] The members of the legislature are also chosen first by the parties (as nominees) and second by the voters (as representatives) in elections that may or may not be held at the same time as the presidential election. In any case, the members of the legislature in a presidential system have terms of office different from that of the president and play no part in his or her selection. Presidential elections are normally considered far more important than legislative elections in a presidential system.

■ **Initiation of Legislation.**   In a parliamentary system, the prime minister and the cabinet can and do initiate legislation. In a presidential system, the president and the members of the administration may initiate new legislation, but only indirectly, working through individual members of the legislature who agree to sponsor such bills. Those bills have no special priority over other bills proposed by the same or other individual members. However, we should not exaggerate the importance of this difference, since in practice the legislative leaders in a presidential system are usually extremely well aware which bills have the backing of the president, and such bills will almost always receive greater and more favorable attention than bills sponsored by ordinary members.

■ **Ceremonial Leadership.**   In a parliamentary system, the ceremonial leader plays a role in establishing the link between executive and legislative powers by calling upon the party leader most likely to gain the approval of the lower house to form a government. The ceremonial leader takes power either by right of birth or by election (but in either case, the choice of that official is far less important than the choices made in legislative elections). In a presidential system, the president is also the ceremonial leader.

■ **Role of Political Parties.**   In a parliamentary system, the political parties choose the candidates for the legislature and choose their own leader in the knowledge that if enough of their legislative candidates are successful, that leader will become the prime minister. They also know that the leader will count on the votes of the successful candidates of the party, not only to take office but also to carry out the party's program. This means that the party plays a far more critical role in parliamentary systems than in presidential systems. Furthermore, the constitutional link between executive and legislative power in parliamentary government forges a link between the party's candidates for executive and legislative power. This normally (but not always) means a more unified party, better able to maintain party discipline in the legislature, and thus better able to combine legislative and executive power in implementing its program. In a presidential system, the political parties choose legislative and executive candidates separately, receive little encouragement from the constitutional system to operate in harmony, and are thus more likely to permit undisciplined voting in the legislature. The end result is that although the voters in a presidential system directly elect the president as well as the legislators, choosing between competing candidates from different parties, they do not have the advantage of knowing that strong and well-disciplined parties will hold their successful candidates responsible to the program on which they campaigned (hence the broken lines in Figure 8.2 from the parties to the presidency and the legislature).

The combined effect of these four differences between a presidential system and a parliamentary system is to make the ties between executive and legislative power much looser in a presidential system. Looser ties in turn tend to leave the determination of which branch is more powerful to other, nonconstitutional factors, which vary from time to time and from nation to nation. The degree of the nation's need for rapid and forceful decision making from its executive, and/or for personal strength or popularity from the occupants of its different offices, thus assumes much greater significance in determining the distribution of power in presidential systems than in parliamentary systems. In times like the present, presidential systems lead to greatly strengthened executive branches, yet the legislative branch may retain enough power to block and frustrate the most powerful president while lacking the internal unity and constitutional authority to take power on its own (see Box 8.2).

The Presidential-Parliamentary System

The **presidential-parliamentary system** is characterized by strong ties between the legislature and the executive and a weak legislature. A constitutional system that has become increasingly common in recent years not only in Europe but also in several of the new African states, it is a blend of the presidential and parliamentary systems, as illustrated in Figure 8.3. At first glance, this system looks very much like a parliamentary system: A president chooses a prime minister, who must win the approval of the legislature's lower house for a cabinet. However, several key differences weaken the power of the legislature while maintaining a strong bond between the two kinds of power. The net result is a much stronger executive.

The first essential difference between a parliamentary system and a presidential-parliamentary system (sometimes referred to as a **quasi-presidential system** or a **parliamentary presidency**) is that the president has the power to appoint anyone at all as prime minister and to remove that person at will.[12] The prime minister need not be a member of parliament, need not be a leader of a major party, and in fact need not even be a member of a political party. The prime minister forms a cabinet, which must be approved by the legislature, but again, cabinet members need not be members of parliament or leaders or members of political parties. It is normal in such a system for the president to be elected directly by the people; the prime minister and cabinet members need not have been elected at all. Such a system permits the president to become a very active player in the game of ministerial musical chairs that takes place when parliamentary cabinets falter and political support declines. When the French people became particularly discontented in the

BOX 8.2
U.S. President Versus Congress: The Separation or Stalemate of Power?

For several years, the United States has been experiencing the downside of the principle of separation of powers: the possibility of stalemate between its executive and legislative branches. For years the problem took the form of Republican presidents versus Democratic majorities in Congress. Then, in 1994 the tables were reversed, as Democratic President Bill Clinton found himself faced with Republican majorities and, in particular, a resolute band of budget-trimming freshmen under the leadership of House Speaker Newt Gingrich. Determined to carry out the unambiguous "Republican Contract" on which they had campaigned and won in the midterm elections, the House Republicans passed bill after bill— on such questions as reforms to the welfare system and the legal system, the weakening of environmental regulations, the battle on crime, and the use of American troops in UN operations— which the president, equally determined, promised to veto.

The president had already responded to the rightward shift of the 1990s by abandoning his plans for reforming the health care system as well as stressing his own interest in trimming the deficit and in reforming the welfare system ("We all know what we need," he said on the last subject, disappointing many of his own supporters with some of his ideas, "we need time limits for welfare recipients, we need strict work requirements, we need very tough child support enforcement, we need more flexibility for states"). By the end of 1995, however, Clinton had reached, at least for the moment, the limit of his own flexibility, and refused to sign a Republican budget bill that included many of the kind of provisions he had earlier announced were unacceptable. The result was that funding for many government services ran out and "the government closed down." (In fact, most offices remained open; the impact was most severe on certain limited groups— and on the public servants who could not be sure when and if lost pay would be made up to them.) Continued negotiations at the White House between the president and congressional leaders produced continued stalemate, as neither side was ready to compromise. When the Republican leadership was ready to agree, the adamant freshmen refused, producing a minivictory for the Democrats, who could then claim the stalemate was the fault of their opponents, unable to agree among themselves. Meanwhile, of course, the problems that the disputed legislation was supposed to resolve remained largely unaddressed. Power was so well distributed it had almost ceased to exist.[11]

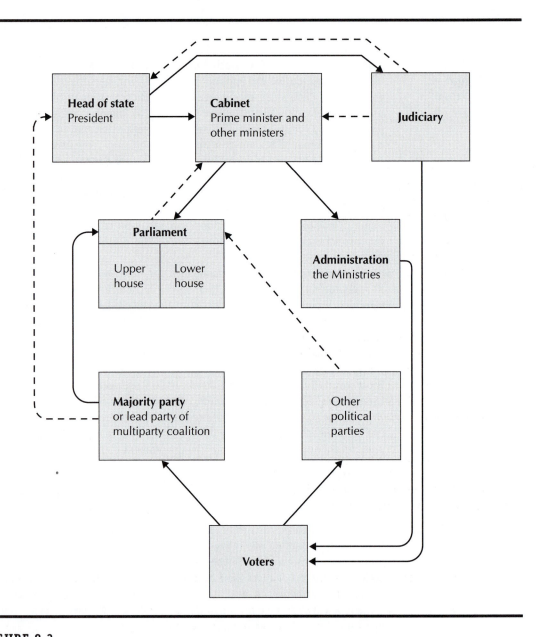

FIGURE 8.3
A Presidential-
Parliamentary
System

spring of 1992 over continuing problems of unemployment and the high cost of living, and manifested that discontent by voting heavily against the ruling socialist party in regional elections, Socialist President François Mitterrand replaced Prime Minister Edith Cresson with Pierre Beregovoy. This action, combined with several other important cabinet changes, temporarily calmed the troubled waters.[13]

The constitution of a quasi-presidential system may also give the president the right to name the highest judges, rule the nation directly during states of emergency, and declare when such a state of emergency exists. These supplementary powers may or may not require the signature of the prime minister; because that official's tenure in office is subject to the will of the president, little restraint on the president's power is implied by such a stipulation in any case. Clearly, in such a system the president is not a ceremonial leader but rather the most powerful figure in the government. But the chief executive's power is not unlimited. The prime minister retains the important powers of setting the government's daily agenda and overseeing both the formulation and the execution of policy—it is the prime minister who plays the most active role, but that role must be played in a way that is satisfactory to the president, to whom the prime minister reports and who has the power to remove him or her from power.

A more serious potential check on the powers of the president in this kind of system rests in the political parties and their elected representatives, particularly if a party other than the president's party gains control of the legislature. In that case, a united and determined majority, following party discipline, will almost certainly refuse to approve the cabinet (including the president's choice for prime minister) until one is appointed that will act in accordance with its will. Even then, a president who fears that popular opinion is shifting against him so rapidly that the next legislative election may produce such a result may decide to dissolve parliament immediately, hoping thus to be able to get a new majority from his own party in place that will last out his own term in office. However, this tactic can backfire, as French President Jacques Chirac discovered in 1997. Opinion polls showed he was slipping badly for having failed to keep campaign promises to improve the lot of the poorer sectors in the French economy, and so he ordered new elections. The result was not the new majority on the French right he sought. It was already too late, and the winners were the socialists, in coalition with the small Green and Communist parties and other leftist movements, leaving Chirac no choice but to name his archenemy Lionel Jospin, leader of the socialists, to the Prime Ministership.[14]

Nevertheless, the president holds most of the trumps in such a system, and this is reinforced by the fact that only the president is elected by all the voters. Thus, the flow of power in a presidential-parliamentary system is almost always that indicated by the arrows in Figure 8.3. The bonds between executive and legislative powers remain strong, but they now serve to hold together the unequal partners of a greatly strengthened executive and a greatly weakened legislature.

REPRESENTATION: LEGISLATORS AND THEIR CONSTITUENTS

We have just examined three versions of the legislature's relationship to the executive branch. Another key difference in legislatures around the world is seen in the relationship that legislators maintain with their constituents. One question all legislators must resolve is whether to act independently on the basis of what they personally believe to be correct principles or to attempt to carry out the will of constituents even when it runs contrary to those principles.

Any attempt to answer the fundamental question is likely to lead to a host of problems. It is often difficult to know the will of constituents with certainty. It is not easy to treat all constituents as equals—some will be better informed and more articulate than others, some will be major contributors to the legislator's campaign fund, and some will be other powerful political leaders who helped the representative secure the nomination in the first place. Sometimes nonconstituents have a claim to legislative attention on the grounds of past favors, promises of future help, or the national importance of the causes they represent. Even if a legislator wishes to be loyal to his or her own constituents, it is often very difficult for that legislator to be sure that the will of the voters truly reflects their own interests. Furthermore, these interests may be extremely varied and not easily compromised. The interests of the whole (the community) are not always in accord with the sum of the interests of the parts (the individual citizens and groups), and both may be in conflict with the interests of the larger polity (the nation) of which they form a part. In such situations, what is the responsibility of the individual legislator to add "best interests of the human polity" to the list of objectives to be served?

Consider, for example, the problems the U.S. Congress has had to wrestle with in helping to determine U.S. foreign policy in China. Many members of Congress have believed, especially since the brutal repression of student demonstrations that took place in China in 1989, but also in response to well-documented reports of repression of religious expression and free speech, persecution of labor organizers, forced abortions to maintain population control, and the torture of prisoners, that the United States must impose economic sanctions on China as well as issue strong statements of disapproval regarding these and other violations of human rights. Others believed, however, that such a move would do more damage to U.S. business interests in China than good to the cause of fostering democracy. By and large, the latter have prevailed in recent years. After supporting a temporary ban on diplomatic visits between the two nations and on new loans to China by the

Hispanic Congresswoman Loretta Sanchez, reelected to a third term in 2000, shakes hands with supporters in Santa Ana, California. When the two do not coincide, representatives must decide whether to act in accord with the will of their constituents or in accord with what they believe is right.
Jonathan Nourok/PHOTOEDIT

World Bank and other international development banks, the policy has been to protest abuses, but expand and strengthen economic ties. By 1998 U.S. businesses had invested $20 billion in the Chinese economy, eight times as much as they had by 1989. Most Favored Nation status was returned to China in 1994 and strong diplomatic ties were established under the Clinton administration. Republican members of Congress were the most outspoken defenders of Chinese human rights during the last years of the Clinton era, but did not demur when President George W. Bush continued the same kind of overtures, especially after the terrorist attacks of September 11, 2001, seemed to make it essential to include China in the new alliances being formed.[15] By that time, China had begun to make some concessions on the issue, but not in response to the U.S. Congress: It was eager to calm UN and NGO critics sufficiently to be allowed to host the 2008 Olympics.[16] In November, 2001, China was admitted to the World Trade Organization (see Chapter 14).

Every representative, and every political scientist writing about the problem of representation, has a slightly different way of trying to resolve the dilemmas of representation. Edmund Burke, the eighteenth-century British statesman and philosopher, wrote at length on this question, and his words are still cited with approbation or contempt, depending on the citer's own views on this important question. Burke believed that the representative should act independently but should remain reasonably aware of his constituents' major interests. He defined interests very narrowly. For him they meant simply that the district one represented might be characterized by a dominant mode of making its livelihood—for example, fishing, raising corn, or mining precious minerals.[17] Burke told his own constituents they could expect no more than this from him; his constituents told him, by way of the vote that removed him from office, that they had a rather different definition in mind.

Hannah Pitkin, a twentieth-century commentator on this problem, has offered a different resolution. She would leave representatives considerable latitude but would insist that their job is to find the best possible way to combine the interests of constituents (which are, for Pitkin, all the individual concerns that are or might be affected by government policy) with those of the nation. When this cannot be done and representatives find it necessary to act contrary to their constituents' will, it is their responsibility to make every effort to explain why and to persuade their followers that the national interest is in fact also their own interest—in short, to attempt to change the will of constituents whenever they cannot follow it. For Pitkin, political representation is never a matter of a single action but rather "the patterns emerging from the multiple activities of many people."[18] She stresses the importance of facilitating representation by having the appropriate institutional framework. The right to vote, sufficiently powerful elected officials, a significant opposition, and a multiple-member lawmaking body are all essential ingredients of representative government, according to Pitkin.

Those of us who have observed representative politics in recent years would probably want to add still further institutional guarantees. In Pitkin's world, representatives are always men and women of principle. They must wrestle with difficult questions, and they do not always resolve them wisely or in the best interests of their constituents, but they never stop trying to do so. Unfortunately, such leadership is not always characteristic of those who take on the tasks of representation. Special interests can and often do pay the bulk of campaign expenses and control the votes of particular representatives, and such interests may operate from outside the legislator's constituency altogether. Nor is a strong opposition always a sufficient safeguard against misbehavior in office. Individuals waiting their turn to take power may be eager to do so on behalf of those same special interest groups rather than on behalf of a wider public. They may well be willing to join those in power in return for a piece of the pie—a tendency Italians call *trasformismo*, meaning a readiness to transform oneself (or, in the British phrase, "cross the carpet"), providing only that the price is right.[19]

A further problem in securing fair representation is the inability of certain groups to elect persons like themselves to serve in their nation's legislative

TABLE 8.1

National Parliaments with Highest Percentage of Women Serving in the Lower or Single House

Rank	Country	Lower or Single House			
		Elections	Seats	Women	% W
1	Sweden	09 1998	349	149	42.7
2	Denmark	03 1998	179	67	37.4
3	Finland	03 1999	200	73	36.5
4	Netherlands	05 1998	150	54	36.0
5	Norway	09 2001	165	59	35.8
6	Iceland	05 1999	63	22	34.9
7	Germany	09 1998	669	207	30.9
8	New Zealand	11 1999	120	37	30.8
9	Mozambique	12 1999	250	75	30.0
10	South Africa	06 1999	399	119	29.8
11	Spain	03 2000	350	99	28.3
12	Cuba	01 1998	601	166	27.6
13	Austria	10 1999	183	49	26.8
14	Grenada	01 1999	15	4	26.7
15	Argentina	10 1999	257	68	26.5
16	Bulgaria	06 2001	240	63	26.2
17	Turkmenistan	12 1999	50	13	26.0
"	Vietnam	07 1997	450	117	26.0
18	Rwanda	11 1994	74	19	25.7
19	Namibia	11 1999	72	18	25.0
20	Australia	10 1998	148	35	23.6
21	Seychelles	03 1998	34	8	23.5
22	Belgium	06 1999	150	35	23.3
23	Switzerland	10 1999	200	46	23.0
24	United Rep. of Tanzania	10 2000	274	61	22.3
25	Monaco	02 1998	18	4	22.2
26	China	1997–98	2984	650	21.8
27	Lao People's Democratic Rep.	12 1997	99	21	21.2
28	Canada	11 2000	301	62	20.6
29	Croatia	01 2000	151	31	20.5
30	Dem. People's Rep. of Korea	07 1998	687	138	20.1

Source: "Women in National Parliaments," *Inter-Parliamentary Union* (12 Oct. 2001). http://www.ipu.org/wmn-e/classif.htm. Reprinted by permission of Inter-Parliamentary Union.

bodies. Sometimes this is simply a matter of voting rights; for example, it is only a short time ago that the majority black population of South Africa achieved full voting rights, but that transition was swiftly followed by the transformation of that nation's legislature as well. Often, however, the problem is social and political rather than constitutional. Take a moment to read Table 8.1, which shows the thirty nations in the world having the highest percentage of women serving in the lower (or single) house of their legislature as of October 2001. The numbers range from 20 to almost 48 percent, and I am sorry to tell you that at least five authoritarian nations in which the legislatures act as little more than rubber stamps for dictatorial decisions are included in the top 30. You will not need my help to note what important nation is missing from the list (it comes in at a tie for 49th place, along with Slovakia).

However representative they themselves may be, many of the world's legislatures have taken significant steps to try to ensure that all their constituents are fairly treated in other agencies of government, often by establishing independent watchdog agencies, such as the office of ombudsman in Sweden. The Swedish Riksdag (parliament) has set up offices of ombudsmen to ensure gender equality, to combat ethnic discrimination, to prevent discrimination because of sexual orientation, to represent children and young people, to help the disabled, and to protect consumers. It has also set up an office of ombudsmen inside parliament, elected by parliament, to supervise compliance with laws and ordinances by all judges, civil servants and military officers.[20] Of course, such agencies do not always work as intended. The laws governing the U.S. Federal Elections Commission, established to weaken the control of large moneyed interests over individual candidates, have, as we discussed in earlier chapters, left loopholes permitting more private money to be funneled into American campaigns than ever before.

Such watchdog agencies are themselves, moreover, part of the government they are expected to monitor and control, and no doubt a stronger safeguard against unequal protection of the laws rests in the existence of a wide range of political organizations outside government. Ironically, however, such organizations can also contribute to the problem. Political action committees and other special interest groups are a case in point, even if some groups (and some parties) may provide elected representatives with helpful reminders of the scope of their responsibilities and the possibility of their removal from office. Furthermore, protecting the right of free assembly that ensures the existence of a pluralistic political system is a task that inevitably devolves on government—that is, on the very officials whose actions we hope to guide and control. Institutions can take us only so far. There comes a time when we must rely on the quality of the men and women inside them.

CAMERAS, COMMITTEES, AND CUSTOMS: OTHER VARIATIONS IN LEGISLATURES

The term *camera* originally referred to a chamber or a room and only later came to mean a device for taking photographs. Thus, when we say that a legislature is *unicameral* or *bicameral,* we are referring to the number of houses (chambers) it has. A **unicameral legislature** has one house; a **bicameral legislature** has two.[21]

Most legislatures have two houses to ensure that different interests— and different principles of representation—will have appropriate arenas of action. Normally the lower house is elected directly by the people, with each representative serving approximately the same number of constituents. Upper houses vary from system to system, but they are usually made up of elder statesmen, elected indirectly (for example, French senators are elected by local and regional government officials) and in office for a longer term than their counterparts in the lower house. In some nations the upper house consists entirely of appointed members and in Great Britain it is composed of "lords," about 90 percent of whom have no claim to glory beyond the fact that they have inherited titles of nobility (others were granted peerages for particular accomplishments; recent reforms make it impossible to pass peerages on to heirs). In *corporatist* states, one or both houses (if there are two houses) will be composed of representatives from different occupations and branches of industry, not from different regions (for example, the Corporazione of Italy under the rule of Benito Mussolini before and during World War II).

In most nations with bicameral legislatures, the lower house is far more powerful than the upper house; the upper chamber deliberates on all bills, but in the event of disagreement, the lower house easily overrides it. There are, however, exceptions. The U.S. Senate—directly elected by the people since 1913—has always been at least coequal with the House of Representatives in the exercise of power.

Another exception was the Supreme Soviet of the former Soviet Union, a bicameral body consisting of the Council of the Union, in which each delegate represented 300,000 inhabitants, and the Council of Nationalities, in which the union and the autonomous republics were represented. The two Soviet houses had equal power, but it would be more accurate to say they were equally powerless, because their activity was normally limited to giving unanimous approval to legislation or decrees that originated in the top councils of the Communist Party.[22] Under former Soviet President Mikhail Gorbachev, the lower house of the national legislature became the Congress of People's Deputies, but once he was seriously weakened by the attempted coup in August of 1991 Gorbachev decided to abolish the Congress and replace it with a single house, an appointed Legislative Council consisting of twenty deputies from each republic. When this and his other efforts did not succeed in stopping the hemorrhaging of power at the top, Gorbachev was forced to resign and Boris Yeltsin, elected president in June 1991, declared, "The Union of Soviet Socialist Republics, as a subject of international law and a geopolitical reality, is ceasing its existence." The new Commonwealth of Independent States left routine lawmaking to the individual republics; policies affecting the entire commonwealth were to be made "cooperatively" by consultations among ministers from the member republics, meeting in a "Council of Heads of State."[23]

Such a situation could not, of course, endure. By the end of 1991, the former superpower had become fifteen sovereign states. Russia, by far the largest and most powerful state, was still technically governed by the shards of the Soviet constitution but was in fact torn apart by internal wrangling over the division of power. In September 1993, President Yeltsin dissolved the parliament, which promptly rejected this act as unconstitutional (it was) and convened itself in the White House (the name of the parliament building). Militant defenders of the legislators launched an armed struggle against the pro-Yeltsin forces, giving the president the excuse to take back parliament by armed force.

A new constitution, giving the president vast powers (including direct responsibility for television and radio and for the foreign, defense, and interior ministries), was ratified by a slim majority in December elections at which the voters (only about half of the registered electorate) also chose a new bicameral parliament with a majority of anti-Yeltsin representatives.[24] When political opposition and ill health forced Yeltsin from power in 1999, his chosen successor, Vladimir Putin, showed little concern for the fact that the Duma (the Russian legislature) was now dominated (see Chapter 6) by the representatives of major commercial interests, some of them openly criminal, working through pseudopolitical parties that shifted constantly and scarcely deserved the name. He did, however, do a far better job of rallying public support for his presidency (see Chapter 9) than Yeltsin had and by now the number of houses of parliament was of little concern to anyone; the question was whether that body could ever be sufficiently reformed to merit a meaningful share of power.[25]

The Role of Committees

Even in systems where the decision-making power of the legislature is weak or nonexistent, the actual work of turning bills into laws can be onerous and time-consuming. The concerns of modern government range far beyond the expertise any single man or woman can acquire, yet legislators are expected to exercise an informed judgment about each piece of legislation that comes before them. This problem has no real solution, but the work of modern legislatures is made somewhat easier by the use of the **committee system.**

There are basically two kinds of committee systems. In some legislatures, such as the U.S. Congress, each committee has a specialized function, and only bills having to do with that specialization may be referred to it. The House Ethics Committee deals only with ethical questions; the Merchant Marine and Fisheries Committee deals with the merchant marine and fisheries. This system of **specialized committees** permits legislators to develop more expertise on particular subjects, since they will consistently be concerned with bills relevant to the same subject matter. However, after every election the memberships of U.S. House and Senate committees—and sometimes the exact nature of what each committee shall cover—change to reflect new political realities. Periodic reforms of the committee system, reducing the power of or replacing committee chairs long in power, can also weaken the relevance of experience.[26] Similarly, when partisan power is equal, as it was in the U.S. Senate immediately after the 2000 elections — or when it shifts in mid-session, as it did in the same body when one Republican senator left his party, putting the Democrats back in power — or when Congressional leaders succeed in taking effective control over the fortunes of the majority party's legislation away from the committees almost altogether, as did House Speaker Newt Gingrich during the mid-1990s, then too committee members' long experience may not translate into effective decision-making power.[27]

In other legislatures a composite committee system exists and members are expected to have expertise across the entire range of possible legislation. In Britain, select committees are set up at the beginning of each session (and often carried forward from session to session; the Public Accounts Committee was first set up in 1861) or may be set up any time, in which case they are *ad hoc select committees,* created to deal with a particular issue. Other committees in the British Parliament are **standing committees** to which different questions may be referred. There are no permanent memberships on the standing committees, which are labeled simply by the letters of the alphabet. Their usual task is to attend to the final details of bills when they have passed their second reading, and they deal mostly with government bills. Since their membership is appointed in proportion to party strength in the House of Commons, "party solidarity is the norm," and they usually work in close collaboration with the minister who is steering the bill through Parliament. Finally, the House of Commons may meet as the Committee of the Whole House to deal with simple bills that can be passed quickly, financial bills requiring an increase in public expenditure, or bills "of a constitutional nature."[28]

In a detailed study of the systems of eight nations, Malcolm Shaw has ranked the relative importance of committees to the work of their legislatures as follows (from most to least important): the United States, Italy (pre-1994), Germany (pre-reunification), Philippines (pre-1972), Canada, Britain, India, and Japan (pre-1993). On the basis of these eight cases, he demonstrates that committees are strongest in political systems where parties are weakest, where presidents are strongest (presidential or parliamentary-presidential systems), and where bills are debated in committee before being given full debate on the floor of the house.[29] Shaw's findings suggest that committees, if given the chance to formulate the terms of debate in the absence of strong party leadership, can be effective ways for legislatures to reestablish some of the power otherwise lost to chief executives.

In any case, it is clear that committee systems are one way to free legislators from having to consider every piece of legislation in depth. Even so, the workload of the individual committee member can be very great. In many legislatures each committee has a paid staff to help the legislators who serve on it. In addition, individual legislators usually have some help from a staff of their own in determining what position to take on any bill that comes before the committees on which they serve or before the full house. Where no such aid is given, or where it is given in inadequate amounts, the individual legislator is inevitably more dependent on others' opinions about the merits of all bills presented. Because they need help in sifting through the masses of materials presented to them, poorly staffed legislators are likely to be more open to lobbying efforts by private groups or by representatives of other branches of the government than are those with adequate help. Lobbyists are always ready to offer interpretations of pending legislation, with supporting documentation, but their interpretations are likely to be anything but objective.

Customs and Mores

There are also significant differences in the customs and mores of the world's legislative bodies. Differences in style may seem to be of little importance, but they can in fact have a strong influence on the course of government. Most African legislators are still influenced by the traditions of palaver (discussing each topic as fully as possible), consensus (doing everything possible to reach a unanimous decision rather than simply abiding by majority rule), and respect (especially for those elders who have achieved the status of "leaders of thought") that were likely to prevail in the decision-making processes of earlier, smaller communities. In some Western legislatures occasional raucous outbursts by opposition deputies protesting government policy are considered acceptable behavior. The British House of Commons is particularly notorious for these spectacles, especially since its proceedings have been on television, a practice that seems to have heightened rather than lowered the intensity of opposing MPs' verbal assaults on one another. At the same time, of course, losing one's temper is regarded as unseemly and counterproductive in many other parts of the world. In some legislatures a certain amount of friendly accommodation, even across party lines ("We'll vote with you on X, if you will help us out on Y"), is seen as essential to good government; in others a tradition of strong party discipline ensures strict partisan voting on even the most minor matters.

It should be pointed out that there is often sharp dissent within a legislature regarding exactly what that body's "customs and mores" require, particularly of the opposition. Republicans in the U.S. Senate were outraged when Linda Chavez was forced to withdraw as President George W. Bush's nominee for secretary of labor because she had paid and sheltered an illegal alien working in her home several years earlier, and again when Democrats characterized the views of the nominee for attorney general, John Ashcroft, as extreme and even possibly racist. "It seems that the confirmation process has ceased to be constructive and has, instead, become entirely destructive," complained William Bradford Reynolds, who had himself been rejected as a nominee of Ronald Reagan for associate attorney general because he was not in favor of affirmative action. But of course Democrats countered that Republican legislators' hounding of President Bill Clinton for the Lewinsky affair had been part of the "most hateful campaign of personal attacks in memory—perhaps in American history."[30] That which one side sees as counter to customs and mores may well be seen as merely responsible performance of legislative duties by the other.

LAWMAKING BY THE EXECUTIVE

The lawmaking powers of formal legislatures have been progressively eroded in many polities. In some cases, legislatures have been devised from the outset to serve only as rubber stamps for decisions made by the nation's leader or leaders. In others, the shift to executive lawmaking has been more subtle, more gradual, and less complete.

Autocratic or Oligarchic Lawmaking

Where legislatures serve merely to formalize decisions made elsewhere about the laws that will govern the citizens of the polity, it is important to find out where laws are really being made and exactly what procedures are being followed. In some polities it is very clear that laws are effectively being made by the chief executive. It is almost part of the definition of charisma that the charismatic leader will have the final word (and sometimes the first and only word as well) on all matters of importance. Hereditary rulers have traditionally felt free to issue new and binding commandments in the form of law, with or without the advice of others. But even modern constitutions may be written to give a particular executive carte blanche in the making of laws (as was done in Ghana in 1966 for Kwame Nkrumah), and other elected chief executives have not always gone through the niceties of seeking constitutional ratification of their usurpation of legislative power. In April 1992, Peru's President Alberto Fujimori, who had already issued some 126 decree laws in his first twenty months in office and was in constant battle with the Chamber of Deputies, simply suspended the nation's democratic constitution, closed down the legislature, dismantled the judiciary, and assumed dictatorial rule. It was an *autogolpe,* which is to say (in Spanish), "a self-coup," and it kept him in power for eight more years.[31]

The term *self-coup* is something of a misnomer, however. It is generally acknowledged that Fujimori's coup could succeed only because he had the support of a majority of military officials, business elites, and even of a large

Autocratic lawmaking. Iraqi President Saddam Hussein makes all major policy decisions for his nation, despite the fact that his is an executive, *not a* legislative, *office.*
AP/Wide World Photos

share of the general population.[32] President Jorge Serrano of Guatemala attempted a self-coup in very similar circumstances in 1993, but in that case the courts, a divided military, the media, civic groups, and international opinion formed a sufficient resistance, the *autogolpe* failed, and Serrano had to leave the country.[33] Dictatorial takeover is in fact always a collective enterprise, not the act of a single person, and certainly requires strong military support. Sometimes, of course, the military acts on its own, staging the coup and setting up a ruling *junta* (team of leaders), which then makes all policy decisions by authoritarian means. When the army took power in Thailand in a military coup in 1991 and placed Prime Minister Chatichai Choonhavan under arrest, the military immediately wrote a new constitution and promised new elections, but made it clear that in the meantime legislative powers—and all others—would remain in its own hands.[34] When the first round of legislative elections in Algeria in December 1991 gave victory to Muslim fundamentalists, the military took power immediately, forced President Chadli Benjedid first to dissolve parliament and then to resign himself, and set up a seven-person Constitutional Council to rule by decree.[35]

Although Bruce Baker has shown that autocratic regimes, once installed, have remarkable staying power, the military does not always have the power to keep its chosen autocrat in power.[36] When the president of the Ivory Coast, Henri Konan Bédié, disqualified one of his more popular ministers, Alasane Ouattara, from running against him in upcoming elections on spurious grounds, the armed forces of that nation placed one of their own, General Robert Guei, in office. Guei was expected to call new elections soon, did so in the fall of 2000, stood for election himself, and then refused to accept the results (which gave clear victory to his opponent, Laurent Gbagbo) and proclaimed himself the president. It did not last long: Ivorians "poured into the street" and "literally chased [Guei] out of office."[37]

Delegated Lawmaking

Legislatures do not always lose to executive takeover or dominion, but neither do they always maintain their powers, even when they may appear to do so. In some polities, a pretense may be maintained that lawmaking is the job of the legislature, but in practice that body may have progressively allowed the executive branch a larger and larger role in the exercise of that function. Such delegation of the lawmaking power may be overt and deliberate, taking place through formal processes and at a specified point in time. The U.S Congress, for example, has formally established independent regulatory commissions and given them the right to issue rulings with the force of law.

In other cases, the delegation of power may take place slowly, almost accidentally, emerging in response to changing circumstances and the strength or weakness of particular leaders and particular institutional constraints. Here, too, the United States provides an example. As Harold Hongju Koh has shown in his analysis of the "national security constitution," the American president's right to issue executive orders with the force of law in matters affecting national security has grown out of the practice of delegating such powers to the chief executive in time of war, a practice never successfully challenged by Congress or the judiciary in peacetime.[38]

Another method that sometimes works where legislatures are weak is for chief executives to carry out their own mandate and to execute the law so selectively as to transform the nature of the rule of law entirely. President Vladimir Putin of Russia did not hesitate, from the earliest days of his term of office, to use Russian law to persecute his enemies. According to Stephen Holmes, "the law is being used . . . as a threat which can be applied or not."[39]

However, legislators do sometimes muster the will to try to take back control over the function of lawmaking that their nations' constitutions have assigned to them, and not to chief executives. This kind of hindsight has occasionally been apparent in the United States regarding the powers the president has taken in the name of national security. The War Powers Act of 1973 required that the president report to Congress any involvement of the

United States in hostilities within forty-eight hours and terminate such involvement within sixty days if Congress should so direct by concurrent resolution. Even this weak effort to retake some control was challenged by the strongest defenders of presidential supremacy as "allowing Congress to tie the president's hands," and in 1991 President George H. W. Bush made it clear that he was asking for congressional *support,* not authorization, when he asked for its vote on whether or not to begin the Gulf War, a precedent President Bill Clinton followed when sending troops to Bosnia in 1995. After the attack on the World Trade Center in September 2001, President George W. Bush simply addressed a joint session of Congress and took its applause as ample support for the "new kind of war" he and his administration planned against terrorism.

Do legislators best serve those who elected them by handing over their powers to presumably more efficient executives in times of national danger? Certainly the practice is fraught with peril; it was, after all, the German parliament that gave Adolf Hitler his unlimited powers. Of course it is true that legislative kowtowing has seldom been so extensive or had such dire results, but still it is important to remember that a nation's legislature is the one arena where representatives of all interests can be expected to meet as equals, struggle to find compromises, and formulate policy acceptable to all. The damage done to the political process by casual self-abnegation of those rights can never be deemed inconsequential.

LAWMAKING BY JUDGES

When rueful legislators do attempt to repossess the powers they have allowed others to usurp, they may well find it necessary to turn to a third branch of government, the judiciary, to adjudicate disputes that arise when they attempt to rectify what now appear to them to have been mistaken delegations of their powers. Similarly, embattled executives may seek judicial endorsement for maintaining powers they have become accustomed to exercising or to keep legislatures from invading what appear to them to be constitutionally protected executive functions.

Whichever side is the plaintiff, the ironic effect is likely to be that the judiciary itself becomes seriously involved in the making of laws. In no other nation is the judiciary so heavily implicated in the lawmaking process as in the United States. In that nation, justices routinely take it upon themselves to decide whether or not legislation conforms to the Constitution, a process known as judicial review. As most students of American history will recall, this power was not explicitly given to the courts by the Constitution but was effectively asserted by the first Chief Justice, John Marshall, in the 1803 case of *Marbury v. Madison.* It was a classic case of executive-legislative struggle in which the winner was the judiciary (see Box 8.3).

BOX 8.3
Lawmaking by Judges: The Case of *Marbury v. Madison*

When President John Adams lost his bid for reelection to Thomas Jefferson in 1800, he did what he could to fill the offices of government with members of the Federalist Party before leaving the presidency. But not all of the new appointments could be made official before he left office. One undelivered commission was the one that made William Marbury justice of the peace for Washington, D.C. Marbury asked Jefferson's new secretary of state, James Madison— whose job it was— to deliver the commission. Madison refused, saying the new government had the right to name its own appointee to fill the post. Marbury went to court, asking for a writ of *mandamus* (a court order forcing delivery of the commission), as was his right under the Federal Judiciary Act of 1789, counting on the partisan sympathy of Chief Justice John Marshall, also a Federalist. But Marshall ruled for Madison, on the grounds that the Federal Judiciary Act of 1789 was itself an unconstitutional invasion of the appointment rights of the executive branch by the legislative branch.

Well satisfied, the new government accepted the ruling and in doing so helped Marshall establish the precedent for judicial review— the right of the courts to review the nation's laws to ensure that they are in accordance with the Constitution. Marshall thereby took for himself and the Court a power far more important than control of the minor office of justice of the peace for Washington, D.C. And he established two great principles with a single blow: one of government (judicial review), the second of politics (be willing to lose a small battle if in doing so you can win a larger one).

The power of judicial review is one that the United States judicial system has continued to develop. The controversy over abortion illustrates the significance the process has assumed in great national debates. When the Supreme Court decided in the case of *Roe v. Wade* in 1973 that there was "a privacy right to abortion" in the Fourteenth Amendment's due process guarantee of personal liberty, state legislatures and lower courts throughout the nation found themselves faced with some very tough questions, defended pro and con by some very tough advocates: May and should a state legislature write laws either making abortion illegal under certain circumstances or reinforcing abortion rights? May and should a court find a particular state law relative to abortion unconstitutional? Should the opinions on this matter of candidates for judicial posts enter in to the decisions of those charged with their appointment? The controversy has become one of the bitterest in the nation's history, and the form it takes is shaped by the right of judicial review in case after case.[40]

In more recent constitutions, the power of judicial review is explicitly included. The Japanese constitution, for example, gives the Supreme Court of Japan the power to determine the constitutionality of any law, order, regulation, or official act, a power it has applied, unequally and unfairly some have argued, to rule on the legitimate size of constituencies for electing the Japanese Diet itself.[41] But in other nations, judges have no place at all in law-making. They are expected to assume that all legislation is constitutionally correct and then simply to adjudicate disputes that arise under existing law. Still other nations allow a modified form of judicial review, as in France, where the leaders of the government (the prime minister, the president, and the presidents of the two houses of parliament) all have the right to ask a nine-person Constitutional Council to rule on the constitutionality of an act of parliament. Unlike the U.S. Supreme Court, the French Constitutional Council is not the highest appellate court (see Chapter 11); it has only limited functions, and it can review the constitutionality of legislation only on substantive, not on procedural, grounds. On the other hand, the Constitutional Council has the right to review acts of parliament before they become law, and its powers are carefully spelled out in the French constitution—two advantages denied the U.S. Court.[42]

Assuming the power to scrutinize the work of the legislature is not the only way judges become involved in the making of laws. Under the terms of many nations' constitutions, the chief executive has the power to appoint the highest-ranking judges. However much it may be denied, it is highly unlikely that such appointments are made with no consideration of the political beliefs of such appointees or that judges who owe their appointments in part to their own expressed values will not act upon them when given the chance. When legislators make laws that later executives deplore, and jurists share the opinions of those executives, the matter is likely to find its way to court and the court to find its way to rule on the "correct" side, setting aside the will of the legislators. It doesn't always happen. But it doesn't always *not* happen either.

LAWMAKING BY POLITICAL PARTIES

Making laws is hard work. The issues are difficult, the solutions hard to find, the reconciliation of conflicting interests tricky to achieve. Yet some legislators appear to get their work done in remarkable harmony, even in unanimity, and are themselves not well-known public figures (or are far better known for their performance in other roles in the political system). In such cases, it is very likely that laws are being written, but not made, in the legislature.

In such cases, where the legislature is obviously merely rubber stamping decisions made elsewhere, the problem is to find out where the lawmaking power truly resides. The first place to look, as the preceding discussion suggests, is in the executive offices. Often enough the search can end right there. Sometimes, however, the chief executives themselves are simply carrying out the wishes of another powerful body, the ruling political party.

At first glance, it may seem inappropriate and even extraconstitutional (see Chapter 5) for a party to be the source of a nation's legislative agenda. But in fact a strong defense for *party government* (see Chapter 6) can be made. Suppose you lived in a system where political parties awarded their nominations only to candidates who were pledged to support the party program. You would have the advantage of knowing not only exactly what the candidates running in your constituency stood for but also what it would mean if the various candidates of a particular party won a majority of the seats in the legislature. It would mean that the program of that party would be carried out and that the business of government could be carried forward relatively smoothly, with a minimum of intraparliamentary squabbling and rancor. Furthermore, it would mean that if the program did not work to your satisfaction you could hold the elected representatives of that party, and the party itself, accountable, and you could vote for the candidates of a different party next time. What is wrong with that?

But party government *is,* at least in part, extraconstitutional government. It means that the decisions on new laws are made outside the legislature, in the conferences of the party as it decides on the content of its program. If the party itself is open and democratically organized, party government can mean the broadest possible democratic participation in the work of government—with citizens joining the local branches of the party they prefer and taking meaningful part in the formulation of issues and the nomination of loyal candidates. But if the party is closed and elitist, party government can make a mockery of any representative pretenses in a nation's constitutional system. Effective power will be exercised by an unelected few behind closed doors at party headquarters rather than by the elected many in the open forum of a legislative body. It all depends on the nature of the party itself.

The danger of nonrepresentative and nonaccountable party government is clearly greatest in single-party systems. In such systems, still found in the remaining Communist states (e.g., China, Cuba, Vietnam), key decisions on new legislation are made in the top ruling body of the party. Although the members of that body are formally elected by the second-highest party body, the Central Committee, a narrow elite normally controls the elections and the flow of power is definitely from the top down. Lower-level organisms of the party serve to educate party members about the necessity and desirability of the new policies, not to discover and reflect popular opinion, and the members in turn play the same educational role in the population at large.[43] The laws thus made may or may not be in the interests of the people governed, but they are certainly not made *by* those people.

SUMMARY AND CONCLUSION

Oliver Wendell Holmes once said, "When I think of the law, I see a princess mightier than she who once wrought at Bayeux, eternally weaving into her web dim figures of the ever-lengthening past—figures too dim to be noticed by the idle, too symbolic to be interpreted except by her pupils, but to the discerning eye disclosing every painful step and every world-shaking contest by which mankind has worked and fought its way from savage isolation to organic social life." [44]

As Justice Holmes's compelling imagery suggests, the law never exists *ab ovo* (a useful Latin term meaning "from the egg"—that is, as if with no other beginning) but is made—and remade—in all kinds of places, for all kinds of purposes. Furthermore, contrary to Holmes (who was, after all, making an address to a bar association dinner and was not above flattering his auditors), we have seen that it is not always made by those with the grace and authority of mighty princesses, nor by those who are constitutionally responsible, nor even by those who are responsive to the needs of ordinary citizens.

We have also seen that even when the lawmaking function is exercised predominantly in representative legislatures designed for that purpose, the exact division of labor is likely to vary. There may be one or two houses, specialized or nonspecialized committees, and a host of customs and mores unique to each nation to determine what laws can be made, how, and by whom.

In all probability, however, the right to make a nation's laws will not be held exclusively by the legislature but will be shared—to a greater or lesser extent—with others outside that body. The executive almost always plays a role in making as well as executing the law, and judges, party leaders, religious authorities, corporation heads, and military chiefs of staff may also join the work of lawmaking when the circumstances make it possible for them to do so.

Furthermore, when legislative power is shared with the executive, the balance of power between the two branches differs according to whether it is a democratic or a nondemocratic system. In a democratic system, it makes a great deal of difference whether we are talking about a parliamentary system, where power may be shared fairly equally; a presidential system, where power is likely to shift back and forth between the two; or a presidential-parliamentary system, where the executive tends to take and keep the upper hand. In all three such systems the question of who shall make the law is decided in part permanently and deliberately, mandated by constitutional provision, and in part temporarily and almost accidentally, as legislators delegate others to perform tasks that were originally theirs—or simply allow such powers to drift into others' hands. In nondemocratic systems, on the other hand, legislators may share the right to make a nation's laws reluctantly and resignedly—or even give up such rights altogether—when an autocratic or oligarchic executive forcibly usurps powers that do not constitutionally belong to that branch.

In pointing out how active a role the executive plays in the making of laws, we have already had quite a bit to say about the executive powers of governments. It is time now to focus directly on that subject. Laws mean little or nothing until someone carries them out. What does it mean to execute the law? The next chapter will be an attempt to answer that question.

QUESTIONS TO CONSIDER

1. What is one of the laws that has been passed in your country in the past year? What is one of the rules of your university or college?
2. What seems to you to be the most important difference between the parliamentary and the presidential systems of making laws? What is the most important advantage each offers as a system of governance?
3. What do you think: Should representatives act independently on the basis of what they personally believe to be correct principles or attempt to carry out the will of constituents even when it runs contrary to those principles?
4. How (specifically) is democracy endangered when lawmaking powers are delegated to or assumed by those not constitutionally responsible for that function? Give an example.

SELECTED READINGS

Blondel, Jean and Ferdinand Muller-Rommel, eds. *Cabinets in Eastern Europe* (New York: Palgrave, 2001). A comparative study of the origins, structure, composition, and activities of cabinets in Eastern Europe since the fall of communism.

Bond, Jon R. and Richard Fleischer, eds. *Polarized Politics: Congress and the President in a Partisan Era* (Washington, D.C.: Congressional Quarterly Press, 2000). Considers how the recent rise in partisan politics has affected congressional-presidential relations. Topics include presidential agenda setting in Congress and lawmaking in a partisan era.

Hickock, Eugene W., Jr. and Gary L. McDowell. *Justice vs Law: Courts and Politics in American Society* (New York: Free Press, 1993). The authors argue that controversial policy issues that should be addressed by Congress are being left to the U.S. Supreme Court to decide.

Laver, Michael and Kenneth A. Shepsle. *Making and Breaking Governments: Cabinets and Legislatures in Parliamentary Democracies* (New York: Cambridge University Press, 1996). A highly theoretical study of how parties create new governments in parliamentary systems and either maintain them in office or replace them.

Rhodes, R. A. W. and Patrick Dunleavy. *Prime Minister, Cabinet and Core Executive* (New York: St. Martin's Press, 1995). An introduction to the roles of the prime minister and the cabinet in British government.

Spitzer, Robert J. *President and Congress: Executive Hegemony at the Crossroads of American Government* (New York: McGraw-Hill, 1993). A historical study of the relationship between presidents and Congress, with a focus on the formation of policy and legislation.

Waldman, Steven. *The Bill: How Legislation Really Becomes Law: A Case Study of the National Ser-* *vice Bill* (New York: Penguin Books, 1995). A behind-the-scenes account of a bill's "inhospitable journey" through the maze of government.

Westlake, Martin. *A Modern Guide to the European Parliament* (London: Pinter Publishers, 1994). An in-depth study of the European Parliament and the changes it has undergone as a result of the ratification of the Maastricht Treaty.

WEB SITES OF INTEREST

1. Governments on the WWW
   http://www.gksoft.com/govt/en/
   Offers links to governmental sites on the Web. Includes institutions of the legislative branch as well as other government-related institutions.

2. Inter-Parliamentary Union
   http://www.ipu.org/
   The Union is the international organization of parliaments of sovereign states, established in 1889 and now working for "the firm establishment of representative democracy." The site lists all parliamentary Web sites and offers information and research on parliamentary democracy.

NOTES

1. National Association of State Boards of Education, "Title IX after 25 Years," *NASBE Policy Update 5*, no. 16, (October 1997), and Leslie Gladstone and Gary Galemore, "Sex Discrimination in Education: Overview of Title IX," *CRS Report for Congress 97–954 GOV,* Congressional Research Service, 14 Jan. 1998.

2. Abdo Baaklini, Guilain Denoeux, and Robert Springborg, *Legislative Politics in the Arab World* (Boulder, Colo: Lynne Rienner, 1999), p. 12.

3. Deborah Sontag, "Flare-Up of Mid-East Violence Continues: Sharon Pushes Effort for a Unity Coalition with the Labor Party," *New York Times,* 12 Feb. 2001, A12; "Kost Effective," *The Economist* (18 Oct. 2000): 31.

4. Michael Laver and Kenneth A. Shepsle, "Government Accountability in Parliamentary Democracy," in Adam Przeworski, Susan C. Stokes, and Bernard Manin, eds., *Democracy, Accountability and Representation* (Cambridge, U.K.: Cambridge University Press, 1999), p. 280.

5. *International Herald Tribune,* 1 Feb. 1996, 3; 2 Feb. 1996, 1, 11; 12 Feb. 1996, A3; 16 Feb. 1996, 5.

6. For a more comprehensive examination of the issue of judicial independence in Britain, see Dennis Kavanagh, *British Politics: Continuities and Change,* 2nd ed. (Oxford, U.K.: Oxford University Press, 1990), pp. 280–81.

7. "A cabinet is a combining committee, a *hyphen* which joins, a *buckle* which fastens, the legislative part of the state to the executive part of the state." Walter Bagehot, *The English Constitution* (London: Oxford University Press, 1867), p. 12. Italics in original.

8. In a comparative study of several presidential and quasi-presidential systems, Matthew Soberg Shugart has shown that the presidents' parties share of legislative seats tends to be reduced after midterm elections and in systems where electoral laws permit legislative candidates to function independently of their parties (that is, are "localizing rather than nationalizing"). "The Electoral Cycle and Institutional Sources of Divided Presidential Government," *American Political Science Review* 89, no. 2 (June 1995): 327–44.

9. "The Case for a US Parliament? American Politics in Comparative Perspective." Paper presented at

the annual meetings of the American Political Science Association, Atlanta, Ga., September 2–5, 1999.

10. The U.S. presidential system has an intermediate step: the Electoral College. Originally each state's voters chose electors, who met and chose the president. Technically, the system remains the same today, except that it is now understood (and in many states, mandated by law) that the electors will all vote for the candidate who won the majority of that state's popular vote.

11. "Political Leaders Make No Progress on a Budget Deal," *New York Times*, 18 Dec. 1995, 1.

12. For a definition of the term *parliamentary presidency*, and an interesting discussion of the type, see Elijah Ben-Zion Kaminsky, "On the Comparison of Presidential and Parliamentary Governments," *Presidential Studies Quarterly* 27, no. 2 (Spring 1997): 221–27.

13. *Le Monde*, 4 April 1992, 1–9. The pacification no doubt worked in part because Cresson, the first woman prime minister in the history of France, was intensely unpopular. The French argue to this day how much that unpopularity was simply the result of her gender; this observer had no trouble at all in being sure the answer was, "A lot."

14. Colette Ysmal, "French Political Parties: A State Within the State," in John Kenneth White and Philip John Davies, eds., *Political Parties and the Collapse of the Old Orders* (New York: State University of New York Press, 1998), pp. 33–54.

15. In one such move, Bush included China in the list of nations exempted from new and higher tariffs on steel imports. See Mike Allen and Steven Pearlstein, "Bush Settles on Tariff for Steel Imports," *Washington Post*, 5 March 2002, A-1. See also "Human Rights and Business as Usual," *The Progressive* (August 1998): 8.

16. Erik Eckholm, "China, With an Eye on Critics, Says It Will Ratify Rights Pact," *New York Times*, 23 Jan. 2001, A3.

17. For a good discussion of Burke's interpretation of interests, see "Representing Unattached Interests: Burke," chap. 8 in Hannah Pitkin, *The Concept of Representation* (Berkeley: University of California Press, 1967), pp. 168–89.

18. Ibid., p. 221.

19. For an interesting recent discussion of these issues, see Laver and Shepsle, op. cit.

20. "The Swedish Ombudsmen," *Fact Sheets on Sweden*, The Swedish Institute, January 2000.

21. This is also the sense of the word behind the phrase *in camera*, referring to proceedings of legislative or judicial bodies held in secrecy.

22. Frederick C. Barghoorn and Thomas F. Remington, *Politics in the USSR* (Boston: Little, Brown, 1986), p. 314.

23. *Time* (23 Dec. 1991): 19–22; *Current Digest of the Soviet Press* 43, no. 51 (22 Jan. 1992): 2–6.

24. Thomas E. Weisskopf, "Yeltsin's Russia: Bleak Prospects for Democracy and Prosperity," *Dollars and Sense* (March–April 1994): 22–25, and Vladimir Orlov, "Government Makeover Boosts Chernomyrdin's Role," *Current Digest of the Post-Soviet Press* 46, no. 2 (9 Feb. 1994): 16.

25. Peter Rutland, "A Flawed Democracy," *Current History* 97, no. 621 (Oct. 1998): 313–18; John M. Kramer, "The Politics of Corruption," *Current History* 97, no. 621 (Oct. 1998): 329–34.

26. Lizette Alvarez, "Honoring Pledge, the G.O.P. Replaces 13 House Leaders," *New York Times*, 5 Jan. 2001, A1, A15.

27. Adam Clymer, "Special Counsel Will Investigate Ethics Case Affecting Gingrich," *New York Times*, 7 Dec. 1995, 1; Richard E. Cohen, "Crackup of the Committees," *National Journal* 31, no. 31 (31 July 1999): 2210–17; Karen Foerstel with Alan K. Ota, "Early Grief for GOP Leaders in New Committee Rules," *CQ Weekly* (6 Jan. 2001): 10–20.

28. Kavanaugh, op. cit., pp. 219–20.

29. Malcolm Shaw, "Committees in Legislatures," in Philip Norton, *Legislatures* (Oxford, U.K.: Oxford University Press, 1990), pp. 237–67.

30. William Bradford Reynolds, "Etiquette for the Senate," *New York Times*, 12 Jan. 2001, A23, and Anthony Lewis, "Perversion of the Process," *New York Times*, 13 Jan. 2001, A31.

31. Maxwell A. Cameron, "Self Coups: Peru, Guatemala and Russia," *Journal of Democracy* 9, no. 1 (1998): 125, 239; Cynthia McClintock, "Peru's Fujimoro: A Caudillo Derails Democracy," *Current History* (March 1993): 112–19.

32. Ibid.

33. Richard L. Millett, "Central America's Enduring Conflicts," *Current History* (March 1994): 124–28, and Maxwell A. Cameron, op. cit.

34. *New York Times,* 2 March 1991, A3.

35. *Washington Post,* 14 Jan. 1992, A16.

36. Bruce Baker, "The Class of 1990: How Have the Autocratic Leaders of Sub-Saharan Africa Fared under Democratization?" *Third World Quarterly* 19, no. 1 (1998): 115–27.

37. Cameron Duodu, "Côte d'Ivoire Deposes a Despot," *World Press Review* (January 2001): 33.

38. Harold Hongju Koh, *The National Security Constitution: Sharing Power After the Iran-Contra Affair* (New Haven, Conn.: Yale University Press, 1990); see especially chap. 2, "Recognizing the Pattern of History," pp. 38–64.

39. Quoted by Michael Wines, "Russia's Latest Dictator Goes by the Name of Law," *New York Times,* 21 Jan. 2001, 3.

40. Linda Greenhouse, "Court Rules That Governments Can't Outlaw Type of Abortion," *New York Times,* 29 June 2000, A1, A20; Joan Biskupic, "Pennsylvania Case Portends New Attack on Abortion," *Congressional Quarterly Weekly Report* 50, no. 4 (25 January 1992): 169–71.

41. Akira Miyoshi, "The Diet in Japan," in Philip Norton and Nizam Ahmed, eds., *Parliaments in Asia* (London: Frank Cass, 1999), pp. 83–102.

42. For a good discussion of the Constitutional Council, see William Safran, *The French Polity,* 4th ed. (White Plains, N.Y.: Longman, 1995), pp. 216–20.

43. For an argument that single-party government creates a "party deficit" and thereby seriously weakens prospects for democratization, see Javier Corrales, "Strong Societies, Weak Parties: Regime Change in Cuba and Venezuela in the 1950s and Today," *Latin American Politics and Society* 43, no. 2 (Summer 2001): 81–113.

44. Oliver Wendell Holmes, "The Law," an address before the Suffolk Bar Association Dinner, 5 Feb. 1885. Reprinted in *Collected Legal Papers* (New York: Peter Smith, 1952), p. 27. "She who once wrought at Bayeux" refers to Joan of Arc.

CHAPTER 9

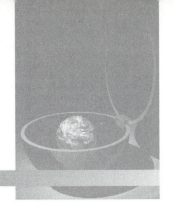

Making Government Work:
Executives and Bureaucrats

Here you are, reading this book, trying to get caught up on your homework. Suddenly it occurs to you (and not for the first time, either): I'd like to stop all this studying and start doing. I'd like to be active in politics and get into government. And I'd like to be a real leader, too, not just one of those bureaucrats.

Well, why not? But let's be practical. Let's think this thing through. So take a piece of paper. First, jot down the steps you might take to get into a position of political leadership. Second, make a list of what you think your duties will be once you have arrived at the top.

Now let's give a little more thought to those poor despised bureaucrats. After all, it could just happen that you might never make it to the presidency, might even find yourself in a bureaucratic job. Isn't that a terrible thought? After all, what did any bureaucrat ever do for you?

Better turn that piece of paper over and add a few more notes. First, get it out of your system: Write down three bad things that never would have happened to you (or a friend or a relative) if it hadn't been for "one of those bureaucrats." Now for the hard part. Write down three good things that never would have happened *for* you (or a friend or a relative) if it hadn't been for "one of those bureaucrats." And, finally, the *really* hard part: Can you think of anything good—for a *polity*—about having a bureaucracy? Put that piece of paper in a safe place, please. And then do me one more favor—read this chapter before you hit the campaign trail.

BECOMING A LEADER

There are four main ways to become a leader: by ascription, by appointment, by election, and by force. Although they may be combined in actual practice, we will look at each separately.

Ascription

In some societies the route to power is open only to those who possess certain characteristics. If they are believed to have those characteristics (that is, if those characteristics are *ascribed* to them), they may become leaders; if not, they cannot. In the most extreme case, the characteristic is something one—and only one—person has by birth. The system of hereditary monarchy, which ensures that only one person can be "next in line," is the most obvious example; there are still over thirty reigning monarchs in the world (see Table 9.1), and almost all are the sons and daughters of former reigning monarchs. In 1999–2000 King Abdallah II of Jordan, King Salahuddin Abdul Aziz Shah of Malaysia, and Grand Duke Henri of Luxembourg all succeeded their fathers.[1] Of course not all "reigning monarchs" really rule, as

TABLE 9.1
Ascriptive Power:
Monarchs in the
Modern World

Bahrain	Sheikh Hamad ibn Isa Al Khalifah (since 1999)
Belgium	King Albert II (1993)
Bhutan	The Druk Gyalpo Jigme Singhye Wangchuk, King of Bhutan (1972)
Brunei	H. M. Sultan Haji Hassanal Bolkiah (1968)
Cambodia	Norodom Sihanouk (1993)
Denmark	Queen Margrethe II (1972)
Great Britain	Queen Elizabeth II (1952)
Japan	Emperor Akihito (1989)
Jordan	King Abdullah II (1999)
Kuwait	Sheikh Jaber al-Ahmad al-Jaber al-Sabah (1977)
Liechtenstein	Hans-Adam II (1989)
Lesotho	King Letsie III (1990)
Luxembourg	Grand Duke Henri (2000)
Malaysia	King Salahuddin Abdul Aziz Shah (1999)
Monaco	Prince Rainier III (1949)
Morocco	King Muhammad VI (1999)
Nepal	King Gyanendra Bir Bikram Shah Deva (2001)
Netherlands	Queen Beatrix Wilhemina Armgard (1980)
Norway	King Harald (1991)
Oman	Sultan Qaboos bin Said (1970)
Qatar	Sheikh Hamad ibn Khalifah Al Thani (1995)
Saudi Arabia	King Fahd ibn Abdul Aziz (1982)
Spain	King Juan Carlos I (1975)
Swaziland	King Mswati III (1986)
Sweden	King Carl XVI Gustav (1973)
Thailand	King Bhumibol Adulyadej (1946)
Tonga	King Taufa'Ahau Tupou IV (1965)

Source: http://www.rulers.org and http://www.infoplease/com/ipa/A0775675.html.

we have seen in Chapter 8. Indeed, many question whether an ascriptive monarchy is appropriate at all in parliamentary democracies where the important decisions are all made by elected representatives.[2]

Furthermore, genuine ascription can take place in presidential systems as well as monarchies. When 29-year-old Joseph Kabila was sworn in as the president of the Congo in January 2001 just ten days after his father, Laurent Kabila, was assassinated, he was unknown to most of his countrymen, having been raised and educated in Tanzania. He was fluent in English and Swahili but not in the languages of the western Congo or in French, still the dominant official language in the country. No election was held. But he *was* the son of the dead president.[3]

Talcott Parsons and Edward Shils, who brought the word into common political science usage, use the term *ascription* more broadly, defining it as a means of assigning people to leadership positions (as well as giving them other forms of differential treatment) on the basis of their attributes (including the groups they belong to and the wealth they possess) rather than on the basis of anything they have accomplished or might accomplish in the future.[4]

As Parsons and Shils point out, all polities—even the most democratic—

specify and abide by some measure of ascription. Age is the obvious example. Despite biblical injunction and the occasional coronation of an infant, no people really allows a little child to lead them.[5] Criteria of race, ethnicity, sex, and geographic community are also very common, even in systems that claim otherwise. Write to me when the United States chooses an Asian woman from the small state of Delaware as its president and I will happily eat my words.

As all this suggests, ascriptive criteria in most cases simply narrow the pool of possible leaders. Moving into a leadership role is still likely to depend on being appointed, being elected, or exercising force.

Appointment

Although some form of election, however rigged or manipulated it may be, is employed in choosing the top leadership of almost every nation, nearly every system fills a large number of its lesser leadership positions by appointment. When this happens, some of the interesting questions are: What kinds of positions are filled by appointment? Who gets to do the appointing? What motivates the appointing party to appoint one person rather than another?

■ Positions Filled by Appointment.
A great deal of variation is found from one polity to the next on the kinds of positions that are filled by appointed officials, but as a general rule we may say that the more specialized the position—that is, the more the job in question requires a high degree of a limited kind of expertise—the more likely it will be filled by appointment rather than by election. The voters of the German state of Hesse may be competent enough to choose their chief executive, the Ministerpräsident, but the Hessian minister of finance must be chosen—or so the reasoning goes in the selection of specialists across the globe—far from the heat of electoral competition, and as much as possible on the basis of expertise rather than personal attractiveness or other characteristics.[6]

There is another rule for determining which positions will be filled by appointment: The more autocratic the regime, the greater the use of the appointment power. The reason for this is obvious; one of the best ways to stay in power is to control who works for you and to make sure they understand to whom they owe their jobs. It is thus not surprising that Jerry Rawlings, who took over the government of Ghana twice by military coup, kept the right to appoint high-ranking members of the civil and police services for himself. Nor are leaders of ostensibly democratic regimes immune to the temptation to enhance their power by using the power of appointment to the utmost. When Vladimir Meciar, head of the Movement for a Democratic

Slovakia, managed to return to the position of prime minister in Slovakia in 1994 after having been removed earlier in the year, he quickly made sure his own supporters were put in charge of all the major appointive offices (including the Supreme and Constitutional Courts).[7]

■ **Who Appoints?**   The simple answer to this question is that *political appointments* are made by those already in leadership positions. As usual, the simple answer is a little bit too simple. In the first place, sometimes the appointment is preordained by law and need not be made by anyone. This is the case when the law states that people who occupy one position are *ex officio* (that is, owing to the office) entitled to occupy another position. The governor of the state of California is always a member of the Board of Regents of the University of California. The voters elect the governor; the fact of being governor secures the incumbent appointment to the Board of Regents.

And even when appointments are made by other leaders rather than by force of law, the answer to the question "Who appoints?" is not always an easy one. It is often the case that more than one leader will be involved in the making—or the blocking—of a major appointment. Watching U.S. presidents anxiously awaiting senatorial confirmation of their choices for their cabinet or for Supreme Court vacancies gives us a recurrent example of appointments that require the concurrence of many individuals beyond the person whose job it is to suggest a nominee.[8]

■ **Motives Guiding Appointments.**   Suppose you have just been elected governor of your state and you have several important appointments to make when you assume office. While the world waits, an inquiring reporter asks you what motives will guide you in your choices. Having just won an election, you are probably smart enough to answer, "I am simply looking for the most capable man or woman to fill every single post." But both you and the reporter know full well there is more to it than that.

This is not to say, however, that finding qualified persons is of no concern to the leader with the power to appoint other leaders. Most elected or appointed officials have agendas they believe in and want the best possible people to help them carry them out. Furthermore, how well or how badly one's appointees perform inevitably reflects on one's own record in office.

But other motives are also at work. We have already considered the motive of enhancing one's own control by filling appointive posts with as many supporters as possible. Appointing a particular person to high position may also send a special signal regarding what the executive intends to have happen next. The appointment by the British of Chris Patten, a "political heavyweight" with the personal backing of Prime Minister John Major, to be governor of Hong Kong shortly before the 1997 deadline for the return of that colony to Chinese control, was seen as a way to send a strong message to the Chinese government regarding the British determination to protect its own interests during the transition.[9]

The power to appoint is also the power to reward. Appointments frequently go to those who have worked hard (or contributed heavily) to secure the election of the officeholder. For many years the office of postmaster general in the United States traditionally went to the chairman of the party whose nominee won the presidency. Ambassadorships are often meted out to the close friends and associates of the chief executive—or to *their* friends and associates. When Pamela Harriman was appointed ambassador to France in 1993, the widow of Governor Averell Harriman of New York owed the honor partly to her reputation as someone who "knew and understood the inner workings of government," but her principal qualification was clearly her status as "the doyenne of Democratic politics and [as] a leading fund-raiser and donor."[10]

Lower-level posts are also open to loyal supporters—the bureaucracies of Italy and Israel are known to be particularly open to political appointment. In the United States, power over patronage has shifted away from the parties and into the White House Office of Presidential Personnel (OPP). This office began with one person in the Truman administration and grew to over 100 persons under the Clinton administration. It now recruits for the cabinet and subcabinet, leaders of independent agencies, and regulatory commissioners, a total of well over one thousand positions. This powerful office has a difficult assignment; according to one of its chiefs ". . . being the head of presidential personnel is like being a traffic cop on a four-lane freeway. You have these Mack trucks bearing down on you at sixty miles an hour. They might be influential congressmen, senators, state committee chairmen, heads of special interest groups and lobbyists, friends of the president, all saying, 'I want Billy Smith to get that job.' "[11]

Today the idea of using an appointment to reward a supporter evokes a mixed response. Having witnessed a series of scandals (ranging from Watergate to Whitewatergate) in the United States, we are only too well aware that the appointment of "cronies" can lead to corruption and inefficiency. Nevertheless, a strong argument can be made that rewarding a supporter with an appointment can lead to good government, *provided that* the appointee meets certain minimal standards of qualification. To test the soundness of this argument, put yourself in the position of the committed supporter. Suppose you have worked long and hard for a candidate and a cause that you believe in with all your heart. You know your work has been good and could be even better in the future. Your candidate wins, and there is an opening that fits your capabilities perfectly. But it does not go to you; it goes to someone from out of state, with more years of education and related experience than you have, but whom you know to be totally uninterested in either the cause or the candidate—someone who is merely looking for the best-paying job. Now who do you suppose would really do better work?

In fact, the answer to that question—even when one is personally involved—may still be uncertain. The point is simply that supporters *may* have qualities of loyalty, trust, and commitment that will make their on-the-job performance more impressive than that of the otherwise better-qualified stranger, and that giving patronage appointments for those reasons to people who have proved their devotion should not be deplored automatically by people who do not know the circumstances of the case.

Finally, an appointment may well be motivated by the desire to co-opt someone whose support one seeks but does not yet have. Co-optation is sometimes used on erstwhile enemies, as when Nelson Mandela, the former president of South Africa, appointed several members of the opposition party to his cabinet, an example followed by his successor Thabo Mbeki in 1999.[12] Former Mexican President Ernesto Zedillo followed a similar strategy in 1995, but his successor, Vincente Fox, who came to office in December 2000, did not. Rather than appoint members of the ousted party, Fox reached out to important business figures in forming his cabinet, reminding us that co-optation can also be extended to those who are neither enemies nor politicians.[13]

One of the advantages—for the appointing officer, not for the appointee—of placing someone in office by appointment is that the process often works both ways: The person appointed can also be removed. When José Lutzenberger, an outspoken spokesperson for environmental causes in Brazil, became a liability—"his outspokenness enraged conservatives and his distaste for administration alienated environmentalists"—he was dismissed from his post as secretary of the environment by President Fernando Collor de Mello just a few weeks before the United Nations Conference on Environment and Development was held in Rio de Janeiro in June 1992.[14]

Election to Office

We have already given some consideration in Chapter 4 to the different rules and regulations that govern voting throughout the world, but our focus then was on what these differences meant to individual participation in the political life of a nation. In Chapter 6 we looked at elections again, this time focusing on political parties and the media. Here our concern is with election as a means of achieving a position of leadership and with how the nature of different electoral systems influence the quality of leadership as well as the quality of citizenship throughout the human polity.

The best way to understand how the circumstances surrounding elections influence the quality of leadership is to imagine yourself a candidate in various systems. Getting elected is not just a matter of getting the most votes.

Write-in candidacies are seldom allowed, and where permitted they are seldom successful. You must get on the ballot to have a good chance of becoming a leader through the electoral process. This usually means that you must meet certain personal standards of age and residency. It may very well mean that you must have been nominated by an officially recognized political party.

Winning a party's nomination means going through a completely separate battle for leadership status before you can even think about competing for government office. If who gets the nomination is controlled by a primary election, your job is to win votes at the polls. But if the party itself decides who its candidate will be—as is the case in most political systems, the American primary election being an exception—then winning the nomination usually means building a record of loyalty to the party and of hard work on its behalf. The party may expect you to have shown you can muster an adequate campaign fund and a personal organization of devoted followers—or perhaps such assets will be seen as liabilities, suggestive of excessive pride and independence. Then there are personal characteristics to consider. Winning the nomination is very likely to mean being a member of the gender, the religious group, and the ethnic group your party is looking for this year. It may mean having the right kind of family life as well as being a good speaker and reasonably attractive to look at. Not to mention being smart enough, educated enough, tough enough, nice enough—and well balanced enough —to endure the ordeals of candidacy without having a nervous breakdown.

Or perhaps you are seeking a nonpartisan post. More than 50 percent of elected officials in the United States have gained their posts through nonpartisan elections—that is, elections in which parties are not allowed to participate. Such elections are particularly common at the local level. In such a case you may still have to show support by presenting a petition signed by a minimum number of your fellow citizens who are willing to assert that the world (or at least Fairview City) will be a better place if you are allowed to run for office. To become a candidate, you must be able to get those signatures. In most countries you must also be able to pay a filing fee, which may or may not be refundable if you win a certain percentage of the vote.

The question of money is, of course, another major consideration. Campaigns are always costly, no matter where they take place. In some systems, those costs are covered, wholly or in part, by the government. In others, the parties are able to cover a major portion of their candidates' expenses. Private interests may fill a candidate's coffers, but as we have seen, they are likely to expect something in return.

As should be clear by now, the preliminary stages of the electoral struggle are likely to eliminate vast numbers of able potential leaders from waging, much less winning, the battle for votes. But let us say that you have nonetheless managed to get on the ballot and amass the funds to run an adequate campaign. At this point, the features of the electoral system we discussed in

Chapter 4 are likely to make themselves felt. If you are campaigning in a system in which extensive personal and impersonal restrictions are placed on the right to vote, you will have to be able to fit your appeal to the relatively narrow interests of the voting population. On the other hand, if you are campaigning in a large and heterogeneous system in which nearly every adult has the right to register and vote, you must be the kind of candidate who can find and take positions with a broad appeal and who is willing to let more divisive issues fall by the wayside.

Similarly, it makes a difference whether you are running in a single-member constituency or under a system of proportional representation (see Chapter 4). If you are one of several representatives to be chosen in your district and the candidate of one party among many, you will be busy calculating what percentage of the vote you or your party will have to win for you to gain office. If you are running in a single-member district, you will want to know if there are provisions for a runoff, and if so, what it will take for you to get into that runoff.

Finally, a feature of the electoral system that can have an overwhelming impact on the quality and performance of elected leaders is the extent to which the system is—and is seen to be—an honest one. Suspicions of dishonest ballot counting hit home in the United States in the fall of 2000, but have tarnished elections throughout the world: Recent examples include Egypt, Peru, Morocco, and Indonesia.

In short, the nature of the electoral system influences the calculations the candidate will make, the kind of campaign he or she will wage, and—given varying abilities to run the necessary kind of campaign—the quality of the leaders who are ultimately chosen.

Force

The reasons that have been given for taking power by force—or for trying to do so—are many and varied; but prime among them, even though rarely mentioned, is likely to be the belief that other routes to leadership are closed. Political systems that pose excessively narrow ascriptive criteria for the pool of potential leaders, that fail to use the powers of appointment to maintain and broaden support, that keep large numbers of voting-age adults off the electoral rolls, or that manipulate election results to suit the purposes of incumbent leaders are clearly more likely than others to be considered illegitimate and thus deserving of overthrow by force.

But not all assassinations, coups d'état, and revolutions have been motivated solely by the ambitions of those who ended up taking power. Sometimes the new leader does not take part in the act of force at all but simply finds a way to turn a complex situation to his or her advantage and then, once in power, shows little sign of sharing the values of those who accomplished the forceful overthrow of the previous government. William Shake-speare's characterization of Mark Antony—as a bystander who publicly laments the murder of Julius Caesar by others while calculating how to turn it to his own advantage—had more than one real-life parallel in the twenti-eth century.[15]

Indeed, assassinating a leader can be just one way to ensure that one's own life will be forfeit and that the dead leader's successor will be someone ready to carry out the existing program. U.S. President Lyndon Johnson, Egyptian President Hosni Mubarak, and Nigerian Supreme Military Com-mander Olusegun Obasanjo all came to power as a result of the murderous acts of others, and all made every effort—at least at first—to carry on the plans of the leaders they replaced. Any innocent successor who shows signs of doing otherwise is likely to be in serious trouble—remember that Andrew Johnson, who came to power when Abraham Lincoln was assassinated and who then began to take a softer line with the defeated South than Lincoln's supporters believed their fallen hero would have done, was the first president to be impeached by the U.S. House of Representatives. The principle applies to leaders in the other branches of government as well. When the Mafia crime syndicate had a well-known Sicilian judge assassinated in 1992 for his unrelenting efforts to bring its leaders to trial and imprisonment, the result was to catalyze anti-Mafia sentiment among the general population of that beleaguered Italian island as never before.[16]

A successful coup d'état or revolution (revolution provokes a far more ex-tensive change than a coup, which is largely confined to changing the top leadership of a regime) is a more effective means of ensuring that leadership will be transferred into sympathetic hands, if not into those that held the gun. Political coups are led by politicians of all political persuasions: Fidel Castro of Cuba, the Ayatollah Ruholla Khomeini of Iran, and Vaclav Havel of the Czech Republic all came to power as the result of successful coups d'état or revolutions. In 1992, the Algerian military backed a coup designed to prevent a Muslim fundamentalist takeover of the democratic govern-ment—but that takeover would have been via democratic elections.[17]

However, coups d'état do not always produce the expected results. One of the most remarkable stories of achieving power by force can be found in the career of Boris Yeltsin, president of the Russian Federated Republic in the new Commonwealth of Independent States during the late 1990s. The force that brought Yeltsin to power was not his; it was, in fact, exercised by per-sons in deep opposition to everything he stood for. But when Yeltsin and his supporters succeeded in rousing sufficient public support to doom the efforts of rightwing plotters to overthrow the government of then Soviet President Mikhail S. Gorbachev, it was he who proved the hero of the day and the ul-timate winner of power, not the visibly shaken Gorbachev, whose inability to predict and prevent his own arrest by the rebels led to the further dimin-ishment of his already declining reputation. In the unraveling of the coup, the government *did* fall, but not into the hands of those who had instigated it.[18]

Wars are seldom fought simply to place certain people in power, but it is not unusual for them to be waged to remove an existing leadership, as the first step to ensuring a more favorable policy toward the invading nation. This was, of course, a principal motive behind the decision of the United States to invade Afghanistan in 2001, and of Russia in putting down revolutionary insurrection in the rebellious region of Chechnya.[19] Iran invaded Iraq in the summer of 1982 with the avowed purpose of "liberating" that nation from the "infidel" rule of President Saddam Hussein, and many believed—erroneously, as it proved—that the United States would not end its intervention in Arab politics during the Gulf War of 1991 until it had finished what Iran had left undone.[20]

In some situations the threat of force is sufficient to change the occupants of leadership roles. A minimum of force was exercised in the ouster of Ferdinand Marcos from the presidency of the Philippines in 1986; the knowledge that the U.S. government expected him to leave and was ready to add its military might to the limited arms of his local opposition if necessary was quite sufficient to persuade the corrupt and unpopular Marcos to depart. Fifteen years later, in January 2001, the military simply made it clear that it would no longer back another Philippine leader, Joseph Estrada, and that defection, plus the well-known approval of the United States, was sufficient to place Gloria Macapagal Arroyo in office, Estrada's loud protests to the contrary.[21]

The departure of the Communist leaders of Eastern Europe was also accomplished in most cases by the threat rather than the exercise of violence against their persons, the 1989 Christmas Day execution of Romanian President Nicolae Ceausescu providing the noteworthy exception.

LEAVING POWER

It seems almost as difficult for some men and women to leave power as to take it. Of course, vacating a post of executive leadership may be so well regulated that there can be no question of when it is time to go. Or departure from office may be ruled by the vagaries of politics, but nonetheless controlled by forces outside the incumbent's power to control. However, sometimes the person or persons in power may find ways to cling to office long after a polity has deemed it is time for a change.

In the Normal Course of Events . . .

Modern democracies set fixed or maximum terms of office for incumbents, but things don't always work out as the constitution suggests they should, as the case of Argentina suggests. As the 1999 presidential elections approached, the economic situation was very bad, and getting worse, with un-

employment up to 18.6 percent, government borrowing on the rise, and drastic reductions in public spending. Social and industrial unrest was rampant and by the time Fernando de la Rua had won a decisive victory (48 percent of the vote in a multiparty system), Argentina has been reclassified by the World Bank as a severely indebted middle-income country. Ever more severe austerity measures were adopted, leading to increased unrest, but also to continued IMF support, albeit with very severe conditions. Public dismay grew, and a massive run on the banks in late November 2001 led the government to clamp down on withdrawals and the IMF to hold back the next loan, which led in turn to looting and rioting that caused the loss of twenty-eight lives, plus hundreds injured, thousands arrested. On December 20 President de la Rua resigned; after a brief interim presidency, Eduardo Duhalde was appointed by Congress on January 1, 2002, to serve out the remainder of de la Rua's term (due to expire in December 2003). The situation grew steadily worse: In April 2002 Duhalde ordered that all bank transactions simply be halted. Whether he would in fact be able to last in office another twenty months was by no means clear.[22]

On the other hand, overtly authoritarian systems may and often do have a simple way of settling the issue of departure. Although elections may be (and usually are) carefully rigged to ensure reelection of the current potentate, who is normally allowed to occupy power until death or retirement, a narrow elite (an *oligarchy*) watches over the situation, often engineers a transfer of power if this is deemed necessary, and, in any case, decides who

TABLE 9.2
Examples of Polities
Where Succession
Is Determined by
a Narrow Elite

Polity	Name of Office	Nature of Elite with Power to Determine Successor
China	premier	political
Iran	velayat faghih*	religious/political
North Korea	president	political
Turkey	president	military/political
Vatican	pope	religious
Zaire	president	political

*Velayat faghih means "religious leader." Under the new Iranian constitution, when it is time to choose a successor to this leader, a council of experts will have the choice of selecting a single leader or a council composed of three or five persons, to be called the Council of Leadership.

Sources: Arthur S. Banks, ed., *Political Handbook of the World* (New York: CSA Publications, 1991), p. 82, and *The Europa World Yearbook, 1995* (London: Europa Publications Limited, 1995). Reprinted with permission.

the successor shall be. This system was used throughout the history of the Soviet Union (the last time was on the death of Konstantin Chernenko in 1985, when the Politburo convened to choose Mikhail Gorbachev as his successor), and can even be used within a military junta: Upon the death of General Sani Abacha in Nigeria in 1998, the ruling junta decided easily enough on another general, Abdulsalam Abubakar.[23] The elite group may vote on the matter, may talk it over and make the choice by appointment, or may exercise force to place its nominee in office—and combinations of all three methods are entirely possible. Table 9.2 offers some examples of polities where a version of the oligarchic solution is used.

Reluctant Departures

When Calvin Coolidge told the reporters gathered for one of his rare press conferences, "I do not choose to run for president in 1928. There will be nothing more from this office today,"[24] he was not only setting a record for brevity of communication. He was also demonstrating that he was one of the very few people with a natural immunity to the dread disease of Caesarism, otherwise known as addiction to power.

Most men and women who achieve positions of great power find it difficult to relinquish that power. No one ever found it harder than Napoleon Bonaparte, who managed somehow to return from defeat and exile on the island of Elba to resume control of his empire; vanquished a second time at the Battle of Waterloo in 1815, he spent his remaining years on the yet more remote island of St. Helena plotting a third conquest of power; some say only murder (by a close associate in the pay of the new French government) was able to call a final halt to his fierce ambition.[25]

Even when leaders accept the necessity of passing on the duties of office to others, they still often seek to determine who their successors will be and to exercise continued control. The Mexican constitution limits the presidency to a single term, but for over seven decades the outgoing president, always the leader of the ruling Institutional Revolutionary Party (PRI), would point out his successor (a signal known as the *dedazo*) and that person was automatically assured of winning—a tradition broken only when the opposition National Action party (PAN) took the presidency in 2000.

Of course, sometimes even a designated successor proves disappointing; in that case, the former leader may try to find a way to return to power. Theodore Roosevelt, dismayed by the protectionist stance taken by his hand-picked successor, William Howard Taft, vainly sought to take back the U.S. presidency four years after leaving it by running as the candidate of the Progressive (Bull Moose) Party in the 1912 election.[26]

Once out of office, it is common for former leaders to expect to be consulted as elder statesmen and to work hard at their memoirs, hoping to influence the history that will be written of their regimes and thereby to maximize the continued power of the ideas they stood for, the laws they made, and the pacts they negotiated with the leaders of other nations. In an extreme case, former President Richard Nixon, discredited, disgraced, and ultimately forced from office by acts so heinous that only his successor's pardon prevented his being charged with criminal behavior, was able nevertheless to maintain a posture of some importance in the United States and international political arena after his resignation from the presidency.

This quite common reluctance to relinquish power can make for difficult problems when a healthy incumbent loses legitimacy in the eyes of the people (or those of the elite holding other posts of power). But every system has its way of saying: Enough! Oligarchic systems may use force or the threat thereof, parliamentary systems can employ the motion of censure, or motion of no confidence, and presidential systems can invoke the process of impeachment.

The parliamentary system for making the desired change is, on the whole, civilized and tidy, permitting as it does the removal of an unpopular prime minister without having to charge that leader with malfeasance in office. Under this system, being removed early on by a disappointed electorate is not pleasant, but carries with it a far lesser stigma than impeachment.

Impeachment: A Variation on Democratic Succession

Presidential systems, however, have no such civilized and tidy way of changing leadership ahead of time; the only recourse is impeachment, and the impeachment process is certainly not a tidy one, as Americans had occasion to see in 1998–1999. Of course the particular messiness of the Clinton impeachment was owing in large measure to the personal behavior of this president, his determination to lie about it openly, and his opponents' determination to make sure that what had been ill concealed became front page news day after day after day.

It was, in any case, a crash course in the impeachment process.[27] Impeachment, as most Americans now know (or at least did for a while) can be used in the United States to remove the president, vice president, and other federal civil officers found to have engaged in "treason, bribery, or other high crimes and misdemeanors." It is the House of Representatives that decides whether to impeach; if it does it must also vote "articles of impeachment" specifying the grounds upon which the impeachment is based, after which the matter goes to the Senate. The Senate decides whether to convict on each of the articles, by a two-thirds vote of those present.[28] In the history of the United States there have been fifteen impeachments, including two presidents, Andrew Johnson (1868) and Bill Clinton (1998), both acquitted by the Senate; eleven judges (seven of whom were convicted and removed from office); one senator (charges dismissed); and one Cabinet member (acquitted).[29]

Although the American media, feeding on the salacious nature of the case, made much of the Clinton impeachment process, when the dust eventually settled there was a general consensus that the lasting consequences for the presidency would be few, if only because public trust in government as a whole had already become quite low.[30] Nor was the current occupant weakened as much as might have been expected. If anything, titillating details and Republican overkill had helped to obscure and confuse the constitutionally more serious charges regarding perjury and suborning witnesses in the sexual harassment lawsuit brought against Clinton by Paula Corbin Jones. The House impeached the president only for lying about and using the powers of his office to "delay, impede, cover up, and conceal" his sexual involvement with a White House aide (Articles I and III of the charges brought by the Judiciary Committee). And on that matter, despite their reputation abroad as being oddly puritanical regarding such matters, a majority of Americans proved perfectly capable of distinguishing between a President's morality and other qualities.[31] (See Figure 9.1.)

When an impeached office-holder is convicted, a vacancy is left and a successor must be found. In the case of the U.S. presidency, the vice president moves into office; other offices are filled by appointments that must be confirmed by Congress. Although far more cumbersome than the parliamentary procedure, which allows the removal of chief executives who have committed no crime whatsoever, the impeachment process, when successful, can lead to a form of democratic succession. However, impeachment provisions are found as well in the constitutions of states whose grip on democracy is still shaky, such as Taiwan and Russia.[32]

FIGURE 9.1

Impeachment and Public Opinion: Perceptions of Clinton as a Strong Leader, Compassionate, and Moral

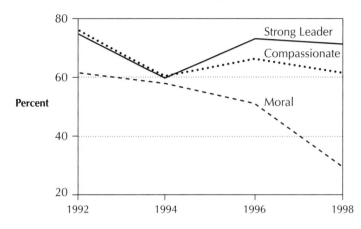

Source: Arthur Miller, "Sex, Politics, and Public Opinion: What Political Scientists Really Learned from the Clinton-Lewinsky Scandal," *PS* 32, no. 4 (December 1999): 724. Reprinted with permission of Cambridge University Press.

WHAT CHIEF EXECUTIVES DO

It is time to turn from the question of how we acquire and remove chief executives to a look at what they do in office. We take it more or less for granted that the most important person in any political system is that nation's chief executive officer, be it president or prime minister or head of the military junta. However, when you stop and think about it, isn't it a little bit strange—at least in democratic systems—that so much emphasis should be placed on that one leader? After all, in democratic systems the chief executive is simply supposed to see to the carrying out of laws that others have made, right?

Wrong. We have already seen that in nation after nation the chief executive plays an important role in initiating and formulating the bills that the legislature will eventually enact into law and in rallying public support for the policies that are explicit or implicit in those laws. The chief executive's role as chief executor of the laws is almost always less significant than his or her role as partner in the making of those laws, especially in peacetime. And it is the combination of those roles—a combination normally found only in chief executives and their immediate staffs—that gives these leaders the power they have.

It is, however, the second aspect, the literal "executing" role of chief executives, that concerns us here. And having said that the executing role is normally less significant than the legislating role, I must immediately make clear that it is nevertheless a far from negligible task. The three principal *ex-*

ecutive tasks of the chief executive are to make appointments, oversee the bureaucracy, and guide public opinion. We have already covered the first (pp. 344–47); we turn now to the other two.

Overseeing the Bureaucracy

Once they have made their appointments, chief executives are responsible for keeping a constant eye on the activities and accomplishments of the people they have appointed. Overseeing that bureaucracy—the public employees whose job it is to carry out the laws of the land—is a task normally shared (not always easily and cooperatively) by the chief executive and the legislative committee responsible for the particular laws being carried out. Carrying his or her share of the surveillance burden can be one of the most difficult and thankless tasks any president, prime minister, or other chief executive must face. Contrary to what might at first be expected, the problem is not just making sure that enough work gets done; it is also trying to keep too much useless work from being done. Bureaucrats are very much like other workers; some simply want to get through the day with as little effort as possible, but others—perhaps the majority—want to do their work well, so well that they will be praised, promoted, and put in charge of other bureaucrats. Hardworking bureaucrats do not want to be overseen, they want to be encouraged to do more of what they think they do best.

These very natural human tendencies are found in nearly every workplace but cause special problems when the workplace is a government office. In government, one important aspect of the normal relationship between management and the workforce is reversed. In private business, the managers have usually been around a lot longer than most of the people they manage; in government, the newcomers are more often found in management and the old-timers in the workforce.[33] The new executives are imposed on the bureaucratic workforce by a powerful outside body that usually has little expertise in the actual business of government—that is, by the voters or the leaders of a coup d'état.

Having the right to bring in new management—which is what voters do every time they elect a new president or change the balance of power in a parliament and thereby force the selection of a new prime minister—is an essential element of the democratic process. Even when the new management is brought in by military force, it can sometimes produce salutary results if the ousted government was more authoritarian and more remote from the people's will than its successors are. In any system, new managers may be more up to date in their area of specialization, more politically sophisticated, and more in touch with the popular will than the managers they replace. On the other hand, the imposition of new management by nonexperts (voters or soldiers) can also mean that inexperienced and temporary top managers will be unable to exercise full control over an experienced and self-aggrandizing workforce.

In any case, chief executives cannot oversee every department personally. There were, for example, 2,749,239 people employed in the U.S. federal government as of 1999.[34] But in a democratic system it is the chief's job to assess the performance of those he or she has appointed to head the key administrative agencies of the government, and to determine when and if changes are needed, either in that leadership or in the entire agency. New agencies are especially likely to be created when new problems must be solved: It was only after the German government had clearly failed to respond quickly enough to the outbreak of bovine spongiform encephalopathy (mad cow disease) in that nation that the German ministry of agriculture was transformed into a new ministry for food, agriculture, and consumer protection in 2001.[35]

Instead of creating a new agency or recombining old ones, a chief executive may prefer to change the leadership of an existing agency, giving it a strong signal that its performance has been unsatisfactory—as when President Vicente Fox of Mexico appointed José Gusman Montalvo the new chief of the federal customs office and Montalvo in turn dismissed 43 of the department's 47 supervisors suspected of committing or condoning crimes.[36]

Guiding Public Opinion

Another chore that falls to chief executives is one for which they are often far better qualified, as the consummate campaigners they have had to be to reach office: rallying the public in support of the decisions they or other government leaders make. Making one's way to any nation's top executive post almost always means mastering the art of persuasion. Richard Neustadt has pointed out the importance of this role for presidents of the United States; an American president must, he says, "be effective as a teacher to the public." Neustadt identifies four ways presidential teaching is different from classroom teaching. First, there is no captive audience; most of the "students" live far away and are preoccupied with their own lives. Second, these students pay attention only when they are already concerned about the matters the president wants to teach them about. Third, the president teaches more by doing (or not doing) than by talking. Fourth, the public's evaluation of the president's past performance always influences how susceptible they will be to the efforts of the chief executive to teach them anything new.[37] Neustadt could have added a fifth difference, one that perhaps seemed too obvious to mention: The position of the presidency gives its occupant a unique combination of prestige, power, and visibility, advantages that go far to overcome the disadvantages suggested in the first four points.

Although Neustadt is probably right that presidents teach more effectively

Executives teach by doing. Here U.S. President George W. Bush shows respect for the religion of Islam and practicing Muslims by visiting the Islamic Center of Washington six days after the attack on the World Trade Center (September 11, 2001), indicating thereby that Americans should carefully distinguish between the need to bring Osama Bin Laden to justice and the right of Muslims to be treated with respect.
© Reuters NewMedia Inc./CORBIS

by doing than by talking, chief executives around the world nonetheless offer a good deal of public explanation, openly explaining the virtues of the policy in question and asking for support. Thus, when Great Britain was about to join the effort to force Iraq from Kuwait in the 1991 Gulf War, Prime Minister John Major personally explained why he believed this to be necessary; the cost of war, he said, would be "less than that of failing to defend principle," and ten years later his successor, Tony Blair, made a similar appeal for a similar alliance, this time against terrorism.[38]

Sometimes the first step a new chief executive must take is to find a gentle way to reduce the expectations he has raised during the campaign that brought him to office. As a candidate, George W. Bush was a staunch supporter of school vouchers, which the parents of students in failing public schools could use at private institutions, but only days after his highly disputed election, he commented, "Others suggest different approaches and I'm willing to listen."[39]

Another public relations task that often needs immediate attention after election is to try to rally the support—or at least reduce the hostility—of important opposing groups. Shortly after his dramatically disputed election, President George W. Bush made numerous visits to various African American communities, no doubt in part because so many African Americans were convinced their votes had not been properly counted and that if they had been, former Vice President Albert Gore would have been elected.[40] He also made early and unusually strong efforts to placate the Democratic leadership in both the House and the Senate, although some doubted these would lead to serious compromise on the issues.[41]

At times the message the chief executive tries to get across has less to do with future policies for which he seeks support than with an effort to place the effects of past policies in the best possible light. This tactic, popularly known as "spin control," depends heavily on creating spectacles that both attract the media (see Chapter 6) and carry the "right" message. It isn't easy to do, since the media are just as likely to make news out of the effort to spin as to carry the message itself—John Anthony Maltese tells how in his early months in office Bill Clinton was castigated as a "tax and spin" president, despite his carefully nonpartisan appointment of Republican commentator David Gergen as his "Communications Director."[42]

But the above examples are the exceptions, not the norm. Much of the routine work of a chief executive is simply to announce—directly or through the appropriate spokesperson and in the appropriate place—what he or she plans to do next, and explain why in terms that can be understood and are likely to win as much support as possible.

Refusing to Execute

In one of those paradoxes that make governments work better while confusing the people who observe them, it is common constitutional practice to give the government officials whose duty it is to carry out the laws the power to refuse to do so. Chief executives very often have the right to refuse to sign—that is, to *veto*—the acts of legislatures as well as to interfere with the carrying out of judicial decisions by pardoning men and women who have been found guilty of crimes and sentenced to imprisonment or capital punishment.

Sometimes the *executive veto* is absolute, but more commonly it can be overridden if the legislature can muster the votes to pass it again by a large enough majority. According to Richard Watson, U.S. presidents have traditionally used the veto to protect the executive against legislative encroachment on its powers, to protect the constitution, or to prevent the introduction of new laws that appear administratively unworkable, fiscally unsound, or simply unwise. He points out that the U.S. Congress has not been reluctant to overrule the president. The record was set during the tenure of Harry Truman, when 37 percent of that president's vetoes were overturned by a second vote.[43]

Vetoing a bill checks the power of legislatures; a pardon issued to someone convicted of a crime checks the power of the judiciary. The executive right to pardon is normally extensive in theory but quite limited in practice. Pardons can be granted to those convicted of ordinary crimes when new and unusual circumstances are uncovered after the sentencing, but under such circumstances it is much more likely that the convict's lawyers will simply seek a new trial. Pardons are more commonly granted for political reasons — either to bring the governmental process into closer accord with public opinion or to curry political favor openly with particular individuals or groups. Although the latter motive is never openly acknowledged, it is often very clear, as when Argentinean President Carlos Saul Menem signed presidential pardons in late 1990 for seven of the men who had been leading protagonists of that nation's "dirty war" of internal repression in the mid-1970s. Menem was under such heavy pressure from the military to free the men that he did so despite the fact that their activities had led to the loss of over 9,000 lives and despite the anger he knew the pardons would provoke at home and abroad.[44]

Pardons may also be granted in return for past favors. Although using the power to pardon thus was surely never intended by the writers of any constitution, it clearly does happen. Almost no one doubted that when outgoing President Bill Clinton pardoned Marc Rich, a commodities trader who fled to Switzerland to avoid certain imprisonment in the United States, the past lavish contributions of his ex-wife to the Clintons and the Democratic Party were a major factor in helping the outgoing president reach the decision to pardon.[45] (For the recent history of pardons in the United States, see Figure 9.2.)

THE BUREAUCRACY

If you are attending a community college, a state college, or a state university, you deal with bureaucrats every time you pay your school fees. Regardless of what kind of college you are attending, you may be paying those fees at least in part with a government loan or with financial aid from the government. You may have been to see government bureaucrats recently to arrange your transportation: to get a driver's license, a student bus ticket, or a license for your bicycle. Many of you have registered to vote. Probably all of you have some identification number, if only a Social Security card. Some of you are paying income taxes. Some of you are married, some of

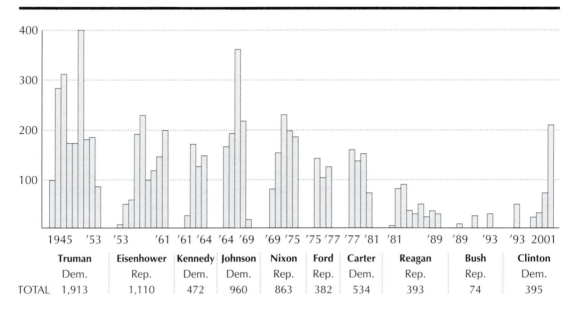

	Truman	Eisenhower	Kennedy	Johnson	Nixon	Ford	Carter	Reagan	Bush	Clinton
	Dem.	Rep.	Dem.	Dem.	Rep.	Rep.	Dem.	Rep.	Rep.	Dem.
TOTAL	1,913	1,110	472	960	863	382	534	393	74	395

Source: "Presidential Pardons" graph from "Rising Numbers Sought Pardons in Last Two Years," by Kurt Eichenwald and Michael Moss from the *New York Times*, 29 Jan. 2001, A1–A16. Copyright © 2001 The New York Times Co. Reprinted by permission.

FIGURE 9.2
Presidential Pardons in the United States, 1945–2001

you are divorced, and some of you have had to register the births of your children. In every case it was necessary to fill out the proper papers with the government.

The same or similar experiences are common to the lives of everyone in the human polity. A young Paraguayan decides to pursue his studies at the National University of Paraguay and fills out the necessary papers. An Indian mother decides to take the rewards offered by her government for joining its sterilization program and signs the appropriate form. A Canadian veteran decides to buy a larger house in Moosejaw, Saskatchewan, and applies for the government loan her military service has entitled her to seek. An Albanian alcoholic agrees to work on his problem and signs himself into the government hospital for treatment.

Not all bureaucratic experiences are initiated by citizens. Some of us get arrested for crimes we may or may not have committed, get drafted into armies we would prefer not to serve in, or have our paychecks garnished for taxes we failed to pay. If we live under a heavily authoritarian government and dare to express dissent, we may find agents of government taking over our property, getting us fired from our jobs, and even subjecting our bodies to confinement and torture.

But even if our experiences have been much less traumatic, few of us can help being annoyed when we have to go through the normal bureaucratic procedures: standing in lines, submitting to interviews, filling out forms, identifying ourselves by numbers, signing everything in triplicate. *Bureaucracy* means, first and foremost, "administration of government," but it also means "governmental officialism," and the adjective *bureaucratic* is usually interpreted to mean "following an inflexible routine." When pressed, we will probably agree that we need government to help us solve some of our individual and collective problems (although we will disagree among ourselves about how much help we need) and also that we believe in "equal protection under the law"—that is, in having the laws applied to all of us in the same way. But shouldn't there be a better way than "inflexible routine" and "governmental officialism" to accomplish these goals?

Before we can consider how the world's bureaucracies might be improved, we need to know more about how they operate now. We need to look at the work of the bureaucrats, considering who they are and how they do their jobs in various nations, before we can properly consider the interesting question of whether or not there is any way to have "administration of government" without "inflexible routine."

Who Are the Bureaucrats?

Although we often think of bureaucrats as white-collar workers standing behind a counter with a grille or seated behind a desk, in fact any employee of a large organization is a bureaucrat, and any employee of government can therefore be called a *government bureaucrat,* including the engineers, teachers, janitors, and other specialized employees who work on the government's payroll. In practice, however, it is more useful to say that a bureaucrat is someone who does the administrative work of government—that is, who has responsibility for interpreting and implementing government policy, whether as the cop on the beat or the highest-ranking minister.

Taking on the role of bureaucrat also means taking on the bureaucratic style. To do their work, bureaucrats have developed a set of norms to guide them. The important principle here is fairness—or the appearance thereof. Whether or not the concept is enshrined in its constitution, as in the case of the United States (see the Fourteenth Amendment), every nation at least gives lip service to the ideal that the laws must be applied with equal force to every citizen; this is the *sine qua non,* the minimal requirement, of bureaucratic fairness. To accomplish this goal, bureaucrats attempt to follow the law to the letter—that is, to carry it out exactly and explicitly. Because most laws are written in language open to a wide range of interpretations, the bureaucratic solution is to write a set of rules detailing exactly how each law is to be carried out, and then to attempt to follow these rules without exception. This can lead to an appearance (and in some cases, a practice) of rigid, inhuman, and even ridiculous behavior on the part of some bureaucrats—the kind of behavior that leads us to use the word "bureaucratic" as a pejorative. When we ordinary citizens want something perfectly reasonable from a government office and are told by a clerk, "I'm sorry, but according to the rules it simply cannot be done," our normal response is to feel angry and frustrated, and to storm out muttering, "Bureaucratic!" as if it were one of the worst terms of opprobrium. But the next time you are tempted to do that, you might stop to consider that this determination to stick to the rules *does* have its positive side, *does* mean that the clerk has been taught to adhere loyally to the principle of equal protection under the laws. There certainly may be better ways to protect that principle, but most of us would agree that protecting it is worth a few inconveniences.

How to Become a Bureaucrat

There are basically two routes to a bureaucratic position: You may be given a political appointment, or you may be hired on the basis of merit. We have discussed political appointments at length (see pp. 344–47). When bureaucrats are hired on the *basis of merit,* a number of different methods may be employed to determine the most meritorious applicant for the job. Years of experience in related tasks, years of education in relevant fields of study, and level of performance on tests designed for the job in question are some of the criteria most commonly employed.

The use of tests was common practice long before the emergence of modern bureaucracy. Passing rigorous examinations was the most honorable path to advancement for administrators in ancient China.[46] Under the Russian Czar Alexander I, the law required candidates to pass examinations in Russian, mathematics, Latin, and modern languages before they could be promoted to "collegiate assessor, the eighth rank, or state councillor, the fifth rank."[47]

Specialized training for government work has become more and more important in the modern age, and without such training the elected official is likely to find it more and more difficult to hold his own with the bureaucrats he is expected to guide. Some polities have established special schools to train those who aspire to high bureaucratic position. France has an entire system of *grandes écoles* (literally, "great schools") for educating its public servants, and those who are able to pass the rigorous entrance examinations for the National School of Administration (ENA) are almost always assured of a high government post upon graduation. Such training has become important for those who seek high elective posts in France as well; almost all French presidents, prime ministers, and major cabinet ministers in recent years have been either "Enarques" (the popular term for ENA graduates) or graduates of other *grandes écoles*.[48]

Success in the bureaucracies of developing nations is also likely to depend on suitable expertise. A background in global economic affairs may be especially useful. Nicephore Soglo, the president of Benin, was himself an official of the World Bank, and, as Victoria Brittain points out, the presidents of Cameroon, Congo, Gabon, Ivory Coast, Senegal, and Zaire have all tended to seek out "techno-politicians" with "years of experience in multilateral agencies" for senior appointive positions.[49]

Of course, appointment by political patronage is still widely practiced in every nation in the world. However, it is rare that the executive making the appointment fails to consider the actual capabilities of the would-be bureaucrat. A new British prime minister is expected to appoint only parliamentary members of his own party to all the paid positions associated with the Cabinet, but M.P.s who lack administrative competence for the post in question are as unlikely to be chosen as those who are deficient in personal loyalty.[50]

The Work of Bureaucracy

As the work of governments grows ever more complex, the world's bureaucratic workforces grow ever more elaborate and specialized. Special agents are required for everything from inspecting nuclear power plants to supervising the artificial insemination of prize heifers on ranches receiving government subsidies. Books must be kept on expenditures of all kinds, for political campaigns in Iowa's First Congressional District, for laying transcontinental gas pipelines in Russia, for shipping kangaroos from Australia to the world's zoos.

The activities of bureaucrats, however diverse, have in common the fact that they all involve the efforts of bureaucrats to *implement* government policy. To accomplish this broader goal, it is not enough, however, simply to do the job called for by policy. Bureaucrats must also gather the funds to pay for the work of government, disburse those funds to the other bureaucrats or private-sector entrepreneurs who do that work, and see to it that no laws or rules are broken in the process. These three more specialized tasks of bureaucrats are worth a closer look.

■ **Collecting Revenue.** Bureaucrats collect the revenue necessary to do the work of government. They write up the tax forms and instruction booklets for all kind of taxes—personal income taxes, corporate income taxes, import and export duties, license fees, inheritance taxes, and taxes on purchased goods are a few of the more common ones. Taxes are levied even on illegal activities; until the practice was recently ruled unconstitutional by the Supreme Court as a form of double punishment, farmers convicted of marijuana farming in Montana were taxed "$100 an ounce or 10 percent of mar-

The work of bureaucracy is never done. Here hundreds of Internal Revenue Service workers check through tax returns at the IRS Service Center in Philadelphia.
© Bettmann/CORBIS

ket value, whichever is greater." [51] Bureaucrats not only levy taxes, they also process the penalties, settle disputes (although, as in the Montana case, final appeal may be made to the judicial branch of the government), and help prepare legislation to change the laws governing the collection of taxes and other revenues.

■ **Disbursing Government Funds.**   Bureaucrats also disburse government moneys. They prepare the government's budget for presentation to the chief executive and, in democratic systems, to the legislature. The policies of these bodies over the years will have been crucial, along with global market forces, in determining the state of the nation's finances, and these may vary rapidly, as the U.S. transition from years of federal deficit to a budget surplus in 2000 illustrated, but whatever the situation, and whatever the final budgetary decisions, it is up to bureaucrats to carry out the plan. [52] Bureaucrats are the ones who purchase raw materials and finished goods (including all those necessary for the nation's defense establishment); pay bills; meet payrolls; process applications for government loans; pay interest on government bonds; give political parties and their candidates whatever help with campaign expenses they are entitled to by law; pay price supports to farmers; pay a wide range of social benefits, from welfare to family allowances to full medical coverage; support the United Nations and its affiliated agencies; send foreign aid to other nations and distribute aid received. They even manufacture the nation's money in the first place. Sometimes goods rather than money are disbursed, as in programs of land redistribution, or the distribution abroad of surplus food from wealthier nations to those suffering from drought and famine.

■ **Preventing or Punishing Infractions of the Law.** Bureaucrats are also expected to see to it that the laws are obeyed and that those who disobey meet with the prescribed sanctions. Some of these laws, such as those determining what acts constitute criminal behavior, apply to everyone; others apply only to those entering into particular relationships with government.

Whether the rule is intended to prevent crime, to protect the environment, or to meet some other social goal, if it is a rule made by government it will be the work of some bureaucrat to see that it is obeyed or to call the malefactor into account. Police officers, prosecuting attorneys, and prison administrators are bureaucrats who try to enforce laws against criminal activity; health inspectors, welfare "snoops," and government safety commissioners are bureaucrats who try to enforce laws concerning other forms of activity that policymakers have decided are desirable or undesirable.

The line between the two kinds of policing is not always easily drawn; serious infringement of rules set to accomplish social goals can lead to prosecution for criminal behavior.

■ **Subdividing the Work of Bureaucracy.** Max Weber, one of the first serious students of bureaucracy, believed that in the ideal bureaucracy all tasks would be assigned carefully on the basis of *specialization* and *hierarchy*. Everyone would do the job for which he or she was best suited, every job would be specific and limited, and every bureaucrat would occupy a clear-cut place in the chain of command, with no confusion as to who had authority over whom.[53]

Even Weber might be surprised if he could see how seriously modern bureaucracies have taken his advice regarding specialization. Consider, for example, the fine distinctions made between the jobs of Oven-Press Tender I and Oven-Press Tender II in the U.S. government (see Box 9.1). States that take direct control of industrial development must make an even broader range of distinctions; consider the posts assigned in the Cabinet of the

BOX 9.1
**Is Too Much
Bureaucracy
Slowing Us
Down?**

573.685-042   OVEN-PRESS TENDER (asbestos prod.) I

Tends hot press and related equipment that hardens asbestos disc pads for use as brake linings; Positions metal die plate on roller-type conveyor, picks up stack of asbestos disc pads from table, and places individual pads into wells of die plate. Discards broken or defective pads. Pushes filled die plates onto racks of hot press. Starts machine that automatically closes press to heat-treat pads for specified time and opens press at end of press cycle. Pulls die plates from press onto conveyor. Removes cured disc pads from die plates, using knockout device that forces pads from plates. Loosens stuck pads with rubber mallet and tosses pads into storage container. Sprays empty die plates with silicone solution, using spray gun, to prevent pads from sticking to plates during heat-treating process. GOE 06.04.19 PD M 08 09 15 17 EC 07 M1 L1 SVP 4 SOC 7675

573.685-046   OVEN-PRESS TENDER (asbestos prod.) II

Tends hot press that hardens asbestos disc pads for use as brake linings; Pushes metal die plates filled with asbestos disc pads onto feed elevator of machine. Presses buttons to open press, move die plates from elevator into press, and closes press. Observes timer lights, dials, and pressure gauges on control panel of machine to determine end of press cycle. Presses buttons at end of cycle to simultaneously open press and move cured disc pads from press onto discharge elevator. Pushes die plates from elevator onto roller-type conveyor, using metal rake. GOE 06.04.19 PD M 08 09 15 EC 07 M1 L1 SVP 4 SOC 7675

Source: U.S. Department of Labor, Employment and Training Administration, *Dictionary of Occupational Titles,* 4th edition supplement (Washington, D.C.: U.S. Government Printing Office, 1986), p. 38.

Chinese government and imagine the vast responsibility of each minister in this nation of over 1 billion citizens (see Box 9.2).

Obviously, overspecialization can hinder effective performance by individuals who dare not step past the limits of their own job description. It can also make meeting Weber's second recommendation—keep the lines of authority clear—very difficult. States with highly specialized bureaucratic structures almost always find it hard to maintain clear lines of authority. The very principle of specialization suggests that the person doing the job knows best how it should be done—better than any alleged superior. As Weber himself noted, "The trained permanent official is more likely to get his way in the long run than his nominal superior [when the latter] is not a specialist." [54] Furthermore, specialization and hierarchy are difficult to combine be-

BOX 9.2
Ministries in the Chinese Cabinet

Agriculture	Public Health
Chemical Industry	Public Security
Civil Affairs	Radio, Film, and Television
Coal Industry	Railways
Communications	State Commission for Economic
Construction	Restructuring
Culture	State Commission for Economic
Electronics Industry	Trade
Finance	State Commission for Education
Foreign Affairs	State Commission for Family
Foreign Economic Relations	Planning
and Trade	State Commission for Nationalities
Forestry	Affairs
Geology and Mineral Resources	State Commission for Physical
Internal Trade	Culture and Sports
Justice	State Commission for Planning
Labor	State Commission for Science and
Light Industry	Technology
Machine Building Industry	State Commission for Science,
Metallurgical Industry	Technology, and Industry for
National Defense	National Defense
Personnel	State Security
Posts and Telecommunications	Supervision
Power Industry	Water Resources

Source: Arthur S. Banks, ed., *Political Handbook of the World: 1993* (Binghamton, N.Y.: CSA Publications, 1993), p. 167. Reprinted by permission of the publisher.

cause those who specialize do not always respond well to proposals that they coordinate their work with that of other specialists. Specialization is thus likely to lead to the proliferation of bureaucratic units with overlapping jurisdictions. Resentful of competition, the person in charge of each unit may well become extremely jealous of his or her own authority, insisting on control of everything that happens within that unit and refusing to cooperate with other units in any way that might impair that authority.

For these and other reasons, the problem of ensuring the correct organization of bureaucracies is one that is never fully solved, and it is not uncommon for new administrations to undertake a complete overhaul of a nation's bureaucracy. The task can be an enormous one. In the reorganization undertaken by Japan at the beginning of 2001, 23 ministries were consolidated into 13,128 bureaus inside those ministries were reduced to 96, and the number of advisory agencies serving them was cut to 89 from 211. Some 540,000 officials were caught up "in a giant game of musical chairs"—and some knew they would lose their chairs in the near future: 235,000 jobs would be cut, "largely through attrition" over the next ten years.[55]

TOO MUCH GOVERNMENT? OR TOO LITTLE?

We human beings are difficult to please when it comes to the operation of our governments. We don't like it when the garbage is not collected, when our roads develop potholes, or when our unemployment benefits run out. We are deeply dismayed when government aid in times of natural catastrophe is slow to arrive, when "nothing is done" about inflation, or when our armies are defeated in foreign wars. On the other hand, we resent seeing our paychecks whittled away by taxes, we don't like to stand in line, we hate to fill out forms, and we detest having to answer the questions of bureaucratic busybodies. And some of us are sure that government benefits are going to all the wrong people—to "welfare cheats" or "exploiting capitalists."

Even when we admit that a bureaucratic system is a necessary part of any modern government, that after all it makes no sense to elect officials to make government policy if no one is in place to ensure that the policy is carried out, still we tend to hold the very idea of bureaucracy in contempt. Is this because we have too much bureaucracy in our lives? Or because the job of bureaucracy is poorly done? Or is it because our expectations of what can and should be done by government bureaucrats are simply unrealistic? As you probably expect, the answer is a combination of all three, and the exact proportions in that combination vary from polity to polity.

Too Much Government

Duplication and waste are found in every domain of human effort. We need only take a critical look around our own homes to find embarrassing examples of waste—food we allowed to spoil, magazines we bought and never read, notes we made and then forgot to consult. And all of us have been known to engage in overkill—making three copies where one would do, printing out ten articles found on the Internet when we knew perfectly well only three of them were likely to be useful for that missing section in the term paper we had to write, or reminding a good friend over and over not to forget an important appointment.

What accounts for such behavior? Without troubling our fellow social scientists the psychologists for an answer, we can speculate that such behavior will be most pronounced when four conditions prevail: relative affluence

www.CartoonStock.com

(we can afford a little waste), a strong desire to reach relatively limited and particular goals (so we give tasks pertinent to those goals excessive energy and attention), nonaccountability (no one else pays much attention to these useless and wasteful activities), and failure to use common sense (we "just didn't think").

All four conditions are all too likely to prevail in the normal bureaucratic setting. First, bureaucrats find themselves in the happy position of spending other people's money—a circumstance that can easily bring a sense of relative affluence. (In a study citing instances of rank extravagance in the Agency for International Development, Sheila Kaplan suggests the ruling motto appeared to be, "Why Pay Less?"[56])

Second, most bureaucrats occupy highly specialized roles. If they are ambitious, their hopes for promotion are likely to rest on demonstrating superior performance of specific tasks. Their jobs seldom require them—or permit them—to consider means of accomplishing overall policy goals that might entail shifting energies and expenditures away from their own narrow domains. Like specialists in any large organization, they seek to use every possible means to create a praiseworthy record of accomplishment, even at the cost of duplication and waste.

BOX 9.3
**One Result of
the Paperwork
Reduction Act
of 1980**

Department of the Treasury

Internal Revenue Service

PAPERWORK REDUCTION ACT NOTICE

The Paperwork Reduction Act of 1980 says we must tell you why
we are collecting this information, how we will use it, and
whether you have to give it to us. We ask for the information
to carry out the Internal Revenue laws of the United States.
We need it to ensure that taxpayers are complying with these
laws and to allow us to figure and collect the right amount of
tax. You are required to give us this information.

Notice 610 (22-81)

Third, bureaucrats are very difficult to hold accountable. Their claims of expertise are often well founded, and their ultimate bosses—temporary elected officials—cannot always deal with them in terms that command their respect. Furthermore, any efforts to improve accountability may simply stimulate greater waste, as reports fly back and forth and efforts are made to meet—or to give the appearance of meeting—standards of efficiency set by those too remote from the tasks being performed.

Finally, it often seems especially difficult for even the best-intentioned bureaucrats to operate according to the dictates of common sense. This difficulty flows in part from two other problems in the bureaucratic world that we have already mentioned: the need to succeed within a narrowly defined domain and the absence of true accountability. Under these circumstances, the typical bureaucrat tends to operate strictly according to the rules, regardless of how patently ridiculous or unproductive the consequences of doing so may be. If in doubt, take a look at Box 9.3.

Too Little Government

It is no paradox to say that we can have both too much and too little bureaucracy. For at the same time that bureaucrats are busily duplicating their activities and wasting their energies, they may also be failing to do what really needs to be done—that is, putting the laws and rules that are supposed to govern the nation into actual practice. Probably more social problems persist because of a failure to implement laws already on the books than because of an absence of such legislation. Yet sometimes the failures of implementation are owing to the nature of the laws themselves. As we saw at the beginning of Chapter 8, laws are merely plans, and, like all plans, they can never be entirely complete, can never foresee all contingencies, and need elaboration and modification when it comes time to carry them out. What we so easily label "bureaucratic inefficiency" may result simply because agency officials are being asked to carry out tasks so large under conditions so difficult that normal standards of efficiency are simply impossible to meet.[57] The failure of the U.S. Food and Drug Administration to take steps to implement serious regulation of the tobacco industry prior to the appointment of David Kessler as its new commissioner in 1990 was an interesting case in point. "We just didn't want to fool with tobacco," said a former official of the agency, stressing the power of two forces: the smoking habit and the industry itself.[58]

It would be naive, however, to deny that bureaucratic misimplementation—or nonimplementation—can also be deliberate. To understand why this is so, it is important to realize that the more power shifts to the executive branch, the more those affected by public policy shift their lobbying efforts to that branch. Bureaucrats are subject to a wide range of temptations to abandon the rules of strict neutrality that supposedly govern their work. They may be bribed to carry out their roles in ways the groups they are supposed to be regulating desire. Or they may simply find that it is suddenly remarkably easy to gain membership to distinguished private clubs or to book good seats for the theater. Perhaps they will be offered a chance of lucrative employment in the private sector when they leave government, if they have done their job "well" in the meantime.

But the most common means lobbyists employ in dealing with bureaucrats is one that is entirely legal and, on the face of it, merely supportive and useful. As already noted in Chapter 5 (pp. 178–79), they simply provide the bureaucrats with information. The information they offer will not be effective if it is too blatantly biased or inaccurate, but inevitably it will be one-sided and partial. Nevertheless, bureaucrats all over the world welcome the help and often depend on it. Close ties develop between the regulator and the regulated; the lobbyists become the "clients" of the regulators, exchanging information and services for a form of policy implementation that is sympathetic to their needs.[59] And like all good merchandisers, the bureaucrats take care of their clients, subtly (and sometimes not so subtly) shaping their interpretations of the law in such a way as to minimize inconvenience to those they oversee, even when the net result is a clear violation of legislative intent. Some have gone so far as to lobby Congress on behalf of those whose behavior they are supposed to regulate, as when U.S. Interior Secretary Manuel

BOX 9.4
U.S. Bureaucratic
Shortcomings

At the beginning of George W. Bush's administration, the report of Comptroller General David W. Walker, head of the General Accounting Office, pointed out the following problems in the U.S. bureaucracy (among others):

The government overpays low-income families claiming earned-income tax credits, because some of these families falsify their income and Social Security numbers and/or overstate the number of children they have.

The Federal Aviation Administration has not followed standard practice in buying computer software for a vast network of radar and communications equipment.

The Health Care Financing Administration has no reliable way to monitor overpayments to doctors, hospitals, and home health-care agencies via Medicare and Medicaid.

The Department of Housing and Urban Development overpaid $935 million to subsidize the rent payments of low-income families who underreported their income or did not report at all.

Source: Robert Pear, "Financial Problems in Government Are Rife, Nation's Top Auditor Says," from the *New York Times,* 18 Jan. 2001, A12. Copyright ©2001 The New York Times Company. Reprinted by permission.

Lujan asked Congress to waive a key requirement of the proposed Endangered Species Act in order to save the lumber industry (instead of the spotted owl).[60] When such a pattern of misimplementation evolves, ordinary citizens suffer from both too much and too little bureaucracy. Too much is done for a privileged few, and too little is done to carry out laws originally intended to apply with equal force to all.

The widespread prevalence of this problem of bureaucratic drift—drift away from control by elected representatives of the people they serve and drift toward control by the very persons and organizations they are expected to guide and supervise—has led to a number of attempted reforms. In the United States, the General Accounting Office (GAO) audits the spending of other bureaus, and the Office of Management and Budget (OMB) has a management section that continually reviews the leadership, organization, and overall effectiveness of all programs submitting requests for funding. (For some of the problems the GAO reported in 2001, see Box 9.4.) Such offices are, however, themselves part of the bureaucratic apparatus and thus are inevitably susceptible to the same viruses that sometimes infect their fellow bureaucrats. More promising means of holding bureaucrats responsible to the general public must come from the public itself. When well informed by responsible news media, well socialized to accept and carry out the duties of citizenship, and well equipped with a strong party system capable of keeping elected representatives aware of and accountable to their interests, the people themselves are the surest means of ensuring bureaucratic responsiveness to the public will, as expressed in the law of the land.

SUMMARY AND CONCLUSION

This may be a good time to take a second look at the notes you made at the beginning of this chapter. How do the answers you gave about political leadership look to you now? Do they hold up pretty well? Which of them would you change, and how? Were you surprised to find that it wasn't, after all, all that hard to find a few good things to say about bureaucrats—if only because, once you think about it, you know so many of them? Perhaps you even began to give the idea of joining the ranks of the bureaucrats some consideration yourself.

In this chapter we have considered the ways of becoming a leader—ascription, appointment, election to office, and force—and the ways of leaving office, examining the problems each entails and the differences between democratic and authoritarian procedures. We have reviewed the key jobs of chief executives and then turned to the bureaucrats, recognizing how many jobs are in fact part of any nation's bureaucracy, examined how bureaucrats gain their positions, and looked at the main tasks they must accomplish. We have puzzled over the problems of knowing how to subdivide their work, and of how to ensure that we have neither too much nor too little government.

We have not, however, paid much attention to the actual policies chief executives and bureaucrats must carry out. That is a large topic, so large we are giving it a chapter all its own, Chapter 10. But first, one last serious word about the question we began with, whether or not you yourself will someday join the ranks of those who carry out your country's business. Although we have tried to uncover deficiencies and problems, do not be deceived: Helping to run a government is one of today's most challenging—and rewarding—professions. Nowhere is there a greater need for well-qualified, well-motivated, and *persistent* men and women. Nowhere are there greater opportunities to bring about change that will have an important and salutary impact on the lives of millions. The fact that the hurdles to doing this are so many and so high only makes the challenge that much more exciting.

Perhaps the real question to ask today is where we will find the men and women ready and able to meet that challenge. You may simply be more certain than ever that political leadership is not for you. But please do not be too quick to dismiss the idea. After all, those who do lead have not yet shown us remarkable success in solving all the problems of the human polity. Leadership is one of the developing arts and sciences, not a fixed craft. You may have more to offer than you imagine, and an ability to acquire the skills and knowledge you currently lack. After all, you *are* a student of the science of politics.

QUESTIONS TO CONSIDER

1. Consider a recent appointment to government office in the news. Who made the appointment and what do you think his or her motives probably were? What evidence do you have?
2. Imagine you have a 13-year-old brother or sister who asks, "What does impeachment mean?" Can you explain it so he or she can understand?
3. Do you agree that respect for the idea of "rule of the law" should make us less quick to condemn modern bureaucracies? Why or why not?
4. What is "bureaucratic drift" and how can it be stopped?

SELECTED READINGS

Abshire, David. *Triumphs and Tragedies of the Modern Presidency: Seventy-Six Case Studies in Presidential Leadership* (Westport, Conn.: Praeger, 2001). Leading presidential researchers and writers examine a multitude of case studies to see what lessons can be learned regarding presidential success and failure.

Casamayou, Maureen Hogan. *Bureaucracy in Crisis: Three Mile Island, the Shuttle* Challenger, *and Risk Assessment* (Boulder, Colo.: Westview Press, 1993). Personal interviews and public testimony are used to illustrate how bureaucratic failures contributed to these two catastrophes.

DeConde, Alexander. *Presidential Machismo: Executive Authority, Military Intervention and Foreign Relations* (Boston: Northeastern University Press, 2000). Argues that the expansion of executive authority began long before the United States became a world power and attributes the phenomenon to the tendency of even weak presidents to manifest "presidential machismo," that is, to seek the status of heroes by waging successful wars.

Foley, Michael. *The Rise of the British Presidency* (Manchester, U.K.: Manchester University Press, 1993). The author argues that personal political leadership has become increasingly important to the role of prime minister in Great Britain. The British prime ministership is compared to the U.S. presidency.

Haggard, Stephan and Mathew D. McCubbins, eds. *Presidents, Parliaments, and Policy* (New York: Cambridge University Press, 2001). Seeking solid evidence regarding the performance of presidential systems in the production of policy (as compared to parliamentary systems), the studies in this volume examine case studies from Asia, Latin America, and central Europe regarding how presidential democracies deal with the challenges of economic reform.

Henderson, Keith M. and O. P. Dwivedi. *Bureaucracy and the Alternatives in World Perspective* (New York: St. Martin's Press, 1999). Examines alternatives to standard bureaucratic practices, such as grassroots initiatives, feminist approaches, the application of ecological perspectives, and a range of case studies from Asia, Latin America, Africa, and the Middle East.

Kernell, Samuel. *Going Public: New Strategies of Presidential Leadership* (Washington, D.C.: Congressional Quarterly Press, 1997). Examines the increasing reliance of U.S. presidents on the practice of appealing for support directly to the public in order to see their programs through an often balky Congress.

Machiavelli, Niccolo. *The Prince* (New York: Appleton-Century-Crofts, 1947). Writing in the early sixteenth century, Machiavelli laid out pragmatic rules for taking and maintaining power without regard for the rights of others or for any other principles of moral behavior.

Neustadt, Richard E. *Presidential Power* (New York: John Wiley, 1960). The classic study of the American presidency, with insights still applicable today.

WEB SITES OF INTEREST

1. Center for the Study of the Presidency
   http://www.thepresidency.org/
   Produces a series of reports on the U.S. presidency, government, and politics.

2. Rulers.org
   http://www.rulers.org
   Lists all heads of state and heads of government, as well as *de facto* leaders; goes back to the eighteenth century in most cases. Also gives recent foreign ministers.

NOTES

1. Georges Marion, "La Succession en Jordanie s'engage à un instant critique pour le royaume," *Le Monde*, 9 Feb. 1999, 5.
2. Michael Elliott, "Why the Monarchy Must Go," *Newsweek* (international ed., 11 Mar. 1996): 24. Not only in the West—and not only in the interests of democracy—have the powers of the monarch been limited: In Cambodia the kingship has traditionally been elective, although the new constitution now says the monarch must be "a member of the Khmer Royal Family, aged at least 30 years, coming from the bloodline of the King Ang Duong, Norodom or Sisowath." William Shawcross, *Cambodia's New Deal* (New York: Carnegie Endowment for International Peace, 1994), p. 53.
3. Norimitsu Onishi, "Joseph Kabila Sworn in as Congo President," *New York Times*, 27 Jan. 2001, A6; "Kabila Is Dead, Long Live Kabila," *The Economist* (27 Jan. 2001): 45.
4. Talcott Parsons and Edward Shils, "Orientation and Organization of Action," in Talcott Parsons and Edward Shils, eds., *Toward a General Theory of Action* (New York: Harper & Row, 1951), p. 82. Their exact definition of ascription is "the normative pattern which prescribes that an actor in a given type of situation should, in his selections for differential treatment of social objects, give priority to certain attributes that they possess (including collectivity memberships and possessions) over any specific performances (past, present, or prospective) of the objects." This is a good example of the use of unnecessary jargon in the social sciences ("social objects" means people!), and I have taken the liberty of providing a translation.
5. See Isaiah 11:6, *The Holy Bible* (Boston: Massachusetts Bible Society, 1965), p. 655.
6. For the Hessian example, see David P. Conradt, *The German Polity*, 4th ed. (New York: Longman, 1989), p. 217.
7. Samuel Abraham, "Early Elections in Slovakia: A State of Deadlock," *Government and Opposition* 30, no. 1 (1995): 86–100. In the past century no one understood and used the powers of appointment for the purposes of autocracy better than Generalissimo Francisco Franco during the thirty-nine years he ruled Spain. Franco selected, appointed, and dismissed the prime minister and all ministers at will and saw to it that the occupants of other significant offices were appointed by his own appointees. Any official who had

significant power to exercise did so only so long as he remained in the favor of the Generalissimo. Since Franco's death in 1975, Spain has adopted a much more democratic constitution, in which appointive offices such as the president's cabinet, high judicial offices, and the Constitutional Court are carefully specified and regulated.

8. No doubt the most dramatic case in your lifetime (at least so far) was in 1991, when Clarence Thomas was finally confirmed as Justice of the United States Supreme Court by a vote of 52 to 48, after days of nationally televised debate over the testimony of law professor Anita F. Hill that Thomas had subjected her to continued sexual harassment when she was his employee. *Congressional Quarterly Weekly Report* 49, no. 42 (19 Oct. 1991): 3026–33.

9. Benedict Brogan, "Heavyweight in Hong Kong Ring," *The Herald* (Glasgow), 25 April 1992, 9; Anthony Blass, "Burke's Heir," *Far Eastern Economic Review* (22 Oct. 1992): 25–26.

10. *New York Times,* 24 March 1993, A7.

11. Pendleton James, President Ronald Reagan's assistant for presidential personnel in 1981–1982, quoted in James P. Pfiffner, "Recruiting Executive Branch Leaders: The Office of Presidential Personnel," *Brookings Review* 19, no. 2 (Spring 2001): 41–43.

12. Frederic Chambon, "Thabo Mbeki a formé un gouvernement de fidèles," *Le Monde,* 19 June 1999, 6.

13. "President Fox and His Cabinet," *World Press Review* (February 2001): 47.

14. *New York Times,* 11 March 1992, A7.

15. "Here comes his body, mourned by Mark Antony: who, though he had no hand in his death, shall receive the benefit of his dying . . ." William Shakespeare, *Julius Caesar,* act 3, sc. 2–ll, lines 45–47.

16. Judge Giovanni Falcone was assassinated in Sicily on May 23, 1992. For the response of the Italian public, see *Le Monde,* 26 May 1992, 3, and *New York Times,* 26 May 1992, A3.

17. Edward Gonzalez, *Cuba Under Castro, The Limits of Charisma* (Boston: Houghton Mifflin, 1974); Amin Saikal, *The Rise and Fall of the Shah* (Princeton, N.J.: Princeton University Press, 1980), and Kim Murphy, "Algeria Struggles to Retain Democracy—But Can It Survive After Being Voted Out?" *Denver Post,* 1 Feb. 1992, 19A.

18. *Los Angeles Times,* 21 Aug. 1991, 1, A8–A16, 22 Aug. 1991, 1, A7; *The Current Digest of the Soviet Press,* 43, no. 51 (22 January 1992): 1–6.

19. David E. Sanger, "President Weighs Who Will Follow Taliban in Power," *New York Times,* 14 Oct. 2001, A1. In the latter case, Russian President Vladimir Putin forbade elections in the province during the course of the civil war there. (David Hoffman, "Putin Places Chechnya Under Kremlin Rule," *International Herald Tribune,* 9 June 2000, 1.)

20. "A Quest for Vengeance: Khomeini's Legions Invade Iraq and Threaten the Whole Arab World," *Time* (26 July 1991): 18–25.

21. Seth Mydans, "Philippines' Ousted President Asserts That He's Still Chief," *New York Times,* 1 Feb. 2001, A10; Calvin Sims, "New Philippine Leader Calls for Unity During Transition," *New York Times,* 21 Jan. 2001, A4; Walden Bello, "Letter from Manila," *The Nation* (19 Feb. 2001): 21–25; *The Economist* (27 Jan. 2001): 18–20.

22. Peter Calvert, "Argentina: The Crisis of Confidence," paper presented at Annual Conference of the Political Studies Association of the UK, Aberdeen, 5–7 April 2002, and Larry Rohter, "Argentine Leader Scrambles to Find His Way Out of a Mess," *New York Times,* 25 April 2002, A12.

23. *Le Monde,* 11 June 1998, 5, and 10 June 1998, 2.

24. William Miller, *A New History of the United States* (New York: Dell, 1968), p. 354.

25. Ben Weider and David Hapgood, *The Murder of Napoleon* (New York: Congdon and Lattes, 1982).

26. Miller, *New History,* pp. 312–13.

27. One never knows what the American public will learn about executive leadership by staying glued to the television set at a time of high political drama: how the mere credible threat of impeachment can drive a president from office (Nixon), how a not-very-popular president can make remarkable gains in the polls during a period of crisis (Bush I and Bush II), how a president can be impeached but stay in office (Clinton), and how the electoral college really works (Gore/Bush)—

just ask your professor how hard it was before the fall of 2000 to interest any of your predecessors in that particular subject, much less actually teach it so it could be understood.

28. Elizabeth B. Bazan, "Impeachment: An Overview of Constitutional Provisions, Procedure, and Practice," *CRS Report 98–186A*, Congressional Research Service (27 Feb. 1998): 1.

29. "The Impeachment Process: Overview of the House and Senate Roles," *Congressional Digest* 78, no. 2 (Feb. 1999): 34–36.

30. Robert J. Spitzer, "Clinton's Impeachment Will Have Few Consequences for the Presidency," *PS* 32, no. 3 (Sept. 1999): 541–545; John M. Broder, "Drawn-Out Impeachment Battle Dealt Its Meager Spoils to All Aides," *New York Times*, 14 Feb. 1999, A1.

31. Arthur Miller, "Sex, Politics, and Public Opinion: What Political Scientists Really Learned from the Clinton-Lewinsky Scandal," *PS* 32, no. 4 (Dec. 1999): 721–29.

32. "Taiwan: Total Recall," *World Press Review* (January 2001): 23, and Lila Shevtsova, "The Problem of Executive Power in Russia," *Journal of Democracy* 11, no. 1 (2000): 32–39.

33. To be sure, private business does hire new executives from time to time and does not always promote from within. But in such cases the new executives are hired by those already in place and can be expected to have similar values and priorities. In government, however, the new executives periodically taking over the top positions are not hired by those already hard at work.

34. U.S. Bureau of the Census, *Statistical Abstract of the United States*, (Washington, D.C.: U.S. Government Printing Office, 2000).

35. Roger Cohen, "Two Named to New German Agency in Shuffle Over Beef Disease," *New York Times* 11 Jan. 2001, A10.

36. "Mexico: Corruption Firings," *New York Times* 2 Feb. 2001, A6.

37. Richard E. Neustadt, *Presidential Power* (New York: John Wiley, 1961), p. 100.

38. *The Times* (London), 16 Jan. 1991, 5.

39. Frank Bruni, "In First Radio Address, Bush Softens on School Vouchers," *New York Times*, 28 Jan. 2001, 15. This no doubt disappointed voucher supporters, but consider the public rela-

tions job faced by the new prime minister of Thailand, Thaksin Shinawatra. Upon his election about the same time as Bush's, the numerous poor people of his nation began besieging hospitals for the low-cost health care he had promised, farmers were refusing to repay loans because of a promised three-year moratorium on such debts, rural hamlets were hastily reconstituting themselves as villages to merit the $23,000 handout promised every one of the nation's 70,000 villages, and businessmen were eagerly expecting the creation of an Assets Management Corporation that would take care of the $12 billion worth of bad bank loans they had defaulted on. (Seth Mydans, "Thai Prime Minister Must Grapple with His Campaign Promises," *New York Times*, 12 Feb. 2001, A13.)

40. Marc Lacey, "Bush Meets with Black Caucus, Continuing a Theme of Outreach," *New York Times*, 1 Feb. 2001, A1.

41. David E. Sanger and Alison Mitchell, "Bush, the Conciliator, Meets with Democrats," *New York Times*, 3 Feb. 2001, A8; Marc Lacey, "Bush Faces Group of Harsh Critics: House Democrats," *New York Times*, 5 Feb. 2001, A12.

42. John Anthony Maltese, *Spin Control: The White Office of Communications and the Management of Presidential News* (Chapel Hill: University of North Carolina Press, 1994), pp. 232–39.

43. Richard A. Watson, *Presidential Vetoes and Public Policies* (Lawrence: University Press of Kansas, 1993), pp. 133–51. For a comparative study of the veto power, see George Tsebelis, "Decision Making in Political Systems: Veto Players in Presidentialism, Parliamentarism, Multicameralism and Multipartyism," *British Journal of Political Science* 25, no. 3 (July 1995): 289–325.

44. *New York Times*, 30 Dec. 1990, A9. "This is the saddest day in Argentine history," said former President Raul Alfonsin, under whose administration the men had been brought to trial and sentenced a mere five years earlier.

45. "An Indefensible Pardon," *New York Times*, editorial, 24 Jan. 2001, A22, and Asha Rangappa, "The Power to Pardon, the Power to Gain," *New York Times*, 3 Feb. 2001, A25.

46. Pao Chao Hsieh, *The Government of China* (Baltimore: Johns Hopkins University Press, 1925),

p. 143; E. A. Kracke Jr., "Region, Family and Individual in the Chinese Examination System," in John K. Fairbank, ed., *Chinese Thought and Institutions* (Chicago: University of Chicago Press, 1959), pp. 251–68.

47. Edward C. Thaden, *Russia Since 1801: The Making of a New Society* (New York: Wiley, 1971), p. 51.

48. William Safran, *The French Polity*, 4th ed. (New York: Longman, 1995), pp. 243–45.

49. Victoria Brittain, "Democracy Takes a Few Steps: The Charismatic Populists are Gone," *World Press Review* (Aug. 1991): 14–16.

50. Dennis Kavanagh, *British Politics: Continuities and Chance*, 2nd ed. (Oxford: Oxford University Press, 1990), p. 203.

51. *Washington Post*, 7 June 1994, A6.

52. For the U.S. shift over the last years of the twentieth century, see Keith Bradsher, "Partnership in the Deficit," *New York Times*, 3 Dec. 1995, 17, and Richard W. Stevenson, "The High-Stakes Politics of Spending the Surplus," *New York Times*, 7 Jan. 2001, WK3.

53. Weber also believed that the rules of bureaucratic behavior should be clearly set, should be impersonal—that is, apply to all without favoritism—should be based on written documents, and should apply only at work; the private and public spheres should be clearly distinct. Max Weber, *Essays in Sociology*, trans. and ed. H. H. Gerth and C. Wright Mills (New York: Oxford University Press, 1958), pp. 196–97.

54. Max Weber, *The Theory of Social and Economic Organization*, trans. A. M. Henderson and Talcott Parsons (Glencoe, Ill.: The Free Press, 1947), p. 338.

55. Stephanie Strom, "Official Japan Does Musical Chairs, and Desks," *New York Times*, 4 Jan. 2001, A3.

56. Sheila Kaplan, "Porkbarrel Politics at U.S. A.I.D.," *Multinational Monitor* (September 1993): 10–15. According to Kaplan, this U.S. agency not only authorizes the payment of excessively high fees for expertise and materials, but also the hiring of "advisers" who are in fact "on the lookout for overseas business" in the nations where they are doling out advice.

57. For general discussions of the problems of implementation, see Cathy Marie Johnson, *The Dynamics of Conflict Between Bureaucrats and Legislators* (Armonk, N.Y.: M. E. Sharpe, 1992), and James W. Fesler and Donald F. Kettl, *The Politics of the Administrative Process*, 2nd ed. (Chatham, N.J.: Chatham House, 1996), pp. 284–315. For a detailed study of the implementation of a single law, see Michael C. LeMay, *Anatomy of a Public Policy: The Reform of Contemporary American Immigration Law* (Westport, Conn.: Praeger, 1994).

58. *Wall Street Journal*, 22 Aug. 1995, A1, A5.

59. Ronald J. Hrebenar, *Interest Group Politics in America*, 3rd ed. (New York: M. E. Sharpe, 1997), pp. 109–10.

60. *New York Times*, 21 Feb. 1992, A12.

CHAPTER 10

Public Policy

WHAT IS A PUBLIC POLICY?

"The doors to this lecture hall close at ten minutes after the hour," announced the mean professor for whom I was working as teaching assistant, "and the teaching assistants will see to it that no one enters after that." There were five of us, and four doors. In those days, I never hesitated to take advantage of gender, figuring gender had certainly taken enough advantage of me: "You guys can do that!" I said to my peers, and to my surprise, they agreed. But I knew the professor had the power to insist the doors be closed and I told the students assigned to my discussion sections that they'd just have to live with it. (And I learned to get to lecture on time myself.)

The professor did not have to do that. But "Attendance is mandatory and shall be considered in assigning final grades," said the University Faculty Guide. So we blocked the doors and we took the roll. He had his way of following university policy.

A rule or a law is a plan; a policy is a general plan. It is a statement about a course of action to be followed, one that is designed to influence and determine relevant decisions and actions. Anyone and any organization can have a policy. A public policy is the policy of a government.

It is almost always easier to state a policy than to follow it. This is certainly true in governments, where leaders change, pressures mount, revenues fall, and bureaucrats may stubbornly keep doing things the same old way no matter what. When we talk about public policy, then, we usually tend to look not at what governments say they will do, but what they actually do do, that is, what laws they pass and implement in a particular domain. When we study policymaking, says Paul A. Sabatier, we study "the manner in which problems get conceptualized and brought to government for solution; government institutions formulate alternatives and select policy solutions; and those solutions get implemented, evaluated and revised."[1] In short, our procedure is more inductive than deductive. We speak of health policy, education policy, and economic policy, and all areas of policy, less as general plans and more as the sum total of government laws and regulations actually made and actually being enforced about a particular problem or sector of society.

We study particular policies not just for themselves but in order to observe the process of public policy, from start to finish, developing general theory from a case or set of cases, or as one author puts it, from "policy stories."[2] Out of such stories we have begun to have some ideas regarding why some procedures work and others fail, and have developed the subfield of public administration (sometimes referred to now as policy studies or public management). The study of public administration includes study of the bureaucratic process, a topic we have covered in the previous chapter. Here we will concentrate first on six factors that play important roles in determining what policy will be and then look at public policies today in the three domains of health, education, and the distribution of wealth.

WHAT DETERMINES WHAT PUBLIC POLICY WILL BE?

As noted, those who study public policymaking tend to concentrate heavily on the process itself. Influential factors outside that process are considered, but normally only within the specific "policy story." Here we look directly at how six characteristics of a system commonly influence its policy decisions: its economic system, its size, its natural resources, the degree of political stability it has, opinions held by the public, and the method of campaign finance. Because of their importance in policymaking and because they have not yet received much of our attention, we will treat economic systems and natural resources at greater length than the others.

Economic System

No single factor has a more important impact on the nature of the policies a nation will adopt than its economic system, that is, its system of producing, distributing, and consuming wealth. The word *economy* comes from the Greek word *oikonomia,* which itself came from the word for "household" and for "managing." Any economic system, whatever its scale, is first and foremost designed to provide for the material well-being of individual human beings, to provide enough food, shelter from the elements, medicine, means of transportation, knowledge, art, and other goods and services to make the human condition at least bearable and sometimes satisfying and happy.

We live in a world in which such resources have never yet been adequate to meet all our needs and desires. Decisions must be made. Policies must be established and carried out. Out of these decisions emerge economic systems; out of further decisions, economic systems change. The relationship between policies and economic systems is so strong and so reciprocal that political scientists have developed the subfield of *political economy* to study it.[3]

Because the economic system we live under affects the policies we carry out so profoundly, we take a moment here to look, briefly, at the characteristics of the four main types that have evolved so far: Pre-Capitalist, Capitalist, Socialist, and Mixed.

■ **Pre-Capitalist Economic Systems.**   The world's first economic systems were a direct response to the exigencies of nature. In most parts of the world, we human beings began as hunters and gatherers, simply taking the materials provided by our habitats, and moving on when local supplies were exhausted. The typical form of organization at this time, the band, was a group of families that moved together and determined together how goods should be shared, what individual behavior was permissible, and what ceremonies were necessary to propitiate the gods and satisfy the eternal longing that "there must be more to life than this." The group established the rules and customs—*made the policies*—that seemed likely to ensure the survival of its members.

The first efforts to raise our own food, rather than take what nature provided, were the beginning of a new economic system, agriculture.[4] When grain crops were discovered, and stored, animal husbandry became possible and increased everyone's chances of surviving the winters, thereby leading to the rapid expansion of the population.[5] It led also to the accumulation of material wealth and often to its concentration in the hands of some families. At that point new policies were needed—policies that would recognize the new realities, yet ensure the survival of the polity. Thus developed the kinship system, a means of ordering socioeconomic and political relationships in which each person's right to use a parcel of land and to own cattle or other property is determined by his or her place in the family lineage.

Over time, the development of mineral wealth meant the development not only of better tools for agriculture but also of better weapons for hunting. And weapons that could be used to hunt one's own game could also be used to take away the goods of others, inevitably an appealing if not a morally commendable way of meeting one's needs under the conditions of scarcity that prevailed.

At the same time, the more goods we were able to produce and the greater their variety, the keener we were to enter into peaceful relationships of trade with one another. The development of trade—coupled with the evolution of more powerful weapons for gaining and guarding wealth—led in turn to the development, in widely distant parts of the globe (but not everywhere), of more specialized polities: market towns, headquarters, villages, cities, even city-states.

As the need for more widely applicable policies evolved, so did the concentration of the power to make them. Now those who could best combine great landed wealth with the intelligent or ruthless exercise of the skills of warfare and intrigue had the advantage. In many places this more concentrated power took the form of *feudalism*, a system whereby large landholders controlled a semi-slave population of serfs to work their land and, when so required, to go to war on their behalf.[6]

The concentrated wealth of feudalism produced a demand for more material comforts, even as it often led the vast majority into ever greater poverty. As the products of craftsmanship became more complex and varied, the work of those who produced them became ever more specialized and the workers themselves ever more independent from the land. As trade expanded and towns prospered, corporate guilds were formed, led by masters who negotiated political as well as economic matters on behalf of the journeymen and apprentices who worked under them.[7]

The forces at work were not to be stopped: Ever more developed economies required ever more centralized institutions capable of making policies designed to ensure order and security, to direct large-scale public works such as the construction of roads and bridges, to set standards for trade and barter, to raise armies and guide aggressive and defensive warfare—in short, to create public policy on a scale not known before. The nation-state was emerging and the great feudal domains began breaking up. The growth of centralized monarchies with greatly expanded responsibilities led in turn to the quest for yet broader markets and for expanded resources. Foreign exploration and conquest began on a scale never seen before.[8]

■ **Capitalism.** Economically, the fifteenth-century voyages of discovery led to a new era of *imperialism*—the conquest and exploitation of others' lands. The practice of imperialism dates back to the ancient Romans, the Moguls of India, and the Ottomans.[9] Earlier imperialists had also ruled over the production of crops on large-scale plantations (*latifundia*) and over the extraction of other raw materials that they took home for processing and sale. Others had forced conquered peoples to work as slaves in life-threatening conditions and brought in more when the local supply was exhausted. What was new now was the geographic extent of European conquest, the immensity of the wealth produced, and the uses to which that wealth was put at home.

Exploitation of others' labor on so vast a scale meant that many goods became cheaper to produce. In response to increased demand, as well as to their growing freedom from feudal domination, the producers of such goods began plowing more and more of their profits back into their businesses in order to expand their productive capacity. This behavior—free entrepreneurs putting a significant share of profits back into capital expenditures in order to be able to produce more and more in response to market conditions—is the essence of capitalism.[10]

Modern capitalism can thus be said to be the child of European imperialism, and imperialism was a policy—indeed the foremost policy—of nations. But the policies directing the growth of capitalism after its establishment changed over the years. In the middle of the seventeenth century, the stronger nation-states adopted mercantilism as the surest means of sustaining the capitalist economy. *Mercantilism* requires the state to use its powers openly to provide the best possible conditions for private entrepreneurs to carry on their business. Uniform monetary systems and legal codes were the positive achievements of mercantilism; permitting the often-inhuman exploitation of laborers at home and abroad was the other side of the coin.[11]

The main point, of course, was that there should be plenty of coins, whichever side one looked at. And the mercantilist nations did prosper, so much so that the steady accumulation of capital provided the base for the eighteenth-century Industrial Revolution. As profits grew and the exploitation of labor worsened, however, the arguments in favor of having a supportive yet interfering partner—the state—began to seem less compelling to those who were developing great wealth. They believed a new policy was needed, one that would set business free to pursue the untrammeled growth that was to characterize the evolution of capitalism in the nineteenth century. That policy was found in laissez-faire individualism.

"Let them do as they will," argued British theorist Adam Smith, asserting that if economic decisions were left to the free play of self-regulating market forces, the best of all possible systems for production and distribution of the world's goods would be found.[12] Laissez-faire economists believe that all government needs to do is ensure sound money (as when it backs the currency with gold deposits), balance its own budget (because a budget deficit represents an unfair incursion of government into the private economy), encourage free trade, and keep welfare expenditures to an absolute minimum. As this suggests, state policy is still very important in a free enterprise system; indeed, as Ray Hudson has pointed out, "the conditions under which capitalist production can be made possible do not occur naturally but need to be secured [and] the state plays a key role in securing them."[13]

By the beginning of the twentieth century, and especially after World War I, the world had changed again. International markets were shrinking, colonized peoples were beginning the long trek to independence, and trade barriers were multiplying as individual nations sought to cushion their separate economies against the spreading Great Depression. The hope that capitalism would automatically provide plenty for all began to fade, and the people whose rewards had so far been limited to such hope began to lose their patience.

■ **Socialist Economies.**   Within the nations on the losing end of these uneven struggles, some began to argue for the introduction of new systems for the production and distribution of wealth, and foremost among those proposed was that of *socialism*. We have discussed the ideology of socialism in Chapter 2 and here we will point out only some of the specifically economic components of this many-sided system of belief.

In its purest form, socialism carries the natural connection of the political and economic spheres to its logical conclusion: It calls for the absolute merger of the two. In the ideal socialist system, the state would control all the means of production and would itself be controlled by the workers. With absolute control, the state would be able to establish and carry out long-range comprehensive economic policies (a planned economy).

Furthermore, knowing that the state made policies only in their own best interests, and that in working for the state they were working for themselves, the workers in the ideal socialist state would no longer be alienated from their jobs. They would therefore produce as well and as much as they possibly could. Either each would "give according to his ability and receive according to his need," or all would be paid equally regardless of the quality or usefulness of their work.

■ **Mixed Economies.** Efforts to put some form of socialist economic system into operation were undertaken in nearly every part of the world once the failings of unrestrained capitalism became apparent. Furthermore, even where the socialist prescriptions were consistently rejected, some form of a *mixed economy*—that is, an economy based on a mixture of public and private ownership of the means of production and on considerable public regulation of the private sector—was likely to be adopted. Soon there was no nation in the world in which every productive enterprise was in private hands, in which no effort was made by the state to consult workers' representatives in making economic policy, and in which the government never undertook to regulate prices or wages. (See Box 10.1 for a discussion of why some states chose socialism altogether while others merely introduced a greater measure of state ownership and regulation into capitalist systems.)

A mixed economy does not always mean nationalizing public utilities and imposing wage and price controls while leaving a large private sector (mostly capitalist) in place, or introducing wage incentives and permitting the market to set prices while maintaining public ownership of the means of production (mostly socialistic). Any economy based on a mixture of public and private control of the means of production may properly be termed a mixed economy. A brief look at another variation, *corporatism*, will help to clarify this point.

A corporatist economy is one in which formal ownership of the means of production remains in private hands but the state requires that all industries and other productive enterprises be grouped into units according to the function being performed. All enterprises devoted to metallurgy, for example, might constitute one *corporation* (the word is used in a broad and general sense), all farmers would belong to another, all seagoing merchants to yet another, and so forth. Even homemakers and students might be assigned to their own units. Under such a system, every corporation has its own ruling body and makes its own policies regarding such matters as what goods and services shall be produced, what wages shall be paid, and what prices shall be charged. However, the state maintains close control over the selection of the leaders in the corporation, and is careful to see that the decisions reached are in accord with state policy. Further liaison between the political and economic spheres is provided by setting up a quasi-legislative body to which the different corporations must send representatives. This

BOX 10.1
**Socialism or
Mixed Economy?**

Why, once the inadequacies of unrestrained capitalism became clear, did some states choose socialism while other states were content simply to introduce certain socialist-type policies into a capitalist system? No single definitive answer is possible, but as a rough generalization, we can say that wherever political leaders were willing, for whatever mixture of self-serving and humanitarian motives, to permit the relatively free development of democratic political processes during the heyday of capitalism — by extending suffrage to ordinary men and women and by permitting the formation of competitive political parties— there it was possible to work out modifications of the capitalist system without abrupt political and economic change. By the end of the nineteenth century, and in many instances long before, the United States, Britain, and most of the nations of Western Europe (Germany, Spain, and Italy are important exceptions) had completely accepted the idea of popular sovereignty. Full rights of citizenship were extended to one group after another, often after determined resistance but never in open repudiation of the basic principles of democracy. Such nations developed and maintained mostly capitalistic economic systems.

On the other hand, in nations like the Soviet Union, many of the Eastern European nations, and China, as well as in the young African states and older Latin American political systems dominated by northern imperialist powers, the increasing concentration of economic power in the early capitalist period was accompanied by authoritarian leadership, either indigenous or imposed from without, that rigorously rejected all demands that political power be shared. In such political systems it was much more likely that political and economic revolution would take place, resulting, when successful, in the establishment of a socialist regime.

economic-based senate takes the place of the more traditional parliament, which, as we know, is based on geographic representation.

Although the corporatist ideal is clearly highly authoritarian in its classic guise and has been strongly discredited by the policies of the French, Italian, and Spanish regimes that experimented with it during the middle of the twentieth century, it continues to appeal as a mode of reducing the painful confrontations among workers, managers, and bureaucrats that we find in less rigidly regulated systems. It is not uncommon today for social scientists to urge a new, presumably enlightened neocorporatism, a kind of capitalist system in which the state exercises its power much less dictatorially but does give official recognition to different interests by establishing boards of representatives to advise the government.[14] Under this version, the neocorporatist state normally closely controls who is appointed to the boards and guides their deliberations by such selective "encouragements" as government subsidies or other supportive legislation on behalf of those who are deemed properly cooperative.

■ **The Current Ascendancy of Capitalism.**   There is one clear truth about economic systems: They change. The corporatist idea comes and goes, and the balance between capitalism and socialism shifts, and shifts again. Even as the more moderate aspects of socialism were being adopted in predominantly capitalist systems, and new, more-or-less fully socialist experiments were being attempted in Central American and African states, the world's political-economic pendulum was starting its swing back in the opposite direction. Elites governing almost all of the states that had opted for the socialist solution in its purest form began to find it personally convenient to restore some characteristics of the much-maligned capitalist system, producing their own form of mixed economy.[15] Those with the greatest power used it to establish policies ensuring themselves significant advantages in wages and other material rewards, new forms of social rank were allowed to evolve, and private enterprises began to flourish here and there, with or without the overt approval of the state. Socialist policy was allowed to founder and capitalist practices to flourish.

The tension thus produced between the proclaimed economic system and economic reality could not endure, especially not when those dutifully carrying out the prescripts of the former were doing so poorly. The Soviet form of socialism fell apart, and the entire former eastern bloc began to shift to openly capitalist economies. The capitalist system is thus now clearly ascendant, although the continued existence of Communist regimes in China, Cuba, Vietnam, and North Korea, and of strong (and sometimes ruling) social democratic parties in much of Western Europe means that socialism is far from dead. Furthermore, as Joseph S. Berliner points out, under the new capitalism "the welfare state has by no means been dismantled" and no capitalist state is carrying out a full return to the laissez-faire tenets of the nineteenth century.[16] Indeed, in some nations the new capitalism may now be evolving toward a new kind of mixed economy, *market socialism,* a system in which market forces are duly recognized and accommodated, but also controlled with comprehensive and extensive social intervention and control.[17]

Although we have now given the nature of the economic system more attention than we will give all the other factors to be considered put together, we have not discussed two of the most important forms of a mixed economy, *colonialism* or *neocolonialism.* However, it seems appropriate to save these for Chapter 14 ("Political and Economic Globalization"), and to turn our attention now to several other important factors influencing national policy-making.

The Size of a Nation

The size of a nation can be measured either as its territorial extent or as the number of citizens inhabiting its territory. Both these measures are influenced by geography as well as economics. Geographic conditions help determine how large a polity will be as well as how many people will seek their living within its boundaries. Climate, natural resources, and the likelihood of natural disasters (such as earthquakes, hurricanes, or floods) determine the suitability of any terrain for habitation. Such natural barriers as mountain ranges or bodies of water help to determine which people live and work together and which are considered "foreigners," with whom intercourse is infrequent and limited.

Once size is established, it inevitably has a profound impact on the course of political life and the policies a government will seek to put into practice. The territorial extent of a nation limits the number of people who can be fed and sheltered, given that society's particular level of development. If the resources within the polity's physical domain are inadequate to its population's needs, then the economic struggle for scarce resources will manifest itself in the struggles over policy. In China, where the total population is well over 1 billion and about 12 million more people are born than die each year, the answer has been the "one family, one child" policy—but the answer to the answer has been to conceal illegal children, making it all but impossible to get an accurate census.[18]

The causal relationship between the economic consequences of geographic size and the substance of policies can work both ways: The size of the nation definitely affects what policies a nation adopts, but policies can also affect the size of the nation, changing territorial extent. Wars shift boundaries outward or inward, governments finance voyages of discovery and conquest, and legislatures grant free land to those who push into the wilderness and statehood or other formal recognition to distant territories. Political decisions also influence the number of citizens a state will have. Deciding to go to war can lead to enormous loss of life, offering government family allowances after such wars can lead to population growth, and pursuing government sterilization or contraceptive programs in nations where the supply of food is inadequate can reduce growth or even cause the population to decline.

Despite the polite fictions of international law, which holds all sovereign states to be equal, small states *are* different from large states. Certainly not all small states are weak: Consider the size of Denmark—or Japan. But small size can make independent survival problematic. When the tiny Baltic states of Lithuania, Estonia, and Latvia first began to clamor for independence from the Soviet Union in 1991, even those most sympathetic to their concerns had to wonder how such tiny states, whose resources had been drained by so many years of Soviet domination, could possibly expect to survive in the modern world. Yet these Baltic Rim states are now doing well, far better than some other ex-Soviet republics that are larger, thanks in part to another geographic factor: location. Their placement along the eastern coastline of the Baltic Sea, bordered to the north by Finland, and to the west and south by Scandinavia and Western Europe, meant that these states played the role of "East-West gateway" even during the years of Soviet dominance, and the ties thus developed have been maintained and strengthened as economic liberalization has followed independence. Foreign direct investments "notably from their Nordic neighbors" have been of major assistance, and it is commonly believed that these states are now moving slowly but surely toward integration in the European Union.[19]

Natural Resources

One of the reasons small states are often at a disadvantage is inadequate natural resources. Yet there is no direct relationship between size and natural wealth; most nations' boundaries were established long before a full inventory of their resources could be taken. Furthermore, resources that may have been adequate in the past may cease to be so, owing to man-made as much as to natural disasters; recurrent famines in Ethiopia are compounded by periodic droughts, but the primary causes are "long-continued bad land use and steadily increasing human and stock population over decades [as well as] soil erosion and massive deforestation."[20]

Geographic location may itself be a resource, as the example of the Baltic states suggests—or a liability. Ricardo Hausmann argues that some nations are simply "prisoners of geography," situated as they are in tropical, landlocked nations with little access to markets and new technologies. He points out that of the 24 nations classified as industrial "not one lies between the Tropics of Cancer and Capricorn, except for the northern part of Australia and most of the Hawaiian Islands," and of the 30 richest economies in the world, only Brunei, Hong Kong, and Singapore are in tropical zones.[21] When to the disadvantages of climate is added a strong propensity for natural disasters—as in the small states of Central America where earthquakes, floods, and hurricanes are common—the first priority of policymakers may be planning in advance for recurrent tragedies and making sure sufficient aid will be rapidly forthcoming.[22]

In any case, what constitutes a "resource" is constantly changing. Yesterday's frustratingly hard earth may have concealed today's uranium mine; to-

Inadequate water, a serious cause of famine, is sometimes caused by poor land use, soil erosion, and massive deforestation as well as by climactic change. Here a Zimbabwean woman attempts to catch termites for protein in her drought-stricken land.
© Louise Gubb/The Image Works

day's thorny patch of scrub brush may turn out to be tomorrow's cure for cancer. As new discoveries of hitherto hidden wealth are made, political forces shift and respond, and new policies are adopted. The expectation that the world's polities will continue to demand ever greater supplies of oil (see Figure 10.1) has offered numerous examples of this truth in recent years. The discovery of oil in eastern Nigeria in the 1960s clearly played a major part in persuading the residents of that part of the nation that they might make a success of the independent state of Biafra—and in persuading a remarkable number of other nations to provide weapons or other assistance to one side or the other in the civil war that ensued, in the hope of having access to that oil when peace was established. The rich deposits of oil offshore from Vietnam were seldom mentioned during that long conflict but cannot have failed

FIGURE 10.1

Growing World and U.S. Dependence on Imported Oil: 1990–2020 (Average daily domestic production vs. demand in millions of barrels per day)

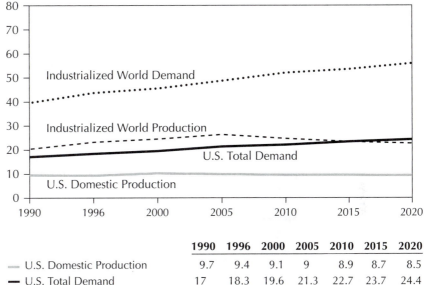

	1990	1996	2000	2005	2010	2015	2020
— U.S. Domestic Production	9.7	9.4	9.1	9	8.9	8.7	8.5
— U.S. Total Demand	17	18.3	19.6	21.3	22.7	23.7	24.4
- - Industrialized World Production	20.1	23	24.7	25.4	24.8	23.7	22.9
••• Industrialized World Demand	39.5	43.4	45.6	48.4	51.1	53.3	55.3

Source: Anthony H. Cordesman with Sarin Hacatoryan, *The Changing Geopolitics of Energy— Part I* (Washington, D.C.: Center for Strategic and International Studies, 1998). Reprinted by permission.

to be a consideration for the policymakers of the nations involved. China uses oil for only about 25 percent of its primary energy consumption, but as industrial development proceeds apace, its total consumption is growing rapidly, forcing the Chinese government to abandon its traditional policy of self-reliance in oil. The need for a dependable external supply is expected by some to "stabilize and moderate Chinese foreign policy."[23]

Middle Eastern oil wealth has long shaped the policies of the nations assembled in the Organization of Petroleum Exporting Countries (OPEC) and of their foreign partners. Iraq invaded Kuwait in 1990 in order to take possession of oil deposits that would help restore her economy after a disastrous decade of war with Iran, and it would be foolish to imagine that the willingness of the United States and her allies to come to the rescue of Kuwait in 1991 was not owing in large part to the need to keep that tiny kingdom's oil flowing in the right directions (and the profits therefrom into the right pockets). The care taken by the United States to widen the antiterrorist alliance formed in 2001 to include as many Middle Eastern states as possible (see Chapter 7) was certainly not owing only to the fact that such states had large and sensitive Muslim populations.

FIGURE 10.2
The Caspian Basin

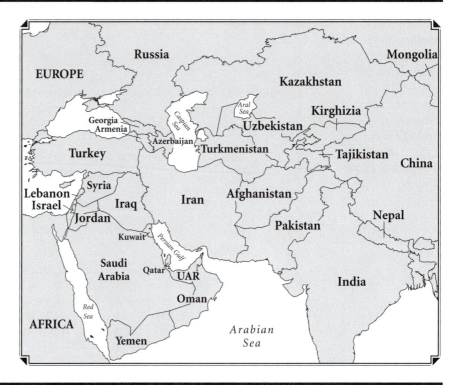

But it is not only Middle Eastern oil that has shaped national policies; in recent years the quest for this all-important resource has shifted heavily northward, into the Caspian Basin. Most of us may have paid little attention to this part of the world prior to September 11, 2001, but not so those interested in oil (Figure 10.2). American oil business executives and government policymakers began an intense investigation in the late 1990s into the prospects, more than a little intrigued by the thought of "proven oil reserves" in the Caspian region ranging from 15 to 30 billion barrels and "unproven reserves" ranging up to 200 billion.[24] The key problem has been how to get them out, given that the area's natural resources are landlocked. An answer that appealed to many was: through Afghanistan. The Afghans were certainly willing, but finding the foreign investors able to do the job was proving an almost impossible task, especially as the American-based corporation most interested in taking part insisted it would not do so as long as the Taliban were in power. As a careful reading of Box 10.2 should suggest, it is unlikely that the war against terrorism is not also, conveniently enough for some, a war *for* oil. (See also Figure 10.2.)

BOX 10.2
What Is a Natural Resource? Who Makes Foreign Policy?

Afghanistan is relatively rich in oil, natural gas, and coal reserves, but poor in the capacity to extract and export this wealth, especially since war with the Soviet Union destroyed much of the nation's productive infrastructure. Petroleum products such as diesel, gasoline, and jet fuel were imported from Pakistan and Turkmenistan and electricity from Turkmenistan. The nation's own economy depended heavily on the production of opium poppies and narcotics trafficking.[25]

For some time prior to the September 11th terrorist attacks on New York City and the Pentagon, Afghanistan had been trying to work out an agreement with Turkmenistan and Pakistan for building a new pipeline, and interest in helping was expressed both by the U.S.-based Unocal Corporation and Saudi Arabia's Delta Oil. John J. Maresca, vice president for international relations for Unocal Corporation, summed up the position of his company in testimony to the House Committee on International Relations in February 1998. The company was interested in far more than Afghanistan's own natural energy resources: "A route through Afghanistan appears to be the best option . . . Unocal envisions the creation of a Central Asian Oil Pipeline Consortium . . . a regional pipeline system that will utilize and gather oil from existing pipeline infrastructure in Turkmenistan, Uzbekistan, Kazakhstan and Russia. . . . The 1,040 mile long oil pipeline, would extend southeasterly through Afghanistan to an export terminal that would be constructed on the Pakistan coast on the Arabian Sea." However, by the end of the century, Unocal abandoned the project because of political turmoil and international outrage over human rights abuses in Afghanistan. Indeed, even in his 1998 testimony, Mr. Maresca had reminded his audience, "we have made it clear that construction of our proposed pipeline cannot begin until a recognized government is in place that has the confidence of governments, lenders and our company."[26]

And then came September 11, 2001, and with it the possibility of another shift in U.S. strategy. Moving the oil through Afghanistan was once again possible to imagine, and it was argued that American military engagement would give the United States "more leverage in working with Central Asian leaders on [a] whole cluster of issues, including ways of avoiding the costs of expensive pipelines running under the Caspian to reach Baku and then go on to Turkey." At the same time Russia was moving strongly into the game, ready to join Washington's antiterrorist campaign in the hope that this would cause the United States to "accept Moscow's role in ensuring the flow of swelling amounts of Caspian oil via the northern route guaranteed by Russia."[27] Everything had changed, and policymakers in all the nations concerned were on the alert to profit from the change.

One way or the other, expect the oil to flow.

As the Afghan story illustrates, even abundant natural resources mean little so long as they remain entirely natural. If they are dramatic or beautiful to see, they may constitute important tourist attractions. They may even contribute to the psychic well-being of a citizenry, and thus indirectly to its productivity. But in most cases, resources, whether natural or imported, must be changed in some way if they are to bring economic rewards. Those changes may be made in the private or the public sector, or by both working together, or they may be made by the citizens of other nations to whom the raw materials are brought for processing. Large-scale foreign investment may lead to local prosperity and a higher standard of living for all or to even greater impoverishment and the destruction of natural beauty. The competition for the right to develop a nation's natural wealth may lead to war and devastation for ordinary citizens, and great wealth for a complicit elite. When does a natural resource become an unnatural liability? What part can a nation's public policies play in preventing this development?

Political Instability

Another factor bound to affect what policies will or can be developed is the political stability of the nation. If there is a fear of civil war, revolution, military coup d'état, or simply widespread strikes and demonstrations that may lead to a peaceful change of power at the next election, decision makers must take those factors into consideration when determining what policies to adopt.

What decisions they make will depend in part on what they perceive to be the causes of the political instability. For some policymakers, those who cause the instability are simply greedy, seeking rewards they have not earned, and the correct response is disciplinary action, if not repression. For others, the grievances expressed must be closely examined on their merits and, if found reasonable, should be substantively addressed. In practice, policymakers often combine carrot and stick, while scholars try to marshal the evidence that would suggest one cause is more likely than the other.

One recent study of 47 civil wars between 1960 and 1999 takes the former point of view and claims that simple greed is a powerful motivation for rebellion. Paul Collier suggests that certain kinds of natural resources—"unprocessed commodities" such as gemstones or coffee—can actually stimulate and prolong civil war: "Rebel groups need to meet a payroll without producing anything, so they prey on an economic activity that won't collapse under the weight of their predatory activities."[28] The perspective of this World Bank author may strike us as rather biased (the world has never seen a good rebellion?), but the economic logic seems reasonable: Presumably George Washington wouldn't have minded being able to buy supplies for the troops at Valley Forge with a few diamonds from a nearby mine. . . .

Political instability affects both specific policy decisions and the state's capacity to make policy at all. Protest demonstrations called by Serbian opposition leaders grew so numerous they helped bring about the fall of the regime of President Slobodan Milošević. Here some 10,000 people rally against Milošević in Belgrade, May 27, 2000.
© AFP/CORBIS

But the American rebellion proceeded nonetheless, without much in the way of handy commodities. It is reasonable to consider as well the grievances of the rebels, their validity, and the desirability (and possibility) of providing remedies. There is no doubt that the most common grievance of all is inequality. Is there a link between income inequality and political instability? Alberto Alesina and Roberto Perotti tested two hypotheses on data drawn from a sample of 71 nations:

1. Income inequality, by fueling social discontent, increases sociopolitical instability.
2. Sociopolitical instability, by creating uncertainty in the politicoeconomic environment, reduces investment.

Ranking those 71 nations from poorest to richest, they gave each a score on their SPI (sociopolitical instability) index. The results of this ranking, shown in Table 10.1 (the higher the figure, the greater the SPI), indicates a positive correlation between poverty and sociopolitical instability. Further analysis showed a high negative correlation between SPI and investment.

TABLE 10.1
Sociopolitical Instability (SPI) and Income Equality (1960–1985). Countries Ranked in Order of Income Equality

Country	SPI	Country	SPI
Tanzania	−0.73	Panama	5.42
Malawi	−2.66	Brazil	−0.19
Sierra Leone	9.11	Colombia	−4.69
Niger	3.42	Jamaica	−11.60
Burma	1.58	Greece	2.41
Togo	6.80	Costa Rica	−11.76
Bangladesh	8.39	Cyprus	−5.55
Kenya	−0.72	Peru	7.46
Botswana	−9.68	Barbados	−11.76
Egypt	1.83	Iran	−1.13
Chad	7.61	Mexico	−4.15
India	−8.92	Japan	−11.68
Morocco	2.41	Spain	−2.77
Nigeria	12.69	Iraq	30.64
Pakistan	9.11	Ireland	−11.37
Congo	21.66	South Africa	−7.08
Benin	30.34	Israel	−11.67
Zimbabwe	−1.76	Chile	0.50
Madagascar	2.42	Argentina	30.54
Sudan	15.09	Italy	−8.10
Thailand	9.31	Uruguay	4.80
Zambia	−3.46	Austria	−11.68
Ivory Coast	−2.74	Finland	−11.76
Honduras	5.00	France	−9.44
Senegal	−0.98	Holland	−11.68
Gabon	4.05	U.K.	−7.63
Tunisia	−2.57	Norway	−11.76
Philippines	−4.14	Sweden	−11.68
Bolivia	44.19	Australia	−11.68
Dom. Republic	8.22	Germany	−11.45
Sri Lanka	−9.91	Venezuela	4.03
El Salvador	7.94	Denmark	−11.76
Malaysia	−11.21	New Zealand	−11.76
Ecuador	19.91	Canada	−11.68
Turkey	2.88	Switzerland	−11.76

Source: Alberto Alesina and Roberto Perotti, "Income Distribution, Political Instability and Investment," *European Economic Review* 40 (1996): 1211. Reprinted with permission from Elsevier Science.

Finding both hypotheses substantiated by their data, Alesina and Perotti then attack the argument that taxation policies that lead to income redistribution are bad for investment because they increase the tax burden on investors. Perhaps so, they say, but on the other hand "the same policies may reduce social tensions and, as a result, create a socio-political climate more conducive to productive activities and capital accumulation."[29]

Public Opinions

As we noted in Chapter 4, there is never a single public opinion, and we are now much better able to know the public's various opinions on any topic of interest, and what proportion of the general public takes each position (including "don't know and don't care"). We have also considered the great importance of opinion polling for successful election campaigning, and how expensive it can be. But the fact that candidates pay attention during campaigns does not tell us whether policymakers, once in office, continue to pay attention.

Some observers of American policymaking argue that all too much attention is paid in the United States. Paul J. Quirk and Joseph Hinchliffe discuss the phenomenon of "plebiscitary policymaking," with leaders dependent on "immediate public approval." With decision-making processes so open, and citizens so ready to express opinions they have arrived at quite superficially on an ever wider range of issues, the result, they argue, is to weaken not only the influence of special interest groups but also that of expert information and judgment.[30] Others are worried that public opinion is not strong enough. Lawrence R. Jacobs and Robert Y. Shapiro find a decline in leadership responsiveness and a rise in opinion manipulation, with the result that the effectiveness of the governing process and the public's confidence in it have declined.[31] In partial corroboration, a study by the Pew Center found that only 31 percent of the members of the U.S. Congress believed that Americans knew enough about issues to make wise decisions about public policy.[32]

Making a careful review of existing studies, Jeff Manza and Fay Lomax Cook arrive at a possible explanation for the different views scholars have regarding the impact of public opinion in the United States. They find that when "measured public opinion expresses a coherent mood or view on a particular policy question (or bundle of policy questions) in a way that is recognizable by political elites" policy is in fact highly likely to move in the direction of public opinion. But they also say the evidence shows that even then "policy entrepreneurs" have considerable room for maneuver, and, given the frequency of disagreement, public opinion normally simply sets "important parameters" on policymaking.[33]

Method of Campaign Finance

However carefully policymakers listen to the public and follow the polls, in many nations they must also make policy in accordance with promises they have made to get funding, legal or illegal, for their election campaigns. As we have already seen, U.S. policymakers are more susceptible to this kind of influence than those of other nations, and the problem is not limited to one side of the partisan fence, as the following examples show. (However, keep in mind that American leaders are not the only ones subject—and responsive—to this kind of pressure.)

U.S. President and Mrs. Bill Clinton raised the art of fundraising to new heights (financially—morally, we might say they dropped it to new lows), personally guiding and guaranteeing the connection between donations and responsive policy. When oilman Roger Tamraz paid $300,000 to spend an afternoon at the White House in 1996 ("there was swimming, there was tennis, there was barbecue, there was the movies. We didn't need to talk about the project [the Caspian Sea pipeline project] because I did not have to"), he told reporters it was a good deal: "It was a good investment . . . it allows you to be in the club of the big boys, it's fine." [34]

The link between donations and actual policy outcomes became even stronger—or at least more apparent—when George W. Bush took office. Over 80 percent of the $314 million contributed to the Bush campaign and the Republican National Committee for his election came from corporations or individuals employed by them. And the payoffs were not long in coming. Within two months of the new president's inauguration, the White House announced he would sign a bill making it tougher for consumers to escape credit-card debt by filing for bankruptcy. What was not announced, but was well known, was that this policy was one that MBNA America Bank, a company that had, together with its employees, given a total of about $1.3 million to the Bush campaign, most hoped to see adopted. That same week the president agreed to a plan to kill the ergonomic regulations designed to protect workers from wrist, back, and other injuries, a wish "high on the priority lists of the U.S. Chamber of Commerce, the National Association of Manufacturers and the National Association of Wholesaler-Distributors," groups that could not legally donate directly to Bush but that had "mounted major grass-roots and advertising campaigns that benefited Mr. Bush and other Republicans in the 2000 elections." Drug companies, tobacco companies, airline companies, and, of course, oil companies all waited confidently for their turn. Tobacco companies were supremely confident the Bush administration would soon kill a massive federal lawsuit ("we are not lobbying on this at all," said the happy Philip Morris spokeswoman after the election) and oil companies had already rejoiced in the addition of Richard Cheney to the Republican ticket ("the GOP's idea of diversity is having two guys heading the ticket from two different oil companies," suggested one irreverent comedian).[35]

Europeans often pride themselves, correctly, on having erected a number of legal barriers against the massive inflow of private moneys into political campaigns and thereby against the control of elected representatives by private interests. But what cannot be done legally in Europe is, unfortunately, often done illegally. One of the cases more shocking to continental sensibilities was the discovery in Germany that millions of corporate dollars had been funneled into the coffers of the ruling Christian Democratic Union (CDU), with the knowledge and blessing of Helmut Kohl, the nation's beloved "eternal chancellor" who had also been the party's leader for 16 years. In exchange for the large sums paid into the secret fund that came to be known by the German press as *Das System Kohl,* numerous state policies had been pursued, including arranging the sale of 36 tanks to Saudi Arabia by a well-known German arms dealer.[36]

PUBLIC POLICIES TODAY

We turn now to specific areas of policy, giving examples and noting some of the problems that arise in each. We begin with health policies, move next to education, and end by going full circle, back to economic questions, this time considering policy problems that arise in connection with the distribution of wealth.

Health

In 2000, the World Health Organization (WHO) carried out a study of its 191 member nations, ranking them from best to worst according to a set of five indicators including overall level of population health. The United States was found to spend a higher portion of its gross domestic product (GDP) on health care than any other nation, but ranked only 37 overall (just after Costa Rica, two notches above Cuba). First place went to France, followed by Italy, Spain, Oman, Austria, Japan, and Singapore.[37]

Perhaps more important than the rankings, however, was the comment by project director Christopher Murray, that "virtually all countries are under-utilizing the resources that are available to them." The principal failings were: not enough attention by health ministries to private sector health care; too many physicians working simultaneously for the public sector and in private practice; widespread corruption, bribery, "moonlighting," and other illegal practices; and failure of health ministries to enforce regulations "they themselves have created or are supposed to implement in the public interest." In short, failures of policy and failures of policy enforcement.

One of the more frustrating aspects of contemporary policymakers' efforts to improve the health of their citizenries has been the emergence of new problems, and the resurgence of those deemed nearly cured. AIDS is the obvious example of the first: By 2001 over 58 million people had been infected with HIV and 22 million had died. Nearly 6 million additional people are newly infected every year and two-thirds of the HIV-positive population live in sub-Saharan Africa, the world's poorest area with the fewest resources for waging an effective campaign against the disease.[38]

"Last October the 120,000 citizens of Punta Arenas, a Chilean town on the southern tip of Latin America, received a very unusual public-health warning. They and the Argentinean citizens of Ushuaia just across the border were warned to stay indoors between the hours of 11 A.M. and 3 P.M.— out of the blistering rays of a southern sun peeking through an ever-expanding hole in the ozone layer. The ozone filter over the South Pole has become so weakened by a mixture of manufactured chemicals— chloro-fluorocarbons, bromine atoms, nitrogen oxides and chlorine— that severe skin damage could occur in just seven minutes."

Source: Richard Swift, "Health Hazard," *New Internationalist* (January–February 2001): 11. Reprinted with permission.

Serious new health problems have also been caused or are at least linked to ecological damage to the planet. One study estimates that "close to one fourth of all disabilities can be traced back to such factors as polluted air and water and unsafe food. More than 3 million people die each year worldwide from water-related diseases."[39] (See Box 10.3.)

Another new factor is the rising cost of health care, particularly drugs. Heavily lobbied by pharmaceutical companies, government officials in the prosperous nations where the companies do business are slow to impose limits on drug costs, with the result that essential medicines are often unavailable to the poor among their own populations, while the problem is even more severe in poorer nations. In the latter case, not only are drugs yet harder to buy, but those available may not address the most common ills— why spend money on research and development of medicines that those who need them cannot afford to buy?[40]

The terrorist attack of September 11, 2001, brought another new problem to the forefront of public attention: how to prepare public health agencies to deal with bioterrorism and other acts of mass destruction. Three years before the attack, D. A. Henderson warned that the threat was real, particularly from smallpox (itself an old problem making a comeback) and anthrax, and that the level of preparedness was shockingly low.[41] Two years later, Joseph Wackerle concurred, pointing out that policymakers had concentrated on programs training firefighters and law enforcement officers to deal with "Weapons of Mass Destruction Events" but had given far less attention to training physicians, nurses, and other health-care professionals.[42] When anthrax attacks began in the United States in the fall of 2001, these assessments seemed well substantiated as the public watched ill-prepared health officials struggle to put together policies and practices that would work.

There are also old problems, seemingly almost vanquished or at least on their way out, now making serious trouble again. In Russia there have been, for example, new outbreaks of cholera, compounded by the refusal of in-dustrial and agricultural interests to clean up lakes and rivers that nurture the bacteria. And Russia offers other examples of old ills becoming newly virulent: The sharp inequalities that have come with the sudden lifting of socialist controls have left the losers in the new economy more subject than ever to alcoholism (half of all deaths in Russia are now owing in part to abuse of alcohol), to cigarette addiction (cigarette production and im-ports have risen 40 percent; 32 percent of all deaths are caused by tobacco-related illnesses), and, for women unable to afford birth-control devices, to death by botched abortions (Russia has one of the highest abortion rates in the world—200.4 abortions for every 100 live births—and in 1993 one report claimed that 15 percent of all female deaths were attributable to abortions).[43]

The challenge to even the most committed policymakers working in a strong and relatively stable economy has been painfully clear in the sad saga of U.S. health care. The WHO report did not come as a surprise; everyone had known for some time that the U.S. health system was in trouble. The Clinton administration came to power in 1993 determined to provide ade-quate health care for everyone and engaged in a complicated and, ultimately, utterly futile set of compromises with the health-care providers and the busi-ness interests (e.g., hospitals and drug companies). The plan failed to win ap-proval, the quality of available health services declined, and, by the end of Clinton's second term in office, 14 percent of the population were still with-out coverage, including 8.5 million children and 9.2 million poor (the poor were far less likely to be insured in all categories—see Figure 10.3).[44]

Education

As in the question of health, so in matters of education it is easy to say to policymakers everywhere: You could do better! Yet here too the problems we would like to see resolved are difficult indeed. To give some idea of the com-plexity, we look first at how serious the need is for educational improvement worldwide and then at some of the policy questions in the struggle over lo-cal versus national control of education now taking place in the United States.

"Everyone has the right to education," says Article 26 of the Universal Declaration of Human Rights (1950), and this declaration has been reiter-ated in many subsequent covenants, such as the International Covenant on Economic, Social and Cultural Rights (1966), the International Covenant on Civil and Political Rights, the Convention on the Elimination of All Forms of Discrimination against Women (1979), the Convention on the Rights of the Child (1989), and the Convention on Technical and Vocational Educa-tion (1989).[45] So, how well are we doing?

FIGURE 10.3 Percentage of U.S. Population Without Health Insurance for the Entire Year of 2000, by Selected Characteristics, Among Total Population and Among Poor

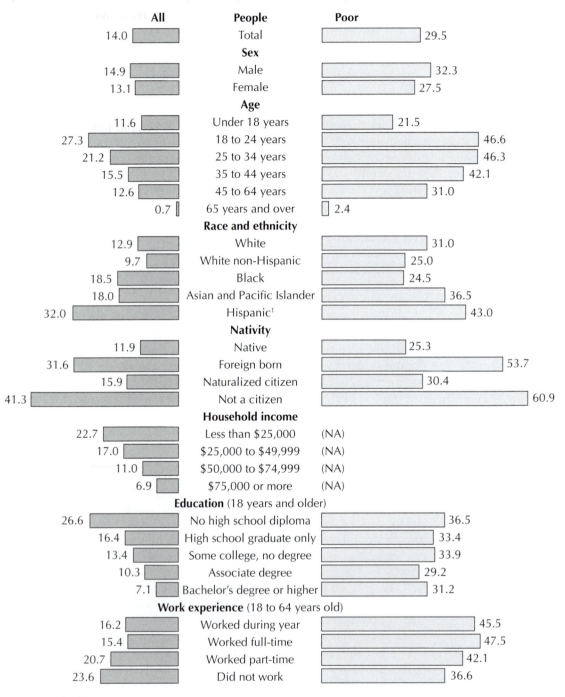

	All	People	Poor
	14.0	Total	29.5
		Sex	
	14.9	Male	32.3
	13.1	Female	27.5
		Age	
	11.6	Under 18 years	21.5
	27.3	18 to 24 years	46.6
	21.2	25 to 34 years	46.3
	15.5	35 to 44 years	42.1
	12.6	45 to 64 years	31.0
	0.7	65 years and over	2.4
		Race and ethnicity	
	12.9	White	31.0
	9.7	White non-Hispanic	25.0
	18.5	Black	24.5
	18.0	Asian and Pacific Islander	36.5
	32.0	Hispanic[1]	43.0
		Nativity	
	11.9	Native	25.3
	31.6	Foreign born	53.7
	15.9	Naturalized citizen	30.4
	41.3	Not a citizen	60.9
		Household income	
	22.7	Less than $25,000	(NA)
	17.0	$25,000 to $49,999	(NA)
	11.0	$50,000 to $74,999	(NA)
	6.9	$75,000 or more	(NA)
		Education (18 years and older)	
	26.6	No high school diploma	36.5
	16.4	High school graduate only	33.4
	13.4	Some college, no degree	33.9
	10.3	Associate degree	29.2
	7.1	Bachelor's degree or higher	31.2
		Work experience (18 to 64 years old)	
	16.2	Worked during year	45.5
	15.4	Worked full-time	47.5
	20.7	Worked part-time	42.1
	23.6	Did not work	36.6

NA Not applicable.
[1]Hispanics may be of any race.

Source: Robert J. Mills, *Health Insurance Coverage 2000: Current Population Reports* (Washington, D.C.: Bureau of the Census, United States Department of Commerce, U.S. Government Printing Office, September 2001), p. 5.

Education means first and foremost learning to read, and in this area not all the news is bad. Yes, there are still many nations with high rates of illiteracy, but what is encouraging are the rates of improvement achieved over the past fifty years: In 1950 over half the nations in the world had adult illiteracy rates of over 50 percent; today only 23 do; the worldwide illiteracy rate was 37 percent in 1970; today it is 21 percent. Some of the success stories have been nothing short of dazzling: China had an adult illiteracy rate of 49 percent in 1970; today the number is 16 percent. Indonesia dropped from 44 to 13 percent in the same period.[46] Adult illiteracy has been significantly reduced in every major region of the world.

However, the problem of illiteracy continues to be strongly concentrated in the less developed regions of the world, and is still a much greater problem for women than for men. Furthermore, important as it is, learning to read does not mean having an education. Years of schooling are a better measure and here too the discrepancies are great. A child in Mozambique gets an average of three years' schooling with a pupil-teacher ratio of 58:1; a child in the Czech Republic goes to school, on average, for 13 years, with a primary school pupil-teacher ratio of 15:1.[47] Girls are less likely than boys to be in school in all regions of the developing world, but the percentage of girls enrolled has risen faster than that for boys during the past ten years, except in sub-Saharan Africa (where the gender gap has widened by 0.7 percentage points).[48] Overall, there have been important signs of progress for both girls and boys, especially in East Asia and Oceania, although again sub-Saharan Africa is an exception (see Figure 10.4; note increase in percentage of primary-school-age children *not* enrolled between 1980 and 2000 and the minimal improvement expected by 2010).

The progress made in providing at least minimum levels of education worldwide is owing in part to an international policymaker, the United Nations, and in particular its foremost social agency, UNESCO, and to the World Bank. In addition, individual nations appear to have welcomed and used this form of aid more effectively than has sometimes been the case in other domains: Literacy is a key factor in development and fortunes cannot be made if workers cannot understand.

But policymakers' problems in the field of education go beyond the task of figuring out how to achieve simple literacy and a minimal education for everyone. Coping in today's ever more technologically advanced, intellectually sophisticated, and internationally competitive world requires not just the ability to read and a certain number of years in school. What state policies work best to encourage ever higher-quality teaching and ever better performance by the students? The questions seem endless and endlessly difficult to resolve. Should there be community participation in the education of children, and if so, what kind, and how can it best be encouraged?[49] Should education be bilingual in communities where a large minority speaks a different language from the majority? Who should pay the costs of education:

FIGURE 10.4

Gender Breakdown of Out-of-School, Primary-School-Age Children in the Less-Developed Regions (1980, 2000, and 2010)

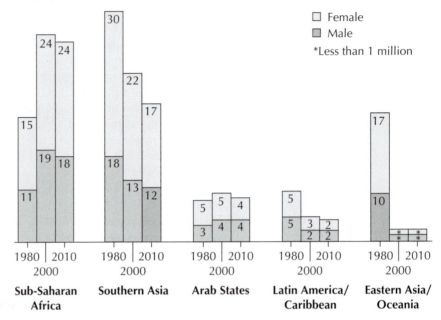

Source: *The Right to Education: Towards Education for All Throughout Life, World Education Report 2000* (Geneva, Switzerland: UNESCO, 2000), p. 47. © UNESCO 2000. Reproduced by permission of UNESCO, www.unesco.org/publishing.

parents or the local community out of local taxes, leading to much wealthier and probably better schools in wealthy communities; or the national government, leading to a loss of local control; or some combination? What about home schooling? What about giving religious institutions control over education, or, in secular nations, some form of support for the private schools they establish? Should all private schools, religious or not, receive some form of public support (such as vouchers)? How much should teachers be paid and what qualifications should they have? Does the state have a right and/or a responsibility to set the curriculum of primary and secondary schools? Of universities? (Does this course meet a requirement your state legislature has set? If not, are you taking one that does?)

Obviously, we cannot explore all these issues here, but let us take a slightly longer look at one that is currently raising a fair amount of controversy in the United States: Should standardized tests be used, and if so who should write them and what penalties should be inflicted on schools that cannot bring their students up to the mark?

In many nations, the question of standardized testing per se is never raised. It is taken for granted in France, for example, that the *baccalauréat* will be a national examination, nationally administered at the completion of sec-

Educational policy is often controversial but few dare deny, as did the former Taliban rulers of Afghanistan, that girls and women have full and equal rights to education. Here Afghan girls, back in school at last, prepare for examinations in March 2002, which will help determine at what level they should continue their schooling.
AP/Wide World Photos

ondary school. It is not a single exam; there are 28 different options and 23 sets of questions.[50] The Ministry of Education must cope with numerous policy questions vis-à-vis the "bac"—questions that are raised, settled, and raised again—such as, are the options well designed, are the exams fair, are the essay questions (of which there are many) interesting and relevant (perhaps *too* relevant?) to today's world, do enough (but not too many) students pass, should passing the exam entitle everyone to at least one year in university? But in my several years of residence in France I never heard anyone ask, "Should we do away with the bac?" One might as well try to abolish the cheese course at dinner.

Similar testing systems are found in England, Germany, and Japan, and indeed in many other nations. In all cases the exams are graded anonymously, and the same standards are applied nationwide. You can fail, but you can take it again next year. Or you might fail only part of the exam, and get a chance to take that part again at the end of the summer. You might pass it with honors, or just by the skin of your teeth. But when you pass it, you have a certificate that means a great deal more than that you stayed in school a fixed number of years. It is a sign of accomplishment, gained by hard work, and it means the same thing whoever your parents were, wherever you come from, and whatever schools you went to—wherever you go in your country. There is little question that it stimulates harder work and leads to a higher level of educational achievement.

There is, however, strong resistance to the idea of a single national test in the United States. Americans worry that "a nationwide exam might ill-serve regional needs and diverse populations," encourage a standardized national curriculum, eliminate the possibility for students to "demonstrate their interests, strengths and potential" in different ways, and lead to "obsessive test preparation" and "drill and kill rote learning." [51] So far, those favoring standardized tests have confined their efforts to individual states. They have had their way in such states as New York, California, Texas, Massachusetts, Wisconsin, and Louisiana. In some cases, their victories have been short-lived or they have been forced to accept serious compromises (such as making the test just one measure among others that help determine if a diploma should be awarded or denied). However, in the midst of this struggle the former governor of Texas took office as president of the United States, firmly convinced that all the states in the nation should follow the Texas example, where the standardized tests were in place and scores (which had been among the worst in the nation) were steadily rising. Bush's education plan suggested that schools that did not measure up to their state's standards should be denied federal funding. But one critic raised a key question: "If Mississippi is doing poorly, are you going to take federal money away from it? And is it going to do more poorly if you do?" [52]

Redistribution of Wealth

The "Mississippi question" relates to our next policy question: What is the responsibility of a nation's government to set policy that redistributes wealth? Mississippi may not be the wealthiest state, but is it right for the national government to ask other states to pay for services that Mississippi cannot afford to give its citizens?

Although conservatives in every nation may strongly advocate reducing the role of government in this regard, almost everyone recognizes that assuring that certain services are available to all citizens works to the benefit of all. Work gets done, gross national product rises, political instability is reduced. Of course, as a government helps pay for education, for health, for the care of the indigent, and for a host of other services, it is in effect redistributing the nation's wealth, taking from tax revenues to give the poor what they could not pay for by themselves. Even when the services go to those who are better off, as well as to the poor, a nation's wealth is being redistributed.

To provide these services, governments raise taxes, and in almost all nations of the world, taxes on income are graduated, that is, the richer you are, the higher the percentage of your income you are expected to pay in taxes (up to a set maximum). Similarly, the taxes one pays on one's home or on rentals of real estate are proportionate to the value of that asset. Gift and estate taxes also fall mostly on the wealthy (repealing gift and estate taxes in the United States "would save the wealthiest 2 percent of Americans about $236 billion over the next decade," calculates one analyst).[53] Other taxes, such as those on goods and services, are not graduated. Often called "indirect" taxes, they do not feel very indirect when you pay them, especially in many European nations where the sales tax is known as the Value Added Tax (VAT) and can be as high as 20 percent (and will soon be set at a common level for all members of the European Union). Nations with high VATs normally provide a far higher level of social services than does the United States, but it is to a considerable extent the VAT, falling more heavily on the rich only because they can afford to buy more, but paid equally by all, that makes such expenditures possible. In the United States, most real estate and sales taxes go to state and local governments. Corporations commonly pay taxes to all levels of government, some based on profits or other graduated measures (e.g., number of employees), some as flat fees for the pleasure of being in business.[54]

But what has been redistributed can be distributed again. Pick up the cards and deal them out again if you don't like the way they came out the first time, but this time add in a joker: the tax loophole. Responding to pressure from various groups of taxpayers (businesses large and small, the elderly, veterans, those working on behalf of various groups with special needs, churches, and, of course, campaign donors), government policymakers are constantly amending tax laws, making fine adjustments, trying hard to leave the cake of financial principle untouched while serving out large slices to those who say, in essence, "That was so good, I'd like some more, please." It is not easy work.

Not all adjustments are made to please special interests of course. Some are made in an effort to slow down an overheated economy, because too much inflation will eventually cut into the buying power of too many customers, or perk up a lagging one, because too many layoffs and bankruptcies will obviously have the same effect. Adjusting interest rates, raising or lowering taxes, paying farmers not to farm, reducing the workweek, and easing or toughening protectionist policies vis-à-vis imports and exports are some of the ways policymakers attempt to keep an economy on the right track; all have the effect of making some people richer and some not so rich as they would be if the policy in question had not been made into law. When the problems are more serious, so are the remedies—see Box 10.4 for Argentinean efforts to save that nation from defaulting on its debts. And no one is ever entirely sure whether such policies will or will not work for the announced purpose. Economist Robert J. Shiller reminds us, "A great embar-

BOX 10.4
Economic Policy in Argentina

In November 2001, President Fernando de la Rua of Argentina announced a new package of economic programs in an attempt to deal with that nation's economic and his own political woes.

The problems:

- A debt of $132 billion to foreign banks.
- A recession in its forty-first month; unemployment at 20 percent.
- A drastic plunge in stock and bond markets.
- A warning from the IMF that there would be no additional funds for that nation until it slashed $1.4 billion from monthly federal revenue-sharing payments to the provinces.
- Provincial governments unable to pay their own employees or their own creditors because the federal government had not met its promises to them.
- An approval rating of less than 10 percent for the government.
- Road blockades by the unemployed around the country and by the trucker's union (the latter at major border points to prevent foreign products from entering and competing with Argentine merchandise.
- An 11.3 percent decline in tax receipts.
- Loss of control of the Argentine congress by the president's *Alianza* coalition.
- Loss of support from the *Alianza* coalition.

The president's plan indicated a remarkably wide-ranging policy response:

- Consumers would receive a decrease in sales taxes if they used credit cards (an effort to fight tax evasion as well as increase spending).

rassment for modern macroeconomic theory is that it has never achieved any consensus on the basic questions of what makes the stock market rise or fall and what ultimately causes recessions."[55]

It is not always easy to tell the difference between what we might call the special interest and the public interest motives for particular adjustments. A key provision in the Republican campaign for office in 2000 was the promise of a major tax cut "to stimulate the economy." Democrats pointed out that as designed, the tax cut would definitely bring far greater benefits to the wealthy than to the less well-off, and might or might not have the desired effect on the economy. The new administration's bill was introduced almost immediately, but the debate went on and on, especially after Republicans lost their majority in the Senate, and often seemed to be characterized by the rawest form of pork-barrel bargaining: my vote for your guys' loophole in exchange for your vote for mine.[56] Meanwhile, although the gap between

BOX 10.4
(continued)

- Five million children and a half million older Argentines would receive monthly cash subsidies.
- The government would swap enough bonds with banks and pension funds for securities with lower interest rates (paying 7 percent instead of 11 percent) to save $4 billion in financing costs.
- The value of the Argentine peso would continue to be pegged to the dollar rather than devalued, to avoid higher inflation rates.
- Income and payroll taxes would be lowered for manufacturers and transportation companies.
- Oil companies would receive tax incentives to expand exploration.
- A new tax would be levied on gasoline.
- Rural provinces suffering from severe flooding would be allowed to issue $1.3 billion in scrip to spur spending.
- Argentina's tax collection agency would be privatized, to fight corruption and tax evasion.

Would it work? One of the president's supposed allies, the major of Buenos Aires, was dubious: "We can change the collar of the dog, but the dog remains the same." Others were harsher still, and called the program a way of defaulting, in fact, on some $95 billion in bonds. Interest rates immediately rose as high as 200 percent. And Argentines quickly withdrew more than $500 million from their bank accounts.

middle- and low-wage workers in the United States grew smaller, that between high- and middle-wage earners grew ever greater.[57] (See Figure 10.5.)

A key and perplexing category among U.S. low-wage earners are those who have been required to go off welfare and into the workforce by the 1996 welfare reform law, the Personal Responsibility and Work Opportunity Reconciliation Act.[58] This law, signed by a Democratic president moving rapidly to the political center, was an effort to reduce welfare costs, that is, to stop distributing quite so much of the federal budget to the poor. Has it been a success? It really depends on whom you ask and what indices you pose as signs of success. Three years after the law went into effect, over 60 percent of those going off the welfare rolls had found jobs, but most such jobs were low paying and offered few if any benefits, and about one-fifth of those who had left welfare had had to return. Former welfare recipients said they were now more likely to get behind on the rent and not to have enough money to

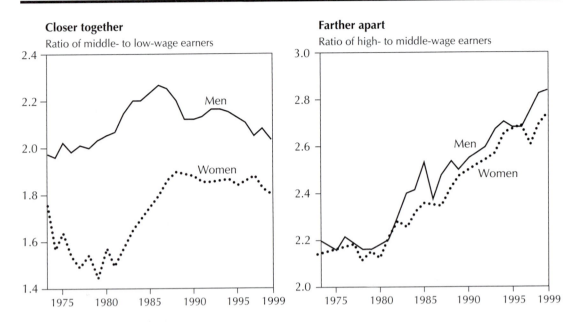

Closer together

Ratio of middle- to low-wage earners

Men

Women

Farther apart

Ratio of high- to middle-wage earners

Men

Women

Note: Each line shows the changing ratio for that group.

FIGURE 10.5

Gap Between High and Middle Class Widens, While Gap Between Middle and Lower Class Lessens, 1975–1999

buy food or medical care, but disagreed strongly when asked if "life was better when you were on welfare." [59]

Single mothers and their children seem to be having the hardest time under the new law, but even here there are conflicting signs. The poorest 10 percent of families headed by single mothers lost an average of about $860 in annual income after the reform. There was no reduction in overall poverty for this group between 1995 and 1999 (the rate moved from 19.2 percent in 1995 to 19.4 percent in 1999), despite a booming economy, an increase in the minimum wage, and improved tax benefits for the poor.[60] But the children of former welfare mothers are more likely to be in school every day and the children of those mothers who earn more at work than they received on welfare now do better in school, according to Judith M. Gueron. Of course, such mothers are often the beneficiaries of expensive alternative government programs offering training, food stamps, help with child care, health insurance, transportation, and/or special tax credits—factors also associated with improved achievement and behavior of the children.[61] So how much is the government really saving? But then again, such expenditures might prove to be the merely temporary costs of transition, as claimed by Tommy G. Thompson, Secretary of Health and Human Services.[62] To understand the complexities, it is important to remember that not all former welfare families are alike. Judith Havemann and Barbara Vobejda find that the "new welfare rules have exacerbated the problems of families whose lives were already chaotic. And they have magnified the strengths of those who were strongly motivated and able to take advantage of new programs."[63]

SUMMARY AND CONCLUSION

Many different factors influence the making of policy in a nation-state, including its economic system, size, natural resources, degree of political stability, public opinions, and method of campaign finance. An economy is a system of producing, distributing, and consuming wealth; no variable influences policy more than the nature of the economic system. This was true when we lived and worked together in hunting bands, in primitive agricultural settlements, in kinship systems, in feudal estates, and in towns with corporate guilds. It is equally true in today's more modern economic systems, be they capitalist, socialist, or mixed economies. Capitalism is a system in which entrepreneurs are free to plow their profits back into capital expenditures. Unbridled capitalism can lead to such inequalities of wealth that a demand will arise for either socialism or some form of a mixed economy. Under socialism, the state controls all the means of production and is itself supposedly controlled by the workers. Nearly every nation in the world, however, has an economy based on a mixture of public and private ownership of the means of production and on considerable public regulation of the private sector.

Size, natural resources, opinions, and pressure from large donors are other important factors influencing policy. The size of a nation affects what policies a nation adopts, but policies can also affect the size of the nation, changing territorial extent. If natural resources are not carefully controlled by government policies, the fruits of their exploitation may benefit foreign investors far more than the local citizenry. Coherent public opinion helps shape policy, but "policy entrepreneurs" can manipulate that opinion; at best public opinion simply sets the parameters for policymaking. Postelection pandering of the victorious to the interests of those who made large contributions is an increasing factor in determining important policy decisions, especially in the United States.

Government policy—or its absence—powerfully shapes our daily lives. In health, education, and the distribution of wealth, the problems facing policymakers are immense: New maladies never seen before and old ones believed under control are recurring; a wide range of controversies over how to improve education make it difficult to give any new method a fair chance; and neither economists nor government officials can come to agreement regarding how to prevent a recession or find one's way out of an existent one.

Yet progress is made, nonetheless, as we have seen in our three examples. Most developed nations of the world now have widely comprehensive health systems in place, and those that do not, such as the United States, at least keep grappling with the problem. Literacy rates have risen dramatically in nation after nation. Recessions do not automatically become depressions, and at least in most of the wealthy nations welfare support is available for those who need it. Let's not be too hard, then, on our policymakers. But then again, let's not be too easy on them either.

QUESTIONS TO CONSIDER

1. What is public policy?
2. What is a mixed economy? Can you give an example of how the economy of your own nation is mixed and how this has influenced a particular public policy?
3. Give some examples of how its natural resources (or lack of them) are important in determining public policy in your country.
4. What change would you most like to see in public policy in the domain of education in your country, and why? Why do you think it has not yet been made?

SELECTED READINGS

Berliner, Joseph S. *The Economics of the Good Society* (Malden, Mass., and Oxford: Blackwell Publishers, 1999). Argues that the welfare state continues under modern capitalism.

Cameron, Rondo. *A Concise Economic History of the World* (New York and Oxford: Oxford University Press, 1997). Offers clear explanations of developing economic systems since the emergence of feudalism.

Caporaso, James A. and David P. Levine. *Theories of Political Economy* (Cambridge, U.K.: Cambridge University Press, 1992). A useful framework for understanding the relationship between politics and economics.

Galbraith, John Kenneth. *A Journey Through Economic Time: A Firsthand View* (Boston: Houghton Mifflin, 1994). Considers the effects of war, revolutions, ideologies, and government policies on the major economic and social events after World War I.

Jacobs, Lawrence R. and Robert Y. Shapiro. *Politicians Don't Pander: Political Manipulation and the Loss of Democratic Responsiveness* (Chicago: University of Chicago Press, 2000). A provocative study of policymaking in the United States today.

Manza, Jeff and Fay Lomax Cook. *The Impact of Public Opinion on Public Policy: The State of the Debate* (New York: Oxford University Press, 2002). The authors present evidence that public opinion still matters in the making of public policy, albeit usually only to set outside limits to what can be done.

Sabatier, Paul A., ed. *Theories of the Policy Process* (Boulder, Colo.: Westview Press, 1999). Public policymaking is conceived as the process by which problems are conceptualized and brought to government for solution, following which governments formulate alternatives, select and implement policies, evaluate them, and revise them.

Scut, J. M. Wildeboer, J. C. Vrooman, and P. T. de Beer. *Worlds of Welfare: Institutions and Their Effects in Eleven Welfare States* (The Hague, the Netherlands: Social and Cultural Planning Office, April 2001). Offers a broad comparative look at the history and effects of welfare systems.

Skocpol, Theda. *Boomerang: Health Care Reform and the Turn Against Government* (New York: W. W. Norton, 1996). Includes analysis of the failure of the Clinton administration to keep the campaign promise of providing adequate health care to all Americans.

The World Health Report 2000 (Geneva, Switzerland: World Health Organization, 2000). In this report WHO ranks 191 member nations from best to worst, giving first place to France and 37th to the United States (just after Costa Rica). Indicators used: overall level of population health; health inequalities (or disparities) within the population; overall level of health care system responsiveness; how well people of various classes find they are served; and the distribution of the costs within the population. Copies may be ordered from *book orders@who.int.*

WEB SITES OF INTEREST

1. Economic Policy Institute
   http://www.epinet.org/
   Offers information on trade and globalization, the government and the economy, education, and labor standards.

2. Center for Economic Policy and Research
   http://www.cepr.net/
   Seeks to promote democratic debate on economic and social issues by presenting those issues in "an accurate and understandable manner."

NOTES

1. Paul A. Sabatier, "The Need for Better Theories," in Paul A. Sabatier, ed., *Theories of the Policy Process* (Boulder, Colo.: Westview, 1999), p. 3.
2. Martin Shapiro, "Public Law and Judicial Politics," in Ada W. Finifter, ed., *Political Science: The State of the Discipline II* (Washington, D.C.: American Political Science Association, 1993), p. 369. For an overview of different contemporary theories, see Edella Schlager, "A Comparison of Frameworks, Theories, and Models of Policy Processes," in Sabatier, op cit., ch. 9.
3. For a good brief discussion of the various and shifting meanings of the term *political economy,* see Eileen R. Meehan, "Rethinking Political Economy: Change and Continuity," *Journal of Communication* 43, no. 4 (Autumn 1993): 105–109. See also James Caporaso and David Levine, *Theories of Political Economy* (Cambridge, U.K.: Cambridge University Press, 1992), and Barry Clark, *Political Economy: A Comparative Approach,* 2nd ed. (Westport, Conn.: Praeger, 1998).
4. Some contemporary anthropologists now believe it was women who were responsible for shifting to a new and more secure mode of ensuring material survival: the cultivation of crops. Made less mobile by childbearing and nursing, women stayed closer to camp (wherever camp was pitched) and had more opportunity to become familiar with the ways of the land, with its cycles of growth and decay, and with the production and planting of seeds. The reproductive functions of their own bodies no doubt helped them, however unconsciously, to understand what was going on in the natural world. Rayna R. Reiter, *Toward an Anthropology of Women* (New York: Monthly Review Press, 1976). See also Rosalind Miles, *The Women's History of the World* (New York: Perennial Library, Harper & Row, 1990), pp. 5–8.
5. It is estimated that the population of Venezuela increased fifteenfold after the inhabitants made corn (which could be dried and stored) rather than roots (which could not) the staple of their diet. *New York Times,* 27 Sept. 1981, 17.

6. For a general study of the feudal era, see J. S. Citchley, *Feudalism* (London and Boston: G. Allen and Unwin, 1978). For the concept of feudalism and its importance in the transition to capitalism, see R. J. Holton, *The Transition from Feudalism to Capitalism* (New York: Macmillan, 1985), chaps. 1 and 6. For the emergence of feudalism from *manorialism* in the eighth and ninth centuries, see Rondo Cameron, *A Concise Economic History of the World* (New York and Oxford: Oxford University Press, 1997), ch. 3.

7. Steven A. Epstein, *Wage and Labor Guilds in Medieval Europe* (Chapel Hill: University of North Carolina Press, 1991).

8. Two good studies of the age of discovery are Carlo M. Cipolla, *Guns, Sails, and Empires* (New York: Pantheon, 1966), and Fernand Braudel, *The Mediterranean* (New York: Harper & Row, 1973). See also Chaps. 5 and 6 in Jan P. Nederveen Pieterse, *Empire and Emancipation* (Westport, Conn.: Praeger, 1989).

9. Bonnie G. Smith, *Imperialism: A History in Documents* (Oxford and New York: Oxford University Press, 2000), p. 10.

10. Interesting recent studies of capitalism include Peter Saunders, *Capitalism* (Minneapolis: University of Minnesota Press, 1995), and Bruno Amoroso, *On Globalization: Capitalism in the 21st Century* (New York: St. Martin's, 1998).

11. Douglas A. Irwin, *Mercantilism as a Strategic Trade Policy* (Washington, D.C.: Federal Reserve System, 1990), and Immanuel M. Wallerstein, *The Modern World System II: Mercantilism and the Consolidation of the European World-Economy, 1600–1750* (New York: Academic Press, 1980).

12. Adam Smith, *Inquiry into the Nature and Causes of the Wealth of Nations* (New York: Modern Library, 1937).

13. Ray Hudson, *Producing Places* (New York and London: The Guilford Press, 2001), p. 48.

14. Howard J. Wiarda, *Corporatism and Comparative Politics* (Armonk, N.Y., and London: M. E. Sharpe, 1997).

15. Alec Nove, *The Economics of Feasible Socialism Revisited,* 2nd ed. (New York: HarperCollins, 1991).

16. Joseph S. Berliner, *The Economics of the Good Society* (Malden, Mass., and Oxford: Blackwell Publishers, 1999), p. 8.

17. James A. Yunker, *Economic Justice: The Market Socialist Vision* (London and New York: Rowman and Littlefield, 1997).

18. Floris-Jan van Luyn, "China's Misleading Census," in *NRC Handelsblad* as reported in *World Press Review* (Dec. 2000): 44.

19. "The Baltic States: A Regional Economic Assessment," *OECD Economic Surveys 1999–2000* (Paris: Organization for Economic Co-Operation and Development, Feb. 2000), pp. 9–19.

20. Marc Lacey, "Front Line of Famine in Ethiopia Is the Soil," *New York Times,* 4 Nov. 2001, A5.

21. Ricardo Hausmann, "Prisoners of Geography," *Foreign Policy* (Jan.–Feb. 2001): 45–53.

22. "Lessons from El Salvador's Tragedy," *The Economist* (20 Jan. 2001): 31.

23. Sergei Troush, "China's Changing Oil Strategy and Its Foreign Policy Implications," *CNAPS Working Paper* (Washington, D.C.: Brookings Institute, Center for Northeast Asian Policy Studies, Fall 1999), and Ted Plafker, "Growth Exposes China to Oil Supply Shocks," *International Herald Tribune,* 30 Oct. 2001, 8.

24. Ian Bremmer, "Oil Politics: America and the Riches of the Caspian Basin," *World Policy Journal* 15, no. 1 (Spring 1998).

25. *Afghanistan Country Analysis Brief* (Washington, D.C.: Energy Information Association, U.S. Department of Energy, Sept. 2001). http://www.ela.doe.gov/ermeu/cabs/afghan.html. For more about other Central Asian nations' interest in Afghanistan, see Larry P. Goodson, *Afghanistan's Endless War: State Failure, Regional Politics and the Rise of the Taliban* (Seattle: University of Washington Press, 2001).

26. John J. Maresca, Testimony to House Committee on International Relations, Subcommittee on Asia and the Pacific, Washington, D.C., 12 Feb. 1998. Not everyone shared Maresca's enthusiasm; see Amy Myers Jaffe and Robert A Manning, "The Myth of the Caspian 'Great Game': The Real Geopolitics of Energy," *Survival* 40, no. 4 (Winter 1998–99).

27. Joseph Fitchett, "War Alters Caspian Equation: U.S. Accepts Bigger Russian Role in Tapping

Non-Gulf Oil," *International Herald Tribune,* 30 Oct. 2001, 9.

28. Paul Collier, *Economic Causes of Civil Conflict and Their Implications for Policy,* World Bank Report, reported in World Bank press release, June 2000. http://wbln0018.worldbank.org/ news/pressrelease.nsf/673fa6c5a2d50a6785256 e200692a7. Collier is strongly opposed to accepting "the conventional grievance account of conflict."

29. Alberto Alesina and Roberto Perotti, "Income Distribution, Political Instability and Investment," *European Economic Review* 40 (1996): 1203–28.

30. Paul J. Quirk and Joseph Hinchliffe, "The Rising Hegemony of Mass Opinion," *Policy Forum* 12, no. 4 (Fall 1999): 1–5.

31. Lawrence R. Jacobs and Robert Y. Shapiro, *Politicians Don't Pander: Political Manipulation and the Loss of Democratic Responsiveness* (Chicago: University of Chicago Press, 2000).

32. *Washington Leaders Wary of Public Opinion* (Washington, D.C.: Pew Center for the People and the Press, April 17, 1998).

33. Jeff Manza and Fay Lomax Cook, *The Impact of Public Opinion on Public Policy: The State of the Debate* (New York: Oxford University Press, 2002).

34. Jim Abrams, "Oilman Claims Contributions All Part of Getting in the Door," *The Associated Press,* 21 Sept. 1997.

35. Tom Hamburger, Laurie McGinley and David S. Cloud, "Corporate Donors Seek Return on Investment in Bush Campaign," *Wall Street Journal,* 6 March 2001. For interesting details about donations from the oil industry to the Bush campaign—and payoffs promised—see Greg Palast, "Bush Energy Plan: Policy or Payback?" *BBC World News,* 18 May 2001. http:// news.bbc.co.uk/hi/english/world/americas/news id_13360000/1336960.stm, and William E. Gibson, "USA: Big Oil, Gas Funding Ads for Bush's Energy Policy," *Orlando Sentinel,* 19 Aug. 2001.

36. Matthew Karnitschnig, "The Kohl Case: Oh, What a Tangled Web," *Business Week* (international ed.) (14 Feb. 2000).

37. "World Health Organization Rates Health Systems," *Populi: The UNFPA Magazine* 27, no. 2 (September 2000). The composite "grade" each nation received was based on five indicators: overall level of population health, health inequalities (or disparities) within the population, overall level of health system responsiveness, how well people of various classes find they are served, and the distribution of the costs within the population. The full report is *The World Health Report 2000* (Geneva, Switzerland: World Health Organization, 2000).

38. Michael Renner, "Overview: The Triple Health Challenge," *Vital Signs 2001: The Trends That Are Shaping Our Future* (New York: W. W. Norton, 2001), p. 2. In some nations, such as South Africa where 4 million are infected, the problem was compounded by reluctance on the part of senior government officials to admit the seriousness of the disease (*The Economist* [28 Oct. 2000]: 31).

39. Renner, op. cit., p. 3.

40. "Only 1 percent of 1,233 new drugs that reached the market between 1975 and 1997 were approved specifically for tropical diseases" (Renner, op. cit., p. 5). See also Robert Weissman, "AIDS and Developing Countries: Facilitating Access to Essential Medicines," *Foreign Policy in Focus* 6, no. 6 (March 2001). Available at http://www .foreignpolicy-infocus.org/.

41. D. A. Henderson, "Bioterrorism as a Public Health Threat," *Emerging Infectious Diseases* 4, no. 3 (July–Sept. 1998).

42. Joseph F. Wackerle, "Domestic Preparedness for Events Involving Weapons of Mass Destruction," *JAMA (Journal of the American Medical Association)* 283, no. 2 (12 Jan. 2000): 252–54.

43. David E. Powell, "Russia's Failing Health Care System," *Current History* 97, no. 621 (Oct. 1998): 335–41.

44. Robert J. Mills, *Health Insurance Coverage 2000: Current Population Reports* (Washington, D.C.: Bureau of the Census, United States Department of Commerce, U.S. Government Printing Office, Sept. 2001). For studies of the Clinton failure and other assessments of the U.S. system, see Theda Skocpol, *Boomerang: Health Care Reform and the Turn Against Government* (New York: W. W. Norton, 1996); Paul Starr, "What Happened to Health Care Reform?" *The American Prospect* 6,

no. 20 (Winter 1995): 20–31; and Robert Kuttner, "Incremental Reform Toward What?" *The American Prospect* 11, no. 7 (14 Feb. 2000).

45. *The Right to Education: Towards Education for All Throughout Life, World Education Report 2000* (Geneva, Switzerland: UNESCO, 2000).

46. Ibid. (UNESCO, The Right to Education, etc.). In an earlier period, in what was called "the largest literacy campaign in history," the Soviet Union reduced illiteracy from 76 percent in 1897 to less than 5 percent for men and to 16.6 percent for women by 1939.

47. *Education Sector Strategy* (Washington, D.C.: World Bank, August 1999).

48. Karin A. L. Hyde and Shirley Miske, *Thematic Studies: Girls' Education,* 2nd ed. (Paris: UNESCO, 2001).

49. For a full discussion of this issue, see Mitsue Uemura, "Community Participation in Education: What Do We Know?" Paper prepared for School and Teachers thematic group of Human Development Network—Education, The World Bank, 1999. http://www1.worldbank.org/education/globaleducationreform/01.PoliticsOfReform/01.01.KeyReadings/polreformkeyread.htm.

50. Mary Morello Shafer, *National Assessments in Europe and Japan* (Washington, D.C.: American Institutes for Research, 1992).

51. Morello, op. cit., and Peter Schrag, "High Stakes Are for Tomatoes," *The Atlantic Monthly* 286, no. 2 (August 2000): 19–21.

52. Diana Jean Schemo, "Bush Pushes Ambitious Education Plan," *New York Times,* 24 Jan. 2001, A1.

53. David Cay Johnston, "Questions Raised on New Bush Plan to End Estate Tax," *New York Times,* 29 Jan. 2001, A1, A20.

54. Staff of the Joint Committee on Taxation, *Study of the Overall State of the Federal Tax System and Recommendations for Simplification* (Washington, D.C.: U.S. Government Printing Office, 2001).

55. Robert J. Shiller, "The Mystery of Economic Recessions," *New York Times,* 4 Feb. 2001, WK17.

56. Richard W. Stevenson, "The Tax-Cut Train Picks Up Steam," *New York Times,* 1 Feb. 2001, A15; Richard W. Stevenson, "Bush's Proposal to Cut Taxes Is Swiftly Introduced in Senate," *New York Times,* 23 Jan. 2001, A15.

57. "The Widening Gap," *The Economist* (3 Feb. 2001): 30. This conservative newsweekly comments wryly, "The rich have certainly got a lot richer."

58. For a discussion of the components of this law, see Christopher Jencks, "The Hidden Paradox of Welfare Reform," *American Prospect* 8, no. 32 (May 1997).

59. Judith Havemann, "Most Find Jobs After Leaving Welfare," *Washington Post,* 27 May 1999, A1. See also Sarah Brauner and Pamela Loprest, *Where Are They Now? What States' Studies of People Who Left Welfare Tell Us* (Washington, D.C.: The Urban Institute, May 1999).

60. Kathryn Porter and Allen Dupree, *Poverty Trends for Families Headed by Working Single Mothers, 1993 to 1999* (Washington, D.C.: Center for Budget and Policy Priorities, August 2001).

61. Pamela A. Morris and Greg J. Duncan, *Which Welfare Reforms Are Best for Children?* Policy Brief No. 6 (Washington, D.C.: Brookings Institution, September 2001).

62. Both Gueron and Thompson are quoted by Robert Pear, "Gains Reported for Children of Welfare-to-Work Families," *New York Times,* 23 Jan. 2001, A12.

63. Judith Havemann and Barbara Vobejda, "Children of Welfare Parents Feel Reform's Help, Hurt," *Washington Post,* 27 Dec. 1997, A1. For a broader, comparative look at the history and effects of welfare systems, see J. M. Wildeboer Scut, J. C. Vrooman, and P. T. de Beer, *Worlds of Welfare: Institutions and Their Effects in Eleven Welfare States* (The Hague, the Netherlands: Social and Cultural Planning Office, April 2001).

Justice Under the Law

In every system of government, three tasks must be performed: Laws must be made, laws must be carried out, and some effort must be made to see that justice is done in the process. Few qualities of human existence are more deeply valued than justice, although we are not always aware how much it means to us. Ask your friends to list eight or ten great goods of human existence in order of importance (give them *love* and *friendship* as examples if they need help getting started), and chances are that most of them will not even mention *justice*. However, this may simply be a sign that people you know have never felt that they have been treated unjustly by the legal system. Suppose, however, that one of your friends happened to be Calvin Burdine of Texas whose court-appointed lawyer slept through several hours of the thirteen-hour trial while the prosecution questioned witnesses and presented its case ("an unconscious lawyer is completely incapable of cross-examination in trial," a new lawyer argued, reasonably enough, in seeking a retrial eight years later for Mr. Burdine).[1] Or perhaps the good friend you ask is Fauzi Saado, a Lebanese refugee in the German town of Huxene, just after he has sat in court listening to Judge Walter Stoy reduce the charges against the three neo-Nazi skinheads who set his home afire, declaring they were "youthful offenders" (the youngest was 18, the others were 19) who had been drunk and had not intended to kill anyone, and sentencing them to a maximum of five years' imprisonment despite the fact the result of their rampage was serious injury to two of the Saado children, leaving one of them deformed for life.[2] Or suppose you asked your question of 27-year-old Jerry Dewayne Williams, who was sentenced in 1995 to twenty-five-years-to-life imprisonment for having stolen a slice of pepperoni pizza from a group of children. The sentence was mandatory under California's "three strikes" law, which applies to any person with two previous convictions (of which one was for a serious or violent felony) who then commits a third crime—Williams the pizza thief "qualified."[3] Might we not expect Mr. Burdine, Mr. Saado, and Mr. Williams to be more likely to include *justice* on *their* lists? We sometimes learn how much we cherish fair treatment under the law only when we encounter what appears to us to be its very opposite.

WHAT IS JUSTICE?

Most of us are likely to say that an injustice has been done when we believe that we ourselves or those for whom we feel compassion have not been treated fairly *by people in positions of authority*. Not all acts of fair treatment are acts of justice, just as not all rules are laws. Justice is a possible result of decisions made by those who have been granted authority to determine what constitutes fair treatment. In the case of governments, *justice* means *fair treatment under the law*. These five simple words contain a wealth of meaning. Only by establishing laws that apply equally to all do those in power gain legitimacy in the minds of those over whom they rule. There can be no belief in the possibility of justice without the prior establishment of the principle of the rule of law. There can be no justice without a body of law to guide the judges.

However, the mere existence of a body of law and of properly credentialed judges in no way guarantees that justice will prevail. No one who has studied the 1857 Dred Scott decision of the U.S. Supreme Court can doubt that those who have been given the authority to determine what is just may make errors of judgment.[4] All we have said so far is that just government is a product that *may* result from the decisions of those who are formally authorized to determine how the laws shall be applied.

What, then, do we mean by *just?* The answer is not easy. What seems just to me may seem highly unjust to you. The citizens of Libya were sure that when Abdelbaset Ali Mohmed al-Megrahi was convicted in 2001 of murder in the bombing of a Pan Am flight over Lockerbie, Scotland, the case had been fixed from the start and their countryman never had a chance.[5] The California State Attorney General saw nothing wrong with sending someone to jail for a minimum of twenty-five years for stealing a slice of pizza: "We at least can think our children can sit down in peace in broad daylight, without a 6-foot 4-inch, 220-pound ex-con threatening them and taking away food from them," said Daniel E. Lungren, and presumably there were other Californians who agreed.[6] Justice is a relative term. A decision is considered *just* if it meets a society's current standards of what constitutes fair treatment under the law.[7] Such standards evolve from tradition, from religious belief, from moral codes, from belief (or, in the Lockerbie case, disbelief) in the legitimacy of the judicial system, and sometimes from simple pragmatic need. It may be just to hang a man for stealing a horse when the community's very survival depends—or seems to depend—on the government's ability to protect cattle ranching.

Are we treading dangerous ground here? Yes, indeed; but then, nobody promised you easy solutions to tough ethical questions when you took up the study of politics—at least I hope nobody did. Most of us do not want to manifest the cultural arrogance of the British colonial authorities who ruled that African chiefs could mete out justice on the basis of native law and custom as long as their decisions were not "repugnant to humanity"—we know that no one people or race has an innate right to determine what is or is not to be considered moral by another. Most of us accept the principle of *cultural relativism*—the idea that each society sets its own standards in accordance with its own culture, and that what is correct in one society may be repugnant in another. But when we apply that principle to our considerations of justice, we may get the uncomfortable feeling that our own values are slipping away as guides to reality. Are we obliged to call laws that sanction slavery just as long as most people in a slave-owning society find them so? Must we agree that torture is an acceptable punishment for political dissent if we know that those so punished would use the same means if they themselves could acquire power? Should we accept as a mere statement of fact the information that in some Arab societies women may be divorced by the simple word of the husband but have no equivalent right themselves—and that there is little or no evidence the women themselves find this practice unjust?

This problem of cultural relativism in the determination of what is just is one of the most difficult problems in the human polity. There is no simple solution to the ethical dilemmas it poses for us, but observing certain precautions can help us find our way. First, we must be careful not to assume that the standards of justice of ordinary men and women around the globe are actually as different as the laws made by the powerful sometimes suggest. Has anyone, for example, really studied the beliefs of ordinary citizens in a slave-owning society, of divorced women in an Arab state, or of the men and women who have been tortured for their political beliefs?

Second, it is important to distinguish between making an evaluation of a given practice and assuming the right to impose change. Surely I have the right to my negative opinion of public whipping as a punishment for adultery, say, whether or not I have the right (or the power) to move in and take the whip away. Third, let us remember that as the world shrinks we may be evolving toward an international code of justice. It may be that your own great-grandchildren, finding this book in the attic and thumbing through it idly, will find this discussion old-fashioned and unnecessary, having grown up in a world in which there are no longer significant differences in what different people find just or unjust throughout the human polity. We ourselves may hasten that day by working with other peoples to create a shared vision of a just world toward which all (ourselves very much included) might resolve to strive. Acknowledging cultural relativism need not mean abandoning hope for a better world.[8]

In the meantime, different conceptions of justice do exist, and different systems have been developed for the administration of justice. Yet even now there are certain similarities across the globe in the way the job is done. Whatever the standards of justice, in every polity there are people whose job it is to make certain that the laws of the land are just, and that they are justly administered. To some extent, this is a job shared by everyone in government. Lawmakers (legislators) and law implementers (executives) are expected to carry out their functions in a manner consistent with those standards. But human nature being what it is, those who make and execute the laws may not always themselves be just. For this reason, most polities have established an institution of government, the judiciary, whose particular function it is to see to it that the citizens receive fair treatment under the law. The job of *assuring* justice is first and foremost the work of judges—not legislators, not executives.

In this chapter we will explore the judicial function. There can be no judiciary without a body of trained, authorized judges, so we will begin with a consideration of the ways judges are chosen throughout the human polity. Then we will explore the question of judicial independence. How free are judges from political intervention, and what are the consequences for the political systems within which they carry out their functions? Then we will review and explain the principal systems of law used in the administration of justice. We will conclude with an overview of regional variations in the rule of law.

CHOOSING CREDIBLE JUDGES

Implicit in the very idea of a judicial system is the conviction that there must be some place where final decisions on political and governmental matters can be made, and made so as to command respect and obedience. For this condition to be fulfilled, the people who make such decisions must know and respect their society's system of law and standards of justice. But it is not enough for them to have this knowledge and respect. They must be believed to have it; they must have legitimacy in the eyes of the public. Such legitimacy is traditionally achieved by three means—by appointing only those whose past careers seem likely to have given them that knowledge and respect, by giving the right of appointment to government officials who are themselves respected because of the importance of the offices they occupy, and by surrounding the judicial role with the physical accoutrements of dignity and stature.

Experienced Judges

In some nations, no one can become a judge who has not followed a clearly defined educational and career path. In others, those who have the power to appoint judges can appoint whomever they please but are expected to choose only those with obviously relevant experience. In Germany, law students must choose at the end of their studies whether to become a judge, prosecutor, civil servant, notary public, or private lawyer. Those who decide to become judges must go through a three-year probationary period, but after completing that successfully they are given a judgeship with lifetime tenure and security. Once made, the decision is fixed—German lawyers do not later become judges, and German judges do not decide to leave the bench and take up lawyering. By the time the German judge achieves appointment

Maintaining judicial dignity during a stressful case with full media attention is not an easy task. Here Leon County Circuit Court Judge Terry Lewis instructs the lawyers for Al Gore and George W. Bush as they present arguments regarding whether or not to continue the recount of ballots in Florida after the presidential election of 2000.
AP/Wide World Photos

to one of the high federal courts, he or she is likely to have acquired a wealth of experience.[9]

In Great Britain, the young man or woman bent on a legal career does not have to decide between being a lawyer and being a judge but rather between being a *barrister*—a lawyer qualified to appear as an advocate in court—and being a *solicitor*—a lawyer qualified to do the paperwork in law offices. Most of those who become barristers have solidly middle-class or upper-class origins and have attended private schools for their secondary education and then the more prestigious universities and law schools (such as Oxford, Cambridge, and the Inns of Court in London). British judges are chosen from the ranks of practicing barristers.[10]

In other nations, however, it is legally possible to become a judge with no formal training or experience whatsoever. This is the case in the federal court system in the United States, where it is not even necessary to be a lawyer to become a federal judge. And in Denmark two ordinary citizens serve alongside one professional jurist as judges in municipal courts and rule on lesser criminal cases; in appeals from municipal court cases to a high court, three citizen judges participate with three jurists.[11]

Respectably Chosen Judges

Who is to say who is to say? Never is it more important to find the right an-swer to this question than in determining who will choose the men and women who are to say what is just. The answer varies a great deal from polity to polity. Nearly all German judges are appointed by the state minis-ters of justice and are considered civil servants, and thus part of the bureau-cratic hierarchy, promoted on the basis of recommendations from superiors. They have middle-class or upper-middle-class backgrounds; only 6 percent come from working-class families. German reunification has played a part in recent judicial recruitment: Many of the judges in former East Germany were considered "poorly prepared for Western styles of judicial and legal practice or . . . compromised by past political connections" and have been replaced by judges from former West Germany.[12]

In other systems, all but the highest judges are appointed by the judges themselves. In Mexico, although the Supreme Court judges are appointed by the president and confirmed by the Senate or the Permanent Committee, they themselves appoint all the judges for the lower courts and elect their own chief justice.[13] In Kenya, a Judicial Service Commission advises the president on whom to appoint to the Court of Appeal of the High Court, and itself appoints all resident magistrates and district magistrates.[14] In Israel a Judges' Election Committee, consisting of the president of the Supreme Court, two other judges of the Supreme Court, the minister of justice (who serves as chair), another minister designated by the government, two mem-bers of the Knesset (the legislature), and two representatives of the Chamber of Advocates, carry out similar functions of appointment, transfer, and dis-missal of judges.[15]

Legislators often play an important role in the appointment of judges. American presidents must get senatorial ratification of all appointments they make to the federal judiciary. When such appointments become controver-sial, not only the senators but also the general public may well become in-volved (see Box 11.1).

Dignified Judges

Making sure that judges have appropriate qualifications and are appointed through time-honored official procedures is clearly a reasonable way of en-suring their credibility. A third method seems less logically defensible yet may be even more effective. It is common practice to surround the judicial office with all possible material attributes of seriousness and high purpose. Almost everywhere, judges are expected to wear special somber apparel, to speak carefully, and to refrain from laughter or other signs of lighthearted-

In October 1991, Clarence Thomas was President George Bush's nominee for Supreme Court justice. From the beginning, Thomas was under serious attack for his relative inexperience, his failure to reveal his position on many issues during the confirmation hearings, and his known conservative stance on many other issues. Still, everyone expected the black nominee to be appointed; the recent retirement of the Court's only other black justice, Thurgood Marshall, dictated a replacement based in part on color, and Thomas's liabilities— viewed as assets by some— seemed unlikely to keep him from the post.

But then an Oklahoma law professor, Anita Hill, decided to speak out. Hill asserted that the judge had sexually harassed her when she was a young employee in his office at the Education Department and at the Equal Employment Opportunity Commission. The professor was black, professional, dignified, and very, very serious. Her testimony was detailed, explicit, and absolutely convincing, not only to many of the senators but also to many who watched her on television.

The hearings continued for several days, with new charges of harassment and new testimony that the judge could not possibly be capable of such behavior. Whom to believe? What to do if one believed the charges? On October 15, 1991, the Senate voted 52 to 48 to confirm the nomination.

But the Thomas case was an exception. Normally, the confirmation process is dignified and relatively uncontroversial (even in the cases where the nominee is not accepted). Sandra Day O'Connor (1981), Antonin Scalia (1986), and Anthony M. Kennedy (1987) were all confirmed unanimously; David H. Souter (1990) by a vote of 90 to 9 and Ruth Bader Ginsberg (1993) by 96 to 3. Ginsberg, the 107th justice and only second woman to be appointed, was hailed as a "consensus" choice. As the then minority leader of the Senate, Robert J. Dole, said, "By any measure, she is qualified to become the Supreme Court's ninth justice."[16]

ness (no matter how humorous or even laughable the proceedings in the courtroom may occasionally be). A sergeant-at-arms or bailiff reminds everyone in the courtroom to rise when the judge enters and to maintain appropriate behavior. In Britain and several other nations in the British Commonwealth, it is still the custom for judges and the barristers who plead cases before them to wear powdered wigs.

Although such practices still prevail, the dignity of the court has nevertheless suffered in recent years from a more modern phenomenon: the invasion of the camera. The difficulty of maintaining a sober atmosphere when a trial is receiving constant publicity and can be followed minute by minute on the screen was made all too amply apparent in the O. J. Simpson case in the United States, when a black sports hero was accused of killing his wife and another man. The knowledge that they were being watched clearly influenced the behavior of everyone in the courtroom. Typical comments were, "There is no question that both the prosecution and defense . . . overtly played to the gallery," and "The judge and the lawyers on both sides seem unable to curb their appetite for attention."[17] The media, often accused of covering trials irresponsibly and biasing the jurors (whose isolation from their coverage is never likely to be complete), defend themselves on the vague grounds of the "people's right to know" and, in the United States, on the basis of the First Amendment. News media cameras and microphones are now permitted in forty-seven states in the United States. The same kind of coverage is possible in Canada, with one important exception: The judge always has the right to order a news blackout if he or she believes the case will be too sensational, and this is often done.[18]

AN INDEPENDENT JUDICIARY: THEORY AND PRACTICE

We often speak with pride of the tradition of an independent judiciary, as if this condition were a long-established and uncontroversial *fait accompli*. But there are, in fact, many questions that are never fully resolved regarding the nature of the ideal relationship between the judiciary and the other branches of government. *Should* the judiciary be fully independent? How independent should it be? By what means should that independence be secured? How well protected is it in practice? And perhaps most difficult of all, can we always be sure when judges are behaving independently and when they are giving in to extraconstitutional pressures to conform?

How Independent Should Judges Be?

> There is no liberty, if the judiciary power be not separated from the legislative and executive. Were it joined with the legislative, the life and liberty of the subject would be exposed to arbitrary control; for the judge would be then the legislator. Were it joined to the executive power, the judge might behave with violence and oppression. There would be an end of everything were the same man or the same body, whether of the nobles or of the people, to exercise those three powers, that of enacting laws, that of executing the public resolutions, and that of trying the causes of individuals.[19]

French political philosopher Charles Montesquieu's eloquent statement is usually taken as the basis for the principle of separation of powers that is embedded in the U.S. Constitution. But his arguments on behalf of separating the judicial branch from executive and legislative functions also have a special cogency here. Judicial independence means that the judiciary is protected—usually by constitutional guarantees—from interference by the other branches of government in the conduct of its work.

As we saw in Chapter 8, even in parliamentary systems—in which the executive and legislative functions are closely joined—the judiciary often maintains a significant measure of independence. The constitution of the Federal Republic of Germany declares without equivocation, "The judges shall be independent and subject only to the law" and are perceived as simply "neutral administrators of the law."[20] Even where such independence has been violated in practice—as in Egypt, where military or state security emergency courts are often given jurisdiction over cases summarily described as threatening national security and where executive authorities sometimes ignore judicial orders altogether—the Constitution nonetheless "provides for the independence and immunity of judges and forbids interference by other authorities in the exercise of their judicial functions."[21] Only openly authoritarian systems fail to offer the judicial process at least a semblance of protection from interference by others in power.

The arguments for an independent judiciary come easily to mind. If judges can be removed from office for unpopular decisions, they are likely to try harder to please the people who have that power of removal than to determine what constitutes the fair application of the law. If judges' decisions can easily be set aside or overthrown, the painstaking, expensive, and time-consuming judicial process becomes an empty exercise. If judges must always rule as instructed by those in high executive office, regardless of the clear meaning of existing law or the principles of fair practice, they will be helpless to foster respect for the law, for those principles, or for the political system itself.

However, there are also some interesting arguments against the establishment of an entirely independent judiciary, even in democratic systems of government. Judges are almost always appointed rather than elected, so it can be argued that they should not be able to set aside the will of the people by selective interpretation of the laws written by the people's elected representatives, an argument often used in the continuing debate on abortion and the question of whether or not the U.S. Supreme Court can, constitutionally, protect a woman's right to make this decision even when state law declares otherwise.[22]

This argument against unlimited judicial independence has inspired some polities to choose judges by election, particularly those at the lower levels of the court system. Although the general public usually approves of judicial elections, the judges themselves would almost always prefer to reach office by appointment, pointing out the difficulties of maintaining accountability to two masters: the voters and the law.[23]

A second argument against absolute judicial independence is that the powers this gives to judges are difficult to limit by law and are consequently likely to be extended ever further. Such *judicialization* or *judicial activism* is most likely in liberal democracies, argues C. Neal Tate, who shows how the process is now well underway in the recently semi-democratized Philippines.[24] The practice of *plea bargaining,* in which attorneys, judges, and defendants arrive at pretrial decisions that permit the defendant to enter an "appropriate" guilty plea to reduced charges, eliminating not only the need for a trial but also, some protest, the defendant's constitutional right of due process, can be viewed from this perspective.[25]

A third and related argument is that there is no guarantee that judges who overstep traditional bounds will always be on the side of the common man, or even on the side of the highest law of the land. Simple racism or sexism may be at work. Certainly no legal code in a modern democracy overtly states that persons of color accused of a crime should be treated differently from whites, nor that women victims of crime should receive less protection than men, but in fact there continue to be constant signs that practice contradicts principle. In the United States, a nation with an incarceration rate four times that of Canada, five times that of England and Wales, and fourteen times that of Japan, the rate of imprisonment for blacks is more than seven times as high as that for whites.[26] Similarly, women's advocates in the United States are still able to cite convincing evidence of judges who refuse to take seriously cases of women assaulted by men, despite a new awareness of the problem since the Simpson case and the Violence Against Women Act passed in 1995.[27]

A fourth (and also obviously related) argument is made on the simple grounds that beneath their impressive robes judges are, after all, mere human beings. There is always the chance that they will begin to manifest the various frailties of the species yet be impossible to remove from power. Some observers of the U.S. court system have suggested a constitutional amendment limiting federal judgeships to a single ten-year term, and indeed in most other nations such limitations do exist.

Finally, as we have already said, what is considered just depends on each polity's particular standards. When those standards change, the society's judges—often socially isolated by virtue of their lofty and engrossing occupations—may be among the last to recognize what has happened. If it is impossible to remove judges who are out of touch with the evolution in the thinking of ordinary men and women, it may be equally impossible to ensure that justice will be done.

Means of Ensuring Judicial Independence

Given the arguments for and against judicial independence, it should not be surprising that great variety can be found in the degree of independence actually accorded to that branch of government and its functionaries in various nations, and in the means employed to ensure that independence.

Challenging the legal system. Zacarias Moussaoui, a French citizen of Moroccan descent, was arrested and charged in the U.S. federal court system in December 2001 on six conspiracy counts related to the terrorist attacks on the U.S. three months earlier. Four of the charges carried the death penalty. Moussaoui declared it was impossible that he would be given a fair trial and insisted on defending himself.
© Reuters NewMedia Inc./CORBIS

One means of protecting judges from political or other interference while maintaining some control over their activities is to give only other judges the power to exercise that control. We have already given examples of this in the matter of appointments, but lawyers and judges often set up self-regulating agencies of their own creation for other purposes as well. When students at Northwestern University in Illinois discovered evidence that a man who had been sentenced to death and was just two days away from execution after 16 years on death row was actually innocent, and the *Chicago Tribune* documented the cases of 12 other men also wrongly convicted but not yet executed, it was a committee of 17 judges that devised a new set of rules requiring better training and experience for defense lawyers handling death penalty cases, and the Supreme Court of Illinois that voted to adopt them.[28]

The second common way of encouraging judicial independence is to make the process of removing judges extremely difficult and complex. United States Supreme Court justices can be removed only by impeachment (as for the president, the House of Representatives brings the charges, the Senate tries the case). Japanese Supreme Court judges are secure in office, but for only ten years: At the end of every decade in office they must be reelected by the people or relinquish office.

Giving judges the right of judicial review (the right to review a nation's laws to ensure that they are in accordance with the constitution; see Box 8.3 on p. 333) is often cited as a means of maintaining judicial independence. If judges can rule legislation or executive decrees unconstitutional, they have (it is argued) a powerful means of warning other officers of government to keep within their proper bounds. However, the right of judicial review is next to meaningless in practice unless other means are used to secure the independence of the judges who exercise that power.

In point of fact, none of the means used to assure a measure of judicial independence is foolproof. Judges may succumb to pressures from leaders secure in office or from those who would replace them no matter what the constitution says. When Alberto Fujimori took power in Peru, one of his first steps was to initiate a process of "judicial reform." The Peruvian judiciary needed reform, but this was not really what Fujimori had in mind so much as turning an already corrupt system to his own advantage. According to César Landa, the then supposedly reformed judiciary applied the law "with an iron fist" against the president's enemies and "with a velvet glove" for his friends.[29]

The continuing independence of the judiciary inevitably depends on the judges themselves, and on the support they receive from the public. The readiness of some judges under pressure to aid and abet certain leaders while blocking the ambitions of others can be—or seem to be—especially apparent during times of transition in the executive branch.

Judicial Dependency: Forced and Complicit

Sometimes judges are clearly *not* independent. They may be working in systems where there is no pretense of judicial independence or where only lip service is given to the ideal, with no adequate protections. Or they may be willingly complicit with power in order to serve their own ambitions or political beliefs.

■ **Forced Dependency.** In openly autocratic regimes, all pretense of honoring the rulings of the regular court system may be set aside. One way to do this is to call for the creation of special courts to enact the will of the leader. During the period of Joseph Stalin's rule in the Soviet Union, political trials were conducted by the office of the People's Commissar of Internal Affairs. Stalin personally appointed the commissar, and when one of them proved "too slow" in ordering executions, Stalin replaced him with another, Nikolai lvanovitch Yezhov, who dutifully inaugurated a period of "tremendous growth in mass repression."[30] In contemporary Iraq, a system of "revolutionary courts" has been set up to try political offenses, narcotics trafficking, and "crimes against God." In these courts the accused are charged with such behavior as "moral corruption," "antirevolutionary behavior," and "siding with global arrogance." There are "virtually no procedural or substantive safeguards," and trials often last less than five minutes.[31]

In other nations, a pretense of judicial independence is made, but other forces may well prevail nonetheless. In China the problem is, says Fu Xiangtao, "draconian officialdom." Xiangtao believes that "with such an immense population to take care of the state genuinely needs a large and reasonably strong body of administrators," but says that the problem has been the excessive power of government officials to interrupt and influence the daily work of the courts. Although reforms have been introduced, including the introduction of the Administrative Procedural Law permitting common people to file suit against officials, judicial independence from the administration remains uncertain in China.[32]

Judges can also lose their ability to operate independently because of political instability. Political violence in El Salvador all but crippled that nation's judicial system throughout the 1970s and 1980s; "the homicide conviction rate . . . dropped as low as 4 percent in rural areas [and] citizens had little confidence in obtaining redress of grievances through the courts."[33] Strong judicial efforts to curb the Mafia in Sicily in the 1980s and early 1990s led to the assassination of judges with little or no effort on the part of the executive branch to do anything about it.

When judicial independence is weak to nonexistent, it is always very difficult to introduce or strengthen it. As Pilar Domingo points out in discussing the efforts being made in various Latin American nations, judicial reforms "are a complex matter and require more than redesigning formal mechanisms that will strengthen political independence and impartiality and enhance accountability and transparency. They also require resources, investment, and a transformation of illiberal habits based on political manipulation, clientelism, and inefficiency that [may] pervade the public sector."[34] But the consequences of failure are far reaching: Successful democratization requires building widely shared perceptions of citizenship and government operating in a context of legal and constitutional accountability. When the judiciary is unable or unwilling to play its part, by protecting basic rights and ensuring the rule of law, such perceptions are unlikely to develop and prevail.

■ **Complicit Dependency.** We turn now to consider a particularly difficult question regarding judicial independence: the willingness of some judges to act complicitly with powerful leaders even when sufficiently protected by law and tradition not to need to do so. What makes this problem especially difficult is that it is often next to impossible to know when judicial rulings that seem suspiciously complicit are truly owing to excessive readiness to please power and/or serve personal political convictions and when they simply represent the judges' own honest interpretation of the law. When Gloria Macapagal Arroyo became the new president of the Philippines in 2001 after the ouster of Joseph Estrada (tainted by corruption scandals and threatened with impeachment but clearly still the favorite of the nation's multitudinous poor), business interests rejoiced and the stock market turned sharply upward. Estrada protested that he had not really resigned and threatened to challenge her takeover, but the nation's Supreme Court had already, with perhaps suspicious speed, ratified her appointment.[35] Questions were raised, but as so often in such cases, never really answered. President Arroyo began her term of office.

Similar questions of judicial motivation arose the same year in France, when jurists in different levels of that nation's court system seemed to be playing political soccer with the question of whether or not French President Jacques Chirac had violated France's very strict regulations regarding campaign finance in his quest for election. Actually, few questioned the president's probable culpability as a candidate; the case was made to revolve around whether or not a sitting president could be indicted while in office, or even questioned as a witness. The nation's highest court, led by a jurist who was himself shortly thereafter expelled from that court for his own scandalous pursuit of financial reward from business interests, said Chirac could not be indicted. Five magistrates then sought to question the French president in related cases; when he refused to appear, a court of appeal said he must, only to be overruled by the highest court in October 2001. Maybe later, said that court, but not while he was in office.[36]

But of course the judicial decisions that attracted the most attention during this political era were made in the United States as the Clinton presidency drew to its more-or-less dismal conclusion. Question after question touched the rawest of judicial nerve endings. Were grand jury investigations into Clinton's legal and personal behavior prior to his impeachment by the House of Representatives politically motivated? Did the Florida Supreme Court do everything it could to twist the law on behalf of Albert Gore in finding grounds for continuing the recount of the vote in that state? Could the five judges on the U.S. Supreme Court—the judicial body whose independence was so highly vaunted, so securely protected—have been indulging in unprecedented Republican and conservative favoritism in writing their tortured and all-but-unreadable majority decision calling that recount to a halt and thereby giving the election to George W. Bush on December 9, 2000?[37] Was it legally sound even if politically convenient for both sides when Clinton was given, on the very last day of his presidency, immunity from further investigation in exchange for admitting he gave false testimony under oath and agreeing to surrender his law license for five years?[38] The first man George W. Bush thanked after his inauguration the very next day was Chief Justice William H. Rehnquist. Rehnquist had just sworn him in, of course, but his votes had also been crucial on December 9 and 12 in making that inauguration possible. Was this thank you a bit more profoundly heartfelt than usual, that is to say, as some certainly did, "not just a formality"?[39]

As is their wont, Americans grumbled/rejoiced/sighed and went forward, most of them hoping never to live through such a set of judicial-political dramas again, and hoping profoundly as well that all three branches of the national government could somehow recover their former dignity and reputation for probity. But the peace was short-lived. The aftermath of the terrorist attacks of September 11, 2001, brought new challenges to the principle of judicial independence: Could an American president simply set aside the domestic court system altogether and call for special military tribunals empowered to try, convict, and sentence foreigners accused of terrorism? President Bush signed such a "Military Order" on November 13, 2001.

The outcry was strong. After all, the United States has often protested the use of military and/or secret trials in such nations as Burma, China, Colombia, Egypt, Kyrgyzstan, Malaysia, Nigeria, Peru, Russia, Sudan, and Turkey.[40] The antiterrorist war had been announced as necessary to protect U.S. democratic values and freedom; surely prime among such values were protections of due process, not all of which were guaranteed in the president's executive order. There was no clear indication that the new tribunals would even conform to international treaties regarding rights of due process.[41] (See Box 11.2.) Some argued that terrorists should be tried as war criminals before an international tribunal such as that established for cases out of Yugoslavia and Rwanda, but others insisted the law of war should not apply to simple criminals.[42] At the very least, members of the U.S. Congress argued, the tribunals should be authorized by Congress and given rules ensuring at least some of the protections normally accorded American citizens.[43]

The question of judicial independence is, as we have seen, puzzling, complex, often fascinating. But we must bear one final thought in mind: Even in nations where judicial independence has legal and ethical status, and is normally well respected, the final judicial word is not always, in fact, the final word. If the chief executives of a state do not respect legal rulings, judges have no independent means to insist on their enforcement. When Germany's Constitutional Court ruled that the state of Bavaria had no right to insist that crucifixes be hung in all classrooms, that state's education minister said, "The crosses are hanging and will remain hanging."[44] Since, when polled, 58 percent of all Germans rejected the ruling, only 37 percent supported

BOX 11.2
**Due Process
Rights in Military
Tribunals**

Article 14 of the International Covenant on Civil and Political Rights sets forth the following due process rights for those accused of crimes:

- A fair and public hearing by a competent, independent and impartial tribunal established by law (but the press and public can be excluded for reasons, for example, of "public order or national security in a democratic society").
- The right to be presumed innocent until proved guilty.
- The right to be informed promptly and in detail in a language the accused understands of the nature and cause of the charge(s) against him.
- The right to have adequate time and facilities for the preparation of his defense and to communicate with counsel of his own choosing.
- The right to be tried without undue delay.
- The right to be tried in his presence, and to defend himself in person or through legal assistance of his choosing.
- The right "to have the free assistance of an interpreter".
- The right not to be compelled to testify against himself or to confess guilt.
- The right to have his conviction and sentence . . . reviewed by a higher tribunal according to law.

Source: Jordan J. Paust, "Military Commissions: Some Perhaps Legal, But Most Unwise," *Jurist,* accessed 18 Nov. 2001 at http://jurist.law.pitt.edu/forum/forumnew38.htm. Reprinted by permission.

it, and the chancellor himself (then Helmut Kohl) criticized it openly, the chances the crosses would come down seemed dim.

GUIDELINES FOR ADJUDICATION: THE KINDS OF KINDS OF LAW

As we noted earlier, normative standards of what is just vary from culture to culture. So do the kinds of law in which those standards are given legal expression—laws that guide the rulings of jurists whose job it is to determine what constitutes fair treatment. We will consider first the different kinds of law that have emerged in human history and then the kinds of law that are dominant in the various "legal cultures" found today throughout the human polity (see Figure 11.1).

Before we begin, however, a word of caution is in order. Trying to understand the different kinds of law can be difficult until we grasp that there are "kinds of kinds"—which is to say, there is more than one way to categorize the kinds of law we human beings have devised. We find out about these different "kinds of kinds" when we ask different questions. If we ask the ques-

Kinds Number 1: Laws are based on:	**Natural Law** Discovered truth	**Positive Law** Commonsense pragmatism
Kinds Number 2: Laws are made by:	**Codified Law** Designated lawmakers writing statutes and devising constitutions	**Common Law** Cumulative judicial decisions regarding the meaning and applicability of other laws and general principles of fairness
Kinds Number 3: Laws govern:	**Criminal Law** Criminal behavior	**Civil Law** Disputes between citizens
Kinds Number 4: Laws apply to:	**Domestic Law** Relationships within states	**International Law** Relationships governed by treaties and covenants

FIGURE 11.1
The Kinds of Kinds of Law

tion, "Are laws based on discovered truth or on commonsense pragmatism?" then we are likely to get an answer that tells us about the difference between *natural law* and *positive law*. But if we ask, "Are laws always written and codified by officially designated lawmakers, or do they emerge more gradually over time, as judges decide thorny questions in the courtroom?" then someone will be ready to explain to us the difference between *statutory law* and codes of law on one hand, and *common* (or "judge-made") *law* on the other. Or perhaps we wonder, "Is there a difference between laws that determine what punishments fit what crimes and laws that are designed simply to settle disputes and provide retribution?" In that case we will be told: Yes, there is *criminal law* and *civil law*. Finally, it may occur to us to ask, "Is there a body of law that governs the behavior within and between nations, separate from laws made within nations?"—thereby stimulating someone to tell us all about the difference between *domestic law* and *international law.*

The task for beginners would be considerably easier if there were well-known names for these kinds of kinds of law, and if scholars would always make clear exactly what kinds they are talking about. Unfortunately, commentators tend to jump about from one kind to the other without raising any signals, and even to use the same terms to identify quite different distinctions. We will try to avoid that pitfall here. To help you find your way, we will take up each kind of kind of law in turn, give them names that signal (even if somewhat roughly) what each is about, and keep our usage of these terms consistent throughout.

Law's Relationship to Truth: Natural Law Versus Positive Law

Life on this planet is sometimes extremely perplexing. How did we get here? Are we here for a reason or just by accident? How should we spend our time here? And what, if anything, happens next? These questions all fall within the domain of philosophy and theology—that is, the domain of metaphysics. However, the third question—"How should we spend our time here?"—is also partly the domain of law, which determines what conduct is not permitted as well as what acts must be performed.

This overlapping of the worlds of law and metaphysics has led some philosophers to believe that philosophy should instruct law. If philosophy or religion can tell us in general how we should spend our time on earth, then we ought to be able to deduce the particular rules we should follow—or so say those who believe there is such a thing as natural law. We ought to be able to discover the laws that already exist in nature, which have been, some would add, implanted there by a divine creator. The idea of natural law can be traced back to the Greek and Roman Stoic philosophers, and particularly to the ideas of Marcus Tullius Cicero, who argued that there was a universal law of nature, discoverable by "right reason" and binding on all.[45] Those who have argued for positive law, or law made by human beings, usually have not denied the various precepts of their society's dominant religion or philosophy. What they *have* denied is the possibility of discovering laws in that way. They argue instead that laws are and must be made pragmatically, to meet given ends. Laws should be clearly *promulgated* (announced), as should the punishments or other sanctions applied to those who transgress them. Such laws should be in accord with the society's moral principles, but they should not be seen as having the weight and authority of absolute truth. They should be recognized, say the positivists, as the instruments of mortal, fallible humans who are simply attempting to establish order on the basis of their empirical experience.[46]

In recent times, the positivist view of law has been dominant in much of the world. But the idea that natural law exists and can be discovered has had great appeal in the past. If it can be argued that the law represents absolute truth of divine origin, then who dares to challenge any law as unjust? Throughout much of human history, the principles of natural law were used to bolster the authority of autocrats. Kings succeeded to power, it was argued, only because it was the will of a divine being that they do so. Thus, their decrees had divine sanction and had to be accepted without question. Even when the "divine right of kings," as this theory is called, led to patently outrageous abuses of power, uncompromising believers in natural law argued that the edicts of kings must be obeyed.

However, such abuses inevitably led other political thinkers to look for arguments that would permit the dethroning of tyrants without denying the existence of natural law. In the seventeenth century, John Locke found such an argument. Natural law was given, said Locke, for the preservation of humankind and to ensure the public good of society. Its commands were binding on sovereigns and legislators as well as on ordinary men and women; when those in power acted in a manner contrary to those purposes, it was a sign that they themselves were contravening natural law. In such a case, it was the right and indeed the duty of the people to replace their rulers with those who would act more in accord with the strictures of natural law.[47]

How Law Is Formalized: Common Law and Codified Law

Many of those who puzzle about the nature of law are content to leave the question of its relationship to truth unresolved and do not feel the need to categorize law as either natural or positive. For them, a more important question is how the law was established. The categories that matter to them are common law and codified law. Other variations in how law is formalized include equity law, statutory law, and constitutional law.

When the Roman Empire grew to include vast numbers of peoples, each with its own established laws, problems developed in maintaining peaceful relationships throughout the land. What was normal practice in one province might be a serious crime in another. Simply imposing Roman law on everyone could have created as many problems as it solved. The Roman answer was to establish special courts to hear cases involving disputes between inhabitants of different territories. The judge (known as a *praetor peregrinus,* or judge for foreigners) would then consider the legal principles of both lands, look for common ground between them, and—failing that—propose a solution based on *equity,* that is, a solution based on an abstract notion of fairness. These decisions frequently served as precedents for succeeding cases. Eventually, in the sixth century B.C.E., Emperor Justinian ordered Roman jurists to codify the body of law that was emerging in this way. The result, known as the "law of the peoples" (*jus gentium*), was the first effort to bring together the pre-existing rules of a polity.[48] (But not the first time laws were written down: Hammurabi created a code of law in Babylon much earlier than that, between 1795 and 1750 B.C.E.[49])

The Roman solution offers good illustrations of several of the ways laws can be established. When the judges for foreigners took it upon themselves to declare what was just, then took note of one another's decisions and treated them as *precedents*—that is, as examples to be followed in succeeding cases—they were building a body of "judge-made law," a kind of law that would later be known as *case law* or *common law*.[50] Common law has both the virtue and the flaw of flexibility. In most systems it is only as fixed as the judges want it to be, which means that unfair decisions can be set aside relatively easily—but so can those that are fair. None of the participants can be certain when the judge's ruling will be *stare decisis* ("let the [previous] decision stand") or when he or she will decide that previous decisions do not really apply to the case at hand.

Today common law is particularly "common" in northern Europe and the United States. The evolution of the legal system of the Republic of Ireland offers an interesting example of the twists and turns possible over the centuries. Some Irish law traces its roots as far back as the customs of the seventh century, when Ireland was composed of separate kingdoms and fiefdoms and the law and its application were in the hands of a small group of teachers and judges. Conquest by the English led, especially after 1800, to a body of English-Irish common law, much of which remained operative after independence was granted in 1922. Beginning with the 1924 Courts of Justice Act, the newly free republic revised its laws to suit itself, but often used English law as its model nonetheless. Since 1973, judges have been influenced by European Community law, but Irish courts continue to be required to follow precedents, so long as the earlier decisions "meet the requirements of aptness and similarity."[51]

Not surprisingly, a body of common law often emerges—or is extended—when a nation must deal with remarkably new and challenging circumstances, circumstances that existing laws simply fail to cover. When, during the Watergate scandal of 1972 to 1974, the U.S. Congress became persuaded that something had to be done about the infusion of large sums of private money into political campaigns, it passed the Federal Election Campaign Act of 1974. This act imposed rigorous requirements for the disclosure of the sources of all political funds and imposed strict limits on both contributions and expenditures for campaigns. It also raised almost as many questions as it answered, such as, When does a contribution become an expenditure? How can spending and contribution limits be reconciled with rights of free speech? The result was a series of court cases, usually brought by people who had been affected by the Federal Election Commission's interpretation of the act. These cases have in turn produced an interesting contemporary example of the building of common law.

Another development in common law is taking place right now, as cases are being brought before the courts of several modern nations that involve the new problems of computer theft and misuse of the Internet. Ingenious *hackers* (computer hobbyists) can now crack code after code and enter the secret systems of governments and business corporations, and the courts are under heavy pressure to interpret existing laws in such a way as to halt such practices.[52] Similarly, governments around the globe are seeking ways to control the flow of information deemed dangerous to the common good, as when a French court ordered the search engine Yahoo! Inc. to prevent French Web surfers from accessing pro-Nazi sites or purchasing Nazi memorabilia through its on-line auction site.[53] Such rulings can extend the reach of the common law or, in nations where that tradition is weak, such as France, stretch the meaning of laws already codified.

Codified law is a body of law that has been set down in writing, as Justinian directed his jurists to do in the sixth century. It may draw on many sources; edicts, treaties, decrees, legislative enactments, and the substance of common law decisions are all grist for the mill of the codifiers, who may themselves write new law to eliminate contradictions or to fill gaps in the material before them. Codified law need not be permanently fixed, but changes in a code of law are usually made more formally than are changes in common law. The Roman code was modified again and again over the centuries until, early in the nineteenth century, Napoleon ordered a new systematization of law throughout the empire he had built for France. The Napoleonic code was built on the Roman code, as were subsequent modifications of that code, such as the code of the German Empire of 1900 and the Swiss code of 1907.[54]

Equity law is a form of law that developed as a way of compensating for another difficulty that arises from common law. Common law can usually be applied only after a crime or a damaging act has occurred. In a typical example of equity law, a judge might decide that waiting for an anticipated act to occur before deciding whether it is legal would do irreparable harm, and might therefore issue an order forbidding the intended act. The act in question might be one performed by a private party (for example, your landlord may plan to install insulation materials to which you are extremely allergic) or by government (for example, the Highway Department's bulldozers are bearing down on your cherished elm tree because they want to widen your street). The most frequent modern legal action invoking equity comes in the form of an injunction issued to suspend proceedings until one party or the other has time to prepare a fuller case. The idea of equity is an interesting and controversial one: Some argue that it goes against the very idea of equal protection under the law, inasmuch as it permits a judge to rule according to what he or she deems fair rather than in strict conformance with statutory law; others insist it simply "allows a judge to rectify the deficiency of a general legal rule that results from the legislature's inability to consider the facts of a particular case when codifying a universal law." [55]

Statutory law includes all legislation, treaties, executive orders, and decrees as well as codes of law. As we have noted, law codes usually incorporate whatever statutory law exists at the time of codification. But other forms of statutory law continue to be written, day after day, year after year. New statutes may or may not be incorporated into an existing code. In some nations, such as Norway, judges have at their command a rich tradition of common law, supplemented by a wide-ranging and ever-changing body of uncodified statutory law. Special forms of statutory law, such as *administrative law* (the rules and decisions of administrative agencies) and *admiralty* and *maritime law* (for cases having to do with shipping and waterborne commerce), are sometimes considered to be altogether separate forms of law.[56]

A *constitution* is itself a special form of law, often referred to as the "highest law in the land." *Constitutional law* is law that has evolved in cases that require independent judicial interpretation of the provisions of a constitution (such as all cases of judicial review).[57] As such, constitutional law can be seen as a form of common law.

Different Law for Different Acts: Criminal Law and Civil Law

Another way to subdivide the kinds of law is to consider the acts of the parties in the case—or rather, the alleged acts. Is someone claiming that a crime against the public order has been committed and must be punished by society? Then the judge must decide the applicability of the appropriate criminal law to the case. Or is someone alleging that one individual has acted unfairly toward another in a way that damages only that individual—not the society at large—and that some form of retribution must be made to the individual who suffered the damage? In that case, the judge will turn to *civil law*.

Civil law covers cases dealing with such matters as divorce, child custody, inheritances, and contracts. Criminal law covers any act that is considered an offense against society, from the most serious cases of rape, arson, or murder to the most petty infraction of parking regulations. The line between civil law and criminal law is not always clear; some acts can be considered simultaneously offenses against society, requiring punishment, and offenses against individuals, requiring restitution. One way to decide which form of law applies is to consider the circumstances. An act that was intentional or reckless may be deemed criminal, while the same act may be subject only to civil law if it results from negligence or accident.[58]

A separate but related distinction is made between crimes with victims and such victimless crimes as gambling and possession of marijuana. It is sometimes argued that "victimless" crimes should be subject to neither criminal penalty nor civil retribution because there is no nonconsenting victim in such cases. However, most polities have decided that at least some of these activities do constitute offenses against the society at large and should be punished as such—that is, under criminal law.

Ordinary citizens who have occasion to deal with the courts are likely to find the distinction between civil law and criminal law more important than any other. The rules of proceeding and the range of possible outcomes vary radically according to whether a civil or a criminal case is under consideration, so much so that it is common to establish an entirely separate system of courts to deal with each. (For the two separate systems in Great Britain, see Figures 11.2 and 11.3.)

The Scope of Law: Domestic Law and International Law

A final categorization of kinds of law derives from the territorial scope of any law. The most obvious distinction here is between domestic law, the body of laws that nations apply only within their territories, and international law, the law that applies in relationships between nations, or between the citizens of one nation and either the government or individual citizens of another nation.

We will examine the provisions of international law more carefully in Chapter 13, but here we will consider two essential differences between domestic law and international law. First, domestic law has much greater legitimacy than international law. Domestic law evolves from the beliefs and the culture of a particular society and is therefore likely to be accepted as reasonable and understandable by most of the members of that society. But international law is not based on the culture of those to whom it applies, and its dictates may draw on notions of fairness that are puzzling, unfamiliar, and even repugnant to those to whom they are supposed to apply.

Second, domestic law is much easier to enforce than international law. The police and the armies of the world are under national, not international, control. European Union law is growing rapidly.[59] Nonetheless, it is often an open question whether its edicts will be obeyed. When the European Court of Human Rights ruled in 1995 that the British Army had illegally killed three members of the Irish Republican Army (who were, ruled the court, clearly trying to surrender) and ordered Britain to pay legal costs to the victims' families, the response of the British deputy prime minister was that that nation would simply ignore the verdict.[60]

Despite such difficulties, both the body of international law and the machinery for arriving at settlements under that law do exist, and they do "work" more often than might at first be expected. Karl Deutsch suggested that international law prevails (when it does) because "it serves the nations to coordinate their mutual expectations and behavior *in their own interest.*"[61] It provides a framework for harmonious interaction between nations, and such interaction is normally easier and less costly than operating in constant conflict or in the anarchy of lawlessness.

There are, of course, also differences in the scope of law *within* nation-states. Municipal ordinances, county rules, state or provincial law, and national legislation all vary in the territorial extent of their coverage. However, local law within nations, a topic we will return to in the next chapter, must always be consistent with national law and, except in rare instances, can always be overturned at the national level. The difference between domestic and international law is in that respect a different kind of difference (a different kind of kind).

REGIONAL VARIATIONS IN THE RULE OF LAW: LEGAL CULTURES

In any given polity we will find aspects of nearly all the kinds of law we have been discussing. Some legal principles will appear to be based on unquestionable truth even in the most pragmatic of cultures. Every society has some form of statutory law, yet every society also has judges who occasionally take it upon themselves to assert a little courtroom inventiveness—and whose decisions earn the flattery of imitation by other judges. Every polity has a way of settling disputes between individuals that is different from the way it punishes crimes against society. And in no part of the world is international law as binding as is domestic law.

Despite this overriding similarity in diversity, however, several distinctive *legal cultures* can be found as we examine how the human polity goes about providing for fair treatment under the law.[62]

The Romano-Germanic Legal Culture

The pattern most widely adopted is the *Romano-Germanic legal culture,* by which is meant those nations (or in some cases, those subunits within nations) in which judicial decisions are based on codes of law based on the Roman tradition. This system prevails in most of Europe, all of Latin America, the nations in west and central Africa that were formerly under French imperial control, and to some extent in the Canadian province of Quebec and the American state of Louisiana. (Both Quebec and Louisiana have strong ethnic and cultural links to France, and thus to the Napoleonic code.) In such cultures, judges are expected not to make law but to exercise the greatest possible care in determining if and exactly how a given law applies to a

FIGURE 11.2
The British Judicial
System: Courts
Exercising *Civil*
Jurisdiction

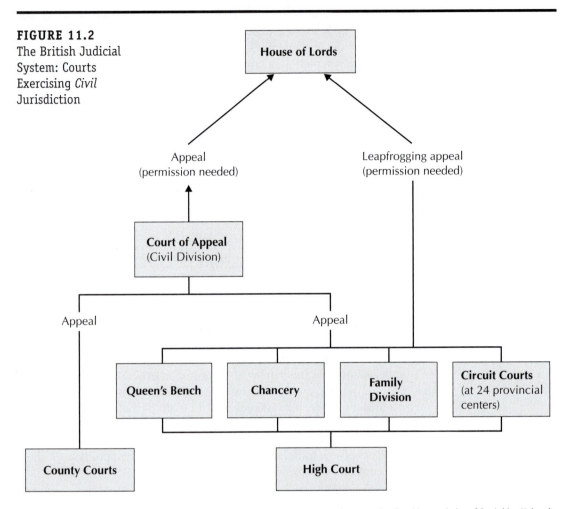

Source: Philip Norton, *The British Polity,* 2nd ed. (New York and London: Longman, 1991), p. 346. Reprinted by permission of Cambridge University Press.

given case. They are not expected to consult other judges' decisions in similar cases; each case is taken up *ab ovo.*[63]

Although the basis of law in the Romano-Germanic legal culture is codified law, not all law is found in the codes. In the Federal Republic of Germany, for example, any legal rule that has been enacted and promulgated by state authorities who are constitutionally entitled to enact and promulgate laws is considered part of statutory law; it is also permissible to refer to custom, defined as "the regular and general public practice of law." Other legal

FIGURE 11.3
The British Judicial
System: Courts
Exercising *Criminal*
Jurisdiction

Source: Philip Norton, *The British Polity,* 2nd ed. New York and London: Longman, 1991), p. 346. Reprinted by permission of Cambridge University Press.

Not all legal systems are the same. Here distinguished Egyptian sociologist Saad Eddin Ibrahim, a professor at the American University of Cairo who led a team of students in an investigation of electoral fraud in his country, covering expenses with a grant from the European Union, is shown on trial for defaming his nation and using foreign funds.
© AFP/CORBIS

systems are heavily influenced by the Romano-Germanic legal culture but do not fully belong to it, as Konrad Zweigert and Hein Kotz argue is the case for the legal systems of the Nordic states of Denmark, Finland, Iceland, Norway, and Sweden. Although they have more in common with a codified than a common law culture, by the time Roman law reached the Scandinavian countries in the seventeenth century, traditional legal institutions had "long been stabilized in provincial and city laws and were being applied in a well-constructed courts system." The mixture is so distinctive these authors insist there is "a special Nordic legal group." [64]

The heavy reliance on codified law in the Romano-Germanic legal culture has the advantages—and the disadvantages—of codification in any sphere of human endeavor. Codification makes it easier to know what should be done but harder to adapt to changes that occur after the code has been established. As a general rule, we can say that nations that adopt this legal culture tend to lose in flexibility what they gain in precision.

The Common Law Legal Culture

The *common law legal culture* exists wherever judges are given wide latitude to interpret existing law and their decisions themselves become part of the law to be interpreted by their successors. The roots of the common law tradition are found in England during the Norman Conquest, when the king's judges traveled throughout the land settling disputes by drawing on local custom, their own often quite rudimentary legal training, and any innate wisdom they might happen to have regarding the tenets of justice. Over the years there slowly emerged what the judges were pleased to refer to as "general immemorial custom of the realm." As Henry Ehrmann pointed out, a jurisprudence based on (or at any rate seeming to be based on) the people's own habits, and built up slowly over the years, is "an excellent means of nation-building." [65] In the English case, it was also a useful way to protect the powerful; the early English judges were closely tied to landowning interests, and in acting as the people's defenders against executive power they were at the same time protecting themselves and other members of their class from incursions by the sovereign on their own wealth and power.

The common law tradition spread throughout the British Empire and is still dominant throughout the British Commonwealth, in the United States, and in other former British colonies. Although it had its beginnings in the days when all law was judge-made law, common law today is everywhere combined with law written by legislatures. The extent to which statutory law has come to supplant custom and judicial precedent as the basis for court decisions varies from nation to nation within the common law legal culture.

English resistance to codification is particularly strong, and in that system the greatest possible respect is paid to the principle of *stare decisis*—that is, to the obligation to abide by preceding decisions, even those the court in question has made itself if the decisions have become well established. [66] African nations, on the other hand, have woven a large measure of respect for their own traditional law, heavily based on custom, into their legal systems, but at the same time they regularly augment and amend that law as the needs of modernization require and the force of public opinion permits.

The American Legal Culture

The extent to which custom and precedent guide American jurists varies considerably, from era to era, and from state to state. A New Hampshire judge once scorned codes of law as "devices of ignorance." California, by contrast, is considered the leading code state. When this Far West state joined the union, common law traditions were thin and Mexican law was often still in place; codification was the answer. In general, the American system is a hybrid mixture of codified law and common law, with heavy emphasis on the latter, especially at the national level of the judiciary.

The mixed nature of the American legal culture is apparent when we follow the course of adjudication on a specific topic, such as relations between the races. The shifting course of race relations in the United States has been matched by a shifting course of judicial decisions, each interpreting the Constitution and statutory law in a manner to suit the sentiments of the judges and the times. In 1896, in the case of *Plessy v. Ferguson,* the Supreme Court declared that racial segregation did not constitute discrimination and that states could require the separation of races as long as equal accommodations were provided for all.[67] This decision was considered progressive at the time because it did establish at least the principle of equal facilities for black and white. However, only two years later the Court ruled in *Cumming v. County Board of Education* that equal protection under the law was not denied when a county provided a high school for white children but none for black children.

Throughout the first half of the twentieth century, the Court continued to rely on the *Plessy v. Ferguson* precedent, interpreting each allegation by black citizens that they had been denied equal protection of the law in light of its "separate but equal" doctrine—sometimes ruling in their favor, sometimes not, but always reaffirming that segregation itself was not illegal. But the U.S. Supreme Court is never absolutely bound by precedent, no matter how many times it has conveniently chosen to pretend to be so. In 1954, the Court abandoned *Plessy v. Ferguson* and ruled, in the case of *Brown v. Board of Education,* that segregation in the public schools was unconstitutional.[68] This new case now became the precedent on which others were to be decided, and in case after case the Court reaffirmed and extended its newfound conviction that segregation was unconstitutional and must not be practiced in any public facility in the United States.

During this period, the U.S. Congress passed the Civil Rights acts of 1957, 1960, and 1964, and the Voting Rights Act of 1965, giving the Court a new body of statutory law to enforce or cite in decisions designed to extend equal protection of the law to all Americans. Working together, the legislature, the executive, and the judiciary gradually pushed back the barriers that had been erected against the nation's African American citizens. By the late 1970s, however, resistance was forming against two practices the U.S. government had widely endorsed as a means of equalizing opportunities for all: affirmative action and busing to achieve school integration. Once again, the Court shifted ground, ruling in *Board of Regents v. Bakke* that programs designed to take affirmative action in improving conditions for blacks or other minorities may not include specific quotas, and declaring in *Milliken v. Bradley* that busing pupils from one neighborhood to another in order to achieve racial integration in the schools could be required only if school authorities had in the past intentionally discriminated against minority students: "Absent an interdistrict violation, there is no basis for an interdistrict remedy." Similarly, in the 1990 case of *Wards Cove Packing v. Antonio*, the Court reversed an earlier decision (*Griggs v. Duke Power Company*, 1971) and ruled that it was up to the plaintiffs to show that an employee's practices were discriminatory rather than the responsibility of the employer to demonstrate that they were not. Although the Court continues to uphold the principles of racial equality, in recent years it has been markedly more conservative in adjudicating disputes that arise over how this goal is to be achieved.[69]

The pattern revealed by this very brief review of major judicial decisions in the area of race relations is repeated again and again in the American legal culture. Sometimes judicial decisions adhere closely to the letter of the law as codified in the Constitution or statute—a practice known as *strict construction*. Sometimes judges treat their own or their predecessors' past decisions as inviolable common law precedent. And sometimes they use their right of judicial review to overrule both legislative statute and court decision (including their own)—a practice known as *judicial activism*. This shifting blend of judicial styles has often produced contradictory and inconsistent decisions, but the net result is a system of justice as heterogeneous and as volatile as the people it serves.

The Socialist Legal Culture

The primary sources of law in Russia under the czars were statutes and codes, supplemented by the personal decrees of the emperor. Alexander II (1855–1881) reorganized the courts of law and declared judges independent of the administrative wing of the government, but the final word in judicial as in other matters was still his own, and this continued under his successor Nicholas II (who also promulgated important reforms).[70]

After the Russian Revolution in 1917, and the creation of the Soviet Union, all reference to the law of the czars was forbidden. At first, the Soviets attempted to settle disputes with no formal law whatsoever, relying on judge-made law. It was not until 1922 that a serious effort was made to modify the existing codes and bring them into congruence with socialist ideology. Peter de Cruz lists some of the ways that that ideology influenced the content of Soviet law and the procedures of its judiciary: The Soviet Union "punished any individual who made profits derived from unearned income which had been gained from private enterprise; it had no separation of powers; its agencies were not allowed to criticize Soviet laws; doctrinal writers could only criticize laws if they were obsolete. . . . The courts simply carried out government policy or the Communist Party's policy . . . [and] the Soviet Codes were regarded merely as a basis for the furtherance of political aims and objectives which would have to be modified, as socialist society changed, in accordance with the building of a truly Communist society."[71]

Since the fall of the Soviet Union, the transformation of its component parts and of the political systems under its sway has included numerous changes in the nature of law. The Russian republics appear to be evolving toward "a novel hybrid system with [coded] law and [common] law coexisting together with remnants of socialist laws." Among the nations of Eastern and central Europe seeking to establish constitutional democracy, only the two separate Czech and Slovak republics are able to draw on fully democratic pasts, and even there the experience was of brief duration (between the two world wars). Two fundamental legal reforms in most of these nations are the extension of constitutional protection to the private realm and the institution of judicial review.[72]

In remaining Communist states such as China and Cuba, socialist-coded law is still in effect and remains subordinated to political purposes. In China the rulings of the Communist Party prevail at every level of government despite the "lack of any clear constitutional or statutory authority for [its] omnipotence." The party controls the National People's Congress, which in turn has the authority to amend the constitution and enact "basic laws" (*jiben falu*).[73] As basic policies shift—"from 'continuing revolution' and class struggle to economic development and modernization, from intractable opposition to the West to active cooperation and promotion of foreign investment"—the law can be and is freely adjusted. When Beijing was made the locus for the United Nations Women's Convention of 1995, the government went speedily to work to adopt a new "Law on the Protection of Rights and Interests of Women." Although the law clearly represented a step forward in a nation notorious for the suppression of women's rights, its mechanisms for implementation and enforcement have been termed "singularly weak," and many see its main function as little more than that of raising the consciousness of Chinese women—one-fifth of the women in the world.[74]

Similarly easy to change, Cuban law was codified in the penal code of 1971 and then thoroughly revised in the penal code of 1987 to bring it more closely in accord with new socialist principles emphasizing reeducation. The new code was written in the belief that "antisocial actions . . . considered [to be] crimes resulted from a lack of civic or political education and from the scarcity of consumer goods due to the economic embargo and blockade imposed on our country by powerful foreign enemies of the revolution." However, shortly after this reform Cuba witnessed an upsurge in criminality, prompting many to seek "repenalization" of acts for which the penalties had been sharply reduced.[75]

The Natural Law Legal Culture

In a *natural law legal culture,* the system of law rests in large part on the precepts of religious and philosophical thought. The Confucian system, which has now largely been replaced by more modern codes in the Asian nations where it once held sway, was until recently one of the clearest examples of a natural law legal culture. Confucianism assigned an elaborate set of rights, responsibilities, and attitudes to each level of society, and this code of ethics provided the basis for Chinese jurisprudence. According to Confucius, "man and God, Heaven and earth, all things living and inert are organic parts of a harmoniously ordered and integrated universe" and "men must so conduct themselves as not to disturb the natural balance of their existing relations." Every citizen was to live in accord with *li,* the rules of proper behavior, and this meant paying strict attention to his or her status within the social system: "The different positions which an individual might occupy by reason of his age, sex, career, family position, employment status, and social prestige were all part of the prescribed natural order and had to be respected."[76] Conflicts should be resolved when possible by the head of the family, drawing on the rules of behavior of the *li,* local practices, and his own experience; if no agreement could be reached the parties to the debate could take their cases to the state courts but this was a long and expensive procedure, and "the imperial magistrates had a reputation for being preoccupied, corrupt and lazy."[77]

Both China and Japan have attempted to move away from the rigid social stratification of Confucianism—the former by adopting a socialist legal culture, the latter moving in the direction of Romano-Germanic coded law—and to de-emphasize the role of religion as the basis of law.[78] However, something of the old religious culture lingers in both systems, not only in the normative content of modern codes of law but also in the continuing tendency to place a heavy emphasis on social pressure and persuasion to ensure compliance with the new norms of behavior.[79]

Natural law legal cultures coexist with—and sometimes conflict with—more modern legal cultures throughout much of the developing world, especially at the local level. Thus, contemporary Indian law is a varying amalgam of ancient Hindu law, going back to the four books of Veda, which came into existence between 4000 and 1500 B.C.E. (depending on which scholar you consult), laws developed and applied under British rule, and the postindependence Hindu Code, meant to establish a single, common statutory standard for all Hindus. Regional variations are allowed, and the rural population (the overwhelming majority) follows local legal tradition, which, according to H. Patrick Glenn, says different ". . . profound things relating to life and death and personal responsibility, which have been passed on for millennia." [80] And, of course, not all Indians are Hindus. Traditional African law, derived from indigenous religions, lives on similarly in the otherwise modernized legal cultures of that continent.

The strongest infusions of natural law in contemporary legal systems are found in Muslim nations. Islamic law, referred to as the Shari'a, is "the manifested will of the Almighty; it does not depend on the authority of any earthly law-giver." [81] As such, it cannot be changed: "Society must adapt itself to the law rather than generate laws of its own as a response to the constantly changing stimulus of the problems of life." Any modifications over time are simply the work of jurists refining the "discovery, understanding, and formulation of a law that *already exists.*" [82] The *qadi* (judge) is expected to reach a decision by considering first "the claims of God"—the rulelike statements of law" contained in the Qur'an (the Muslim holy book)—and second the Traditions, statements about what the prophet Mohammed actually said or did in determining justice. The judge then seeks to discover how the present case is analogous to a situation cited in these basic texts and rules accordingly. [83]

Even in the branches of Islamic law that have been heavily westernized, such as contract law, Muslim codes often urge judges to have recourse to the Qur'an in difficult cases. But as is the case in all religions, the same religious texts do not always receive the same interpretations. For the Ayatollah Ruhollah Khomeini of Iran, the Shari'a made it clear that Salman Rushdie, the author of the novel *The Satanic Verses,* and his publishers must be sentenced to death because the book blasphemously employed Islamic myths and Qur'anic motifs in contemporary and futuristic settings. [84] In Iraq, Saddam Hussein has defended punishing criminals by amputating hands, feet, or ears as consistent with Islamic law. [85] In contemporary Egypt, on the other hand, there is far less agreement "regarding what Shari'a means or what form its application should take." Some would pursue the example of more conservative Islamic states, but "liberal and secularist" Egyptian intellectuals argue that Islamic texts and legal opinions can and should be used "to establish reason as the guiding force in modern society." For them, the true aim of the Shari'a is to build an honest and just society in which freedom and dignity are enhanced. [86]

CONVERGENCE OF LEGAL SYSTEMS

As you have no doubt noticed, the distinctions among legal cultures are by no means precise and fixed. As globalization proceeds and nation-states become ever more interdependent, it is natural that such distinctions should become even more blurred, a process legal scholars refer to as *convergence.* Peter de Cruz describes the tendency of common law systems like England to rely more on regulations "as a means of speedy implementing of legal reforms rather than [allowing] the courts to develop the law as they have been doing for several hundred years." At the same time, German constitutional courts and French administrative courts—examples of judiciaries in coded law systems—are more and more likely to make their decisions on the basis of case law. According to de Cruz, three important developments contributing to convergence are the spread of American business law to the rest of the world, especially Europe but also in the Far East; the fall of the Soviet Union and the consequent westernization of the legal systems formerly under its control; and the proliferation of international and regional agreements such as the European Human Rights Convention, the UN Convention on the Rights of the Child, and similar treaties of wide extent.[87]

SUMMARY AND CONCLUSION

As we have seen, the meanings and means of justice vary throughout the human polity. In general, we may agree that justice means "fair treatment under the law," but in practical terms justice is whatever a particular society believes it is. Still, it is important not to exaggerate the differences among various systems' notions of justice; the ordinary men and women of the world may have more shared beliefs about what is just than their systems of law would suggest. Even when we do not agree with one another, our new interdependence forces us to understand and accommodate one another's conception of justice—if only to permit us to do business with one another. Nevertheless, we can reserve the right to apply our own standards in evaluating other systems, once we have made a serious effort to understand why and how other polities have developed their own values about law and justice, acknowledged their right to do so, and firmly rejected the ethnocentric assumption that we ourselves know all the answers and therefore have the right to impose our views on others.

The means of establishing just government also vary. Every nation tries to choose credible judges by appointing only experienced people to that post, by giving the right of appointment to people who are themselves respected by virtue of the office they occupy, and by surrounding the judicial office with the physical accoutrements of dignity and stature—but each nation determines for itself what constitutes appropriate experience, respectable officeholding, and sufficiently impressive judicial insignia. Similarly, despite the obvious connection between keeping judges free from political restraint and protecting individual rights, there is no widespread agreement that the judiciary should be independent of the other branches of the government, or if so, how independent it should be. Where judicial independence is deemed desirable, various means are used to secure that independence—from giving only other judges the power to discipline judges to making the process of removing judges extremely difficult and complex. Giving the courts the power of judicial review is not, however, a dependable means of ensuring judicial independence.

Enforcing justice is often as difficult as ensuring fair adjudication. Executives have a number of motives and means for failing to carry out the will of the courts—or pressuring judges to rule as they themselves wish—political circumstances may make it impossible to conduct normal peaceful judicial processes, international or regional bodies may have the power to contradict rulings made within a single state, and the judges themselves, too eager to reduce the workload on an overburdened system or too guided by their own racial or gender biases, may sometimes be guilty of setting aside their own nation's principles of justice.

In carrying out their work, the judges of the world draw on several kinds of kinds of law. Sometimes law is categorized according to how close it is believed to be to absolute truth, sometimes according to the process by which it is created and formalized, sometimes by the kind of act to which it applies, and sometimes by the territorial extent of its coverage. Some aspect of every kind of law is likely to be present in any given polity, but most systems tend to have a dominant legal culture. The Romano-Germanic legal culture relies heavily on codified law, the common law legal culture on "judge-made" law, the socialist legal culture on statutory law made to fit the particular exigencies of state control of the economy, and the natural law legal culture on the guidance of religious precept, more or less formally enshrined in written law.

Despite these differences, however, there is a contemporary trend toward *convergence* of the world's legal systems, a process consistent with our growing interdependence and speeded on by the downfall of the Soviet Union, the spread of American business law, and the proliferation of international treaties.

In every nation, the application of the law is inevitably uneven, whether by deliberate intent (more common in hierarchical systems) or by the accidents of interpretation (more common in democratic states). The application of the law becomes more personal, as well as more arbitrary, the closer we move to the local level. Indeed, most people have direct experience of government of any type only at that level. To broaden our understanding of the nature of that experience, we turn our attention now to local and regional government.

QUESTIONS TO CONSIDER

1. What is meant by "cultural relativism" and how does it apply to the study of what is just?
2. How independent do you think judges should be? Which arguments against unlimited judicial independence seem strongest to you, and why?

3. Has anyone you know been involved in a court case? (If not, use a recent case in the news for your example.) Was it a matter of civil law or common law, and how can you tell?

4. What is distinctive about the American legal culture?

SELECTED READINGS

Belliotti, Raymond. *Justifying the Law: The Debate Over Foundations, Goals, and Methods* (Philadelphia: Temple University Press, 1992). A critical survey of the works of leading legal minds and of the different schools of legal thought.

de Cruz, Peter. *A Modern Approach to Comparative Law* (Boston: Kluwer, 1993). Provides an introduction to the comparative study of law and legal systems.

Edelman, Martin. *Courts, Politics and Culture in Israel* (Charlottesville: University Press of Virginia, 1994). The author examines Israel's many legal systems and the difficulties such multiplicity causes for the development of a modern democracy, and urges their reconciliation in a written constitution that includes a bill of rights.

Jacob, Herbert, et al. *Courts, Law, and Politics in a Comparative Perspective* (New Haven, Conn.: Yale University Press, 1996). Compares the interactions between politics and legal practices in the United States, England, France, Germany, and Japan, focusing on how constitutional courts function, the procedures of criminal justice and the processing of civil disputes, and making an effort to show how ordinary citizens and large corporations use the courts.

Litan, Robert E., ed. *Verdict: Assessing the Civil Jury System* (Washington, D.C.: The Brookings Institution, 1993). Essays on the civil jury system in the United States, providing historical background as well as a thorough analysis of the contemporary system.

Lobban, Michael. *The Common Law and English Jurisprudence 1780–1850* (Oxford: Clarendon Press, 1991). Discusses the intellectual history of law and the formation of the legal framework in Britain in the late eighteenth and early nineteenth centuries.

Russell, Peter H. and David M. O'Brien, eds. *Judicial Independence in the Age of Democracy: Critical Perspectives from Around the World* (Charlottesville: University Press of Virginia, 2001). This collection of studies examines the problem of judicial independence from an international and comparative perspective, beginning with a general theory of the concept.

Smith, Christopher E. *Courts and Public Policy* (Chicago: Nelson-Hall, 1993). Synthesizes scholarly arguments and findings on judicial policymaking. Discusses the constitutional scope of judicial authority and practical questions about the policymaking capabilities of the court.

Tate, C. Neal and Torbjorn Vallinder. *The Global Expansion of Judicial Power* (New York: New York University Press, 1995). A study of the increasing power of the judiciary throughout the world.

WEB SITES OF INTEREST

1. American Society of International Law
   http://www.asil.org/
   Dedicated to advancing the study and use of international law for nearly a century, the society now provides resource materials and a nonpartisan forum for debate and discussion on issues of law, international relations, and the increasing role of international law in public affairs.

2. Findlaw: Supreme Court
   http://www.findlaw.com/casecode/supreme.html
   A searchable database of U.S. Supreme Court decisions since 1893.

NOTES

1. Rick Bragg, "New Trial Is Sought for Inmate Whose Lawyer Slept in Court," *New York Times,* 23 Jan. 2001, A12.

2. Tamara Jones, "Germany's Troubles," *Los Angeles Times,* 7 March 1993, 14.

3. *New York Times,* 5 March 1995, 21. The California law is now under review by the U.S. Supreme Court. The Ninth Circuit Court has already held that the Constitution "does not permit the application of a law which results in a sentence grossly disproportionate to the crime." (*Lockyer v. Andrade,* no. 01–1127; Charles Lane, "Court to Review 'Three Strikes'," *Washington Post,* 2 April 2002, A-2).

4. In 1857 the Supreme Court ruled that Dred Scott, a slave who had claimed freedom after being taken to a free state, was nevertheless still a slave and furthermore said that Congress could not deprive persons of any kind of property anywhere in the United States and that the Missouri Compromise, which had set boundaries to slavery, was itself unconstitutional. Edward S. Greenberg and Benjamin I. Page, *The Struggle for Democracy* (New York: HarperCollins, 1996), pp. 457–59.

5. Neil MacFarquhar, "Homeland Sees Political Motive in Guilty Verdict," and "Lockerbie Verdict Tainted by Politics, Qaddafi Says," *New York Times,* 1 Feb. 2001, A9, and 6 Feb. 2001, A10.

6. Just for the record, let it be noted that Mr. Williams was in fact 6 feet 5 inches tall and weighed 185 pounds. *New York Times,* 5 March 1995, 21.

7. See John Rawls, *A Theory of Justice* (Cambridge, Mass.: Belknap Press of Harvard University Press, 1971), pp. 1–16.

8. For an interesting contemporary discussion of this age-old problem, see Christina M. Cerna, "Universality of Human Rights and Cultural Diversity: Implementation of Human Rights in Different Socio-Cultural Contexts," *Human Rights Quarterly* 16, no. 4 (Nov. 1994): 740–52. Cerna concludes that "international norms dealing with rights that affect the private sphere of human activity will take the longest time to achieve universal acceptance" (p. 752).

9. David P. Conradt, *The German Polity,* 5th ed. (New York and London: Longman, 1993), p. 179.

10. "Judicial System," in F. M. Leventhal, ed., *Twentieth-Century Britain: An Encyclopedia* (New York: Garland Publishing, 1995), p. 417.

11. Stanley Anderson, "Lay Judges and Jurors in Denmark," *American Journal of Comparative Law* 38, no. 4 (Fall 1990): 839–64.

12. Conradt, *The German Polity,* p. 179, and Thomas Reynolds and Arturo Flores, "Germany" in *Current Sources of Basic Codes and Legislation in Jurisdictions of the World: Western and Eastern Europe,* vol. 2, no. 33 (Littleton, Conn.: Rothman AALL, May 1995), pp. 3–4.

13. Tim L. Merrill and Ramon Miro, *Mexico: A Country Study* (Washington, D.C.: Federal Research Division, Library of Congress, 1997).

14. Graeme Newman, Adam C. Bouloukos, and Debra Cohen, *World Factbook of Criminal Justice Systems: Kenya* (Washington, D.C.: U.S. Department of Justice, Bureau of Justice Statistics, 1996).

15. Gloria M. Weisman, *World Factbook of Criminal Justice Systems: Israel* (Washington, D.C.: Bureau of Justice Statistics, U.S. Department of Justice, 1996).

16. Joan Biskupic, *Washington Post,* 4 Aug. 1993, A4; *Congressional Quarterly Weekly Report* 48, no. 40 (6 Oct. 1990): 3228, and 49, no. 42 (19 October 1991): 3026–33.

17. Charles S. Clark, "Courts and the Media," *C.Q. Researcher* (23 Sept. 1994): 819–35, and Marc Fisher, "Simpson Ad Nauseam? Tell It to the Judge," *International Herald Tribune,* 23 May 1995, 1, 3.

18. Clark, "Courts and the Media," p. 831.

19. Charles Secondat Montesquieu, *Spirit of the Laws,* ed. Franz Neumann, trans. Thomas Nugent (New York: Hafner, 1949), pp. 151–52.

20. Conradt, *German Polity,* p. 179. On the other hand, the Constitutional Court, which has the

power of judicial review, is seen by Conradt as having an "explicitly political character" since "both state and party/political factors" play an important role in the selection of its members (p. 183).

21. *Country Reports on Human Rights Practices 2000: Egypt* (Washington, D.C.: Bureau of Democracy, Human Rights, and Labor, Department of State, 2001).

22. Thomas P. Carr, Karen J. Lewis, and Michael J. Matheron, "Waiting for Roe II," *Congressional Research Service Review* (Sept. 1991): 5–6.

23. *New York Times*, 12 Feb. 1992, A1.

24. C. Neal Tate, "The Judicialization of Politics in the Philippines and Southeast Asia," *International Political Science Review* 15, no. 2 (1994): 187–97.

25. Aogán Mulcahy, "The Justifications of 'Justice': Legal Practitioners' Accounts of Negotiated Case Settlements in Magistrates' Courts," *The British Journal of Criminology* 34, no. 4 (Autumn 1994): 411–30. Mulcahy believes those who favor plea bargaining in fact favor "crime control" over "due process" (p. 427).

26. *New York Times*, 28 Oct. 1994, A1, A9. As of the end of 1993, 2,432 African Americans out of every 100,000 were in prison; the number of whites per 100,000 was 203. Great Britain seems to go in the opposite direction—judges are allowed to increase a punishment if they detect racist motivation behind the criminal act—yet it is also true that in that nation blacks frequently receive harsher sentences than whites for the same crime (*The Economist* [18 June 1994]: 62–63).

27. Ted Gest with Betsy Streisand, "Still Failing Women?" *U.S. News and World Report* (19 June 1995): 54–55.

28. Things had gotten pretty bad in Illinois: In 33 of the cases investigated, the defendants had been represented by lawyers who had been disbarred or suspended. *New York Times*, 24 Jan. 2001, A12.

29. César Landa, "The Scales of Justice in Peru: Judicial Reform and Fundamental Rights," Occasional Paper No. 24, Institute of Latin American Studies (London: University of London, 2001).

30. Samuel Kucherov, *The Organs of Soviet Administration and Justice: Their History and Operation* (Leiden, The Netherlands: E. J. Bull, 1970), p. 691.

31. "Iran" in House Committee on Foreign Affairs, *Country Reports on Human Rights Practices for 1993* (Washington, D.C.: U.S. Congress, 1994), pp. 1176–83.

32. Fu Xiangtao, "Battling Bureaucracy Through the Ages," *China Today* (April 1993): 41–43.

33. Richard A. Haggerty, *El Salvador: A Country Study* (Washington, D.C.: Department of the Army, 1990), pp. 251–52.

34. Pilar Domingo, "Judicial Independence and Judicial Reform in Latin America," in Andreas Schedler, Larry Diamond, and Marc F. Plattner, *The Self-Restraining State: Power and Accountability in New Democracies* (Boulder, Colo., and London: Lynne Rienner, 1999), pp. 151–75.

35. "After the B Movie, A New Main Attraction for Filipinos," *The Economist* (27 Jan. 2001): 37.

36. Thierry Bréhier, "Le conseil constitutionnel attribue à M. Chirac une immunité pénale," *Le Monde*, 26 Jan. 1999, 5, and Suzanne Daley, "Court Shields President Chirac from Corruption Inquiries," *New York Times*, 11 Oct. 2001, A3.

37. Vincent Bugliosi, "None Dare Call It Treason," *The Nation* (5 Feb. 2001): 11–19.

38. Neil A. Lewis, "Leaving His Post, Clinton Accepts an Immunity Deal," *New York Times*, 20 Jan. 2001, A1.

39. Elizabeth Becker, "An Inaugural Thanks Was Not Just a Formality," *New York Times*, 21 Jan. 2001, A15.

40. "Past U.S. Criticism of Military Tribunals," *Human Rights Watch*, Nov. 28, 2001. http://www.hrw.org/press/2001/11/tribunals1128.htm.

41. Jordan J. Paust, "Military Commissions: Some Perhaps Legal, But Most Unwise," *Jurist*, 18 Nov. 2001. http://jurist.law.pitt.edu/forum/forumnew38.htm.

42. Jennifer Elsea, *Trying Terrorists as War Criminals*, (Washington, D.C.: American Law Division, Congressional Research Service, The Library of Congress, 29 Oct. 2001).

43. Elizabeth Bumiller with Katharine Q. Seelye, "Bush Defends Wartime Call for Tribunals," *New York Times,* 5 Dec. 2001, A1, B7.

44. *New York Times,* 8 Sept. 1995, A10.

45. *de Re Publica, de Legibus* by Marcus Tullius Cicero, with an English translation by Clinton Walker Keyes (Cambridge, Mass.: Harvard University Press, 1966), *passim.*

46. One of the earliest proponents of positive law was John Austin, in his *Lectures on Jurisprudence* (London: J. Murray, 1869). This view of the law emerged simultaneously with a more positive approach to all social phenomena—using the word *positive* with its dictionary meaning of "concerned only with real things and experience; empirical; practical." In this regard, see the work of the nineteenth-century philosopher Auguste Comte, in Gertrud Lenzer, ed., *Auguste Comte and Positivism* (New York: Harper & Row, 1975).

47. See John Locke, *Two Treatises of Government* (New York: Hafner, 1947), pp. 188–94; and Richard Hooker, *Of the Laws of Ecclesiastical Polity* (New York: Dutton, 1958), pp. 187–201. For an interesting discussion of these questions, see Lloyd L. Weinreb, *Natural Law and Justice* (Cambridge, Mass.: Harvard University Press, 1987).

48. W. W. Buckland, *The Main Institutions of Roman Private Law* (Cambridge, U.K.: Cambridge University Press, 1931), pp. 1–24; and H. F. Jolowicz, *Roman Foundations of Modern Law* (Oxford: Clarendon Press, 1957), pp. 6–21.

49. "On the Books," *Foreign Policy* (January-February 2001): 103.

50. Michael Arnheim, ed., *Common Law,* vol. 6 in Series on Legal Cultures from the International Library of Essays in Law and Legal Theory (New York: New York University Press, 1994).

51. Reynolds and Flores, "Ireland" in *Current Sources of Basic Codes and Legislation in Jurisdictions of the World: Western and Eastern Europe,* vol. 2, no 33 (Littleton, Conn.: Rothman AALL, May 1995), pp. 1–5.

52. Of course, existing criminal law amply covers those who use such tactics to obtain other persons' credit card numbers and personal security codes for automated bank teller machines, a new form of fraud now costing credit card corporations hundreds of millions of dollars per year. *New York Times,* 9 April 1992, A25.

53. Jonathan D. Glater, "Hemming in the World Wide Web," *New York Times,* 7 Jan. 2001, WK5.

54. Codified law is sometimes also referred to as *civil law,* although that term is commonly used to identify law developed to settle disputes (as distinguished from criminal law). To avoid confusion, I will use *civil law* only in its most common meaning.

55. Eric G. Zahnd, "The Application of Universal Laws to Particular Cases: A Defense of Equity in Aristotelianism and Anglo-American Law," *Law and Contemporary Problems* 59 (Winter 1996): 263–95.

56. Lisa L. Abrams, *The Official Guide to Legal Specialties: An Insider's Guide to Every Major Practice Area* (Chicago: Harcourt Legal and Professional Publications, 2000), pp. 170–90 (administrative law); pp. 1–10 (admiralty and maritime law).

57. E. M. Barendt, *An Introduction to Constitutional Law* (Oxford: Oxford University Press, 1998).

58. Political scientists, following the work of Gabriel Almond, sometimes refer to the judicial function as the "adjudication of disputes." (See Chapter 1.) A moment's careful consideration of the kind of cases that fall under criminal law, however, should make it obvious that such a definition trivializes the work of the courts. Unless you think deciding culpability in cases of murder, rape, grand larceny, and mayhem is just a way to settle "disputes."

59. Peter de Cruz, *Comparative Law in a Changing World* (London: Cavendish Publishing, 1999). See Chapter 3, "European Community Law," pp. 139–81.

60. *New York Times,* 28 Sept. 1995, A7.

61. Karl Deutsch, *The Analysis of International Relations* (Englewood Cliffs, N.J.: Prentice Hall, 1968), p. 162.

62. There have been many efforts to classify the world's different ways of legally regulating behavior and no doubt there will be many more. Scholars are not yet agreed whether to call these types legal cultures, families, systems, or orders, much less what the exact subdivisions are. For repre-

sentative recent summaries, see Chapter 5, "The Style of Legal Families," in Konrad Zweigert and Hein Kotz, *Introduction to Comparative Law,* trans. Tony Weir, 3rd ed. (Oxford: Clarendon Press, 1998); and Chapter 19, David Goldberg and Elspeth Attwooll, "Legal Orders, Systemic Relationships and Cultural Characteristics: Toward Spectral Jurisprudence," in Esin Örücü Elspeth Attwooll, and Sean Coyle, *Studies in Legal Systems: Mixed and Mixing* (The Hague, London, and Boston: Kluwer Law International, 1996). My own breakdown draws from several and is no more definitive than theirs; it just seems reasonable to me.

63. *Ab ovo* (introduced in Chapter 8) means "from the beginning."

64. Zweigert and Kotz, *Comparative Law,* pp. 276–85.

65. Henry Ehrmann, *Comparative Legal Cultures* (Englewood Cliffs, N.J.: Prentice Hall, 1976), pp. 22–23.

66. For comments on the importance of the idea of *stare decisis* in U.S. jurisprudence, see Harld J. Spaeth and Jeffrey A. Segal, *Majority Rule or Minority Will: Adherence to Precedence on the U.S.* (Cambridge, U.K., and New York: Cambridge University Press, 1999).

67. Brook Thomas, ed., Plessy v. Ferguson: *A Brief History with Documents* (Boston: Bedford Books, 1997), pp. 1–34; 169–78.

68. James T. Patterson, Brown v. Board of Education: *A Civil Rights Milestone and Its Troubled Legacy* (Oxford and New York: Oxford University Press, 2001).

69. Opoku Agyeman, "The Supreme Court and Enforcement of African American Rights: Myth and Reality," *The Black Scholar* 21, no. 3 (Summer 1990): 22–28.

70. de Cruz, *Comparative Law,* pp. 189–90.

71. Ibid., p. 188.

72. Peter de Cruz, *A Modern Approach to Compara-* *tive Law* (Deventer, The Netherlands: Kluwer, 1993), pp. 328, 333–34.

73. James V. Feinerman, "Economic and Legal Reform in China," *Problems of Communism* 40, no. 5 (Sept.–Oct. 1991): 62–75.

74. Lisa Stearns, "The New Chinese Women's Law," 19, no. 1, *WIN News* [a publication of the Women's International Network] (Winter 1993): 54.

75. Raul Gomez Treto, "Thirty Years of Cuban Revolutionary Penal Law, *Latin American Perspectives* 18, no. 2 (Spring 1991): 114–25.

76. Zweigert and Kotz, *Comparative Law,* p. 288.

77. Ibid, p. 291.

78. Bureau of Public Affairs, "Japan," in *Background Notes* (Washington, D.C.: U.S. State Department, 1990), pp. 1–8.

79. Ibid., p. 94.

80. H. Patrick Glenn, *Legal Traditions of the World: Sustainable Diversity in Law* (Oxford and New York: Oxford University Press, 2000).

81. Zweigert and Kotz, op. cit., p. 304.

82. Ibid.

83. Lawrence Rosen, *The Anthropology of Justice* (Cambridge, U.K.: Cambridge University Press, 1990), pp. 41–42. Rosen notes, however, that the *qadi*'s decision must also have "the general agreement or consensus of the community" since the prophet is believed to have said, "my community will not agree in error."

84. "The 'Satanic' Furor," *Maclean's* 102, no. 9 (27 Feb. 1989): 16–19, 22, *New York Times,* 15 Feb. 1989, A1, A10, and 23 Feb. 1989, A15.

85. *Time* (6 Feb. 1995): 46.

86. Fauzi M. Najjar, "The Application of Shari'a Laws in Egypt," *Middle East Policy* 1, no. 3 (1992): 62–73.

87. de Cruz, *Modern Approach to Comparative Law,* pp. 332–37.

CHAPTER 12

Levels of Government Within the State

"**T**ake me to your leader," says the charming but obviously well-armed extraterrestrial visitor. Assuming you decide to comply, what do you do next?

> Take her home to meet Mother?
> Take her to the chief of police, the mayor, or the county commissioner?
> Take her to the governor?
> Take her to the president?
> Take her to the United Nations Secretary General?

Of course you would like to take her to the president, but chances are you will decide to settle for a local government official. When we need government in a hurry, for a particularly urgent problem, we turn to local government. Ask yourself what level of government you would turn to in the following slightly more realistic emergencies:

> You see the sky filling with black smoke a few blocks from your home.
> You see a stranger taking valuables from your absent neighbor's home.
> Your rural county's only doctor has collapsed of a heart attack on your doorstep.
> You find a lost child.

If you think these examples are too carefully chosen, try this exercise: Make your own list of the first twenty emergencies, common to the human condition, that come to mind. Cross out the ones you would try to deal with without contacting any government agency (but be careful—hospitals are often city or county owned and operated). Then figure out in what percentage of the remainder you would be likely to turn to *local* government agencies. Even in this day of vastly expanded federal power, I will bet you a subway token that in well over 50 percent of the emergencies that require government assistance your first move will be to contact a local government body.

THE NATURE OF SUBNATIONAL GOVERNMENT

Subnational government is any government less broad in its extent and applicability than an entire nation. Only in the twentieth century has the distinction between national and subnational government become worldwide, or nearly so. When human beings lived in small communities, all government was local, and those who led the government were likely to be leaders in other domains as well, such as religion and hunting. Even today many nation-states have populations no larger than those of cities—and rather small cities at that (see Table 12.1).

Most nations, however, are too large to be served by a single level of government. Some problems cannot be solved the same way throughout the

TABLE 12.1
World's Largest
Cities and Smallest
Nation-States,
by Population

Largest Cities	Population	Smallest Nations	Population
Tokyo	26,444,000	Tavalu	11,000
Mexico City	18,131,000	Nauru	12,000
Bombay	18,066,000	Palau	19,000
São Paulo	17,755,000	San Marino	27,000
New York City	16,640,000	Liechtenstein	32,000
Lagos	13,427,000	Monaco	32,000
Los Angeles	13,140,000	Saint Kitts and Nevis	39,000
Buenos Aires	12,560,000	Antigua and Barbuda	66,000
Shanghai	12,887,000	Andorra	67,000
Calcutta	12,918,000	Marshall Islands	68,000

Source: *The World Almanac and Book of Facts 2001,* World Almanac Education Group, Mahwah, N.J. 07495, pp. 860–61. Reprinted by permission.

realm. Some problems do not manifest themselves everywhere. And above all, some problems require attention from people on the scene who are well acquainted with the local community.

All this is simply common sense. But these obvious and noncontroversial statements inevitably raise questions that may lead to debate and confusion. First, what specific kinds of problems require the attention of subnational units of government? Second, what should be the division of power among the various levels of government in a nation-state? Third, what kind of intermediate levels of government are required to meet a society's needs for governance? Fourth, what kind of institutional structures are appropriate to local government? Fifth, how can the quest for grassroots citizen involvement, most easily accommodated where local government structures are strong, be balanced against the need for centralized planning and allocation of resources, a function that must fall to the national government? Sixth, how can we make sure that the geographic borders of *constituent units,* that is, of the units that compose the state, will be accepted by those thus divided from—or combined with—each other?

Different nations have given different answers to these questions, and individual nations do not always give the same answers in every era—or region. One way to address the first two questions—what kinds of problems to refer to subnational governments and how much power to give these governments to handle those problems—is to adopt a unitary, federal, or confederal system of government. In the next section we will examine the difference between these three ways of dividing the work of government. In the two following sections we will examine some of the answers that have been given to the third question—what kind of intermediate structures are needed —and the fourth—what institutional structures are appropriate for local governments. The problems of how to establish the right relationship between national and subnational governments and how to fix the borders of constituent units will be discussed in a final section.

Before we begin, however, let us clear up two matters of terminology. Political scientists sometimes use the word *local* to refer to any subnational government body and sometimes to refer only to the governments of cities or still smaller units. We will follow the latter practice here and label *intermediate* or *provincial* any government body that is narrower than an entire nation yet wider than a city in the scope of its coverage—such as the American state, the French *departement,* or the Swiss *canton.* The term *subnational* will refer to both intermediate and local units of government.

The use of the word *federal* can also be confusing, since Americans often refer to the federal government when what they really mean is the national (or central) government. We will try to avoid that common yet understandable error. Here, *federal* will have only the meanings assigned to it in the next section.

UNITARY, FEDERAL, AND CONFEDERAL POLITICAL SYSTEMS

We may agree that it is necessary to have more than one level of government to meet our immediate national and international needs for the exercise of collective power, but we still have to decide which tasks to assign to each level and how much power to give them. In a unitary system all the powers of government are reserved to the central government. That government may delegate the exercise of those powers to such subunits as counties or departments, but any such delegation can be revoked at any time. In a federal system of government, on the other hand, certain powers are reserved to the central government, but others are constitutionally reserved to the governments of the nation's constituent parts—that is, to the states, provinces, or cantons. Finally, in a confederal system, the units are actually independent states that have decided to join together in a formal alliance, acting as a single unit for some limited purposes but not for others.

All three systems have clear advantages and disadvantages. In a federal system, the national government is, at least in theory, freer to deal with national issues. Citizen participation is made easier by the existence of several levels of government, some close at hand. Governmental experiments (primary elections, welfare aid, and abolition of the death penalty are examples in the United States) can be tried out and modified in a limited setting. And when new groups seek statehood or cantonhood, additional units can be added with no disruption of the system.[1]

In a unitary system, on the other hand, laws are much more likely to be uniform throughout the nation and representation is more likely to be equal throughout the nation (with no "federal" provisions for equal representation of every constituent unit regardless of the number of its inhabitants, as in the case of the U.S. Senate, for example). It is less likely that some parts of the nation will have greater tax revenues than others. Finally, in a unitary system, no sphere of independent power is capable of blocking the execution of national policy, and there is no difficulty keeping the lines of authority clear.

A confederal system lacks most of the advantages of either federal or unitary government. It does, however, provide a structure for harmonious interaction on a limited number of matters for peoples for whom single nationhood is not yet—or is no longer—tolerable. It is often a transient system, for systems on the way to greater unity or greater independence, but as such can provide an extremely useful set of institutions.

Which system a nation adopts is likely to depend far less on the careful weighing of such pros and cons than on the conditions prevalent at the time the new nation comes into existence. If the demands for unified action in the face of a hostile world are extreme and if authoritarian leadership is accepted as the norm—two conditions prevailing when most of the older nations of Europe and Asia were formed—a unitary system is likely even when the peoples joining together have very different backgrounds and customs. When a number of Gallic tribes united under the bold leadership of Vercingetorix in an effort—vain, as it proved—to resist the advance of Julius Caesar and his armies in 52 B.C.E., that was the beginning of modern France. The forceful imposition of nearly forty years of Communist rule on most of eastern Europe was maintained by creating unitary states, with power strongly concentrated at the top. China is another example of a unitary state created by force in which all power is exercised at the center. According to that nation's constitution, each province's government is the administrative arm of the central government; whatever powers it has may be revoked at any time. National bodies have the power to annul "those local regulations or decisions of the . . . provinces, autonomous regions and municipalities . . . that contravene the Constitution, the statutes or the administrative rules and regulations" of the central government, as well as "to exercise unified leadership over the work of local organs at different levels throughout the country."[2]

This is not to say, however, that all unitary states have come into being as the result of the exercise of force—either by others who threaten from outside or by homegrown tyrants who seize control—over disparate peoples who would otherwise prefer to remain apart. Most of the nations of the world are unitary, and many have formed their governments out of a sense of shared identity and geographical common sense. And even when originally compelled to unite out of fear, most modern unitary states have evolved a strongly shared sense of identity and nationhood.

If a nation-state is to be created out of what have been largely independent units, each with a separate political culture and separate bases of economic and military power, if the motive to join together is strong but no unit or individual has the force to impose unity against the will of the others, and, finally, if not everyone is sure that a single polity is possible or desirable, federalism may be the answer. Federalism is a complex form of government, but that very complexity may be what it takes to make government work in a complex situation. Consider the proposals made to resolve the problems in Afghanistan (see Box 12.1).

In any case, once the decision is made to adopt a federal system, some powers must be allocated to the national government and others to the constituent units, and this must be spelled out carefully in a written constitution. In some federal systems, specific powers are assigned to the national government and all other powers are reserved to the constituent units—a solution adopted by the United States, Australia, and Switzerland, for example. In Switzerland, a majority of the 26 cantons and half-cantons as well as a majority of all votes cast are required for constitutional amendments (which may be initiated for submission to referendum by as few as 100,000 Swiss citizens), and as few as eight cantons (or 50,000 citizens) may demand that a law passed by the bicameral Federal Assembly be submitted to a national referendum. The cantons are responsible for law and order, education, culture, and public works, whereas the central government's domain covers defense, foreign affairs, the postal service, and most of the railway system.[3] In other federal systems, such as Canada's, the powers of both units are specified in separate lists.

Whatever the formal distribution of power, however, in most federal systems the trend has been for the central government to take on ever greater responsibilities. Population growth, the development of large cities, nationwide and worldwide communication and transportation systems, and the emergence of multinational corporations have contributed to the growth in the powers of central governments, even in federal systems. Such developments produce problems that are at least national in scope and often beyond the capabilities of constituent units to solve, whatever the constitution may say.

The problem of adjusting to a shifting balance of power between central and provincial powers is apparent in Canada. When first formed in 1867, the Canadian federal system allowed the provincial governments considerable autonomy, but it is now much more common for the national and provincial governments to cooperate in development schemes, particularly in the areas of health, welfare, and transportation. When a new airport is built, for example, the nearest city, the province, and the central government all have carefully specified roles to carry out. When originally established, the intent of these development schemes was to give the provincial governments the power to select the programs, to initiate plans for projects, and to administer them once adopted. However, it soon became normal for the national government to take the lead role, in the interests of improved efficiency and "nation building." Recognizing that nation building meant centralization, Canadian provinces have recently begun to make serious efforts to limit federal use of its spending powers and to regain their own lost powers. In Quebec, as we have seen, this concern has led a very large minority to

BOX 12.1
**Would Federalism
Work in
Afghanistan?**

The 26 million Afghans are divided as follows:

- 40 percent are Pashtoons, speak Pashtoo, and live in eastern and southern Afghanistan. They are internally divided into tribes and clans. They are the dominant political community and their laws proscribe intermarriage with other groups.
- 33 percent are Tadjik, speak Dari (or Afghan Persian), and live in valleys and mountains north and northeast of Kabul.
- 8 to 9 percent are Hazaras, speak a version of Persian called Hazaragi, and live in central Afghanistan.
- 8 to 9 percent are Uzbek, speaking Uzbeki.
- 9 to 11 percent are numerous other ethnic and linguistic minorities.

Most Afghans are Sunni Muslims, but the Hazari are Shiite. Islamic thought is further divided according to the Sufi tradition, emphasizing tolerance and peaceful coexistence with other religions, and the intolerant Wahabi tradition, followed by the Taliban (and the multinational followers of Osama bin Laden).

Experts on federalism suggest that that form of government might work better in Afghanistan than the kind of strong central government with a multiethnic administration put in place as an interim government at the end of 2001. Federalism, says Reeta Chowdhari Tremblay, can maintain a "fragile equilibrium . . . between indestructible union and indestructible units." When it works well, adds David Cameron, it "disperses conflict by shifting it to state and local levels; it generates conflict *within* ethnic groups, as different factions battle for control of sub-national governments; it can foster cooperation across ethnic lines, as groups of sub-national provinces or states form coalitions to demand, support or oppose policies formulated at the center; and, finally, it can free up the creative energies of local communities which possess control over their own educational systems, social services, and regional bureaucracies." First, however, peace must be fully restored, international support including peacekeeping must be in place, the warring parties must "want to make a new start" and the process of building the new constitution must itself build consensus by ensuring full participation of all groups. Then, and then only, says Cameron, the "federal moment" may arrive.[4]

Source: *Federations* (October 2001), special issue on Afghanistan.

TABLE 12.2
Ten Major Federal
Systems

Nation	Number and Name of Units
Australia	6 states, 2 territories
Brazil	26 states, 1 federal district
Canada	10 provinces, 2 territories
Germany	16 states
India	25 states, 7 union territories
Mexico	31 states, 1 federal district
Nigeria	30 states, 1 federal capital territory
Russia	21 autonomous republics, 49 oblasts, 6 krays
South Africa	9 provinces
United States	50 states, 1 federal district

Source: *The World Almanac and Book of Facts 1996,* World Almanac Education Group, Mahwah, N.J. 07495, pp. 740–831, passim. Reprinted by permission.

seek total separation, but other provinces have also tried—usually without success—to block the growth of national power.[5]

Although they cover nearly half of the world's land surface, and about 40 percent of the world's population, only 24 of the 180 politically sovereign states are federations.[6] Table 12.2 lists ten major federal systems and their constituent units.

The confederation is a form of limited unification that is now in the process of being reinvented. Until the recent astonishing transformations in the map of the world—especially in Europe—the standard example of a confederation was drawn from history. The thirteen American colonies were far from certain they wanted to be even as closely allied as federalism requires, and the first U.S. constitution, the Articles of Confederation, called only for a partnership among nearly independent equals. The earliest U.S. political parties were named, significantly, the Federalists and the Antifederalists—those who argued for and against a "more perfect union." The Swiss provided another historic example, having joined together in the thirteenth century as a loose confederation of cantons, but they too eventually decided to form a federation, in 1848.[7]

Lately, however, we have witnessed the emergence of new confederations. The European Union (EU) itself seems to be assuming the form of a confederation, and perhaps on some not-too-distant day will become a true federation, a United States of Europe. (See Chapter 13 for a full discussion of the EU.) The breakup of the Soviet Union brought movement from the opposite direction: A nation that was a federation, the Soviet Union of Socialist Republics—consisting of fifteen union republics, twenty autonomous republics, six krays, 120 oblasts and eight autonomous oblasts—sought to turn itself into a confederation, the Commonwealth of Independent States (CIS), consisting of Armenia, Azerbaijan, Belarus, Georgia, Kazakhstan,

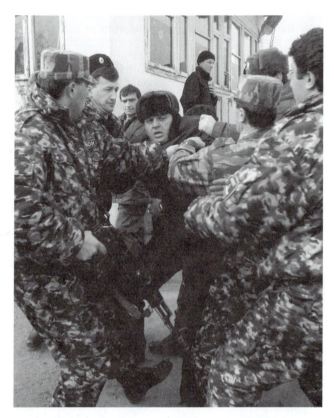

*Fighting to leave a federalist state. Not every federal system works well for all par-
ticipants. Chechnyans want out of Russia; Russia is determined to keep them in.
Here a Chechen man seeks to fight his way through the Adler Checkpoint in In-
gushetia but is stopped by Russian soldiers (January 20, 2000).*
© Reuters NewMedia Inc./CORBIS

Kyrgystan, Moldava, Russia, Tajikistan, Turkmenistan, Ukraine, and Uzbekistan.[8] The nation of Czechoslovakia provided a third kind of transformation, from a unitary state into a loose confederation consisting of just two
states.

In fact, however, neither of these latter two efforts proved successful: The
CIS is simply an extremely loose association of separate nations. It has no
capital, no independent budget, and in effect no government. The hopes for
coordinated activity among its members have not been met, except to a
slight extent in the realm of banking.[9] Similarly, the pretense of confederalism in Czechoslovakia very rapidly gave way to the creation of two separate
states, the Czech Republic and Slovakia.

We should not, however, be too quick to dismiss these efforts at confederation building. The move to confederalism was no doubt a good way to ease the process of separation. Consider the comments of the Slovak leader Vladimir Merciar at the time of the transition: "We are not going to fight, we are not going to dispute. We will try to understand each other. There was a great risk of not understanding each other, leading to destruction. We drew nearer together. We are satisfied we have arrived at a means of negotiation." [10] These carefully chosen words reveal how complex it is to change the relations between whole peoples, and how a seemingly weak and indecisive form of union, the confederation, can provide exactly the structure needed in difficult times, however briefly it may endure.

Before leaving this topic, we must note that not every contemporary state fits clearly into one of the three categories of unitary, federal, or confederal. The new Russia is an interesting example in that regard. Theoretically, Russia contains twenty-one "autonomous" republics, designated as "independent participants in international and foreign economic connections," a

Federalism is not an easy system of government to establish. Here a Russian cheerfully explains the traffic jam: "We have pluralism! One light is for the city, one for the region, and one for the country!"
SovFoto/EastFoto

status that comes very close to suggesting a confederation. In practice, however, it has become clear that these republics (which account for 29 percent of the nation's territory and 15 percent of its population) are not at all autonomous. Neither Tartarstan nor Chechnya has ever opted to be part of Russia, and the military response to the efforts of the latter to break away and form a genuinely independent state has made clear how little independence has actually been granted to these units. During his time in office, President Boris Yeltsin seesawed on the question of regional powers, attempting to curry the favor of regional leaders in his struggle with the Russian parliament and other opponents in Moscow.[11] His successor, President Vladimir Putin, has been more single-minded. Once he rallied sufficient political support (especially in pursuing the battle against the Chechnyan rebels), he moved to consolidate national power. One important step was to change the basis for selecting the two representatives from each region who serve on the Federation Council, the upper house of the Russian Parliament. In July 2000 Putin convinced the Council itself to eliminate the automatic appointment of elected regional governors, apparently partly by threatening the governors with criminal investigations if they did not comply. Representatives to the Council are now appointed by the regional assembly and the regional executive (one each), a change that weakens both the Council and the regions. More recently, the two houses of parliament have given the 89 governors the right to serve eight additional years if reelected—but at the same time Putin has gained the power to fire governors summarily.[12] Under this president it begins to seem that Russia more closely fits the definition of a unitary state, despite its technically federal character.

INTERMEDIATE LEVELS OF GOVERNMENT

What kind of intermediate levels of government are required to meet a society's needs for governance? The answers given have been many and varied. Choosing between a federal and a unitary system is only the first step. Both federal and unitary states require subnational units. True, only in federal systems do such units have complete responsibility in certain domains, and in actual practice national governments are increasingly exercising broader control over subnational units even in federal systems. Nevertheless, there remains a significant scope for the exercise of state (or cantonal or provincial) power in every federal system. Furthermore, even though the policy-making powers granted subnational units in unitary systems can readily be revoked, in practice such units typically have a considerable measure of independence as long as they operate within national guidelines. And in both federal and unitary systems, subnational governments bear the heavy burdens of administering policies made either by themselves or at the national level.

Provincial Government

Much of the real work of government is carried on at intermediate levels. All but the world's smallest nations have some level of intermediate government between the central government and municipal government. In federal systems they are usually called states, provinces, or cantons. In unitary systems the more common name is department. Be careful, however—the name itself is not a sure guide to the kind of system under study. The French, for example, whose government is strictly unitary, use the word *canton* to refer to the constituency from which are elected representatives to the *departmental* level of government (there is no cantonal level of government any more than there is a congressional district level of government in the United States), and when they talk about life in "the provinces," they do not mean "in the *departements*" but rather anywhere in France that is not Paris. And of course, throughout the world the word *state* is often used to refer to the nation-state, as is the word *republic* (but the latter was also the name for the subdivisions of the Soviet Union). To keep confusion down to a minimum, here I will use the term *provinces* to mean all intermediate governments that are directly above the local level yet still below the level of the national government, trusting you to remember that this includes American states, Canadian provinces, Israeli administrative departments, Swiss cantons, French *departements,* British counties, and numerous other units.

Whatever its name and whatever its powers, the provincial government occupies a difficult position in any nation's hierarchy of governmental bodies. Normally it has come into being because its inhabitants have some qualities or needs in common that are not shared by the rest of the nation. The provincial government must strive to protect its inhabitants' interests, whether the system is federal or unitary. The government of the Canadian province of Quebec seeks to maintain a fair balance between its majority population, which is of French extraction, and the British-descended minority, while at the same time ensuring that the rights of its French-speaking people are protected within Canada at large. Even where the boundaries have been drawn by imperialistic conquest, breaking up formerly united peoples, as in Africa, or by nature, following rivers or mountain ranges, or by ruler-wielding bureaucrats (look at the straight-edge boundaries of the American state of Colorado), a sense of common identity often builds within the unit. With that identity comes a shared set of goals requiring purposeful government action.

At the same time, the provincial government often lacks both the powers and the resources to meet those goals. It must struggle with both central and local governments to recruit the leadership, acquire and keep the rights of taxation, and rally the degree of popular support that will permit it to meet the demands placed on it by those governments as well as by its own inhabitants. Its struggle with national government is likely to be particularly difficult and frustrating, as that body becomes ever more powerful and uses its powers of taxation to redistribute a nation's wealth in accordance with national policy.

On the other hand, provinces seldom accept the yoke of central control without a struggle. If the situation becomes intolerable, and circumstances suggest the plan is plausible, a province may even seek to set itself up as a separate nation, as has been the case with the Republic of Chechnya in the new Russian Federation.[13] More commonly, when a provincial government, or one of its agencies, is particularly dissatisfied, it seeks to gain the support of one branch of the national government in curbing what it views as the excesses of another. In the United States, the courts often play a particularly important role in this regard, adjudicating disputes between the levels of government. Another approach that may work is to rally public opinion against national policy. For example, when a local environmental protection agency in Siberia opposed the Russian government's agreement to give Weyerhaeuser Corporation, a U.S. timber company, access to some 1 million hectares of Siberian forest land, it was able to gain sufficient international publicity for its cause to slow the project down. Still, when the province is up against international business as well as its own national government, as in this case, the scales may seem unfairly weighted against it. Weyerhaeuser has undertaken its own extensive public relations campaign and is now providing funding for a local research institute that was originally one of the strong opponents of the logging plan.[14]

Provincial governments also struggle with each other in their incessant quest for a greater resource base. This aspect of the problem is further complicated by the fact that needs, goals, and even political identity patterns are constantly shifting among constituent units. States that were on opposing sides in a historic civil war may find themselves embattled partners in the struggle to get a fair share of revenue allocation from a burgeoning oil industry now developing in other states—states that may themselves have been enemies but are now united in their efforts to protect a new source of wealth.

Regional Government

One answer to the shifting dilemmas of provincial government is to establish yet another intermediate level of government: the *region*. A region is usually formed by grouping provincial units. It is intermediate government just below the level of the national government and above the level of the province. Occasionally a region is formed *within* a single province, but even then it usually is responsible only to the national government. There are two kinds of regional government, distinguished by the scope of their coverage and also to some extent by how permanently each appears to be embedded in the nation's political system.

■ **Structural Regionalism.**   In the first kind, structural regionalism, provincial units are grouped in regions by constitutional fiat. Regional assemblies, normally composed of elected representatives from the provincial level, meet to deal with matters of regional significance and concern. This kind of regionalism is normally established by constitutional amendment, and the regions thus created are expected to be permanent additions to the body politic. As an example, under the Fifth Republic, France has been divided into twenty-two regions, most of which are made up of several of the republic's ninety-six departments. Each region has its own council, charged with "assuming the burden and receiving the benefits of [the region's] share in the national economic plan." [15] Established by the followers of Charles De Gaulle when the Fifth Republic was created in 1959, the new regions were considerably strengthened by the Socialists when they came to power in 1981. The Socialist government quickly moved to establish direct elections to the regional councils and to eliminate the requirement that they submit all their deliberations to a regional prefect for approval. These changes have been maintained even during periods when the Gaullists were again in control of the French parliament (from 1986 to 1988, from 1993 to 1995, and again in 2002).

Structural regionalism has also been used to permit minority nationalities living in compact communities to exercise some degree of autonomous power. China has five autonomous regions: Guangxi Zhuang, Nei Menggu (Inner Mongolia), Nijgxia Hui, Xinjiang Weiwuer (Uighur), and Xizang (Tibet). Although power is still rigorously controlled from Beijing, regional identity permits symbolic remnants of cultural-historical distinctiveness— such as the "Nine Leagues and Forty-Seven Banners" of Inner Mongolia— to be retained.[16] Although few in number, these regions occupy an important place in the Chinese scheme of government (see Figure 12.1).

■ **Functional Regionalism.**   The second kind of regional government, functional regionalism, is more limited in scope. It is usually not a permanent structure established constitutionally but rather a short-term statutory solution to current problems that may or may not endure. Such regional governments are normally established to deal with only a single problem, such as the development of electricity, the conservation of water resources, or

FIGURE 12.1
Local Government
in China

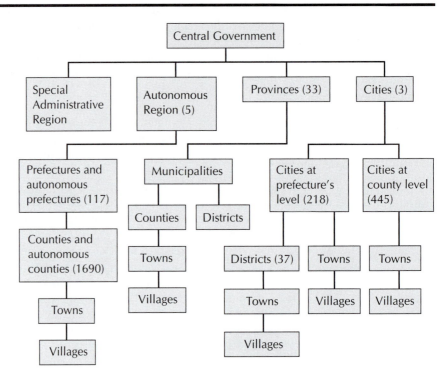

Source: "Country Paper: China," in *Local Government in Asia and the Pacific* (a joint publication of the Economic and Social Commission for Asia and the Pacific, Asian and Pacific Section of the International Union of Local Authorities, and Korea Local Authorities Foundation for International Relations, 1999).

other specific policy areas not easily accommodated by municipal, provincial, or national centers of government. The Bay Area Air Quality Management District (BAAQMD), established to limit air pollution and offensive odors in the San Francisco Bay Area, is an example of such particularized regionalism. The district maintains a professional and effective staff, and investigates some 7,000 pollution complaints per year. It maintains a toll-free complaint hot line and investigates all complaints, if possible within 45 minutes of the call.[17]

Public transportation is another governmental function likely to require regional solutions, as both goods and people move regularly across municipal and provincial borders. Regional transportation authorities, ranging from New York's Metropolitan Transportation Authority (MTA) to the Metropolitan Atlanta Rapid Transit Authority (MARTA) to the San Francisco Bay Area Rapid Transit District (BART) are all government bodies empowered to deal with transportation problems within their special jurisdictions.

One of the problems with functional regional governments, however, is the difficulty citizens (and sometimes even other government officials) may have in remembering that they exist. Portland Metro, a regional government responsible for land-use and transportation planning in the 1.5 million person metropolitan area around the city of Portland, Oregon, is the nation's only directly elected regional government: Presumably its citizens know it is there. However, assuming you do not live in Portland or its environs, what would you do if you were annoyed by one of the following problems?

- Private contractors are trying to take over your favorite park for a housing development.
- The subway is *always* late.
- That strange smell in your neighborhood is getting stronger and stronger.
- Traffic control on the bridge you drive across is poorly designed and is costing you precious study minutes every day; ferry service, however, is much too sporadic to be a reasonable substitute.

In all these cases, it might well be that the best way to draw attention to the problem—especially if you live in a large metropolitan area—would be to register a complaint with the appropriate functional regional government. Would you know which one to call? Take a look at the list in Box 12.2. Pick one of the problems just listed and imagine yourself living in Oakland, California. Which agency would you call?

The reasonable answer, regardless of which problem you selected, is probably, "None of them." Your first call should almost certainly be to your own local city hall, in order to find out whom to call next. However, functional regionalism is definitely on the rise. David Rusk suggests that although they will never replace local governments as primary providers of local services, their powers affecting such vitally important domains as land-use, transportation planning, affordable housing, and fiscal disparities within metropolitan areas will become ever more important to our collective well-being.[18] And one of your questions to city hall should probably always be: "Is there a regional agency that handles matters like this?"

Local Government

The structures of local government are, if anything, even more varied than those of intermediate or national government. Human beings live in all kinds of aggregations, from isolated hermitages to small farms, from compounds or small villages to suburban settlements, from towns to medium-sized cities to major metropolises of several million inhabitants. With such immense variety, what does it take for government to be "local?" Is a nearby city hall serving millions more local than a distant county seat serving a mere handful of ranchers?

Here we shall interpret local government to mean any government that

BOX 12.2
Regional Government in the San Francisco Bay Area: Agencies and Purposes

Alameda— Contra Costa Transit District (AC Transit). Purpose: Public bus transit

Association of Bay Area Governments (ABAG). Purpose: Areawide comprehensive planning; cooperative action among Bay Area governments

Bay Area Air Quality Management District (BAAQMD). Purpose: Air pollution control

Bay Area Dischargers Authority (BADA). Purpose: To collect data on aquatic wildlife and quality of water; to assess the effect of pollution on San Francisco Bay

Bay Area Rapid Transit District (BART). Purpose: Rail rapid transit system

Bay Conservation and Development Commission (BCDC). Purpose: Regulate filling, dredging, and changes in existing uses of the Bay and shoreline

East Bay Dischargers Authority (EBDA). Purpose: Wastewater disposal

East Bay Municipal Utility District (EBMUD). Purpose: Water supply, wastewater treatment, management of public use lands

East Bay Regional Park District (EBRPD). Purpose: To provide open space, regional parks, trails, recreational opportunities, and environmental education for the public

Golden Gate Bridge, Highway and Transportation District (GGBHTD). Purpose: To operate and maintain Golden Gate Bridge, bus, and ferry systems

Metropolitan Transportation Commission (MTC). Purpose: Comprehensive regional transportation planning; allocation of state and federal transportation funds

Midpeninsula Regional Open Space District (MSORD). Purpose: Acquisition and preservation of open-space lands for low-intensity recreation and greenbelt

Regional Water Quality Control Board (RWQCB). Purpose: To protect the quality of surface and ground water

Water Transit Agency. Purpose: Plan additional ferry service around Bay

Source: From *Decision Makers: Directory of Regional and Inter-County Agencies 1995–1997,* 15th ed. (Lafayette, Calif.: League of Women Voters of the Bay Area Education Fund, 1995). Reprinted by permission of League of Women Voters of the Bay Area.

can be physically known to each and every citizen. Local government is government that citizens can quite literally get in touch with—and vice versa. It may be a hard day's drive away, but the ordinary citizen can achieve some degree of personal access to local government, if only to hand over his or her tax payment to a bored bureaucrat. It may be possible for some citizens to acquire the same degree of access to other levels of government, but local government is close and accessible to everyone. (That being the case, you may find it useful to take a break in your reading and go visit some unit of local government yourself. Attending a town meeting, interviewing a mayor or city manager, or just watching your local board of education in action is an excellent way to learn how meaningful this level of government can be to citizens affected by its action.)

Local governments, like provincial and national governments, have rule-making, rule-applying, and rule-adjudicating functions to carry out. However, local government is typically under the control of provincial government (even in federal systems). Consequently, the form local government takes must normally meet the approval of national and/or provincial governments, and mayors, chiefs, councils, and boards all carry out their functions only at the sufferance of higher authorities.

The most common rule-making body at the local level is the elected board or council. Each French commune has its *conseil municipal*. Each Chinese county has a County People's Congress. The Republic of Kiribati (formerly Gilbert Islands) includes twenty-one inhabited islands, and for each one of these there is an island council.[19]

These local legislative bodies normally make rules (commonly referred to as *ordinances*) that apply to the local matters over which the central government has delegated them the authority to rule. Of course when national matters assume deep importance locally, a local council may feel obliged to act even while waiting for instruction and assistance from above, as was often illustrated in the actions taken by American cities immediately after the terrorist attacks of September 11, 2001.[20]

The chief executive responsible for carrying out the law at the local level may be a traditional *chief* entitled to his post by his place in the kinship system, a *mayor* elected by the people or by the rule-making council, a *city manager* hired by that council, or a *civilian* or *military administrator* appointed by the national government or by the government of a conquering nation. The powers of each of these leaders may be extensive or merely ceremonial.[21]

The bureaucratic apparatus available for carrying out local rule is similarly varied. City hall may be an elaborate edifice such as the Hotel de Ville in Paris or the kitchen table of a part-time mayor in an Appalachian town. Public service may be more or less personal, more or less efficient, and more or less humanitarian.

■ **Problems of Local Government.** Whatever the formal arrangements, the most serious problem facing almost every local government is how to acquire the resources to finance the programs they would like to carry out under the powers and responsibilities they have. The tax base of local governments is always limited, but the demands of citizens for local government response to their daily needs are not. Local communes constantly seek new

*A town hall meeting in Swanzey, N.H., March 12, 2002. The most common prob-
lem facing local government bodies is how to acquire the resources they need to
finance the programs they would like to carry out.*
Keene Sentinel/Steve Hooper.

sources of revenue to finance programs that higher levels of government have
assigned to their domain

In Norway, for example, local government is responsible for providing
day care centers, basic education, and primary health care for the elderly.
However, the local authorities rely on grants from the central government
and income taxes for almost all their revenue, and it is the national government that determines what the income tax rate shall be. Property taxes provide 10 percent of total revenue, but these too are limited by national law.
Thus when national growth rates in the overall economy decline or stagnate,
the tax base is weakened and central government grants are reduced. At such
times, local governments in Norway find it difficult to meet their obligations;
they bear the responsibilities for key aspects of social welfare but lack the resources to carry out their functions well.[22]

In poorer nations, the problems are of course that much more severe. The
slums of Mumbai (formerly Bombay) in India are known and deplored
throughout the world, despite the fact that this enormous city (population
of 8,243,000) employs 4.6 million people and per-capita income in the state
of Maharashtra is approximately $370 per annum, relatively high by Third

World standards. Income is, of course, very skewed, but has been rising steadily, especially in Mumbai. According to K. C. Sivaramakrishnan, the problem is that an average of 87,000 new families per year move into the metropolitan area, while housing has grown by only 47,000 units per year. Even a slum dwelling is a desirable asset: These are "the most expensive slums in the world" and the 6 million people living in them cannot help but consider themselves better off than the estimated 33,000 "households" living on pavements beside commuter railway lines, under bridges, "and in other outdoor locations." India's national government has tried to help by providing loans and subsidies to state governments for constructing apartment blocks and the World Bank has provided financial support for a program known as Affordable Low Income Shelter, designed to interest entrepreneurs in a "public-private partnership." But although such plans have

Housing for ever growing urban populations is one of local government's most intractable problems, nowhere more so than in Bombay, India, where an average of 87,000 new families per year move in, creating "the most expensive slums in the world."
Ilene Perlman/Stock, Boston, LLC.

BOX 12.3
Local Government Rule Making in Northern California

The problem to be resolved at the November 1994 meeting of the Point Arena City Council seemed a simple one: whether or not to buy the "intrinsically safe" radio (a radio that does not spark and can be used at incidents involving hazardous materials) requested by Fire Chief Nyal Thomas. But Public Safety Commissioner Judy Beier, whose approval was required, was opposed, because, she said, the fire chief had not gone through the proper channels. Harbormaster and Director of Emergency Services Bill Pettigrew was so incensed he offered to resign his position, saying he "could not work with a commissioner who was uninformed about firefighting and public safety issues and was unwilling to listen to those who were." Beier replied, "I resent the fact that you say I'm uninformed and untrained. I don't think you're giving me credit for my talent and skills." Council member Richie Wasserman urged the parties to get over personality conflicts and work together: "You are all irreplaceable." Fire Chief Thomas wondered if they weren't "burnt out" trying to solve the fire protection problem. Beier offered another reason for holding back on the radio purchase: The California Department of Forestry and Fire Protection would soon be inventorying the city's firefighting equipment and giving the Council a list of the items the City should buy. "Under our contract with CDF," said Beier, "we are obligated to meet this cost." Mayor Raven Earlygrow did not take part in the discussion; he was listening to local election returns on his pocket radio. The matter unresolved, the council moved on to the next item on the agenda.

Source: Lisa Walker, "City Council Tackles Dispute Among Safety Officials," *Independent Coast Observer* 16, no. 33 (11 Nov. 1994), 1, 10.

been helpful, the demand for new housing grows ever greater, and international, national, and local resources combined have not been sufficient to reverse the trend.[23]

The tension between demand and capability can be found in the struggles of local government in the simplest rural community (see Box 12.3); the problem of skewed income and shocking poverty can be found in the wealthiest big cities of the wealthiest nation (in the ten largest U.S. cities, the income of the richest fifth of the population has grown to 14 to 21 times as much as that of the poorest fifth; see Figure 12.2).

■ **The Search for Solutions.**   How should local governments respond to the problems they face? Robert Putnam argues that it makes a great deal of difference whether or not the community has strong traditions of civic en-

FIGURE 12.2
Difference in
Income in the
Ten Largest
U.S. Cities[a]

New York	$5,237 EARNED BY POOREST FIFTH	
RATIO 21.04	**EARNED BY RICHEST FIFTH** $110,199	
Los Angeles	$6,821	
18.05	$123,098	
Chicago	$4,743	
18.27	$86,632	
Houston	$5,591	
17.44	$97,536	
Philadelphia	$4,745	
15.74	$74,664	
San Diego	$8,611	
12.07	$103,921	
Detroit	$3,109	
20.47	$63,625	
Dallas	$6,478	
16.59	$107,475	
Phoenix	$7,357	
11.86	$87,279	
San Antonio	$5,041	
14.63	$73,739	

[a] Median annual incomes of the poorest fifth and richest fifth, with difference expressed as a ratio.

Source: *New York Times,* 26 Dec. 1994, A20.

gagement of any kind. According to Putnam, when citizens routinely take part in their community life—such as reading the local newspapers, joining music or literary societies, or taking part in a soccer club—local government is likely to work well. Civic engagement produces social capital, a reservoir of trust, and makes it possible to get things done even when resources are limited. Anticipating an argument, Putnam insists such communities "did not become civic simply because they were rich. . . . They have become rich because they were civic." [24] He seems to suggest that solutions to the problems of local communities lie in their own hands, regardless of levels of national or provincial funding or any history of political oppression.

A more promising approach to improving the effectiveness of local government may be contemporary efforts that combine local and provincial or national government resources and expertise to combat a local problem experienced in numerous communities throughout a nation. The recent history of the struggle against violence by and against urban young people illustrates what can be done—and how hard it is to know what will succeed, and for how long.

Urban youth violence became a very serious problem in the United States in the late 1980s and early 1990s. During that period, the adolescent homicide rate doubled, gunfire became a leading cause of teenage death, and more than 60 percent of persons arrested and charged with crimes were between the ages of 13 and 29.[25] By the late 1990s the overall crime rate was dropping, but youth violence, particularly homicide, had reached shocking proportions.

National attention naturally focused on the shocking instances of multiple murders in schools, such as the Columbine High School shootings in 1999.[26] But in fact the problem is more widespread than many have realized, and the role of guns—and their easy availability—is indisputable. Just between 1985 and 1992, the number of murders by juveniles in which a gun was involved doubled, while the number committed without a gun did not increase. The rise in the use of guns is associated with the recruitment of youth to sell drugs, the need other young people felt to carry guns to protect themselves from armed drug sellers, and the growing belief among adolescents that guns provided status and power.[27] Although the possession of handguns by juveniles is illegal by federal law, allowing some to argue that all that was needed was better enforcement, neither the federal government nor most states restrict the purchase and ownership of long guns, which includes semi-automatic AK-47s, AR-15s, and other assault rifles.[28] Nor can there be much doubt that the continued easy availability of handguns for adults increases the opportunity of young persons to obtain such weapons for themselves, illegal or not.

The failure of the U.S. Congress and most states to pass more effective gun laws thus placed much of the burden of reducing youth violence on the states and cities. Some of the efforts have been impressive, in both design and effect. California spent over $35 million to set up the Violence Prevention Initiative (VPI), which works via the media, community action, and individual leadership. First evaluations of this program showed positive changes in attitudes toward gun safety and regulations, greater use of violence prevention skills, and a decrease in violent crime at rates better than those in comparable communities without VPI. In other state- or city-level initiatives, the state of Missouri set up an Intensive Case Monitoring program to assign (and pay) college students to tutor, counsel, and "keep a close watch" over juvenile delinquents; the state of Washington created fourteen violence-prevention projects funded with a combination of federal, state, and local resources; and the city of Boston set up Operation Ceasefire, otherwise known as the Boston Gun Project. In the two years following the beginning of the

Boston project, which focused police efforts on reducing illegal gun trafficking among youth, deterring gang violence, and responding immediately when violence occurred, youth homicides decreased by 63 percent.[29]

Recently, however homicide rates have taken another jump, and the increase in Boston was particularly shocking: back up by more than 60 percent in 2001. Teenagers continue to be "the age group most prone to crime." A declining economy, the number of inmates recently released from state and federal prisons, the increase (1 percent per year) in the number of teenagers, and post-September 11 trauma were all cited as possible causes.[30]

■ **Local Justice: The Role of the Police.** Whether the local crime rate is high or low, no question of local government is more sensitive than the resolution of disputes. When crimes are committed, reputations are besmirched, or contracts are violated, tempers flare and the human heart reaches out for help—social help. Whether or not that help will be available depends in large part on the local judicial apparatus.

Technically, the local police are not part of that apparatus; their job is simply to carry out the rules. In practice, however, the police are often both the first and the last agency of local justice with which the citizen comes into contact. Typically, police officers arrive on the scene, attempt to calm tempers and impose order, and suggest solutions. Although most police are careful to carry out these duties within the limits of the law, some are not; police racism, brutality, and corruption are widespread evils. The agency Human Rights Watch recently issued an overview of incidents of police brutality in fourteen major American cities. They found that "police brutality is persistent in all of these cities; that systems to deal with abuse have had similar failings in all the cities; and that, in each city examined, complainants face enormous barriers in seeking administrative punishment or criminal prosecution of officers who have committed human rights violations." Although it is true that the officers involved are normally a small minority of the force, they are routinely protected, says the report, "by the silence of their fellow officers and by flawed systems of reporting, oversight and accountability." The agency recognizes that mistakes are unavoidable and that policing is a dangerous job, but insists the abuses described could have been prevented with a better system of oversight.[31]

Of course, the police do not always have the final judicial word, and it matters a great deal what other, more formally juridical bodies are available at the local level. In many villages, especially those more remote from large centers of population, the lowest level of the judicial branch is a local notable with minimal training and credentials who has been assigned to "keep the peace" by settling minor disputes. In American small towns this may be the justice of the peace; in Papua New Guinea, Village Courts respect traditional processes of dispute resolution and seek to use mediation, compromise, and compensation before referring any case to the more adversarial system of criminal procedure followed at higher levels; and in the more remote villages of both Kenya and Ghana, local chiefs and councils of elders still provide "an informal, customary criminal justice system." [32]

What if the matter is too weighty for such relatively informal adjudication, or the decision seems unsatisfactory and unfair to one of the parties? At this point almost every government provides some way of linking local judicial functions to the national court system. Whether the dispute goes to a municipal criminal court, a small claims court, or a nearby national appeals court, a line is being crossed—away from relatively autonomous local justice and into a national network of courts, appeals, higher courts, and "courts of last resort" (which may not be courts at all; chief executives sometimes personally fulfill that function). Nations that cannot establish such links from local to national systems of justice are not, finally, sovereign states. They are little more than loose confederations—otherwise they would not leave final authority in such an important domain in the hands of local fiefdoms. The effort in the United States to eliminate "vigilante justice"—that is, justice administered by bands of armed men self-appointed to hold others accountable to what they conceived society's norms of righteous conduct to be—was thus a key step in nineteenth-century nation building. [33] Similarly, the Constitutional Council of Nigeria had to find a way to persuade northern Nigerian authorities that citizens in their region had the right to appeal decisions of the Islamic local courts to the secular national court system. Making such links is no easy matter. American vigilantes often had to be treated as criminals themselves before the authority of the national system could be established; in Nigeria the Constitutional Council had to agree that the national courts would include judges well versed in Islamic law, and even then consent was tacit and grudging during that nation's most recent experiment with civilian rule.

Submunicipal Government

Not all local government is at the level of the municipality. When the municipality in question is extremely large (see Table 12.1), smaller ruling bodies are sometimes formed. Most common is a system in which the city is subdivided into *wards*. In such systems each subunit has its own offices, complete with bureaucratic functionaries and executive authority, but operates strictly within the limits set by higher levels of government. These offices are where citizens go to register births, get married, sign children up for school, pay taxes, request and receive social benefits, and register deaths. In a normal, law-abiding, and uncontentious lifetime, a citizen may never come into contact with any higher level of government.

Such decentralization often works well for the citizen as subject, but what about the citizen as participant? To meet the need for citizen participation in local government in large metropolises, still other structures have been devised. One of the most common is the *neighborhood council*, often established in response to national government restrictions that permit such groups to appeal for and employ national funds, or to be consulted when such funds are secured by others for local purposes. Since the councils must normally meet certain standards of institutionalization (for example, having elected officers and regular meetings) to qualify for this kind of involvement in the work of government, they quite naturally develop a permanent identity and become a rallying place for other, more political forms of local activism.[34]

Another form of submunicipal government is the *workers' council*, located in the factory, office, agribusiness, or other large-scale economic enterprise. In France, all the larger corporations are required by law to set up workers' councils, which have the right to help determine such matters as working conditions and fringe benefits problems that are frequently the subject of national government policy.[35] Is this local government? As is often the case, the line between private and public domains is blurred. The businesses in question may be in either the private or the public sector (a large share of French economic enterprise is under state control), and the matters being resolved by the workers' councils are matters that might otherwise be resolved by private employers without government interference or advice. Does the fact that the state requires the formation of the councils make them government bodies? The answer is not clear.

In other, more defined socialist systems, the role of workers' councils as official submunicipal units of government is considerably more obvious. In Cuba, *consejos de trabajo,* composed only of workers, were set up in 1965 and given the power to rule on problems of discipline and violations of labor law. Although these councils originally had a significant degree of power, it was power that the government had given and thus could take away, which is exactly what it did in 1980 with Law 32, a law that transferred most of the workers' power back to management. Since then, not surprisingly, "an overwhelming atmosphere of weariness" characterizes the work of the councils, according to one sympathetic observer.[36]

DILEMMAS OF SUBNATIONALISM

Whatever the domain of action, there are no easy answers to many of the problems modern nations refer to lower layers of government. But the dilemmas of subnationalism go beyond the question of what local policies will work, how to get them made into law, and how to pay for them. The effort to maintain effective lower levels of government is constantly plagued by two other problems: the struggle between center and periphery, and the frequent difficulty of fixing borders and powers of constituent units that will actually hold.

Center Versus Periphery

The question of the proper relationship between the national government and subnational units is often posed as a struggle in which the "center" (the national government) tries to achieve power over the "periphery" (provincial and local governments), and the periphery fights to maintain its right to exercise power independently.

The language itself has a touch of bias. Why should the national government be the center rather than the local city hall, where we achieve our most immediate and often most significant contact with the world of government? Indeed, from the citizen's point of view the national government often rests on the periphery of consciousness, not quite real until it is time to pay taxes or go to war. The terminology used contains an unfortunate hint that it is somehow always better to have expanded central control.

Be that as it may, there are interesting arguments on both sides of the center versus periphery dispute. National governments exist to make cooperative endeavor across a wider expanse than the municipality or province possible. Doesn't that mean that therefore there must be national agencies able to engage in centralized planning and allocation of resources? On the other hand, if everything is decided at the center, how can local needs be adequately understood and addressed, and how can the local populace have any sense of involvement and citizenship? In fact, it must be separately determined in each case whether greater national (central) control over local and provincial (peripheral) arenas of political power is desirable—or if the contrary is what is needed. And even then it is not always easy to tell. In the 1990s, for example, the new government of South Africa established urban environmental policy initiatives designed to provide clean drinking water and adequate sanitation to all South Africans, but little was accomplished in Cape Town, where one-third of the 3.1 million population were homeless, one-third were "poorly housed," and the very conditions the new policy was designed to eliminate were rampant. Curious to know why, David McDonald found that the municipal bureaucrats of Cape Town were often unenthusiastic, as well as uninformed, about the new policies. Most of the city's senior bureaucrats were white and were holdovers from the apartheid era —their jobs had been protected by the national government in order to encourage them to "become part of the transition process" rather than obstructionist. However, the strategy may not have succeeded. When interviewed by McDonald, they were able to make few connections between protection of the environment, which they were more likely to see "as an abstract concept of nature, somehow detached from human beings" and the conditions in which two-thirds of their fellow citizens, mostly non-white, were forced to live—even worse, many of them made openly racist remarks when asked to consider that connection.[37] In this case, was the center or the periphery more to blame for the failure of local government? Which level should have taken a stronger role?

Subunits in Flux

The many shifts in national borders resulting from the defeat of communism following the fall of the Berlin Wall in 1989 have accustomed us to the idea that former provinces may themselves become independent states, setting up new levels of subnational government, and following the seemingly hopeless efforts of Israel and Palestine to fix the borders between themselves and to live in peace teaches us how difficult and dangerous it can be to design new states where others ruled before (see Figure 12.3).

As of 1887 all but 5 percent of the population between the Mediterranean Sea and the Jordan River was Arab. Under British rule, which began in 1920, the Jewish population steadily grew, from one-tenth to one-third the population of the area. In 1947 the United Nations proposed a partition, which Arabs rejected. The ensuing war left the newly created Israel with all of the land except the West Bank and the Gaza Strip. These territories were occupied by Israel in the 1967 Arab-Israeli war, and Israel built 16,800 settlements in them over the next two decades, despite UN peace terms calling for Israeli withdrawal from the territories in exchange for Arab recognition of Israel's right to exist. The Palestine Liberation Organization did not endorse the UN peace terms until 1988, when it called for an independent Arab state. In 1993, the two sides agreed to talk, and over the next seven years Israel both carried out negotiated withdrawals from some parts of the territories and continued building settlements there. In 2000, Israel proposed a new partition: a smaller West Bank, split into three sections separated by Israeli territory, plus the Gaza Strip would be the new Palestine. The PLO rejected the proposal and violence began again.

We are usually somewhat less aware, however, of how often borders shift inside states that themselves remain relatively constant and, even more commonly, how often the status of constituent units may change, and how passionately such change may be sought—or deplored. (See Box 12.4 for a first example.)

Even groups within states that have been granted greater autonomy than the nation's other constituent units consistently ask for more, sometimes seeking absolute independence and sometimes using violent means to make their point. Native Americans often seek more land—or at least fiscal com-

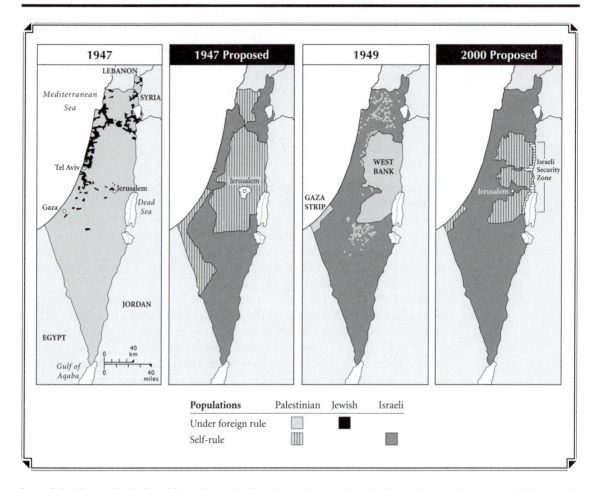

Populations	Palestinian	Jewish	Israeli
Under foreign rule			
Self-rule			

FIGURE 12.3
The Shifting
Boundaries of
Palestine

pensation for land they claim is theirs, as in the case of the Oneida people of New York who believe that some 200 years ago state and local governments in central New York unlawfully acquired 270,000 acres of their land—and that that land is now worth more than $1 billion.[38] Many Basques and Catalonians demand full independence from Spain despite significant grants of special rights, and a militant movement among the former has often engaged in acts of violence and terror to pursue their cause. When new borders are created in response to ethnic strife they do not necessarily hold: A band of ethnic Albanians has waged guerrilla warfare in an effort to annex parts of

BOX 12.4
Is It Good for Hawaii to Be a State?

Hawaii's status changed dramatically when it became the fiftieth state of the United States, but if Haunani-Kay Trask, a professor at the University of Hawaii and the leader of the movement known as Ka Lahui Hawai'i, had her way, a significant portion of the islands would drop that relationship and achieve "native sovereignty." The movement seeks not only a status "very like the nation-within-a-nation status that recognized American Indian nations have," but also greatly reduced tourism, which Trask identifies as "the single greatest cause of homelessness" on the islands because it has forced real estate costs to rise well beyond the reach of most indigenous Hawaiians. She points out that "most tourists who visit Hawaii have no sense of our history. The perception is a very romanticized and false one that we were willing natives who wanted our archipelago taken over by the U.S. The truth, of course, is that the U.S. . . . invaded and took our country. . . . The taking of Hawaii is the first great push of U.S. overseas imperialism." Native Hawaiians suffer racial discrimination and are "exiles at home," says Trask. Her friendly advice: "If you're thinking about Hawaii, don't come."[39]

Serbia to newly independent Kosovo.[40] Colombia has actually ceded a region of land as large as Switzerland to the largest guerrilla group in the nation, not permanently but as a first (and so far unsuccessful) step toward luring it into peace talks, and may cede another, smaller area, to another rebel group.[41]

Examples illustrating the frequency and the destabilizing effects of unfixed subunits exist throughout the world; we conclude with the example of the Kurds, a people who are culturally, linguistically, and religiously distinct and united, and who live contiguously, yet have been unable to achieve either nationhood or provincial autonomy in today's world. Most of them live in one of three Middle Eastern nations: Turkey, Iran, and Iraq. The 13 million who live in southeastern Turkey do not have even a province to call their own; of the 4.5 million living in Iran, 1.4 million live in that nation's province of Kurdistan where their governor, also a Kurd, has driven the Kurdish nationalist movement out of the country and into Iraq; and of the 4 million living in Iraq, over half live in a condition of "de facto independence" in a U.S.–protected enclave. This last group survives in large part by smuggling goods between Iraq and Turkey and consequently fears improved ties between Iraq and Turkey (which would make such trade legal and direct) almost as much as they fear the possibility of a successful attack by Saddam Hussein.[42]

SUMMARY AND CONCLUSION

Subnational government is government we cannot do without, even if it is also government we cannot always make work in comfortable tandem with national politics. Most polities are simply too large and too complex to be served adequately by a single level of government. It always helps, and is often essential, to have local authorities who understand and can respond to purely local needs, even if the resources must be obtained from higher levels of government.

In a unitary system, all the powers of government are reserved to the central government but may be temporarily delegated to such subunits as states. In a federal system, certain powers are constitutionally reserved to the government of the nation's constituent parts, although the tendency in recent years has been for the national government to assume an ever stronger role. In a confederal system, largely sovereign states maintain a loose association that permits coordinated action on a limited number of matters.

A federal system can free the national government to deal with the more important national issues, allow citizens more meaningful participation at a lower and more immediate level of government, permit governmental experimentation on a limited basis, and allow for the addition and subtraction of constituent units with relatively little turmoil. A unitary system often provides its citizens with more uniform laws, provides for more equal representation and disbursement of government moneys, has clearer lines of authority, and avoids the development of independent spheres of power. A confederal system sometimes offers a useful transitional structure as peoples move closer together or further apart.

Whichever kind of larger system they belong to, intermediate levels of government are often caught between the devil of national power and the deep blue sea of local needs and demands. One answer is to establish an additional layer of intermediate government, the region, either as a permanent constitutionally prescribed body of government or as a more particular and possibly less enduring functional agency.

Local government is government that can be physically known to each and every citizen. Its rule-making functions are normally carried out by elected bodies acting within the constraints imposed by higher levels of government—particularly the economic restraints of a severely limited power to tax or otherwise raise revenues adequate for the services their constituents demand. Local justice is often rendered by an executive agency, the police, and that agency may be responsible to national rather than local authorities, further complicating the relationship between the two. Once the more formal local judicial system is brought into a dispute, the crucial question becomes the nature of the link between that system and the national judiciary.

Establishing some such link is essential for maintaining the sovereignty of the state at large.

In larger municipalities the more accessible local government may be sub-municipal. Wards, neighborhood councils, and workers' councils are some of the more common examples.

Other, broader problems complicate the study of subnational government. The question of the proper relationship between the national (central) government and local (peripheral) government is difficult to resolve in theory and often impossible to implement in practice. Knowing how to establish and maintain the borders and the powers of constituent units of government can be as difficult as fixing borders between nations.

As we have seen, subnational governments are essential components of the human polity. Indeed, because they are the governments we have most immediate access to, they are the governments we would most like to see assume a truly human face. But local and provincial government officials occupy a difficult terrain, caught between the multitudinous hopes and aspirations of the citizens they live among and the distant centers of national power whose purposes they must serve to serve their own. If they do not always respond as we might wish, there is nothing to stop us from scorning them in private, and those of us living in systems with free elections may do so openly—blithely throwing the rascals out from time to time. However, before grasping the momentary satisfactions of democratic empowerment, we might sometimes do well to consider the limitations under which they labor, and ponder whether those we propose to send to city hall or to the provincial capital in their stead will be any better able to overcome the restraints inherent in the very principle of divided government power.

QUESTIONS TO CONSIDER

1. Why is the confederal system sometimes used *temporarily?*
2. Do you have some form of functional regionalism in your city or state? What good does it do? Do you know how to get in touch with it?
3. What are the responsibilities of your own local government? What services are they supposed to provide and do they do so adequately (in your opinion)? Be specific (you may want to make a phone call to get some answers).
4. Have you ever witnessed an example of police brutality? How would you go about determining if this is or is not a problem (and how significant a problem) in your community?

SELECTED READINGS

Beer, Samuel Hutchison. *To Make a Nation: The Rediscovery of American Federalism* (Cambridge, Mass.: Belknap Press, 1993). A readable study of the origins of federalism in the United States.

Bennett, Robert J. *Local Government in the New Europe* (New York: Halstead Press, 1996). Examines local government systems and the process of political decentralization throughout Europe.

Burgess, Michael, ed. *Canadian Federalism: Past, Present and Future* (New York: Leicester University Press, 1991). Essays on the evolution of Canadian federalism.

Freire, Mila and Richard Stren. *The Challenge of Urban Government: Policies and Practices* (Washington, D.C.: World Bank, 2001). Examines the wide-ranging issues confronting cities, such as metropolitan management, city strategy and governance, financing urban infrastructure, and urban poverty.

Lewis, Norman. *Inner City Regeneration. The Demise of Regional and Local Governments* (Buckingham, Pa.: Open University Press, 1992). Argues that local governments in the United States suffer from a "legitimation deficit" and lack of the power and resources to cope with the socioeconomic decline of older cities.

Mabileau, Albert, et al. *Local Politics and Participation in Britain and France.* (Cambridge, U.K.: Cambridge University Press, 1990). A collection of essays exploring the ways in which reforms in local government and administration have changed opportunities for the French and British citizen to participate in government.

McKay, David. *Designing Europe: Comparative Lessons from the Federal Experience* (New York: Oxford University Press, 2001). Examines existing federations with a view to identifying those arrangements that hold lessons for emerging European federalism.

Michelmann, Hans J. and Panayotis Soldatos, eds. *Federalism and International Relations: The Role of Subnational Units* (Oxford: Clarendon Press, 1990). Essays on the performance of federal systems as actors in international relations. Cases include Australia, Austria, Belgium, Canada, Germany, and Switzerland.

Smith, Michael Peter. *Transnational Urbanism: Locating Globalization* (Malden, Mass.: Blackwell, 2001). This author treats globalization not as an accomplished fact, but as an unfinished project of social and political practices and looks at such questions as how and why transnational migrants, refugees, diasporas, ethnic formations, entrepreneurs, political activists, and institutional networks locate and actively maintain relationships across national borders.

WEB SITE OF INTEREST

Local Government Commission
http://www.lgc.org
A forum and technical assistance program to enhance local governments' ability to create and sustain healthy environments, healthy economies, and social equity.

NOTES

1. The Brazilian federal constitution allows the states of that nation to divide or join with others freely, a right that is quite frequently exercised— as recently as 1988 a former Brazilian territory, Fernando de Noronha, became part of the state of Pernambuco. See "Brazil," in Arthur S. Banks,

ed., *Political Handbook of the World* (New York: CSA Publications, 1991), p. 82.

2. Article 67, sec. 8, and Article 89, sec. 4, General Principles of the Constitution of December 1982 adopted by the Fifth Session of the Fifth National People's Congress. From "The People's Republic of China," *The Europa World Year Book,* vol. 1 (London: Europa Publications Ltd, 1994), pp. 781, 783.

3. "Country Report: Switzerland," *Economist Country Briefings,* 10 Oct. 2001. http:// www.economist.com/countries/Switzerland, and Daniel J. Elazar, "Switzerland as a Model for Constitutional Reform in Israel," Jerusalem Center for Public Affairs, 18 Dec. 2001. http:// www.jcpa.org/dje/articles2/switz.htm.

4. David Cameron, "A Role for Federalism in Afghanistan After the Taliban," and Reeta Chowdhari Tremblay, "A Federal Arrangement for Afghanistan," both in a special issue on Afghanistan, *Federations* (October 2001): 3–4, 9.

5. Hamish Telford, *The Federal Spending Power in Canada: Nation-Building or Nation-Destroying?* (Kingston, Ontario: Institute of Intergovernmental Relations, Queens University, 2001).

6. Ronald L. Watts, *Comparing Federal Systems,* 2nd ed. (Montreal: McGill-Queen's University Press, 1999), p.4.

7. There have been two subsequent major revisions to the constitution, in 1874 and 2000. *Economist Country Briefings,* op. cit.

8. Minton F. Goldman, *Commonwealth of Independent States and Central/Eastern Europe* (Guilford, Conn.: Dushkin, 1992).

9. Colin Campbell, Harvey Feigenbaum, Ronald Linden, and Helmut Norpoth, *Politics and Government in Europe Today,* 2nd ed. (Boston: Houghton Mifflin, 1995), p. 430.

10. *Le Monde,* 21–22 June 1992, 3. See also *The Economist* (27 June 1992): 55.

11. Campbell et al., *Politics and Government in Europe Today,* pp. 496–99.

12. Michael McFaul, "Putin in Power," *Current History* (October 2000): 307–14; and "Russia's Regional Bosses Can Dig In," *The Economist* (3 Feb. 2001): 55.

13. Andrei Shoumikhin, "The Chechen Crisis and the Future of Russia," *Comparative Strategy* 5, no. 1 (1996): 1–10.

14. Divish Petrof, "Siberian Forests Under Threat," *Ecologist* (Nov./Dec. 1992): 167–70.

15. Henry W. Ehrmann and Martin A. Schain, *Politics in France,* 5th ed. (New York: HarperCollins, 1992), pp. 370–84.

16. Eileen Martin Harloff and Cuiyi Wei, "Present Day Local Government in China," *Planning and Administration* 16 (1989): 115.

17. Noga Morag Levine, "Between Choice and Sacrifice: Constructions of Community Consent in Reactive Air Pollution Regulation," *Law and Society Review* 28, no. 5 (1994): 1051–53.

18. David Rusk, "Growth Management: The Core Regional Issue," in Bruce Katz, ed., *Reflections on Regionalism* (Washington, D.C.: Brookings Institution Press, 1999), p. 104.

19. *The World Factbook 2001* (Washington, D.C.: Central Intelligence Agency: Superintendent of Documents, U.S. Government Printing Office, 2001).

20. William Glaberson, "Local Officials Scramble to Develop Antiterrorism Plans of Their Own," *New York Times,* 5 Oct. 2001, B8, and Amy E. Smithson, "To Bioterror a Local Response," *New York Times,* 20 Oct. 2001, A21.

21. In earlier times, African chiefs sometimes ruled autocratically, but they were more often limited by the knowledge that they could be removed from power if they went too far beyond the will of those they governed. Ashanti chiefs, for example, always knew they could be "destooled"— that is, have the symbol of power, typically a three-legged stool on which no one ever actually sat, taken from them. In contemporary Africa, the chief has often become a merely ceremonial figure, although that status in itself may help him achieve appointment as a modern paid administrator.

22. Rune J. Sørensen and Arild Underdal, "Coping with Poverty: The Impact of Fiscal Austerity on the Local Budgetary Process in Norway," *Scandinavian Political Studies* 16, no. 1 (1993): 58, 59. See also Gunnar Rongen, "Efficiency in the Provision of Local Public Goods in Norway," *European Journal of Political Economy* 11 (1995): 253–64.

23. K. C. Sivaramakrishnan, "Managing a Metropolis: The Challenge of Low-Income Housing and Neighborhood Redevelopment in Mumbai (Bombay), India," *Global Outlook: The International Urban Research Monitor* (August 2001): 30–32. http://wwics.si.edu/NEWS/glout0801.htm.

24. Robert D. Putnam, "The Prosperous Community: Social Capital and Economic Growth," *Current* (October 1993): 4–9.

25. Carla Nielsen et al., "Youth Violence," *State Government News* (August 1994): 20–35. Although we pursue the U.S. example here, the phenomenon of increased urban violence by young people is found throughout the world. See, for example, Nancy Cardia, *Urban Violence in Sao Paulo* (Washington, D.C.: Woodrow Wilson International Center for Scholars, Comparative Urban Studies Occasional Papers Series, 33), 2000.

26. Barron, James and Mindy Sink, "Terror in Littleton: In a Violent Instant, Routine Gives Way to Panic," *New York Times,* 21 April 1999, A3.

27. Alfred Blumstein, *Youth Violence, Guns, and Illicit Drug Markets* (Washington, D.C.: National Institute of Justice, U.S. Department of Justice, June 1996).

28. "Gun Laws Work, Loopholes Don't," Brady Campaign to Prevent Gun Violence, 20 Dec. 2001. http://www.bradycampaign.org/facts/issuebriefs/loophole.asp.

29. For the California and Boston projects, see "Youth Violence in Urban Communities" a seminar held at Harvard University May 11–12, 2000, part of the university's ongoing Urban Seminar Series on Children's Health and Safety. http://www.urbanhealth.org.

30. Fox Butterfield, "Killings Increase in Many Big Cities," *New York Times,* 21 Dec. 2001, A1, A16.

31. *Shielded from Justice: Police Brutality in the United States* (New York: Human Rights Watch, June 1998). The fourteen cities examined were Atlanta, Boston, Chicago, Detroit, Indianapolis, Los Angeles, Minneapolis, New Orleans, New York, Philadelphia, Portland, Providence, San Francisco, and Washington, D.C. Of course, police brutality is not only an American problem. For stories regarding abusive behavior by police in Japan, Canada, and Mexico, see *Washington Post,* 30 April 1990, A13, A19; *Christian Science Monitor,* 31 July 1991, 4; and *New York Times,* 1 April 1992, A3.

32. Sinclair Dinnen, *World Factbook of Criminal Justice Systems: Papua New Guinea* (Washington, D.C.: U.S. Department of Justice, Bureau of Justice Statistics, 1996); Graeme Newman, Adam C. Bouloukos, and Debra Cohen, *World Factbook of Criminal Justice Systems: Kenya* (Washington, D.C.: U.S. Department of Justice, Bureau of Justice Statistics, 1996); and Obi N. I. Ebbe, *World Factbook of Criminal Justice Systems: Ghana* (Washington, D.C.: U.S. Department of Justice, Bureau of Justice Statistics, 1996).

33. For a contemporary example of vigilantism, this time in Venezuela, see Diana Jean Schemo, "Lynch-Mob Justice Growing in Poor Sections of Caracas," *New York Times,* 12 May 1996, A4.

34. Jeffrey Berry, Kent E. Portnoy, and Ken Thompson, *The Rebirth of Urban Democracy* (Washington, D.C.: The Brookings Institution, 1993), p. 65.

35. William Safran, *The French Polity,* 4th ed. (New York: Longman, 1995), p. 30.

36. Janette Habel, *Cuba: The Revolution in Peril* (London and New York: Verso, 1991), pp. 81–85.

37. David McDonald, "Neither from Above, Nor from Below: Municipal Bureaucrats and Environmental Policy in Cape Town," *Canadian Journal of African Studies* 30, no. 2 (1997): 315–40.

38. James Dao, "Anxiety Growing Over Indian Claim in New York State," *New York Times,* 13 Jan. 1999, A1, A22, and Beverly Gage, "Indian Country, NY," *The Nation* (27 Nov. 2000): 11–18.

39. David Barsamian, "The Progressive Interview: Haunani-Kay Trask," *The Progressive* (Dec. 2000): 36–40.

40. Steven Erlanger, "Multiplying Albanian Insurgents in Yugoslavia Threaten Belgrade's New Democracy," *New York Times,* 21 Jan. 2001, 10.

41. Juan Forero, "Colombia, in Risky Move, Plans to Cede Zone to 2nd Rebel Group," *New York Times,* 27 Jan. 2001, A1, A5.

42. "Iran's Kurds: The Lucky Ones?" and "Bush's Kurdish Fans," both *The Economist* (23 Dec. 2000): 56.

PART FIVE

Governing the World

International and Regional Governments

"I have a hard time remembering where Sacramento is," said the distressed student staying after class to speak to me, "And you expect me to think about *Brussels.*" Oh dear. Perhaps it is now asking too much to go directly from a chapter on local government to one on international and regional governments. However, we have all had much more practice lately in learning, in good ways and bad, how the local is never that far from the global, and vice versa. Even our vocabulary is bending north and south, east and west—just consider "a global village," "think globally, act locally," and even "glocal." The two levels do indeed have brand new ways of coming together. When we finally find our way to Sacramento, a state capital, watch out: Brussels, a national capital housing many international offices, may have got there first.

Our purpose in this chapter is not, however, to trace the impact of international governing agencies on local affairs, but rather to look at those agencies in their own right. True, it is not so very long ago that mentioning "world government" was considered the next thing to being unpatriotic, the words themselves almost taboo in the classroom. And now arguments against globalism come from the left as well as the right; fears of the future are strong and some are indisputably well founded.[1] Nonetheless, although the world is still far indeed from having a single government, international and regional agencies are so numerous and are constantly growing so much stronger, that honoring that taboo would leave us as exposed as the hindquarters of the proverbial ostrich. Whatever opinions we hold, we need to know what they are, what they do, and how they are changing. Political science encompasses the study of evolving world government.

The chief motive for trying to build international institutions is national. Every nation seeks to gain some mastery over its own destiny, and to minimize unpleasant and disconcerting intrusions from the outside world. Gathering good intelligence and maintaining diplomatic relations—topics covered in Chapter 7—help reduce the element of surprise and improve a polity's chances of responding effectively to sudden crises. But another way the nations of the world attempt to gain some mastery over the course of history is by making pacts with one another—agreeing to engage in certain activities or promising to do so in the event of certain other developments. Such pacts, ranging in scope from very broad to very narrow, are the very fabric of international government. They may be made between as few as two nations, as many as 180. They may take the form of treaties or of fixed organizations—and organizations formed by pacts may make and remake the terms of their relationship with further pacts, further organizational initiatives.

We begin this chapter by looking briefly at the historical development of international institutions prior to 1945, continue with an overview of the major changes beginning with World War II that produced an entirely new and ever-changing international system, and then take a more detailed look at the post–World War II evolution of treaties, of regional governments, and of the UN and other international bodies. We conclude with a consideration of whether or not it is possible to establish democratic accountability at the world level.

THE HISTORY AND TYPES OF INTERNATIONAL GOVERNMENT

In this section we consider the pre-1945 development of international relations, focusing on three ways nations attempted to establish agreements and procedures that would increase the chance of living in harmony with one another: the treaty; fledgling regional organizations; and one effort to build international government, the League of Nations.

Treaties: Types and Historical Examples

Treaties are made for a wide range of purposes. There are four main types: *conflict prevention treaties,* made in an effort to reduce the chance of war or lesser conflict by setting the terms for peace after a war, resolving border disputes, agreeing on arms limitations, or merely stating a common commitment to keep the peace; *trade treaties,* designed to facilitate economic exchange among nations; *defense treaties,* designed to offer assurance to the signatories that if one of them is attacked the others will come to its aid; and, finally, what we may call *geosocial and humanitarian treaties,* designed to protect the quality of our shared life on the planet. A specific treaty may in fact combine particular types, endeavoring, for example, to prevent a resumption of hostilities at the end of a war by setting up mutually beneficial terms of trade or promising the conquered people protection of individual rights.

A fifth kind of treaty is the pact that forms a regional organization or international organization. However, because this kind of treaty is just the first step in the creation of the second and third ways we seek to control international relations, we will not treat it separately here.

Historical examples can be found for all the main types of treaties. Indeed, of the three peaceful ways of seeking to resolve or avoid international conflict by international cooperation—treaties, regional organizations, and international organizations—the treaty has the longest and most variegated history.

■ **Conflict Prevention Treaties.** The most common—and best known—kind of conflict prevention treaty is the peace treaty that ends a war. The earliest such agreement we know about is the Stele of Vultures, a document that records the terms of peace insisted upon by Eannatum of Lagash in Babylonia after he defeated the city-state of Umma, written nearly 4,500 years ago.

Another well-known ancient peace agreement is the treaty made 3,200 years ago by the Hittite king Hattusilis III and Ramses II of Egypt after the battle of Gadesh.[2] An extremely important pre-1945 peace treaty was the 1648 Treaty of Westphalia, which ended a long era of religious wars in Europe, and brought into being the modern system of sovereign territorial states. In fact, conflict prevention treaties have been made at the conclusion of almost every war since ancient times.

Although peace treaties almost always are presented as conflict prevention treaties, the means adopted have not always been well chosen. Sometimes they have simply spelled out the terms of dominion of one nation over another, as when the Fulani people conquered the Mande people of West Africa in the middle of the eighteenth century and demanded that the Mande respect the laws of Islam or turn over their land to those who did.[3] The provisions in the Versailles Treaty ending World War I, which assigned Germany and its allies blame for causing the war and called for massive reparations that made recovery and the return of stability impossible to achieve, were, many believe, a major cause of World War II.[4]

Another form of conflict prevention treaty with pre-1945 antecedents is an agreement among nations at peace to remain so. The Locarno Conference of 1925 brought the former combatants of World War I together to sign an agreement renouncing force and committing themselves to "a system of peaceful resolution through mediation, reconciliation and judicial settlement."[5] Signatories of the Kellogg-Briand Pact (or Pact of Paris) of 1928 agreed that states should no longer have the right to wage war in any form.[6] Although these agreements came to naught during the rise of Nazi Germany in the 1930s, they did establish a pattern for regional and subregional security arrangements.

■ **Trade Treaties.** Trade treaties have also been made throughout most of human history, but assumed much greater importance at the end of the nineteenth century and thereafter. In 1860 Britain and France signed the Cobden-Chevalier treaty, in which each nation agreed to lower a broad set of tariffs to the other. When this put other exporters at a decided disadvantage in the French market, they too began seeking, and obtaining, similar treaties with France; by 1866 most European states had entered into a widespread network of Most Favored Nation (MFN) treaties.[7]

Although treaties focused only on trade are common now, for much of human history important changes in conditions of trade were more likely to evolve from what appeared at the time simply to be treaties of peace. Such was the case for the Treaty of Nanking in 1842, bringing to an end the first Opium War in China, but also transferring the desolate and unpopulated island of Hong Kong into the hands of the British. No one recognized that the one great asset of the island, a magnificent harbor, would turn it into the center of trading, banking, shipping, and shipbuilding it was to become, nor did anyone predict how refugees from the Communist takeover of the mainland in 1949 would build on that base by bringing with them the necessary capital and know-how to create a vast array of light industrial enterprises.[8]

■ **Defense Treaties.** Defense treaties create *defense alliances,* usually among nations combining in order to counter the superior or growing power of a common foe, as when the French and British agreed to struggle together to hold the Russian Revolution of 1917 in check.[9] The 1939 Pact of Neutrality and Non-Aggression between Germany and the Soviet Union was not so much an alliance as an agreement not to attack each other; under its cover the two nations seized Poland, each taking a portion for itself; however, two years later Germany attacked the Soviet Union.[10]

Even when they do not self-destruct quite so rapidly, defense alliances produce another problem: They breed counteralliances. Thus, when France, Britain, and Russia formed the Triple Entente before World War I, Germany, Austria-Hungary and Italy retaliated by forming their own Triple Alliance.[11]

■ **Geosocial and Humanitarian Treaties.** The end of the nineteenth century and beginning of the twentieth saw several examples of geosocial and humanitarian treaties. A very important set of such treaties focused on ending slavery. The General Act of the Brussels Conference of 1889–1890 pronounced itself in favor of "putting an end to the traffic in African slaves," the Convention of Saint-Germain-en-Laye of 1919 called for "the complete suppression of slavery in all its forms and of the slave trade by land and sea," and the Convention to Suppress the Slave Trade and Slavery in 1925 vowed "to prevent and suppress the slave trade" and "to bring about, progressively and as soon as possible, the complete abolition of slavery in all its forms." [12]

For an example on the geosocial side, we find serious international efforts to regulate the management of wildlife beginning in 1900, with what must be the most awkwardly titled treaty in history: the London Convention Designed to Ensure the Conservation of Various Species of Wild Animals in Africa which are Useful to Man or Inoffensive. This treaty was never ratified by all signatories and so never came into effect, but a subsequent 1933 London Convention Relative to the Preservation of Fauna and Flora in their Natural State was somewhat more successful, setting up provisions controlling the export and import of wildlife.[13]

Types of Regional Government and Historical Examples

The earliest regional governments were *empires,* "vast unifying polities" spreading outward, "insatiable in their appetite for expansion," certain they were "worthy of dominating all those peoples with whom they came into contact." [14] An empire was not a modern state; it was a kind of regional government under the control of a state, usually led by a single autocrat, which took power by force and ruled the conquered peoples from its own capital city. Examples include Egypt under the Pharaohs, beginning in 3100 B.C.E.; Mesopotamia under Sargon; Assyria; Persia, the empire of Alexander the Great; the Chou dynasty; India under Chandragupta and Asoka; the classical Roman Empire; and the empire of the Mongols, which came to an end only in the fourteenth century.

Beginning in the sixteenth century, major European powers reached out to build their own version of empires. Now new modes of transportation made geographical contiguity less important, but communication systems were still sufficiently primitive that distant peoples inevitably maintained some powers in their own hands. Great Britain, France, Germany, Belgium, Spain, and Portugal conquered and controlled, in the name of empire, some of North America, most of Africa and Latin America, and vast portions of Asia. Prior to World War II, these conquests were officially colonies or territories within their respective empires, although many had begun to regain considerable autonomy. In 1926 Great Britain decided to create a new form of regional government, the Commonwealth, as a way of maintaining a modicum of control. Australia, Canada, the Irish Free State, Newfoundland, New Zealand, and South Africa were all now to be considered "autonomous Communities within the British Empire, equal in status, in no way subordinate one to another in any aspect of their domestic or external affairs, though united by a common allegiance to the Crown and freely associated as Members of the British Commonwealth of Nations." [15]

Other pre–World War II regional organizations emerged from treaties. Often even the simplest treaties entailed the establishment of some form of organization to carry out their provisions, and such structures could sometimes inspire the formulation of further treaties and further structures. In the nineteenth century, increasing economic exchanges between nations constituted another stimulus for the development of cooperative organizations that went beyond the skeletal commissions established by economic and defense treaties.[16] In some cases, the process thus begun led to the formation of new states, as formerly distinct entities moved from functional cooperation to national integration. Italy, Germany, and Switzerland were each formed after long periods of treaty making between independent principalities.

Types of International Government and One Historical Example

No dream has held greater appeal for humankind than the dream of a united world. Here we may distinguish two types: those that do not get beyond the realm of dreams and those that do. Historically, the dream was often dreamt:

Confucius imagined a "Grand Union," Dante yearned for a world monarch, the anarchist Mikhail Bakunin called for a "United States of the World" based on "the right of voluntary union and the right of voluntary separation," and Marxists hoped that "the International Republic of Soviets" might one day be established.[17]

Only one organization provides a pre-1945 example of the second type: the League of Nations, founded at the Paris Peace Conference in 1919. The covenant establishing the League could be described as a conflict prevention treaty and a defense treaty rolled into one, calling as it did for members to preserve each other's territorial integrity and political independence against aggression (Article 10) and setting out procedures for resolving international conflicts when they did develop (Articles 11–16). It even prescribed punishments: Those who used armed force contrary to the covenant would be subject to economic sanctions imposed by all other member states. But what moved the League from the status of treaty to that of international government was that it set up both an assembly and a council of permanent members, plus various bureaus and committees to deal with specific problems. It became an organization.

Because the United States never signed the Treaty of Versailles (in which the covenant establishing the League was embedded) and because the organization was unable to act effectively against Japan, Italy, Germany, and the Soviet Union when they engaged in acts of aggression during the 1930s, the League of Nations is often viewed as an utter failure. However, Kalevi J. Holsti points out that prior to its dissolution in April 1946, the League actually considered sixty-six disputes and conflicts and produced compromise outcomes for thirty-five of them, a "level of achievement . . . substantially higher than the record of the UN since 1945." Holsti notes as well that the League's numerous bureaus and committees made real contributions in the areas of health, communications, arms traffic, slavery, drugs, and the conditions of workers, women, and children, and that it set up a mandates system, giving control of Germany's overseas colonies to the victors of World War I and itself the responsibility for monitoring this "trust." [18] Not too shabby a record for the first time out.

HOW INTERNATIONAL RELATIONS CHANGED AFTER WORLD WAR II

The nature of international relations changed drastically with the conclusion of World War II in 1945—and has continued to change up to and including the present time. A quick review of the most important of these changes is useful before we look at more contemporary examples of treaties, regional governments, and world government.[19]

The first changes to examine are those that were caused by the war itself. The battle against fascistic totalitarian governments and recognition of the danger they posed to all democracies prompted a determination on the side of the victors to build stronger institutions of peace, and helped spur the creation of the United Nations at the war's conclusion. But defeating fascism had also led to the development of nuclear weaponry. Although dropping atomic bombs on the civilian populations of Hiroshima and Nagasaki in 1945 may have speeded the end of the war, it also inspired an arms race that rapidly became a desperate contest between the United States and the Soviet Union, with the latter reaching near parity by the 1970s. The emergence of two nuclear giants created a world in which two superpowers, locked in fierce ideological warfare that constantly threatened to erupt in cataclysmic military battle, endangered the security not only of each other, but of everyone on the planet. Paradoxically yet also reasonably, both the threat of fascism and the deadly dangers of the "Cold War" had strengthened almost everyone's awareness that there *was* a human polity, and that we needed to protect it with stronger instruments and institutions dedicated to peace than had hitherto ever been possible to build. That recognition failed to prevent either the Korean War in the 1950s or the war in Vietnam in the 1970s, but did play an important part in avoiding the escalation of these and other localized conflicts into wider wars.

However, what was required to keep the peace—or at least avoid a third world war—changed as other forces gained momentum. One of these was the disappearance of imperialistic empires and the emergence of a great many more independent nations—up to 130 from 60 in the thirty years between 1945 and 1975.[20] These new nations added a new dimension to the struggles between the U.S. and the USSR, as each sought to incorporate as many of them as possible in its own power bloc. They also added new members to international and regional systems (and created several new regional organizations themselves), new causes for strife as civil and border wars within and among them erupted, and new claims on the humanity of those whose wealth had so long been built at least in part on the resources of these lands. Such developments inevitably shifted and expanded the work of international governance.

Another enormous change was the end of the Cold War and the fall of communism at the end of the 1980s.[21] The new nations emerging from the Soviet bloc became candidates for membership in organizations formerly designed at least in part to struggle against that bloc (NATO, the European Union) and older alliances crumbled and fell apart. These nations were not only potential new allies of the west, however—they were also subject to disintegration and internal conflict on a massive scale, as illustrated in the struggles between the member communities of the former Yugoslavia and in the battle of Chechnya for independence from Russia. The result was more new nations, more new battles, and many more new burdens for those who seek to prevent the outbreak or soften the blows of war.

And all along, other sources of violent conflict were gathering force. Sporadic acts of terrorism were nothing new, nor was violence on behalf of religion. That there was a worldwide network of terrorism building was known to many. Yet the attack on the United States in September 2001 somehow produced a difference not merely of degree but of kind. So bold and so successful a blow, directed against such a proud and powerful nation, galvanized not only that nation but the world. Suddenly "world war," so long deemed unimaginable, reappeared. The vastly different form it took as the U.S. began to retaliate—strategic bombing of the weak by the strong in pursuit of the diabolic, with a promise to pursue the last wherever they could be found—posed yet new challenges to the structures working for international harmony.

These massive changes in the international system—and so far we are not even mentioning the forces of increasing economic globalism, a topic we will explore in detail in the next chapter—have produced a very different world. What treaties, what regional organizations, and what international bodies are in place to cope with these dramatic developments? Can they possibly measure up to the job required of them?

THE CONTEMPORARY INTERNATIONAL SYSTEM

As the relations between nations have changed, so have the institutions designed to keep those relations peaceful and beneficial to all of humanity. And although dreams of true world governance continue, the real work has continued to be carried out via treaties and supranational agencies of considerably more limited scope.[22]

Contemporary Treaties

Treaty making has certainly not abated in the nearly six decades since the conclusion of World War II. Now there is even a treaty about treaties (see Box 13.1).

Keeping track of all the treaties is a major job, one the United Nations has taken on by establishing the United Nations Treaty Collection. It is not always easy to know which documents to include. Although here we are using only the general term "treaty," there are in fact now a wide variety of international "instruments" that fall under that general category: statutes, covenants, accords, agreements, conventions, protocols, memoranda of understanding, *modus vivendi,* and exchange of notes are some of the terms used. Such instruments undergo a variety of processes in their gestation: The UN's own alphabetical list, "not presumed to be exhaustive," includes Adoption, Acceptance or Approval, Accession, Act of Formal Confirmation, Amendment, Authentication, Correction of Errors, Definitive Signature, Deposit,

BOX 13.1
**A Treaty About
Treaties**

The 1969 Vienna Convention on the Law of Treaties is partly a codifi-cation of customary international law and partly a development in in-ternational law regarding what constitutes a treaty and under what cir-cumstances it shall be considered binding. It defines a treaty as "an international agreement concluded between states in written form and governed by international law, whether embodied in a single instrument or in two or more related instruments and whatever its particular desig-nation." It accepts that a fundamental principle of international law is *pacta sunt servanda* (treaties must be kept) but says that whether or not a specific agreement is to be considered a treaty under international law depends on "1) the intention of the parties to be bound under interna-tional law, 2) the significance of the agreement, 3) the specificity of the agreement, and 4) the form of the agreement" and it lays out precise con-ditions that must be met in applying all four criteria. It says that treaties which violate key principles of international law render themselves void. Such principles are peremptory norms of general international law such as "rules prohibiting genocide, slave trade and slavery, apartheid and other gross violations of human rights." If a new overriding norm emerges after the signing of the treaty, with which it conflicts, then the parties to the treaty are released from any further obligations. If present conditions are so radically different from those existing at the outset of the treaty as to render it impossible for either party to continue honoring the terms of the pact, that is another acceptable reason for terminating a treaty (and is known as *rebus sic stantibus*).

The United States signed the convention, but the U.S. Senate refused to ratify it. This was in large part because of uncertainty regarding what exactly were the "peremptory norms" of the international community and who would have a right to determine them, but also because it was un-clear that the United States could ever claim that it was not bound by an agreement on the grounds that although the convention may have been signed by American officials, it had not received ratification by the Senate.

Source: *Treaties and Other International Agreements: The Role of the U.S. Senate.* U.S. Senate Committee on Foreign Relations, 106th Cong., 2nd sess., S. Rpt. 106–71 (Washington, D.C.: U.S. Government Printing Office, 2001).

Entry into Force, Modification, Notification, Objection, Provisional Application, Ratification, Registration and Publication, Revision, Signature, and Referendum.[23] In any case, with this rich treasury of documentation, it is not difficult to find examples of all the kinds of treaties discussed above.

■ **Conflict Prevention Treaties.** Perhaps the most important conflict prevention treaties since 1945 were the series of arms limitations agreements between the United States and the Soviet Union, culminating with the agreement to eliminate all multihead intercontinental ballistic missiles and to reduce by two-thirds the number of nuclear warheads each possessed.[24] Although the 1972 Antiballistic Missile Treaty was abrogated in 2001 by the United States, when President George W. Bush argued that the development of a missile shield was essential to protect the nation against "future terrorist or rogue-state missile attacks," at the time they were reached all these agreements had played a key part in bringing the Cold War to an end and reducing the threat of nuclear holocaust.[25] On the other hand, the peace treaty at the conclusion of the Gulf War, when little more was actually demanded of Iraq than its withdrawal from Kuwait and its leader Saddam Hussein was allowed to remain in power, scarcely fits the terms of "conflict prevention" at all, especially when Iraq refused to allow inspections to ensure it was not producing weapons for nuclear or biological warfare and the United States maintained control of the skies in order to protect Kurdish refugees.[26]

■ **Defense Treaties.** Many important defense treaties were signed in the years following the end of World War II. Two of the most important were (1) the North Atlantic Treaty, signed by the United States and eleven other nations in 1949, in which the partners agreed to consider an armed attack against one or more of them in Europe or North America an attack against them all; and (2) the Warsaw Pact, signed by the USSR, Albania, Bulgaria, Hungary, the German Democratic Republic (East Germany), Poland, Romania, and Czechoslovakia on May 14, 1955. The Warsaw Pact was designed to counter NATO (discussed at greater length below) and also to justify continuing Soviet military presence in the other nations joining the Pact—indeed, when Hungary sought to opt out in 1956, it was prevented from doing so by Soviet force.[27]

■ **Trade Treaties.** The scope of trade treaties in recent years has often been broad indeed; the principal signatories (Canada, the United States, and Mexico) of the North American Free Trade Agreement (NAFTA), which came into effect in 1994, have a combined population of 370 million people

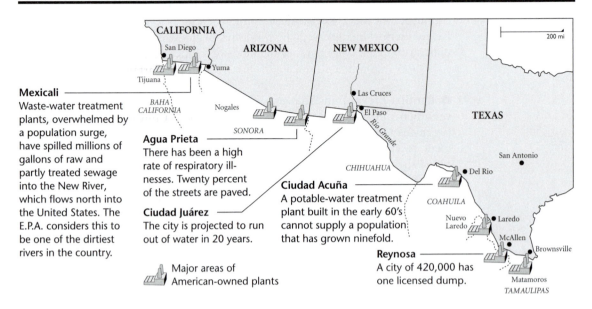

Mexicali
Waste-water treatment plants, overwhelmed by a population surge, have spilled millions of gallons of raw and partly treated sewage into the New River, which flows north into the United States. The E.P.A. considers this to be one of the dirtiest rivers in the country.

Agua Prieta
There has been a high rate of respiratory illnesses. Twenty percent of the streets are paved.

Ciudad Juárez
The city is projected to run out of water in 20 years.

Ciudad Acuña
A potable-water treatment plant built in the early 60's cannot supply a population that has grown ninefold.

Reynosa
A city of 420,000 has one licensed dump.

Major areas of American-owned plants

Source: Ginger Thompson, "Chasing Mexico's Dream into Squalor," *New York Times,* 11 Feb. 2001, 1, 6. Copyright © 2001 The New York Times Company. Reprinted by permission.

FIGURE 13.1
The Mixed Blessings of a Trade Agreement: NAFTA and the *Maquiladoras*

and a gross domestic product of $6.8 trillion.[28] The main provision in NAFTA is a schedule of tariff reduction on manufactured goods that will lead to their total elimination by 2009. Since the treaty was signed, Mexico's exports to the United States have been growing at around 20 percent a year, but much of the production takes place in foreign-owned manufacturing plants, known as *maquiladoras,* located near the border. These factories provide jobs and pay more than Mexican factories normally do, especially in the south: More than 1 million people migrated to them from southern Mexico in the first five years of NAFTA. However, wages and living conditions in the towns where these factories are concentrated are nonetheless shocking by U.S. standards: Mexican workers make less in a day than their American counterparts earn in an hour, and unpaved shanty towns with inadequate clean water and worse than inadequate sewage systems have sprung up all along the border.[29] (See Figure 13.1.)

■ **Geosocial and Humanitarian Treaties.** A wide variety of treaties having nothing to do with war, peace, or trade have been put into practice since World War II, seeking to improve the conditions of life for all the citizens of the human polity. Some of the most important have focused on protecting the planet, others on protecting individual human rights.

Since the early 1970s Multilateral Environmental Agreements (MEAs) have established a wide range of treaties seeking to eliminate the kinds of damage done to the planet that cannot be solved within single nations. Some recent examples include the Climate Change Convention of 1992, the Convention to Combat Desertification of 1994, and the Cartagena Protocol on Biosafety of 2000. Others have been limited to particular regions, such as the Convention on the Protection and Use of Transboundary Watercourses and International Lakes of 1992 and the Inter-American Convention for the Protection and Conservation of Sea Turtles of 1996. More and more frequently, MEAs include institutional arrangements designed to supervise implementation and compliance with the treaty.[30]

The impetus for new agreements in the area of human rights was actually provided by World War II, when the Nuremberg Trials charged many of the leaders of Nazi Germany with crimes against humanity, specifically genocide. This was the first time the victors in a war asserted that individuals—not only states—could be held responsible for violations of human rights during times of war. Soon after the trials concluded the Universal Declaration of Human Rights was passed by the UN General Assembly in 1948; this document was not legally binding but was followed by five conventions that

The Maquiladora. *New trade agreements make it possible for U.S. and other foreign producers to recruit Mexican laborers making less in a day than American workers make in an hour for their factories near the U.S. border. This factory is in Tijuana.*
© Annie Griffiths Belt/CORBIS

were (when signed and ratified). These dealt with genocide, racial discrimination, discrimination against women, political and civil rights, and economic and social rights; disappointingly, they have so far been ratified by only about half the nations in the world.[31]

Regional Organizations

The chief regional organizations of today are listed in Box 13.2. Here we will look at four: the European Union (EU), the African Union (formerly the Organization of African Unity or OAU), the Association of Southeast Asian Nations (ASEAN), and the North Atlantic Treaty Organization (NATO).

■ The European Union.

A condition of the American Marshall Plan, initiated after World War II to assist in the rebuilding of Europe, was that the recipients work out a single plan for the distribution of any aid received. In response, French Foreign Minister Robert Schumann proposed the creation of a single authority to control the production of coal and steel. In 1952, France, former West Germany, Italy, Belgium, Luxembourg, and the Netherlands signed the European Coal and Steel Community Treaty. This was no simple treaty; although its terms covered only coal and steel, the well-known intention of at least some of the signers was to develop eventually a wider-ranging European Common Market—and possibly even a single European nation, roughly equal to the Soviet Union and the United States in territory, population, and natural resources.

In the first years of the ECSC's existence, the partners made rapid progress toward these goals—so rapid that in 1957 the Treaty of Rome was signed, creating the European Economic Community (EEC). The EEC abolished all customs duties among the member countries and established a Council of Ministers, an Executive Commission, and a Court of Justice. Ten years later, in 1967, a European Parliament was added. However, for the first twelve years of its existence the European Parliament was a nonelected body with no legislative functions. Representatives were appointed by the member nations as they saw fit, and the Parliament's function was simply to oversee the work of the Executive Commission. The Parliament had the power to force the resignation of the commission by a two-thirds vote, and in 1975 it gained the power to amend any draft budget submitted to it by the Council of Ministers. But not until 1979 did Europe hold its first direct elections to this parliament, and many of those elected had campaigned by promising to prevent any expansion of the Parliament's power that might threaten national prerogatives or sovereignty.

Thus it was almost the end of the twentieth century before whatever hopes the European community held for a united Europe could be viewed as any-

BOX 13.2
Major Regional Organizations Formed Since World War II

1945	League of Arab States
1947	Economic Commission for Europe (EEC)
1947	Western European Association
1948	Organization of American States (OAS)
1949	North Atlantic Treaty Organization (NATO)
1949	Council for Mutual Economic Assistance (COMECON)
1952	Australia, New Zealand, United States Security Treaty Organization (ANZUS)
1955	Warsaw Treaty of Friendship, Cooperation and Mutual Assistance
1957	European Economic Community (the Common Market)
1959	Inter-American Development Bank (IADB)
1960	Central American Common Market (CACM)
1960	Organization of Arab Petroleum Exporting Countries (OPEC)
1961	Organization of Economic Cooperation and Development (OECD)
1963	Organization of African Unity (OAU) now African Union
1967	Association of Southeast Asian Nations (ASEAN)
1973	Caribbean Community (CARICOM)
1975	Economic Community of West African States (ECOWAS)
1991	Commonwealth of Independent States (CIS)
1991	Southern African Development Community (SADC)
1991	Southern Cone Common Market (MERCOSUR) (Argentina, Brazil, Paraguay, Uruguay)
1992	Council of the Baltic Sea States (CBSS)
1992	European Union (evolved from European Community)
1995	North American Free Trade Agreement (NAFTA)
1995	Organization for Security and Cooperation in Europe (OSCE)

Source: *The World Factbook 1995* (Washington, D.C.: Central Intelligence Agency, 1995), pp. 485–521 and *Europa Yearbook, 1987*, vol. 1 (London: Europa Publications, 1987), pp. 90–211. Reprinted by permission.

thing but that: hopes. The worldwide economic recession that began with the oil shortages of 1973 was sharply felt by most of the member states (by then including Denmark, Greece, Ireland, Portugal, Spain, and the United Kingdom as well as the original six). It also had the effect of worsening economic relations among them. Former patterns of protectionism began to reestablish themselves, and the members' commitment to free trade among themselves was marred by quarrels over wine, sheep, fruit, and other "sensitive items" as individual governments tried to protect native producers against cheap imports.

By the end of the 1980s, however, the twelve partners had agreed that as of 1992 they would eliminate all internal commercial, financial, and customs barriers, thereby creating a truly common market. And when the time came, they may have faltered a bit, but they moved ahead determinedly, producing the Maastricht Treaty that in fact went far beyond the trade agreements originally envisaged, laying out in detail the steps to be taken toward a new Economic and Monetary Union (EMU) and a new political union (the European Union, or EU). In the very near future, said the treaty, Europe would have a single currency, a common foreign and defense policy, and common citizenship.

It was not easy to get all the representatives to agree on the details. Spain, Portugal, Greece, and Ireland had to be reassured with promises of *cohesion,* meaning that all EU members should be of roughly the same economic strength, and that the richer states should make contributions as necessary to the poorer ones, to achieve that end. Once cohesion is achieved, the next step was to be *convergence:* Germany, the member state most concerned with financial stability and responsibility, insisted that the new Economic and Monetary Union should not be formed until at least seven of the members had "converged," meeting fixed criteria regarding rates of inflation, interest rates, national budget deficits, public debt ratio to GDP, and currency stability, and new states were to be admitted only when they too met these criteria. (See Figure 13.2.) The common currency, the euro, was not to be introduced until 2002.

To reassure the British, always the problem child, the treaty gave strong promises to respect *subsidiarity*—that is, to guarantee that no European laws would be made except in the domains specifically set aside for the community or when the objectives could be better realized at the supranational level than by the states acting individually. (To make this promise more secure, the treaty specified that on many subjects, especially those of a fiscal nature, decisions could be made only by unanimous vote.) Also to please the British, the treaty spoke of *opting in:* Only those nations who wished to would be obliged to share in joint making of social policy on such issues as working conditions, equal rights for men and women, social security, and treatment of immigrants. Eleven states immediately "opted in," and Britain's John Major went home happy to report that he had been able to sign without giving up his government's determination to subordinate social needs to what it believed were the overriding needs of the British economy.[32]

The new treaty had to meet the test of several referenda and failed the first by a narrow margin, when the Danes voted against it on June 2, 1992.[33] The Irish voted yes by a very large margin a few weeks later, but the positive French vote in September was by a very slim majority. Some important changes were made in the treaty, and Denmark reversed its vote in the following year. One by one, the others signed on, always excepting Britain. In 1994, four other nations voted whether or not to seek to join the Union: Austria voted yes heartily (66.4 percent approving), Finland was reasonably enthusiastic (56.9 percent in favor), Sweden agreed but rather reluctantly

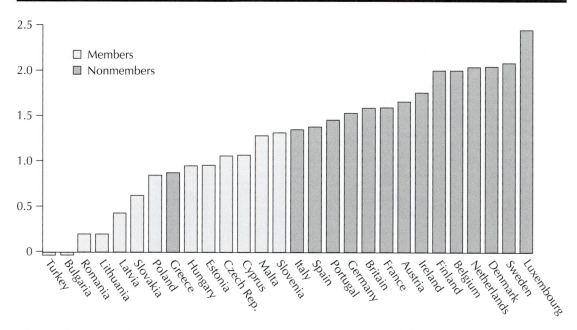

This graph estimates the readiness of "candidate countries" (at the beginning of 2001) to meet the official criteria for joining the EU, ranking them along with the fifteen then-existent members (Austria, Finland, and Sweden having joined in 1995).

FIGURE 13.2
Index of Suitability
to Join the EU

(52.2 percent), and Norway, in a vote that raised a new record for voter turnout, said "no" (by 52.3 percent).[34] Austria, Finland, and Sweden were admitted in 1995, bringing the total to 15. In 1999 the new European Central Bank began to function, and banks across Europe began carrying out all noncash transactions in euros and offering those customers who wanted them euro bank accounts.[35] As of January 1, 2002, euro currency and coins were being used in twelve of the fifteen member states (Great Britain, Sweden, and Denmark opted out but Sweden was expected to change its mind soon); by the end of the year it would no longer be possible to spend francs, lira, pesetas, schillings, escudos, drachmas, punts, marks, or any of the other old forms of cash in those twelve nations.[36]

The EU was also showing itself stronger and more united in other domains. The European Court of Justice, acting as an international court, an administrative court, a civil court, an administrative tribunal, and a transnational constitutional court, has steadfastly and successfully asserted the supremacy of EU law over national law.[37] After the terrorist attacks of

Europe's new currency, the euro, came into general usage January 1, 2002, replacing national currencies in twelve of the fifteen member states. Here a 10-euro note is being offered for a newspaper in Berlin.
© Reuters NewMedia Inc./CORBIS

September 11, 2001, on the United States, the EU proved itself able to move rapidly to respond, as its judicial and interior ministers quickly agreed to propose radical changes to European law enforcement, eliminating extradition procedures, setting up common definitions of what were "terrorist crimes," agreeing on length of prison terms, and enabling judges to issue arrest and search warrants that could be enforced across the continent.[38]

The road to unity is obviously not an easy one and there have been important setbacks, most noticeably in the inability of the members to agree on and pursue a single policy vis-à-vis the conflicts in former Yugoslavia and in the evidence of financial fraud practiced by some EU officials at very high levels.[39] Further institutional development is clearly necessary for the EU to meet the demands of greater accountability to its composite citizenry; there has even been talk of giving the Union a true constitution.[40]

But although the road is long and sometimes rocky, progress is clearly being made. Ignoring dire warnings from a cynical new world that the effort to combine social protection with economic progress and fiscal stability is hopelessly out of date in an era of unrestrained free-marketeering, the so-called Old World continues to build a yet newer world, a united Europe. It is true that as of the beginning of the new millennium, very few of the 373 million citizens of Europe thought of themselves as purely European. However, in every nation except Britain, about 50 percent told pollsters that although they were their own nationality first, they were "European second."[41]

■ **The African Union (formerly the Organization of African Unity).** The Organization of African Unity (OAU) was formed in 1963, when thirty-one heads of African states met in Addis Ababa, Ethiopia. There was little agreement at this first meeting as the dignitaries present argued among themselves about whether the new organization should immediately form a common market and work to establish some form of pan-African union, take a much more gradual approach toward the same ends, or focus primarily on lending "unconditional support" to the African peoples still under colonial rule. The last position ultimately prevailed, as eloquently stated by Algeria's president, Ahmed Ben Bella: "Let us all die a little, so that the peoples still under colonial domination may be free and African unity may not be a vain word." The OAU took this mission as its prime reason for existence.[42] By 1983, twenty more nations had gained independence—many of them significantly aided by efforts of OAU member states—and joined the organization; and by 2001 there were fifty-three member states in the OAU.

Although generally credited with rendering strong service to the cause of liberating the continent from overt political domination by former colonial powers (economic domination often persists), the OAU was not as effective in other domains as many would have wished. Among these is the problem of how to bring lasting peace to the continent. It established a Crisis Management Center that sent military observers to Rwanda, Burundi, and the Comoros, and made repeated efforts to broker peace between Eritrea and Ethiopia. At a Heads of State Summit in Algiers in 1999 it adopted a resolution "denouncing coups and barring from future summits any regime that comes to power by force of arms."[43] Most observers, however, believe the organization has not done enough in this regard: "The OAU has been missing in action in recent crises, in Sierra Leone, Liberia, Guinea, Ivory Coast, the Congo," says Peter Takirambudde.[44]

The OAU organized meetings on other problems of special import, often in conjunction with the United Nations.[45] One such meeting was the International Symposium on Refugees and Problems of Forced Population Displacements held in Addis Ababa, Ethiopia, in 1995. There are now approximately 7 million refugees in Africa, ten times the number twenty-five years ago. The OAU identified the root causes as including not only armed conflict and arms proliferation, but also natural disasters, the failures of governments, and poverty so severe that about two-thirds of Africa's population lives below the poverty line and thirty of the poorest countries in the world are on that continent.[46]

The problem, says Strobe Talbott, is that the OAU has always been "overburdened, overextended, undersupported, and underequipped."[47] It is therefore little wonder that the organization has found it difficult to meet its own past commitments in all domains. Yet many insist the organization could have done more in the nearly four decades of its existence. Africa has the poorest record of any region in the world in the fight against poverty, its AIDS crisis continues unabated, and serious electoral abuses have made true democracy impossible to achieve in many of its nations—these are problems, say the critics, on which the OAU could and should have tried to do more.[48] For some, the problem is that the OAU is just "a private club for friends," interested only in preserving the interests of African heads of state. Others say too much should not be expected of "an intergovernmental organization of the weakest states in the world."[49]

In any case, change is in the offing. In July 2001, at a final summit meeting held in Lusaka, Zambia, the OAU took the dramatic step of deciding to transform itself into the African Union, using the European Union as its model, and this was done in mid-2002. Its members plan to give themselves broader powers and press for "real political and economic integration" among Africa's fifty-three nations, creating a common parliament, a central bank and a court of justice, and a single currency.[50]

Meanwhile, most of the states belonging to the OAU have also pursued their goals through other bodies, such as the United Nations' Economic Commission for Africa (ECA) and several smaller regional associations. There are now more than thirty regional associations in Africa. Among the most important are the sixteen-member Economic Community of West African States (ECOWAS), focusing almost exclusively on economic ends, and the nine-member Southern African Development Coordination Conference (SADCC), still dedicated first and foremost to the independence of all African peoples (see Box 13.3).

■ **The Association of Southeast Asian Nations (ASEAN).** The Association of Southeast Asian Nations (ASEAN) was created in 1967 by Indonesia, Malaysia, the Philippines, Singapore, and Thailand in the hopes of removing serious tensions among themselves, reducing the influence of other states, and promoting their own socioeconomic development. Although the organization grew slowly at first, the reunification of Vietnam under Communist rule in 1975 and the subsequent invasion of Cambodia in 1978, spurred its development, and the new focus of the organization became re-

BOX 13.3
African Regional Associations[a]

African Development Bank
Central African States Development Bank
East African Development Bank
West African Development Bank
West African Economic and Monetary Union (WAEMU)
Economic Community of West African States (ECOWAS)
Economic Community of Central African States (ECCAS)
Mano River Union (MRU)
Council of the Entente States
Central African Economic and Monetary Community (CAEMC)
Economic Community of the Great Lakes Countries (CEPGL)
South African Development Community (SADC)
Inter-Governmental Authority on Drought and Development (IGADD)
South African Customs Union (SACU)

[a] List does not include Arab regional associations.

Source: Arthur S. Banks, ed., *Political Handbook of the World* (Binghamton, N.Y.: CSA Publications, 1987), pp. 747–54; *The World Factbook 1991* (Washington, D.C.: Central Intelligence Agency, 1991), p. 371.

sisting the further spread of Communist rule, in Cambodia and elsewhere in Southeast Asia. Such a cause enlisted international support; however, in 1991 the Paris Peace Agreement, signed by all members of the UN Security Council, achieved a resolution of the Cambodian issue, and the members of ASEAN became concerned that the end of the Cold War and the consequent lesser involvement of the United States in the area might leave them subject to domination by larger Asian powers such as Japan and China.[51] These anxieties were a stimulus to further expansion of their operations and greater efforts to increase their membership. The ASEAN Free Trade Area (AFTA) was established to lower intra–ASEAN tariff barriers and ASEAN members worked to be the dominant body within the larger (twenty-one-member) ASEAN Regional Forum (ARF) established in 1994. Since then, Vietnam, Burma (Myanmar), Laos, and Cambodia have been admitted, in that order.

In 1997, however, the rapidly growing economy of the region collapsed, beginning with the disastrous effort of Thailand's central bank to fight off speculators exploiting a downturn in the nation's economy by floating the country's currency. Almost overnight, other currencies failed and "what had been one of the world's most dynamic regions became dependent on billions of dollars in bailouts from the International Monetary Fund."[52]

One result of the crisis was to cause some members to challenge the organization's low-key and nonconfrontational decision-making process. Following traditional Asian practice, decisions are made by consensus, and where consensus cannot be reached, member states go their own ways, pursuing cooperation in other areas. Typically, meetings "have no formal agenda and approach sensitive security issues in an oblique and non-confrontational manner."[53] Such an approach allows the individual members to keep their options open while working as collectively as they can; however, after the 1997 debacle, some officials and analysts began to ask whether it might not have been a good idea to have intervened to stop Thailand's policy mistakes. Thailand itself and the Philippines have challenged the principle of "noninterference" with respect to instability and bloodshed in Burma (Myanmar), thereby provoking that government to label their statements "presumptuous."[54]

However, effective interference in each other's internal affairs is made difficult by the organization's lack of political integration—it has no supranational bodies comparable to the European Commission and the European Parliament and is not composed only of democracies. It does, however, now have a Secretary-General, who has a five-year term in which to "initiate, advise, coordinate, and implement ASEAN activities." Its highest decision-making organ is the Meeting of the ASEAN Head of State and Government; an ASEAN Summit is convened every year. Ministerial-level meetings are held on a variety of subjects, ranging from agriculture and forestry, to transnational crime, to tourism, and some 29 committees and 122 technical working groups have been formed to support these ministerial bodies.[55] Most of these are recent developments, suggesting that times are truly changing. Regional government may well be on the march in Southeast Asia.

■ **The North Atlantic Treaty Organization (NATO).** The North Atlantic Treaty Organization was founded in 1949 to include Belgium, Canada, Denmark, France, Iceland, Italy, Luxembourg, the Netherlands, Norway, Portugal, the United Kingdom, and the United States.[56] Greece and Turkey joined in 1952, Germany in 1955, Spain in 1982, and three former Warsaw Pact members—the Czech Republic, Hungary, and Poland—in 1999. Its purpose was first and foremost to form a defense alliance, in which all members promised to maintain the security of the North Atlantic area by coming to each other's aid. However, its members also promise, in Article 2, to pursue the "further development of peaceful and friendly international relations by strengthening their free institutions, by bringing about a better understanding of the principles upon which these institutions are founded, and by promoting conditions of stability and well-being."[57]

During the Cold War the primary focus of NATO was to contain the Soviet Union and assure U.S. commitment to the defense of Europe. But with the fall of communism a new Partnership for Peace was established, setting up closer relations than heretofore with a number of other former Warsaw

Pact members, former Soviet republics and neutral or nonaligned states: Albania, Armenia, Austria, Azerbaijan, Belarus, Bulgaria, Estonia, Finland, Georgia, Kazakhstan, Kyrgyzstan, Latvia, Lithuania, Macedonia, Moldova, Romania, Russia, Slovakia, Slovenia, Sweden, Switzerland, Tajikistan, Turkmenistan, Ukraine, and Uzbekistan. Most of these "Associates" are considered candidates for eventual membership.

Since the 1990s efforts have been made by the United States to reduce its participation in NATO and by European nations to take greater responsibility for their own defense, not necessarily through NATO. The EU has sought to give the Western European Union (WEU) a stronger role on defense matters for the European Union, and to develop an "extended European security order."[58] Some scholars have argued that NATO is not well suited to nonmilitary missions such as promoting democracy: Dan Reiter claims that "the EU is likely to be equally if not more effective than NATO at democratizing Eastern Europe, without the costs or the geopolitical risks incurred by enlarging the alliance."[59] Others expect NATO to continue to play an important role but agree it should strengthen its "European pillar."[60]

NATO did take a major role in 1999, waging the seventy-eight-day bombing war against Yugoslavia to guarantee the freedom of Kosovo. However, it was widely understood that it did so under very strong American leadership. Less than two years later the Bush administration argued strongly for reduced American participation in the Kosovo peacekeeping effort (where U.S. troops represented about 13 percent of the total).[61] And the following year the United States entered Afghanistan on its own, but brought its NATO allies, as well as other friendly nations, into an ad hoc defense alliance. Thus, at the very time that many speak of greatly enlarging NATO, others have been far less enthusiastic, and its strongest partner, the United States, has become less and less constrained by the other members, preferring either to control operations of the organization at limited cost to itself or to take action unilaterally, wherever it sees fit to do so, and with whatever partners. NATO is a regional organization in a time of tension and flux. What members it will have, what role it will play in international affairs, and how it will interact with other nations and institutions, are questions yet to be answered.

The United Nations

The men and women who drafted the United Nations charter were conscious of the need to recognize the continuing strength of nationalism and thereby avoid the fate of the League of Nations.[62] The new charter made it clear that no nation would be expected to commit its forces to a military action without internal deliberations and assent. It wished to avoid repeating what it believed had been another mistake of the League: granting all nations equal voting power. The UN Charter therefore gave the five major world powers at the time (the United States, the Soviet Union, China, Great Britain, and France) permanent membership in the organization's strongest "action body," the Security Council, and gave each the right of veto.[63]

The Charter, adopted in San Francisco in 1945 by fifty-one member states, is thus not a blueprint for a world state, nor is it intended to function as one. It is instead a set of rules governing an *international* organization, in which each nation's sovereignty is recognized and accepted. That organization was established to help preserve international peace and to foster international cooperation in addressing the social and economic problems that plague the human polity. To accomplish this mission, the UN has six governing organs and a wide range of committees, programs, and agencies (see Figure 13.3).

■ **The General Assembly.** All 189 member states of the United Nations are entitled to representation in the General Assembly. This body is "the main deliberative body," with the right to discuss and make recommendations on "any questions or any matters within the scope of the present Charter," to control the budget, and to elect members to the five other governing organs. It requires a two-thirds majority to decide on the most important matters, such as peace and security, admission of new members, and budgetary matters.

The work of the General Assembly is done by six "main" committees: First (Political and Security); Second (Economic and Financial); Third (Social, Humanitarian, and Cultural); Fourth (Special Political and Decolonization); Fifth (Administrative and Budgetary); and Sixth (Legal), as well as by many other specific committees addressing such issues as peacekeeping, crime prevention, and the status of women.[64]

Until 1970, the United States and its Western allies effectively controlled the General Assembly. When checked by Soviet vetoes in the Security Council, this bloc of nations could usually manage to have its way on major issues by going through the Assembly. For the next twenty years or so, however, power in the Assembly shifted away from the Western world, and decisions were often made by blocs and counterblocs of small, medium, and large states as the body moved from issue to issue. Then, with the end of the Cold War, power shifted again, in part back to a now more harmonious Security Council, in part to other subsidiary bodies. By 1996, according to one analysis, the General Assembly was no longer being consulted in constructive ways and its impact on policy decisions had seriously diminished.[65]

■ **The Security Council.** The official role of the Security Council is to maintain international peace and security. It functions continuously (a representative of each member state must be present at UN headquarters at all times). Besides its five permanent members (China, France, Russia, the United Kingdom, and the United States), the Security Council has ten members elected for nine-year terms according to rules that ensure geographic representativeness.

The composition of the Security Council is hard to defend logically today. As Richard Falk notes, "To retain permanent seats on the Security Council for both Great Britain and France, while denying such a presence to India and Brazil, or Japan and Germany, is to mock the current distribution of influence in world politics." But as Falk also mentions, it has so far proved impossible for the UN to agree on how to change the membership of this body.[66]

The Council has the right to discuss any situation that threatens international peace, to make recommendations for the resolution of disputes, to require members to apply sanctions against other states, and to make recommendations concerning the regulation of national armaments. It is the Council that sends peacekeeping forces to "help reduce tensions in troubled areas, keep opposing forces apart and create conditions of calm in which peaceful settlements may be sought," an action it has taken more than fifty times. It can suspend a member state against which such action is being taken (as it did in the case of Yugoslavia in 2000).[67]

The Council works through two standing committees and as many special ad hoc committees as it deems necessary. On substantive matters, all five permanent members plus four other member states must vote affirmatively—that is, each permanent member has the right to veto any proposal before the Council.[68]

■ **The Economic and Social Council.**   The function of the Economic and Social Council (ECOSOC) is to promote international cooperation in economic and social matters. The fifty-four members of this body are elected by the General Assembly for three-year terms and here, too, every effort must be made to ensure geographic representativeness. ECOSOC is assisted by a large number of functional and regional commissions, such as the Population Commission and the Western Asia Commission, and by a wide range of specialized agencies, such as the World Health Organization (WHO), the International Monetary Fund (IMF), the United Nations Educational, Scientific, and Cultural Organization (UNESCO), and the World Trade Organization (WTO), as indicated in Figure 13.3 (the IMF and WTO will be further discussed in Chapter 14). Over 1,500 nongovernmental organizations (NGOs) maintain consultative status with the Council.[69]

In recent years, beginning in 1992, the United States and other nations have worked to strengthen ECOSOC, giving it new responsibilities in economic, social, and related fields. This has improved the UN's ability to respond to humanitarian crises around the world. It was, for example, ECOSOC that established the UN program on HIV/AIDS in 1996, bringing

FIGURE 13.3 The United Nations System

International Court of Justice	Security Council	General Assembly

Military Staff Committee
Standing Committee and ad hoc bodies
International Criminal Tribunal for the Former Yugoslavia
International Criminal Tribunal for Rwanda
UN Monitoring, Verification and Inspection Commission (Iraq)
United Nations Compensation Commission
Peacekeeping Operations and Missions

Main committees
Other sessional committees
Standing committees and ad hoc bodies
Other subsidiary organs

Programs and Funds

UNCTAD
United Nations Conference on Trade and Development

  ITC
  International Trade Center (UNCTAD/WTO)

UNDCP
United Nations Drug Control Program

UNEP
United Nations Environment Program

UNHSP
United Nations Human Settlements Program (UN-Habitat)

UNDP
United Nations Development Program

  UNIFRM
  United Nations Development Fund for Women

  UNV
  United Nations Volunteers

UNFPA
United Nations Population Fund

UNHCR
Office of the United Nations High Commissioner for Refugees

UNICEF
United Nations Children's Fund

WFP
World Food Program

UNRWA*
United Nations Relief and Works Agency for Palestine Refugees in the Near East

Other UN Entities

OHCHR
Office of the United Nations High Commissioner for Human Rights

UNOPS
United Nations Office for Project Services

UNU
United Nations University

UNSSC
United Nations System Staff College

Research and Training Institutes

INSTRAW
International Research and Training Institute for the Advancement of Women

UNICRI
United Nations Interregional Crime and Justice Research Institute

UNITAR
United Nations Institute for Training and Research

UNRISD
United Nations Research Institute for Social Development

UNIDIR*
United Nations Institute for Disarmament Research

*Report only to the General Assembly.

Source: United Nations Department of Public Information, DPI/2079/add.l, 1/02. Reprinted by permission of the United Nations.

| Economic and Social Council | Trusteeship Council | Secretariat |

Functional Commissions
Commission for Social Development
Commission on Human Rights
Commission on Narcotic Drugs
Commission on Crime Prevention and Criminal Justice
Commission on Science and Technology for Development
Commission on Sustainable Development
Commission on the Status of Women
Commission on Population and Development
Statistical Commission

Regional Commissions
Economic Commission for Africa (ECA)
Economic Commission for Europe (ECE)
Economic Commission for Latin America and the Caribbean (ECLAC)
Economic and Social Commission for Asia and the Pacific (ESCAP)
Economic and Social Commission for Western Asia (ESCWA)

United Nations Forum on Forests

Sessional and Standing Committees
Expert, ad hoc and related bodies

Related Organizations

IAEA
International Atomic Energy Agency

WTO (trade)
World Trade Organization

WTO (tourism)
World Tourism Organization

CTBTO Preparatory Commission
Preparatory Commission for the Comprehensive Nuclear-Test-Ban-Treaty Organization

OPCW
Organization for the Prohibition of Chemical Weapons

Specialized Agencies
ILO
International Labour Organization
FAO
Food and Agriculture Organization of the United Nations
UNESCO
United Nations Educational, Scientific and Cultural Organization
WHO
World Health Organization
World Bank Group
IBRD International Bank for Reconstruction and Development
IDA International Development Association
IFC International Finance Corporation
MIGA Multilateral Investment Guarantee Agency
ICSID International Centre for Settlement of Investment Disputes
IMF
International Monetary Fund
ICAO
International Civil Aviation Organization
IMO
International Maritime Organization
ITU
International Telecommunication Union
UPU
Universal Postal Union
WMO
World Meteorological Organization
WIPO
World Intellectual Property Organization
IFAD
International Fund for Agricultural Development
UNIDO
United Nations Industrial Development Organization

Secretariat

OSG
Office of the Secretary-General
OIOS
Office of Internal Oversight Services
OLA
Office of Legal Affairs
DPA
Department of Political Affairs
DDA
Department for Disarmament Affairs
DPKO
Department of Peacekeeping Operations
OCHA
Office for the Coordination of Humanitarian Affairs
DESA
Department of Economic and Social Affairs
DGAACS
Department of General Assembly Affairs and Conference Services
DPI
Department of Public Information
DM
Department of Management
OIP
Office of the Iraq Programme
UNSECOORD
Office of the United Nations Security Coordinator
ODCCP
Office for Drug Control and Crime Prevention
UNOG
UN Office at Geneva
UNOV
UN Office at Vienna
UNON
UN Office at Nairobi

together the resources and expertise of the World Health Organization, UNICEF, UNDP, UNFPA, UNESCO, and the World Bank.[70]

■ **The Secretariat.**   The Secretariat is the bureaucratic apparatus of the United Nations. It is headed by the secretary-general, who is appointed by the General Assembly on the recommendation of the Security Council, for a five-year, renewable term, and is assisted by a worldwide staff of 8,600 persons drawn from 170 nations. These international civil servants take an oath "not to seek or receive instructions from any Government or outside authority." In addition to staffing UN headquarters in New York City, the Secretariat maintains important offices in Geneva, Vienna, and Nairobi.[71]

■ **The International Court of Justice.**   The fifteen judges of the International Court of Justice, all of whom are always from different nations, are elected by the General Assembly and the Security Council for nine-year terms and meet in The Hague, the Netherlands. The Court's job is "to settle in accordance with international law the legal disputes submitted to it by States, and to give advisory opinions on legal questions referred to it by duly authorized international organizations and agencies."[72] Only states (not individuals) may be parties in cases before the Court, and the Court has jurisdiction only over cases the members agree to refer to it.

The Court has sought to establish a reputation for fair and expert deliberation and thus to win compliance with its decisions, but has not been entirely successful in either respect (the United States has been among those nations choosing to comply with World Court rulings only when convenient). In making its decisions it is guided by international treaties and conventions in force, international custom, and the general principles of law.

The United Nations has also backed the creation of an International Criminal Court (ICC), intended to have jurisdiction over abuses resulting from international conflict, such as war crimes and crimes against humanity and genocide. The treaty proposing this body (the 1998 Rome Treaty on the International Criminal Court) has been signed by over 130 nations, including the United States, but only twenty-seven of the necessary sixty nations have actually ratified it.[73]

■ **The Trusteeship Council.**   The Trusteeship Council was established to assume the role formerly held by the League of Nations Mandate System after World War I. Eleven territories taken from Germany, Italy, and Japan after World War II (by no means all the world's colonies) were placed under its supervision, and this council was directed to promote their political, economic, social, and educational advancement while fostering "their progressive development toward self-government or independence." This body's work was completed with the admission of Palau to the UN in December 1994, at which time the Trusteeship Council suspended its activities.[74]

■ **Other UN Agencies and Programs.** As you can see in Figure 13.3, the "UN family" contains many other very important programs and agencies. The work of the UN Children's Fund (UNICEF), the UN Development Program (UNDP), the International Atomic Energy Agency (IAEA), the World Food Program (WFP), the Food and Agriculture Organization (FAO), the World Health Organization (WHO), the Office of the UN High Commissioner for Refugees (UNHCR), the Office of the UN High Commissioner for Human Rights, the International Labor Organization (ILO), and the UN Environment Program (UNEP) are among the agencies that, while they do not always gain as much attention as UN peacekeeping efforts, nonetheless make a major difference, working in a multitude of ways, to improve the conditions of life for all members of the human polity.

■ **How Successful Is the United Nations?** Any evaluation of the United Nations, as of most human labors, is likely to be based on the evaluator's hopes for it. Those who believed the United Nations would be a means of keeping perfect peace have been disappointed. Belligerent parties have often ignored its recommendations. Open acts of aggression have been condoned and even encouraged. The organization has never had an enforcement capability sufficient to serve as a genuine deterrent to aggression. It played almost no role in ameliorating or resolving the most serious conflict that has emerged since its birth, the Vietnam War. Its peacekeeping mission in the former Yugoslavia was widely ruled a failure. In other conflicts the UN has found itself enmeshed in situations it can neither leave nor resolve.

But by their very nature, peacekeeping (or, perhaps more accurately, peace-establishing) missions are risky, complicated, costly, and unsure and it is important to note that real successes have also been achieved. The UN has made key contributions to a number of arms control measures: the partial nuclear test ban treaty, the banning of nuclear weapons from outer space and the seabed, and the Nuclear Nonproliferation Treaty. The UN Observer Mission in El Salvador (ONUSAL) monitored a cease-fire and was involved in the entire restructuring of that nation's governing and socioeconomic structures at the end of its civil war. The UN Transitional Authority in Cambodia (UNTAC) supervised and verified the withdrawal of Vietnamese forces in 1992 and helped repatriate and resettle some 350,000 displaced Cambodians; it also eliminated millions of landmines, monitored human rights, and organized and supervised a national election in which 90 percent of the registered voters were able to take part. The UN has also monitored national elections in Nicaragua, Namibia, Liberia, and eastern Slovenia. Despite heavy American control, Operation Desert Storm, forcing Iraq to withdraw from Kuwait in 1991, was a UN operation. And in recent years the UN has taken on major new responsibilities for governing "postconflict societies" such as Kosovo and East Timor, as well as for resolving boundary issues, eliminating threatening weapons capabilities, prosecuting violations of international humanitarian law, and seeking compensation for victims of conflict.[75]

The United Nations has also disappointed those who had hoped it would do more to improve the world's economic and social conditions, especially in the global South. Part of the problem has been financial, not only in the sense of limited resources but in disagreement over how resources should be spent: "Poor states argue that needs should determine expenditure levels rather than the other way around. Major contributors, sensitive to the amounts asked of them and the purposes for the funds, are hesitant to pay for programs they oppose."[76] Even when there is agreement on what should be done, many are critical of the means employed and the limited success achieved. Take a look in your university's library under "United Nations" and note how many of the books and articles about the organization are catalogs of its failures, replete with recommendations (often conflicting, of course) for its improvement.

Yet here, too, accomplishments have often been impressive and there are those who recognize that in many respects the organization has "a distinguished and action-packed history."[77] The World Health Organization virtually eradicated smallpox by 1980. The UN Relief and Works Agency has helped millions of refugees. The UN Commission on the Status of Women, ECOSOC, the General Assembly, the UNHRC, and the UNDP Governing Council have all been active in working to improve the condition of women around the globe. The UN Human Rights Commission investigates situations in countries where human rights violations are believed to occur and other UN agencies are also active in this domain. Indeed, every agency listed in Figure 13.3 has important humanitarian and/or pragmatic accomplishments to its credit.

Furthermore, as important as its own contributions have been, the UN has also done a great deal in all these (and other) domains to raise the world's consciousness of problems otherwise often easy for the more comfortable nations of the global North to ignore. This has been particularly true in the area of human rights and the environment: The UN has organized or hosted numerous international conferences stimulating North-South rich-poor dialogue on such issues.

But although every nation in the world has benefited in one way or another from such activities, the United Nations has nevertheless been disappointing to many. The shifting terms of the global economy naturally produce confusion and anger, and sometimes that anger is directed against the

United Nations as well as against competing nations. Those who are negatively affected argue that the UN should broaden its interpretation of "unfair trade practices" and act to restrict practices in other nations that are making the old terms of trade impossible to maintain.[78] Others are simply ready and eager to make the most of the new opportunities and would like the UN to work in ways that are useful to them. Yet another group is concerned that the emerging global economy is creating a global underclass containing the less fortunate members of all our polities and believes that the UN must work against that development.

Meanwhile, despite its sometimes disappointing performance, the United Nations continues to win strong support across the globe. An important accolade came in 1988 when the body won the Nobel Prize for peace, and again in 2001 when its Secretary-General, Kofi A. Annan, was so honored. It may be something of an exaggeration to claim that there has always been "general agreement by [the] peoples of the world that the United Nations is the only hope for international peace and security and that it is an essential institution for the advancement of social and economic development," but that the UN is "truly a symbol and instrument for peace and human progress" seems difficult to deny.[79]

SUMMARY AND CONCLUSION

Efforts to achieve international harmony date back as far as recorded human history can tell. In ancient times the peacekeeping treaty between states was the preferred means. The four most common types of treaty are convention prevention, defense, trade, and geosocial and humanitarian. If we include the empire as an example, regional governments also date back far before the modern age.

Although one effort was made in the first half of the twentieth century to establish a worldwide organization capable of securing peace and promoting international development, World War II marks a clear watershed in the evolution of international relations. Understanding the dangers of a fascistic takeover, the victors established the United Nations, only to fall into Cold War hostility among themselves. The fall of communism and the rise of terrorism provoked further far-reaching changes.

The result has been a near-explosion in the number of treaties and regional organizations, and suborganizations of the UN itself, as we have sought ways to establish harmony and alleviate suffering in an ever more complex and ever more rapidly changing global polity. The European Union, the African Union, ASEAN, and NATO have been among the most important new regional organizations, and the UN's six main governing bodies have gained in significance (excepting the now-suspended Trusteeship Council), as have an ever-proliferating number of subagencies and associated organizations. We are now bound to one another in an interconnecting web of economic, cultural, and defensive agreements and organizations.

Despite all our work, however, wars continue to erupt, populations are decimated by famine and conflict, human rights are still widely abused, and the planet cries out for succor from our selfish and short-sighted exploitation of its riches. Will we ever really be able to put our shared home in order?

Yet when we are tempted to despair, it may help us to remember that we have only been working on the task of settled, social civilization for 5,000 years. If anthropologists are correct that our species took its present form about 120,000 years ago, then it took us 115,000 years (give or take a millennium) just to get to that point and our accomplishments in the past 5,000 years do not seem so paltry.

Still, however rapid our recent progress has been when viewed metahistorically, we may not have a great deal of time left. Given the success of the perverse efforts we have made to develop the means of destroying ourselves altogether, it is possible that the advances we have made in the last 5,000 years may prove to be too little, too late. Then again, the very magnitude of the dangers we face may force us not only to save ourselves but also to create a stable and harmonious international order while we are at it.

QUESTIONS TO CONSIDER

1. What three methods did nations use to try to improve international relations prior to World War II? Can you give one example of each?
2. What changes during and in the fifty years after World War II affected the nature of international relations, and how?
3. Do you think the changes that have been taking place are leading to a better world? A worse one? Or just a very different one?
4. How would you evaluate the work of the United Nations so far? Why?

SELECTED READINGS

Aust, Anthony. *Modern Treaty Law and Practice* (New York: Cambridge University Press, 2000). A comprehensive treatment of the law of treaties, with examples of practical problems as well as legal disputes that arise in their implementation. Describes the treaty-making and treaty-using processes from the point of view of a practitioner with 30 years of experience.

Bass, Gary Jonathan. *Stay the Hand of Vengeance: The Politics of War Crimes Tribunals* (Princeton, N.J.: Princeton University Press, 2000). Exploring particular cases such as the prosecution of the Armenian genocide and of war crimes in Bosnia, the author examines the politics behind international war crimes tribunals, including how leaders from David Lloyd George to Bill Clinton have wrestled with the moral dilemmas such tribunals pose.

Diehl, Paul Francis. *International Peacekeeping* (Baltimore, Md.: Johns Hopkins University Press, 1993). Provides a historical background to international peacekeeping and examines recent peacekeeping operations to determine the elements necessary for success.

Goldman, Kjell, Ulf Hannerz, and Charles Westin, eds. *Nationalism and Internationalism in the Post-Cold War Era* (London and New York: Routledge, 2000). Anthropologists, political scientists, sociologists, philosophers, and historians consider what the term "post–Cold War" really implies, including changes in the world market economy and the strengthening of regional units.

Kaplan, Robert D. *The Coming Anarchy: Shattering the Dreams of the Post Cold War* (New York: Random House, 2000). An unflinching look at the disappointments and tragedies of the post-Communist world, including environmental degradation, the spread of famine and disease, violent wars of "fierce tribalism and trenchant regional-

ism," growing crime, and ever greater political apathy in the world's most advanced democracies.

Lundestad, Geir and Odd Arne Westad. *Beyond the Cold War: New Dimensions in International Relations* (Oxford: Oxford University Press, 1993). A collection of writings on the future of world politics.

Schabas, William A. *An Introduction to the International Criminal Court* (New York: Cambridge University Press, 2001). Reviews the history of international criminal prosecution, the drafting of the Rome Statute of the International Criminal Court, and the principles of its operation, including the scope of its jurisdiction and its procedures.

Schiavone, Giuseppe. *International Organizations: A Dictionary and Directory* (New York: St. Martin's Press, 1993). Provides profiles of over 200 international organizations.

Ulph, Alistair, ed. *Environmental Policy, International Agreements and International Trade* (New York: Oxford University Press, 2001). Explores the role of international trade agreements in developing environmental policy. Considers how to design policies and institutions for the solution of transfrontier environmental problems and issues of industrial location and trade.

WEB SITES OF INTEREST

1. United Nations
   http://www.un.org/
   Reporting on the work of the UN and its more than 30 affiliated organizations, this site is a compendium of information on the work being done internationally to promote respect for human rights, expand food production, stabilize financial markets, protect the environment, fight disease, foster development, reduce poverty, improve

the safety and efficiency of transportation, improve telecommunications, and fight drug trafficking and terrorism.

2. United Nations Treaty Collection
   http://untreaty.un.org/
   Prepared and updated regularly by the Treaty Section of the Office of Legal Affairs of the UN; offers access to over 40,000 treaties and international agreements.

NOTES

1. See, for example, the comments of Robert Kaplan in Robert Wright and Robert Kaplan, "Debate: Mr. Order Meets Mr. Chaos," *Foreign Policy* no. 124 (May–June 2001): 50–60.

2. J. A. Thompson, *The Ancient Near Eastern Treaties and the Old Testament* (London: Tyndale Press, 1963), pp. 9, 11.

3. Ousmane Poreko, "Evolution sociale chez les

peuls du Fouta-Djalon," *Etudes Guinéennes, Les Recherches Africaines* 4 (Oct.–Dec. 1961): 78.

4. Samuel Williamson Jr. "World War I," in Joel Krieger et al., ed., *The Oxford Companion to Politics of the World*, 2nd ed. (Oxford and New York: Oxford University Press, 2001), p. 928.

5. "Vladimir Petrovsky: The Spirit of Locarno Is Cause for Hope for Multi-Lateral Diplomacy," United Nations Press Release, 16 March 2001. http://www.unog.ch/UNOG01/Files/PDF/Press Release/Dg0108e.pdf.

6. Charles W. Kegley Jr. and Eugene R. Wittkopf, *World Politics: Trend and Transformation*, 6th ed. (New York: St. Martin's Press, 1997), p. 75.

7. David Lazer, "The Free Trade Epidemic of the 1860s and Other Outbreaks of Economic Discrimination," *World Politics* 51, no. 4 (July 1999): 447–83.

8. Hugh D. Baker, "Hong Kong: A View from Both Sides," *Asian Affairs* 26 (February 1995): 10–19.

9. Michael Jabara Carley, "Episodes from the Early Cold War: Franco-Soviet Relations, 1917–1927," *Europe-Asia Studies* 52, no. 7 (2000): 1275–1305.

10. David N. Farnsworth, *International Relations*, 2nd ed. (Chicago: Nelson Hall, 1992), p. 80.

11. Bruce Russett and Harvey Starr, *World Politics: The Menu for Choice* (New York: W. H. Freeman, 1992), p. 92. See pp. 91–100 for a discussion of alliance tactics and strategy.

12. *League of Nations Convention to Suppress the Slave Trade and Slavery September 26, 1925*, 2 Jan. 2002. http://www.yale.edu/lawweb/avalon/league/lea001.htm.

13. Peter H. Sand, "Whither CITES? The Evolution of a Treaty Regime in the Borderland of Trade and Environment," *European Journal of International Law* 8, no. 1 (1997): 19–58.

14. Seyom Brown, *New Forces, Old Forces and the Future of World Politics* (New York: Harper-Collins, 1995), p. 20. Brown does not call these polities regional governments; he says they were "universal empires," not because they ruled the planet but because they were worlds unto themselves, "single and essentially contained." But they extended their sway only over certain areas, and so were in fact regional governments.

15. "Commonwealth Origins," *British Politics* (4 Jan. 2002); see also *The World Factbook 2001* (Washington D.C.: Central Intelligence Agency, 2001). After World War II Britain expanded the Commonwealth to include most of its former colonies; in 1961 it expelled South Africa for its policy of apartheid. The Commonwealth endures to this day: In 1997 it adopted a set of economic principles focusing on promoting economic growth while protecting smaller member states from the negative effects of globalization.

16. Joan Edelman Spero, *The Politics of International Economic Relations*, 4th ed. (New York: St. Martin's Press, 1990).

17. Gerard J. Mangone, *The Idea and Practice of World Government* (New York: Columbia University Press, 1951), pp. 3–9. See also the selections in Chapter 34, "The World Society Approach" in Evan Luard, *Basic Texts in International Relations* (New York: St. Martin's Press, 1993).

18. Kalevi J. Holsti, "League of Nations," in Krieger, *The Oxford Companion to Politics of the World*, pp. 491–92.

19. For a useful summary, see Geir Lundestad, *East, West, North, South: Major Developments in International Politics 1945–1990*, trans. Gail Adams Kvam (Oslo: Norwegian University Press, 1991).

20. Frederic S. Pearson and J. Martin Rochester, *International Relations: The Global Condition in the Twenty-First Century*, 4th ed. (New York: McGraw-Hill, 1998), p. 67.

21. See the introduction to Hans-Henrik Holm and Georg Sørenson, eds., *Whose World Order?* (Boulder, Colo.: Westview, 1995) for a thoughtful consideration of the magnitude of the changes.

22. For one example out of many of works focusing on the prospect of true global governance, see Meghnad Desai, "Global Governance," in Meghnad Desai and Paul Redfern, eds., *Global Governance: Ethics and Economics of the World Order* (London and New York: Pinter, 1995), pp. 6–21.

23. *United Nations Treaty Collection: Treaty Reference Guide* (New York: United Nations, 1999).

24. For a summary of the first Strategic Arms Limitation Treaties (SALT) see Hoyt Purvis, *Interdependence: An Introduction to International Rela-*

tions (Fort Worth: Harcourt Brace Jovanovich College Publishers, 1992), pp. 148–49.

25. "Bush Offers Arms Talks to China as U.S. Pulls Out of ABM Treaty," *New York Times,* 14 Dec. 2001.

26. For relevant articles on Iraq's continuing military power after the war, see *International Herald Tribune,* 30 June 1991, B1; and *New York Times,* 16 April 1992, A3, A20.

27. Raymond L. Garthoff, "Warsaw Treaty Organization," in Krieger, *The Oxford Companion to Politics of the World,* pp. 900–901. Although usually referred to as the "Warsaw Pact," the organization created pursuant to the treaty was in fact the Warsaw Treaty Organization.

28. Andreas Falke and Hung Q. Tran, "NAFTA and the European Union: Two Important Economic Regions with a Solid Basis for Cooperation," *Deutschland* (Oct. 1994): 18–21; John Ross, "Mexico: Historic Turning Point," *Global Exchanges* (Summer 1994): 1–6. NAFTA is an example of how an important treaty can lead to the development of a regional organization, and then to other treaties with the prospect of other organizations.

29. "Fox and Bush, for Richer, for Poorer," *The Economist* (3 Feb. 2001): 37–38; Ginger Thompson, "Chasing Mexico's Dream into Squalor," *New York Times,* 11 Feb. 2001, 1, 6.

30. Robin R. Churchill and Geir Ulfstein, "Autonomous Institutional Arrangements in Multilateral Environmental Agreements," *American Journal of International Law* 94, no. 4 (Oct. 2000): 623–59.

31. Pearson and Rochester, op. cit., pp. 356–57.

32. *The Economist* (14–20 Dec. 1991): 51–54, and (29 Jan. 1991): 64; *Le Monde,* 8 Feb. 1992, 1, 6, 8, 9.

33. *Le Monde,* 16 June 1992, 7.

34. Pertti Pesonen, "Three Nordic Referenda on EU Membership," *Scandinavian Review* 82, no. 3 (Winter 1994): 4–11.

35. Edmund L. Andrews, "11 Countries Tie Europe Together in One Currency," *New York Times,* 1 Jan. 1999, A1, A8.

36. Edmund L. Andrews, "A Smooth Debut Lifts Euro's Value in Money Markets," *New York Times,* 3 Jan. 2002, A1, A18.

37. Peter de Cruz, *Comparative Law in a Changing World* (London: Cavendish Publishing, 1999), pp. 168–69.

38. Donald McNeil, "Europe Moves to Toughen Laws to Fight Terrorism," *New York Times,* 20 Sept. 2001, A11. Final adoption would take several more steps, but the speed with which these key EU officials reached agreement, just ten days after the attack, was impressive.

39. Ian Budge, et al., *The Politics of the New Europe* (London and New York: Addison-Wesley-Longman, 1997), pp. 49–50, and John Peterson, "The European Union: Pooled Sovereignty, Divided Accountability," *Political Studies* XLV (1997): 559–78.

40. "Our Constitution for Europe," *The Economist* (28 Oct. 2000): 21–22, 27–28.

41. "More-or-Less European Union," *The Economist* (26 Aug. 1995): 46. One analyst pointed out that Europeans are after all accustomed to a sense of dual nationalism (for example, the Welsh who are British, the Bretons who are French, and the Basques who are Spanish) and that it may be easier for them than it might be for others to accept the idea of divided loyalty and divided sovereignty.

42. Seth Kitange, "Towards a Pan-African Community," *Africa News* 20, no. 13 (28 March 1983): 5.

43. Strobe Talbott, "The Crisis in Africa: Local War and Regional Peace," *World Policy Journal* 17, no. 2 (Summer 2000): 21–25.

44. Takirambudde, the Uganda executive director of the Africa division of the Human Rights Watch, is quoted in Noramitsu Onishi, "African Bloc Hoping to Do Better as the 'African Union'," *New York Times,* 12 July 2001, A3.

45. The terms of association between the OAU and the UN were formalized in UN Resolution 48/25 in November 1993. See Department of Public Information of the United Nations, "Cooperation Between OAU and the UN System," *Yearbook of the United Nations 1993,* vol. 47 (Dordrecht, the Netherlands: Martinus Nijhoff, 1993), pp. 304–6.

46. Peter Tran, "The OAU/UNHCR International Symposium: Refugees and Problems of Forced Population Displacements in Africa," *Migra-*

tion World Magazine 23, nos. 1–2 (Jan.–April 1995): 23–27.

47. Talbott, op. cit.

48. Tran, op. cit., cites the World Bank's pessimistic view of African poverty: "the only region in the world likely to experience an increase in absolute poverty."

49. Comments by interviewees quoted in Onishi, op. cit.

50. Ibid.

51. Shaun Narine, "Institutional Theory and Southeast Asia: The Case of ASEAN," *World Affairs* 161, no. 1 (Summer 1998): 33–47.

52. Peter Eng, "Transforming ASEAN," *Washington Quarterly* 22, no. 1 (Winter 1999): 49–65.

53. This language was used in a 1995 "Concept Paper," laying out broad guidelines for ARF meetings. Narine, op. cit.

54. Eng, op. cit.

55. *Association of Southeast Asian Nations: An Overview,* ASEAN, 31 Dec. 2001. http://www .aseansec.org / view.asp?file = / history / overview .htm.

56. France withdrew from the alliance's integrated military command structure in 1966 but is still a member of NATO and a full participant in the North Atlantic Council.

57. Paul R. Viotti, "North Atlantic Treaty Organization," in Krieger, *The Oxford Companion to Politics of the World,* pp. 605–7.

58. Martin A. Smith and Graham Timmins, "The EU, NATO, and the Extension of Institutional Order in Europe," *World Affairs* 163, no. 2 (Fall 2000): 80–89.

59. Dan Reiter, "Why NATO Enlargement Does Not Spread Democracy," *International Security* 25, no. 4 (Spring 2001): 41–67.

60. John Gerard Ruggie, *Constructing the World Polity: Essays on International Institutionalization* (New York: Routledge, 1998). See especially Chapter 9, "NATO and the Transatlantic Security Community."

61. Steven Erlanger and Michael R. Gordon, "Allied Aides Say U.S. Kosovo Role Is Still Crucial," *New York Times,* 16 Jan. 2001, A1, A10.

62. In fact, the League's language calling for collective action against aggressor states was extremely

vague and required near unanimity among the members. As a result, the clauses were seldom invoked, and never successfully in any major conflict.

63. Charles W. Kegley Jr. and Eugene R. Wittkopf, *World Politics: Trend and Transformation,* 6th ed. (New York: St. Martin's Press, 1997).

64. *Background Notes: United Nations* (Washington, D.C.: Bureau of International Organization Affairs, U.S. Department of State, July 2000).

65. *The United Nations and the Twenty-First Century: The Imperative for Change: Report of the Thirty-First United Nations of the Next Decade Conference* (Muscatine, Iowa: The Stanley Foundation, 1996), p. 31.

66. Richard Falk, "World Prisms: The Future of Sovereign States and International Order," *Harvard International Review* 21, no. 3 (Summer 1999): 30–35.

67. *Basic Facts About the United Nations* (New York: Department of Public Information, United Nations, 2000).

68. The ten nonpermanent members of the Security Council must include five members from Africa and Asia, one from Eastern Europe, two from Latin America, and two from Western Europe and other areas.

69. *Basic Facts,* op. cit.

70. *Background Notes,* op. cit.

71. *Basic Facts,* op. cit.

72. *Basic Facts,* op. cit. The five other organs and sixteen specialized UN agencies are the only bodies at present authorized to seek such opinions; the Court has issued twenty-four since 1946, taking up such questions as reparation for injuries suffered in the service of the United Nations, the territorial status of southwest Africa (Namibia) and western Sahara, and the legality of the threat or use of nuclear weapons.

73. Steven Lee Myers, "U.S. Signs Treaty for World Court to Try Atrocities," *New York Times,* 1 Jan. 2001, A1, A6.

74. *Background Notes,* op. cit.

75. Michael J. Matheson, "United Nations Governance of Postconflict Societies," *American Journal of International Law* 95, no. 1 (Jan. 2001): 76–85.

76. Kegley and Wittkopf, op. cit.

77. Stanley Meisler, *United Nations: The First Fifty Years* (New York: Atlantic Monthly Press, 1997).

78. Jagdish N. Bhagwati, *The World Trading System at Risk* (Worcester, U.K.: Harvester Wheatsheaf, Simon & Schuster, 1991), p. 20.

79. Fred Babi, Gerhard Haensel, and F. Lwanyantika Masha, "Public Opinion in the World About the United Nations," *Review of International Affairs* 42 (10 May 1991): 12–15.

CHAPTER 14

Political and Economic Globalization

534

Prague is the capital of the Czech Republic, the larger and more western part of what used to be Czechoslovakia, in central Europe. It is a very old city that has weathered many crises, and many battles. A great old castle looms on a hilltop on its western edge, and the river Vltava runs through it. On the eastern side of the river is the Old Town, and further east yet is the New Town. Franz Kafka, whose novel *The Castle* tells far more about the negative aspects of modern bureaucracies than you found in Chapter 9, lived in Prague—you can go there and visit his tiny house, just below the castle. And when you roam around the city, you will see some of the world's most dazzling examples of every form of architecture: Roman, Gothic, Baroque, Rococo, Neoclassical, Art Nouveau, Modernist, and contemporary.

But if you drop your eyes down from the castle heights, and down too from the turrets, towers, and spires of the bridges, churches, and other wondrous buildings, what you will see in Prague today is: A hot dog stand. A young man selling toys. A shop selling souvenirs. A tour guide inviting you for a boat ride on the river. And yourself, the traveling student, multiplied a thousand thousand times. Prague is open to the world, and the world has discovered Prague—again. Capitalist enterprise runs rampant in its streets and up the sides of neon-lighted hotels. The city is alive, the money flows, the times are good.

Or thus it appears in the center of Prague. The rest of the Czech Republic does not look quite the same. As your train chugs in from the west, you are immediately struck by how utterly decrepit the rail yards are, and although the countryside is green and beautiful, the small towns you wind through on your way do not look much better. The people you see seem poor, but you notice they do not look sad or oppressed, just matter-of-fact as they go about their lives. Later someone may tell you, as someone did me, "Regimes come and go; the Czech peasant knows how to take it all in stride."

Regimes come and go, but never in the history of the human polity, not even in the times of the Roman Empire, have so many been guided so strongly by a single force. That force is globalization. And what is being globalized is Western-style democratic capitalism.

For many authors globalization simply means growing economic interdependence among nations. However, the spread of democracy—or quasi democracy—is an important element in the current era of globalization, and so is the spread of Western values and culture. Furthermore, it is very clear that all of these are linked, that the forces of globalization are themselves interdependent. Hence here we define globalization as: *growing social, political, and economic interdependence and resemblance among the nations of the world*. Note the word *growing*, please: Globalization is an ongoing phenomenon, not something that has been completed, far from it, and not something that is inevitably going to be completed in the future. This is particularly true when we speak of "resemblance"—although the (often partial and tentative) shift to democracy and the widening influence of Western culture are important aspects of globalization, it would be very wrong not to recognize that for the present the differences among the nations of the world are still far more striking than their similarities in all three domains.[1]

As do most others offering definitions, we deliberately leave out the question of agency; although certain institutions can be identified as very strong players indeed in the process of economic globalization (we will discuss them in some detail below), in fact *all* of us are taking part in the globalization now going on. Even those who do not approve and protest in one way or another against it, and even those who lead lives seemingly remote from the forces at work, are helping to shape the new world of nations. Naming all the agents of globalization, and saying exactly *how* responsible they are, is impossible at present; future historians may be able to be more precise.

In any event, this era of globalization is an era of massive change. It is deeply affecting our social life and our political life, as well as our economic life. Societies are shifting, from communism to democracy and capitalism, but also from single-party authoritarianism to multiparty democracy and capitalism, and sometimes just from single-party authoritarianism to multiparty authoritarianism in polities where capitalism has long prevailed. And accompanying these political and economic transitions are vast cultural changes.

In this final chapter our purpose is to investigate two of these three changes, emphasizing first the political—is the shift to democratic politics really happening? Then we add in the economic, considering three different combinations of politico-economic changes, three kinds of transition. Next we look more closely than we have before at four major international institutions facilitating (some would say forcing) these transitions: the IMF, the World Bank, the World Trade Organization, and G-7 (now G-8). Our final section explores the impact of economic globalization on nations, both those that are less and those that are more developed, and considers the various proposals for reform now being made.

PROSPECTS FOR GLOBAL DEMOCRACY

The most striking characteristic of contemporary change is the fall of communism in state after state and the establishment of capitalism. The second most widespread change is the transformation of non-Communist but nonetheless authoritarian states into multiparty political systems, making them at least quasi-democratic. More than thirty nations began the move to democracy between 1974 and 1990.[2] There are now more than one hundred nations with competitive elections in which at least some civil and political

Joining democracy? Here Russian Prime Minister Vladimir Putin joins the G-7 (making them G-8) in Okinawa on July 21, 2000. But just how democratic the new Russia really is remains open to question.
© Fujifotos/The Image Works

rights are protected.[3] This is, therefore, a time of massive *political* change and the direction of the change is toward democracy.

But shifting to democracy cannot be done merely by deciding to do so. Many questions about democracy have never been fully resolved. What, after all, is a democracy? What can we count on a democracy to do? Can a democracy be established anywhere, given the determination to do so, or are there essential preconditions? What roles must be played by elites to make the effort a success? Is there anything outsiders can do to help? Once everything is set in motion, will the process be unstoppable, or will some of the new democracies falter and fail, littering the global landscape like half-finished homes planned by overly ambitious and underfinanced developers?

These important questions are being posed with ever greater urgency by political scientists and other scholars watching this era's events unfold. A brief look at some of the answers they offer will help shape and sharpen our investigation.

What Is a Democracy?

As our earlier discussions have presumably made clear, democracy is a political system, not an economic one. Although often present together, democracy and capitalism are far from synonymous, and indeed some scholars argue that the latter necessarily limits the possibility of fully achieving the former. In any case, the literal meaning of democracy is simply "rule by the people." In contemporary practice, it is often assumed that the way people rule is by voting in "free" elections—that is, under conditions of universal suffrage, adult citizens are free to vote in elections with a secret ballot and more than one political party in the competition. A typical definition reflecting this certainty that free elections are all but synonymous with democracy is the one offered by Philippe Schmitter and Terry Lynn Karl: "Modern political democracy is a system of governance in which rulers are held accountable for their actions in the public realm by citizens, acting indirectly through the competition and cooperation of their elected representatives."[4]

Other authors have been much more demanding. In addition to free elections, Robert Dahl lists effective participation, control of agenda, and enlightened understanding as necessary criteria.[5] Peter Merkl agrees that parties and elections are "common structural attributes and criteria" of democracy, but adds civil, political, and social rights: Citizens in democracies have the right to petition government, to exercise free speech (including access to a free press), and to assemble and organize for democratic political purposes.[6] George Munda Carew, focusing on regime changes in the multiethnic political communities of Africa, points out that free elections are not sufficient to prevent unfair treatment of minorities; a true democracy must also respect "the fairness principle" and function within a "culture of solidarity, fellow feeling and fair play."[7]

What Can We Count on a Democracy to Do?

Even when a regime meets the more difficult criteria set for democracy, we should not expect heaven on earth. Overall, the physical quality of life is clearly better in democracies (see Figure 14.1), but many have argued that the quality of life permits the establishment of democracy, not vice versa. Democracy does not guarantee social or economic equality, nor even a decent standard of living for all. It does not eliminate immorality or corruption: "Democratic politics involves, almost always, lots of unsavory characters, people whose views one finds unattractive, even antidemocratic, certainly unpalatable."[8] There is no solid evidence that democracies are more efficient economically or administratively than other forms of government, nor are they likely to "appear more orderly, consensual, stable or governable than

FIGURE 14.1
Patterns of
Democratization
and the Physical
Quality of Life

Patterns of Democratization	Scores of the Physical Quality of Life Index 0 10 20 30 40 50 60 70 80 90 100	Number of Countries
Consistently nondemocratic		10
Inconsistently nondemocratic		59
Inconsistently democratic		23
Consistently democratic		23

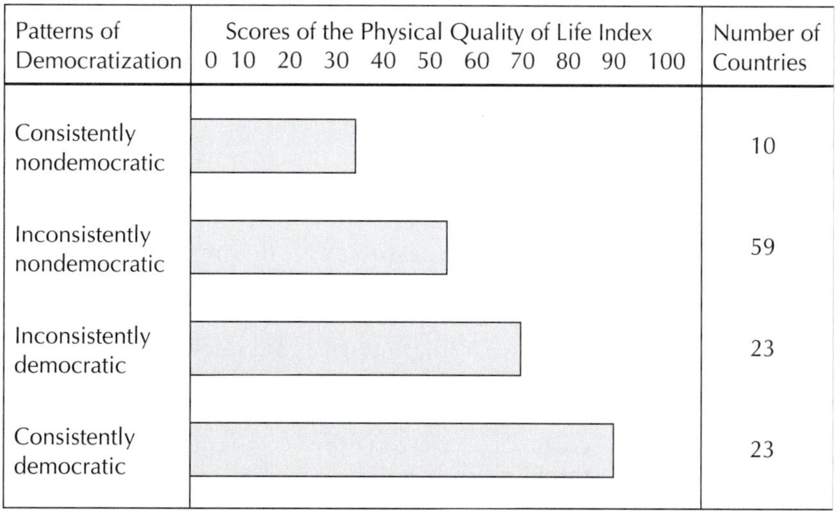

Source: Doh Chull Shin, "Political Democracy and the Quality of Citizens' Lives: A Cross-National Study," *Journal of Developing Societies* 5 (January–April 1989): p. 37. Leiden, The Netherlands: E. J. Brill, 1989. Reprinted by permission.

the autocracies they replace."[9] Ensuring freedom of choice does not ensure its exercise; democratic government is not enough to protect us from the pressures of social conformism.

Democracy does, however, have two indisputable advantages over other forms of government. First, the idea of democracy is appealing; it is highly satisfactory to believe we are able to participate in creating and running our own government.[10] Second, and more substantively important, democracy provides a more peaceful way of processing conflict and effecting change than can be found in other systems: "Democracies have the capacity to modify their rules and institutions consensually in response to changing circumstances"—when we are on the losing side, the processes of democracy help us to "lose peacefully."[11] Stable democracies are considerably less prone to civil conflict than are societies in political transition, and somewhat less so than harshly authoritarian states where civil peace is kept by the harsh exercise of force: "the most reliable path to stable domestic peace in the long run is to democratize as much as possible."[12] The contribution democratic processes make to the peaceful adjudication of disputes carries over into the international arena; although democracies go to war, they rarely fight each other: one author goes so far as to assert that since 1816 "no democracy has fought another democracy."[13]

Are There Preconditions for Establishing a Democracy?

There is now a widespread conviction that all nations should adopt the democratic model. Is this a realistic hope? Can any nation become democratic "if it tries?" Or must certain conditions be in place before democracy can flourish? Georg Sørensen finds that four sets of preconditions have been posited by different authors—and that none of them holds absolutely true. Some have associated the development of democracy with modernization and wealth, others argue for the importance of having a political culture that emphasizes egalitarianism and tolerance, still others think a strong middle class is an essential precondition, and a final argument is that external factors (such as the amount of aid received or the extent of foreign control over a nation's economy) will inevitably play a powerful role in determining whether or not democracy is possible. Sørensen finds exceptions for every claim: "For every factor seen as conducive to democracy, counterexamples can be put forward" and reminds us as well that "in many countries, different preconditions may exist that point in different directions." [14] According to Doh Chull Shin, most scholars now recognize that "no single factor is sufficient or necessary [and that] the emergence of democracy in a country is the result of a combination of causes." [15]

The Role of Elites in Establishing Democracy

The readiness to acknowledge that the birth of each new democracy may be the result of a different combination of factors has also permitted scholars to give more attention to the important role often played by specific actors—or kinds of actors—in the process. Although those who struggle to establish democracy are usually eager to attack the power and privileges of dominant groups, we should not, Laurence Whitehead reminds us, "just single out the heroic strain in democratic leadership. There are also late converts, accidental leaders, and figures who arouse expectations that they are entirely unsuited to fill." [16] Furthermore, even members of an existing authoritarian elite sometimes see democracy as a means for taking power away from the more dominant members of their own group. Indeed, a number of "transitologists" believe that most of the transitions to democracy in recent years have been set up as a result of negotiations with dominant elites in the former regime. [17] This in turn provokes a further question: If the pay-off to such elites is too great, and permits them to stay in power, how genuine is the new democracy?

What Can Outsiders Do to Help?

Is there a role for those who live and work in established democracies to play in helping other nations make this kind of regime change? The experts are, on the whole, dubious. Charles Tilly wonders if trying to promote democracy is not like trying to change the weather: "We can more or less understand the weather and its wide variation in different times and places, perhaps even affect it in small ways. However . . . no one seriously talks about promoting good weather." He believes external efforts are likely to have a chance of success when they take the specific circumstances of a particular system into consideration and are coordinated with internal activities working toward the same end. But he adds that it might be useful to have a "rapid strike force" capable of intervening to facilitate democratic change whenever an authoritarian system enters into a period of crisis.[18] Sidney Verba is equally cautious: "We do not know how to manage change, we do not know how in any precise way to create democracy out of nondemocracy . . . we can provide support, but whatever grows probably has to grow uncontrolled and grow outside our control in ways that are sometimes negative . . . I suppose what we do is to help and to hope for the best."[19]

Is Democracy Unstoppable Once Begun?

Here the answer from the scholars is unambiguous: no. They soberly remind us that the consolidation of democracy is a long and difficult business. To John Higley and Richard Gunther, consolidation means elite consensus on procedures plus extensive mass participation in elections; Juan Linz says it means that none of the major actors thinks there is any alternative to the democratic process as a way to gain power; and to Guy Hermet it means that a society can "no longer imagine any other possible regime."[20] In any case, no one thinks consolidation happens easily. Doh Chull Shin finds that the presently democratizing nations "tend to lack many factors that facilitate the process of democratization"; it is "uncertain," he says, "whether these democracies will continue to consolidate or whether they will regress into authoritarian rule."[21] Georg Sørensen is also pessimistic about the chances for what he calls "democratic deepening." He worries that the negotiations made with preexisting elites have made the new democracies "frail and unconsolidated and plagued by acute social and economic problems"; he allows a few exceptions (South Korea, Taiwan) but concludes that "the odds seem to weigh heavily against the further development and consolidation of the frail democratic openings that have taken place in recent years."[22]

Will the passionate striving of the human spirit for the right to control its own destiny overcome the dire foreboding of the experts? Will the economic gains possible when governments (and the massive resources they control, either directly or by the impact of the laws they write and enforce) change hands regularly be sufficient to motivate elites to continue the struggle to install this system of governance? Will international businesses provide the motive power, in their eagerness to foster the worldwide establishment of a kind of regime that is basically stable and thoroughly familiar? It is certainly too soon to know which, if any, of these forces may give the lie to our pessimistic pundits. But while we wait to find out, we can take a closer look at some of the actual transitions that have been taking place, and their impact on us all.

KINDS OF TRANSITIONS

As we have already pointed out, the major form of political change in recent years has been from authoritarian to democratic governance. This change has taken place in two kinds of authoritarian systems, Communist and non-Communist; in the former it has been accompanied by a change to a capitalist economic system. But not all political change has been to democracy; as we will see, in some cases Communist states have shifted a long way toward free market capitalism while making little or no political change. And we will take another look at the case of Peru here (see pp. 553–55) to remind ourselves that political change can still go in many different and surprising directions.

Transitions from Communism to Democracy and Free Market Capitalism

The changes produced by the fall of communism beginning in 1989 have been the most dramatic and have seized the lion's share of the world's attention. All the component states of the Soviet Union and all the former satellites of that state in Eastern and central Europe introduced the beginnings of capitalist economic systems and announced the introduction of democracy.

What does this mean in practice? In all cases, it means the overnight introduction of apparently competitive elections with a multiparty system and the introduction of at least a partial market economy. What it does not mean is that true democracy has been established or that all the former elites have been banished from power. Some of them have never left power, whereas others have begun to find their way back under new party labels. The changes have been radical, but the changes themselves have changed. At the same time, those Communist nations that have so far resisted overt radical regime change—China, North Korea, and Vietnam as well as Cuba—have also been making some surprising changes in the nature of their economies. Let us examine this complex pattern of change in somewhat closer detail.

■ **Political and Economic Change in Eastern and Central Europe: The Polish Case.** Of course, every case is different, but a brief examination of the recent history of Poland will give us some interesting illustrations of the kinds of changes that have taken place in Eastern and central Europe.

Poland is an interesting case because the move toward democratization began long before the fall of the Berlin Wall in 1989 and the rapid sequence of revolutionary overthrow of other Communist regimes in the succeeding months. The trade union Solidarnosc and the Catholic church had been putting pressure on the Communist leadership for many years, and that leadership had been making concessions, finally introducing quasi-free elections in June 1989. Lech Walesa, the leader of Solidarnosc and an electrician by trade, became the president of the new regime in 1990 and the new Sejm (the lower house of the Polish legislature) was turned over to a strong anti-Communist majority; the nation embarked on a vigorous pro-market reform program. However, a mere three years later, in September 1993, the parties with roots in Solidarnosc were soundly defeated and in the presidential elections of 1995, Walesa himself lost his bid for reelection and was replaced by Aleksander Kwasniewski, a former Communist.[23]

What caused the shift back to leaders and ideas that seemed to have been so thoroughly discredited? First, Solidarnosc lost in victory the cohesion it had had in opposition; internal power struggles were tearing it apart. Second, the new electoral system, commendably open and democratic, allowed almost anyone to form a party; by 1992, Poland had over 132 parties; by 1995, the number had grown to over 200. "Only" twenty-nine parties won seats in the 1991 elections to the Sejm, but the strongest of these had only 12.31 percent of the vote and sixty-two seats. Third, and probably most important, the new economic system, rather than bringing the optimistically expected instant improvement to the lives of the Polish people, imposed new rigors on most of them. Price controls were eliminated and the market became the basis of all major economic activities; by 1995 the private sector accounted for 45 percent of the country's gross domestic product (GDP), employed 60 percent of the labor force, and included 1.5 million firms. Positive results were readily apparent: Inflation was reduced to a "mere" 38 percent by the end of 1993 (having reached 640 percent at the beginning of 1990) and economic growth moved into the highly respectable 4 to 5 percent range. Foreign aid was pouring in, 50 percent of the nation's foreign debt was canceled, and the International Monetary Fund (IMF) was offering some $700 million in loans.

But as we have seen in other cases, what looks like national economic recovery to outsiders may look like something very different to those inside who are struggling to make ends meet. There were more goods available, but less money to buy them with: By 1993, the average real wage was 25 percent below the 1989 level, public employees' wages were fixed (regardless of inflation), unemployment was at 15.7 percent and a third of the people, many of them elderly, were living below the poverty line.[24] Nor was privatization always what it appeared to be: Public businesses were sometimes allowed to fall into the hands of former state-employed managers and extensive state support for favored private firms continued.[25]

By 1993, the political tide had turned, and on May 28 the Sejm voted the existing cabinet out of power. President Walesa called for new elections and in September the two former Communist parties, the Democratic Left Alliance (SLD) and the Polish Peasant Party (PSL), took a majority of the seats in both the Sejm and the Senate.[26]

The overall improvement in the national economy continued: By 1995, annual Polish exports were at $20 billion, imports at $23 billion, and Western foreign investment at $1 billion. The situation for some of the general population also improved: By the end of 1994, unemployment fell slightly (to 14 percent), real wages rose slightly (by 3.4 percent), and inflation was down to 22 percent.[27] But this was not enough to keep Walesa in office, and at the end of 1995 Kwasniewski, the leader of the Democratic Left Alliance, became Poland's new president.[28] He was reelected in 2000, and in 2001 his party retained control of the Sejm.

Had Poland returned to communism? Not at all, says Kwasniewski: "Communism is a thing of the past. It is not possible for it to return and there is no sense in its coming back."[29] Kwasniewski, described as a "deep-dyed, deideologized pragmatist," claims he is too young (41 years old at the time of his first election) to be held responsible for the errors of the past regime, and has an upper middle-class family income. He is, he says, a social democrat. Although he favors reducing unemployment, building inexpensive municipal housing, and "taking into account the interests of labor veterans," he also supports the entry of Poland into NATO and Europe, free market reforms, the reduction of state spending, some privatization and more foreign investment.[30] "Now we can expect the long dominance of the post-Communists in Polish political life," says Polish sociologist Edmund Wnuk-Lipinski.[31]

Although the details vary greatly, the general picture is very much the same in other Eastern and central European states formerly under the rule of the USSR. New parties led by former Communists took power in Hungary and Bulgaria, and the governments of the Czech Republic and Slovakia are increasingly dependent on support from former Communists and/or social democrats.[32] In all these nations, former Communists now present themselves as reformers who will ensure that the burden of reform is more equitably shared, not as unregenerate believers determined to turn back the clock. At present writing, only the Hungarians have moved back toward the right.[33]

What about the former Soviet Union? Unlike most of the Eastern European states, most of the nations that formerly constituted the Union of Soviet Socialist Republics had no past history of democratic constitutions or strong civil societies to draw upon nor strong leaders interested in developing a democratic polity. Michael McFaul identifies three post-Communist regime types: dictatorships (the regimes of central Asia, Belarus, Azerbaijan, and "maybe Armenia"); quasi-authoritarian electoral democracies (e.g., Russia, Ukraine, Georgia, and "perhaps Moldova,"), and true consolidated democracies "with some lingering transitional problems" (as in Estonia, Latvia, and Lithuania).[34]

In Russia itself there has been far more emphasis on the transition to capitalism than on that to democracy, and even the former has been far from smooth. The ruble went into steady decline after the fall of communism and the government had to pay up to 18 percent interest on government bonds to keep itself afloat. Nevertheless, the transition proceeded and soon Russia had some 2,500 licensed commercial banks, 600 investment funds, and 40 million shareholders. Nearly 16,000 medium-sized and large enterprises were privatized in less than two years, and by 1994 the private sector produced 62 percent of the nation's officially recorded gross domestic product, a proportion higher than that in Italy. President Vladimir Putin is said to be truly committed to market reform, but far less committed to consolidating democracy: "his advisors speak openly of building a 'managed democratic' system that is far more 'managed' than democratic, and he has yet to discourage them."[35] One close observer describes what is going on as "robber capitalism. It's lawless, but at the same time very vital and viable." Another is less optimistic, expecting those "robber barons" who are making their fortunes in these early stages to "lobby the state for regulations to protect their gains," which will in turn "cause long-term stagnation . . . increase income inequality . . . cause social conflicts. Then you would have a serious danger of a radical, totalitarian revolution."[36]

Transitions from Communism Toward Free Market Capitalism

The pressures for change exerted by an ever-stronger international market economy are also being felt in still-Communist nations like China, North Korea, Vietnam, and Cuba. In these nations massive political regime change has not yet taken place, but economic changes have been profound.

Such changes began in the three Asian states long before the fall of the Berlin Wall. The beginning of China's economic reform dates back to 1978, and in fact 1989 brought a three-year setback, as the Tiananmen Square uprising on behalf of democratic politics in June of that year persuaded Chinese leaders to adopt more conservative economic policies as well as to heighten political oppression.[37] Despite this temporary slowdown, the economy of the People's Republic of China grew at the average annual rate of 9.7 percent between 1979 and 1999, with particularly spectacular growth since 1991 (see Table 14.1).[38]

TABLE 14.1
China's Average
Annual Real GDP
Growth Rates:
1960–2000

Time Period	Average Annual Percent Growth
1960–1978 (pre-reform)	5.3
1979–1999 (post-reform)	9.7
1990	3.8
1991	9.3
1992	14.2
1993	13.5
1994	12.7
1995	10.5
1996	9.7
1997	8.8
1998	7.8
1999	7.1
Jan.–June 2000	8.2

Source: Wayne M. Morrison, *China's Economic Conditions* (Washington, D.C.: Congressional Research Service, Issue Brief 98014, September 21, 2000).

The decision to compete in the world market has brought massive change to China, but so far it has not brought serious political change.[39] The Communist Party-state still rules. This means, in turn, that the economic system has not simply become a free enterprise system; it is what the Chinese call a "socialist market economy." Foreign investment has grown, and so has the private sector, but according to David S. G. Goodman, the most spectacular growth has been in what is known as the "collective sector." This sector includes collectively owned enterprises that are heavily controlled by—but for the most part not owned by—the state. They now account for 35.7 percent of the gross value of industrial output (the state accounts for 52.9 percent, private enterprise for 5.7 percent, and "other and foreign-involved" for 5.7 percent). Goodman identifies six kinds of collectives, from large-scale enterprises like the West Lake District Dragon Well Tea Company (see Box 14.1) to local government collectives to share-based cooperatives. What they have in common is that "each must operate within the market economy but is also inextricably part of the party-state."[40] This dual identity shapes every form of economic development in China: acquiring raw materials, securing bank credits, and finding markets still depends on personal connections with state officials.

China's "socialist market economy" thus appears to be a transitional hybrid economy resulting from the effort of a massive Communist system to maintain total political control while effecting the transition to capitalism and making itself competitive in the world market. In recent years it has made several major economic reforms and promised others; in November 2001 the 142 members of the World Trade Organization gave formal approval for its admission.[41]

BOX 14.1
The Workings of a Large-Scale Collective in a Socialist Market Economy: China's West Lake District Dragon Well Tea Company

[A] successfully reformed large-scale collective is the West Lake District Dragon Well Tea Company. The Hangzhou green tea plantations are famous throughout at least the Chinese speaking world, and Dragon Well Tea is probably the most famous of Hangzhou's teas. Tea in East China can be compared with wine in Burgundy, both in appreciation and in its cultivation and production. Many small producers in a very few select and nominated areas are the only ones able to produce Dragon Well Tea. Before 1949 there were some twelve villages that produced Dragon Well Tea, but by 1980 this had declined to only two. Nonetheless, those two villages maintained the traditions of tea cultivation, including the intergenerational transfer of knowledge.

The Tea Company, very much like a Burgundian *négociant,* buys the tea from the growers, which it then processes and markets. By the early 1980s the local tea industry had been badly rundown despite any lingering reputation. In 1984 the local Dragon Well villages decided to engage in reform on their own behalf. They appointed a native son, trained tea taster and producer previously working in the Trade Section of the Village Government, to reorganize the collective in order to develop and market Dragon Well Tea and the local industry. By any standard, the enterprise has been a great success. In 1984, 13 persons were employed in the company itself, which had a turnover of 210,000 yuan RMB. By 1991, the collective employed 134 people and had a turnover of more than 10 million yuan RMB. More significant is the collective's impact on the local economy: the number of tea villages has already increased to five, and there are plans to replant still more former tea areas.

(continued)

The tendency for the state to maintain a very high level of both ownership and control while steadily pushing the economy toward the market and away from central planning is also found in Vietnam, North Korea, and Cuba.[42] In the latter two cases, special factors add further complications: In North Korea, the expectation of eventual reunification with fully capitalist South Korea overshadows everything, especially since the death in 1994 of "Beloved Leader" Kim Il Sung; in Cuba, the efforts of the state to improve its condition after the loss of Soviet support by permitting a measure of growth in the private sector (with an emphasis on tourism) have been all but canceled out by the deleterious effects of the U.S. embargo and the passage in 1995 of the Helms-Burton law that levies such punishments as cancelation of U.S. visas on foreign investors who profit from properties expropriated from American citizens or companies after Fidel Castro took power in 1959.[43]

BOX 14.1
(continued)

The funding of the Tea Company is of particular interest. Initially, it had been structured as an early reform-era form of the "share-based cooperative" introduced later. As a collective with local government support the Tea Company was successfully able to negotiate a 30,000-yuan RMB loan from the Agricultural Bank. The remaining 20,000 yuan RMB of the original capital was to be provided by the workforce. The collective agreed to pay the workforce a dividend, which would be higher than the prevailing bank interest. Unfortunately for the implementation of any collectivist ideology, the Tax Office insisted that tax had to be paid before any dividends were declared. In the first year of operation there was insufficient profit to ensure the dividend payout, and as a result the workers withdrew their capital.

The Tea Company is now funded on a system of workers' pledges. All members of the workforce are assigned a proportion of the total enterprise capital according to their position in the company and their wage. Local government fixes a target for the enterprise profit in the coming year which is calculated according to a three-year moving average. If the target is 25 percent met, the workforce then shares the next 27 percent of the profit target before taxes are paid. If the target is not met, the workforce must compensate the local government. In either case reward or compensation is calculated according to the individual worker's pledge, or notional share of the total enterprise capital.

Source: David S. G. Goodman, "Collectives and Connectives, Capitalism and Corporatism: Structural Change in China," special issue on "Enterprise Reform in Post-Socialist Societies," *Journal of Communist Studies and Transition Politics* 11, no. 1 (March 1995): 19–20. Reprinted by permission of Frank Cass, publisher.

Transitions from Non-Communist Authoritarian Rule to Democracy

Transitions from non-Communist authoritarian rule to democracy have taken place in Italy and Germany after World War II, and in Portugal, Spain, and Greece more recently.[44] Here, however, we will look at this form of transition only in Africa and Latin America.

■ **In Africa.**   In the first twenty years (roughly 1960 to 1980) after achieving political independence from colonial rule, most of the new African states were ruled by single-party or military dictators, often supported by the former colonial powers in exchange for continuing privileged access to these nations' cheap labor and raw materials. But in the 1980s regime change

came to Africa, and by the mid-1990s multiparty elections had been introduced in a majority of African political systems.[45]

What caused the change? Certainly world opinion played a part. So did
domestic opinion as "declining living standards . . . arbitrary and bad government, corruption and a breakdown of law and order" caused Africans to
lose patience with their rulers.[46] But this is a good time to remember those
transitologists who insist that what causes the introduction of democracy is
the determination of the powerful to establish it (see p. 540).

In the African case, two sets of the "powerful" were at work. The first
were the organizers of the structural adjustment programs of the World
Bank and IMF (see below, pp. 556–60). The second were the internal elites
whose grip was becoming shaky as their nations' increasing fiscal decline reduced the resources they required (such as foreign exchange, local currency,
and government contracts) to make the necessary patronage rewards to their
supporters.[47] In exchange for massive loans from the first, the second readily agreed to economic liberalization, improving conditions for foreign investors and at least a facade of political liberalization as well.

Although the dramatic events in Eastern Europe and the Soviet Union and
the more gradual shift from military to parliamentary rule in Latin America
heightened the hopes of many that "democracy and capitalism are progress-
ing irresistibly, and in tandem," close observers have pointed out that in
Africa as elsewhere in the world there are reasons to doubt that the truth is
as cheerfully simple as that.[48]

First, the move to democracy in these regimes is not only led by elites, it
has often been less than popular with the general population, because it is
linked with the imposition of rigorous austerity programs demanded by the
IMF and the World Bank. Second, although particular leaders may change,
the African elite, consisting of lawyers, university lecturers, bankers, businessmen, professionals, and former officials of international institutions, still
dominate the new governments and parties.[49] Furthermore, elections do not
necessarily produce leadership change. Clever autocrats know how to make
"their own adjustments." When protests escalated in his country in 1990
and international pressures grew, the late Félix Houphouet-Boigny of the
Ivory Coast moved swiftly to master the new situation. He "announced a
suspension of many of the planned austerity moves, legalized opposition
parties, and called presidential and legislative elections for October and November. . . . Thanks to this swift initiative, [his party's] advantages as the
state party, and the opposition's fragmentation, [he and his party] won the
elections handily." [50] Similar tactics worked to keep the autocratic rulers of
Ghana, Uganda, and the Sudan in power, as the transition to multiparty systems was made. Ghana's leader, Flight Lieutenant Jerry Rawlings, simply
waited until three weeks before election day to announce his own candidacy,
by which time the opposition was hopelessly divided.[51] In Uganda President
Yoweri Museveni allowed political parties to form and offer candidates, but

not to raise funds or hold meetings.[52] And in the Sudan General Omar Ahmed al-Bashir gave candidates only twelve days to campaign in a nation one-fourth the size of the United States, allowed one piece of campaign literature and a single 15-minute spot on the state-owned television and radio station for each candidate for the presidency, and encouraged officials in polling places to "help" voters make their choices.[53] All three were chosen by comfortable percentages to remain in power by the "free" elections that followed.

Even the most dubious observers admit, however, that things have changed in Africa. Openly autocratic rule is no longer acceptable in most nations, opposition parties do exist, the press seems freer to criticize those in power, and associations such as trade unions and women's groups are taking a renewed interest in the political game. It may still be only a game, and one that has little real meaning yet for the vast majority of Africa's population. Continuing and severe economic hardship plus ethnic rivalries that can erupt in mass violence make the task of democratic consolidation more difficult here than in Europe.[54] But something has changed. It is too soon to be certain the change will hold, and deepen, but it is also too soon to be certain that the change will fail.

■ **In Latin America.**   The situation in Latin America is similar to that in Africa in several respects. As in Africa, this continent also experienced a massive turn away from dictatorship in the 1980s; over two-thirds of the Latin American people were living under military rule in 1979, but by 1993, "not a single military regime remained in Central or South America or the Spanish-speaking Caribbean"[55] (see Table 14.2). As in Africa, a severe need for economic bailout (here owing largely to the impossibility of keeping up payments on foreign loans) helped convince endangered elites they would have to accept neoliberal economic strategies of reducing government regulation, privatizing public enterprises, and shrinking the size of the state in order to qualify for further foreign aid and loans.[56] As in Africa, democracy has been "pared to the bone" and is largely limited to its "electoral dimension" leaving social needs "at the bottom of the agenda."[57] As in Africa, certain groups, generally those already better placed in the social system, have prospered with the change while the poor have grown poorer. As in Africa, intermediary representative groups (opposition parties, trade unions, other associations of civil society) have not yet gained sufficient strength as "channels of interest mediation [to be able to] renegotiate with society the terms of political representation."[58] And finally, as in Africa, although the overall results have been dubious and disappointing, one can find some grounds for hope, as we will see.

There is, however, one key difference in the nature of Latin American re-

TABLE 14.2

Transitions to Civilian Government in Latin America

Ecuador	1979	Uruguay	1984
Peru	1980	Brazil	1985
Honduras	1982	Guatemala	1986
Bolivia	1982	Chile	1990
Argentina	1983	Paraguay	1993
El Salvador	1984		

Source: Brian Loveman, "'Protected Democracies' and Military Guardianship: Political Transitions in Latin America, 1978–1993," *Journal of InterAmerican Studies and World Affairs* 36, no. 2 (Summer 1994): 106.

gime change, and that is the far more powerful role of the military, both before and after the changes that have taken place. Although military regimes were in power in many nations on both continents throughout the 1960s and 1970s, those in Latin America were far less limited by poverty and the inhibiting conditions of postcolonial trade and aid than their African counterparts; at the same time, these nations were far more determined to "obliterate the political left and roll back decades of labor gains" (few such gains had yet been made in Africa).[59]

The exceptional power of the Latin American military did not come to an end with the introduction of formal democracy, and the new governments have been described as keen to avoid "any policy initiative that might provoke a new military coup." Although they have sometimes reduced the size of the military, they have often granted, explicitly or tacitly, immunity to members of the armed forces known to have engaged in extreme acts of oppression during their time in power, have incorporated many of the antidemocratic and anti-civil libertarian institutions and practices of the past regimes into contemporary constitutions, and have given the military a range of powers that more established democracies would never countenance. The result, according to Brian Loveman, is that these are "protected democracies" —which is to say, regimes in which the military is given the role of "protecting" the new system from its own excesses and/or in which the civilian authorities have accepted military definitions of what constitutes such an excess. Loveman concludes that in most of these nations military coups are no longer a threat, but that is because they are not necessary: "Protected democracy provides a handy legal rationale for the military to assert themselves in a variety of acceptable ways. . . . Beneath the veneer of elected civilian government, both authoritarian legal institutions and a political mission for the armed forces have been consolidated"[60] (see Table 14.3).

Nevertheless, as in Africa, the new regimes do provide some grounds for hope. They may not have had "any significant effect on the great and increasing inequalities of their economies or societies," and it may be true that "the dice are probably loaded in favor of repeated iterations of shaky and

TABLE 14.3
Military Limitations
on Transition to
Elected Government
in Selected Latin
American Nations

Argentina	Least successful case for military controlling transition, but gradual reassertion of military presence as civilian governments make concessions after mutinies and coup attempts 1985–1992.
Bolivia	Military retains basic prerogatives; no trials for human rights violations, except prosecution of ex-President García Meza and 47 collaborators on various charges.
Brazil	Military maintains almost all prerogatives and relative service autonomy; no Defense Ministry permitted. Intelligence agencies (SNI) and National Security Council also retain much autonomy despite later name changes and reorganization. Military fails to control transition election entirely, but active participation in elaborating 1988 Constitution ensures broad constitutional mission, participation in policymaking affecting "national security" (e.g., labor and agrarian reform policy), and continued relative autonomy.
Chile	Transition according to 1980 Constitution. Small concessions to opposition in 1989 reforms, but also implementation before President Aylwin takes office of *leyes de amarre* (group of laws, decrees, and organic laws that further limit authority of incoming government in many policy areas, including new organic laws for armed forces and national police just prior to transition).
Ecuador	Military monitors plebiscite on alternative constitutions; impedes participation of certain candidates in transition election; manipulates recount on first round of 1978 presidential election; assures respect for institutional prerogatives of armed forces and participation in naming defense minister.
El Salvador	Army retains most prerogatives; country under state of siege for most of 1984–1993, involving broad military jurisdiction over civilians. Minimal civilian authority over military. Peace Accord between government and FMLN in 1992 calls for civilian role in reforming military education through a new Consejo Académico Cívico-Militar and in reviewing cases of officers accused of human rights abuses for their dismissal (*depuracíon*).
Guatemala	Military creates *Tribunal Supremo Electoral* to control transition election and devises new election laws. Calls constituent assembly (1984) to adopt a new constitution. Obtains confirmation of decrees of junta and guarantees against trials for human rights abuses. President Cerezo claims he has "30% of the power" (the army has the rest).
Paraguay	Military retains all previous prerogatives; 1991 armed forces law stipulates "autonomy" of armed forces, Congress cannot pass laws on military unless previously approved by president; pre-election rumors that if *Colorado* party candidate Carlos Wasmosy lost, the armed forces would seize power. Various election irregularities.
Uruguay	Military vetoes candidacy of most popular presidential candidate; key opposition leaders in jail; informal guarantees of military prerogatives; SIFA (Armed Forces Intelligence Service) continues surveillance of civilian politicians, activists, labor leaders, and media.

Source: Drawn from Brian Loveman, "'Protected Democracies' and Military Guardianship: Political Transitions in Latin America, 1978–1993," *Journal of InterAmerican Studies and World Affairs* 36, no. 2 (Summer 1994): 120–21.

relatively short-lived democracy and ever uglier authoritarian rule," as Guillermo O'Donnell sadly observes.[61] Yet O'Donnell himself is willing to hope he may be wrong and bases that hope on the fact that "most political and cultural forces of any weight now attribute high intrinsic value to the achievement and consolidation of political democracy." He reminds us that when democracies are first established anywhere, it is usually with a great deal of pessimism, uncertainty, and even reluctance. Like others, he points out the importance of the motives of elites—it is, he says, when the main political, social, and religious forces conclude "that the costs of trying to eliminate each other [exceed] the costs of tolerating each other's differences" that true democracy has a chance.[62] Although the grounds for hope seem slight indeed, perhaps that moment is on its way in Latin America.[63]

A Transition from "Protected Democracy" to Authoritarianism and Part Way Back Again: The Case of Peru

The difficulty of deepening Latin American democracy has been given striking illustration in the case of Peru. As we have noted earlier, shortly after being elected president, Alberto Fujimori announced an *autogolpe* ("self-coup") on April 5, 1992, giving himself the power to rule by decree. The constitution was suspended and the legislature was closed down. Fujimori had become impatient with the reluctance of the Peruvian Congress to implement the economic austerity measures required by the IMF and the World Bank, or to take the counterinsurgency measures he had urged against Shining Path, a revolutionary movement that seemed to be growing stronger every day.

The hesitation of the lawmakers to pass the economic legislation sought by Fujimori had clearly been linked to the condition of the Peruvian people. With only 15.6 percent of the economically active workforce employed full time at the minimum wage or above and half the population living below the poverty level, many members of the legislature doubted that further cuts in public spending could be made. It was also not difficult to understand their reluctance to adopt the counterinsurgency measures Fujimori had proposed, linked as these were to efforts to give the armed forces dangerous new powers in many areas.[64]

In the days following his coup, Fujimori took these and similar steps on his own (including dismissing thirteen members of the Supreme Court and more than 100 judges and prosecutors).[65] But to his surprise, the fact that he was following policies the international community had recommended did not bring a positive response from that community. On the contrary: The United States suspended aid, the IMF postponed a $222 million loan, and other South American governments suspended cooperation with Peru.

Fujimori soon learned what was wrong—it was his open repudiation of democracy. His methods were too blunt.[66] The president was a quick study—before his first month in dictatorial power was up, he had announced that he would hold a plebiscite within six months and called for a "national dialogue for peace and development."

Fujimori's own party, Cambio 90, won a majority of seats in the new assembly in the November elections, partly because two other major parties boycotted the election, but also because so many Peruvian voters had been disappointed by the performance of the previous ostensibly democratic government and believed that Peru needed "stronger government to deal with the chaos, insecurity and corruption that had become a part of daily life."[67]

Once given this supposedly democratic ratification for the abolition of democracy, Fujimori could pursue his program. The United States offered a debt-restructuring plan (the Brady plan), reducing the total foreign private debt by nearly half. In April 1995 Fujimori was elected to a second term by a vote of 64 percent; and his party took 67 of 120 seats in the new legislature. (These impressive electoral results were owing in part to clever strategies used to encourage opposition candidates and new parties—the thirteen competitors for the presidency and the nineteen opposition parties seeking legislative seats thoroughly divided the opposition vote.)[68]

There were some signs of real progress at first: Inflation, which had run at 40 percent per month, was down to 15 percent per year by 1994; and economic growth was up to 12.9 percent that year.[69] Privatization of the economy moved along rapidly, often into the hands of foreign investors, thereby helping to build foreign exchange reserves of $7 billion. But not all the signs were positive. The country's growth rate, although still strong, had fallen to 6.7 percent by the mid-1990s and was expected to keep falling; the economy went into a recession produced by major cuts in public spending. Most important, there was little if any positive change in the condition of the ordinary people of Peru, aside from some improvements in the availability of electricity and water. As of mid-1996, 85 percent of the workforce still did not have full-time jobs, 55 percent lived in poverty, and "the influx of foreign companies and investment into Peru [had] produced no perceptible job growth."[70]

Popular unrest continued to grow, and the president relied more and more on a greatly strengthened armed forces and National Intelligence Service (SIN). In July 2000 Fujimori won a third term, contrary to constitutional term limitations, in elections widely deemed fraudulent. However, the revelation (complete with televised video) that his national security adviser had offered a bribe to an opposition party member to switch loyalties, and that high-ranking military and intelligence officials had been involved in selling guns to the Revolutionary Armed Forces of Colombia, brought the president down a mere two months later: Fujimori announced that he would hold new

From auto-coup to auto-flight. The career of Peruvian ex-President Alberto Fuji-
mori from elected president to self-named dictator to re-election by fraud to self-
exile illustrates how difficult achieving democratic transition can be. Here Peru-
vians demand the extradition of Fujimori from Japan.
© Reuters NewMedia Inc./CORBIS

elections and not be a candidate.[71] In June 2001 Alejandro Toledo won election as the new president, "promising to root out deep-seated corruption of the Fujimori regime and restore Peruvians' faith in elected government." A first step was the effort to bring Fujimori back from Japan (to which he had fled) to face charges of crimes against humanity, for allegedly endorsing a death squad that had killed 24 persons.[72]

As Maxwell Cameron has pointed out, Peru is a good example of the importance of giving attention to the quality of the democracy that is being established in transition regimes. It is not enough to have multiple parties and elections if power remains centralized in the hands of the executive, the judiciary lacks independence, and the military maintains important political powers; we must, says Cameron, "avoid creating polities in which the demos [the public] hates democracy."[73]

INTERNATIONAL AGENTS OF ECONOMIC GLOBALIZATION

Three international government organizations heavily involved in facilitating the economic and political changes now under way are the International Monetary Fund (IMF), the World Bank, and the World Trade Organization (the WTO, which has evolved from the General Agreement on Tariffs and Trade, GATT). All boast virtually universal membership and are playing a strong role in shaping and reshaping the economies of both old and new regimes, and the interdependence between them. A fourth institution, also new but much more limited in membership, is the Group of Eight (G-8), which takes the form of periodic meetings of the leaders of the world's eight most powerful nations: the United States, France, Germany, Great Britain, Italy, Japan, Canada, and Russia.

To understand the power of these organizations to drive the engines of globalization, we need to take at least a brief glance at the history of their development. When the Great Depression of 1929, which began in the United States but soon reverberated throughout the world, began to subside, the affected nations were determined not to be caught again. Their first response was self-protective: Each pursued policies of economic nationalism and isolationism, seeking to curb imports and strengthen exports, and each acted with only its own immediate benefits in mind.

Although the spread of protectionist policies had some short-term benefits, it also had serious and obvious negative effects. Costs of production rose (as industries were forced to pay higher than world market prices for protected manufactured goods they needed for their own production) and productive efficiency declined.[74] Such policies also helped create the conditions of competition and hostility that played a key role in the outbreak of World War II.

In an effort to prevent the recurrence of such a response to domestic economic problems, the major Western nations created three important international institutions after the war: the World Bank and the IMF in the Bretton Woods agreement of 1944 and GATT in 1947. All of these institutions have assumed new importance and new functions in recent years; to give a necessarily brief explanation of these developments, we begin with the last, GATT, which, as noted, has now been folded into a new institution, the World Trade Organization (WTO).

The purpose of GATT was to promote international trade that would be as free as possible from protectionist limitations. This goal was interpreted as meaning, in essence, mutual reduction of tariffs and equal treatment by each nation of all other nations in matters of trade (in accordance with the *most favored nation principle,* which meant that no nation would be treated any less well than the nation with whom the most favorable conditions of trade are arranged). As a result, tariffs were significantly reduced across the globe, and, partly because of these reductions, world exports increased from

$94 billion in 1955 to nearly $2 trillion in 1982, while global GNP grew from $1.1 trillion to $11.4 trillion.[75]

Partly in response to the conditions created by GATT, transnational corporations flourished in the postwar years, no longer so impeded by isolationist policies, and began moving enormous liquid assets from country to country, taking advantage of changing interest rates, currency fluctuations, and other marginal shifts in financial conditions that can mean production advantages that are anything but marginal. The rise of transnational corporations included multinational—or transnational—banks (TNBs). During the 1970s, loans made by such banks came to account for nearly 70 percent of all international finance, and the rate of return was impressive (Citibank, for example, earned 20 percent of its profits in the late 1970s from loans to a single nation, Brazil).[76]

The 1980s were, however, a time of reckoning. Many of the debtor nations, especially in Latin America, were unable to make their payments on these loans and defaulted. Defaults in Mexico (1982), Brazil (1983), Venezuela (1983), and Peru (1985) were serious enough to produce a massive international debt crisis. By the end of 1990, Western commercial banks were owed $350 billion by debtor countries in the developing world.[77] The response of the TNBs was to reduce and refinance foreign debts, providing lower interest rates and longer-term loans, in exchange for which the debtor nations improved opportunities and conditions for foreign investments.[78]

Although such bargaining helped the delinquent nations to avoid default and even resume growth, the problems were far from resolved. It became clear that the foundering economies would need larger scale bailouts than private banks, even the mightiest, could supply. It is at this point that the IMF, the World Bank, and the G-8 began to play a far larger role.

The role of the IMF, a key specialized agency of the United Nations, is to promote international monetary cooperation, stabilizing exchange rates and providing exchange funds for needy states. It maintains a central fund of hard currency reserves that can be made available to countries with periodic deficits. Member governments deposit assigned shares of gold and currency in a central fund and then are entitled to borrow from the fund at times when they are short on foreign exchange holdings.[79] It has more than 180 members and operates with no public or professional scrutiny; its meetings are closed and the minutes are not made public—even the amount of money the fund has to lend is never announced.[80] Since 1989 the number of countries seeking IMF funds to rehabilitate their economies has risen from 63 to 94.

The World Bank (which is actually the International Bank for Reconstruction and Development) is a bank created and owned by governments. It is "the chief global institution in the capital sector of the international economy" and has over 170 members.[81] Its mission is to ensure "an open international trading system and global financial stability . . . [by] using public loans for economic developments."[82]

Opportunity for change or photo opportunity? Here the G-8 leaders have their picture taken at the summit in Kananaskis, Alberta, Canada, on June 26, 2002. From left: Italian Prime Minister Silvio Berlusconi, German Chancellor Gerhard Schroeder, U.S. President George W. Bush, French President Jacques Chirac, Canadian Prime Minister Jean Chrétien, Russian President Vladimir Putin, British Prime Minister Tony Blair, and Japanese Prime Minister Junichiro Koizumi.
AP/Wide World Photos

Both the World Bank and IMF are dominated by the world's wealthiest nations, because in each institution the number of votes a state has is determined by its financial contributions—to the central fund of currency reserves in the case of the IMF, to the capital reserves of the World Bank. The United States is the largest single contributor, closely followed by the other members of the G-8.

The origins of the G-8 go back to April 1973 when the finance ministers of the United States, West Germany, France, and the United Kingdom first met in the White House library to discuss current problems in the international economic order. They decided the discussions were useful enough to be continued on a regular basis, and Japan and Italy were brought in in 1975, Canada in 1976, and Russia in 1998.[83] (Because the first seven continue to hold some meetings that exclude Russia—the only nation among them that is dependent on IMF financing and is only partially converted to capitalism—the organization is sometimes referred to as "G-8/G-7.") In addition to ministerial meetings, the G-8 heads of state also hold periodic summit meetings, accompanied by hundreds of bureaucrats and other government officials.[84] Together, the G-8 control about two-thirds of the world's economic output, and their powers of global governance have become formidable indeed: "Most of the world's major economic and security initiatives are discussed first by the G-8/G-7 leaders and their ministers before the other multilateral organizations take action."[85] According to one author, they are nothing less than "the board of directors for the free world."[86]

The powers of all these institutions of global governance have greatly increased in recent years. Both the IMF and the World Bank now require indebted countries to adopt "structural adjustment programs" modifying their interest rates, exchange rates, and wage and trade policies in ways that increase their chances of having the funds with which to repay their loans. Specifically, this means privatizing a significant portion of the public sector, stopping the subsidization of inadequately profitable businesses, liberalizing trade agreements with other nations, and pursuing export development projects rather than focusing on domestic consumption.[87] Such agreements not only make the indebted nations deserving of funding but also give foreign investors new incentives to move their businesses (and their jobs) abroad. In theory, everyone prospers—although of course much of the profit from any economic growth thus achieved flows into foreign bank accounts.

Whatever the result for others (a topic we discuss below), one effect of the increased number of loans was to help bail out Western commercial banks from the trouble their inadequately cautious lending practices had got them into in the 1970s and 1980s. Between 1984 and 1990 $178 billion flowed from the Third World to commercial banks through loan repayments.[88] Nor were the institutions themselves losing money, as Herman Daly and John B. Cobb Jr., explain in the case of the World Bank:

> The fact is that the World Bank will almost always be repaid, even if the project or policy it finances produces only losses. This is because the Bank lends to sovereign governments that have the power to tax and print money. They cannot print foreign exchange, but they can buy it by printing more of their own money and accepting the consequences of inflation and devaluation—or they can tax their people honestly, rather than by inflation. In either case they can pay back the World Bank, and

nearly always will do so rather than default and lose their credit rating. ... [R]epayment flows on past loans are now so large that there is a 'negative net flow' of funds to the South from the Bank [that is, the Bank is receiving more than it is giving out].[89]

As both the IMF and the World Bank became, under the control of the G-7, and then the G-8, ever stronger forces for economic globalization, GATT did not lag far behind. At the Uruguay round of negotiations in 1994, the nations present brought trade in agricultural and textile products into "regular GATT discipline," and transformed GATT itself into the World Trade Organization (WTO), giving the member states a far more elaborate institutional structure (a secretariat, a director general, and a staff) than it had in its first fifty years of existence.[90] The WTO thus became the fourth major international institution shaping economic globalization, differing in one interesting respect from the other three: decisions are arrived at by consensus among those participating in any set of agreements. Their relative strength naturally influences the outcome of those agreements, but within the WTO itself there are no procedures for coercing consent.

IMPACT OF ECONOMIC GLOBALIZATION ON NATIONAL ECONOMIES

As we saw in Chapter 1, the impact of economic globalization on individuals varies enormously, as the world divides itself into new sets of winners and losers. But the more positive theorists of globalization hope that in the long run all these "adjustments" will surely work for the "greatest good for the greater number." Individuals may suffer, but reorganized economies will prosper. Eventually individuals beyond the tiny class of fortunate elites will prosper as well. Can it be true?

Of course no one can fully predict the future. But in an effort to begin to answer this all-important question we look at the results thus far and the assessments of knowledgeable critics. We examine first the impact of economic globalization on underdeveloped economies, secondly on those supposedly developed, and then conclude this section with a consideration of proposed reforms.

Impact on Less Developed Economies

The first thing to say about the impact of globalization on less developed economies is simple enough: They have, overall, been getting poorer. Net expansion in world trade does not bring equal benefits to all nations, and poorer nations are not well placed to prosper from the world trade conditions fostered by the WTO. The most favored nation principle makes it impossible to protect the less developed nations from the competition of more affluent nations, and their standing in the international economic arena has fallen rather than improved. According to one assessment, "households in Latin America were poorer in 1990 than they were in 1980, in sub-Saharan Africa [poorer than in] 1960"[91] India, Russia, and most of the nations of Eastern Europe are now major debtors as well. Since the World Bank initiated its new lending practices in the early 1980s, the Third World's debt burden has risen from $785 billion to $1.5 trillion.[92]

Globalization was expected by some to lead to income convergence around the world, but the opposite appears to be the case. The income gap between the fifth of the world's people who live in the richest countries and the fifth in the poorest rose to 74 to 1 in 1997 (as compared to 60 to 1 in 1990, 30 to 1 in 1960—and 3 to 1 in 1820!). The luckiest fifth have 86 percent of the world's GDP (the bottom fifth have 1 percent), 68 percent of foreign direct investment (bottom: 1 percent), and 74 percent of world telephone lines (bottom: 1.5 percent). The world's 200 richest people doubled their net worth between 1994 and 1998. The assets of the top three billionaires are greater than those of the 600 million people living in the least developed nations.[93]

Economic globalization means the increasing integration of national economies "through trade, finance, production and a growing web of treaties and institutions," with the result that "the national market is being increasingly displaced by the international marketplace."[94] But it is a marketplace that demands highly skilled labor in industry and science (and in sports and entertainment as well). Workers who qualify can now relocate much more easily when times at home are bad; unskilled or lesser skilled workers are ever more vulnerable to local winds of change. (See Box 14.2.)

Child laborers have been among the hardest hit. By the end of the last century the WTO had come out in favor of "core labor standards" that would prevent any country from using child labor, prison labor, bonded labor "and all the other ingenious variants of slavery that persist in the modern world" but "the negotiations broke up in disorder and acrimony": Families whose real income is steadily shrinking are not about to give up the help of younger family members "tending cattle, gathering fodder, collecting water, harvesting rice, cutting sugar-cane, or spreading pesticides on family farms."[95]

Furthermore, there is a growing body of evidence that the development projects financed by the World Bank seldom work out as planned. At the end of a soberly empirical assessment of efforts made under structural adjustment programs made in Ghana, Uganda, Tanzania, Kenya, Mozambique, and Zambia, Peter Gibbon, Kjell J. Havnevik, and Kenneth Hermele conclude "while there have been significant problems encountered in the implementation of adjustment programs, insofar as they have been implemented, the accompanying trends are not encouraging. Where it has occurred, growth has been generally low and/or temporary. In those few cases where

BOX 14.2
The "Iron Rice
Bowl" Comes
Up Empty

Wang Xiujun is 38 years old, a mother of one tireless nine-year-old boy, and jobless. A former technician at Shanghai's China Record Factory, she was laid off during the summer of 1992. Her voice quakes with frustration from countless months of not finding new employment. "This is unfair," she insists. "I was supposed to be a lifetime employee."

She recalls when there were as many as 1,600 workers at the China Record Factory. Today, management wants to maintain a staff of 400 to 500. There are only two executives remaining in Wang's workshop.

"These managers are arrogant," she complains. "They're . . . sitting in their Mercedes-Benzes, and they don't care whether the workers . . . have jobs or not."

For Wang, and hundreds of thousands like her, the "iron rice bowl" has cracked apart in China's economic reform and enterprise restructuring. According to the Ministry of Labor, urban unemployment stands at 2.6 percent, or 4 million of the total urban workforce. Although this number is low by Western standards, it conceals a statistical time bomb. At least 10 million of China's 74 million state-enterprise workers are now considered surplus.

The mammoth Wuhan Iron and Steel Corp. is in the midst of shedding two-thirds of its employees, or 80,000 people. China's textile industry, which as of 1993 employed 7.5 million workers, is planning to "switch" 4 million employees to other sectors within the next three years. Mean-

it has been higher or more sustained, the results seem to have little to do with adjustment . . . a moratorium is probably merited, in which other options are explored." [96]

Impact on More Developed Economies

But globalization has also not been as kind as one might expect to the economies (and citizens) of developed nations (for an example, see Box 14.3). The desire to keep profits and wages at levels that can be sustained only by continued growth has produced widespread inflation, or rise in price levels, in many of the world's more developed economies. Keeping profits up by cutting out jobs altogether has led to serious unemployment: By the end of the twentieth century there were about 34 million unemployed persons in the seven countries of the Organization for Economic Cooperation and De-

BOX 14.2
(continued)

while, the central government is cutting its own bloated workforce by 25 percent, or 8.5 million employees.

The problem is how to take care of them. The socialist state enterprise has functioned as a social-welfare institution. It is the sole provider of housing, medical care, and retirement pensions for more than half of the urban labor force. "As things stand now, we can't let these insolvent factories just close down," one trade-union official says. In Shanghai, workers at insolvent state enterprises are being encouraged to retire early and find other work to supplement a reduced income.

Unemployment subsidies in Shanghai vary widely depending on the factory involved, but they seldom amount to more than 210 yuan ($24) a month, and are usually much lower. In a city where per-capita monthly income averages 324 yuan ($37), the difficulties faced by the unemployed are apparent to anyone who has tried to manage a household budget.

While those with technical training and manual skills have an easier time finding new or part-time employment, workers who are middle-aged and lack education must hit the streets and try their luck at parking bicycles, selling papers, or peddling fruit and clothing.

"I'm good at repairing houses," one laid-off machine operator says. "So I have been working for friends rather steadily. But others from my factory are out on the street selling eggs and spices."

Source: T. S. Rosseau, "Eastern Express" from *World Press Review* (July 1994): 12. Reprinted by permission of "Eastern Express," Hong Kong, and *World Press Review* magazine, New York.

velopment (OECD), that is, in the world's wealthiest nations. When workers are laid off, those who find new jobs almost always do so at lower levels of pay. The United States has established a $10 billion budget for work-related education and training, but Ethen B. Kapstein estimates that at least another $39 billion is needed and sees retraining as only a partial solution in any case: "If the concern is income inequality, policies should be adopted to close the income gap. If the concern is unemployment, more jobs should be created. Training . . . is not by itself a solution."[97]

The poorly paid, underemployed, and unemployed workers of the developed nations are obviously unable to serve as eager consumers, and lowered demand leads to still lower growth, to more layoffs, more unemployment, and to business failures. Efforts to curb inflation by setting higher interest rates and making money harder to attain may slow the rate of price increases, but they also put another brake on growth in many sectors of the economy, and they do not make the goods produced by the na-

<table>
<tr><td>

BOX 14.3
**Japan: A
Developed
Economy in
Trouble**

</td><td>

After World War II, Japan moved steadily forward to world economic leadership, based in large part on successful management techniques and careful long-range planning that produced startling technological achievements the rest of the world was willing to pay for. But the news of late has been less impressive. Shaken first by a sudden stock market slump and then by the high costs of the Kobe earthquake, the long-buoyant economy has run into serious trouble despite public bail-out expenditures that have totaled over $546 billion since 1992.[98] Prices and profits have all been falling precipitously, as the yen has grown steadily stronger in the world market. A $127 billion trade surplus and currency that buys more per yen every day sounds fine, but not when it makes it more difficult to sell Japanese products abroad, not when it is more profitable to import cheaper foreign goods and sell them at home than produce your own (a practice severely limited by Japan's continuing protectionist tariffs), and not when more and more domestic firms find that the only way to stay afloat is by cutting their workforce, selling off assets, and reducing production.

If Japan's market-driven deflation continues unchecked, economists worry that this period of stagnation will turn into a period of prolonged recession for that country.

</td></tr>
</table>

tions that attempt this solution significantly more competitive on the world market.

The difficulty of selling goods to consumers with fewer jobs makes access to the world market all the more important, but goods that are too costly at home are even more overpriced for the world market, where other nations, paying their workers lower wages and/or relying heavily on automation to save on labor costs, are able to offer their goods at lower prices. Moving production facilities to less developed nations or investing in their indigenous enterprises under the favorable conditions created by IMF or World Bank "adjustments" may be a fine solution for those who can afford to do so (see Box 7.3 on p. 270), but of course weakens the home economy all the more.

The governments of the world's industrialized nations have attempted to solve the problems posed by slowed growth, inflated prices, and unemployment with a range of solutions as diversified as the range of their political and economic systems. Conservative capitalist systems such as the United States and Great Britain have experimented with raising and lowering interest rates, in the hope that the "supply side" of the free enterprise system will produce the necessary adjustments. Nations with more mixed economies such as France, the Scandinavian nations, and most of southern Europe still try to make traditional welfare state responses to the problem, buying up major private businesses, pouring government funds into job-creating projects, and (sometimes) increasing the taxes of the wealthy. In the more authoritarian capitalist systems of Asia and Latin America, the response to slowed growth is commonly a severe austerity program at home combined with improved conditions for investments from abroad. "Tax competition" has become the norm, as such nations "lower tax rates on income earned by foreigners within their borders in order to attract both portfolio and direct investment." [99] The Asian economic crisis of the late 1990s, combined with government economic reforms designed to woo foreign business investments (and producing an influx of higher paid foreign workers), has meant that in Singapore "globalization is in and a welfare state is out." As a result, however, the income gap between rich and poor has widened dramatically: In 1998 wages of lower-income groups plunged by 34 percent, households in the top 20 percent earned 18 times more than those in the bottom 20 percent, and 44 percent of those age 40 and over were unemployed.[100] Yet this tiny state is the ninth richest country in the world by per-capita income and has been ranked by one study as the world's most global nation (owing to its high trade levels, heavy international telephone traffic, and steady stream of international travelers).[101]

Although each of these approaches has brought about some change, particularly in the reduction of inflation, growth rates in many nations have remained unimpressive and unemployment figures stubbornly unresponsive.

What Is to Be Done?

Almost everyone is now ready to admit—or indeed to shout—that globalization has not yet shown many signs of meeting all the hopes once held for it. We are now at the stage of analyzing the problems and recommending solutions.

For some the answer is relatively simple: Stop the world and get off, that is, dismantle the international financial organizations altogether. Herman E. Daly and John B. Cobb Jr. argue that the problems produced by globalization are so great that the real answer is simply to return to national control of indigenous economies.[102] Alain Touraine would seem to agree: The problem, says this leading French sociologist, is that "the triumph of financial power" has been met by "the inaction or incomprehension of governments and nations" whose main political institutions, such as parliaments and trade unions, have been utterly overwhelmed. Some way must be found to "rebuild political control of the economy" and he believes that means bringing the economy back under the control of the states, a task for "large-scale and long-term social and political movements." [103]

Such movements do in fact appear to be forming, as has been seen in the demonstrations against recent meetings of the World Trade Organization, beginning in November 1999. Organized via the Internet by a coalition composed largely of a revived international labor movement, students demonstrating on their campuses, environmentalists, and "other left forces," these protesters are challenging global corporations and international economic institutions, and "raising fundamental issues about class power and international solidarity among workers."[104]

Others are more inclined to accept that a corner has been turned, and that there is no turning back. They are more interested in shaping the new forces than seeking ways to eliminate them. Some focus on reform of the global financial institutions. Jessica Einhorn, a former managing director of the World Bank, acknowledges that its emphasis "on markets and stable macroeconomic policies [has] impoverished the poor" and its "willingness to deal with almost any government [has been] wholly insensitive to human rights and other democratic values" while "the closed nature of its deliberations and restricted circulation of its reports . . . [have] precluded the poor's participation." She believes the bank has overextended itself and must learn to recognize the limits to what even so powerful an institution can accomplish."[105]

But the IMF is even worse, says Joseph Stiglitz, because it gives in constantly to the pressure exerted by the finance ministers of the advanced industrial nations and because "IMF experts believe they are brighter, more educated, and less politically motivated than the economists in the countries they visit," whereas in fact the latter are often better educated and more knowledgeable.[106] Others believe the IMF's loans in times of financial crisis create a "moral hazard," encouraging reckless financial behavior by both borrowers and lenders.[107] Several authors are disappointed in the G-8/G-7 meetings and condemn them as unwieldy and overly elaborate "photo-ops," in which the participants are unable to focus on the very serious problems now confronting the human polity.[108]

For others the villains of globalization are not the international financial organizations but the national financial institutions that direct their activities on behalf of private national financial interests; William Greider singles out the U.S. Treasury for special blame and claims it over-responds to demands from private banking and finance, mainly the major U.S. banks and brokerage houses. He would dismantle the IMF and replace it with a "new, more democratic institution."[109] But businessman David Rothkopf, while agreeing that "we have not come close to perfecting global capitalism" insists that "the genius of capitalism is . . . that it continually reinvents itself" and that the remedy is not to give up but to use globalization to reform local systems "so that the disenfranchised have access to . . . capital, education, legal institutions, market efficiencies and other benefits." According to him, it is not Western business elites and not the international financial agencies that are causing the problems; it is local elite control of limited national assets.[110]

Others worry that the new war on terrorism initiated in the fall of 2001 makes reform less likely, and that the IMF and the World Bank will become pawns in that war, as they respond to political pressure to lend to countries that are allies in that war, regardless of their policies at home.[111]

Finally, there are those who think the answer lies neither in limited reforms of specific institutions nor in dismantling them nor in extensive decentralization. Their solution would be: accept internationalization and take charge of it.

Eva Etzioni-Halevy makes the argument for improving global accountability by reviewing the "linkage deficits in transnational politics," at the regional as well as the international level, and showing how these mean that "the weaker parts of the public are unable to make transnational elites promote their interests." [112] For Joseph Nye the "democratic deficit in the global economy" is what brought the otherwise very diverse Seattle protesters together; he fears that creating a true global democracy with majority rule would mean less not more protection for international environmental and labor standards, but urges citizens to work harder through their own governments to insist upon and strengthen openness (transparency) and accountability.[113] More boldly, Richard Falk and Andrew Strauss declare it is time to begin creating a global parliament, and create true international governance capable of regulating the regulators.[114] And Maria Claudia Drummond would not stop there. It is time, she says, to "devise instruments for the promotion of democratic, global citizenship. . . . Globalization has created unparalleled concentrations of autocratic power that must be brought under democratic control; otherwise they will produce poverty and despair for countless millions." The United States and the UN should take the lead in creating a new "global civil society." [115]

CONCLUSION

The immensity of the changes taking place in the human polity over the past fifty years has made the beginning of the new millennium a time for deeply serious reflection. Ours is not an era in which simple remedies can be easily deduced from any single ideological approach. The satisfaction of seeing whole nations suddenly commit themselves to "our way" must necessarily be accompanied by sober thoughts of how to make "our way" work. Political scientists who know how to confront the complexity of the relationships between economic and political developments have an important role to play in this vital task.

But it is part of human nature to enjoy even the most difficult challenges, and to find a way to tackle them. There must be a way out of the complex and interwoven dilemmas that have followed so swiftly and sometimes dishearteningly on the massive changes that initially promised such a brave new world. There must be something the individuals who make up the human polity—like you, like me—can do to insist that change be followed by change, that the problems that have emerged must be solved, and to help find the solutions. What must we do? What can we do?

Our first job, it seems to me, is to know what our values are and figure out which of them matter the most. Can you make a list of your values? Can you figure out which comes first, which last? Are you willing to sacrifice one on behalf of another that is higher on your list?

A second, and equally important, job is for us all to develop a new and deeper respect for the truth, as well as we are able to determine what that strange animal may be. "Reason from evidence" is easy to say, not so easy to do. We need to act on our values, of course, but we must not let serving them cause us to deny obvious realities or entertain unreal hopes that all our woes will somehow magically just go away. There is real work to be done.

That being so, the next thing to do is to choose a task and choose a way to work on it. We cannot all do everything, but every one of us can make some kind of contribution. Really working on one small part of one small problem is surely better than thinking about working on everything. Maybe you will join others who are trying to do the same thing—that's a good way to learn what works and to maximize the effect of the work you do. But you may be a loner, at least for now, and that's okay. Everyone can find a way to help.

But suppose the public service work you decide to do just makes the job chosen by that guy who sits on the other side of the classroom harder to do? We don't all have the same values; we do sometimes work at cross-purposes. There is no total cure for this, but there are a couple of partial ones. Keeping respect for the truth means hearing what "that guy" has to say and basing your defense of what you are trying to do on the most solid facts you can find. You two may find you can work together after all.

The other partial cure for the tendency of human beings to cancel each other out is for us all to learn to keep a new thought constantly in mind: *connectedness.* By this I do not mean only that the human polity consists of all the world's peoples, ever more dependent on one another for their well-being (so therefore be nice). I mean something a bit more tangible than that. To see what connectedness means, pick up a copy of today's newspaper and make a list of all the headlines having to do with national or international news. Then ask yourself what each one has to do with all the others. Anything? Everything? Try it and see. Then think about how the problem you have decided to work on is connected to other problems and other efforts (not all of them benign). If you do this, chances are you will find a way to work on your problem that is less likely to be at cross-purposes with the work of others who share your general hopes for a better and fairer world.

While you are doing all this, you may as well give some thought to what you think the role of international governance institutions should be and how to get them to play it. Which reforms seem most important to you? How can we move toward making them? What role might you yourself play in aiding that effort?

Whatever you decide and whatever you do, a final thought to keep in mind, or so it seems to me, is the need to work where and when we can. This is a tricky one. Whether they end up working in the schools, the government, or the business world, political scientists have tough work to do that may or may not be related to saving the world. Academic freedom is all well and good, but no department head is going to hand out many accolades or promotions to teachers or professors whose work seems biased and oblivious of different points of view. No senior government bureaucrat or elected official needs to hear daily lectures from junior staff about how important it is to build international governance institutions that work, given the frailty of the nation-state. And no boss in private business is likely to keep paying a junior employee who insists day after day that the company has a social responsibility to avoid layoffs at home and make sure its investments abroad are creating jobs with good pay and good working conditions and not extracting unreasonable profits. No matter what their field of employ, most junior employees do well to soft-pedal their sociopolitical activism at work and keep most of it for after hours. Otherwise, they may end up having only after hours.

But you are not always going to be a junior employee, are you? Someday you will be that tenured teacher, that senior bureaucrat, or that boss, right? And what then? Well, for one thing, by then you should have a yet better idea what kinds of recommendations and activities on behalf of your beliefs are reasonable and appropriate in your line of work. If you say, "None," then answer me this: How will the behaviors of governments or businesses ever improve if living and breathing social scientists, bureaucrats, elected officials, and businessmen and women take no responsibility beyond that of earning a living wage? Let us hope that when you reach a more senior position, you will make a point of taking connectedness seriously, in every aspect of your own life as well as in the way you read the headlines.

Who can tell if you will? Not I. But I can hope. And only thus, it seems to me, can any of us hope for the creation of a human polity in which all humanity has a home. This new ethic—this very old ethic—must somehow be made to grow and thrive in all our connected worlds. Making this happen is a tremendous challenge. And an absolute necessity.

QUESTIONS TO CONSIDER

1. Given what you now know (and knew before, on your own or from other courses), what do you believe are the prospects real democracy will be established world-wide in your lifetime?
2. Why is it important to think about the processes of building world government even if we "don't believe in it"? And how do you personally feel about the question?

3. What criticisms are most often made of the IMF and the World Bank and what can be said in their defense?

4. How can thinking about the "connectedness" of world events help you determine what your own role might be in working for a better human polity? What plans do you have for trying to help in that endeavor?

SELECTED READINGS

Danaher, Kevin, ed. *Democratizing the Global Economy: The Battle Against the World Bank and the International Monetary Fund* (Monroe, Maine: Common Courage Press, 2001). Activists and academics examine the mounting protests against the World Bank and IMF and the ways in which an international grassroots movement is seeking to build a more democratic global economy.

Gagnon, Alain-G. and James Tully, eds. *Multinational Democracies* (New York: Cambridge University Press, 2001). A collection of studies examining the complex character and internal tensions of democratic societies that comprise two or more nations, and seeking to draw understandings from the established democracies of the United Kingdom, Spain, Belgium, and Canada that may be useful in the diverse societies now struggling toward democracy.

Gilpin, Robert. *Global Political Economy: Understanding the International Economic Order* (Princeton, N.J.: Princeton University Press, 2001). Argues that the significance of economic globalization has been exaggerated and misunderstood, and that national policies and domestic economies remain the most critical determinants of economic affairs. Stresses the importance of economic regionalism, multinational corporations, and financial upheavals.

Hadenius, Axel. *Institutions and Democratic Citizenship* (New York: Oxford University Press, 2001). Contributes to the debate on democracy's preconditions, concluding that democracy is not the product of social and economic forces but rather of prevailing institutional conditions, that is, the nature of the state.

Horowitz, Shale and Uk Heo, eds. *The Political Economy of International Financial Crisis: Interest Groups, Ideologies and Institutions* (Lanham, Md.: Rowman and Littlefield, 2000). Focusing on the effects of the world financial crises at the end of the twentieth century on thirteen different nations in East Asia, Southeast Asia, Latin America, and Eastern Europe, the studies collected here illustrate how policymaking coalitions are formed and how political institutions mediate the pressure of rival coalitions.

Keohane, Robert O. and Joseph S. Nye. *Power and Independence,* 3rd ed. (New York: Longman, 2001). Explores the relationships between economics, politics, and patterns of institutionalized international cooperation. Analyzes the effects of new technologies and growing globalism on power and interdependence today.

Korten, David C. *When Corporations Rule the World* (Bloomfield, Conn.: Kumarian Press, 2001). Argues that economic globalization has concentrated the power to govern in global corporations and financial markets detached from accountability to human interests; presents a policy agenda for "restoring democracy and rooting economic power in people and communities."

Markoff, John. *Waves of Democracy: Social Movements and Political Change* (Thousand Oaks, Calif.: Pine Forge Press, 1996). An attempt to locate current efforts of democratization within a historical context, giving special emphasis to the role of social movements in this process.

Stubbs, Richard and Geoffrey R. D. Underhill, eds. *Political Economy and the Changing Global Order,* 2nd ed. (New York: Oxford University Press, 2000). Specialists in politics, economics, and international relations from ten different nations show how rapid change is the norm of the new international political economy.

Widner, Jennifer A., ed. *Economic Change and Political Liberalization in Sub-Saharan Africa* (Baltimore, Md.: Johns Hopkins University Press, 1994). A discussion of the economic crisis in Africa beginning in the 1980s and continuing to the present

time. Analyzes the effects of structural adjustment and economic reform programs.

WEB SITES OF INTEREST

1. International Forum on Globalization
   http://www.ifg.org/
   An alliance of activists and scholars seeking to provide a forum for the discussion of the current restructuring of global politics and economics.
2. World Bank
   http://www.worldbank.org
   Provides information on the World Bank's activities in more than 100 developing economies, including how the World Bank liaises with government and civil society.
3. International Monetary Fund
   http://www.imf.org/
   Current reports of the work of the IMF in its efforts to "promote international monetary cooperation, exchange stability and orderly exchange arrangements; to foster economic growth and high levels of employment; and to provide financial assistance to countries to help ease balance of payments adjustment."
4. Globalization Issues
   http://globalization.about.com/
   Provides links to Web sites about the history, process, and pros and cons of globalization.

NOTES

1. A thoughtful discussion of the importance of including the spread of democratic ideas in discussions of current globalization can be found in Katherine Fierlbeck, *Globalizing Democracy: Power, Legitimacy and the Interpretation of Democratic Ideas* (Manchester, U.K., and New York: Manchester University Press, 1998).
2. Georg Sørensen, *Democracy and Democratization: Processes and Prospects in a Changing World* (Boulder, Colo.: Westview Press, 1993), p. 31.
3. Carole Pateman, "Democracy and Democratization," *International Political Science Review* 17, no. 1 (1996): 5–12. As Pateman points out, "Never before has democracy been so popular."
4. Philippe C. Schmitter and Terry Lynn Karl, "What Democracy Is . . . And Is Not," in Larry Diamond and Marc F. Plattner, *The Global Resurgence of Democracy* (Baltimore, Md.: Johns Hopkins University Press, 1993), p. 40.
5. Robert A. Dahl, *Democracy and Its Critics* (New Haven, Conn.: Yale University Press, 1989), pp. 106–15.
6. Peter H. Merkl, "Which Are Today's Democracies?" *International Social Science Journal* 136 (May 1993): 257–58.
7. George Munda Carew, "Development Theory and the Promise of Democracy: The Future of Postcolonial African States," *Africa Today* 40, no. 4 (1993): 46–50.
8. Sidney Verba, "A Research Perspective" in "Threats to Democracy: Plenary Session IV," Commission on Behavioral and Social Sciences and Education, National Research Council, *The Transition to Democracy: Proceedings of a Workshop* (Washington, D.C.: National Academy Press, 1991), p. 78.
9. Schmitter and Karl, "What Democracy Is," p. 49.
10. Philippe Braud, *Le Suffrage universel contre la démocratie* (Paris: Presses Universitaires de France, 1980) et *Le Jardin des délices démocratiques* (Paris: Presses de la Fondation Nationale des Sciences Politiques, 1991).
11. Schmitter and Karl, "What Democracy Is," p. 51; Jane Mansbridge, "Politics," in "What Is a Democracy? Plenary Session I," Commission on Be-

havioral and Social Sciences and Education, *Transition to Democracy,* p. 6.

12. Havard Hegre, Tanja Ellingsen, and Scott Gates, "Toward a Democratic Civil Peace? Democracy, Political Change and Civil War, 1816–1992," *The American Political Science Review* 95, no. 1 (March 2001): 33–48.

13. Mansbridge, "Politics," p. 5. Mansbridge bases this statement on unpublished data from the Yale Human Relations Area Files on 186 societies. She notes it requires us to presume that Germany was a monarchy in World War I and a dictatorship in World War II and that Lebanon in 1967 was a military regime. We might add that the statement also requires us to ignore civil wars within democracies and the readiness of other democracies to come to the aid of one side or the other in such internal battles.

14. Sørensen, *Democracy and Democratization,* pp. 25–28.

15. Doh Chull Shin, "On The Third Wave of Democratization: A Synthesis and Evaluation of Recent Theory and Research," *World Politics* 47, no. 1 (October 1994): 151.

16. Laurence Whitehead, "The Drama of Democratization," *Journal of Democracy* 10, no. 4 (1999): 84–98.

17. For example, see Sørensen, *Democracy and Democratization,* pp. 29–30. For Sørensen, such negotiations mean that the new regimes' ability to introduce social and economic reform measures—measures that might harm the interests of the elites—will necessarily be restricted.

18. Charles Tilly, "Overview," in "Comment and Synthesis: Plenary Session III," *Transition to Democracy,* pp. 60–61; see also p. 25.

19. Verba, "Research Perspective," pp. 82–83.

20. These authors are cited by Shin, "On the Third Wave," pp. 144–45.

21. Ibid., p. 137.

22. Sørensen, *Democracy and Democratization,* pp. 40, 61–62.

23. *New York Times,* 21 Nov. 1995, A14.

24. Kenneth Ka-Lok Chan, "Poland at the Crossroads: The 1993 General Election," *Europe-Asia Studies* 47, no. 1 (1995): 125–27.

25. "Eastern Europe's Capitalism: Who's Boss Now?" *The Economist* (10 May 1995): 65–67.

26. "Nostalgia Wins the Day in Poland," *New Statesman and Society* (1 Oct. 1993): 20–21.

27. Ray Taras, "The End of the Walesa Era in Poland," *Current History* 95, no. 599 (March 1996): 127.

28. "Kwasniewski Wins: Political Lessons Explored," *The Current Digest of the Post-Soviet Press* 47, no. 47 (1995): 15–17.

29. *New York Times,* 6 Nov. 1995, A3.

30. "Kwasniewski Wins," *Current Digest,* pp. 16–17.

31. Quoted in Peter Finn, "Grim Outlook at Polls for Poland's Solidarity," *Washington Post Foreign Service,* Sunday, 2 Sept. 2001, A23.

32. For some representative accounts, see Patrick H. O'Neil, "Hungary's Hesitant Transition," *Current History* 95, no. 599 (March 1996): 135–39; Barnabas Racz and Istvan Kukorelli, "The 'Second-Generation' Post-Communist Elections in Hungary in 1994," *Europe-Asia Studies* 47, no. 2 (March 1995): 251–79; "Bulgaria, Back Under Ex-Communism," *The Economist* (7 Jan. 1995): 43–44; Samuel Abraham, "Early Elections in Slovakia: A State of Deadlock," *Government and Opposition* 30, no. 1 (1995): 86–100; "Czechs Prepare to Vote," *The Economist* (25 May 1996): 58.

33. Information regarding current regimes may be found at http://www.electionworld.org/.

34. Michael McFaul, "Ten Years After the Soviet Breakup: A Mixed Record, An Uncertain Future," *Journal of Democracy* 12, no. 4 (2001): 87–94.

35. McFaul, op. cit.

36. Both are quoted in "Russia's Emerging Market," in "Survey on Russia," *The Economist,* 8 Apr. 1995, 3–5.

37. Kate Hannan, "Reforming China's State Enterprises, 1984–93," special issue on "Enterprise Reform in Post-Socialist Societies," *Journal of Communist Studies and Transition Politics* 11, no. 1 (March 1995): 33–55.

38. Wayne M. Morrison, *China's Economic Conditions* (Washington, D.C.: Congressional Research Service, Issue Brief 98014, 21 Sept. 2000). See also David S. G. Goodman, "Collectives and Connectives, Capitalism and Corporatism: Structural Change in China," special issue on "Enter-

prise Reform in Post-Socialist Societies," *Journal of Communist Studies and Transition Politics* 11, no. 1 (March 1995): 12–32.

39. Shen Tong, "The Next Revolution," *New York Times,* 1 Sept. 1992, A15.

40. Goodman, "Collectives and Connectives," p. 19.

41. Paul Blustein and Clay Chandler, "WTO Approves China's Entry: Move Expected to Speed Beijing's Transition to Capitalism," *Washington Post,* 11 Nov. 2001, A47.

42. Melanie Beresford, "The North Vietnamese State-Owned Industrial Sector: Continuity and Change," Special Issue on "Enterprise Reform in Post-Socialist States," *Journal of Communist Studies and Transition Politics* 11, no. 1 (March 1995): 56–76.

43. "Kim Jong Il's Inheritance," *The Economist* (16 July 1994): 19–21; Susan Hurlich, "Letter from Havana: Capitalist Ways—Cubans Dabble in Free-Enterprise Markets," *Macleans* (21 Aug. 1995): 22–23; Joel Simon, "Despite U.S. Coercion, Cuba Dips Toe into Capitalist Zones," *Christian Science Monitor,* 16 July 1996, 1, 18.

44. Some of these cases are treated in Guillermo O'Donnell, Philippe C. Schmitter, and Laurence Whitehead, eds., *Transitions from Authoritarian Rule: Prospects for Democracy* (Baltimore, Md.: Johns Hopkins University Press, 1986).

45. "Democracy, African-Style," *The Economist* (3 Feb. 1996): 17.

46. "Democracy in Africa," *The Economist* (22 Feb. 1992): 17–20.

47. Jeffrey Herbst, "The Dilemmas of Explaining Political Upheaval: Ghana in Comparative Perspective," in Jennifer A. Widner, ed., *Economic Change and Political Liberalization in Sub-Saharan Africa* (Baltimore, Md.: Johns Hopkins University Press, 1994), p. 194. Herbst highlights urban populations and military and security forces as the two groups whose interests must be addressed for African leadership to stay in power.

48. Ernest Harsch, "Structural Adjustment and Africa's Democracy Movements," *Africa Today* 40, no. 4 (1993): 8.

49. Ibid., p. 23.

50. Ibid., p. 19.

51. Herbst, "Dilemmas," p. 185.

52. James C. McKinley Jr., "After a String of Dicta-

tors, Ugandans Vote Once Again," *New York Times,* 10 May 1996, A3; Susan Linnee, "Incumbent Wins Big in Uganda," *San Francisco Chronicle,* 11 May 1996, A8.

53. *New York Times,* 11 March 1996, A5, and "Sudan," *Defense and Foreign Affairs* (March 1996): 14.

54. John F. Clark, "Elections, Leadership and Democracy in Congo," *Africa Today* (third quarter 1994): 41–60.

55. Brian Loveman, "'Protected Democracies' and Military Guardianship: Political Transitions in Latin America, 1978–1993," *Journal of Inter-American Studies and World Affairs* 36, no. 2 (Summer 1994): 105–89. Quote from p. 105.

56. Ibid., p. 114.

57. Loveman, "'Protected Democracies,'" p. 115; Carlos M. Vilas, "Latin America in the 'New World Order': Prospects for Democracy," *International Journal of Politics, Culture and Society* 8, no. 2 (1994): 275. For a case study of minimalist democracy in Central America, see the special issue on Guatemala, *Journal of InterAmerican Studies and World Affairs* 42, no. 4 (Winter 2000).

58. Frances Hagopian, "After Regime Change: Authoritarian Legacies, Political Representation and the Democratic Future of South America," a review article in *World Politics* 45 (April 1993): 464–500. Quote from p. 500.

59. Ibid, p. 467. In general, Hagopian stresses the need to examine each regime separately, particularly when attempting to assess the impact of the period of military rule.

60. Loveman, "'Protected Democracies,'" pp. 123–25, 157–58.

61. Guillermo O'Donnell, "Introduction to the Latin American Cases," in Guillermo O'Donnell, Philippe C. Schmitter, and Laurence Whitehead, eds., *Transitions from Authoritarian Rule: Prospects for Democracy* (Baltimore: Johns Hopkins University Press, 1986), pp. 14–15.

62. Ibid., p. 15.

63. Scott Mainwaring is another author who rejects all-encompassing pessimism, assessing democratic reforms in Chile as successful and pointing to some gains in Brazil and Uruguay. Mainwaring appears to accept, however, the truncated version

of democracy that other authors cited here repudiate. See his "Democracy in Brazil and the Southern Cone: Achievements and Problems," *Journal of InterAmerican Studies and World Affairs* 37, no. 1 (1995): 113–79.

64. Maxwell A. Cameron, *Democracy and Authoritarianism in Peru* (New York: St. Martin's Press, 1994), p. 149.

65. The significance of trying civilians in military courts was brought home to the U.S. public in early 1996 when New Yorker Lori Helene Berenson, whose trial was closed to the public and whose lawyers were not allowed to cross-examine witnesses or challenge key evidence, was convicted of treason in Peru by such a court, and sentenced to life in prison. *New York Times,* 14 Jan. 1996, 4, 6.

66. As one senior U.S. State Department official put it, Peru would have to "get that democratic feeling back." Quoted (anonymously) by Cameron, *Democracy and Authoritarianism,* p. 155.

67. Ibid., p. 145.

68. David Scott Palmer, "'Fujipopulism' and Peru's Progress," *Current History* (February 1996): 73, 75.

69. Ibid., pp. 70–75.

70. *New York Times,* 19 May 1996, 4.

71. Coletta A. Youngers, "Peru: Democracy and Dictatorship," *Foreign Policy in Focus* 5, no. 34 (Oct. 2000).

72. Scott Wilson, "Fujimori's Long Shadow: New Leader in Peru Seen as Distracted by the Many Probes of His Predecessor," *Washington Post Foreign Service,* Monday, 17 Dec. 2001, A19.

73. "Presidential Coups d'État and Regime Change in Latin American and Soviet Successor States," paper delivered at 1998 meetings of the Latin American Studies Association, Chicago, Ill., September 24–26, 1998. See also Maxwell A. Cameron and Philip Mauceri, eds., *The Peruvian Labyrinth: Politics, Society and Economy* (University Park: Pennsylvania State University Press, 1997).

74. José M. Gonzalez-Eiras, "International Trade and Economic Nationalism," in Antonio Jorge, ed., *Economic Development and Social Change: United States–Latin American Relations in the 1990s* (New Brunswick, N.J.: Transaction, 1992), pp. 9–10.

75. John H. Jackson, "The World Trade Organization, Dispute Settlement, and Codes of Conduct," in Susan M. Collins and Barry P. Bosworth, eds., *The New GATT: Implications for the United States* (Washington, D.C.: The Brookings Institution, 1994), pp. 63–83.

76. Stuart Corbridge, ed., *World Economy* (New York: Oxford University Press, 1993), p. 27.

77. Ibid., p. 28.

78. See, for example, Kenneth N. Giepin, "Brazil in an Accord with Large Banks on Cutting Its Debt," *New York Times,* 16 April 1994, A1.

79. Frederic S. Pearson and J. Martin Rochester, *International Relations: The Global Condition in the Twenty-first Century,* 4th ed. (New York: McGraw-Hill, 1998), p. 491.

80. Jeff Gerth and Elaine Sciolino, "I.M.F. Head: He Speaks, and Money Talks," *New York Times,* 2 April 1996, A1.

81. Pearson and Rochester, op. cit., p. 495.

82. Jessica Einhorn, "The World Bank's Mission Creep," *Foreign Affairs* (Sept./Oct. 2001).

83. Tom Barry, "G8 and Global Governance," *Foreign Policy in Focus* 6, no. 27 (July 2001) http://www.fpif.org.

84. Peter R. Weilemann, "The Summit Meeting: The Role and Agenda of Diplomacy at Its Highest Level," *NIRA Review* (Spring 2000): 17–20.

85. Barry, op. cit.

86. William J. Antholis, "Pragmatic Engagement or Photo Op: What Will the G-8 Become?" *The Washington Quarterly* 24, no. 3 (Summer 2001): 213–26.

87. Herman E. Daly and John B. Cobb Jr., *For the Common Good* (Boston: Beacon Press, 1994), p. 440.

88. Ibid., p. 11.

89. Ibid., p. 440.

90. John H. Jackson, "The World Trade Organization, Dispute Settlement, and Codes of Conduct," in Collins and Bosworth, *The New GATT,* pp. 63–83.

91. Corbridge, *World Economy,* p. 29.

92. Walden Bello and Shea Cunningham, "Reign of Error: The World Bank's Wrongs," *Dollars and Sense* 195 (Sept./Oct. 1994): 11.

93. "Globalization with a Human Face," *Human Development Report* (New York: Oxford University Press, 1999).

94. Jeffrey D. Sachs, "International Economics: Unlocking the Mysteries of Globalization," *Foreign Policy* 110 (Spring 1998): 97–111.

95. Jeremy Seabrook, "Invisible Children of the South," *New Statesman* 129 (26 June 2000): 14–15.

96. Peter Gibbon, Kjell J. Havnevik, and Kenneth Hermele, *A Blighted Harvest: The World Bank and African Agriculture in the 1980s* (Trenton, N.J.: Africa World Press, 1993), pp. 128–29.

97. Ethen B. Kapstein, "Workers and the World Economy," in *Foreign Affairs Agenda, The New Shape of World Politics: Contending Paradigms in International Relations,* rev. ed. (New York: Foreign Affairs, 1999), p. 197.

98. "That Sinking Feeling in Japan," *Business Week* (8 May 1995): 52–54.

99. Reuven S. Ayi-Yonah, "World-Class Tax Evasion," *American Prospect* 11, no. 13 (22 May 2000): 28–30. For a further discussion of the importance of tax policies in the process of globalization, see Tanzi Vito, "Globalization and the Work of Fiscal Termites," *Finance and Development* 38, no. 1 (March 2001): 34–37.

100. S. Jayasankaran, "A City Divided: Growing Disparities in Household Incomes May Alienate Those Who Have the Least," *Far Eastern Economic Review* 163, no. 41 (12 Oct. 2000): 26–27.

101. "Measuring Globalization," *Foreign Policy* no. 122 (Jan.–Feb. 2001): 56–65.

102. Daly and Cobb, op. cit.

103. Alain Touraine, "The Good Fight Against Capitalism," *Le Monde,* 27 Nov. 2001, translated and reprinted by *World Press Review* (Feb. 2002): 20.

104. "Toward a New Internationalism: New Era of Protest Against Globalization," editorial, *Monthly Review* 52, no. 3 (July/Aug. 2000): 1–10.

105. Jessica Einhorn, "The World Bank's Mission Creep," *Foreign Affairs* (Sept./Oct. 2001). Others argue that not only the international financial institutions but the UN itself is trying to accomplish goals that could be better met at the regional level; a measure of decentralization is in order. See Bruce Russett, "Global or Regional:
What Can International Organizations Do?" in Toshiro Tanaka and Takashi Inoguchi, *United Nations Global Seminar 1996, Shonan Session* (New York: United Nations, 1996). See also Edward D. Mansfield and Helen V. Miller, "The New Wave of Regionalism," *International Organization* 53, no. 3 (Summer 1999): 589–627.

106. Joseph Stiglitz, "The Insider: What I Learned at the World Economic Crisis," *The New Republic* (17 April 2000).

107. Ricki Tigert Helfer, "Rethinking IMF Rescues," *Brookings Institution Conference Report #1* (August 1998). http://www.brook.edu/pa/conferencereport/cr01.htm.

108. William J. Antholis, "Pragmatic Engagement or Photo Op: What Will the G-8 Become?" *The Washington Quarterly* 24, no. 3 (Summer 2001), 213–26; Peter Weilemann, "The Summit Meeting: The Role and Agenda of Diplomacy at Its Highest Level," *NIRA Review* (Spring 2000): 17–20; and Tom Barry, "G8 and Global Governance," *Foreign Policy in Focus* 6, no. 27 (July 2000).

109. William Greider, "Time to Rein in Global Finance," *The Nation* (24 April 2000).

110. David Rothkopf, "After This, Whatever Capitalism's Fate, Somebody's Already Working on an Alternative," *Washington Post,* 20 Jan. 2002, B01. Rothkopf is chairman and CEO of Intellibridge Corporation.

111. Paul Blustein, "A Tighter Hand in Doling Out Global Aid? IMF, World Bank Principles Face a New Policy Threat," *Washington Post,* 30 Sept. 2001, H1.

112. Eva Etzioni-Halevy, "Linkage Deficits in Transnational Politics," *International Political Science Review* 23, no. 2 (2002): 203–22.

113. Joseph S. Nye Jr., "Globalization's Democratic Deficit: How to Make International Institutions More Accountable," *Foreign Affairs* 80, no. 4 (July/Aug. 2001): 2–6.

114. "Bridging the Globalization Gap: Toward Global Parliament," *Foreign Affairs* 80, no. 1 (Jan.–Feb. 2001).

115. Maria Claudia Drummond, "Guide Globalization into a Just World Order," *Washington Quarterly* 24, no. 3 (Summer 2001): 173–83.

Glossary

A teacher I know has an answer for students who complain that he sometimes uses words they don't understand: "I'm sorry," he says sympathetically, "I just wish there were a book somewhere that could tell you the meanings of all the words in the English language."

Unlike a dictionary, a glossary is not comprehensive and does not give all possible meanings of the terms listed. But this glossary *will* help you understand each term as it is used in this book. For a fuller definition, please do consult your dictionary.

Ad hoc coalition. A temporary organization created to allow several political organizations to pool their resources in a joint effort in which all are interested.

Administrative law. The rules and decisions of administrative agencies.

Admiralty and maritime law. Law governing shipping and water-borne commerce.

Aggregation of interests. The gathering and compromising of different points of view on a topic in order to facilitate the making of policy. Often seen as a prime function of political parties.

Alienation. The condition of being withdrawn and detached from oneself and/or society. A concept developed by Karl Marx describing the tendency of factory workers to see themselves as mere extensions of their machines.

American government. The subfield of political science devoted to the study of the political processes and institutions of the United States.

Amorphous groups. Groups of individuals who share an interest and act on its behalf in a way that indirectly affects government policy.

Anarchism. An ideology stressing belief in the ability of men and women to establish functioning social communities without need for the apparatus of the state and dedicated to the overthrow of existing states by revolution.

Anomy. The condition of being without values; normless.

Apartheid. The South African system of strict racial segregation, maintained by that nation's minority government of white supremacists. Under apartheid, black Africans were required to live in isolated "homelands" and other nonwhite populations were confined to particular neighborhoods within the cities.

Apathy. The condition of being without interest, unconcerned, indifferent.

Apprentice. A person who works in a trade or an art for a more experienced tradesman or artist in return for instruction.

Arms control. Using diplomacy in order to obtain international agreements that limit the production and/or use of nuclear weaponry.

Ascription. A basis for leadership recruitment, specifically, the placing of persons in positions of leadership because their possession of other characteristics (e.g., placement in a lineage system) leads one to believe they must have the necessary qualities to rule.

Associational group. A fully organized group

formed specifically to represent the interests of its members.

Attitudes. General, often unverbalized sets of feelings that incline the person holding them to adopt particular specific beliefs and opinions.

Authoritarian system. A political system in which the power of the rulers is virtually unlimited, although this power is not always exercised in all domains. See also *totalitarian system.*

Authority. The right to exercise the power and influence of a particular position that comes from having been placed in that position according to regular, known, and widely accepted procedures. A person in such a position.

Authority figures. Persons whose positions carry such authority—the boss, the landlord, the military commander—that they may continue to shape political choices for us in adulthood as they did in childhood.

Balance of payments. The relationship between the payments received by a nation for goods it exports to other nations and the payments made to other nations for goods it imports.

Balance of power. The theory that the best way to prevent war is to ensure that the major nations of the world remain roughly "balanced" in the power each has to wage war successfully. See also *deterrence.*

Band. A nomadic group of families that live and move together and that determine together how goods shall be shared, what individual behavior is permissible, and what religious ceremonies shall be performed.

Behavioral approach. A way of studying politics that focuses on how an individual acts politically and that seeks explanations for that behavior within that individual.

Belief. The conviction that a certain thing is true or false. See also *opinion.*

Bicameral legislature. A legislature with two houses, usually an upper house and a lower house. See also *unicameral legislature.*

Bureaucracy. The administration of government through departments and subdivisions managed by sets of appointed officials following fixed rules of procedure.

Bureaucrat. A government employee responsible for carrying out some aspects of the administrative work of government according to fixed rules of procedure.

Bureaucratic. A tendency to follow rules closely, without regard for differences in rank or circumstance of the persons to whom they apply. Often used pejoratively to refer to someone who insists on following a routine in a mechanical way, insisting on proper forms and petty rules.

Bureaucratic drift. A movement of bureaucracies away from control by elected representatives of the people they serve.

Cabinet. A body composed of the heads of the most important subdivisions of a nation's executive branch and led by the nation's chief executive. Its functions are normally to advise the chief executive and to assist in the formulation of legislation to be proposed to the national legislative body. In a presidential system the cabinet is under the control of the president and is responsible to that leader, whereas in parliamentary and presidential-parliamentary systems its ultimate responsibility is to the legislature.

Cadre parties. Political parties with small, loosely affiliated memberships, a co-opted elite leadership with little control over the base, and weak communication links.

Capitalism. An economic system in which individuals are free to invest their savings (capital) as they wish, to purchase goods and hire labor in order to develop private enterprise, and to reinvest profits (also capital) in such businesses or in those of other citizens.

Cartel. Associations of businesses formed in the early twentieth century to establish national or international monopolies over particular raw materials or manufactured goods.

Catchall party. A party that makes concrete, pragmatic short-range promises to fulfill the immediate interests of as many voters as possible.

Center-periphery relations. Relations between a polity's central government and the governments of provincial and local units. See also *periphery.*

Ceremonial leader. See *chief of state.*

Charisma. Having the gift of leadership and being recognized as having that gift.

Chief executive. The most powerful leader in a

given polity's executive branch—usually the most powerful leader in the state. Normally a prime minister or president.

Chief of state.   The official who performs the ceremonial roles of government leadership. Normally a hereditary monarch or an elected but relatively powerless president. In a presidential system, the functions of chief of state and chief executive are combined.

City-state.   An early form of political community, a polity seldom larger in population or area than a medium-size city of today but constituting at the same time a sovereign state.

Civic culture.   A culture in which citizens combine a commitment to moderate political participation with a belief in the legitimacy of officialdom and a tendency toward parochialism.

Civic training.   Teaching the facts about a political system and the procedures for participating in that system as a citizen. See also *political indoctrination.*

Civil law.   Law governing unfair (but not criminal) behavior that affects only other individuals, not the community. Civil law calls for retribution to the offended party, not punishment on behalf of the public order.

Civilian supremacy.   The principle that civilian leadership shall be maintained over the armed forces of a polity.

Class.   A kind of group identity, normally based on differences in level of income, level of education, and kind of occupation, sometimes also based on differences in accent, dress, and kinds of material acquisitions desired and purchased.

Clientelistic linkage.   The connection between citizens and political leaders that takes place when the former offer electoral support in exchange for material rewards provided by the latter.

Clientelistic parties.   Parties in which leaders make sure their followers receive certain material benefits for their support but do not encourage them to express opinions on matters of policy.

Codified law.   Laws that have been set down in writing in conjunction with other laws. Edicts, treaties, decrees, legislative enactments, and judicial precedents are among the forms of law that may be codified. See also *statutory law.*

Colonialism.   The system by which a nation maintains control over a distant territory in order to exploit that territory's resources. See also *neo-colonialism.*

Committee system.   The use of specialized or standing committees by legislative bodies to organize and facilitate their work.

Common law.   Law made by using the rulings of judges in earlier cases as precedents. Sometimes referred to as "judge-made law." See also *precedent.*

Common law legal culture.   The making of judicial decisions by reference to previous judicial decisions. Dominant throughout the British Commonwealth, in the United States, and in other former British colonies.

Communications media.   A term referring to the technical devices employed in mass communication, typically including newspapers, magazines, radio, and television. Commonly known as the media.

Communism.   A form of socialism emphasizing the absolute abolition of private property, economic equality, rule by the workers (the proletariat), and access to power by armed revolution. Subcategories of communism include Marxism, Leninism, and Maoism.

Comparative government.   The subfield of political science devoted to the study of foreign polities, using the comparative method.

Confederal system.   A system of government in which the units are independent states that have decided to join together in a formal alliance, acting as a single unit for some limited purpose, but not for others.

Confederation.   A system of government in which nearly all powers are reserved to the constituent units of the nation—that is, to the states, provinces, or cantons.

Conservatism.   An ideology that stresses conserving what exists; takes a nonegalitarian view of human nature; and holds order, continuity, loyalty, protection of individual freedoms, piety, and nationalism as its highest values.

Constituency.   All the people, especially voters, served by a particular elected official, especially a legislator. The district of such a group of voters.

Constitution. A set of rules prescribing the institutions and procedures of government and having precedence over all other rules in a given polity.

Constitutional law. A nation's constitution and the body of judicial rulings about the meaning of the constitution. The subfield of political science devoted to the study of the institutions and procedures of government as these are formally prescribed in constitutions and explicated in judicial rulings.

Co-optation. Granting prestigious appointments or other benefits to one whose support is sought but not yet certain, as a means of securing that support.

Corporate guilds. Organizations formed in Europe in the sixteenth century to regulate the social, economic, and political affairs of craftsmen when such workers—masters, journeymen, and apprentices—found themselves able to live independently from the feudal system.

Corporatism. An economic system in which formal ownership of the means of production remains in private hands, but the state requires that all industries and other productive enterprises be grouped into units according to the function performed. See also *neocorporatism*.

Coup d'état. A French term meaning overthrow of the state, normally by armed force. A coup is different from a revolution in that it usually entails replacement of the top leadership of a regime by another narrow elite, and is not based on a mass movement.

Criminal law. Law governing crimes. Criminal law views an act of crime as an offense against the public order and therefore deserving of punishment by society.

Cultural relativism. The idea that each society sets its own standards in accordance with its own culture, and that what is correct in one society may be repugnant in another.

Cultural values. Values shared by a group of people.

Culture. The ideas and customs of a given people in a given period.

Decentralization. The process of breaking up the concentration of power in the central government and allocating some portion of that power to provincial and local units.

Decree. A rule issued by a leader in a given polity's executive branch and having the force of law.

Delegation of power. The practice of ceding to one branch of government powers that are constitutionally assigned to another, most commonly from the legislative branch to the executive branch.

Demagogue. A person who gains public office by appealing to fears and prejudices, and then uses the power of office for personal gain.

Democracy. Rule by the people. A system of government in which all adults not disqualified by criminal behavior or mental incapacity have the right and the means to exercise some form of genuine control over government. The means of ensuring democratic government normally include the protection of individual liberties, free elections, and political equality.

Democratic socialism. An ideology espousing the principles of socialism but stressing the need to achieve and exercise power democratically.

Deterrence. The theory that the best way to prevent nuclear war is to build up such a massive and threatening arsenal of nuclear weapons that no other nation will dare to attack. See also *balance of power*.

Dialectical materialism. The Marxist theory that human history is evolving through stages characterized by different modes of production and different allocations of power to control the means of production. Movement from stage to stage is by dialectics: The status quo is the thesis, the effort to impose its opposite is the antithesis, and the eventual compromise between old and new is the synthesis—which becomes, in turn, the new thesis.

Dictatorship. A political system in which power is concentrated in the hands of a single individual and is maintained by the autocratic exercise of that power; often characterized by the development of a cult of personality around the dictator.

Diplomat. A representative of a government who conducts relations with another government in the interests of his or her own nation.

Diplomatic corps. The group of diplomats for each country.

Direct democracy. Government immediately by the people, as contrasted to government by elected representatives or by charismatic or dictatorial autocrats.

Directive linkage. The connection between citizens and political leaders that exists when the latter maintain control over the former, either by coercion or by manipulation.

Directive parties. Parties that link voters to government by helping the government maintain coercive control over its subjects.

Division of labor. The assignment of different tasks to different persons in a community.

Domestic law. The body of laws that nations apply within their own territories.

Economic and Social Council. A United Nations organization whose function is to promote international cooperation in economic and social matters.

Economic development. The transformation of natural resources (the nation's own or those imported from other nations as raw materials) into ever more valuable processed goods, the improvement of services, and the marketing of those goods and services in order to enhance the material well-being of the nation's people.

Economic equality. The condition that exists when all citizens have approximately the same amount of material wealth.

Economy. A system of producing, distributing, and consuming wealth.

Elected board (council). The most common rule-making body of local government.

Electoral system. The rules and regulations governing how citizens vote in a polity.

Empire. A polity composed of numerous smaller polities that maintain their own identities but have come under the sway of another polity, usually through warfare.

Equality. Having the same fundamental needs as well as the same rights under the law. Such rights may be political, economic, and/or social.

Equity law. Law designed to supplement the common law by providing relief when the operation of the law will wreak irremediable harm; an example is the injunction.

Espionage. The act of gathering information about another nation that the nation prefers not be known; spying.

Ethnic group. A self-identified group with distinctive racial and/or national characteristics and a shared set of beliefs and values.

Executive veto. A veto by the person in the highest government position.

Extraconstitutional forces. Forces outside the formal government of a polity that are nevertheless strong enough to shape public policy.

Extraconstitutional power. Power exercised by the government when groups external to the government are able to pressure the agents of the government into a situation in which they feel they have no choice but to comply.

Fascism. A far-right ideology based on the principle that race, nationalism, and absolute obedience to authoritarian leadership are the highest values.

Federal system. A system of government in which certain powers are reserved to the central government but others are constitutionally reserved to the governments of the nation's constituent parts —that is, to the states, provinces, or cantons.

Feedback. A term used in political systems analysis to denote the transmission of information, rewards, or punishments from one element of a system to another, as a form of response to input from that element. See also *input*.

Feudalism. A system in which the political leaders, large landholders, and the serfs who worked the land were linked by mutual political and economic dependency. Wealth, and thereby political power, was based on agricultural production.

Freedom. The condition of being able to act without restraint.

Functional regionalism. A form of regionalism, often temporary, established to deal with a single problem; more limited in scope than structural regionalism.

General Assembly. The organization of the United Nations to which each of the member states sends a representative and which has the power to make recommendations in the name of the United Nations if a two-thirds vote can be obtained.

Government. The institutions responsible for making and carrying out the laws of a polity and for adjudicating disputes that arise under those laws.

The arena in which political choices are made manifest. In political systems analysis, the decision-making apparatus that receives inputs and emits outputs.

Guerrilla warfare. The attempt to accomplish political change by training and arming a band of revolutionaries who live in hiding, preferably in difficult and well-forested terrain; who attempt to recruit others to their cause; and who make only limited attacks on the forces of the state until the balance of power between themselves and the state is sufficiently equal to permit open warfare. See also *terrorist organization.*

Head of state. In a parliamentary system, the nation's monarch or president.

Hegemonic party system. A system in which there is more than a single party but one party has established pronounced and continuing dominance.

Ideological party. A party of true believers who gradually rally others to their cause.

Ideology. A comprehensive set of beliefs and attitudes about social and economic institutions and processes.

Imperialism. The policy and practice of forming and maintaining an empire by the conquest of other countries and the establishment of colonies.

Indirect election. An election in which only those who have already been elected to another post are entitled to vote.

Indoctrination. Overt instruction in a body of beliefs.

Industrialism. A social and economic system characterized by large industries, machine production, and the concentration of workers in cities.

Inflation. An increase in the amount of money in circulation, resulting in a relatively sharp and sudden fall in its value and a rise in prices.

Influence. The ability to affect the behavior of another. See also *power.*

Initiative. A provision in a polity's electoral system that permits citizens to vote directly on specific proposals for new legislation, provided a certain number of citizens petition for the opportunity to do so.

Injunction. A court order issued to prevent an action until the offended party has had time to prepare and present a fuller legal argument that the action should not take place.

Input. A term used in political systems analysis to denote the support and demands coming to governments from such forces as public opinion, interest groups, and political parties. See also *feedback.*

Institution. A structure with established, important functions to perform; with well-specified roles for carrying out those functions; and with a clear set of rules governing the relationship between the people who occupy those roles.

Intelligence agency. A government office assigned the task of gathering information about other nations in order to assist a nation's decision-makers in the formulation of foreign policy and the safeguarding of national security.

Interest. A clearly identified personal stake in a decision or the outcome of an event.

Interest group. An organization whose main purpose is to affect the operation of government by persuading key persons in government to act in accordance with the group's interests.

International Court of Justice. The judicial branch of the United Nations, with jurisdiction only over cases the members of that body agree to refer to it. Sometimes called the World Court.

International law. The law that applies in relationships between nations, or between the citizens of one nation and either the government or the individual citizens of another nation.

International relations. The relationships between nations. The subfield of political science devoted to the study of relationships between nations.

International terrorism. Terrorism directed by citizens of one or more nations against another nation.

Iron law of oligarchy. According to Robert Michels, the natural tendency of people in organizations to divide into those who lead and those who follow.

Journeyman. A craftsman who has completed an apprenticeship and is now a qualified worker for another craftsman.

Judicial activism. The use of judicial review to overrule both legislative statute and court decision.

Judicial independence. The protection of the judiciary, usually by constitutional guarantees, from interference by the other branches of government in the conduct of its work.

Judicial review. The power of a judiciary to review legislative and executive enactments in order to decide whether or not they conform with a polity's constitution and to declare such enactments null and void where they are found not in conformance with that constitution.

Judiciary. The branch of government concerned with punishing criminal acts and adjudicating disputes that arise under the law.

Justice. Fair treatment under the law. As such, justice is the possible (but not inevitable) result of decisions made by those who have been granted authority to determine what constitutes fair treatment.

Kinship system. A means of ordering sociopolitical relationships in which each person's right to use a parcel of land and to own cattle or other property is determined by his or her place in the family lineage.

Laissez faire. A French term meaning "let them do as they will." A laissez-faire economy is one in which government stays out of the world of business as much as possible.

Law. A regulation established by public authorities and backed by the collective power of the polity to which it applies.

Left. A term used to describe political ideas comparatively. Those on the political left tend to take a more positive view of human nature and to be convinced that change and progress are necessary and possible to improve the human condition. See also *right*.

Legal cultures. Regional variations in the evolution and application of the law.

Legislature. A body of persons given the responsibility and power to make laws for a polity.

Legitimacy. The condition of being considered correct and proper. See also *political legitimacy*.

Liberalism. An ideology that sees the role of government as protecting individual liberties while at the same time ensuring everyone the chance to lead the best possible life and to fulfill his or her individual potential.

Liberty. The absence of constraint.

Linkage. The connection between one political unit (e.g., citizen, political organization, level of government, nation-state) and another.

Lobbying. Seeking to influence public officials by direct personal contact; often attempted in the lobbies of public buildings by the paid representatives (lobbyists) of groups or individuals.

Local government. Subnational government that is under the jurisdiction of provincial and national (and sometimes regional) government and that is within the reach of the citizens it governs.

Mass parties. Political parties with large, dues-paying memberships. These parties are centralized, are bureaucratic, and have strong communication links running throughout the organization.

Master. A sixteenth century leader of a corporate guild who negotiated political and economic matters on behalf of those who worked under him.

Material benefits. Goods and services made available to an interest group's members.

Mercantilism. A theory urging that the state use its powers openly to provide the best possible conditions for private entrepreneurs to carry on their business, thereby identifying the interest of the state with that of private business.

Minister. A high officer appointed to head a segment of government.

Minority government. In a multiparty parliamentary system, a cabinet composed of representatives of parties that have, altogether, only a minority of seats in the legislature.

Mixed economy. An economy based on a mixture of public and private ownership of the means of production, and on considerable public regulation of the private sector.

Model. An imitation of something that is or that is thought to be or that may someday come to be; a representation of the essence of the subject.

Moderate pluralism. A system in which numerous parties are only moderately differentiated from each other ideologically.

Motion of censure. A motion made in parliamentary and presidential-parliamentary systems to remove a prime minister and his or her cabinet from office.

Multiparty party system. A party system with more than two parties.

Municipal council. A body of individuals, usually elected, whose duty it is to make the laws (ordinances) of local government. Sometimes also responsible for electing a mayor or appointing a city manager.

Municipal law. Collective name for local ordinances.

Nation. A relatively large group of people who feel they belong together by virtue of sharing one or more traits such as race, language, culture, history, or a set of customs and traditions.

Nationalism. A collective identity shared by the citizens of a polity; the belief that national interests are more important than international considerations.

Nation-state. A polity in which all citizens share a sense of common identity (nationhood) and in which subunits, if any, are wholly or partly under the domain of a central government. See also *state.*

Natural law. Law based on laws that already exist in nature and that have been, according to some philosophers, implanted there by a divine creator. Those who believe in natural law believe it is discoverable by "right reason" and is binding on everyone. See also *positive law.*

Natural law legal culture. Basing judicial decisions on the precepts of religious and philosophical thought. Found throughout the Islamic world and often also found in coexistence with more modern legal cultures, especially at the local level, as in many villages in India and in non-Islamic African nations.

Natural resources. The material wealth that can be drawn from a nation's natural environment.

Neighborhood association. A group of citizens who gather together to seek to influence government to make changes of benefit to their immediate neighborhood—or not to make changes that will be detrimental to their neighborhood.

Neocolonialism. A system for maintaining the economic dependence of one state on another while permitting it to acquire or maintain its political independence. The usual methods are the establishment of cooperative political leadership in the dependent nation, backed up by the promise of military assistance from the dominant nation, and the creation of trade agreements beneficial to the dominant nation and to the indigenous elite. See also *colonialism.*

Neocorporatism. An economic system in which the state gives official recognition to different interests by establishing boards of representatives to advise the government and grants subsidies or enacts supportive legislation favoring those that are cooperative with the state. See also *corporatism.*

Norms. The values or standards that an individual, a group, or a social system decide to apply to the facts of a situation.

Oligarchy. Rule by the few, usually in their own behalf. The iron law of oligarchy is the tendency of all organizations to divide into those who lead and those who follow.

OPEC. The Organization of Petroleum Exporting Countries. An international organization formed to promote the interests of the world's major oil-producing states. Its members include Algeria, Ecuador, Gabon, Indonesia, Iran, Iraq, Kuwait, Libya, Nigeria, Qatar, Saudi Arabia, Venezuela, and the United Arab Emirates.

Opinion. The conviction that a certain thing is probably true, often combined with an evaluation. See also *belief.*

Order. The condition of peace and serenity, in which everything appears to be functioning properly.

Ordinance. A ruling made by a local government body; sometimes referred to as municipal law.

Organization. A body of persons working together in a structured way to achieve a specific purpose.

Ostracism. The exclusion of an individual from a group.

Outputs. A term used in political systems analysis to denote the work produced by governments: laws (including ordinances and proclamations), the steps taken to implement laws, and the decisions made to settle disputes that arise under the law.

Pardon. The constitutional right of a chief executive to cancel punishments decreed by jurists, including those in military tribunals.

Parliament. A national legislative body, normally composed of an upper house and a lower house. See also *parliamentary system.*

Parliamentary system. A system of government in which the national legislature (parliament) is linked to the national bureaucracy by the fact that both are ruled by the same body, the cabinet, which is itself responsible to the legislature. See also *cabinet* and *parliament.*

Parochialism. The tendency to withdraw into the private sphere; to be concerned only with matters in one's own immediate area and to take a narrow, limited, and provincial outlook on life.

Participatory democracy. Self leadership; a government ruled immediately by the people, not by their representatives.

Participatory linkage. The connection between citizens and organizations (including governments) that exists when the former are directly involved in the decision-making processes of the latter.

Participatory parties. Political parties in which members are aided in participating directly in policymaking processes.

Particularistic party. A party that identifies completely with the interest of a particular social group.

Party primary. An election held to choose the person who will stand as a political party's nominee for an elective post.

Party system. Political system defined by the number of parties that operate within it.

Patronage. Jobs, honorary positions, or other material rewards given in exchange for political support. Sometimes referred to as "the spoils of office."

Periphery. Provincial and local governments, as contrasted to the "center" (the national government).

Phenomenology. An approach to the study of politics that focuses on change and the events (the *phenomena*) that led up to that change. It is an inquiry into the causes of a significant change in a political system.

Planned economy. An economy guided by the state in accordance with a general plan.

Pluralism. A condition in which all groups within a control have an equal right and opportunity to form, put forward their points of view, win adherents, and influence decision makers. Under such circumstances, polity is the result of a pluralistic struggle for power. Pluralist theorists argue that such a condition actually exists in western democracies and, further, that the net result is the fairest possible form of government.

Polarized pluralism. A party system in which the parties are ideologically separated by vast distances.

Policy-responsive linkage. A connection between citizens and political leaders in which the decisions of the latter are responsive to the views of the former.

Policy-responsive parties. Parties in which members work to ensure that policy is made in the interests of their supporters, but that are not directly under the control of those members.

Political appointment. An appointment to government office that is made by someone already serving in another government position.

Political behavior. The subfield of political science devoted to the study of political attitudes and acts.

Political bias. Partiality on the part of the media, expressed through the media's deliberately shaping the content and presentation of the news so as to favor certain political interests, actors, practices, and/or ideas over others.

Political consultant. Political operatives who help candidates deal with all aspects of campaign politics.

Political culture. A set of political values, beliefs, and attitudes that is widely shared throughout a polity.

Political documents. Forms of the written word that are studied by political scientists; namely, constitutions, statutory laws, judicial decisions, party statutes and platforms, leaders' speeches and memoirs, records of legislative proceedings, newspaper accounts of political happenings, and the like.

Political economy. The relationship between economic conditions and the political choices we make. The subfield of political science devoted to the study of the relationship between economic and political factors.

Political equality. The condition that exists when all citizens have an equal right to participate in the political process and to be treated equally in it.

Political event. An event that affects the right to allocate scarce resources in a polity.

Political indoctrination. Teaching a specific political ideology in order to rationalize and justify the behavior of a particular political regime. See also *civic training*.

Political legitimacy. The condition of being considered correct and proper in the exercise of political power. See also *legitimacy*.

Political organization. An organization that is not itself a government agency but whose main purpose is to affect the operation of government. The subfield of political science devoted to the study of nongovernmental organizations that seek to influence government.

Political party. An organization that seeks to place representatives in government by nominating candidates to stand for election, claiming that power so won will be exercised in the public interest.

Political party system. The identification of political systems according to the number of parties they have and the concentration or dispersion of power among the parties. Common types include the one-party system; the hegemonic party system (more than one party, but one is dominant over all the others); the two-party system; and the multiparty system.

Political socialization. The ongoing processes through which citizens acquire—and amend—their personal views of the political world.

Political system. A structure with interdependent parts that deals with political matters.

Political systems analysis. An analytical framework that treats political units (particularly political organizations and nation-states) as systems composed of interdependent parts and explores the relationships among those parts.

Political theory. The subfield of political science devoted to the study of political philosophy, including the formulation of concepts, categories, and logical explanations of political phenomena.

Politics. The process that determines who shall occupy roles of leadership in government and how the power of government shall be exercised. The authoritative allocation of scarce resources throughout a polity.

Polity. A state, or any society with an organized government. Any group of persons who have some form of political relationship with one another. The interdependence of human beings around the globe has created a worldwide polity, the human polity.

Polls. Studies of the opinions of the public, or of selected portions thereof, normally based on interviews with a random sample of the group in question.

Positive law. Law made by humans, pragmatically, to meet specific needs. See also *natural law*.

Power. The ability to control the behavior of others by threatening and/or carrying out severe sanctions if that behavior is other than compliant. See also *influence*.

Pragmatic-bargaining party. A party that aggregates interests through negotiations, which reach unconcernedly across conflicting values.

Precedent. A court case used as an example to be followed in succeeding similar cases. See also *common law*.

Precinct. An electoral subdivision of a city, usually comprising a few blocks. See also *ward*.

Predictions. The content of well-founded speculation on the part of political scientists about the feared or hoped-for events of the future.

Presidential-parliamentary system. A system of government in which the chief executive is elected directly by the people and in turn appoints a prime minister who must be approved by the parliament (the national legislature) before taking responsibility, with his or her cabinet, for carrying out the laws of the land and developing legislative proposals to put before the parliament. In this system, the prime minister is responsible to both the president and the parliament. Sometimes referred to as a quasi-presidential system.

Presidential system. A system of government in which the chief executive is elected directly by the people, is responsible for carrying out the laws of the land, and has only advisory powers with respect to the actual content of those laws, which are made by a separate legislative body whose members are elected independently of the president.

Pressure methods. The means groups use to exert pressure on government.

Pressure points. The levels and branches of government that groups seek to influence.

Prime minister. The chief executive in a parliamentary system and the second in command in a presidential-parliamentary system. A prime minister is chosen by the ceremonial chief of state in the former system and by the president in the latter. He or she must be approved by parliament in both systems and normally leads the party with the most seats in parliament.

Progress. The condition of advancing toward a better state; improvement.

Proportional representation. An electoral system

that gives each political party contesting an election a number of seats (usually in a legislature) roughly proportionate to the number of votes its candidates received in combination.

Protectionism. The policy of sheltering domestic producers—both agricultural and industrial—by adopting government policies that shield them from the competition of the world market. The favored methods of protectionism are the imposition of high tariffs on imported goods, the establishment of price supports for domestic goods, insistence on trade agreements favoring domestic businesses, and setting quotas on the amount of certain foreign goods that may be imported.

Proximate forces. Forces we encounter in person, such as family, teachers, and bosses (as contrasted to nonproximate forces, such as historical figures, political leaders, and the media).

Public administration. The subfield of political science devoted to the study of the bureaucratic processes and institutions of government.

Public agenda. The list of political issues that are normally of concern to almost everyone in a nation during a political campaign.

Public interest group. A group that claims to work for a cause that is in the public's interest, not its own. See also *special interest group*.

Public opinion. The collective nature of a body of individual opinions.

Public opinion poll. A study of the opinions held by a representative sample of the entire population.

Purposive benefits. The satisfaction some members of interest groups get from working on behalf of a value or cause in which they believe.

Quasi-presidential system. See *presidential-parliamentary system*.

Recall election. A special election held when a sufficient number of voters petition to remove an official (usually an elected official) from office.

Recruitment. The process of finding, persuading, and training candidates to run for electoral office. Often seen as a major function of political parties.

Referendum. A provision in a polity's electoral system enabling a group of citizens to "refer" a piece of legislation passed by the government to the voting public, provided a sufficient number of citizens petition for the right to do so.

Regionalism. A level of intermediate government below the level of the national government and usually (but not always) above the level of the province. See also *structural regionalism* and *functional regionalism*.

Representative leadership. Leadership based on the right of the people to choose certain individuals to attend to matters of state on their behalf.

Revolutionary one-party system. A single party that is used as the chief instrument for taking over an existing political system and effecting revolutionary change in all social, economic, and political relationships.

Right. A term used to describe political ideas comparatively. Those on the political right place greater stress on the importance of maintaining tradition and order than those on the political left. See also *left*.

Romano-Germanic legal culture. The making of judicial decisions by reference to codes of law based on the Roman tradition. Common in most of Europe, all of Latin America, the nations of West and Central Africa formerly under French dominion, and in the Canadian province of Quebec and the American state of Louisiana.

Rule of law. The principle that the regulation of social behavior shall take place under laws that apply equally to all.

Ruling. An interpretation, usually by a judicial body, of a regulation, decree, ordinance, or law.

Secret society. A group of lay persons who share a common religion, who hold secret ceremonies to reinforce the sense of solidarity with the group, and who commonly engage in social, charitable, and/or political activities they believe to be consistent with their religion.

Security Council. The organization of the United Nations in which the United States, Russia, China, Great Britain, and France have permanent membership, each with the right of veto.

Separation of powers. The constitutional establishment of three branches of government—legislative, executive, and judicial—each with separate and independent bases of support, terms of office, and powers of office.

Simulation. A process in which computer technology is used to gather all available information about a subject, form a model of that subject, and then manipulate that model by introducing other factors and examining their impact on it. See also *model*.

Single-party system. A political system in which only one political party is allowed.

Social equality. The condition that exists when every citizen has the right to be treated as a social equal, at least with respect to one's basic characteristics and needs.

Socialism. An ideology that holds that human beings readily engage in cooperative social activity and that the state, controlled by the workers, should own or at least control the means of production. An economic system in which the state controls all or most of the means of production.

Socialist legal culture. The making of judicial decisions by reference to the law code of the former Union of Soviet Socialist Republics, a code characterized by its explicit use of the law to serve political purposes.

Socialization. The process by which values are passed on clearly and persuasively by those who hold them to those who do not; the inculcation of values.

Sociocultural values. Values derived from membership in a particular social group, such as pride in a way of life, in shared traditions, and in the group culture.

Solidary benefits. The benefits provided by an interest group when it gives its members a sense of belonging, a chance to socialize with others, and/or improved social status.

Sovereignty. The power of a polity to make decisions that cannot be overruled by any other body.

Special interest group. A group that works exclusively for the interests of its own members. See also *public interest group*.

Specialized committee. A legislative committee that is responsible for bills having to do with a specific area of policy, such as agriculture or health. See also *standing committee*.

Spontaneous groups. Groups of organized individuals who act together politically and deliberately, but in an unconventional and often violent fashion.

Stagflation. An economic condition in which prices are inflated yet at the same time growth is slowed.

Standing committee. A legislative committee that is not limited in scope, to which different kinds of bills may be referred. See also *specialized committee*.

Stare decisis. A Latin phrase meaning "let the decision stand," referring to the practice in common law legal cultures of basing decisions in contemporary cases on those made in earlier similar cases.

State. A structure that has the legal right to make rules that are binding over a given population within a given territory. See also *city-state* and *nation-state*.

Statutory law. Written law, including legislation, treaties, executive orders, decrees, and codes of law. See also *codified law*.

Strict construction. The judicial practice of adhering closely to the letter of the law as found in a constitution or statute.

Structural-functional approach. A way of studying politics that focuses on the political functions that must be carried out in every political system and that seeks to discover which structures do, in fact, perform these tasks.

Structural regionalism. A form of regionalism in which provincial units are grouped in regions by constitutional fiat and are expected to be permanent additions to the body politic. See also *functional regionalism*.

Structure. A set of patterned role relationships.

Subnational government. Government below the level of the nation; regional, provincial, and local government.

Subversion. Any act designed to interfere with an established government by covert means, usually with a view to accomplishing its destruction.

Suffrage. The right to vote in political elections.

Surrogate. A person who takes the place of another and stands in for that person. In politics, surrogates often stand in for the chief executive in public ceremonies or for political candidates in election rallies.

Syndicalism. An ideology that argues that the trade union should replace the state, allowing workers to assume control of their own affairs, and that this should be accomplished via a general strike of nationwide proportions.

System. A structure all of whose parts are interrelated, so that a change in one part means a change in all.

Technocratic elite. Leaders in government and the private sector with high level and up to date skills in production and/or management.

Technological development. The use of high level and up to date skills to improve processes of transforming natural resources into useful goods and services.

Terrorist organization. An organization that attempts to change the operation of government by using violence to induce fear of the consequences of *not* changing and/or provoking the authorities to respond so oppressively as to lose legitimacy in the eyes of the general public.

Theocracy. A government ruled by religious leaders who claim to have divine authority for their edicts.

Totalitarian system. A political system in which the authorities have unlimited power and attempt to exercise it over all domains of life; authoritarianism carried to the ultimate extreme.

Transnational corporation. A cluster of businesses located in several different nations but commonly owned and managed. An independent network of fiscal, research, productive, and distributive institutions, often with gross annual sales larger than the gross national products of many nations.

Treaty. A document signed by representatives of two or more nations that sets the terms for relations between those nations with regard to particular matters.

Two-party system. A system in which two parties compete for an absolute majority that is within the reach of either.

Unicameral legislature. A legislature with only one house, as in the state of Nebraska in the United States. See also *bicameral legislature*.

Unitary system. A political system in which all the powers of government are reserved to the central government. That government may delegate the exercise of those powers to subunits but can revoke such delegation at any time.

Urban politics and government. The subfield of political science devoted to the study of politics and government in cities.

Value. A serious and deeply held normative principle with wide applicability.

Veto. The constitutional right of a ruler to reject bills passed by a legislative body.

Vote of confidence. A vote taken in a parliamentary or presidential-parliamentary system to demonstrate the legislature's continued confidence—or lack of confidence—in the prime minister and his or her cabinet. Usually called for by the prime minister during a period of crisis. If the vote is lost, the government is normally dissolved, and new elections are held.

Ward. An electoral and sometimes also an administrative subunit of a city. See also *precinct*.

Workers' council. A council of workers' representatives, usually elected, whose duty it is to take an active part in management decisions, particularly as these affect the interests of the workers. Established by the company and often (especially in socialist systems) mandated by the state, the workers' council should not be confused with the independent trade union, although the two may have shared leadership.

Xenophobia. The fear or hatred of anything foreign or strange.

Zero-sum. A term taken from game theory, used to describe a situation in which the gain of one player (e.g., politician or nation) can only be at the expense of another player.

Index